Praise for *The Balkans* and Misha Glenny

"Misha Glenny is the wisest and most reflective of all the Western journalists who have covered this part of Europe in the past two decades. . . . This was an enormously ambitious book to undertake, but it is the book which Europe and America need."

—Neal Ascherson, *The Observer* (London)

"His book covers an amazing amount of historical and geographical ground, ranging from early nineteenth-century Greece to Kosovo the day before yesterday. . . . This is popular history of the Norman Davies school, conceived on a large scale, highly readable, accessible, full of the music of the past. Its great strengths are evocation, fascinating detail and narrative sweep. A great achievement."

—Timothy Garton Ash, *The Mail on Sunday* (UK)

"Above all, the book is justified by the insights which add up to a convincing picture of the problems."

—Felipe Fernandez-Armesto, *The Sunday Times* (London)

"An endeavor which deserves extraordinary admiration and as yet has no rival." —Jonathan Steele, *The Guardian* (London)

"Compelling . . . Glenny's book should be required reading for all those wishing to know what has gone wrong with the region."

—Jonathan Eyal, *The Irish Times*

ABOUT THE AUTHOR

Misha Glenny was born in 1958 and educated at Bristol University and Charles University in Prague. His coverage of the fall of communism in 1989–1990 was widely acclaimed and led to the writing of his first book, *The Rebirth of History*. During the Yugoslav crisis of the early 1990s, he was the Central Europe correspondent for the BBC World Service. In 1993, he won a Sony Award for his coverage of Yugoslavia. Glenny's *The Fall of Yugoslavia* (1993) won the Overseas Press Club Award for Best Book on Foreign Affairs. His other books include *McMafia: A Journey Through the Global Underworld* and *DarkMarket: Cyberthieves, Cybercops and You*.

He has written for most major news outlets in Europe, North America, Africa, and Asia and has lectured around the world, most recently as a visiting professor at Columbia University.

THE BALKANS

Nationalism, War, and the Great Powers
1804–2011

Misha Glenny

◆◆◆

PENGUIN BOOKS

PENGUIN BOOKS
Published by the Penguin Group
Penguin Group (USA) Inc., 375 Hudson Street, New York, New York 10014, U.S.A.
Penguin Group (Canada), 90 Eglinton Avenue East, Suite 700, Toronto,
Ontario, Canada M4P 2Y3 (a division of Pearson Penguin Canada Inc.)
Penguin Books Ltd, 80 Strand, London WC2R 0RL, England
Penguin Ireland, 25 St Stephen's Green, Dublin 2, Ireland (a division of Penguin Books Ltd)
Penguin Group (Australia), 250 Camberwell Road, Camberwell,
Victoria 3124, Australia (a division of Pearson Australia Group Pty Ltd)
Penguin Books India Pvt Ltd, 11 Community Centre, Panchsheel Park, New Delhi – 110 017, India
Penguin Group (NZ), 67 Apollo Drive, Rosedale,
Auckland 0632, New Zealand (a division of Pearson New Zealand Ltd)
Penguin Books (South Africa) (Pty) Ltd, 24 Sturdee Avenue,
Rosebank, Johannesburg 2196, South Africa

Penguin Books Ltd, Registered Offices: 80 Strand, London WC2R 0RL, England

First published in the United States of America by Viking Penguin,
a member of Penguin Putnam Inc., 2000
Published in Penguin Books 2001
This edition with a new epilogue published 2012

1 3 5 7 9 10 8 6 4 2

THE LIBRARY OF CONGRESS HAS CATALOGED
THE HARDCOVER EDITION AS FOLLOWS:
Glenny, Misha.
The Balkans: nationalism, war, and the great powers, 1804–2011 / Misha Glenny.
p. cm.
Includes bibliographical references and index.
ISBN 0-670-85338-0 (hc.)
ISBN 978-0-14-242256-4 (pbk.)
1. Balkan Peninsula—Politics and government—19th century.
2. Balkan Peninsula—Politics and government—20th century.
3. Nationalism—Balkan Peninsula. I. Title
DR43.G58 2000
949.6'028—dc21 99–089564

Printed in the United States of America
Set in Stempel Garamond

To my mother and Jack for everything

Warkworth. Before NORTHUMBERLAND*'s Castle. Enter* RUMOUR, *painted full of tongues.*

RUM: Open your ears; for which of you will stop
The vent of hearing when loud Rumour speaks?
I, from the orient to the drooping west,
Making the wind my post-horse, still unfold
The acts commenced on this ball of earth:
Upon my tongues continual slanders ride,
The which in every language I pronounce,
Stuffing the ears of men with false reports.
I speak of peace, while covert enmity
Under the smile of safety wounds the world:
And who but Rumour, who but only I,
Make fearful musters and prepar'd defence,
Whilst the big year, swoln with some other grief,
Is thought with child by the stern tyrant war,
And no such matter? Rumour is a pipe
Blown by surmises, jealousies, conjectures,
And of so easy and so plain a stop
That the blunt monster with uncounted heads,
The still-discordant wavering multitude,
Can play upon it. But what need I thus
My well-known body to anatomize
Among my household? Why is Rumour here?

From the prologue to *Henry IV, Pt. 2*

CONTENTS

ACKNOWLEDGEMENTS

I occasionally wonder whether I would have ever embarked on writing this book if I knew how much work it was going to require and what a lonely endeavour it would be. Friends and colleagues were always on hand to restore my morale.

The first of four years' writing was spent at the Woodrow Wilson Center for International Scholars in Washington DC. I am deeply grateful to all who assisted me at this exceptional institution. In particular, Professor John R. Lampe first suggested that I consider going to the Wilson Center. Without his help and encouragement, this book would never have gone beyond the embryonic stage. I also wish to thank Kristin Hunter for her unstinting support and friendship during my time at the Wilson Center.

I am pleased to acknowledge the generous assistance of the Royal Institute of International Affairs and the encouragement offered by its former director, Sir Timothy Garden, and George Joffé.

Professor Gale Stokes waded stoically through many drafts of the early chapters of this book, lending me the benefit of his great experience as a historian of the Balkans. His stern criticism was invaluable in focusing my attention on many weaknesses which I hope I have gone some way towards rectifying. Liam McDowall has not only been the firmest of friends but a remarkable source of information and ideas that only come with years of first-hand experience of the Balkans. Grenville Byford demonstrated faith in my work when I encountered my greatest doubts. His wisdom and kindness pulled me through. Throughout the past four years, Ivan Vejvoda's calming influence has been an inspiration in helping me steer through the Balkan rapids. Fatos Lubonja provided great insight in our discussions on Albania.

Many others have read the text in various states. The following people have offered valuable observations: Keith Brown (who also acted as a librarian of rare texts), Professor Richard Crampton, Snežana Ćurčić, Aleksa Djilas, Paddy Glenny, Tamara Glenny, Mark Mazower, Milorad Pupovac, Professor Maria Todorova and Bill Schwarz. Their collective intelligence has improved the book immeasurably although any outstanding errors are my responsibility alone. My sincere thanks are also due to Herb Okun, Robert Silvers and Susan Woodward. As always I was able to rely on Imma Palme, Hans Ljung and Braca Grubačić to help out at a moment's notice.

Melissa Llewelyn-Davies offered the most detailed and encouraging criticism of the work in progress. She, Rosa Curling and Richard Curling provided invaluable humour and goodwill at times of extreme pressure.

My greatest debt is to Neil Belton, my editor, friend and most forthright critic. The effortless dexterity with which he wields the tools of his trade have lent this book a coherence which I could never have provided on my own. Any confidence I have in my work is due solely to Neil.

My mother, Juliet Sydenham, has not only given me support beyond words but also contributed her considerable editorial skills.

I have one regret about this project. It has deprived me for far too long of the company of my children, Miljan, Alexandra and Callum.

The Balkans, 1804

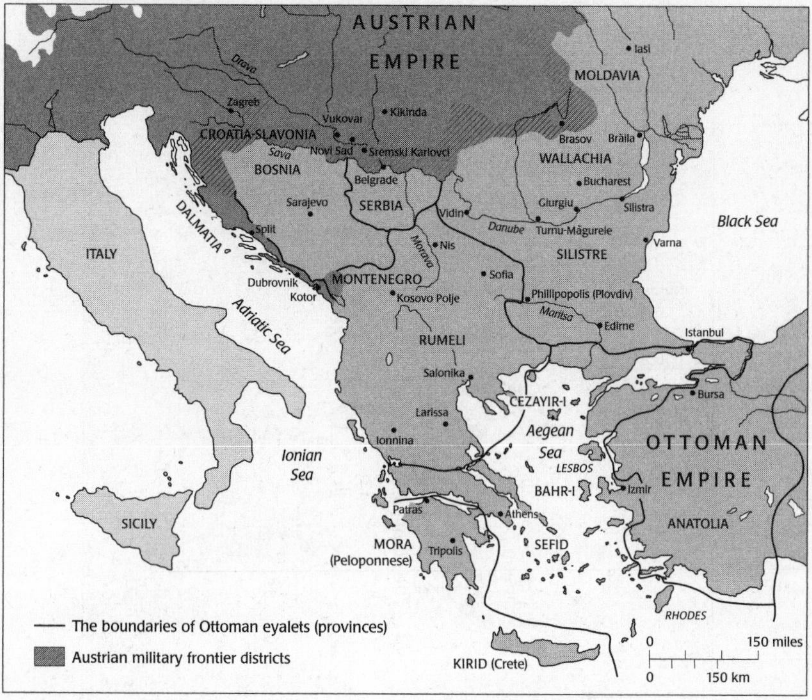

— The boundaries of Ottoman eyalets (provinces)

Austrian military frontier districts

The Belgrade Pashalik, 1804

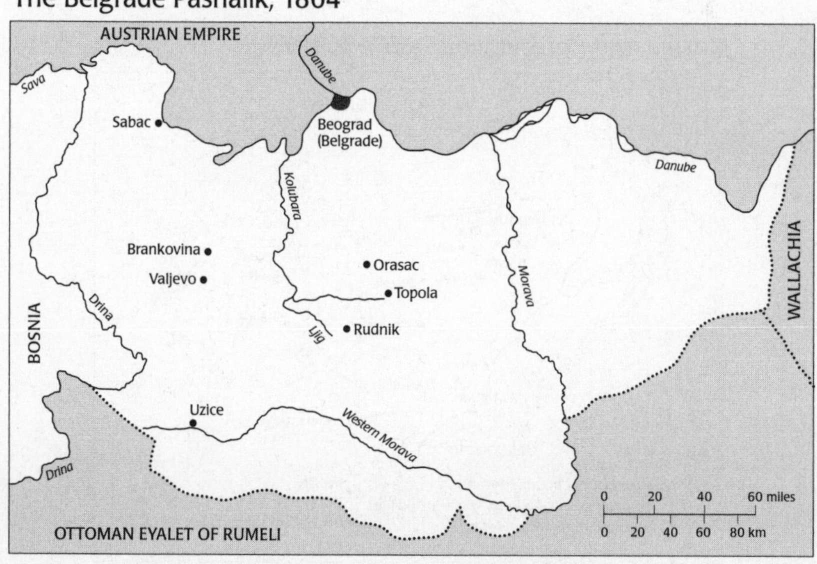

The Greek War of Independence, 1821–30

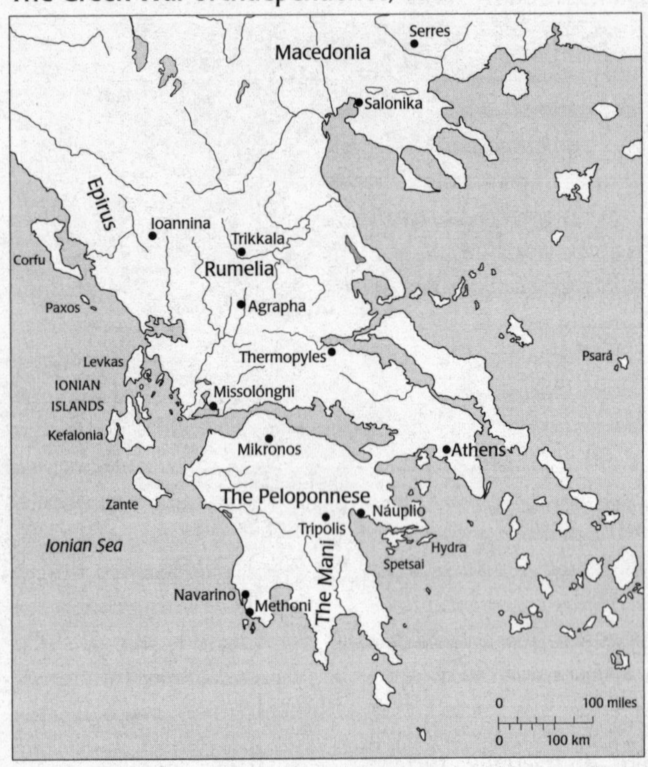

Bosnia and Hercegovina, 1850–2, 1875

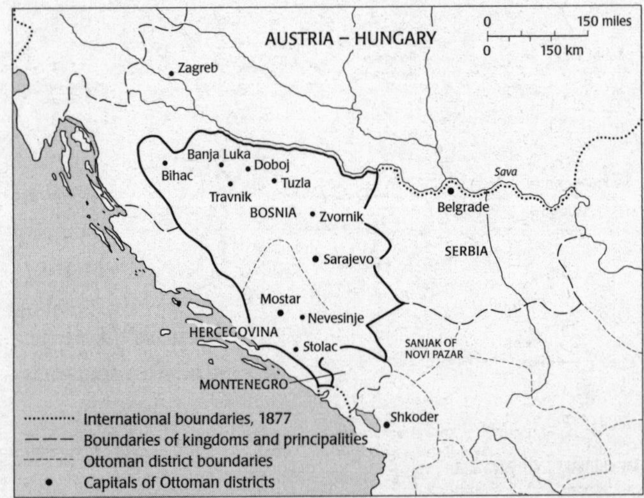

The Treaty of San Stefano, 1878

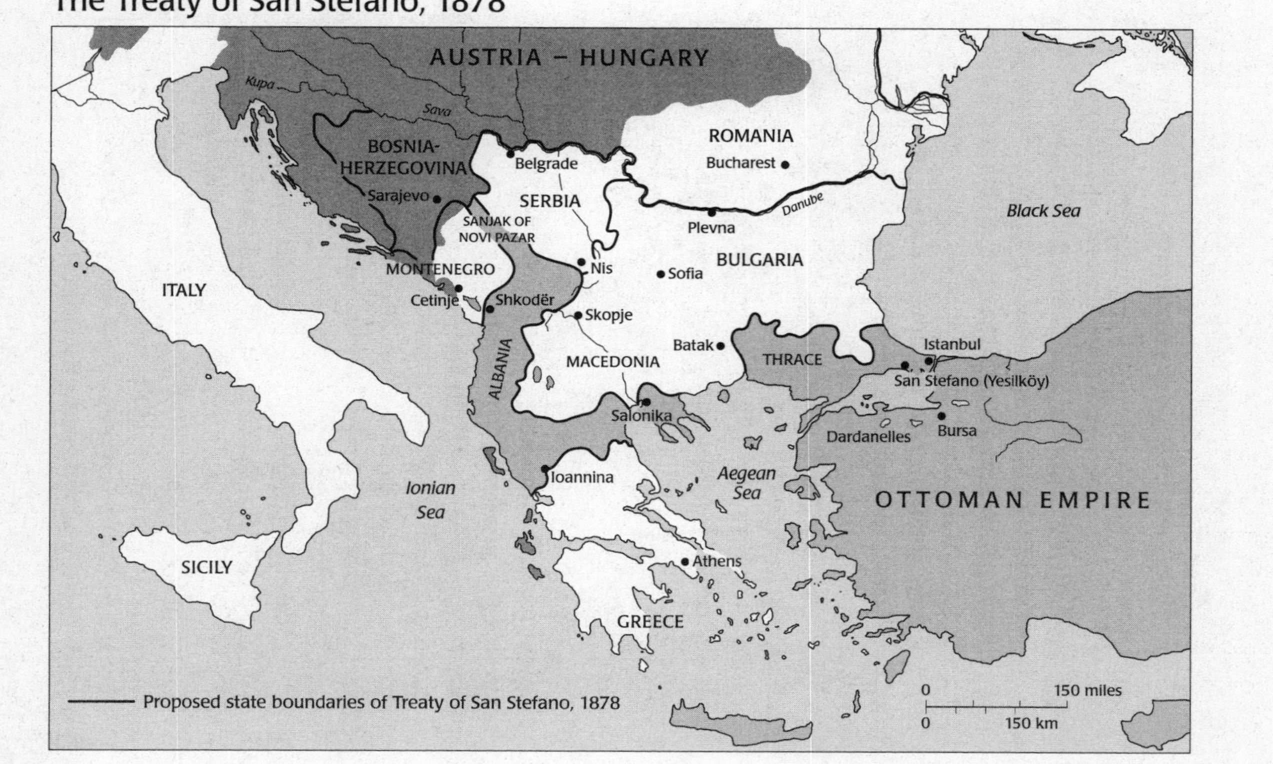

The Berlin Treaty, 1878

The Balkan Wars; Croatia and Bosnia

World War I

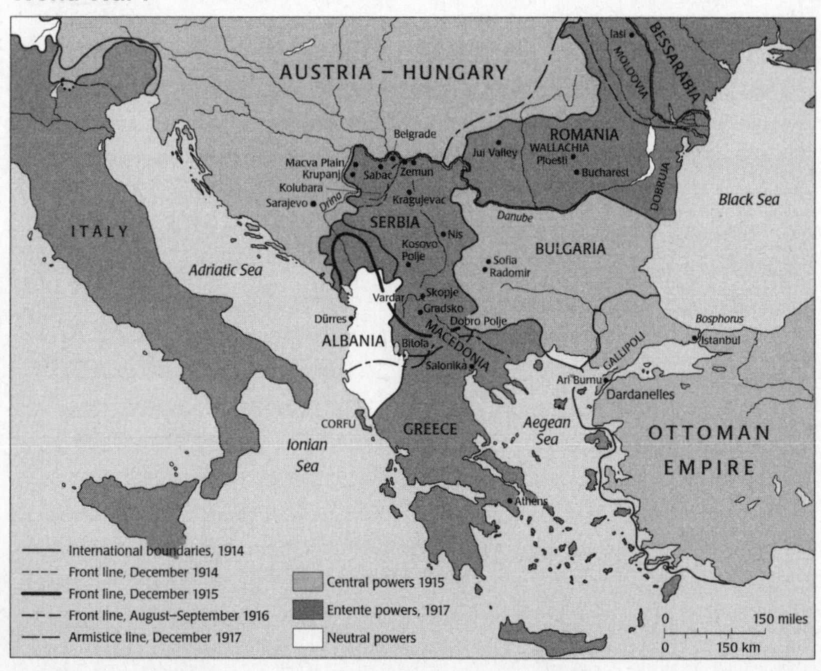

The Balkans and the Paris Peace Conference

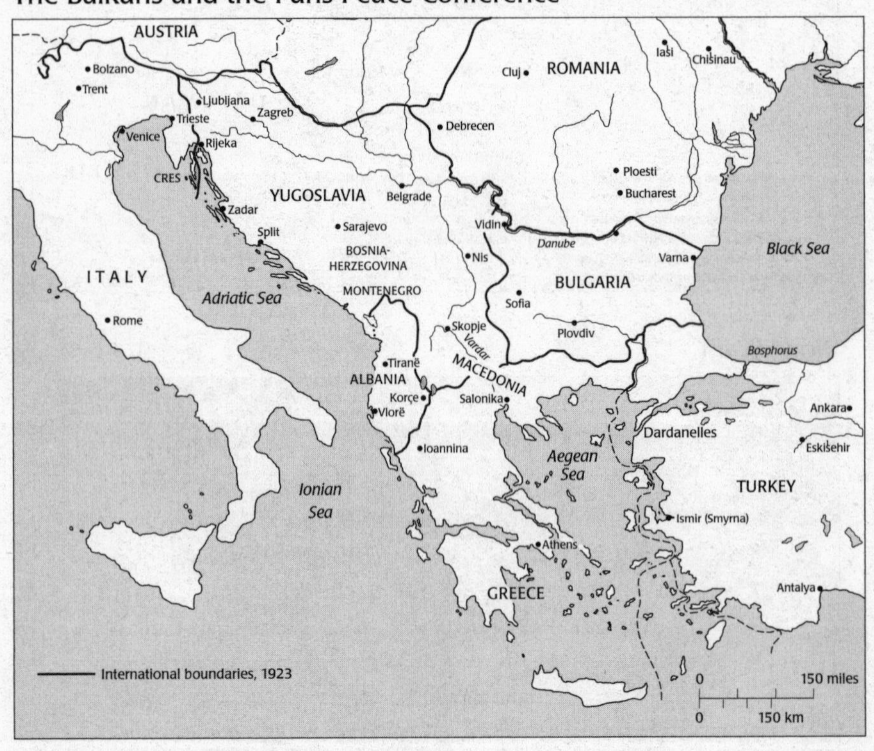

The Balkans under Nazi influence

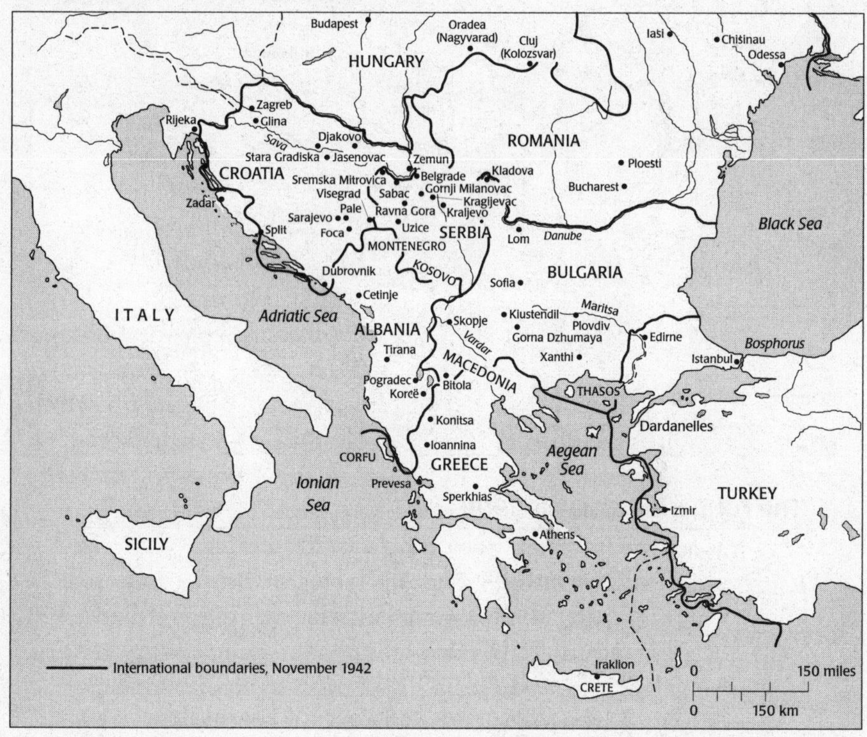

The Balkans, 1945–89

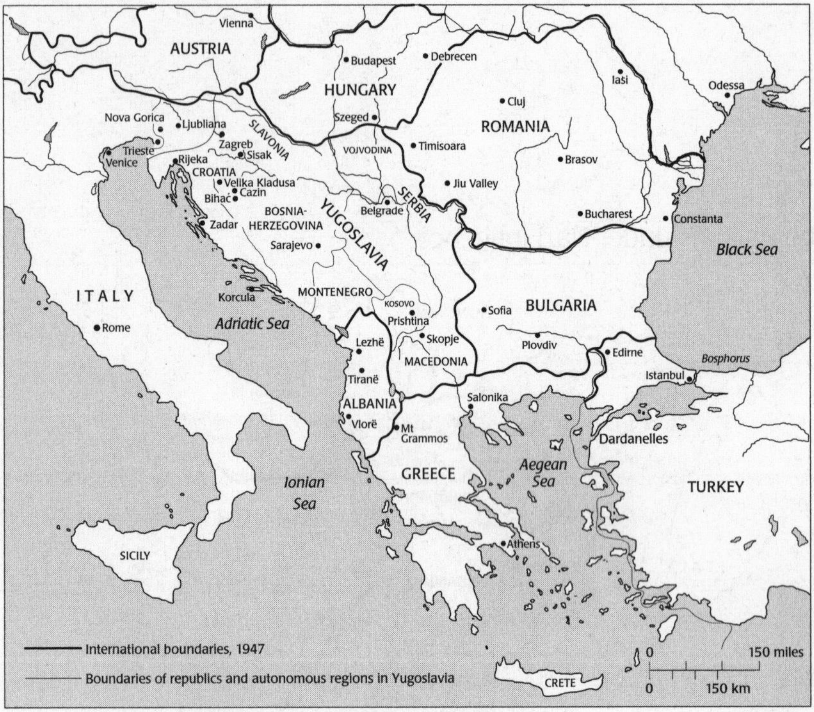

International boundaries, 1947

Boundaries of republics and autonomous regions in Yugoslavia

The Former Yugoslavia, 1999

INTRODUCTION

'Kosovo', the British Prime Minister, Tony Blair, informed his public in early April 1999, 'is on the doorstep of Europe.' Yet no geographer would consider Kosovo and its neighbours part of Asia. If neither in Europe nor in Asia, where does the Balkan peninsula lie? Perhaps Mr Blair has been influenced by Bram Stoker's *Dracula* in which the Balkans occupied 'the centre of some sort of imaginative whirlpool', where 'every known superstition in the world is gathered'. For many decades, Westerners gazed on these lands as if on an ill-charted zone separating Europe's well-ordered civilization from the chaos of the Orient.

Today the language of observers is less romantic but the sentiments that distance and mythologize the Balkans persist. It is in fact only recently, since the turn of the 20th century, that the world has adopted the adjective 'Balkan' and derivatives like 'Balkanization' as pejorative terms. If somebody displays a 'Balkan mentality', for example, it implies a predilection for deceit, exaggeration and unreliability. As Yugoslavia began to disintegrate in 1989, generalizations about the peoples who inhabit the region, and their histories, were spread by media organizations that had long ago outlawed such clichés when reporting from Africa, the Middle East or China. The Balkans apparently enjoy a special exemption from the rules against stereotyping.

The truth is that even the contours of these mysterious lands between two continents are obscure. Many scholars have claimed that the Danube represents the northern border of the peninsula. This would all but exclude Romania, a country that features not just in most Western studies of the Balkans but even in Romanian histories of the Balkans as well, despite the country's reluctance to be grouped with its southern neighbours. After the First World War, American and West European politicians frequently referred to Hungary as belonging to the peninsula; yet since 1945 the designation has atrophied. Many Croats have long insisted that their culture is foreign to Balkan traditions and that their identity is exclusively Central European. Few historians have agreed. The Aegean and Ionian islands of Greece draw upon a Mediterranean heritage and yet the country's second largest city, Thessaloniki, has a history as central to the Balkans as that of Sarajevo.

The fog that shrouds these lands lifts from time to time, revealing unexpected features, before it descends again to create a new and complex landscape. Any serious consideration of the Balkan peninsula runs up against the unanswerable question of borders. Which countries belong there? A still more sensitive question is – which peoples does it embrace? Countless scholars, politicians, diplomats and journalists have offered definitions, underpinned variously by geographical, political, ethnic and historical arguments, some of them measured, some preposterous. But a consensus has never been found, nor could it be.

Like all other books on the Balkans, the definition of the peninsula that this book uses is a mixture of the geographical, historical and political. The core regions considered are mainland Greece, Serbia, Croatia, Romania (although Transylvania's role is secondary), Turkey and the Ottoman Empire, Bulgaria, Bosnia and Hercegovina, Montenegro, Macedonia and Albania. Inasmuch as they occasionally impact on those areas, the peripheral territories of Slovenia, Vojvodina, Hungary, Moldavia, Anatolia, Cyprus and the Greek Aegean and Ionian islands are also briefly discussed.

The difficulty in defining the Balkans arises from the conflation of political and geographic descriptions that are themselves problematic. The term Balkan peninsula is modern, coined by the German geographer, Johann August Zeune, in 1808. It arose from a long-standing misconception that the Balkan mountain range, the backbone of present-day Bulgaria, did not taper out in eastern Serbia (as is the case) but stretched unbroken from the Black Sea to the Adriatic. It took a century for this inaccurate description to eclipse other classical or geo-political names, like Turkey-in-Europe or the Near East, as the preferred choice in most European languages. The more neutral term South Eastern Europe persists as an also ran in both English and German to this day.

As a synonym for the Balkans, 'Turkey-in-Europe', those regions of the Ottoman Empire which lay to the West of the Bosphorus, raised questions as to the nature of the northern periphery – parts of Hungary, Croatia and even Austria had at one time been under the control of Ottoman armies. Would this mean that if a territory became detached from the Ottoman Empire, it would lose its Balkan status? Are the former Ottoman provinces of Bosnia and Hercegovina excluded from the Balkans because they were annexed by the Austro-Hungarian Empire in 1908, before the Ottoman collapse?

It was not until the end of the Great War that a new layer of meaning was imposed on the term. 'Balkanization' was first used by journalists and politicians not to describe the political fragmentation of the Balkan peninsula but the emergence of several small new states to replace the Habsburg and Romanov empires. It would have been just as accurate to label this process the East Europeanization or even the Balticization of Europe.

But the most enduring definition of the word Balkans has its origin in the assassination of Archduke Franz Ferdinand in Sarajevo in 1914. In 1940, the American journalist, John Gunther, wrote in his immensely popular book *Inside Europe* that

> It is an intolerable affront to human and political nature that these wretched and unhappy little countries in the Balkan peninsula can, and do, have quarrels that cause world wars. Some hundred and fifty thousand young Americans died because of an event in 1914 in a mud-caked primitive village, Sarajevo. Loathsome and almost obscene snarls in Balkan politics, hardly intelligible to a Western reader, are still vital to the peace of Europe, and perhaps the world.*

* Quoted in Maria Todorova, *Imagining the Balkans*, Oxford, 1997, p. 119.

Gunther's contempt reflects a solid body of Western popular opinion that regarded and still regards the Balkans as a toxin threatening the health of Europe. The chemistry of this toxin is assumed to be too complex for any known antidote. In the absence of a cure, the West found that one solution was to isolate it and forget about it. This is what happened during the Cold War, when the northern Balkans were lost in the cultural black hole of Soviet imperialism; the socialist renegades, Yugoslavia and Albania, were placed under the rubric of the 'Eastern Adriatic'; and the southern Balkans were transformed into the strategic NATO region of the Eastern Mediterranean. The politically loaded term, the Balkans, would resurface only on rare occasions when murder and intrigue cast a shadow over the otherwise placid order of south-eastern Europe. One notable example was when agents of the Bulgarian government murdered the BBC Bulgarian Service journalist, Georgi Markov, with a poison-tipped umbrella on a bridge over the River Thames.

Balkan politics could only be isolated because they were assumed to be static. So powerful and long-standing were the traditions of enmity in the Balkans, it was argued, that they had lodged themselves in the genetic makeup of the region's inhabitants. Western Europeans conceded that the Balkans belonged to Europe (although Tony Blair's remark about Kosovo being on its doorstep reflects how reluctant a concession this was). But with at best a foot in the door of civilized Europe, the Balkan peoples had followed a different evolutionary path, in which blood and revenge were the preferred forms of political discourse.

The conflict in the former Yugoslavia from 1991 onwards appeared to confirm this essentialist interpretation of the Balkans. These people, wrapped in their 'ancient hatreds', as another British Prime Minister, John Major, has described them, seemed incapable of learning from history. Sarajevo in 1992 was merely a novel form of the tinderbox that had sparked war in 1914.

Consistently and conspicuously absent from Western reflections on the Balkans since the latter half of the 19th century has been any consideration of the impact of the West itself on the region. The great powers, or 'the international community', as they are now known, have always been 'dragged' into Balkan conflicts as apparently unwilling partners to local disputes whose nature has eluded them. The Balkans were thought to be impervious to the civilizing processes which the European empires claimed to have introduced elsewhere in the world. Yet when the great powers extracted themselves from some Balkan entanglement, they rarely investigated the consequences of their intervention.

I began my own journey through the Balkans equipped with much of the prejudicial baggage that other outsiders carry and would not pretend to have discarded it all. My original decision to write a history of the Balkans was prompted by the realization that I was, along with many other observers of the wars in Yugoslavia during the 1990s, obliged to make judgements about Yugoslav and Balkan history when I had only the vaguest acquaintance with the subject. It has been my firm intention, in what follows, to avoid reading or refracting Balkan history through the prism of the 1990s but on a few occasions I have felt it worthwhile to remark on echoes, continuities or discontinuities.

From the beginning, I was convinced that to understand Yugoslav history, it was necessary to look at the history of the entire region. I was then confronted with the voluminous material on the region published over the past two centuries. This history has itself been 'Balkanized', to further abuse the term. Synthetic studies of the Balkans are rare; in contrast, academic monographs, eye-witness accounts and documentary collections on particular countries or events are legion. This applies as much to work that has emerged from the region as it does to 'external' history. I was also struck by the absence of any broad history that seeks to trace the relationship between the great powers and the Balkans over the past two centuries. As this book suggests, the influence of the great powers on the Balkans since the beginning of the 19th century has contributed substantially to a history that is not static – in which age-old enmities are doomed to permanent repetition – but breathtakingly dynamic.

Had I pursued a strict narrative line, this book would quickly have become a calendar of wars, coronations and changes of government. Although my account is broadly chronological, I have chosen to concentrate on those events and processes within and without the Balkans which have, I believe, played a significant role in the shaping of the region and our perceptions of it.

At the turn of the 18th century, when the present narrative begins, the region was in many respects unrecognizable to the twenty-first century reader. There were very few towns and three or four cities at most; the latter were usually Ottoman garrisons where few non-Muslims lived with the notable exceptions of Bucharest, Salonika and Istanbul itself. Everywhere there was a very low density of population and a much higher percentage of the land was covered with forest. The overwhelming majority of people in the Balkans made their living from subsistence agriculture; there was no industry to speak of, while the trading networks ran along the coastal periphery. Life was extremely slow; armed conflict inside the Ottoman Empire most infrequent; ethnic hostility rarely sprang the boundaries of localized disputes.

In the two decades following the French revolution, serious rebellions broke out in four corners of Europe – in Ireland (1798), Poland (1796), Spain (1808–1812) and Serbia (1804–1830). These were all peasant societies with significant economic grievances, and in each case the uprisings were peasant *jacqueries* – but only in part. All four rebellions assumed a nationalist character as well. The first three broke out in Christian empires – the rebels were all Catholics. They drew support from influential sections of the middle class and the intelligentsia and they were all bloodily repressed. The Serbian Uprising of 1804 was different, in that the rebels were Orthodox Christians in a Muslim state. The revolt in the pashalik of Belgrade was not at first the rising of a powerful national group against a foreign oppressor. It broke out in protest against the weakness of the state. Far from starting as a nationalist revolution, the Christian rebels aimed at the restoration of Ottoman rule in their province. Yet of the four peasant rebellions in Europe at the time, it was the only one that succeeded. At the start of the 19th century, national consciousness was probably weaker on the Balkan peninsula than anywhere else in Europe. It is a significant paradox that after the French Revolution gave birth to the age of nations, the nationalism of peoples excluded from history found its first home in two of Europe's most underdeveloped regions – Serbia and Greece.

CHAPTER 1

A CONFEDERACY OF PEASANTS

Rebellion and revolution, 1804–66

The slaughter of the knezes: the Serbian Uprisings and the Ottoman Empire, 1804–30

On a freezing morning in late January 1804, Mehmed-aga Fočić saddled one of his Arabian horses and headed south-west out of Belgrade in the direction of Valjevo. Fočić would not risk travelling alone so he left with a retinue of 200 janissaries, nominally members of the Sultan's elite guard. In reality, these janissaries eschewed loyalty to Selim III in far-off Istanbul in favour of their local masters, the four *dahi* – Fočić, Kućuk-Alija Djevrljić, Mula Jusuf and Aganlia. The unrestrained brutality with which these janissary commanders ruled over the northern edge of the Ottoman Empire had made them many enemies among the Christian Serb peasants and even among their fellow Muslims. By 1804, the *dahi* never left the fortress of Belgrade without armed protection.

The province of Belgrade was sparsely populated and covered with thick forest where Serbian farmers grazed their pigs. But the forest also hid bandits, Serbs who had given up working the land to live off plunder. In the first years of the nineteenth century, the ranks of these outlaws had grown steadily as men fled the misrule of the *dahi*.

Fočić's first stop was the village of Ljubenino Polje, thirty miles south-west of Belgrade. Here he was greeted warily by Aleksandar Nenadović, the knez or local Serb chieftain. The two men then set off for Valjevo. Relations between them seemed friendly enough, but Nenadović had fallen into an elaborate trap. The janissaries had received intelligence that he and his family were smuggling weaponry across the Sava from the Habsburg Empire, and were preparing for rebellion. On the way to Valjevo from the village, Fočić's men seized Nenadović and his companion, Ilija Birčanin, and clapped them in irons.

Valjevo was the centre of conspiracy among the Serb peasantry, and Fočić had in his possession a letter from Nenadović's son that proved the chieftain's complicity in the gun-running. The janissary commanders had agreed amongst themselves to strike against the leadership of the Christian revolt before it started, and the Nenadović clan was the first target. Aleksandar and Birčanin were hauled in front of a large crowd of onlookers, Christian and Muslim. 'This letter has killed Aleksa', cried Fočić, holding up the incriminating document. 'He conspired with the Germans [Habsburgs] and denounced us, the janissaries, to our own sultan. It would be a sin to leave his head upon his shoulders. Cut it off!'[1] After the decapitations, the bodies were dumped on an open meadow by the River Kolubara. Panic seized the Muslim and Christian populations of Valjevo. The Muslims locked their doors, fearing the reaction of Serb villagers; the Serbian men grabbed their weapons and took to the forest.

Many more heads rolled in the next few days. One outlaw, the Serbian monastic priest, Hadži-Ruvim, escaped Fočić's squadron of executioners and sought refuge with the Greek bishop of Belgrade, Leontius. Under pressure the bishop handed him over to Fočić's most sadistic colleague, Aganlia. In an attempt to extract details of the rebellion, Aganlia stripped the flesh from Ruvim's body with a pair of pliers. When the priest still refused to talk, his head was cut off in a public ceremony at the city gate. This was the beginning of the 'slaughter of the knezes' (*seća knezova*). The pre-emptive assault 'precipitated what the Janissaries most hoped to avoid – a general uprising of the Serbs'.[2] The rebellion marked the beginning of modern history on the Balkan peninsula.

In late 1801, the four janissary commanders had murdered the popular governor of Belgrade province, Haci Mustafa, a trusted lieutenant of the reformist Sultan, Selim III (1789–1807). His death was no isolated incident; the Sultan's authority over the Empire's peripheral territories had declined so dramatically in the second half of the eighteenth century that soldiers, governors and landowners had scrambled to fill local power vacuums as they appeared.

The Ottoman elite's refusal to adjust its social and military structures to the economic and technological developments in other European empires had caused this sclerosis. Cocooned in privilege, the conservative majority – the 'wise men' of the Islamic hierarchy, the *ulema*; and the bloated officer classes in the army – resisted the encroachment of European ideas and administrative systems, seeing in them a threat to Ottoman tradition. Although the Empire was a well-established prop on the international stage, its sultans and viziers declined to play an active role in the drama. Watching from the wings as Spain, Britain, Holland and France developed their great commercial empires, they ignored the influx of large amounts of gold and silver into European markets. Such fundamental shifts in the global economy, they assumed, were of no concern to the protected markets of the empire. This was a serious miscalculation. In the two centuries since the colonization of the New World, the impact of European mercantilism promoted inflation, famine and political instability in the Ottoman Empire.

There were voices at the Sublime Porte* advocating modernization. They argued that if the leadership refused to adopt the latest advances in science and engineering, then the army, the key to Ottoman power, would corrupt beyond repair. In the last decade of the eighteenth century and the first six years of the nineteenth century, the young Selim III allowed these voices to be heard.

For much of his youth, Selim had been literally locked up in the Golden Cage at the Imperial Palace; but he was permitted contact with a few peers who convinced him of the need for reform and innovation. When Selim emerged from his seclusion, he had no practical experience of the world, but he was already a zealous proponent of change. He was determined to restore the domestic authority of the state and to rehabilitate it as a great power.

---

* The Imperial Palace in Istanbul whose name became synonymous with the government.

During the first four years of his reign, the Ottoman Empire was at war with the Habsburgs. This was not the time for Selim to introduce reforms. He waited until 1794 before revealing his plans to establish the *Nizam-i-Cedid* (New Order). This had at its core a small, modern army trained in the latest techniques, mainly by French officers. Led by the janissaries and senior army officers, the Empire's privileged classes launched a sustained campaign to undermine the New Order. Western influence in the military, they believed, was the thin end of the wedge that would crack open and eventually destroy their privileged world.

The janissaries were the Sultan's most resolute opponents. Three and a half centuries earlier, the military prowess of this imperial guard was the foundation upon which the great Ottoman Empire had been built. The janissaries, who were culled as boys from the Sultan's subject peoples, were not permitted to marry or have children to ensure they remained loyal to the Sultan. But by the time Selim assumed the throne in 1794, the force had degenerated into a corporation dedicated to self-aggrandizement. Its members now took wives and built up minor dynasties. Friends, relations and hangers-on shared the privileges of a once exclusive organization. Of 12,000 names registered in the janissary rolls of Istanbul in 1790, only 2,000 rendered the military service that in theory entitled them to membership. The New Order directly threatened their interests; an efficient competitor would expose their indolence. To undermine the reform, they signed up new members in huge numbers, for which the Sultan was obliged to pay. By 1809, there were almost 110,000 registered janissaries in the Empire, a fourfold increase since the creation of the New Order.

Had the janissaries been the only problem facing Selim, the Sultan could have dealt with them. But at the turn of the century, he had to confront the pashas, a much more serious challenge to his authority. These regional governors formed the crucial link in the chain of command between Istanbul and the mass of imperial subjects. The Ottoman Empire stretched from Bosnia, Belgrade and Bucharest in the north to the Maghreb, Mesopotamia and Palestine in the south; the Sultan's control over these enormous holdings had always been guaranteed by the pashas and the janissaries. At the turn of the nineteenth century, Selim III found he could no longer rely on either as they accrued ever greater autonomy at the expense of a weak Porte.

Two men proved a particular threat – Paşvanoğlu Osman Paşa of Vidin (now in north-western Bulgaria) and Ali Paşa of Ioaninna (in the north-western Greek province of Epirus). On the surface, both Ali and Paşvanoğlu were despots whose unrestrained rule merely reflected the extent of Ottoman decay. But they also constructed proto-modern states that acted as a bridge between the Ottoman Empire and the nation states which eventually emerged on the peninsular.

Paşvanoğlu Osman was still in his teens when his father lost the family's hereditary estates around Vidin in a vendetta. Paşvanoğlu saw service in the imperial army during the Austro-Turkish war of 1789–92 before returning to Vidin, determined to avenge his family's loss. Within a year, he had built up an army of brigands, janissaries and disaffected imperial troops. When the governor of Vidin, who was loyal to Selim, sent a force to deal with them, Paşvanoğlu's men routed it.

The rebellion at Vidin had an electrifying impact on the Ottoman Empire. Mercenaries and militants flocked to join Paşvanoğlu – Albanian irregulars, janissaries from Bosnia and Serbia, and perhaps the wildest units of all, the *kircali*, nomadic bandits who offered their services to the highest bidder. Their horses, decorated with gold and silver, and their female slaves, who dressed as men and were forced to satisfy their captors sexually as well as accompany them to the battlefield, added a touch of freakish theatricality to the Vidin enclave.

Paşvanoğlu organized raiding parties across the Danube from Vidin into Wallachia (now southern Romania) where the wretched population were already suffering the extortionate practices of their local prince. Paşvanoğlu's proto-state penetrated into southern Bulgaria, where he disrupted the imperial collection of grain and tax; and in 1795, he declared his independence from the Sultan. This challenge provoked a swift response. Selim sent a powerful army to besiege Vidin, but just as he appeared to be restoring his grip on domestic affairs and preparing to consolidate his reform programme, Napoleon Bonaparte betrayed him.

The French invasion of Egypt in 1798 took most in Europe by complete surprise. For Selim and his circle of reformers, it was a psychological and practical disaster. The Sultan was a great admirer of France and its progressive intelligentsia, and had developed a warm relationship with the revolutionary government in the last decade of the eighteenth century to counter the territorial ambitions of Austria and Russia in the Balkans. Although the logic of the French Revolution undermined everything that the Ottoman Empire stood for, the Sultan and his advisers presumed that this far-away struggle between republicans and monarchists would have no impact on Ottoman power.

The invasion of Egypt, however, was a warning to Selim that France under Napoleon remained an opportunistic power. The Sultan diverted troops from Vidin to meet this new challenge. With the main Ottoman armies engaged in Egypt, Haci Mustafa could no longer enforce the expulsion order on the janissaries that he had proclaimed earlier, with Selim's approval. They returned to Belgrade from their refuge in Vidin in 1798. For three years, the *dahi* attempted to undermine Mustafa's authority, finally avenging themselves on the governor by murdering him.

The struggle that erupted in the Belgrade *pashalik* in February 1804 did not, as might be expected, set Muslim overlord against Christian peasant.* On the contrary, the peasantry and the *sipahi*, the established Ottoman landlords, cooperated openly with Selim's modernizing agents against the violence of janissary reaction.

So close were the ties binding the Christian peasantry and the murdered reformer, Haci Mustafa, that he was known reverently as the 'mother of the Serbs'. This trust extended so far that in 1799 Selim issued an unprecedented *firman* (imperial decree), permitting the Christians to carry weapons – a rifle, two pistols and a *yatagan*, a long, curved Turkish knife. The peasants then formed armed units to aid the *sipahi* and supporters of Selim against the janissaries. This landmark decision by Selim offended the theological establishment in Istanbul for whom religious affiliation defined moral and legal rights; the janissaries considered it a declaration of war. Their leaders, the four *dahi*, launched a counter-attack against the Christians, unleashing the slaughter of the knezes in 1804. (The *dahi*, strange as it might seem in the light of modern ethnic nationalism, were probably all Slavs themselves: Aganlia had started life as a bargee in

* See chapter 2 for a discussion of the relationship between Muslims and Christians.

Bosnia, while Kućuk-Alija came from Rudnik in the central Serbian region of Šumadija.)

The alliance between the Muslim landlords, the *sipahi*, and their Christian peasantry was strong at first. Indeed, relations between them were much better in the Belgrade *pashalik* than elsewhere in the Ottoman Empire. The Serbs were organized in extended family units, the *zadruga*. A group of families would elect a representative to the *knežina*, a kind of district council that in turn elected the knez or chieftain. The knez dealt with the landlords and Ottoman administrators. This did not amount to political or economic autonomy but it encouraged the development of a tolerably stable agrarian system based on the *sipahi* rights as the owner of a *timar*. On these large estates, the peasants enjoyed hereditary rights and even some protection in law. In exchange, they would render labour services and pay a fixed tax every year. Beyond this, the peasants were at liberty to keep the produce they farmed. This was a relatively enlightened arrangement, even by west European standards.

During the late eighteenth century, however, the *timar* system was eroded by the more ruthless form of estate management known as the *čitluk*, which reduced the peasant to the role of debt-ridden sharecropper. Vuk Karadžić, the father of Serbia's literary revival, who was born in 1787, famously described the *čitluk* as 'the worst Turkish institution in Serbia'. The *sipahi* in the Belgrade *pashalik* sought to retain the *timar* system against the janissaries who began increasing their profits by introducing *čitluks*.

The greed of the janissaries also impinged on the interests of a peasant aristocracy of pig farmers which had emerged among the Serbs during the late eighteenth century. The Belgrade *pashalik* had twice fallen under the control of Austria. The large Serb merchant community in Vojvodina (the mixed Serb/Hungarian province in the Habsburg Empire to the north of Belgrade) was a vital link in establishing this trade and satisfying the Habsburg Empire's insatiable desire for pork. Even after the *pashalik* reverted to Ottoman control in 1791, the pig trade continued to flourish.

The election of the knezes was an egalitarian tradition, but during the eighteenth century a barely perceptible shift saw the wealthier families, especially those associated with pig-farming, assuming the function of the knez in many regions. The knezes were also responsible for tax collection, which could yield attractive profits.

The dispute between the established *sipahi* and arriviste *dahi* was bitter, but it was the Serbian peasantry that bore the brunt of janissarial wrath. The regular weapons searches made by the Muslim police inspectors were often violent. But the *dahi*'s most serious error was the imposition of draconian taxes on livestock, especially swine.

The *dahi* grew anxious as the flow of weapons coming across the Danube from the Habsburg Empire increased. By the end of January 1804, 'cartloads of Christian weapons were reaching Belgrade'.[3] Large numbers of the Serb bandits, the *hajduci*, had served in the Austro-Hungarian army during the Habsburgs' war with Turkey of 1789–92. Contacts between these men and the Habsburg military and police remained close, ensuring logistical support for Serbs at the turn of the century even though the government in Vienna was trying to cut the supply of arms to avoid the accusation that it was interfering in Ottoman affairs.

The *dahi*'s pre-emptive strike did not go entirely according to plan. Although the janissaries succeeded in eliminating between 70 and 120 knezes and hundreds of hapless peasants, a large number of Serb notables escaped. One janissary unit failed to kill Djordje Petrović, or Karadjordje (Black George), who soon assumed military command of the First Serbian Uprising.

A former member of the volunteer Habsburg forces, Karadjordje took to the forests of his native Šumadija on his return from the Austro-Turkish war to become a *hajduk*. He then became one of the most successful pig farmers in the Belgrade *pashalik*. Thanks to his connections in the Austrian Empire, he grew rich, at least by Serbian standards. His profession, his greed, his military skills and his foul temper would all have an impact on the emergence of modern Serbia.

Following the janissaries' attack, the Serbian Uprising assumed the form of a peasant rebellion. Its initial aim was to rid the countryside of the *dahi*'s armed police. Afterwards, the Serbs turned on the janissary strongholds – the fortified towns – a military operation that required much greater coordination. The coalition of the *sipahi* and Christians sought the restoration of imperial authority and a return to the benign rule epitomized by the late Haci Mustafa. From May 1804 to July 1806, the leaders of the Uprising repeatedly petitioned the Sultan, expressing their unquestioning loyalty to the Porte.

*

The *dahi* upset a social order in the Belgrade *pashalik* that had changed little during the previous three centuries. During this time, Christians and Muslims led separate lives, meeting only in the collection of taxes and tributes by the Ottoman ruling classes. The division between the two communities was stark. Almost all the 300,000 or so Serbs in the *pashalik* lived in the countryside whereas the 20,000 Muslim administrators, soldiers and tradesmen inhabited the towns.* Aside from the different ethnic characteristics of Slavs and Muslims, who were mainly Turks, they were each easily identifiable by their dress. The Christians were forbidden to wear brightly coloured clothing, which explains in part why to this day Serb villagers, especially women, prefer long black dresses. To challenge such regulations, the *hajduci* took to wearing blue or green jackets adorned with silver coins. They also rode horses in defiance of the Ottoman rule which denied Christians the right to mount 'horses or dromedaries'.

Life in the villages was generally well ordered, patriarchal and monotonous. Men went out to work, while women stayed at home, although they were required to help in the fields at harvest time. The *zadruge* consisted of extended families who would share a central room used for work and recreation, with sleeping chambers leading off on all sides. Family ties were at the heart of Serbian society and the peasantry would be loath to break up a *zadruga* even when it became crowded, preferring to expand their dwellings so that it was 'not unusual for one house to form an entire street'.[4] The great nineteenth-century German historian of the Serbs, Leopold Ranke, summed up the central role of the family by noting how these households, 'supplying all their own wants, and shut up each within itself – a state of things which was continued under the Turks, because the taxes were chiefly levied upon the households – formed the basis of Servian nationality. Individual interest was thus merged, as it were, in that of the family'.[5]

Aside from marriage, Serbs could enter into a familial relationship

* While this pattern is now barely visible in Serbia, it was a central feature of the war in Bosnia-Hercegovina which began in 1992. The strategy pursued by the rural Serbs of besieging towns where Bosnian Muslims were concentrated, and then expelling or murdering the population once the defences were breached, was identical to that developed by Karadjordje in the First Serbian Uprising.

in two other ways. Most important was the institution of the *kum*, whose first function was as the bride or groom's personal witness at the wedding. The *kum* immediately became an integral part of the new family and assumed special duties as a protector of the family's interests. The betrayal of *kumstvo* was an unpardonable sin.

Slightly less authoritative a bond than *kumstvo*, but imbued with mystical properties for obvious reasons, was the forging of blood brotherhood. This involved the actual exchange of blood (usually from the wrists) of two friends whose relationship was thus transformed. Like *kumstvo*, the blood brotherhood could be found throughout the Balkan peninsula in both Christian and Muslim communities (it was not, however, common among the ruling Turks). The vendetta and blood feud, however, which were common in the southern Balkans, were rare in the Belgrade *pashaliks*. Here, the Christian peasants were poor, but they enjoyed a relatively stable social and political organization, partly for geographical reasons. The blood feuds of Montenegro, Albania and Greece prevailed in mountainous areas dominated by pastoral farming. The *zadruge* and the *knežine* of the Šumadija, the forest land of central Serbia, provided a framework for the arbitration of disputes. An additional disincentive to taking the law into one's own hand was the hefty blood tax imposed by the Turkish authorities when a Christian murdered another Christian (murdering a Muslim brought swift and nasty capital punishment). Life was relatively less violent in the Belgrade *pashalik* than it was in some of the more remote areas of the Ottoman Balkans.

Above all, the *zadruga* preserved the social and cultural traditions of the Serbs and did so more effectively than the Orthodox Church. The Church is often erroneously assumed to have been the sole bearer of Serbian identity during the three and a half centuries of Ottoman rule that separated the collapse of the medieval Serbian empire and the First Serbian Uprising of 1804. In fact, its role was limited, especially since it did not use the vernacular but Slaveno-Serbian, a variation of Old Church Slavonic that none of the illiterate peasantry understood. The monasteries could at least lay claim to the guardianship of the iconic traditions of the medieval Serbian empire. But the senior hierarchy had been dominated by Greeks since the abolition of the Serb patriarchate in 1776, and the Greek hierarchy increased the alienation of Serbs from the official

Church. During the First Serbian Uprising, the bishops, who were trapped in the besieged towns, supported the Turkish authorities, thus deepening resentment among Serbs.

The local priests in the *pashalik* were often uneducated appendages to the *zadruge* and *kneževine*, doing little more than officiate at weddings, funerals and baptisms. They were usually appointed by the local knezes to whom they owed what standing they had. They exerted little doctrinal influence on the peasantry, if indeed they had the slightest understanding of doctrine themselves.

The most highly developed cultural form among the Serbs was the epic poem. Sung or recited by itinerant performers and shunned by the Church, the poems dwelt on the great themes of Serbia's pre-Ottoman history. The stories about the Serbian defeat at the battle of Kosovo Polje of 1389 and other events from the medieval period became the cornerstone of modern Serbia's national mythology. (Kosovo Polje is frequently presented as the end of the Serbian medieval empire, its army vainly defending Christendom. In fact, Serbian power splintered and collapsed gradually over the next sixty years. The fortress of Belgrade did not fall under Ottoman control until the early sixteenth century.) The uprisings at the beginning of the nineteenth century were represented as the revival of the Serbs' struggle against the all-conquering Ottomans at the end of the fourteenth century. Through these poems and songs, modern Serbia claimed a vital continuity with a romanticized past as a means of underscoring its claims to disputed territory. The singers were entertainers, but their tales also encouraged an imagined, mythicized historical consciousness. Rich in natural imagery, most of the songs contained stark moral messages. The epic poem bore evidence of cultural exchange, both in its musical base and as a literary form, especially with the literature of the Bosnian Muslims and to a lesser extent with the more stylized poetry of the Dalmatian coast and other parts of Croatia. The First Serbian Uprising signalled a change in the function of the epic poem. Singers such as the blind Filip Višnić, a Serb from Bosnia, used the medium to record and glorify the achievements of the rebels, most famously in *The Beginning of the Revolt Against the Dahi* which has been taught in Serbian schools ever since.

The Serbian peasantry at the beginning of the century lived, at least by modern standards, in a stable and self-contained society. When the janissaries disturbed it, they provoked a reaction so fierce that it swept away Muslim control of the countryside. By August 1804, the Serb rebels and a large army sent to Bosnia by the Sultan combined to destroy the armed resistance of the janissaries in the fortified towns. But the struggle had aroused new aspirations among the knezes, and in their leader Karadjordje in particular. With 20–30,000 men under arms, the Serbs had transformed themselves into an extraordinary anomaly – a powerful, Christian military force within the boundaries of the Islamic empire, fighting alongside the Sultan's regiments.

Karadjordje's soldiers were not organized as a regular army. They were made up of hundreds of small bands, herded together by the *hajduci* and the knezes, whose first operations involved burning and looting Turkish properties in the countryside and forcing the Turkish populations into the fortified towns. The brutality of this type of warfare was accentuated by the influx of Serb refugees from Bosnia and Vidin who were themselves the victims of reprisals in their home territories. They formed irregular units known as the *beskućnici* (the homeless), who, with nothing left to lose, became ferocious guerrillas.

Discipline was a permanent problem. The Serb commanders had difficulty motivating their irregular troops to sustain the sieges. Many regarded battles as moonlighting, a means of enriching themselves, albeit modestly: 'One man would take a cauldron or something similar as booty, and go off home with it', Vuk Karadžić observed during the siege of Šabac, a pivotal action during the first phase of the Uprising. 'Someone else would capture a cow or mare from the Turks, and take that home; another would buy some of the booty and go away and sell it; yet another would get bored at just sitting with nothing to do, and go off home to reap the corn or look after the rest of the harvesting.'[6]

To counter indiscipline and the reluctance of many peasants to risk their lives and livelihoods by going to war, the rebel leadership opted for coercion. Those who were not for the Uprising were against it, as Prota Matija Nenadović described in his memoirs:

> whatever knez does not stand firm and keep his army together that knez shall die in torments; and whatever soldier shall not be found in his place, that soldier shall be impaled before his

> door. So do not play with your lives; let each who can carry a gun go to his unit . . . Gospodar George* will send his men secretly through the villages and whomsoever they find at home they will kill him and break him on the wheel and burn his house.[7]

In an attempt to forge loyalty and cohesion, Karadjordje and his followers appropriated the symbols and icons of the Serbian medieval empire. In speeches exhorting his followers to battle, he invoked the spirit of Kosovo Polje. He had a seal made, bearing the inscription 'With the mercy of God, Georgije Petrović, [in the name] of all the people of Serbia and Bosnia'. The cross decorated with four Cyrillic Cs – one of the symbols of the medieval Serbian – reappeared together with the double-headed eagle on Karadjordje's coat of arms.

The Serb rebels captured and executed the *dahis* by August 1804. Janissary units resisted for another year while the Sultan became increasingly concerned at the growing strength and independence of the Serb forces. The Sultan insisted on a restoration of his authority but the Serb leaders first demanded guarantees to insure themselves against the return of misrule. By the summer of 1805, Selim decided to deal with the Serbs as rebels, dispatching a large army to Niş where the Serbs won an unexpected victory. Karadjordje and his allies were no longer fighting miscreant janissaries; they were at war with the imperial order.

For the first time in Ottoman history an entire Christian population had risen up against the Sultan. As the military confidence of the Serbs grew, so did their political awareness. The agricultural elite among the Serb rebels, as typified by Karadjordje, gradually encroached on the economic privileges of the Muslim *sipahi*. In petitions to Istanbul, Karadjordje requested that he be recognized as chief of the Serbs with an exclusive right to administer and tax the country. Turks would be permitted to settle only in Belgrade unless they received the express permission of both the nominal Ottoman governor and Karadjordje himself. The customs service and judiciary would be staffed only by Serbs, while the fortresses of the

---

* Karadjordje.

pashalik would be garrisoned by equal numbers of Ottoman and Serb troops.

By the autumn of 1806, the Sultan was prepared to concede almost all the Serbian demands. At this point, however, war broke out between Turkey and Russia. Until then, the outside world had shown little interest in this regional Ottoman dispute. Suddenly, the Serb cause was thrust into the maelstrom of the Napoleonic Wars. This internationalization of a crisis within the Ottoman Empire set the pattern for the next two centuries in the Balkans – great-power politics has almost always decisively influenced the course of state formation. As a recent historian has said:

> The entrenchment of French troops in the western Balkans, the incessant political crises in the Ottoman Empire, the growing intensity of the Austro-Russian rivalry in the Balkans, the intermittent warfare which consumed the energies of France and Russia and the outbreak of protracted hostilities between the Porte and Russia are but a few of the major international developments which directly or indirectly influenced the course of the Serbian insurrection. The Serbs frequently were put in the position of reacting to events over which they had absolutely no control. In a very real sense the fate of the Serbian people was placed in the hand of capricious rulers in the major capitals of Europe.[8]

Napoleon's victorious campaigns against the Third Coalition culminated in the battle of Austerlitz in December 1805. The peace treaty signed later that month in Pressburg (Bratislava) conferred on France the status of an Adriatic power for the first time. Austria was forced to hand over Venice and Istria, as well as the Dalmatian coast, including the bay of Kotor. As a result, Napoleonic expansion began to encroach on the Balkans, bestowing overnight a greater strategic importance on the *pashalik* of Belgrade.

In October 1806, Russia intervened in the Ottoman crisis. St Petersburg was unmoved by the struggle between the Serbs and the Porte – until the actual declaration of war in December 1806, the Russian Foreign Ministry was urging both Karadjordje and Selim to make peace within the framework of Ottoman sovereignty. Instead, the Russians were angered by events in the Danubian Principalities,

Wallachia and Moldavia (roughly, present-day southern and eastern Romania and Moldova), where the Porte had engineered the dismissal of two Greek princes favoured by St Petersburg.

In the struggle for influence between Russia and Turkey in the Balkans during the nineteenth century, the Danubian Principalities played a key role. These border territories of the Ottoman Empire paid tribute to their sovereign, the Sultan, but enjoyed extensive administrative autonomy presided over by two princes. The princes, called *hospodars*, were drawn from the Greek Phanariot community, so-called because they originally hailed from the Phanar district of Constantinople. Elections to the office of Danubian prince were fiercely contested as the post invariably brought its holder rich rewards. Romania's indigenous aristocracy, the boyars, were jealous of the *hospodars*' political monopoly; the peasantry also loathed the Greek princes. Most Wallachians and Moldavians regarded them as self-seeking overlords, no better than the Turks.

Russia's influence in the Principalities grew steadily in the second half of the eighteenth century. In 1774, the Treaty of Kuchuk Kainardji between Russia and Turkey granted St Petersburg an unprecedented role as spiritual protector of the Ottoman Empire's Orthodox subjects, as well as increased diplomatic representation. A close relationship developed between the Russian Foreign Ministry and the princes of Wallachia and Moldavia. The Treaty of Iaşi (now in north-eastern Romania) in 1792 then gave Russia control of the territory between the Bug and Dniestr rivers (now in southern Ukraine), thus bringing the Ottoman and Russian empires face to face in the north-eastern corner of the Principalities.

When the Porte replaced the two Russian-backed princes in Wallachia and Moldavia in the autumn of 1806, Tsar Alexander ordered the invasion of the Principalities. In December, the Porte declared war and the Serbs exploited the situation by pressing home their advantage in Belgrade which had been under siege for much of the Uprising. France encouraged the Ottomans to resist both the Serbs and the Russian incursion into the Principalities. The Serbs now found themselves in the middle of a dangerous Balkan sideshow just when Napoleon was planning another major campaign in the main European theatre of war. Karadjordje forged an alliance with St Petersburg – not an unreasonable choice, but henceforth, the success of the uprising was dependent entirely on the presence of Russian troops in the Balkans. By throwing in their lot with the Tsar and declaring their determination to cast off Ottoman domination, they became vulnerable to the fragile position of Russia within the broader context of the Napoleonic Wars.

When the Tsar finally decided to withdraw his forces in 1812 to face the looming threat of Napoleon's Grand Army, it was only a matter of time before the Serbians collapsed under attack from a reinvigorated Ottoman Empire. The end came in the autumn of 1813, when three mighty Ottoman armies converged on the *pashalik*. Karadjordje fled to Austria.

Karadjordje's political authority had been sustained for nine years by military success and Russian support. But his role in the *pashalik* never went unchallenged by other regional strongmen. He had been elected by an assembly of knezes held at Orašac (central Serbia) in the middle of February 1804, following the 'slaughter of the knezes'. Eye-witness accounts suggest that the assembly was a tense theatrical event. Two knezes turned down the leadership of the rebellion before Karadjordje himself rejected the offer twice. He argued that his bad temper rendered him ill-suited for the job as he would order the death of those who crossed him. Apparently this admission made him all the more popular with his fellow chieftains.

Although the Serbs had a large number of men under arms, these were organized in strong regional units whose primary loyalty lay with their local knezes. The strongmen did not challenge Karadjordje's position as supreme military commander, but from the beginning, they resisted his attempts to centralize political and economic power. Jakov Nenadović, who had replaced his brother Aleksander as Valjevo knez following the latter's murder by Mehmed-aga Fočić, told Karadjordje that he was not welcome in western Serbia. Eventually, in 1810, his four main rivals organized a conspiracy and in the same year, Milenko Stojković, who ran both eastern Serbia and an extensive harem, organized a rebellion against Karadjordje. Although no rebellion succeeded during the First Serbian Uprising, Karadjordje never felt safe. None of the Serb leaders was literate and their arguments frequently ended in shooting matches. Karadjordje himself had a terrifying reputation. He justified the warning he issued at the time of his election in Orašac, executing among others his own stepfather and brother, whose body was left hanging in front of Karadjordje's house as an unambiguous reminder to others.

Behind the drama of intrigue, shoot-outs and murder lay a serious struggle concerning the constitutional nature of the Serbian proto-state. Karadjordje wanted to establish a system of monarchical centralism while his baronial opponents were fighting for an oligarchy in which each leader would reign supreme in his own locality. A third, weaker force was made up of tradesmen and intellectuals from Vojvodina in the Habsburg Empire. They argued for an independent judiciary and other institutions to curb the power of both Karadjordje and the regional commanders. The modernizing influence of the Vojvodina Serbs was restricted to the town of Belgrade where their brightest intellect, Dositej Obradović, a writer and educationalist, founded the first Serbian high school in 1808. Karadjordje made sure, however, that their political influence was strictly limited. This was not only because the indigenous Serbs were uninterested in the revolutionary ideas of the Enlightenment fostered by Obradović and his compatriots. The Vojvodina Serbs often alienated the Serbs of the *pashalik* who were risking their lives in armed conflict and had little time for the theorizing of intellectuals. As one of the most important writers on the Balkans has described:

> The transriparian Serbs regarded themselves as distinguished bearers of Western culture, destined to administer the illiterate and 'half-savage barbarians' of the Principality. Dress, language and outlook divided them from the native Serbs. The new 'men of the pen' looked down upon agricultural or manual labour, demurred against teaching their sons a craft or marrying their daughters to a craftsman, and for several years wore 'German' clothes instead of the Serbian national dress. Instead of the 'thee' and 'thou' in the homespun manner of the Principality, they employed the German habit – ridiculous-sounding to Serbian ears – of addressing each other in the third person. Finally, they refused to call Serbians 'brother' in the customary fashion of the patriarchal society in Serbia.[9]

In 1807 the chieftains did bow to pressure from leading Vojvodina Serbs by consenting to a Governing Council. Like the new civilian courts, however, the Council never challenged the authority of the Serb military commanders, especially in time of war. In their own fiefdoms, the chieftains often ruled with unchecked brutality.

The peasantry began to view the squabbling knezes with contempt as having merely usurped the function of the *dahi*. The new elite adopted the dress style of the Turks, donning embroidered green silk and wearing turbans, and extracting profits just as their Turkish predecessors had. Building a strong, stable and balanced state out of such unrefined socio-economic material in a state of permanent warfare was to prove a daunting task.

After the failure of Milenko Stojković's rebellion in 1810, Karadjordje, a year later, engineered what amounted to a constitutional *coup d'état* with tacit Russian support. But his decision to emasculate several of his rivals backfired. The exile or disfranchisement of these chieftains critically weakened the Serbs' ability to resist the Ottoman army after St Petersburg and Istanbul assigned sovereignty over the *pashalik* of Belgrade to the Porte at the Treaty of Bucharest in 1812.

Within a few months, Ottoman forces had overrun the territory and many of the leaders of the Uprising had fled to Austria. The first attempt to build a Serbian state had foundered on a conflict between centralism and regional particularism. This would be a recurring problem for state-builders throughout the Balkans.

The Christian peasants of the Belgrade *pashalık* fought courageously when they could no longer tolerate the oppressive regime of the *dahi*. Despite the remarkable achievement of Karadjordje and his forces, the Uprising exposed the difficulties facing the backward and illiterate Christian communities of the Empire as they tried to invent new constitutional arrangements to replace the Sultan's waning power.

The final defeat of the First Serbian Uprising was signalled by Karadjordje's flight to Austria on 3 October 1813. Those of his peers who stayed in the *pashalik* were determined to make capital out of this apparent act of cowardice. At first the new Governor, Süleyman Paşa, favoured reconciliation with the Serbs. With the exception of the most wanted chieftains, a general amnesty was granted, and many thousands of peasants who had fled from the Ottoman army returned. But Süleyman then ordered the reimposition of a harsh feudal regime. Opposition to these measures soon grew among a Serbian peasantry that had developed new aspirations since 1804. The Governor's attitude hardened and by the spring of 1814 the bad old days seemed to have returned:

> Men were roasted alive, hanged by their feet over smoking straw until they asphyxiated, castrated, crushed with stones, and bastinadoed. Their women and children were raped and sometimes taken by force to harems . . . Outside Stambul Gate in Belgrade, there were always on view the corpses of impaled Serbs being gnawed by packs of dogs.[10]

So vindictive was the restoration of the Porte's authority that within two years the Serbs launched the Second Serbian Uprising in 1815 under the leadership of Miloš Obrenović. The younger brother of one of Karadjordje's fiercest rivals, Miloš was, like Karadjordje, an illiterate pig farmer. Born into extreme poverty in a village near Užice in west-central Serbia, as a teenager he moved east to Rudnik to assist his brother in building up a livestock business. After the death of his brother in 1811, he replaced him as chieftain.

In 1814, assuming that Serbian resistance had been broken, Selim III's successor as Sultan, Mahmud II (1808–39), withdrew most of his army from the *pashalik*. Miloš took advantage of this to launch a new rebellion in spring 1815 and soon the chieftains controlled most of the *pashalik*. Miloš had learnt some important lessons from the course of the First Uprising. His political ambition was identical to Karadjordje's – he sought absolute power over all other Serbs in the Belgrade *pashalik*. But his tactics were very different. In contrast to Karadjordje, he made every effort to avoid sustained military confrontation with the Ottoman armies, putting all his energy into striking a bargain with Istanbul. The agreement reached with the Porte in October 1815 guaranteed Miloš's pre-eminence in Serbia in exchange for loyalty to the Porte. Any attempt by other Serbian chieftains to unseat Miloš was henceforth to be seen as an attack on the Sultan.

In 1817, Karadjordje returned to Serbia in secret. His presence was betrayed to Miloš, who ordered his execution and then sent his rival's head to the Sultan to demonstrate his obeisance. The incident is often cited as an example of the Serbs' fratricidal barbarity, but this interpretation obscures the cold political calculations behind Miloš's action. Karadjordje was sent to Serbia as an agent of the Philiki Etairia (Friendly Society), the Greek revolutionary organization that aimed to destabilize Ottoman Europe in preparation for an armed rebellion. Karadjordje's presence not only threatened the internal stability of the *pashalik*, but his role as a Friendly Society agent could have undermined the entire basis upon which Miloš was building an independent Serbia – in agreement with his unwitting partner, the Sultan himself.

For Miloš was engaged in a complex and clever game. He was steadily chipping away at the foundations of Ottoman power in Serbia by making Istanbul ever more dependent on him economically. By the agreement of October 1815, large parts of the administration of the territory were handed over to Miloš. He used his control of the Serbian economy to buy further political and economic concessions from Istanbul. Within a decade he had become the largest livestock exporter in the province, using his political power to guarantee a virtual monopoly on the trade. He raked off vast sums from the population, having bought the rights to all tax revenue in exchange for a paltry annual tribute to the Sultan. As Miloš became richer, the Porte, engaged in debilitating wars first against the rebellious Greeks and then against Russia, turned to him with ever greater frequency for financial help. By 1830, he bought the right to hereditary rule for his family in perpetuity, an important step forward in the struggle for independence and an even more important step forward for the Obrenović family. When he came to power in 1815, 'Miloš didn't have two pennies to rub together', Vuk Karadžić noted in 1832. 'He has enriched himself to such a degree that . . . he can pay the Sultan a ton of sovereigns for the hereditary principle . . . build palaces all over Serbia, and live like some God on earth.'[11] He had become one of the wealthiest men in Europe.

Although Miloš professed obedience to the Sultan, he maintained close relations with Russia, the official protector of Orthodox interests in Serbia since Miloš's agreement with the Porte in 1815. He also found he could use the relationship to put further political pressure on the Turks. The Russo-Turkish war of 1829 was fought to the east of Serbia in Wallachia, and along the Danube. The fighting cut off the rest of the Ottoman Empire from its main supply of salt in

Wallachia. When Mahmud II asked Miloš to supply the Ottoman armies with grain, he did so in exchange for the exclusive right to import salt from Wallachia into the Empire. Because of his warm relations with Russia, he was permitted to load the barges that had carried grain to the Ottoman armies with salt from behind Russian lines for the return journey. This economic arrangement, which benefited both warring parties, permitted Miloš's agents to travel throughout the theatre of war. As an additional favour to St Petersburg, he supplied the Russian army with detailed information about Turkish troop movements. 'In this way, he was able to carry out his obligations to Russia, his protector, and his obligations to Turkey, his suzerain.'[12]

The great loser in Miloš's dazzling diplomatic game was the Serbian peasantry. Although Obrenović's rule restored order throughout the province, he was more systematic in his economic exploitation of the Serbs than the Ottomans had ever been. His reign, which lasted until his abdication in 1839, was punctuated by rebellions. At first these were organized by jealous chieftains like Karadjordje, but increasingly they attracted the support of the peasantry. The latter rose against Miloš for the first time under the leadership not of a chieftain, but of a trader, Miloje Popović Djak:

> Djak's rebellion . . . was a massive demonstration of peasant opposition to a new order that they detested . . . The Serbs were discovering that rule by their own leaders did not in itself bring liberty and well-being. Djak's followers also discovered how weak a popular uprising could be when confronted by the organized power of a centralized state. Nor was the lesson lost on Miloš. As a result of this rebellion he devoted more effort than ever to the organization of a standing army and a larger state apparatus.[13]

This vigilance against the people, the enemy within, was to be a constant preoccupation of Serbian rulers down to the present.

After surviving the Second Serbian Uprising, the Porte had to face rebellion among the Greeks of Thessaly and the Peloponnese. This crisis led to the first major conflict between the great powers after the Congress of Vienna, and drew the excited attention of the most prominent representatives of European Romanticism. It also led to the establishment of the first new nation-state in Europe, albeit under great-power sponsorship, since the French Revolution.

The Greek War of Independence: Greece and the Ottoman Empire, 1821–30

Being Greek at the beginning of the nineteenth century was no simple matter. Greek-speakers were spread across the Ottoman Empire. They lived in the Empire's Near Eastern territories in today's Syria, Lebanon and Israel; they were settled in large areas of Anatolia, especially close to the Black Sea littoral. Istanbul and the west coast of what is now Turkey was teeming with Greek-speakers; Crete and the Peloponnese had large numbers of Muslims whose tongue was Greek. The Greek Phanariot notables were the hereditary administrators of the Danubian provinces, Wallachia and Moldavia. And the uprising of Greeks in 1821 began in what is now Romania.

The Orthodox Church, under the jurisdiction of a patriarch and a largely Greek hierarchy, extended to every corner of the Empire. Until well into the nineteenth century, non-Greek-speaking Orthodox Christians were habitually referred to in all western diplomatic communications and newspapers as 'les Grecs', because they were identified as members of the Orthodox Church, not as separate national groups. To complicate matters further, native Greek-speakers identified themselves as either Christians (Χριστιανοί), Romans (Ρομιοὶ) or Greeks (Γραικοί). It was only at the turn of the century that the word Hellenes (Ἑλλένηδες) rapidly re-established itself after a long absence from active use.

This exceptional diversity gave rise to enormous differences in attitudes and circumstances. A much larger number of Greeks had a stake in the Ottoman Empire, as compared to their Slav co-religionists like the Bulgarians and Serbs. The Greeks of Constantinople were the beneficiaries of a rich cultural tradition associated with the Byzantine Empire. In particular, their skills as linguists afforded them special privileges as dragomans, the official Ottoman interpreters. Over the centuries, the office of chief imperial dragoman, invariably held by a Phanariot Greek, developed into what was effectively a Foreign Ministry. From Selim III's reign onwards, it assumed a real political significance as the consuls of the great powers began to play a greater role in Ottoman politics. Throughout the Greek War of Independence (1821–30), the dragoman of the imperial fleet was a Greek, directing operations against the Greek insurgents. Like the Phanariot princedoms in Wallachia and Moldavia, these offices brought prestige and substantial opportunities for financial gain.

The island Greeks dominated maritime life in the Ottoman Empire. The bulk of the Ottoman military and merchant fleets were manned by Greeks and Albanians. From the seventeenth century onwards, some families built up large private fleets, acquiring considerable fortunes and laying the foundations for the Greek shipping lines of the nineteenth and twentieth centuries. The Turks excluded themselves from trade as it conflicted with both their sense of propriety and their religion; the majority of the Slavs and Romanians were firmly rooted in their modest peasant lives. This left the commercial market in the European part of the Empire open to the talents of Greeks, Jews and Armenians. The island Greeks and the seafarers from the coastal regions were distinguished by their peculiar ethnicity (many were of mixed Albanian-Greek origin); by their dialects and traditions; and above all by their industrious approach to commerce, which encouraged a greater understanding of the outside world than the continental Greeks displayed. Indeed, during the War of Independence, the military, economic and ideological influence of the maritime Greek community was to prove decisive in smashing Ottoman rule.

Greek merchants benefited substantially from the diaspora that stretched deep into the Caucasus, along the Black Sea coast of southern Russia and, in the other direction, through the Venetian territories into western Europe. These émigré communities provided the Greeks of the Empire with economic connections and a cosmopolitan source of knowledge and intelligence. As pressure built up inside the Empire in the first two decades of the nineteenth century, the ideas of the French Revolution affected a much larger and more influential segment of Greeks than could possibly have been the case among the Serbs of the Belgrade *pashalik*.

Of course, peasants as illiterate as their Slav counterparts made up a very large section of Greek society in the Empire. They lived lives of drudgery, generating income for their Turkish and Greek landlords. For many of the so-called notables or primates in the southern Balkans were Greeks who indulged in exploitative tax-farming. Like their Serbian counterparts, they would pay a fixed sum to Istanbul for the right to collect all taxes in a particular area. A notable was free to keep this income, so it was in his interest to extract as much money and as many goods as possible from the villages and towns in his catchment area. Known as the *kocabaşi*, these proto-aristocratic Greeks were deeply resented by the peasantry:

> The khoja-bashi imitated the Turk in everything, including dress, manners, the household. His notion of living in style was the same as the Turk's, and the only difference between them was one of names: for instance, instead of being called Hasan the Khoja-Bashi, he would be called Yianni, and instead of going to mosque he would go to church. This was the only distinction between the two.[14]

When imperial authority began its slow decline in the seventeenth century, the Porte granted ever greater policing powers to local notables. In Bulgaria and Rumelia, lawlessness seriously damaged transport and communications. To combat the problem, Istanbul established the office of the *armatalos* among the Empire's Christian subjects. The *armatoloi* were recruited from local brigand groups and persuaded to exchange their criminal activity for a legal role in the Ottoman state. They received money for guarding roads and policed a number of villages which would also pay the *armatalos* protection money. This encouraged a complex and corrupt network of patronage. Combined with the exactions of the primates, this laid the foundations for a clientelist system that has plagued Greek society for most of its modern history. In the Ottoman Empire, however, the system functioned to the mutual advantage of both peasant and ruler. The chief opponent of the *armatalos* was the brigand, or *klepht*. In character and background, the *armatolos* and *klepht* were indistinguishable and there was a regular exchange of personnel between the two groups. The *klephts* and *armatoloi* were both experienced in small-scale armed warfare.

Following the fall of Selim III in 1806, his two successors, particularly Mahmud II, restricted the authority of the *armatoloi* in an attempt to restore central power. An apparently reasonable strategy, it backfired on two counts. First, it provoked a new wave of men leaving the Sultan's service and taking to the mountains as *klephts*. Second, it bolstered support for Âli Paşa, the Sultan's great enemy in Ioannina, who recruited many disaffected *armatoloi* into his army.

The Orthodox Church was the most important institution defining Greek identity but it was also the most conservative. The extent of Greek influence at the Porte became evident in 1766 and 1777 when the Sultan agreed to close down the autonomous churches of the Serbs and Bulgarians, so that the Greeks dominated not just the Greek-speaking Orthodox Christians but the Slavs as well. As far as the Orthodox Church and the Ottoman state were concerned, religion took precedence over culture in defining one's Greekness.

In addition to the class and cultural differences among the Greek-speakers, different regions had developed distinct traditions by dint of the specific relationship they enjoyed with the Porte. In Rumelia, the collection of mountain villages known as *Agrapha* (Unwritten), for example, were so remote and difficult to subdue that they were not recorded for tax purposes and were more or less untouched by the Ottoman authorities. The Greek notables in the Peloponnese enjoyed extensive autonomy from Istanbul, encouraging administrative skills which were far in advance of those demonstrated by the Rumeliots to the north. Rumelia itself could boast the highest concentration of *armatoloi* and *klephts* and a tradition of guerilla warfare.

Throughout Rumelia, the Peloponnese and the islands, there were large Albanian communities – most of them Orthodox Christians although Muslim Albanians predominated in the Epirot centre of the rebel pasha, Âli Paşa. Many Albanians underwent a process of Hellenization that was accelerated by their participation in the War of Independence. The Koundouriotes, for example, the most powerful maritime family on the island of Hydra, who led a substantial faction during the war, were of Albanian origin.

Many of these Greek-speaking groups had grievances against the Empire. But most also reaped some benefits from their standing in society. The Phanariot Greeks, in particular, were deeply complicit in imperial corruption and resistant to radical change. The imperial Greeks' combination of intellect, wealth and military prowess was of critical value to the insurgents once the rebellion broke out. Yet it frequently complicated matters. The Greeks suffered from the same local particularism that eventually destroyed Karadjordje's leadership of the Serbian Uprising. Theirs was a more challenging ideological struggle than the Serbs', as the Greeks were obliged to address the question of their historical and contemporary identity. For despite their intellectual and social wealth, the Greeks did not know who they were.

In 1814 a group of failed Greek merchants founded a secret society, the Philiki Etairia (Friendly Society), with a simple political objective – 'the liberation of the Motherland'.[15] None of the conspirators had the first idea of the geographical contours of the Motherland, or of who belonged in it. The Society was based not in the Ottoman Empire but in Odessa, the Russian Black Sea port.

The Society's vague goals reflected the uncertain nature of Greek identity. But this uncertainty also allowed it to react quickly to developments, because the Society was not bound by a specific strategy. The Philiki Etairia became an excellent organizer. Its members were imbued with an invigorating Romantic passion but also well disciplined by conspiratorial rules. Within a few years, it had gained adherents throughout the Ottoman Empire and beyond. The majority of its members were Greek-speakers but its pan-Christian sentiment also attracted Russians (many of them working directly on behalf of the Tsar), Romanians, Serbs (Karadjordje, for example, went through the initiation ceremony), Albanians and even some disaffected Turks. Members were sworn to silence about their activity and gradually inducted into a complex hierarchy of secret signals. Any order from the mysterious Arkhi, or chief council, was disseminated in code with a seal displaying sixteen compartments and sixteen sets of initials. Members were forced to place their loyalty above any other tie, including kinship, committing themselves to slaying their closest relative if the Society so ordered. Many of the leaders of the War of Independence were Society initiates. Its first president was Alexander Ypsilantis, a Greek officer from a Phanariot family who was serving in the Russian army. Ypsilantis planned and led the first, disastrous rebellion in the Danubian Principalities.

In the decade prior to the rebellion, many *klephts* sought refuge on Corfu and other Ionian islands, which were at the time under British control. The majority served in British units through which membership of the Society spread rapidly, soon infecting the mainland Peloponnese and Rumelia. The majority of the Peloponnesian clergy joined the Society against the express wishes of the Orthodox hierarchy in Istanbul, which considered the organization subversive and dangerous. The Patriarch, Gregorias V, was not just a stubborn reactionary. With good reason, he feared retaliation against vulnerable Christians in the Ottoman capital if these revolutionary activities gained momentum.

The influence of the Friendly Society reflects a marked difference between the Greek War of Independence and other Balkan rebellions. The Greek rebellions of 1821 were not spontaneous reactions to deteriorating social and economic circumstances, like the First and Second Serbian Uprisings. They were the result of a conscious plan to destabilize the Ottoman Empire.

By 1820, Ali Paşa was no longer able to sit cross-legged because of obesity, but he ruled over *pashaliks* stretching from Elbasan in the north (now in central Albania) to Trikkala to the south of the Pindus mountains. This bizarre individual had come close to establishing his own independent state through a combination of butchery, extortion, an intelligent foreign policy and dynastic manoeuvring. Notwithstanding his use of terror, he also attracted a loyal following among his Ottoman subjects by dint of shrewd clientelist politics.

His political base was more diverse than his reputation for despotism would suggest. Although an Ottoman official, he never learnt more than a few words of Turkish, but was fluent in Greek and his native Albanian. Throughout his career, he demonstrated great skill in playing off the religious and class differences among his subjects and enemies against one another. Until the Greek rebellion launched by the Philiki Etairia in March 1821, Mahmud II, who had succeeded Selim III in 1806, and the Porte administration had dismissed the organization as inconsequential. According to them, the chief obstacle preventing the restoration of Ottoman authority in the Balkans was Ali Paşa. In contrast, Ali had realized the significance of the Greek revolutionary movement and had begun to explore possible cooperation with it. As the Sultan advanced preparations for a frontal assault on Ali's stronghold in the town of Ioannina in southern Epirus, the Pasha underwent an opportunistic conversion to Hellenism. 'The Greek revolution', one historian has noted, 'broke out because the Ottomans mistakenly decided to humble the one man – Ali Pasha – who could have prevented it.'[16]

In the early spring of 1820, some 20,000 Ottoman troops assembled before Ioannina. Bolstered by a growing number of Greek *armatoloi*, Ali's forces offered tenacious resistance and held out until the following winter. The failure of the Ottoman commander prompted Mahmud to send garrisons from the Peloponnese northwards to Ali's stronghold. Meanwhile, the leader of the Friendly Society, Alexander Ypsilantis, launched his disastrous uprising in the Danubian Principalities on 6 March 1821, by crossing the River Pruth from Russian territory. Three weeks later, the Greeks of the Peloponnese, exploiting the absence of the Ottoman garrisons, raised the revolt. The Greek War of Independence had begun.

The Ottoman Empire exploded. In Istanbul, Mahmud II accused Patriarch Gregorias of failing to restrain the Orthodox population in the Danubian Principalities, the Peloponnese, Rumelia, Macedonia and Thrace. In early April, the janissaries and the Turkish mob were let loose on the city's Greek population. Robert Walsh, the chaplain to the British Embassy, witnessed how a young man 'was forced upon his knees by two Turks pressing on his shoulders, and in that position a third came behind him with his kinshal . . . With a single horizontal stroke he severed his head from his neck; his body was thrown into the puddle in the middle of the street for passengers to trample on, and his head was laid contemptuously between his thighs. The executioners then hastily passed on, leaving both to be torn by the dogs who were gathering around'. On Palm Sunday, in a desperate attempt to halt the atrocities, Gregorias announced the excommunication of all Greeks rebelling against the Ottoman state. This did not satisfy Mahmud, and six days later the Patriarch was seized by a group of Ottoman police while celebrating Mass and hanged from the gate of the Phanar. The killing of Gregorias was the start of a murderous purge of the Orthodox hierarchy in several parts of the Empire. In Smyrna, the Greek population was decimated by the mob, which also slaughtered the city's chief mullah and several Turkish notables when they attempted to intervene to save the Christians.

In the Peloponnese and Rumelia, meanwhile, a reciprocal orgy of violence had broken out. The Greek insurgents, who outnumbered the local Muslim population* by a ratio of ten to one, embarked upon a series of uncontrolled massacres; tens of thousands of Muslims died. This campaign culminated in the sacking of the main fortified town in the Peloponnese, Tripolis. George Finlay, the first great historian of modern Greece and a committed philhellene, was nonetheless appalled by the behaviour of the Greek rebels:

> Human beings can rarely have perpetrated so many deeds of cruelty on an equal number of their fellow-creatures as were perpetrated on this occasion . . . Women and children were frequently tortured before they were murdered. After the Greeks had been in possession of the city for forty-eight hours, they deliberately collected together about two thousand persons of every age and sex, but principally women and children, and led them to a ravine in the nearest mountain where they murdered every soul.[17]

These outbursts of extreme violence were not restricted to intercommunal fighting. The weakness of the Ottoman forces in the Peloponnese, in particular, but also in parts of Rumelia, led to a power vacuum that sucked the rebels into a disastrous internecine struggle. The extreme diversity of interests among the Greeks was accentuated by the vagueness of the uprising's goals. To be sure, there was the common cause of removing the Ottomans; but once this had been achieved, there was no clear vision of what should take the Empire's place. Ironically, this civil conflict was alleviated by the swift defeat of the rebellion in Thrace and Macedonia.

To the north of the Peloponnese and Rumelia, Ali's defences in Epirus were finally breached in February 1822. He met his death at the hands of a fellow vizier. It had taken almost two years of bitter struggle to remove one of the most extraordinary figures of the Ottoman Empire. But the political costs of the Sultan's victory were high. The Peloponnese, the three islands of Hydra, Spetsai and Psara, and Crete had been liberated from Ottoman rule as had large parts of Rumelia in continental Greece. In addition, the *klephtic*

---

* The majority Ottoman population in the Peloponnese and Crete were Greeks who had converted to Islam. Their mother tongue was Greek.

and *armatolic* warriors had full or partial control over the strategic passes, Mikronos in the west and Thermopyles in the east.

Rebel authority was steadily eroded in Rumelia by the military advances of the Turks, which culminated in 1824 in the siege of Missolonghi, during which Lord Byron died of tuberculosis. But the Peloponnese, which enjoyed the naval protection provided by the islanders, was to remain in Greek hands until early 1825, when Ibrahim Paşa, the son of Mehmed Paşa of Egypt, landed with a crack force at Methóui in the south-west of the peninsula.

Between 1822 and 1825, the enormity of the task facing the Greeks in their aim of establishing an independent state revealed itself. The liberated areas slid into the quagmire of civil war. The illusions of Greek émigrés and of the growing number of Philhellenes arriving from Britain, France, Germany, Italy and the United States were often rudely shattered by the struggle between the competing factions.

The divisions stemmed from regional differences among the Peloponnese, the islands and Rumelia, although power bases also emerged in both eastern and western Rumelia. Very soon after the outbreak of revolution, three representative bodies emerged: the first was the council of primates in the Peloponnese, which was able to adapt existing power structures to secure the privileges they enjoyed under the Ottomans. The second, based at Missolonghi in western Rumelia, was the fiefdom of Alexander Mavrokordatos, a Phanariot Greek who had arrived there from the Danubian Principalities. Another Phanariot, Theodore Negris, established a council in eastern Rumelia. But within each geographical area, there were numerous other conflicts, some of them microscopic, others with far-reaching implications for the course of the Greek struggle. The tendency of the divisions to overlap makes it difficult to align the regional differences with the social and ideological splits separating the fighters. For the purposes of tracing an embryonic Greek national consciousness, however, it is important to focus on two aspects of the crisis.

The most significant operational dispute was the gulf separating the engine of the revolution, the *klephtic* and *armatolik* military leaders known as the *kapoi*, and the civilian leadership, whether primates or Phanariots. The primary concern of the *kapoi*, beyond the defeat of the Turks, was the consolidation and expansion of their local power. The *kapoi* had the vaguest notion of a Greek national identity and certainly no concept of a nation state. The *klephts* and the peasantry made up less than 10 per cent of the membership of the Philiki Etairia, even though they comprised the bulk of the population where the revolution actually succeeded. The main insurgent force was thus far removed from the conspiracy that had inspired the war. The *kapoi* were a long way, too, from the image of romantic heroes imposed on them by later Greek writers and historians. 'The ordinary klepht was a wretched and hunted fugitive of law seeking temporary refuge in the klephtic band',[18] a revisionist Greek historian has written; the *klephts* were ready to dispense their own rough justice on rich Turks and Greek primates, but equally given to preying on the miserable Christian peasantry.

Having played the leading role in the massacre, expulsion and plundering of the Turks, the *kapoi* resumed a life of banditry or established local fiefdoms which they guarded jealously against rival colleagues and against any encroachment from the emerging regional governments in the Peloponnese or Rumelia. They wanted simply to take the place of the Turks or the Greek primates. The institutions of the Ottoman Empire – the pashas, the agas and the tax farmers – represented an immutable order for these largely uneducated men, especially those ignorant of the ideology unleashed on Europe by the French Revolution. They were equally unaware of the Hellenic revival inspired by the Greek diaspora and fostered by the philhellenes. The eighteenth-century Greek scholar, Koumas, tells of a visit he made to one of the most influential *klephts*, Nikotsaras. In order to show respect, Koumas addressed the *klephtic* leader as Achilles. Nikotsaras retorted angrily: 'What rubbish are you talking about? Who is this Achilles? Handy with a musket, was he?'[19]

The bands were dependent on the flocks of goats and sheep which they tended and these herds were often the cause of serious skirmishes between various militia groups. The strength of each group depended on the ability of its leader to sustain its warriors and expand their numbers. One frequent method of recruiting new members was to operate a scorched-earth policy, depriving the peasantry of their livelihood and forcing the menfolk to join the band.

This fusion of terrorism and guerrilla warfare could operate on very different scales. A village, for example, might fend off marauders, especially when the villagers could use the mountains for cover. At the other extreme, men like Teodoros Kolokotrones or Petrobey, the leader of the feared Mavromichalis clan which controlled most of the isthmus of the Mani, could deploy hundreds or thousands of irregulars. Their tactics led to severe economic disruption in the regions under Greek control, especially in the production of food. Travelling across the Peloponnese in 1823, two British philhellenes, Edward John Trelawny and J. Hamilton Brown, recorded how there was 'scarcely a vestige of habitation or cultivation'. Now and then, they would encounter a shepherd tending a small, emaciated herd of sheep or goats. Beyond Tripolis, instead of grazing land they found grouped 'in a narrow space, five thousand or more skeletons of men, horses, mules and camels: vultures had eaten the flesh and the sun had bleached the bones'.[20] In 1825, the Sultan dispatched Ibrahim Paşa's army to crush the rebellion in a country already devastated by *klephtic* warfare.

The unsophisticated *kapoi* mirrored the political primitivism of Karadjordje and the *hajduk* armies of the Serbian uprisings. However, the Greek notables and intelligentsia were a more powerful force than their Serbian equivalents. They acted as a serious counterweight to the peasant military leadership. This had a paradoxical impact: on the one hand it deepened the rifts which plagued the Greek side in the war, but it also helped push the Greek revolutionary struggle beyond the confines that had hemmed in the Serbian insurgents and towards the formation of a nation state.

The second significant factor dividing the insurgents was cultural. This was the schizophrenia of the Greek heritage: oriental and byzantine on the one hand; occidental and romantic-revolutionary on the other. Each Greek would tend towards one of two different worlds although between the illiterate *klepht* and the French-educated revolutionary there was a large, less clearly defined population. Many contemporary observers dismissed all Greeks as stubbornly anti-western in the patronizing, oversimplified fashion that has become a hallmark of Anglo-Saxon commentary on the Balkans in the past two centuries. Here is William Mure, writing in 1842: 'Politically speaking the Greeks were Asiatics, and all their oriental ideas, whether social or political, required to be corrected or eradicated, before they could be expected to form a civilized people upon civilized European principles.'[21]

Naturally, many travellers and philhellenes were shocked at the Greeks' lack of sophistication, and the absence of a physical resemblance to the Hellenes of their classical imagination. 'All came expecting to find the Peloponnesus filled with Plutarch's men', Colonel Leicester Stanhope explained, 'and all returned thinking the inhabitants of Newgate more moral'.[22] Yet Stanhope and the others failed to notice the steady erosion of backward social and political attitudes under the influence of the Greek diaspora. No other Christian nation in the Balkans could compete with the intellectual and mercantile resources at the disposal of the Greeks. Greek books and schools had proliferated across the Ottoman Empire; while there were but timid literary stirrings among the Slavs and Albanians. Byron remarked in 1811 that 'it is impossible to discover any nation with so great a proportion of books and their authors as the Greeks of the present century'.[23] Greek students and printing presses were to be found well beyond the borders of the Empire – in Padua, Paris, Venice and Vienna. The sailors of the Greek fleets had often acquired foreign languages. Due to the Russian, French and British influence in the Ionian islands, many refugees from Ali Paşa's rule and from the Empire itself had come into contact with modern military techniques. After the rebellions broke out, many educated Greeks headed for the Peloponnese and Rumelia. Three of the most influential leaders to emerge were Phanariots – Mavrokordatos, Negris and Demetrios Ypsilantis. Due to the conservatism of both the primates and the *kapoi*, such educated, well-organized outsiders, had an opportunity to promote Enlightenment ideas.

They did, of course, meet resistance. The westernizers wanted four things: a written constitution; a secular state; a codified judicial system; and a regular army. All these threatened the vital interests of three groups: the Church; the primates; and the *klephts*. This common interest acted as a brake on the economic and social forces driving these three groups apart. To this must be added a powerful, indignant xenophobia among the peasantry, and confusion among the westernizers as to how they might achieve their aims. Under such conditions, the task of directing the independence war away from a peasant rebellion with fratricidal undertones, and towards the creation of a functioning republic, appeared formidable. What force would be powerful enough to turn the Greek insurgents into heralds of modern European nationalism?

The event that secured the ultimate success of the Greek War of Independence was the battle of Navarino on 20 October 1827. The destruction of the Ottoman fleet, anchored in a bay in the south-western corner of the Peloponnese, left Ibrahim Paşa in an unwinnable military situation. The support of the British, French and Russian navies for the Greek insurgents violated the Treaty of London of July 1827 by which the three great powers had committed themselves to securing an armistice between the Ottomans and the Greeks 'without taking part in the hostilities between the contending parties'. Egged on by the philhellenic sentiments of Stratford Canning, the British consul in Istanbul, Vice-Admiral Sir Edward Codrington, the commander-in-chief of the British fleet in the Mediterranean to whom the French and Russian commanders were subordinated, had little choice but to use his guns when Ibrahim Paşa and the Sultan refused to implement the Treaty. In three and a half hours of a 'hard pounding, gentlemen',[24] as the Duke of Wellington later put it, Ottoman naval power was brought to an abrupt end, and with it effective control over a large swathe of the Empire's original European territories.

The finest hour of the philhellenic movement, it would seem, had come. This was surely a noble culmination of the selfless toiling by hundreds of young idealists who had forsaken the comforts of home to revitalize the corrupted Greek nation with the forgotten spirit of Hellenism; and to expose the indifference of their own governments to the suffering of the Greeks. Had their heroism and their moving appeals not finally persuaded cynical governments to act? Was not the battle of Navarino the final admission of the three great European powers that they could no longer stand by as the despotic Turk oppressed a Christian nation?

Until well into the twentieth century, this was how the philhellenic intervention in the Greek War of Independence was understood, obscuring both the real nature of that intervention and the key role played by a single section of Greek society. In fact, the philhellenes' contribution to the Greek cause was questionable. Just five months before the battle of Navarino, Lord Cochrane, more a mercenary than a professed philhellene, almost wrecked the Greeks' military prospects in a campaign which resulted in the loss of the Acropolis to the Turks. Most of the philhellenes' activity was characterized by incompetence, personal greed and witless pontificating. All observers, Greek and non-Greek, exempt Lord Byron from this criticism. Aside from the fact that Byron was in a league of his own as a writer and poet, he demonstrated a rare understanding of the complexity of the Greeks' nascent modern nationalism and the problems of identity associated with it. Byron did not expect the Greeks to conform to a mythical image of antiquity. He was open in his disgust at Greek treatment of Turkish prisoners, particularly during the siege of Missolonghi. He was also adamant that the Greeks would have to solve their internal disputes before they could expect any substantial aid from outside. He had understood, however, that Turkish rule over parts of Greece was no longer viable.

In the five months which he spent on the Ionian island of Kefalonia before his final journey to Missolonghi in late 1823, Byron was inundated with requests from the leaders of the various Greek factions, who were about to plunge into civil war, to give his support to their particular cause. Some factions, like the Souliots and the Mavromichalis clan from the Mani, merely wanted to get their hands on his money, but most considered the approval of the legendary 'Veeron', as they called him, to be of great symbolic significance.

Byron's death inspired a wave of sympathy both for his contribution to the liberation of Greece but also for the Greek cause itself. The tributes paid to him by politicians and literary figures throughout Europe galvanized the flagging cause of philhellenism, pressuring the British government in particular to adopt the more interventionist stance that eventually culminated in Navarino. Byron's influence was significant in a further respect. His support for the London Greek Committee, which was formed in March 1823 and included a large number of prominent public figures, provided a link between the Greek westernizers and British reformers and radicals, whose politics was henceforth partly defined by solidarity with the Greeks. But the London Greek Committee was formed long after similar bodies in several major European cities, and it was a poor fundraiser – within six months of the American Committee's foundation, the city of New York alone secured more money than the London Committee had raised in a year and a half.

The motives of the most active members of the London Committee were pragmatic. Some, like the philosopher, Jeremy Bentham, and the economist, David Ricardo, were clearly convinced of the justice of the Greek cause, but a majority of members saw the Committee merely as a way of embarrassing the British government. Given that only five of the first eighty-five members had been to Greece and that most of the others demonstrated no particular knowledge of the Greek struggle, it has reasonably been argued that most of the Committee were simply involved in furthering their political ambitions in England.[25] The Committee distinguished itself in two respects – it was the motor behind the international loan, initially suggested by Byron, which was raised on behalf of Greece's revolutionary government. In addition, it persuaded the British government in 1823 to respect the blockade that the insurgent naval force had imposed on Turkish supplies to its army in Greece. This conferred *de facto* recognition on the insurgents as legitimate combatants. The loan also established Greece as an independent international subject, ensuring that Britain, France and Russia would eventually intervene, however reluctantly, in a dispute that began the break-up of the Ottoman Empire. The Eastern Question was no longer a hypothesis. A grand rehearsal for one of the great nineteenth-century power games had begun.

All the European powers had shunned the Greek war when it first erupted. In 1820, rebellions in Spain and Naples had disturbed the symmetry of the European concert, composed in Vienna in 1815. Having expended so much military and diplomatic energy on restoring a reactionary balance of power, the allies who had defeated Napoleon had no wish to see it unsettled by the impetuous Christians of the Ottoman Empire. The British government was especially unwilling to aid the Greeks until the battle of Navarino. (The Duke of Wellington, appointed Prime Minister immediately after the battle, was infuriated by Vice-Admiral Cochrane's action at Navarino and never let the commander forget it.) Britain's commitment to the Ottoman Empire was born of fear of Russian expansionism, which might disturb Britain's trade routes to the East. In addition, several members of the London Greek Committee were successful merchant adventurers who had made substantial fortunes trading with the colonies. In their judgement, the emerging Greek state was set to become the most influential maritime force in the Mediterranean, and so they considered support for the Greeks a sound business investment.

This highlighted an aspect of the Greek War of Independence that has not always been given due weight – the importance of the maritime Greeks. Time and again, the navy of the three islands, Hydra, Spetsai and Psará, saved the Greek rebellion when it teetered on the brink of collapse – either because of Ibrahim Paşa's superiority on land or because of the internecine struggles on the mainland. The tactical ingenuity of the Hydriot naval leadership when engaging the better-equipped vessels of the Ottoman fleet was remarkable. Although Spetsai and Psará both fell in 1826, Hydra remained unconquered throughout the war. The Greek maritime families played a key economic role as well. Profits from their commercial and piratical activities financed the war effort when the mainland population was no longer able to feed itself. The maritime force also provided intelligence from abroad as well as maintaining links with the diaspora and sympathizers in the rest of Europe. The authoritative historian of early modern Greece, John Petropoulos, has written that 'without their naval and financial contribution, the Revolution could not have succeeded'.[26] Although the three great powers were the guarantors of the Greeks' final success, they would not have become involved in the first place had the Greek islanders not sustained the struggle for as long as they did.

Navarino may have won the war for the Greeks, but it did not solve their political problems. For now, in addition to the regional, social, personal and philosophical splits among them, they were also burdened by a new crisis, encapsulated in the names of three groupings, the 'English', 'French' and 'Russian' parties. For some time, the various factions had been courting and been courted by London, Paris and St Petersburg in a struggle for influence in the new Greece. In February 1830, the three foreign mentors established an 'independent' Greece at the London Conference. The new state, although it was obliged to pay Istanbul an indemnity, would rely on the guarantee of the three contracting powers, who had still to define the borders of Greece and elect a monarch. There were no Greek representatives at the London Conference and the country's leaders were not consulted about the Treaty. The constitutional heart of the new state was non-Greek, an ominous beginning that would have far-reaching consequences. The reliance of domestic parties on competing foreign powers has remained a congenital weakness of Greek politics. It also set a dispiriting precedent for other Balkan nationalisms as they emerged during the nineteenth and twentieth centuries – success was only guaranteed if a powerful foreign sponsor could be found. In the absence of consensus within a particular national group as to which power should play that role, domestic strife and, on occasion, civil war have followed.

The civil strife that engulfed Greece at its birth in 1830 and degenerated into civil war after the murder of the country's first President, Ioannis Kapodistrias, was an early and violent example of this tendency. After Navarino, Kapodistrias, a Greek nobleman who had served for many years as Russia's Deputy Foreign Minister, embarked on a programme of centralizing political power with the aim of lending some coherence to the new state. His motives were sound: the country was devastated and needed political stability if it was to carry any credibility in the outside world. Kapodistrias, however, was accustomed to the delicate intrigues of the Vienna Congress and not the more brutal world of the Peloponnesian vendetta. Although he attempted to integrate the various factions into his system of authoritarian government, he underestimated the strength of particularism. All sides distinguished themselves by their appalling behaviour. The Hydriots, who had excelled themselves during the war, mounted an insurrection in August 1831 so bitter that they preferred to scuttle their entire fleet, the only real source of independent Greek power, rather than see it come under central government control. By imprisoning Petrobey, the Maniot leader of the Mavromichalis family, Kapodistrias sealed his own fate. The President was shot dead in October 1831 while leaving the church in Greece's first capital, the pretty harbour town of Nauplio.

The civil war that followed the assassination and ended in 1834 has been described as 'the longest and most damaging of any yet known in Greece'.[27] It was cynically exploited by the great powers vying for greater influence in their newly born protectorate. The immaturity of Greek political consciousness was demonstrated by the willingness with which the political factions subordinated national interests to those of their foreign patrons. The bloodshed ended when the Russians, French and British agreed to impose on the Greeks the young Bavarian prince, Otto (1832–62), son of the philhellenic Ludwig. He would guarantee the controlling interest of the great powers over the young state. The autocratic Bavarian bureaucracy he brought with him was determined to impose its will on the factions. But the formally liberal constitution failed to diminish the jealous traditions of clientelism. 'The grafting of the forms, but not the substance, of western constitutional government onto an essentially traditional society', Richard Clogg has remarked, 'was to create within Greece a fundamental political tension that has continued for much of its post-independence history.'[28]

The First Serbian Uprising began over half a century before the unification of Italy; the first modern Greek state was proclaimed forty years before the unification of Germany. But the national identities of Serbs and Greeks were ill-defined. Both national movements owed their success more to Ottoman decay than to their own inherent strength. To compensate for their political and economic weakness, the national elites sought support for their aspirations from the European powers. Herein lies the start of the Balkan tragedy – these were peasant societies poorly equipped to assimilate the ideas of the Enlightenment, and located at the intersection of competing absolutist empires. The result was a stunted constitutional development whose shortcomings would inevitably be exploited by the great powers as competition between them intensified in the region in the second half of the nineteenth century.

Two faiths, one blood: Croatia, Vojvodina, Austria, Hungary, 1848

On 5 June 1848, excited crowds lined the streets leading to Zagreb's baroque town centre to cheer the entrance of Baron Josip Jelačić of Bužim. They had high expectations of this respected commander of the imperial forces which were stationed in the Banija region of the Habsburg's Military Frontier Zone, thirty miles south of the Croatian capital. Since Kaiser Ferdinand had appointed him two months earlier, Baron Jelačić had stiffened the resolve of Croatia's growing national movement by issuing a forcefully worded proclamation: 'Until the parliament of the united Croatian kingdom meets, every region and every district should administer its own affairs. They shall accept official orders from nobody and from nowhere but from me, His Majesty's representative.'[29] At last, his supporters thought, a leader with imperial authority and military power had rejected the pretensions of the Hungarian national movement. In March 1848, a new, revolutionary Hungarian government had effectively thrown off the rule of the Kaiser in Vienna. Since then, it had strengthened its control throughout the Hungarian crown lands of St Stephen, including Croatia and Slavonia. Jelačić, as the Kaiser's Viceroy (or Ban) and as the political embodiment of the Croatian cultural awakening, was determined to resist the Hungarian programme.

Mounted on a tall white horse, Jelačić was dressed in a white braided waistcoat, a thick red overcoat, blue breeches, short Croatian boots and a Turkish sabre tied by a silken sash. For the ceremonial installation of the new Viceroy of Dalmatia, Croatia and Slavonia, Imperial Adviser, Field Marshal and General Commander in Croatia, the recently invigorated Croatian parliament was meeting under a pavilion on Catherine Square. As Jelačić took the oath, he held the hand of the Patriarch of Sremski Karlovci in Vojvodina, Josip Rajačić, the highest spiritual dignitary of the Serbs in the Austro-Hungarian Empire. Rajačić had been invited to the ceremony at the express wish of Jelačić. In order to underline his commitment to the 'single-blooded nation of two faiths', Jelačić celebrated his investiture first with a Holy Catholic Mass and then with a service of thanks in the Orthodox Church.

In a memorable address, Jelačić, flushed with the spirit of revolution and liberalism, occasionally broke from the text prepared by Ivan Mažuranić, to the delight of the assembled deputies:

> Our homeland has had its heroic and celebrated Viceroys. History has testified to this and now I testify to it. But I doubt that any Viceroy was more joyous than I . . . Brothers! Freedom has become the truth; for can anyone now doubt that freedom is not our property? . . . For let any danger descend, the whole nation will be one hand, one heart and one invincible hero . . . [I] am obliged to tell and warn you that with regard to our relations with Hungary we stand by the principle of an alliance with the king of Hungary . . . But in the unhappy case that the Hungarians continue to prove them-

> selves to act not as brothers to us and our people in Hungary but as oppressors, let them know . . . that we are ready with sword in hand![30]

The Viceroy was lifted high by the delirious crowd. The same honour was extended to the Serb, Rajačić. In a matter of months, Jelačić had been transformed from middle-ranking officer in the Military Frontier to a beacon of hope, not just for Croats but for many Serbs as well. 'In those days', one of Jelačić's closest confidantes recorded,

> Zagreb looked just like an eastern city for you could not only see Croatian national dress but Serbian and Turkish as well. St. Mark's Square and the gates of the Viceroy's palace were permanently full of deputations from all corners of the land, from Bosnia, from Bulgaria and from the other Slav regions of Austria. They all came to greet the beloved popular Viceroy. Prince Petar Petrović II sent the Viceroy two Montenegrin senators and offered to supply him with weaponry. Because all awaited an armed march on Hungary.[31]

On his deathbed, Jelačić spoke of that period: 'the Slav peoples expected me all the way to Istanbul'. Almost half a century after the outbreak of the First Serbian Uprising, the Croats had risen against their Hungarian overlords in their own right but also in the name of their fellow Slavs, in particular the Serbs.

Modern nationalism in Croatia and Slovenia emerged from a curious sideshow of the Napoleonic Wars. In 1809, Napoleon created the 'Illyrian Provinces' from territory ceded by the Austrians. This French foothold in the far western Balkans comprised a part of Slovenia, a part of Croatia, a part of the Military Frontier* and Dalmatia. Napoleon introduced the legal code and administrative practices of the French Republic into the Provinces. This gave the Croats and Slovenes first-hand experience of the new economic and

---

* This special militarized zone stretched from southern Croatia in the west as far as Transylvania in the east. It was governed directly by Vienna and policed by garrisons who could both defend the Austro-Hungarian Empire from attack by the Ottomans and operate as an offensive force.

political liberties that had inspired western Europe. In addition, the French allowed people to use the Slovene and Croatian languages (for official purposes the language of political communication at the time was still Latin).

The 'Illyrian Provinces' referred back to 'Illyricum', the name of the western Balkans in classical antiquity. Building on the Napoleonic Illyria, the movement of Croat national awakening assumed the name 'Illyrianism'. The heart of the Illyrian movement was Zagreb. Its followers were mostly Croats. Nonetheless, the choice of name underlined the pan-Slav and pan-Yugoslav (or southern Slav) sentiments that informed the Illyrians' writings. They did not claim the superiority of Croats over other parts of the south Slav community. The name also helped to elide problems posed by the regional differences among the Croats themselves, although in some instances this did not always succeed, notably in Dalmatia where people considered themselves Dalmatians rather than Croats.

The Croats were beset by peculiar problems of identity born of language, geography and history. The medieval Triune Kingdom of Croatia comprised Dalmatia, Croatia (roughly the regions around the capital Zagreb) and Slavonia. But jurisdiction over these three regions was divided under the Habsburgs. The Empire was split into the Habsburg crown lands and the Hungarian crown lands of St Stephen. In theory, the Czech crown lands and the Croatian crown lands were also entitled to their own administration but this right had atrophied. Croatia and Slavonia came under the domination of the Hungarian kingdom. After the Habsburgs had wrenched Dalmatia from Venice, it was placed under the direct control of Vienna. Furthermore, the Military Frontier, which included parts of all three Croat provinces and was inhabited by a mixture of Serbs and Croats, also lay under the immediate jurisdiction of Vienna. The Illyrians considered the Croats to be unfairly divided even within the Empire.

As the Illyrians emerged in the 1820s and 1830s, Hungary's vigorous national movement sought to establish complete autonomy for the lands of St Stephen. As these included Croatia and Slavonia, the Illyrians were *ipso facto* an obstacle to these plans and, furthermore, a tool that Vienna might use in its struggle against the Hungarians. Austrian absolutism itself was, of course, also a determined opponent of the growth of national movements anywhere in the Empire. Metternich realized that to maintain his system, confirmed at the Congress of Vienna in 1815, he had to play one national group off against another. So it suited Metternich to encourage the Illyrians when he wished to intimidate the Hungarians. He also used the Croat national movement as a counterweight to the Italian *risorgimento*, since the Venetians nurtured a claim to Dalmatia.

The outstanding figure of the Illyrian movement, Ljudevit Gaj, symbolized some of the Croats' identity problems. He was the son of a first-generation German father and second-generation German mother, and as an adolescent his Croatian was so poor that his high-school professor in Varaždin permitted him to write his homework in German. Gaj nonetheless identified himself entirely with Croatian culture and became a fluent Croatian speaker, adopting the local dialect known as *kajkavština*.* In 1835, however, he made a decisive move towards the creation of a literary Croatian by adopting *štokavština* as the standard dialect in his newspapers, *Horvatzke novine* and *Horvatzka danica* (*Croatian News* and *Croatian Dawn*. A year later, he succeeded in replacing the adjective 'Croatian' with 'Illyrian'). This meant that both the Serb and Croat national movements had adopted roughly the same dialect for their literary language.

Croatian nationalism had begun its oscillation between two extremes. The first, pan-Slav, pro-Serb (or rather pro-Yugoslav), would periodically give way to its pro-Austrian, anti-Serb and central European alter ego. The multiple cultural and civilizational influences that had influenced the Croats over many centuries were inevitably reflected in Croatian political nationalism.

Illyrianism represented one of the high points of the Yugoslav stream of Croatian nationalism that claimed the unity of all south Slavs. Carried away by his vision of south Slav brotherhood, Gaj announced in December 1835 that the land of Illyria would be 'a

* There are three main dialects in Croatia named after the word for 'what'. *Kajkavština* is spoken in Zagreb and the surrounding regions; *čakavština*, the least widely spoken, is heard in Rijeka and the Istrian peninsula; *štokavština* dominates to the east of Zagreb, in Slavonia and Bosnia. Importantly, most Serbs speak the third form.

harp fashioned between three corners', northern Albania, eastern Bulgaria and southern Hungary. 'The unbreakable strings on this harp' would encompass all of today's Bulgaria, parts of Austria, Italy, Albania and all that was Yugoslavia until 1991.

This was the ambitious romanticism that fired the idealism of young Croats, especially those studying at the high schools and university of Vienna. They were destined to play a significant role in the Revolutions of 1848, strengthening the solidarity that emerged among Polish, Czech, Serb and Slovak nationalists in the Habsburg Empire. But Gaj's pan-Slav vision did not fit easily with the aims of the main political class in Croatia and Slavonia, the lesser gentry, who had supported Illyrianism since the 1820s. Its primary concern was to reassert the economic and administrative influence lost during the eighteenth century to the landowners of Hungary.

In 1841, the Illyrians formed their own political party, the *Narodna stranka* (National Party). Its programme paid rhetorical homage to the unity of the south Slavs, but the Party's vision focused ever more narrowly on the goal of autonomy for Croatia and Slavonia and the unification of these provinces with Dalmatia, within a reformed Austro-Hungarian Empire. Gaj also attempted to spread his pan-Slav message among the Empire's Serbs. He had some success in the Military Frontier: in Banija, Kordun, Lika and Kninska Krajina, where Serbs and Croats mixed closely, interest in Illyrianism and the National Party grew quickly. Cut off from mother Serbia and nurturing a range of grievances against their overlords in Vienna, the Serbs of the Military Frontier became enthusiastic supporters of the Croatian national movement in 1848.

Until the explosion of that year, however, the Serbs of the Habsburg Vojvodina had little use for the new national ideology of the Illyrians. Their national consciousness was already further developed than that of the Croats. Although notable differences existed between the Vojvodina Serbs and the Serbs in the Principality of Serbia, the politics and territorial aspirations of the latter exerted much greater influence in the Vojvodina than the vague romanticism of the Illyrians, since the Serbs already claimed a tradition of statehood before the Croats had properly charted the contours of any future nation state. The irredentism of the Vojvodina Serbs was actually discouraged by the government in Belgrade which was at pains not to offend the imperial government in Vienna, despite the cultural and economic links that had flourished between Novi Sad (the principal town of Vojvodina) and Belgrade since the First Serbian Uprising.

The Croats were the first nationality to experience the disadvantages that the uneven development of national consciousness imposed on the Balkan peninsula. The idealistic Illyrian movement had only just been born when statesmen from Serbia and Greece were already formulating their hardheaded plans for the expansion of their respective states.

In January 1844, the Greek Prime Minister, Ioannis Kolettis, addressed the constitutional assembly in Athens:

> The kingdom of Greece is not Greece; it is only a part, the smallest and poorest, of Greece. The Greek is not only he who inhabits the kingdom, but also he who lives in Janina, or Thessaloniki, or Seres, or Adrianople, or Constantinople, or Trebizone, or Crete, or Samos, or any other country of the Greek history or race . . . There are two great centers of Hellenism, Athens and Constantinople. Athens is only the capitol of the kingdom; Constantinople is the great capital, the City, *I Polis*, the attraction and the hope of all the Hellenes.[32]

Until it came crashing down after a disastrous war with Turkey in 1922, the *Megali idea* (the Great Idea), as outlined by Kolettis, became the ideology above all others driving the Greek state. The geographical boundaries of the *Megali idea* were drawn freely from an imaginative reconstruction of Byzantine and classical Greek polities. As a programme for territorial expansion, it contained the potential for conflict not just with the Turks of the Ottoman Empire but with the Bulgarians, Albanians and even the Serbs. The Greek claim was 'historicist', in that it referred back to earlier Greek states. As the Austro-Hungarian and Ottoman empires began to fragment, historicist arguments such as the *Megali idea* and plans to resurrect the medieval Serb and Bulgarian empires came into conflict ever more frequently with the modern demographic, linguistic and cultural realities of the peninsula.

A few months after Kolettis's announcement, Ilija Garašanin, the most capable and influential Serbian politician of the mid-nineteenth century, secretly sketched out his ambition for the expansion of the

Serbian state. The *načertanije* or Plan, as Garašanin's project was known, was informed by a historicist approach, recalling the supposed halcyon days and territorial boundaries of Tsar Dušan's medieval Serbian empire, and by a linguistic-cultural criterion. The sentiment underlying the *načertanije* seemed to imply that where there was any doubt, it could be assumed that a south Slav was a Serb, whether he knew it or not.

Garašanin had good cause to concentrate on the future territorial development of the Serbian state. Although independent in all but name, Serbia still had to pay close attention to the Ottoman Empire. Politically, the Serbs were dependent on the Porte's goodwill and overdependent on the protection of Russia. Economically, the country relied on the transit routes and markets of the Ottoman Empire. Like most Serbian notables, Garašanin's family had extensive interests in the pig-farming trade, and although a supporter of the free-trade agreement struck between Serbia and the Habsburg Empire in 1837, he was worried about the leverage this deal gave Vienna over Serbia. He was convinced that land-locked Serbia needed an outlet to the sea. One large obstacle stood between Serbia and its dream of a port – the vilayet (province) of Bosnia. In order to guarantee Serbia's economic independence, Bosnia needed to be incorporated into Serbia. The idea of a Greater Serbia had been born.

If Serbia were to attempt to expand northwards into the Austro-Hungarian Empire, Garašanin knew that Vienna and Budapest would crush the challenge. Bosnia and Hercegovina, attached to a declining Ottoman Empire and home to a large, disgruntled Orthodox Christian peasantry, offered a much greater prospect of success. As one of Garašanin's closest aids put it in conversation with Ban Jelačić, 'The entire future of Serbia lies in the Balkan peninsula while events in Austria affect her only indirectly.'[33] This was in April 1848. Two weeks later, events forced Garašanin to think differently.

After Louis-Philippe fled France for England in February 1848, revolution ripped eastwards through Europe, touching first Frankfurt and the German Confederation before heading south to Vienna. Within days, revolts in Saxony, Berlin and Bavaria forced princely or kingly rulers into concessions or collapse. On 24 March,

Sardinia promised Lombardy armed assistance against the Habsburgs. The Vienna system, designed to protect both absolutism and the balance of power, was in ruins, and its architect, Prince Metternich, joined Louis-Philippe in English exile. The Holy Alliance that bonded Prussia, Russia and Austria in their crusade against liberalism was paralysed.

Revolution seized Vienna on Monday, 13 March. The city descended into chaos. In a desperate effort to stabilize the situation, Kaiser Ferdinand V announced a series of concessions, including full freedom of the press and the right of regions to form their own militias. The Hungarians were swift to exploit Ferdinand's weakness. In a state of political and psychological shock, the Kaiser immediately granted demands for the creation of a Hungarian cabinet to rule the lands of St Stephen. Count Lajos Batthyány was appointed Prime Minister. He and his progressive colleagues, notably Lajos Kossuth, seized their moment and implemented a wide range of social and economic reforms.

Ferdinand did, however, counter the Hungarian push towards autonomy with one key decision – the appointment, on 23 March, of Josip Jelačić as Ban (Viceroy) of Croatia, thereby establishing an alternative centre of authority inside the Hungarian crown lands. The choice of Jelačić was disputed at the court in Vienna. He was not a general and had to be promoted two ranks in order to assume the title of Ban, which angered senior officers in the Habsburg military. The conservatives in Vienna viewed him as a dangerous revolutionary, but thanks to Archduchess Sofie, Ferdinand's conspiratorial aunt, the Kaiser agreed to his appointment. In fact, as Sofie and her clique had hoped, he turned out to be the ideal candidate. Although sympathetic to the Croatian national movement, Jelačić was absolutely loyal to the Kaiser and his Empire.

The initiative to appoint Jelačić had originated in a petition to the Kaiser, signed jointly by representatives of Croatia's gentry and its aristocracy. They had been prompted to do so by the vigorous peasant rebellion that swept through Croatia and Slavonia in March 1848. They saw Jelačić as a guarantor both of greater autonomy and of law and order against a restless peasantry, potentially the most powerful revolutionary force in Croatia during 1848. His appointment was also the first move in a complicated game played by the court in Vienna to set Hungarian and Croatian nationalism against each other. The resulting collision played a key role in the defeat of revolution in the Empire.

Ferdinand's decree on the press and the national guard was insufficient to halt the breakdown in authority. Instead, a variety of ideological and professional groups began pressing their demands through a series of mass meetings. One of the most radical organizations was the Croat student body. Ljudevit Gaj, who had raced to Vienna from Zagreb as soon as the news of revolution reached Croatia, made contact with these revolutionary students. They were, however, still unclear whether to agitate on behalf of Croats or Slavs in general. At their opening assembly, they issued a proclamation to the people, called *Greetings to our Brothers in Croatia, Slavonia and Dalmatia*. The title suggested an appeal to Croats. But its content proposed a broader pan-Slav, and specifically anti-Hungarian, agenda:

> Half the Empire is made up of Slavs but time and again we are squeezed and tortured like no other people . . . The self-seekers will tell that you already have freedom of the press and a national guard so stop making a fuss. Do you know what freedom is without nationality? A body without a soul. A dead thing. We want living freedom! Do you not realize that in Pozsony [Bratislava, where the Hungarian parliament met] they wanted to annihilate you in the name of that dead freedom, to annihilate the name of our people, our national colours, our national heraldry and our language?[34]

Croat students believed reaction was already defeated. Yet Metternich's political demise signalled the beginning of a bloody and self-destructive competition between the new liberal elites of the Empire. At the centre of this struggle lay Hungary.

Liberals and progressives throughout western Europe and the United States welcomed the Hungarian revolution as the crowning moment of that momentous year – and there is no doubt that the Hungarians offered the most serious challenge to the *anciens régimes* of the Holy Alliance. Kossuth and the Hungarian government played their cards with great dexterity, especially in building wide political support for their programme among Hungarians.

After the appointment of Batthyány as Prime Minister, the new government had to overcome three hurdles. First, it had to strike a political bargain with Vienna. It did not even raise the possibility of separating from the Empire; the Kaiser was to remain as monarch, and Vienna would be able to call on the services of the Hungarian army. Second, it had to establish a strong social base among Hungarians in support of the reformist programme. The Hungarian Liberals around Kossuth were wary of the revolutionary potential of a peasantry still locked in feudal penury. 'We could either crush the revolution', explained Ferenc Deák, one of the leading rebels, 'or we could place ourselves at its head thereby preventing civil war between us and the peasantry.'[35] One of the first reforms enacted by the Hungarian parliament immediately after the revolution was the abolition of all feudal obligations. The landowners were to be paid compensation and a new, more equitable tax system introduced. Mutual suspicion between the landowners and the peasantry was still strong but the land reform, combined with the developing sense of Hungarian national identity, was sufficient to limit social unrest.

The third obstacle was formed by the national minorities. Freed from Habsburg rule, the minorities immediately acquired a new oppressor in the Hungarian administration. The modernizing and centralizing aspects of the reforms were underpinned and reinforced by nationalism – it could hardly have been otherwise. Nonetheless, although Hungarian historians generally insist that efforts were made to induce the minorities to cooperate with the Revolution, the Liberals' offers fell far short of what was needed to prevent a revolt against Hungarian rule.

And a general revolt is what they got. Instead of wooing Jelačić, Battyhány attempted to have him dismissed on 10 June. The challenge to the Hungarian government duly came – not from the Croats, but from the Serbs.

Novi Sad was the largest and most influential urban centre of the Serbs. Its economy and culture were far in advance of Belgrade's. Until the early 1840s, the Serbs of Novi Sad and the Banat region had enjoyed rising living standards due to their role as middlemen in the trade between Serbia and the Austro-Hungarian Empire. As the Hungarian Liberals encroached on Vienna's authority during the 1840s, the influence of the Serb population on public affairs was marginalized. By 1848, the policy of exclusion had degenerated into arbitrary repression.

In March of that year, the Serbs presented a petition to the Hungarian government, demanding the restoration of autonomy for the Orthodox Church and the recognition of Serbian as a state language. In exchange, the Serbs said they would back the Hungarian struggle against Vienna. Kossuth dismissed their demands with a brusque warning that 'only the sword would decide this matter'.[36] In doing so he sealed the unspoken alliance between Serbs and Croats – the 'one-blooded nation with two faiths' – and, as a result, the fate of the Hungarian revolution.

On 2 April, a Serb delegation in Vienna appealed for the unification of the Banat and Bačka (two provinces within Vojvodina) with Croatia, Slavonia and Dalmatia. With the approval of Serbia's Prince Alexander Karadjordjević, who had come to power in 1842, and Ilija Garašanin in Belgrade, Serb leaders in Novi Sad decided to convene a Serb National Assembly. At the beginning of May, Serbs from all over the Banat streamed into Sremski Karlovci, the former seat of the Orthodox Church in the Habsburg Empire. Joined by Croats, Czechs, Poles and Slavs, they gathered in the streets and began chanting 'Rise up, Rise up, Serbs!' Through popular acclamation, the government of the Serbian Vojvodina was proclaimed, headed by Colonel Josip Šupljikac, the supreme Vojvoda (Military Leader or Duke).* Rajačić was named Patriarch of the restored seat in Karlovci. Conspicuously, the new assembly did not rescind allegiance either to Vienna or to the Kingdom of Hungary. But the concluding words of the proclamation breathed life into the Yugoslav idea for the first time: 'Before all else, we demand resolutely a true and genuine union with our brothers of the same blood and tribe, the Croats. Long Live Unity! Long Live the Triune Kingdom!'[37]

At the same time, the Hungarian government envoy in Vojvodina, Petar Čarnojević, himself a Serb, established summary courts throughout the region, sentencing many Serbs to death and hanging dozens of them. They were allegedly preparing an uprising although the evidence against them was often very slim. Serbs in the town of Kikinda rose in protest, sparking off a series of small but

* Although a much liked figure, Šupljikac was at the time serving with the Habsburg forces in Italy. The Serbs lost crucial time in organizing their forces awaiting his return.

gruesome conflicts. The Serbs lynched both Hungarians and those Serbs who declared their loyalty to the government in Pest.* Units of the Hungarian army responded by launching counterattacks on the towns and villages.

On 12 June, the Hungarian commander, General Hrabovsky, mobilized his forces in the garrison of Petrovaradin and began to bombard the patriarchal seat of Sremski Karlovci. In response, Djordje Stratimirović, the operational commander of the forces of the Serbian Vojvodina, mobilized all Serb males in the province. The Hungarians dispatched Čarnojević for talks but, as Stratimirović later wrote, 'with this fervour that had gripped both Serbs and Hungarians, all these attempts at peace had become academic. In Novi Sad . . . bloody fighting had broken out; Serbs and Hungarians took up arms'.[38] The Revolution of 1848 was transformed into civil war. Thus began

> the most curious of all wars, in which troops on both sides flew the same flag, claimed loyalty to the same ruler, and treated their opponents as traitors and rebels . . . Many officials believed sincerely that his majesty was on their side; others were Magyar or Serbian nationalists; the majority were desperate and confused. The mutual reluctance of many combatants did not prevent the war in the South from deteriorating into general brutality. In the extraordinary ethnic mosaic of the Banat . . . where Serbian, Hungarian, Romanian, German, Slovak and Bulgarian settlers of the Catholic, Orthodox and Protestant faiths *had lived in peace for centuries*, people were massacring one another in the name of nationality [emphasis added].[39]

This was a modern conflict, triggered by imperial collapse and the nationalist rivalry of two liberal bourgeoisies. It was not an explosion of ancient tribal hatreds, as is so often claimed. And the Serbs and Croats, after all, were fighting side by side as brothers.

The struggle in the Vojvodina was passionate and confusing.

---

* In the Vojvodina, Slavonia and Croatia, significant numbers of gentry, Serb and Croat, keenly supported Hungarian rule. Known as Magyarons, they considered the Hungarians to be more reliable as patrons of their class.

Units of the Military Frontier, whose job in theory was to defend the border against the Turks, were pulled in every direction. Some Serb and Croat units fought with the Hungarians. Others, which included Hungarians, fought with the Serbs. In Budapest, Batthyány and the Hungarian Catholic Church advanced the theory that the Serbs were luring the Croats into an alliance in order to impose the Orthodox faith on the Catholic Croats. In some areas, this Hungarian ploy succeeded and battles broke out between Serbs and Croats.

In general, however, the outbreak of war provoked a great wave of sympathy for the Serbs in Croatia and Slavonia. Dozens of patriotic songs and poems were written praising the brotherhood of Serbs and Croats, poems like *Vojnica* (War Lament) which describes how Patriarch Rajačić immediately appealed to Ban Jelačić for support after the outbreak of civil war:

The fire was lit in Kikinda,
The wild Magyars are hanging my sons.
Vukovar and Petrovaradin
Are in their hands; a knife is in our back.
And Hrabovsky, the man of the hornbeam head:
*The fiend, the plague of the Slav people**
Has led the charge on Karlovci.
The Serbs respond in kind.
I handed weapons to our children,
For our people is soaking in blood.
We cannot resist alone.
Help from the Croats is needed forthwith.[40]

On 11 June, the day before Hrabovsky's artillery assault on Sremski Karlovci, the people of Prague rioted in support of the creation of an independent Czech army. Students and workers joined together and fought running battles with imperial grenadiers in the centre of the Czech capital. A week later, Prince Alfred Windischgrätz, the imperial commander in Bohemia and Moravia, issued orders to bombard Prague to force the closure of the pan-Slav congress, which was meeting there. Prague's beautiful baroque façades took a heavy

* Hrabovsky was himself a Slav.

pounding while bloody skirmishes between the Czechs and the imperial army resulted in over 350 deaths.* The Czechs surrendered their capital city after a few days.

The outcome in Prague represented the first success of a reactionary group at the imperial court. These conservatives believed the time was ripe for counterrevolution. Like Windischgrätz, most were senior commanders of the Austrian army. At the end of July, their confidence grew still greater with the victory of General Radetzky over the Piedmontese at Custozza.

By the late summer of 1848, the following, stupefyingly complex, military and political situation obtained in the Austro-Hungarian empire:

1 In the Vojvodina or southern Hungary, the Serbs of Vojvodina and Hungarians were at war.
2 The Croats, under Jelačić, were preparing to invade Hungary.
3 The Hungarians faced outbreaks of rebellion among the Slovaks in the north of their crown lands.
4 After the Pest government proclaimed the Union of Transylvania with Hungary, the Romanians of Transylvania organized a rebellion.
5 In Italy, military errors and political disunity resulted in the collapse of the Piedmontese-led war to liberate Lombardy and Venice from the Austrian Empire.
6 In Vienna, the liberal revolutionaries were demanding unification of the Austrian Empire with the Germans of the Frankfurt parliament to create a Greater Germany under a constitutional monarchy. This was fuelled by German nationalism, putting the Viennese revolutionaries at odds with their Czech and Hungarian counterparts.
7 With the exception of the Italians, none of the nationalist movements actually supported the dismissal of the Kaiser as their monarch.
8 The imperial court, resident in Innsbruck, had meanwhile approved the suppression of the Czechs and backed Radetzky's campaign in Italy. It also gave tacit support to the Croats and the

* These included Windischgrätz's wife who the Prince had rather injudiciously left in their Prague apartments. A mob broke into the residence and murdered her.

Serbs in their struggle against Hungary. This move was a key component in the imperial strategy of 'divide and rule'.

9 Under pressure from the political and intellectual elite in the principality of Serbia, Ilija Garašanin permitted the formation of volunteer units from Serbia proper to fight in the Vojvodina. Serbia was also supplying weaponry to the Vojvodina Serbs, and offering money and logistical support to the Croats.

10 Russia had assembled a substantial army on the River Pruth. Tsar Nicholas I was ready to attack the Hungarians in defence of the Holy Alliance with Vienna.

11 The following active or tacit alliances existed:
The Italians and Hungarians supported each other's movements.
The Croats and Czechs attempted to coordinate their activities.
The Serbs of Vojvodina and the Croats formed an informal military alliance with the aim of south Slav unification.
Serbia proper discreetly supported this alliance.
The imperial court gave apparent backing to the Serbs and the Croats but secretly remained resolutely opposed to either group's national demands.
Tsar Nicholas supported the Kaiser.
Serbia feared an alliance between Hungary and Turkey.
Hungary was confident it could defeat Jelačić, but feared, with good reason, the Tsar's army on the Pruth.

If Windischgrätz were to defeat the court's main enemy, the Hungarians, he needed to channel Croatian and Serbian nationalism against Budapest. It was time to reap the benefits from Jelačić's appointment. With the Hungarians facing challenges on so many fronts, Jelačić elected to march on Hungary, hoping that this would secure autonomy for Croatia. But above all, he wanted to demonstrate his loyalty to the imperial court and therefore allowed himself to be co-opted by Windischgrätz's counterrevolution. The Croats, poorly equipped and lacking sufficient forces for the campaign, were halted by the Hungarians at the battle of Pákozd on 29 September. The imperial military leadership had promised Jelačić reinforcements, but they never came, and some Croatian historians have argued convincingly that Windischgrätz withheld this support intentionally.[41] In this way, the leader of the counter-revolution steadily drained Jelačić's authority within Croatia while sapping the strength of the Hungarian military. Jelačić's Achilles' heel was his devotion to the monarchy. After Pákozd, he retreated not to Croatia but to Vienna where he assisted Windischgrätz in the campaign to drive the revolutionaries out of the imperial capital. Though he may have appeared weak and indecisive he faced a difficult dilemma and one cannot be too harsh on him. His illusions about the imperial court were shared by many Croat patriots. Indeed, only a small group on the left of the *Narodna stranka* articulated the need for an alliance with the Hungarians, which would have been a formidable challenge to Vienna. But the government in Pest contributed substantially to the collapse of the revolution by refusing to accommodate the Croats or other minorities.

The second factor that undermined the Croats was the failure of their leaders to resolve the question of the peasantry. The Croatian Sabor had been very reluctant to abolish the peasants' feudal obligations, and even when they did, much later than the Hungarians, Croatia's landowners were reluctant to implement the new regulations. Throughout the summer of 1848, spontaneous peasant uprisings broke out in Croatia and Slavonia and were suppressed by the Zagreb authorities. The peasantry's attitude towards the Croatian political reform was therefore ambivalent at best. Some Croatian landowners were even inclined to support the imperial counter-revolution to re-establish their authority over their peasants. This division was conspicuously absent in Hungary where the revolution had a wider social base.

The Hungarian revolution assumed still more radical forms. In December, Windischgrätz forced the abdication of the weak Kaiser Ferdinand, who was succeeded by the eighteen-year-old Franz Joseph. The Habsburg authorities had already abolished the Hungarian government and warned all who refused to submit to imperial rule that they would be considered traitors. The Hungarians countered by withholding recognition of Franz Joseph and establishing instead a revolutionary National Defence Committee under the leadership of Kossuth.

The Hungarians drove the imperial forces out of the country. At this point in the summer of 1849, Tsar Nicholas I offered his services to Franz Joseph in the name of the Holy Alliance. Two Russian armies, one stationed east of the Pruth in Bessarabia, the other east of the Vistula in Russian-controlled Poland, swept across and down into Hungary and finally smashed the revolution in August.

Reaction had triumphed throughout the Habsburg Empire. In Hungary, the newly restored Austrian authorities exacted a terrible retribution against the rebels. Elsewhere in the Empire, the demands of other national communities, especially the Croats and Serbs, who had contributed significantly to the exhaustion of the Hungarian forces, were simply ignored by the Kaiser. Liberal nationalism had apparently suffered a catastrophic defeat.

In one respect, the Hungarian claim to primacy in the challenge to Habsburg absolutism is justified – it almost succeeded in destroying half an empire. But the emphasis that many western historians have placed on the path-breaking role of Kossuth's movement has obscured the debilitating impact of mutually exclusive national claims on the events of 1848. In its drive for modernization, liberal constitutionalism had too often become inseparable from national intolerance.

The war in Vojvodina, in particular, demonstrated the grim potential for violence that exists when power vacuums emerge in a region where two or more nascent national groups compete to replace the retreating authority. This has been the most common cause of war in the Balkans since the beginning of the nineteenth century. Serbia's response to the conflict in the Vojvodina is also instructive. Garašanin neither wanted nor expected the Serbs in Vojvodina to rebel. Like most others, he was convinced that the conditions for an uprising were riper in Bosnia-Hercegovina. For this reason, Garašanin invested time and money in establishing a network of secret agents in Bosnia. Should unrest break out there, he intended to direct the course of revolution. The Serb rebels in Vojvodina deflected attention in Serbia proper away from Bosnia towards a region in which Serbia was reluctant to get involved. Serbia was now a *de facto* state; as such the responsibilities and calculations of its political elite had changed. Its primary aim was to guarantee the security and economic well-being of the state and to develop the mechanisms and institutions of a constitutional monarchy. Expansionist adventures would only be embarked upon if there was a good prospect of success. There was little chance of victory in Vojvodina. Serbia's involvement indicated that in this age of maturing nationalism a community on the periphery, like the Vojvodina Serbs, could exert an influence on the policy of a mother state disproportionate to its value. Ultimately, however, the interests of state, rather than the struggle of the community outside its borders, were paramount.

The events in Croatia of 1848 demonstrated that the Croats faced an uphill struggle for liberation. In addition to the divisions and weaknesses in Croat society, Croatia faced a serious topographical problem. The Triune Kingdom – Croatia, Slavonia and Dalmatia – had a weird shape. The Ottoman strategic bastion of Bosnia-Hercegovina jutted into the Kingdom like an intrusive arrow. This made the journey from the port of Split in Dalmatia to eastern Slavonia unnecessarily long and awkward. The early leaders of the Illyrian movement all recognized this anomaly by proposing that any future Croatian state should include, at the very least, Bosanska Krajina in north-western Bosnia or preferably the whole of Bosnia-Hercegovina. The Serbs assumed that Bosnia belonged to them. In 1848, the Muslim landowners and administrators of Bosnia still thought it was theirs. Given that the Serbs were well advanced in their project of state-building, the Croats were faced with an awkward dilemma. Either they would need to cooperate with the Serbs, and accept a subordinate role, or oppose them and face the consequences.

Despite the importance of 1848 for the northern Balkans, it remains a short, ferocious storm in a long period of relative calm. After the storm had subsided, the new Balkan elites returned to the problem of state-building. In this they demonstrated a surprising degree of energy and enterprise.

In the grip of progress: the Danubian Principalities, 1820–66

Romania's road to independence was marked by such unexpected twists and turns that it might have been drawn by M.C. Escher. In January 1821, Tudor Vladimirescu, a minor boyar and former soldier in the Russian army, led an uprising of militiamen whose primary aim was to depose the Greek prince, the *hospodar*, and banish Phanariot rule from the two Principalities, Wallachia and Moldavia. Throughout the eighteenth century the *hospodars* had sucked the cultural and economic lifeblood out of the Principalities, as illustrated by the mutation of the Greek word *kiverneo*, meaning 'to govern', into its Romanian derivative *chiverniseala*, which means 'to get rich'.[42] Subordinate to the Porte, the *hospodars* administered an economic regime that forced Romania's indigenous aristocracy, the boyars, to sell a large part of their produce to Constantinople at prices fixed below the value of the goods in western Europe. At a time when the Ottoman Empire's ability to harvest declining resources was under pressure, the *hospodar* system, which ensured the steady flow of annual tribute, commodities and tax revenue, was extremely useful.

The Vladimirescu uprising was driven by hostility to Greeks. Herein lies a bizarre paradox: carried out by Romanians in the heart of Wallachia, the uprising was conceived and executed as the first act of the Greek Revolution. It was intended to soften up the Principalities' defences to facilitate Alexander Ypsilantis's invasion from Russia into Moldavia. The affair was planned by the Philiki Etairia whose leadership hoped it would trigger a wave of instability through the Empire, leading to the eventual liberation not of the Romanians but of the Greeks.

Vladimirescu and Ypsilantis failed to ignite a broader revolution because they did not receive the expected support from Russia. St Petersburg and Istanbul were old enemies, but Tsar Alexander was deeply conservative and felt obliged to resist revolution wherever it occurred, whether in Russia or in neighbouring empires. While it was legitimate to beat the Turk on the battlefield, it was not done to subvert him from within. Thus the first lesson from the débâcle was that no revolutionary movement in the Principalities could succeed without the backing of a great power. Between 1711 and 1829, seven major wars were fought on the territory of Moldavia and Wallachia. The Principalities stood at the intersection of the Russian, Austrian and Turkish empires, and acted as the land bridge which Russian armies had to cross into the Balkan peninsula. In the eyes of St Petersburg, their strategic importance among the proto-states of the Balkans was unparalleled. The fate of such a crucial region could not possibly be left to the people who happened to live there.

Disillusioned with Ypsilantis and the Etairia, Vladimirescu nonetheless found himself in control of Bucharest. Here he assumed the role of revolutionary Prince to replace the *hospodar* who had been poisoned by Vladimirescu's co-conspirators. But Vladimirescu soon found himself in trouble with his own people. The peasants around Bucharest seized this revolutionary moment to make their own demands, mainly to abolish the hated feudal obligation, the *clacă*, which obliged the peasant to work an unlimited number of days for his landlord every year. When the Turkish army crossed the Danube to restore order, the Romanian landowners were greatly relieved.

The Turks did agree to do away with the *hospodars*, who had become too unreliable. The boyars were happy to continue collecting the tribute for the Porte while augmenting their economic power with political influence. For the peasantry, however, a greedy Romanian oligarchy had replaced a Greek kleptocracy. Landowners did not pay taxes, peasants did. In Greece and Serbia, the peasants had formed the backbone of the military force that shook Ottoman rule, and while this did not eliminate tension between the emerging elites and the peasantry, it did mean that peasant interests were not ignored. In Wallachia and Moldavia, it never entered the boyars' heads that the peasants had any legitimate demands whatsoever.

Nonetheless, French revolutionary ideas were transmitted to Romania more swiftly than to anywhere else in the Ottoman Empire because of the close linguistic affinity between Romanian and French. The sons of rich boyars, especially from Wallachia, were sent to study in Paris where they quickly adopted French political culture as their own. During the reign of the *hospodars*, the hitherto hereditary title of boyar had been devalued by regulations allowing its sale. The proliferation of noble titles created a new type of boyar, less wedded to the countryside but eager to exercise political influence. This urban boyar became first the agent of western ideas in the Principalities and later the backbone of the Liberal party, just as the landowning boyar would later support the Conservatives.

The works of Montesquieu, Voltaire and Rousseau flooded into the private and public libraries of the Principalities, particularly Wallachia. Boyars, intellectuals and merchants from Bucharest and Iaşi made the pilgrimage to Paris. The appearance of Romanian cities was transformed over a twenty-year period from the mid-1820s. The boyars embarked on the large-scale cultivation of wheat, which was sent up the Danube to western markets. The barges returned loaded with clothes, furniture and cigars. Fashion changed dramatically, as the Ottoman robes of the east were discarded in favour of the hats and suits of St Petersburg and Vienna. One contemporary commentator noted in 1829 how Bucharest had been struck by 'the disease of love'. Divorce, affairs, elopement and rape appear to have been part of the staple culture of the Wallachian capital's nobility.

With their awakened passion for national revival, the boyars established the principle of joint citizenship for the people of Wallachia and Moldavia. The idea of being Romanian, with a common heritage, was invented in its modern form. The demand for the unification of the Principalities was heard ever louder, especially in Bucharest where people regarded the city as the natural centre of power in a future Romanian state. Although dramatic, these changes affected a small proportion of society. As the leading historian of modern Romania puts it, the boyars had listened to only one part of the revolutionary messages from France, 'the foreign policy and the revival of nationalism, completely ignoring its democratic aspect, social equality'.[43]

Four peculiar circumstances – an absentee landlord, the Sultan; an indigenous landlord class; proximity to Russia and Austria; and the growing influence of Enlightenment ideas – allowed the Principalities to stumble into autonomy in the late 1820s. Unlike the Serbs and the Greeks, the Wallachians and Moldavians did not have to run the gauntlet of full-scale armed insurrection against the Muslim overlord. The boyars continued much as before, accommodating themselves to the vagaries of great-power politics.

The decisive event came in 1829 with the Treaty of Adrianople, which concluded the Russo-Turkish war and drove the Ottomans from the Principalities in all but name. Although the Principalities were still obliged to pay an annual tribute to the Porte and recognize the Sultan as sovereign, Russia now dominated Wallachia and Moldavia, creating a quasi-constitution, known as the Organic Regulations, for each Principality. The boyars were no longer restricted to the Ottoman markets – they could sell their produce wherever they wanted.

The Regulations did not transform the Principalities overnight into a paradise of *laissez-faire* commercial activity. Having lost a substantial chunk of its European territory in the Greek War of Independence, the Ottoman Empire was still determined to milk both the Principalities and Serbia within the framework of their new autonomous status. So although the boyars could choose their markets in principle, they still had to trade under a punitive tariff regime; and their new-found autonomy was seen as a threat by Russia to its own economic interests. Austria-Hungary, for its part, regarded the loosening of ties between the Principalities and the Porte as an excellent opportunity to extend its commercial influence in the region. Thus, Moldavia and Wallachia had sailed out of the Empire's stagnant economic lake into the turbulent sea of great-power strategic and commercial interests.

Despite these difficulties, Romanian trade expanded. In accordance with the Treaty of Adrianople, the Ottoman army had evacuated its three fortresses defending the Danube basin in Turnu-Măgurele, Giurgiu and Brăila. This extremely fertile area was now open to cultivation, providing the foundations for a boom in cereal production. In 1831 the amount of land under cultivation stood at only 370,000 hectares, which was roughly the same as it had been a century earlier. By 1865 this had grown to 1,415,000 hectares while in 1912 the figure stood at 5,180,000. This astonishing growth also saw a sharp rise in the cultivation of wheat and a relative decline in corn production, so that on the eve of the First World War, the Principalities had become the fourth largest wheat producer and exporter in the world after the United States, Canada and Russia. Such a mighty achievement was not always advantageous: wheat production rocketed throughout the world during the nineteenth century, leading to a drastic fall in prices, so that even though Romania was producing a great deal more wheat, the growth in its income was relatively low.

Before the landowning boyars could exploit the country's growing agricultural potential, they had to overcome the problem of transport. Road-building did not begin until the 1840s, creating great difficulties for the transport of perishable goods. It was more expensive to send grain 320 kilometres from northern Moldavia to the Black Sea coast than it was to ship it from the Black Sea to Britain. Russia saw wheat cultivation in Romania as a threat to its own harvests in southern Russia, much of it sold on to Britain and France. If the Principalities were able to modernize the port facilities on the Danube and the Black Sea, they could begin to undercut the price of Russian wheat on world markets. To throttle this competition, Russia exploited its position as protector of the Principalities by allowing the mouth of the Danube to silt up. Russia's interest in the Principalities was essentially strategic. St Petersburg wanted a pliant satellite, not an economic competitor.

The period of Russian domination in the 1830s and 1840s left both the landowning boyars and the growing urban elite unhappy. The former resented Russian foot-dragging on the economy, while the latter was frustrated by the slow progress of political reform and the obstacles it faced in developing the country's industrial base, especially in Wallachia where the greatest concentration of factories lay. The Russians, however, had created an important constitutional voice through which the boyars could articulate their dissatisfaction, namely the assemblies of Wallachia and Moldavia. Democracy this was not. The assemblies were elected by about 800 boyars, who were hostile to any hint of liberal reform. The assemblies were in turn subordinate to a prince who was also elected by an extremely limited franchise. The prince ruled for life and although the assemblies did not have the right of recall, they were able to make their influence felt through control over the budget. The Principalities were thus ruled by a reactionary oligarchy. Their opposition to Russia was not born of hostility to absolutism but to the specific economic restrictions which Russia imposed on them.

A perennial grievance was the continuing separation of the two Principalities, an issue taken up by the rising class of lesser boyars. They shared the landowners' antipathy to the Russian protectorate, and they resented their exclusion from political life. Tired of floating in this constitutional purgatory, liberal Romanians exploited the European wave of discontent in 1848 by mounting their own revolution – the only uprising that year in territories under Ottoman suzerainty.

The rebellion began in the Moldavian capital, Iaşi, but soon petered out there. Then, in late June, a group of young liberals deposed the ruling prince in Wallachia, Gheorgiu Bibescu, and established a revolutionary government in the capital, Bucharest. The victorious conspirators were dominated by a new and impressive breed of Romanian intellectuals and politicians. Many were the Paris-educated sons of rich boyars. The events of 1848 were a stormy baptism for this young and inexperienced group, which later became the most forceful proponent of liberalism in Romania. Paradoxically, the revolution was not a carnival of anti-Ottoman sentiment. The rebels realized that the Ottoman Empire was politically impotent in the Principalities. Indeed, they showed imagination by securing the backing of the Ottoman government for their revolutionary constitution. This support was only withdrawn under extreme pressure from Tsar Nicholas.

While wooing the Porte, the revolutionaries vented their wrath against the oligarchy and the Russians by publicly burning the Organic Regulations. The boyars were the chief beneficiaries of the Regulations while the Russians were their main sponsors. It was Nicholas I who persuaded Sultan Abdülmecid (1839–61), and not the other way round, to join his forces in occupying the Principalities in September 1848 and suppressing the revolution.

A central goal of the revolutionaries had been unification of the two Principalities, but they faced internal opposition. A broad political division separated the Moldavian and Wallachian elites, symbolized by the different intellectual influences in their two capitals, Iaşi and Bucharest. Among intellectuals in the Moldavian capital, the influence of German Romantic nationalism, especially the ideas of J.G. Herder, was paramount. Herder's work suggested that the essence of national identity was transmitted through popular language and culture. During the nineteenth century, his theories were adopted by conservative nationalists who believed that national identity could not be learnt, but only transmitted through blood. In contrast, the Bucharest intellectuals had imbibed the French conception of nationhood which saw commitment to a particular culture as the central requirement in establishing a person's national identity. (Everyone could be considered French provided they accepted French culture – unless, of course, they had yet to attain 'civilization', like the Algerians.) For this latter group, anyone, regardless of origin, could join the Romanian national struggle by accepting its goals (but, as we shall see, Romania's Jews were excluded from this liberal embrace).

Bucharest intellectuals, like Ion C. Brătianu and C.A. Rosetti, who established the revolutionary government of 1848 and would later inspire the founding of the Liberals, were the first to advance the theory that Romanians formed the last outpost of western culture in south-eastern Europe. Their ethnic identity and autonomous traditions, they believed, meant that they shared much more in common with French and English culture than with the 'Asiastic' values of the other regions of the Ottoman Empire.

Of course, the lines separating these two intellectual trends in Romanian nationalism were hazy, particularly where they overlapped with political allegiance. The regionalist sentiment in Moldavia dovetailed with the interests of the dominant landowning boyars in the Principality. Many rejected unification as they feared, with good reason, that a centralizing government might interfere with their comfortable economic arrangements in the countryside. The Moldavian boyars and intellectuals tried to scupper the union of the two Principalities in 1866. That year saw the establishment of a Romanian monarchy which effectively secured the country's unification and marked an important step on the road to full independence. But before the supporters of unification were able to find a foreign prince willing to take on the task of running an obscure Balkan proto-state, they needed one of their regular strokes of luck. This came in the form of the Crimean War, one of the most futile wars of the nineteenth century, which greatly benefited the Romanians even though they did not participate in it.

Such an outcome did not seem likely in July 1853 when Russian troops occupied the Principalities, allegedly to protect Christian shrines in the Holy Land. The usual abuses accompanied the Russian occupation. The two princes of Moldavia and Wallachia were forced out of office and fled to Vienna. The Russian authorities introduced a harsh military regime and suppressed political organizations. In October, the Porte declared war on Russia, citing the occupation of the Principalities as the *casus belli*. In fact, the occupation was a mere symptom of the conflict and not a substantive issue. Nonetheless, it was serious enough to provoke the Austrians into forming a coalition with the Turks and forcing out the Russians. The Russians were prepared to go to war with Turkey but not with both Turkey and Austria. The Romanians were overjoyed at the departure of the Russian troops, but less pleased with the immediate occupation of the Principalities by Austrian and Ottoman forces, which were to remain until the end of the conflict.

The defeat of Russia in the Crimean War was serendipitous for Romania. Nicholas I was forced to relinquish his role as protector of the Principalities. No great power considered restoring the Ottoman Empire's authority over them, not even the Porte itself. Romania's future status was to be guaranteed by an international coalition. Wallachia and Moldavia found themselves in a peculiar power vacuum, and a majority of the boyars, including a substantial number of the conservatives, decided to exploit the situation by pushing for unification. They received considerable support for the idea from Napoleon III who supported the Romanians' maximalist programme – unification of the two Principalities under a foreign prince.

Piedmont, eagerly trying to establish its credentials as an embryonic great power, offered the Romanians full support, partly out of ideological solidarity and partly because it knew that a united Romania would create an extra security problem in a region of the Habsburg Empire far away from Italy. Franz Joseph was worried that unification would exert a powerful attraction on the large Romanian population of Transylvania and so he, together with the Porte, resisted all attempts to extend the Principalities' autonomy. Vienna and Constantinople received backing from London which regarded unification as a threat to the Ottoman Empire, whose tottering status Britain had, after all, been defending in the Crimean War. This provoked a rift between Britain and France which Russia decided to encourage by warming suddenly to the idea of Romanian unification.

During this manoeuvring by the great powers, the politicians and intellectuals of the Principalities displayed a sensitive touch, considering their lack of experience in the labyrinthine game of great-power diplomacy. Given how little leverage they enjoyed, they achieved a remarkable success when in 1859 they persuaded their guarantors to permit the election of a single prince, Alexander Cuza, a rather dull army officer from Moldavia, to reign over both Principalities for his lifetime.

The triumphant Romanian elite then turned upon itself in a series of damaging internal squabbles. The Liberals and the Conservatives, two nascent political parties, were emerging from the confusion. Cuza, the new prince, was beset by exasperating conspiracies and peculiar coalitions. These brought Liberals and Conservatives, Moldavians and Wallachians, pro-western and pro-Russian factions together in brief, querulous alliances.

Cuza was a reformer who had been active in the 1848 revolution in Bucharest. He was frustrated not just by Conservatives, who were suspicious of his political programme, but by his jealous Liberal allies. This created a dilemma for him – and he soon concluded that if he were to succeed in his reforms, he would have to assume autocratic powers.

Matters reached a climax over the crucial issue of agrarian reform. Throughout the 1850s, peasant dissatisfaction with the ever increasing *clacă* obligations was growing. The landowners, however, remained intransigent, and Cuza, appreciating that something had to be done about the plight of the peasants, decided to overrule the landowners by force. In 1864, he mounted a military coup, and then issued a decree on agrarian reform.

Unfortunately, the agrarian reform was hastily executed and would exercise a malign influence over Romanian society in the course of the next century. The decree abolished feudal relations in the countryside, but it also destroyed any protection that the peasants had enjoyed. Some 30 per cent of the cultivated land (over 2 million hectares) was distributed to 511,896 peasants. It was not long before the peasants discovered that their small plots were not sufficient for them to turn a profit, so they were forced to enter into ruinous contracts to work the boyars' lands. In order to maintain profit levels, the boyars imposed devastating conditions on the peasants and the gulf between the two classes widened still further. Although the reform actually benefited the landowners in the short term, they nonetheless considered Cuza's decree an outrageous incursion on their privileges. The most honest attempt of the nineteenth century to remove the causes of social tension in the Romanian countryside had merely sowed the seeds of future discord.

Part of the opposition to Cuza coalesced around the growing belief that if the Principalities were to secure both unification and independence, it was essential to establish a constitutional monarchy headed by a foreign prince. The preoccupation with the establishment of a royal line drawn from one of Europe's principal dynasties was intensified by the relative success of the experiment in Greece. Although riven by clientelism and intrigue, Greece's independence was never in doubt. Not only was its status backed by a great-power coalition, there was an instinctive reluctance on the part of the great powers to tamper with a recognized monarchy. Looking to their immediate neighbour, Serbia, the Romanians saw a fragile Principality that had not succeeded in gaining full independence. In addition, Serbia could not boast the prestige of a prince connected to a great imperial house of Europe. Worse still, they had two princely lines, the Obrenović and Karadjordjević, who were in permanent and sometimes bloody competition. Factional disorders at the court infected the country much more than in Greece, exposing the Serbs to manipulation by foreign powers.

In February 1866, the Romanian conspirators, gathered in what was called 'the monstrous coalition', made their move and sent a group of disaffected army officers to arrest Cuza in his bed. He abdicated without resistance to seek solace in the bottle and the arms of his mistress.

The search for a foreign prince turned out to be a delightful mix of daring and farce. Agents were sent to scour Europe for unemployed princes. Some of these were offered the job and turned it down, but eventually Carol of Hohenzollern-Sigmaringen, a sub-branch of the Prussian royal family, was chosen. He accepted in principle, but he and his backers in Bucharest had to overcome resistance inside the Principalities and abroad.

Whether by chance or guile (nobody knows who suggested Carol be offered the throne), the choice of a German prince was particularly advantageous. The Romanians believed that Napoleon III would support both unification and the establishment of a constitutional monarchy. Austria-Hungary, Russia and Turkey, the Principalities' immediate neighbours, would doubtless object and might have prevented a foreign prince's accession to the throne; but Carol had the support of Germany.

Resistance to the project in Moldavia was spawned by a combination of regional patriotism, conservatism in political and religious circles, and fear of invasion by the 60,000 Russian troops mustered on the border. As plans for Carol's appointment accelerated in the spring of 1866, there was talk of the peculiar prospect of civil war among Romanians before they were united in a single state. Moldavians warned that Carol would erode the national character of any future state by placing his German bureaucrats in key positions. Carol's Catholicism fired the wrath of Moldavia's Orthodox hierarchy while the forced abdication of Cuza, who was from Moldavia, was regarded as a further attempt to diminish the power and significance of Iaşi in favour of Bucharest. In April 1866, the Moldavians took to the streets of their capital to demonstrate against Carol and unification. 'Down with Union', 'Long Live Moldavia' and 'Revolution: Fear Not, Hold on a Few Hours, the Russians Are Coming to Our Aid.' For half a day, civil war reigned in Iaşi. However, the demonstrators were unable to persuade the army units to join their ranks. Seventeen protestors were killed and four wounded. Although many Moldavians believed the events signalled a general uprising against Wallachia, it proved to be a last stand against Bucharest. Although opposition to the King by no means collapsed, it was too weak to resist the growing logic of centralization in the embryonic nation state.

The army's commitment to unification was crucial and well understood by Carol. He was elected by the joint assembly of Moldavia and Wallachia on 13 May and took office a week later, the day he arrived in Bucharest. With creditable diplomacy, Carol immediately made moves to placate Moldavian hostility to his election; but with an eye to future security, he began reforming the army and establishing close ties with its leadership. Balkan armies in general were aware that they could have little impact in conflicts involving the great powers, but most politicians appreciated how important their role was in the domestic political balance.

The great powers watched the process of Romanian unification closely. At first glance, it is perhaps astonishing that the Romanians achieved this union without being crushed by foreign intervention. Their three great neighbours, Russia, Austria-Hungary and the Ottoman Empire, were in principle opposed to it taking place. But Istanbul's desire to restore its authority in the Principalities, which after all still owed fealty to the Porte, was cancelled out by Russia's determination to exclude the Turkish army from the region.

Austria had considered intervening in Romania unilaterally. But the move towards union and the enthronement of Carol matured during one of the most fateful periods of European history. In the summer of 1866, Prussia, under the guiding hand of Otto von Bismarck, the most accomplished European politician of the nineteenth century, humbled the Habsburg Empire at the battle of Königgrätz. In the same year, with the blessing of Napoleon III, Italy exploited Vienna's weakness by absorbing Venetia into the new kingdom. Bismarck had allotted a minor role to Romania in this enormous upheaval in the European balance of power. Through private channels, he encouraged Carol to accept the throne. A unified Romania with a German royal line represented a distinct setback to Austria-Hungary's plans for expansion in south-eastern Europe. In addition, a Romanian state was likely to become a magnet for the Romanian population in Transylvania, further unsettling the Habsburg borderlands.

The exclusion of Austria from the politics of north-central Europe and the success of German unification were to have a decisive impact on the development of nationalism and nation states in the Balkans. Although the German state created in 1871 was an empire and its creator a political conservative, it seemed profoundly modern, successful and attractive. It represented a threat to the imperial structures of the Romanovs and Habsburgs, not to mention the military power of France and the industrial superiority of Great Britain. The victory of a centralizing state with a clear Teutonic identity in northern Europe was seen by politicians and intellectuals throughout the Balkans as a vindication of their struggle to establish constitutional monarchies based on the aspirations of a single nationality. Among the southern Slavs, the question of what actually constituted a single nationality was still extremely confused; but this was not yet the main cause of conflict in the Balkans. The 1860s and 1870s saw the Ottoman Empire slide into deep financial crisis. The ever more uncertain balance of power in the Balkans ensured that even minor uprisings of Christian peasants, which had proliferated since the late 1850s, could have momentous consequences for the European balance of power.

CHAPTER 2

THE REALM OF RUINS

Reform and decay, 1839–78

The Tanzimat: The Ottoman Empire, Bosnia-Hercegovina, 1839–75

The Ottoman Empire was vast. It straddled three continents and bordered seven seas. It was guardian to the holiest shrines of the three great faiths of Europe and the Near East, Judaism, Christianity and Islam. The Sultan was at once both Emperor and Caliph, Allah's chosen representative on earth. From the fourteenth to the sixteenth century, the imperial army swept all before it, one of the most successful machines of military conquest in history. In its wake, the Ottoman military left not only scorched earth but a unique social and political system. This was sometimes brutal but often more equitable and predictable for its subjects than the early modern monarchies of Europe. Until its final collapse in the early twentieth century, the Empire remained overwhelmingly rural in character. Elsewhere in Europe, towns and cities became the driving force behind first a mercantile and then an industrial revolution. For the most part, the Ottoman economy slept through these far-reaching changes. Some merchants, traders and craftsmen were alert to the processes of technological advance and economic modernization. They were rarely Muslims with influence over the government, but Greek, Jewish, Armenian and, later, Bulgarian businessmen with no particular interest in preserving Ottoman power.

By the late 1830s, the population of this economic backwater was a mere thirty-six million. The majority, some twenty-one million, were Muslims. Most of the roughly eleven million ethnic Turks did not yet regard themselves as Turks. They were either Ottomans, the administrative and military elite, or miserable Anatolian peasants. The other Muslims were Arabs (six to eight million), a million and a half Albanians and perhaps a million Kurds. The Christians included around six million Slavs speaking a wide variety of south Slav dialects and professing different faiths (there were also small Muslim populations among the Slavs of Bulgaria and Macedonia, as well as the larger community in Bosnia); four million Romanians, two and a half million Armenians and two million Greeks (certainly more than lived in Greece itself).

Imperial subjects were divided into *millets.* A *millet* gathered all members of a faith whose origins lay in the Old Testament – the three largest were the Muslim, the Greek Orthodox and the Jewish *millets*. The religious hierarchy was responsible for the spiritual welfare of its particular *millet*, but it also had broad jurisdiction in legal matters affecting two or more parties in the same *millet*, and oversaw social and educational life. The word *millet* means nation. For the Ottomans, nationhood meant religious affiliation, so that Bosnian, Turkish and Albanian Muslims, for example, would all speak different languages and enjoy widely different cultural traditions but would still be part of the same 'nation'. This also held true for the diverse peoples gathered in the Orthodox *millet*. The western practice of referring to them all as 'les Grecs', whether Greeks or not, was not so absurd as it may appear two centuries later. Marriages between orthodox Greeks and orthodox Albanians, Vlachs or Slavs were not uncommon and created no difficulties for the men and women involved. Marriage to a Catholic Greek, however long his or her Hellenic heritage, was impossible, unless one of the parties converted. As far as the religious hierarchies and the Ottoman state were concerned, religion always took precedence over culture, language and race in defining one's identity.

During the first four of the Ottomans' five-century domination of south-eastern Europe, serious disturbances among and between the *millets* of the Empire were rare. The complex hierarchy of social relations was mostly based on unwritten law and edicts proclaimed by the *ulema*, the leading Islamic clerics. These rules governed the type and style of dress reserved for different *millets*. There were 'countless traditions urging the Muslims to distinguish themselves, even in appearance, from the infidels and to avoid imitating their habits in dress as well as all else . . . The turban is the barrier separating belief and unbelief'. 'He who imitates a people, becomes one of them.'[1] Christians were obliged to dismount from their horses whenever they encountered a Muslim. For a non-Muslim to bear arms was a most serious violation of the elaborate code. The ownership of land, or its stewardship on behalf of the Sultan, was restricted to members of the Muslim *millet* although trading, money-lending and tax-farming were frequently the prerogative of the others – notably the Jewish and Armenian *millets* but also the Orthodox, especially in Bosnia-Hercegovina.

The Empire's borders were guarded by the great Ottoman armies. But internal peace and stability were chiefly the product of this ordered *millet* system that reproduced itself generation after generation. For the majority, whether Muslim, Christian or Jewish, life comprised little more than being born, reproducing and working oneself to an early grave. Yet in return for this mundane existence each individual enjoyed a degree of security and the certainty of being able to identify his or her place in the Empire.

Even within this stable system, not everybody, of course, would choose to follow a predictable path. The *devşirme*, the culling of Christian children to serve in the janissaries or the administration; the life of a travelling merchant; or, for Christians and Jews, conversion to Islam, all held out the possibility of social advance. But most Ottoman subjects were more than content to exchange such adventure for the security of a highly defined social hierarchy. Mutual respect and peace between the *millets* was in theory guaranteed to anybody who accepted Islam's supremacy.

Two crises on the periphery of the Empire, the Serbian Uprisings and the Greek War of Independence, shattered the complacency of the Ottoman elite and underlined the necessity of reform at the dawn of the nineteenth century. The *millet* system was clearly no longer sustainable in a world where the products of modern industry reached every part of the globe, and had an enormous effect on every local economy. The Ottoman Empire, in order to survive, had to absorb those advances from the West that had created such a discrepancy in the vitality of the European and Ottoman systems.

Reform of the *millet* and economic modernization were, however, mutually incompatible. Western commercial practices implied dynamic social change. To accommodate this, the *millet* system would have to be abolished – and with it the peculiar essence of the Ottoman Empire. A group of brave and extraordinary men, known collectively as the Men of the Tanzimat, the *tanzimatçılar*, attempted to reconcile economic change with the reform of the *millet*. The experiment was doomed to heroic failure. Nowhere was the problem they addressed more acute than in the vilayets (provinces) of Bosnia and Hercegovina.

By the early nineteenth century, chronic poverty, strained social relations, arbitrary official cruelty and bitter resentment towards Istanbul flowed through the Ottoman Empire like poisoned blood, but no other province could match Bosnia and Hercegovina for the severity of its symptoms.* Seen from the end of the twentieth century, dazzled as we are by clichés about Balkan tribalism and other modern mythologies, it is worth noting that nationalism was probably the least important force pushing Bosnia steadily towards centre stage of the Balkan drama. This would culminate between 1875–78 in the Great Eastern Crisis – the most fateful period in the peninsula's nineteenth-century history.

The poverty of force

> Victims of despotism and violence in their own countries, they [Polish and Hungarian refugees serving with the Ottoman army in Bosnia] became the tool with which the sultan crushed all movements and unrest in Turkey, regardless of their aims, aspirations or origins; and they served and died in campaigns which in fact only accelerated the inexorable drift towards collapse of this doomed and exhausted empire for which there was no medicine. Because both the medicine and the disease were equally fatal for it.
>
> Ivo Andrić, *Omerpaša Latas*[2]

* The one area which came very close was, unsurprisingly in retrospect, the Lebanon.

To understand the origins of the Great Eastern Crisis it is necessary to go back almost four decades before the Bosnian Uprising of 1875. In early November 1839, Sultan Abdülmecid invited a select audience, including foreign representatives, to the Gülhane, the leafy Rose Garden that once looked out onto the Bosphorus from below the Topkapi palace. Mustafa Reşid, the father of reform in the Ottoman Empire, announced the *Hatt-ı şerif* of Gülhane, the Noble Rescript of the Rose Garden. This was the earliest scripture of the *Tanzimat-ı Hayriye* – the Auspicious Reorderings – that eroded the special privileges of the Muslim *millet*, and were, in consequence, anathema to the ruling Ottoman class in Bosnia and Hercegovina. Their introduction sparked one of the longest political struggles ever to afflict the Ottoman Empire. In Bosnia, they pitched the ruling landowning and administrative class of Bosnia against the three great standard-bearers of reform and modernization, Mustafa Reşit Paşa, and his two protégés, Âli Paşa and Fuad Paşa.

These three gifted administrators formed the core of the group of cautious revolutionaries behind the Tanzimat. All had served in embassies abroad where they embraced progress, but with characteristic scepticism. They were, however, adamant as to the need for change in provincial Ottoman affairs. Their paramount aim was to rein in the *de facto* autonomy of Bosnia. Over the centuries, investment in the region had been vast, in order to ensure a bulwark against imperial Christian designs on the Sultan's lands. Bosnia had also been an important and often lucrative source of raw materials, notably salt, silver and timber. In the halcyon days of the janissaries and the *devşirme*, Bosnia and Hercegovina had provided the Empire with many of its most influential military and political figures. They had in turn endowed the provinces with great mosques, elegant bridges and charitable foundations. Together with Macedonia, Bosnia was the most diverse Ottoman province in Europe, where Islam had succeeded in establishing deep roots, and simultaneously the most isolated and closed society in the western part of the Empire.

But by the middle of the nineteenth century, its strategic value loomed the largest. Russia's influence in Serbia and the Danubian Principalities had squeezed the Sultan's authority to the north and east. A strong Bosnia was essential to ward off the predatory instincts of Vienna, whose interest in acquiring leverage over the Ottomans' western territories was fired by Russia's encroachment.

From the 1840s onwards, Serbia's awakening interest in the fate of fellow Serbs in neighbouring provinces threatened Bosnia's integrity. Were the idea of a Greater Serbia to prosper, it could excite irredentism and nationalism throughout European Turkey. Sultan Abdülmecid had been aware of this problem since ascending the throne in 1839. Reşid Paşa, the new Foreign Minister, convinced the new Sultan to continue the work of his father, Mahmud II, who had laid the foundations of reform by his courageous abolition of the janissaries in 1826. Abdülmecid embraced reform but had not inherited his father's determination – Reşid, Âli and Fuad could never trust him to force reforms through if he felt he was under pressure from other factions at court. He did agree, however, that his government should at least confer declarative equality on the Christian *raya* to appease nationalist aspirations and great-power pressure. (In reality, very little actually changed in the Christians' social position.)

The Christians certainly had a long list of complaints. The *haraç* (the head tax on non-Muslim males paid in lieu of military service) was a perennial source of discontent. The decision in 1839 to abolish the tax and allow Christians to serve in the army was never seriously implemented and the *haraç* was quickly reintroduced albeit with a new name. Most burdensome of all were the requirements of labour service which the peasantry was obliged to render to its feudal masters. In judicial matters, the chief grievances concerned the issue of Christian testimony, which in cases involving Muslims was considered invalid. Additionally, in the event of physical injury or murder perpetrated by a Muslim on a Christian, the former did not have to appear in court but was simply obliged to pay a 'blood tax' to the family involved, set invariably at low levels by the local *kadi* or judge.

Political issues were the least contentious. The Christian peasants were poorly represented by their churches. The Franciscan community in central and western Bosnia and in Hercegovina was an exception, and defended Catholic rights where it could. The leadership of the Orthodox Church was much weaker. The hierarchy, dominated by Phanariot Greeks, showed little interest in those under their spiritual jurisdiction and fluttered an obsequious eyelid at the Muslim authorities, with whom they were entwined in a mutually advantageous relationship.

After the Serb Foreign Minister, Ilija Garašanin, set his secret course of expansion in 1844, small conspiratorial groups and individuals, some sponsored by Serbia, engaged in revolutionary activity in Bosnia. Yet these clandestine cells did not agitate publicly for an improvement in the conditions of a peasantry that itself demonstrated little interest in politics. Any political demands were therefore modest, restricted to petitioning for the right to build churches, to sound church bells, to worship without hindrance, and to establish and run schools. Most of these complaints were specifically addressed by the reforms in the *Hatt-ı şerif* and subsequent *firmans* – but nothing had been done about them in practice.

Distasteful though they were, the concessions made to the Christians did not at first unsettle most Ottoman Muslims. For the Bosnian Muslim elite, it was a different matter. Especially since the Austrian conquests at the end of the seventeenth century, when many Muslims retreated into Bosnia from Hungary, the Bosnian Muslims had represented the firmest bastion of Ottoman power in Europe. The Habsburg monarchy had left them with especially bitter memories of Christian Europe. More recently, they had provided refuge to many thousands of Muslims who had been forced to evacuate the Belgrade *pashalik* during the First and Second Serbian Uprisings. It is unsurprising that they viewed the Gülhane decree as the thin end of the wedge even if it was commonly assumed that the Porte had no means of enforcing its reforms. The Bosniak elite was so determined to resist change that it was even prepared to wage a sustained war against the Sultan.

Although the Tanzimat appeared to be an open assault on the regime in Bosnia and elsewhere, the reformers were careful to couch their intentions in modest language and, where possible, to identify difficulties upon which everyone could agree. Included in the proposals for a complete overhaul of the tax system was a recognition of the damage caused by the widely disliked tax farmers. Despite the bold proclamations, the Empire did not have the resources either to police the activity of the tax farmers or to establish an alternative administration. The tax farmers remained, and indeed grew richer at the expense not just of the population but of the state's authority as well. While individual commercial monopolies were broken down as promised by the Noble Rescript, the Sublime Porte replaced them with state monopolies in order to increase revenues. As the visiting

Austrian consul to Sarajevo and Mostar noted in 1844, the reforms had the opposite of the desired effect in Bosnia:

> The impressions which I took with me on departing Bosnia are, if it is possible, worse than those which greeted my arrival. The [authorities in Istanbul] had shaken up the old forms, the old system with its entrenched practices, with its age-old traditions, with its eternal political and religious patterns of behaviour and thought. But they had attacked these without being able to replace it with anything specific or thorough . . . They only had one consequence: they made everybody unhappy.
>
> . . . So now trade is depressed and poverty on the increase. Every time the Pasha sends a fiscal contribution to Constantinople, which is now about once a week, people start to growl and say that the country is being bled dry.[3]

The *begs* of Bosnia reacted in time-honoured fashion to this intolerable insult to their life styles. They ignored central government, forcing a succession of weak pashas to halt the flow of money to Istanbul while conscription to the army was reduced to a trickle. This was an explicit challenge to the authority of the Sultan in his province. After repeated warnings, the Porte finally decided in the spring of 1850 that the time had come to crush the Bosnian overlords. To meet the Bosnian sedition, the Sultan called on his greatest military commander – Omer Paša Latas.

The conflict between the Bosnian Muslim elite and the Porte, as represented by Omer Paša, revealed an unexpected paradox. Of all the communities in the Ottoman Empire (excluding those in the Serbian and Danubian Principalities, and Egypt), the Bosnian elite had quite the most developed sense of their own *national* identity. Despite belonging to the most conservative section of the Muslim *millet*, they regarded Ottoman law increasingly as a foreign imposition. They saw quite correctly that the Tanzimat might lead in the end to an erosion of what they held most dear – their ownership and control of land.

Just after Omer Paša's arrival in Sarajevo in May 1850, the most powerful *begs* held a conspiratorial meeting to devise a strategy to defeat him. It was presided over by their doyen, Ali Stočević

Rizvanbegović, the vizier of Hercegovina and a determined opponent of reform. Ali warned that should the Tanzimat succeed, it would lead to 'the expulsion of *Bosniaks* from Bosnia'.[4] Unless Omer Paša were defeated, Ali continued, 'Bosnia would cease to be Bosnian in thirty years'.[5] The primary loyalty of the *begs* was not to the Sultan or the Muslim *millet*, although these were important, but to the local conditions underpinning their privileges.

By the middle of the nineteenth century, the term *Bošnjaci* or Bosniaks was commonly used both in Bosnia and in Istanbul to mean the Bosnian Muslims who also spoke Serbo-Croat as opposed to Ottoman Turkish. Their self-identity was one of the most complex in the Empire. Politically, the Ottoman state was their ultimate guarantor against interference from Christian great powers. Yet reformers at the Porte were also a threat. On a cultural level, they shared a confession with the other Muslims of the Empire but a language with the Christians and, in many respects, a hybrid culture as well. The relative prominence of these various identities, on the surface apparently mutually exclusive, depended on the particular circumstances at any given time. The Bosniaks' cultural identity could not flower into a full-blown political consciousness because they could not reach beyond their class, except to the tiny minority of Muslim peasants. Nonetheless, the rebellion of the *begs* against the Porte and Omer Latas Paša was the most important event in the development of a modern identity by the Bosnian Muslims in the nineteenth century. Omer Paša represented a reactionary authority attempting to impose progressive reforms. In Bosnia, the *ancien régime* found its temporary defender in nationalism and its enemy in a modernizing absolutism. This paradox could not be reconciled; both the *begs*' economic aspirations and the Ottomans' political strategy were doomed.

> The Imperial *serasker* [military commander] enters Sarajevo with a large, well-equipped army, with sweeping powers, and with the task of smashing and rooting out not the rebellious *raya* or foreign enemy but those who had for centuries ruled Bosnia and who until yesterday were called the Sultan's sons: the begs, the primates and members of the most respected families 'of Turkish ear' . . . He is not come as governor to rule and to arbitrate but to wage war and to punish. And, to cap it all,

> this *serasker*, who has crushed many rebels around the Empire, is nothing other than an erstwhile Christian from Lika,* an Austrian cadet, who has sought refuge in Bosnia a quarter of a century ago, has converted to Islam and then by his trade, by his cunning and through his personal achievements has succeeded in acquiring the highest military position in the Empire . . .
>
> [The primates] also know that he is not one of those old-fashioned Ottoman executioners, with ceremonial guns and a personal retinue of hundreds, with little knowledge of the real world and local conditions, but a real soldier and commander, with modern weapons and uniformed troops, with properly trained officers, Turkicised and a careerist, with the zeal of the mercenary and the arrogance of the unbeliever and foreigner.[6]

Omer Paša's entrance into Sarajevo in May 1850 was spectacular. He had insisted that the seat of government be transferred from Travnik, which the *begs* had always preferred because of its relative remoteness. His triumphant entry into the new home of the Bosnian vizier was designed specifically to reinforce his intention of eradicating resistance to the rule of the Sultan. He brought with him 30 senior officers (mostly Islamicized Poles and Hungarians who had fled the Austrian Empire in 1849), 8,000 troops of the regular army, 2,000 feared Albanian irregulars and, most imposingly, 34 of the most modern cannon. The regular troops included a special unit, known as the *murtad* (traitors') battalion, made up exclusively of Poles and Hungarians.

Surrounded by the symbols not of pomp but of war and violence, Omer Paša read out the Sultan's *firman* requiring the *begs* of Bosnia to accept and implement the Tanzimat. This was effectively a declaration of war on the recalcitrant *begs*. It remained to be seen who would submit and who would resist. The split among the most influential families was roughly even, which may be explained partly by regional rivalries and partly by the old trick of placing bets both ways.

---

* Now a region in Croatia, north of the Kninska Krajina; then part of the Habsburg Empire's Military District.

Almost two years of brutal civil war ensued. Three months after Omer Paša's arrival, the *begs* rose up in the Posavina region, in the Tuzla-Zvornik district under the leadership of Mahmud Paša Tuzla and in Hercegovina, where Rizvanbegović had withdrawn after Omer Paša had released him from house arrest in Sarajevo. Posavina, north of Sarajevo, was easily suppressed but Mahmud Paša put up much tougher resistance. The Tuzla region was especially important for Omer Paša as traditionally conscription had never applied here. The new *serasker* was determined to assert the Porte's right to cull soldiers from the population, and after some bloody struggles Omer Paša succeeded in taking Tuzla in the middle of December 1850.

Tens of thousands of people had participated in the battles for the Tuzla region and much blood was spilt on both sides. Establishing a precedent, Omer Paša unleashed a ferocious retribution against the rebels. The two local chiefs, Mahmud Paša Tuzla and Hafiz Paša, escaped into Austria and Serbia respectively. In a typically grim gesture of triumphalism, Omer Paša wrote to the Ottoman military commander in Belgrade, 'Send my regards to my dear "friend" Hafiz-paša and tell him to avoid eating, for a little while, fish from the Sava. For they have been feeding on Bosniak flesh which I drove into the river Bosnia at Doboj.'[7] On their return to Sarajevo through Posavina, Omer Paša's troops, who had been augmented by the wildly undisciplined Albanian irregulars, embarked on a spree of plunder and pillage against all the villages, whether Christian or Muslim.

This set the pattern. The inability of the *begs* to establish proper strategic cooperation allowed Omer Paša to pick them off, launching a massive assault on Rizvanbegović's strongholds in Mostar, Buna and Stolac in Hercegovina before moving on to deal with the rebels in Jajce, Banja Luka, Prijedor and Bihać. After his surrender, Rizvanbegović, who was ninety years old, was forced to walk in chains some 150 kilometres before he was 'accidentally shot dead' on the road to Jajce.[8] Towns which had been held by the rebels were liable to huge punitive fines when they surrendered to Omer Paša. By the middle of June 1851, his temporary military headquarters at Travnik had become 'one enormous prison. One sees Turks of every rank, mullahs, kadis, begs, wandering around the streets in chains or dragging around materials to repair the roads'.[9] Omer

Paša's systematic policy had led to 'the crushing of the entire Bosnian aristocracy, its most noble and influential members. Not a single office of state is now held by a Bosniak'.[10]

This, of course, was the real aim of Omer Paša and his masters, Mustafa Reşid, Âli Paşa and Fuad Paşa. In the wake of his military victories, Omer Paša introduced a comprehensive reorganization of Bosnia and Hercegovina's administrative structures.[11] All this, however, cost the Porte vast sums of money, and funds from Istanbul soon dried up. Payment of Omer Paša's troops and officers fell into chronic arrears, and so the *serasker* resorted to requisitioning. An entire Catholic community of several hundred families was moved out of Travnik to accommodate soldiers during the summer of 1851. The population, Christian and Muslim, was obliged to feed the army and in the most damaging move of all, livestock and horses were confiscated without payment. The Austrian consul, Demeter Atanacković, was on the whole sympathetic to Omer Paša's attempts to restore order and authority in Bosnia and Hercegovina. But he could see that the policy of reform was caught in a vicious circle:

> Sarajevo is dead. Trade and commerce is utterly flat. Last weekend, very little food was brought into the town for sale. You don't see any beasts of burden anymore – either because they have been already requisitioned by the military or because the peasantry have fled to the mountains to avoid having them confiscated . . . As I have so often permitted myself to point out the peasantry, Muslim and Christian alike, is so downtrodden with all manner of burdens. They have to hand everything over to the military, food and fodder, against no payment. And if that weren't enough both the regular army and the insurgents vie with each other in plundering and laying the country to waste.[12]

Omer Paša's ultimate loyalty was to the Sultan and he firmly approved the reformist course. He appears to have been close to both Fuad Paşa and Âli Paşa in Istanbul. But he was originally a Serb who had fled the Austrian military in mysterious circumstances. He believed that part of his job in Bosnia was to improve the lot of the Christian population. This would also persuade the *raya* to support his campaign against the *begs*. He praised the Christians' behaviour during the civil war, made the occasional magnanimous gesture (such as exempting Christians from the punitive fines levied against rebel towns) and insisted to Atanacković that their religious and political rights must be guaranteed. Yet although the Christian population supported him, their allegiance was tempered by fear of what might happen once he left Bosnia. And if there were any doubt about Omer Paša's loyalty to the Sultan, he systematically disarmed the Christians after he had destroyed the *begs*.

As the fighting dragged on, the Christians felt that if anything matters were getting worse for them. They had been forced to bear the intolerable behaviour of armies and irregulars while failing to benefit from the reforms. For, despite all the cash, the bloodshed and the administrative revolution, Omer Paša's programme was tangled up at the middle and lower levels of bureaucracy. By the middle of 1851, the Orthodox population had resorted to petitioning the Sultan, begging for the introduction of real reforms to make life more tolerable. Omer Paša had no answer to this – despite his evident commitment to the Christians, the punishing war against the *begs* had left him exhausted, with neither the resources nor the will to do anything for the *raya*.

This was not how the Muslims and the *begs* in particular saw his crusade. Even before his arrival, Omer Paša was regarded as doubly pernicious, a man of central government and a *poturice*, a convert to Islam whose sympathies were thus automatically under suspicion. He further alienated himself by arriving in Sarajevo with his hard-drinking desperadoes from Poland and Hungary, most of whom could speak neither Turkish nor Bosnian and whose attachment to Islam was questionable.* Omer Paša embodied everything that the *begs* despised about their Empire – he was a foreigner, a professional and a reformer.

By the autumn of 1851, Omer Paša had succeeded in crushing the power of the *begs*. But in doing so, he had devastated Bosnia. He

* In 1851 the Islamic hierarchy in Bosnia insisted that the converts be circumcised. Rather than face the cut, about half of the *murtad* battalion decided it was time either to emigrate to America or to take their chances back in the Habsburg Empire.

had introduced a new administrative mechanism and smashed the autonomist tendencies of the Bosnian elite. But he had failed to secure his two central economic aims – a regularization of conscription and tax collection. And like a lizard's tail, the economic order of the indigenous ruling class grew back almost as soon as Omer Paša had chopped it off. Within a year of his departure, the tax farmers were back in the fields gathering their lucrative harvest while the chief families re-established themselves and once more refused to send their contingents to the Bosnian army. They had lost control of the administration, which was now run by Muslims from outside Bosnia, but their feudal economic regime remained intact. The two sources of Ottoman authority in the province, the Sultan and the local *begs*, continued to dream of two different, mutually exclusive Bosnias. Over the next twenty-five years, this tension resulted in political stagnation.

The conflict highlights one of the Tanzimat's central weaknesses, one that helped reinforce contemporary western perceptions that the reform was merely an oriental ruse, and not, as was actually the case, a serious attempt to rejuvenate the ailing Empire. The reformers devised all manner of projects that left bold imprints throughout the Empire. But the key issue of agrarian relations was barely addressed. These deteriorated steadily, and the misery of the Christian peasantry in Bosnia increased. Over the next twenty years, the territory would be tormented by spontaneous rebellions. These were no longer clashes between competing parts of the fissiparous Ottoman elite. Instead, they were expressions of rural – and hence almost entirely Christian – despair. In Bosnia, this peasant violence – directed at the tax farmers and Muslim landlords – led to a rapprochement between the Bosnian landowners and the reformers at the Porte. Under the pressure of the most serious uprising, in 1858 (ironically this was quelled by Omer Paša Latas on a return visit), the Bosnian Muslims agreed to a gradual introduction of the Tanzimat. They made several important concessions to the Christian populations over their religious rights; and they ceded much of their political sovereignty (and with it their specific political identity) to the Porte. This gradual process went on throughout the 1860s during the long administration of the intelligent reformer, Topal Osman Paša. But Topal's work was too late. The fundamental cause of peasant grievances, the feudal labour obligations, was never tackled by any reformers from Istanbul.

In itself, peasant discontent could not have destroyed the Ottoman Empire. But the twenty-five years separating Omer Paša's arrival in Sarajevo and the outbreak of the Hercegovina uprising in 1875 was a period of tremendous change within Ottoman society as a whole. This transformation, as the great Bosnian novelist Ivo Andrić noted, was both overdue and fatal.

The *tanzimatçılar* put considerable effort into their central strategy of modernization in the fifteen years following the publication of the Gülhane decree. But Sultan Abdülmecid lacked a steady hand. Until the outbreak of the Crimean War in 1853 (which saw France and Britain fighting alongside the Ottomans to prevent Russian control of the Black Sea Straits, which would have threatened the Allies' interests in the Mediterranean), he vacillated between the first great man of the Tanzimat, Reşid Paşa, and more conservative figures who were less able and ever more determined to foil Reşid's plans. The reformers' diagnosis was undoubtedly correct: the Ottoman Empire's only hope for survival lay in a thorough overhaul of the mechanisms of state. But the causes of decline were many and complex, ensuring that implementation of the Tanzimat was haphazard even after victory in the Crimean War had consolidated the authority of the *tanzimatçılar*. Nonetheless, the shocks they administered to the well-defined pecking order of the Empire were real enough; and they led not to modernization but to chaos.

The European yoke

The Crimean War was an enormous waste of resources for the three great-power combatants, the Russians, the French and the British. Nonetheless, it provided a welcome fillip to the Men of the Tanzimat. Under the terms of the Treaty of Paris which concluded the war on 30 March 1856, the Empire, as a victorious power, was granted the dubious privilege of membership in the Concert of Europe. France and Britain, the victorious European powers, insisted on the Empire's elevation but equally demanded of Abdülmecid that he guarantee further concessions to his Christian populations.

The Sultan and his reformers had already obliged in February that year by promulgating the second great document of the

Tanzimat, the *Hatt-ı Hümayun*. Satisfied with these commitments to the equality of peoples, the British, French and Austrian delegations to the Paris negotiations agreed in Article IX of the Paris Treaty to recognize 'the high value' of the new decree. They committed their governments to abstain from interfering 'either collectively or individually in the relations of the Sultan with his subjects or in the internal administration of the Empire'. In addition, they signed a tripartite treaty 'guaranteeing joint and several defense of Ottoman independence and integrity'.[13] Stratford Canning, the experienced British consul and most powerful foreigner in Istanbul, lamented the latitude this gave the Porte, noting bitterly, 'I would rather have cut off my right hand than have signed that treaty'.[14]

However, the defeat of Russia dealt a severe blow to the Ottoman conservatives. Eventually it proved to be a pyrrhic victory for the Men of the Tanzimat. Success in the Crimean War fused with the energy of the *tanzimatçılar* to produce two unexpected outcomes – the accumulation of the Ottoman debt and the reorganization of the *millet* system.

The failure of agrarian reform, the accumulation of the debt and the breakdown of the confessional social order destroyed the Ottoman Empire. Equally important, however, they encouraged in a very short space of time the beginnings of a modern national consciousness among the Turks themselves – a consciousness of which there had been no significant sign before the 1860s.

There were no financial houses under the Ottoman state's influence until April 1840 when an imperial *firman* announced the establishment of a bank, subsidized by the government, in order to compete with the Armenian and Jewish money lenders. The following year, the government issued a paper currency for the first time. Called *kaime*, they have been more properly described as promissory notes. To keep interested parties guessing as to the amount of *kaime* in circulation, the government decided against numbering them. A cunning ploy in theory, perhaps, but in practice a disaster because the notes were easy to forge. It was an inconspicuous début in the world financial market.

The Crimean War had imposed a huge burden on the imperial treasury. The Ottoman government had to host the British and French forces in Istanbul and on the Black Sea coast. The Empire's primitive banking system did not have sufficient funds to cover the costs of the war, and so in a momentous first step on the path to eventual financial ruin, the Porte negotiated in August 1854 a loan of three million pounds sterling with the British and French governments. The two western allies backed this first loan for political reasons, and approved a second for five million pounds in 1855. They stipulated in the agreement that the monies would be 'devoted to the pursuits of war'.[15] Britain and France actively encouraged Istanbul to take out the loans in order to further their own strategic and political aims in the Near East.

But in the immediate aftermath of war, the Empire found itself in need of yet more cash, both to pay off the interest and capital of the wartime loans and to alleviate its budgetary problems. By 1858 not even the interest accrued had been paid, so Reşid requested a further loan. The creditors were less accommodating this time, and were 'able to force the empire to accept such onerous conditions of interest and discount that it had to pay as much as 60 percent on this loan alone, a process that continued with depressing regularity in subsequent years'.[16]

Once the *tanzimatçılar* discovered that they could contract a new foreign loan every time the Empire ran out of cash, they found it a very difficult habit to kick. Their suppliers were keen to feed their addiction. The Turkish loan soon developed a reputation as being one endless free lunch for investors. At the time, the British investment market was saturated with capital. Average returns on investments in domestic industry and public utilities stood at between 4 and 5 per cent. The Turkish bonds, backed in part by the British and French governments, offered a 9 or 10 per cent return.

One of the most successful get-rich-quick schemes in history, the debt imposed a ruinous burden on the Ottoman economy, already steadily corroded by competitive pressure. As the great powers, particularly Britain and France, became more closely involved with the Ottoman economy in the first half of the nineteenth century, they sought to secure maximum economic and commercial advantage by treaty. The substantial profits made from the loans were the icing on a rich cake. The central ingredient was the tariff system. The Porte was forbidden to raise the uniform import duty on goods from western Europe above 5 per cent. To compensate for the pitiful income which this generated, the Porte increased export tariffs to the punitive rate of 12 per cent, on top of the various internal taxes levied for the transportation and sale of goods *within* the Empire. This policy of economic self-flagellation allowed the manufactured goods of western Europe to swamp the Ottoman Empire at the expense of the more primitive indigenous produce, so that as a historian of the Tanzimat has noted, 'Bursa, under such conditions, was full of Bursa towels made in Manchester'.[17]

After the politically motivated loans of the Crimean War period, the involvement of the British and French governments declined while that of private capital grew. At the beginning of this period, the British government did not consider its interests identical with those of venture capitalists and entrepreneurs; but in large part due to the sudden explosion of economic involvement in the Ottoman Empire, this attitude began to change: 'What had been an embarrassment to Castlereagh, a subject to be virtually shunned for Canning, was appearing to Palmerston as an opportunity and as a right to be employed with discretion, and was forshadowed [sic] as a possible national duty.'[18]

For twenty years the government in London insisted that the debt was the best way to secure the stability of the Ottoman Empire and thereby prevent the expansion of Russian influence. Prussia observed the whole process with greater dispassion. A letter from the Foreign Ministry in Berlin to its representative in Istanbul, Count Goltz, in August 1860 clearly predicts where the debt policy would end:

> Evidently any sum of money, no matter of what proportions, will accomplish no good, if it is delivered to an administration which has neither adopted nor put into execution the fundamental principles of political economy and continues its original system. It can be stated with certainty that such an administration would not only be unable usefully to employ the product of the loan, but also it would not be long before the necessary means would be lacking to meet interest and sinking fund charges. This act would place the governments of Europe in the difficult alternative of themselves meeting the obligations of the Ottoman Empire, or of taking coercive measures which would place the Empire in the greatest danger, and which would form a singular contrast to their good intentions.[19]

Within five years of the first loan being taken out, all escape routes from bankruptcy had been closed off except for one narrow alley – the slashing of expenditure. In a memorably apoplectic pamphlet published as the full extent of the great debt crisis of 1876 was becoming clear, J. Lewis Farley outlined the chronic venality of the Sultan and his ministers:

> No matter what their origin, however, the first thought of modern Turkish statesmen is to amass money. They know their tenure of office is insecure, and they seize the opportunity. It is true, there was always peculation and corruption at the Porte, but these habitual vices were, to some extent, kept in check by Fuad and A'ali. Since the latter's death, however, all control has ceased, and corruption is the rule from the highest to the lowest. Their creed is: 'The country is going hopelessly to the dogs; let us *take care of ourselves.*' . . . In England, the richest country in the world, the Prime Minister receives 5000l. per annum; in Turkey, the poorest country in Europe, the Grand Vizier draws 30,000l. a year, while the Civil List, and the salaries of all the high officials are vastly more than those of the Queen and Ministers of Great Britain.[20]

While issuing frequent warnings to the Sultan and the Porte about the level of expenditure, however, the British and French governments simultaneously encouraged the Ottoman state to purchase their goods. After Abdülmecid's death in 1861 onwards, London was keen to indulge the passion of the new Sultan, Abdülaziz (1861–76), for modern warships, the 'ironclads'. In the ten years before his downfall in 1876, the Sultan purchased twenty of these expensive monsters for his navy. While the British establishment frequently complained about the grossly corrupt system of economic administration in the Empire, less publicity was given to the growing complicity in it of British financial houses. The brokers, Dent, Palmer & Company of London, arranged more loans to Turkey between 1853 and 1876 than any other house. Such was the influence wielded by Mr Palmer in Istanbul that he organized the removal of at least one Grand Vizier when the latter refused to contract yet another loan in an attempt to stem the tide of Ottoman indebtedness. Happily, the new head of government proved more amenable to Mr Palmer's desires.

The mess was worsened by the incompetence of an administrative system that for centuries could rely on income and expenditures which fluctuated very little. The sophisticated accounting techniques required to manage the dramatically altered financial condition of the Empire simply did not exist. A Ministry of Finance was not even established until 1839. Although the Ministry began to publish budgets in the 1840s, these were vague speculations, since no mechanism existed to ascertain accurately either income or expenditure.

The Porte attempted to overcome the problem by increasing its income. Tax farmers had succeeded in re-establishing their rights within three years of being banned in 1839. But in 1855 their privileges were officially restored and even enhanced, inflicting a new regime of arbitrary cruelty on the peasantry. Livestock and cereal requisition became commonplace, especially during the regular outbreaks of urban famine. The traders, like the peasantry overwhelmingly non-Muslim, also had to endure sharp tax increases.

Taxing the peasantry was easy; extracting money from the landowners of the Empire was anything but. In the mid-1860s, Midhat Paşa, another energetic supporter of reform, emerged as a skilled provincial administrator. His reorganization of the vilayet of Niş, comprising much of Bulgaria and northern Macedonia, led to a growth in income from the region and a uniquely prosperous peasantry. Partly due to Midhat's efforts, overall revenue from this area showed a steady increase throughout the period of the debt crisis.

But income from most other parts of the Empire stagnated or declined. The landowners seized on a legal loophole by declaring as much as three-quarters of all arable land in the empire as property of the *vakif*s, charitable trusts which were partially tax-exempt. Needless to say, the Ottoman administration had no means of dealing with such blatant tax avoidance. As a result of this and the persistent rescheduling of payments, the debt consumed a larger wedge of annual income year on year. The Porte's dependence on new foreign loans increased, until by 1875 it devoured 43.9 per cent of all revenues (after the deaths of Fuad and Âli in 1869 and 1871 respectively, any pretence of controlling expenditure was given up). This figure is all the more staggering when one considers that of the £180,259,836 issued to the Ottomans on the London market between 1854 and 1874 some £170,874,420 was unredeemed. The figure excludes a special Railway Construction Loan, drawn in 1870, for another £31 million so that the actual sum owed was nearer £200 million. A massive default was inevitable.

In October 1875, the crisis erupted. Nedim Paşa, the then Grand Vizier, announced the suspension of payments on the debt, 'in effect a declaration of bankruptcy'.[21]

It was clearly never the conscious intention of either Britain or France to ravage Turkey by allowing the Empire to accumulate debt. Indeed, both countries were keen to preserve the Empire at all costs. But it remains true that a combination of European fiscal recklessness and Turkish profligacy played an important role in sparking off the Great Eastern Crisis. It would provoke both xenophobia and a novel, if confused, patriotism among the class of Turkish intellectuals and professionals, themselves a product of reform; and it would lead to the New Ottoman movement, the first stirring of modern Turkish nationalism.

Osmanlılık – Ottomanism

There have been several attempts to construct a supranational identity in modern Europe. The most enduring is to be found in Switzerland, although maintaining harmony in this highly devolved, affluent Alpine state has been less easy than is sometimes assumed. Belgium continues in existence despite the often venomous relationship between its two main constituents, the Vlaams and the Walloons. The concept of 'Soviet man', which claimed to represent a civilizational breakthrough, was one of the best publicized of the supranational identities. Yet it was often a convenient disguise for Great-Russian chauvinism; and it eventually crumbled to dust in 1989. As we shall see, the Yugoslav identity – the brotherhood of the south Slavs – was still more complex.

The most ambitious effort in the nineteenth century to engineer a multi-ethnic civic identity was a product of the *tanzimatçılar*, whose idea of *Osmanlılık*, Ottomanism, was a necessary corollary of their administrative reforms. Yet, however desirable and inventive *Osmanlılık* may have been, the attempt to build this identity had to compete with a powerful alternative from abroad – the victory of unifying nationalisms in Italy and Germany. The Christians of the Empire inevitably sought to emulate the Italians and Germans. On the other hand, many Muslims regarded Ottomanism as a sign of weakness – a retreat of Islam in the face of a rising assertiveness among Christian peoples.

Both the *Hatt-ı şerif* of 1839 and the *Hatt-ı Hümayun* of 1856 had broken the most fundamental rule upon which the Ottoman Empire was constructed – they had confirmed the equality of all the Sultan's subjects, regardless of the *millet* to which they belonged. It thus implicitly denied the superiority of Islam. The *ulema* understood quickly just how severely the two main scriptures of the Tanzimat damaged its position. The *Hatt-ı Hümayun* was promulgated at the grandest of ceremonies in Istanbul and completed by a request for God's blessing. 'Oh Allah! Have mercy on the people of Mohammed', intoned the imam. 'Oh Allah! Preserve the people of Mohammed.' The attendant Minister of War muttered to his neighbour that 'he felt like a man whose evening-long labours on a manuscript were ruined through [the] careless upsetting of the inkpot'.[22]

The *Hatt-ı Hümayun* was bound to undermine the *millet* system. Equality implied that the Christians and Jews would relinquish the self-regulation that was an integral part of the system:

> The Ottoman statesmen were thus justified in believing that a surrender of these communal privileges should be the price paid for the establishment of an Ottoman nationality under which everyone would fully enjoy the benefits of state services as well as the equal protection of the laws. As matters turned out, these statesmen were never allowed an opportunity to carry out such ideas in practice, since they were under constant pressure from the Great Powers to grant at one and the same time equal rights of citizenship and special community privileges.[23]

This pressure did not bring sudden relief to the Christians. It did, however, fuel resentment among the Muslims. As Cevdet Paşa, a leading member of the Young Ottomans and the father of Turkish legal reform, noted, 'Many Moslems began to grumble: Today we lost our sacred national rights which our ancestors gained with their blood. While the Islamic nation used to be the ruling nation, it is now bereft of this sacred right. This is a day of tears and mourning for the Moslem brethren.'[24]

It certainly was difficult to convince the Muslims that yielding their political and social primacy was the only way to advance their vital interests. At the same time, the reformers could not allow the Christian *millets* to exploit their new status to strengthen irredentist claims. To judge by both their deeds and words, the four great *tanzimatçılar*, Reşid, Âli, Fuad and Midhat, understood this clearly. They concurred that the only possible way of allaying Muslim suspicions and accommodating Christian aspirations was to foster the development of *Osmanlılık*, an identification with the modernizing Empire. Identification with the *millet*, or religious community, would thus be replaced with the more secular, west European concept of the state as provider of individual rights and the recipient of duties and loyalty.

The reformers had no illusions about the problems this posed. The *millets* were based both on a specific interpretation of the Koran and on traditions peculiar to the Ottoman Empire. In order to dismantle or adapt them, the *tanzimatçılar* needed to find a new structure capable of lending legitimacy to *Osmanlılık*. Probably the only available political tool was constitutionalism. And therein lay the problem. At the beginning of the Tanzimat, there were no economic or political interest groups able to force the adoption of a constitution from the ground up. More than any other movement in the nineteenth century, this was a revolution from above.

As we have seen, the Ottoman landowners had little incentive to foster change. Trade was firmly in the hands of non-Muslims who had no experience of political activity outside the confines of their own *millet*. The strict social hierarchy of the Empire and its isolation from European social trends had left it bereft of an independent intelligentsia. Ziya Bey, one of the new breed of thinkers and writers who emerged during the Tanzimat, estimated dolefully in 1868 that a mere 2 per cent of Muslims in the Empire were literate while one of his colleagues noted that the rest were 'without tongue and without pen'.[25]

The reformers themselves resisted the idea of a constitution for several reasons: they were scared of provoking a reaction in conservative circles, especially the *ulema* and the more powerful regional oligarchies; they were worried that any devolution of political power would weaken their authority to implement change; and in Âli's blunt opinion, the principle of representation promised chaos:

'The Ottoman Empire numbers twelve to fourteen nationalities, and unfortunately, as a result of the religious and racial hatreds which divide, above all, the Christian populations, each one of these nationalities does not as yet show great inclination to grant just and necessary concessions. If the representatives which they would nominate by way of elections were to be brought together today, such a national assembly would instantly give rise to all scandals imaginable.'[26]

The prospect of constitutional rule also seemed certain to encourage the growth of nationalist demands among the Christian populations. To be sure, the reformers expanded the consultative bodies of government but any widening of the decision-making process was slow in coming. The reformers conceded the desirability of a constitution in some distant future; for the present the idea frightened them as much as it did the *ulema*.

The erosion of the *millet* system combined with the failure of the *tanzimatçılar* to instil Ottomanism in either the Christian or the Muslim populations created a political void. The Ottoman state no longer regarded its subjects as Muslims, Christians or Jews, nor yet did they recognize them as Serbs, Bulgarians or Turks. *Osmanlılık* had little attraction for the population and so they turned instead to the alternative offered by the Italians and Germans – nationalism and the nation state. Identity was defined in the first instance by confessional affiliation. But this was complicated by language, by social and economic considerations, and by the construction of historical myths. The Orthodox Church splintered into several national Orthodox churches – Serbian, Bulgarian and Romanian. Among the Muslims, language separated the Albanians and Bosniaks from the Turks. Lacking the dense network of social and economic relationships of a France or Britain, the young elites among both Christians and Muslims seized upon exclusivist nationalism as a means of ensuring the survival of the imagined nation. To join the national community implied subordination of class or regional interests to those of the embryonic state.

At first, the young national movements aimed to undermine or even bring down the great oppressor – the Sultan, his bureaucrats and his generals. But migratory patterns in the Empire had been fluid for almost five hundred years. Conversion to Islam had also divided ethnic communities. Catholic, Orthodox and Muslim

Albanians lived in communities as far apart as Wallachia and Egypt. There were Muslims who only spoke Slav or Greek; in many areas Greeks, Turks, Albanians, Jews and Slavs lived together, sometimes mixing with one another, sometimes remaining isolated. The Habsburg Empire was another such Babel, if slightly less noisy. Given this complexity, it was likely that at some point the emerging nations would no longer need to fight the imperial oppressor but would turn against one another. The ideology of exclusive nationalism in the Balkans, invariably encouraged and even defined by great-power politics, contained the seeds of tragedy.

Confessional cleansing

Even under favourable conditions, the effect of the Tanzimat would have tested the most able politicians. But from the 1830s to the 1870s, the Ottoman Empire also experienced a substantial and destabilizing demographic shift. During this period over one million people, almost all Muslims and mostly from the Caucasus, sought refuge in the Empire. A precedent had already been set when the victims of Russia's expansion southwards in the eighteenth century resettled in Ottoman lands. In the first half of the nineteenth century, Tsarist forces swept deep into the Caucasus and Central Asia. Another huge movement of people was triggered by Russia's defeat in the Crimean War. Fearing retribution, hundreds of thousands of Tartars fled the country for the Ottoman Empire.

Traditionally, the Empire had always welcomed persecuted peoples. The magnificent Sephardic community in southern Europe with its centre in Salonika was founded in 1492 by the Jews who fled Spain. The majority of these Jews eventually fell victim in the twentieth century not to Islamic fundamentalism but to a peculiarly perverted ideology from a Christian culture. The Islam of the Empire excluded nobody on grounds of faith, a fact often obscured by twentieth-century western perceptions of Islam. In the nineteenth century, there was even a substantial flow southward of Poles and Hungarians, whose descendants can still be found in Anatolia, escaping the tyranny of Russia and Austria.

When a Christian monarchy like Russia expanded to the south, the Muslims living in the conquered territories naturally turned to Turkey. Those who arrived after the Crimean War, in particular, had suffered considerable violence at the hands of the Russians. They assumed that as members of the dominant *millet*, they would be suitably privileged. The government did indeed introduce a beneficial code regulating the status of refugees in 1857. According to this, the destitute among them (i.e. the great majority) would receive a small amount of capital and exemption from tax and military conscription for twelve years if they settled in Anatolia and for six years if they chose the Balkans.

The majority chose the lengthy Anatolian tax break but about one-third migrated to the Balkans, a few to Bosnia but most to Bulgaria, Macedonia and Thrace. Here they encountered a large population of Christians. In a series of unpleasant incidents, the new arrivals visited the violence they had suffered at the hands of the Orthodox Russians on to the Orthodox Bulgarians, many thousands of whom fled to Russia.*

The influx of refugees into this region is a relatively obscure episode in Ottoman history. Yet it had a significant impact both on the Tanzimat and on the longer-term relations between Christians and Muslims in the area. From the 1830s onwards conditions had improved in the Bulgarian-populated areas of the southern Balkans as nowhere else in the Empire. In addition the eyalets (provinces) of Niş, Vidin and Silistra were the focus of a systematic attempt at administrative reorganization by the *tanzimatçılar*. In 1864 these three eyalets were transformed into the much larger Tuna, or Danube, vilayet under the last great man of the Tanzimat, Midhat Paşa, the most fervent promoter of *Osmanlılık*. Midhat channelled money into the construction of roads, bridges and tunnels. He founded agricultural cooperative banks which advanced loans to the peasantry. To a degree, he is still regarded among contemporary Bulgarian historians as a progressive influence, although their admiration is tempered by dismay at Midhat's uncompromising suppression of any movement smacking of separatism.

Since the Romanians and Serbs had achieved economic independence from the Porte, Bulgaria, Macedonia and Thrace had become the main wheat suppliers to the Empire, the central reason

* A majority of these Bulgarians later returned after ascertaining that life with their fellow Orthodox Russians was even less rewarding than the unpredictability of the Empire.

why living standards were improving in these regions. Nonetheless, Bulgarian revolutionary committees were proliferating and receiving active support in both Serbia and Romania. Midhat combated the influence of the revolutionaries by implementing a series of enlightened policies. Apart from modernizing the transport and economic infrastructure, he also inaugurated a system by which local disputes would always be resolved after discussion with both local Muslim and Christian leaders. In the Tuna vilayet, more than anywhere else in the Empire, Christians were integrated into the legal and political process.

But Midhat's reforms were undermined by the last great migration into the Empire which occurred in 1864 when hundreds of thousands of Circassians abandoned their mountainous strongholds as Russia finalized its conquest of the Caucasus. Their arrival in the Empire led to one of the nineteenth century's great humanitarian crises (which never even touched the European conscience). About 400,000 Circassians sought refuge in Anatolia, Bulgaria and Macedonia. Starving, they headed towards Bulgaria's Danubian border with Romania and the land border with Serbia. Homeless, exhausted and smitten by smallpox and typhoid, thousands fell ill and died in the open. The insanitary conditions spread the epidemics among the local Bulgarian and Turkish populations. The Circassians had travelled to the border areas because, after the creation of the Danube vilayet, Midhat had agreed to an expansion of military forces to defend the new province. The Porte, lacking money as always, used the influx of refugees as an expedient and declared that the new soldiers should be recruited from the Circassians and Tartars. Both by decree and by *force majeure*, Christians were evicted *en masse* from their homes and villages to accommodate the new arrivals. The refugees began to terrorize parts of the countryside and thousands of Christians fled into Romania (some also went to Serbia). The émigré Bulgarian revolutionaries acquired many new recruits. Midhat's efforts to neutralize Bulgarian nationalist sentiment were nullified.

The problems between refugees and the settled population consolidated the pattern of arbitrary violence associated with displaced populations that was to become such a hallmark of warfare and civil conflict in the Balkans. One historian, generally sympathetic to the Muslims and Turks of the Empire, noted that the refugees from southern Russia 'began to take vengeance on their non-Muslim neighbors in a manner hitherto unknown in the Ottoman Empire'.[27]

It had been over sixty years since the peasantry of the region had been subject to the unbridled terror of Paşvanoğlu and his shock troops, the *kircali*. But the conflict in the 1860s was different in one key respect. However terrifying Paşvanoğlu's regime was, the *kircali* did not discriminate among their victims according to faith or race. And Bulgarians, Bosniaks, Serbs, Albanians, Turks, Greeks and Vlachs all participated in the troops' murderous activity. Nobody could mistake, however, the confessional contours of the conflict between the Caucasian refugees and the peasantry from the Tuna vilayet. As the Empire struggled under ever greater pressure from abroad and domestic economic failure, the lines of confessional conflict, first drawn during the First Serbian Uprising, came into much sharper relief. The Tanzimat, whose aim had been to dissolve national difference through *Osmanlılık*, had precisely the opposite effect.

The realm of ruins

Reşid, Ali and Fuad had all been influenced in their thinking by time spent at the Ottoman embassies in Austria, Germany, France and England. Other Ottomans had also started to travel abroad and acquaint themselves with intellectual life in western Europe. One result of this was the belated establishment of newspapers and the beginnings of a debate about public affairs in the Empire. As with the idea of a constitution, the free dissemination of opinions posed problems for the *tanzimatçılar* (rather like the relationship between *perestroika* and *glasnost* for Mikhail Gorbachev over a century later). Economic reform brought with it new ideas. From an early stage, the English-language newspaper, the *Levant Herald*, specialized in exposing graft in the Ottoman administration as well as providing commentary on the mounting debt crisis. More ominously for the Porte, a group of young intellectuals, several educated in Europe, started publishing Turkish newspapers and journals.

This group of publicists and commentators formed the nucleus of the first Muslim political opposition in the Ottoman Empire. In certain respects the dilemmas these people faced reflected the dualism that continues to affect Turkish nationalism in the twentieth century. As one student of the period put it a century after this movement emerged, 'there is hardly a single area of modernization in Turkey today, from the simplification of the written language to the idea of fundamental civil liberties, that does not take its roots in the pioneering work of the Young Ottomans'.[28]

While embracing the ideals of west European romantic nationalism and constitutionalism, their patriotism was necessarily designed to appeal to the Muslim *millet*. Bravely but unsuccessfully, they attempted to reconcile the secular ideals that inspired them with the more conservative precepts of political Islam: to harmonize Europe with Anatolia; a liberal constitution with the *şeria*; a modern economy with the traditional Ottoman hierarchy.

The Osman virtues old are all, alack, undone;
The ancient Osman zeal abideth in ne'er an one;
The Osman glory of yore is past and gone;
The Osman State is come into such a plight that none
The signs and portents sad of approaching doom can see.[29]

Ziya Bey, the writer and bureaucrat, was a reluctant supporter of the Tanzimat. His lament reflected the deep underlying traditionalism of the New Ottomans. It was written in 1868 as the Porte was still struggling to pacify an uprising in Crete and a year after the Ottoman Army had agreed in a humiliating move to withdraw its last seven garrisons from the (still) autonomous principality of Serbia. Despite Ziya's conservatism, he was well aware that expressing such thoughts even twenty years previously would probably have resulted in his execution. For although they clung to a romantic image of an Ottoman past, the critics of the Tanzimat also embraced, in varying degrees, many of the reform's fundamental aims: *Osmanlılık*; educational reform and the drive to increase literacy rates; economic modernization; and above all, the expansion of consultative political structures. But the Men of the Tanzimat would not risk a constitution. Imperial absolutism was to be replaced by an oligarchy, i.e. themselves, not by representative government. In the 1860s, the New Ottomans finally articulated what they considered must be the logical goal of the Tanzimat – the promulgation of a constitution and the regulation of the Sultan's authority. It was not only through articles in journals that the New Ottomans advanced their cause. Istanbul was suddenly vibrant with drama, poetry and novels, the majority striking a tone of patriotism and of critical loyalty to the Sultan.

The greatest figure to emerge from this flowering of Ottoman cultural life was Namık Kemal. The development of his thinking, as reflected in his journalism, poetry and plays, neatly reflects the intellectual and political puzzle facing these harbingers of Turkish nationalism. In 1865, Namık and his friends founded a secret society, explicitly modelled on the Italian nationalists, the Carbonari. Such structures, and the New Ottomans' support for a constitutional monarchy, reflected the profound influence of western liberal thought on the movement. But its ideology was complicated.

In Ottoman society, the words 'Turk' or 'Turkish' were essentially derogatory. A member of the elite would consider himself an Osmanli, while the language he would speak was Ottoman, a highly stylized version of Turkish with a considerable Arabic influence. *Kaba türkçe*, coarse Turkish, was the tongue of the Anatolian peasantry who were known as Turks.[30]

Both the *tanzimatçılar* and the increasingly populist New Ottomans found Ottoman Turkish an obsolete tool. The Arabic script had been awkwardly adapted to the phonic system of Turkish while there were nine competing calligraphic systems in existence. The language itself was high-falutin and elaborate. Combined with the primitive state of education, this places the appallingly low literacy rate in the Empire in its proper context.

As the Empire started to buckle under the combined pressure of its self-confident Christian neighbours and the disaster of the debt, Namık Kemal's commitment to *Osmanlılık* began to harden into a passion for *vatan* – fatherland. The words 'Türk' and 'Türkistan' began to be used for the first time alongside or in place of 'Ottoman' and the 'Ottoman Empire'. The steady shift towards populism and away from the elitist methods of the *tanzimatçılar* was fuelled by the dissatisfaction of the Muslim population with the increasingly obvious influence of Europe in the life of the Empire. The New Ottomans were drawn into an alliance with more conservative elements, particularly the *ulema* but also the *softas*, or religious students. The alliance was cemented by a certain shared xenophobia but also by the fear that dependency on Europe was eroding the social fabric (the debt was the object of especially fierce and entirely justified criticism). Yet the association was confused, as the New

Ottomans never abandoned their demands for a constitution and some form of representative government, which was anathema to the religious conservatives.

Matters came to a head after the deaths of Fuad in 1869 and Âli two years later. Midhat thus assumed the mantle of the Tanzimat. Unfortunately, Midhat was a relative outsider, enjoying much less influence in Istanbul than his predecessors. Abdülaziz was tiring of the Tanzimat, particularly as it affected his ability to spend vast sums of money on luxuries. Âli's replacement as Grand Vizier was Nedim Paşa, whose cupidity was matched only by his gullibility. Within two years, all the good work of the *tanzimatçılar* began to unravel. The global economic crisis of 1873 accelerated the crumbling of the Sultan's authority. An astonishing variety of political forces competed to fill the political vacuum and the rush provoked civil unrest, rebellion, regicide and war. Returning to the Ottoman Empire after one of his extended visits to Europe, Ziya Bey expressed himself in typically gloomy terms:

> *I passed through the lands of the infidels, I saw cities and mansions;*
> *I wandered in the realm of Islam, I saw nothing but ruins.*

The great crash of 1873 had a swift and debilitating impact on the Ottoman Empire as the Austrian banks trading in Istanbul collapsed and were refused aid by the Habsburg government. Most of the small private Ottoman banks were swallowed up in the wash of the sinking Austrian banks. Europe's major lending houses began repatriating capital from various parts of the world. Most slammed the door in the face of the Porte when the Ottoman government, once the pampered guest of the European financial markets, came calling for additional loans.

In response to the crisis, the Sultan and his government made no serious attempt to cut expenditure. Instead, the regional authorities were required to redouble their tax-collecting efforts. The previous year Anatolia suffered a severe drought, which had provoked a sudden increase in the price of grain. Production in the Danubian Principalities dropped by almost 50 per cent from the year before, while huge locust swarms attacked the fields of Cyprus. The Porte felt obliged to impose a ban on the export of wheat from the

Bulgarian provinces in the hope of staving off shortages in the towns. Even more severe was the crop failure in areas populated by the Turkish peasantry. The scarcity of food was compounded by the most brutal winter in over seven decades. If they were in a position to do so, the peasants began to hoard food for their personal consumption. The Empire's ailing transport infrastructure literally crumbled under the weight of the snows. The result was urban famine on a vast scale.

Hundreds of dead bodies lay on the streets of Istanbul as wolves moved into the outskirts of the capital, preying on the inhabitants. Tens of thousands died of hypothermia and starvation while the extreme flooding which followed the hard winter ensured that the famine continued well into the spring. By this time, 90 per cent of livestock reserves in Anatolia and the southern Balkans had been slaughtered, leading to disruption in supplies for several years. One observer witnessed how 'in the Kayseri district [of Istanbul] a camel forty days dead was torn apart by the hungry; when the vali ordered it buried, the people dug it up and ate the rotting flesh, some dying in consequence'.[31]

Outbreaks of unrest had increased throughout Bosnia and Hercegovina from 1871. After 1873, they became endemic, and were no longer restricted to the Orthodox peasants. Muslims and Catholics joined their compatriots on several occasions to present lists of grievances to the Porte. In 1874, the Catholics of western Hercegovina began to resist the tax demands of the local governor. Although making up a much smaller percentage of the population than the Orthodox *raya*, the Catholics were blessed, in the radical Franciscans, with a canny and resourceful group to defend their interests. The Franciscan clerics negotiated skilfully with local authorities while maintaining close contacts with the Habsburg state and monitoring the changes in European politics as these affected their position.

Germany's unification after the defeat of the Habsburg forces at Königgrätz in 1866 was followed by the even more spectacular humiliation of France in 1871. The Russian government exploited the drama of the Franco-Prussian war by unilaterally releasing itself from some of its obligations under the Treaty of Paris of 1856. It made clear that it would launch its ships on to the Black Sea once more. This effectively reopened the Eastern Question.

Austria-Hungary had lost the power game in central and northern Europe, and now faced the prospect of renewed Russian moves into the Balkans. Vienna cast its acquisitive gaze with ever greater urgency on Bosnia and Hercegovina. Mindful of these circumstances, the Catholic hierarchy in Bosnia appealed to the Habsburg army commander in Dalmatia, General Rodić, for help. It recognized that ultimately political status depended not on the strength of popular feeling but on the actions of the great powers. Its energies were more fruitfully expended in agitating at a powerful neighbour's court than among its own flock. And it knew that if its cause were taken up by the neighbouring Empire this would embolden the faithful. The Ottoman authorities had already banned the import of Austrian newspapers into Bosnia and Hercegovina because of their relentless reporting of the Christian peasantry's misery. Austria's annexation of Bosnia and Hercegovina looked increasingly likely.

Because of these shifts in Europe's geo-politics, when the Hercegovinian and Bosnian uprisings broke out in 1875, the Porte no longer saw them as irritating domestic disorders but as an acute strategic threat.

An inconspicuous event

In 1874 the crop failed throughout most of Bosnia and Hercegovina. As in Anatolia the previous year, a harsh winter compounded the effect. A bad harvest not only threatened the provinces' peasantry with starvation. It ensured that the tax farmers, ably supported by the *zaptiehs* (gendarmes) and if necessary the regular army, would pursue their work with even greater zeal. The tax farmer had no fixed schedule; he would arrive with his armed retinue at an unspecified time after the crop had ripened. Until the tax farmer had arrived, estimated the harvest's value and then confiscated his share, the peasants were not permitted to bring in the fruits of their labour. The most profitable and widespread crop was maize, the primary target for the revenue collectors. In Hercegovina, however, the poor rocky soil could rarely sustain maize and instead tobacco and grapes were the main cash crops.

As winter approached in 1874, the grapes of Hercegovina were rotting on the vine. Most peasants could wait no longer for the tax farmer and began to sell their produce. The tax farmers did not turn up in the Nevesinje area of eastern Hercegovina until January 1875. The chief collector was Stanko Perinovo, who like many tax farmers was not a Bosnian Muslim but a Serb from the nearby town of Mostar. As the Russian traveller, Alexei Gilferding, had observed, the Christian tax farmers and traders were the object of especial loathing: 'Many Orthodox traders buy up the right to collect the tithe . . . and woe betide those peasants who fall into their hands: the Orthodox traders plunder them worse than the Muslims.'[32] When Perinovo made extortionate demands of his Orthodox compatriots in the Nevesinje area, they refused to pay. Instead, most fled to Montenegro while the *zaptiehs* started plundering their villages in lieu of tax.

The six months that followed were like a mummers' play which introduced many of the domestic and foreign characters in the roles that they would adopt to more devastating effect over the next three years. Skirmishes between the Serb peasants and Ottoman troops were followed by retreat into the mountains; hostage-taking became common; the Austrian Emperor made an ostentatious tour of Dalmatia, carefully taking in the border areas with Hercegovina to underline Vienna's dishonourable intentions towards the neighbouring Ottoman territories; the mischievously adept Russian consul in Istanbul, Count Nikolai Pavlovich Ignatiev, began pushing both the Ottoman government and the Serb peasantry now towards confrontation, now towards rapprochement; and secret organizations in Serbia stepped up their revolutionary activity in Bosnia.

In late June 1875, a caravan of Muslim traders was making its way from Mostar across the inhospitable countryside of eastern Hercegovina towards Nevesinje. According to Serb villagers in the region, the traders were transporting supplies to local military garrisons that had recently received troop reinforcements. Other histories discount this version, maintaining the merchants' business was purely civilian, albeit with gendarmerie protection. It was mid-morning as the caravan emerged from the forest on to an open plain, Četna Poljana. Pero Tunguz, the most notorious *hajduk* leader in the Nevesinje area, was lying behind a hillock, his gun aimed at the Muslim commander, Captain Karminić. Karminić fell lifeless to the ground. The first of the Nevesinje Rifles had been fired. Tunguz's *četa* (band) of some fifty men routed the Muslims, killing about ten of them, before making off with the caravan's load of guns, ammunition, sugar and coffee. On hearing the news, Selim Paşa, the local governor, immediately ordered units of the Ottoman army to fan out among the largely Orthodox villages to apprehend the criminals. The *hajduci* had of course already disappeared into the mountains, but there were still plenty of Serb villagers to intimidate.

Pero Tunguz is still regarded as a folk hero among the region's Serbs, fêted in the local epic poetry. But the Serbs of eastern Hercegovina would pay dearly for this opening shot of the Uprising. Because the Nevesinje Rifle was fired too soon – against the express wishes of the local knezes and, more importantly, against the urgent advice of Knez Nikola of Montenegro, the tiny mountainous principality which was the main 'international' sponsor of the Nevesinje Serbs. By provoking conflict between the peasantry and military authorities before the harvest had been brought in, Tunguz had ensured that the rebels would have no supplies during the coming winter.

The Nevesinje rebellion was different from the countless acts of armed resistance in Hercegovina and Bosnia over the previous decade. It had been at least a year in preparation. While the local leaders were aware that the stability of the Ottoman Empire had deteriorated rapidly in the past five years, they could not understand, as Knez Nikola did full well, that insurrection in Bosnia and Hercegovina might lead to a crisis of much greater proportions. Both Nikola and his nationalist allies in Serbia wanted to get the timing right. Tunguz's attack caught everybody off guard. The echo from the Nevesinje Rifle travelled well beyond Hercegovina, first into Bosnia and then St Petersburg, the Hofburg at Vienna and the Topkapı palace in Istanbul.

The Muslim peasantry suffered conditions almost as miserable as those under which the Serbs laboured while the wealth of the landowners, the *begs* and *ağas*, was being steadily drained by the government in Istanbul, desperate to feed its debt. Even the tax farmers themselves were beginning to moan that life was becoming uncomfortable for them. It was now dangerous, they complained, to collect taxes in certain areas because of attacks by *hajduci* or the violent hostility of the locals. In short, the social, economic and political system in Bosnia-Hercegovina was on the verge of explosion and the incident at Četna Poljana, insignificant in itself, was sufficient to light the fuse.

The governments in St Petersburg and Vienna were alerted by their local agents to the worsening situation in Hercegovina. The Porte immediately sent a high-level commission to investigate the events in the hope of averting conflict. But, as the first historian of the Bosnian Uprising has noted, 'blood had already been spilled. Preventing a general conflict between the Christians and Turks would now be extremely difficult'.[33] The *zulum* (outrage or atrocity) was about to engulf much of Hercegovina. It was a matter of weeks before it reached Bosnia. This was the prologue to the Great Eastern Crisis – the most significant period in nineteenth-century Balkan history, and one that would change the peninsula beyond recognition.

From 1873 onwards, more symbols of imperial pride and power fell into Ziya Bey's realm of ruins. Economic collapse was bringing with it political intrigue and turmoil. Christian rebellion brought with it international condemnation and threats. The pan-Slavists hurled insults at the Islamic state and taunted the Turks with the impending Russian conquest of Istanbul. It is no surprise that the resonant confessional overtones of nationalist struggle in the Balkans provoked a backlash of pan-Islamic sentiment. Just as romantic nationalists and liberals were mobilizing European public opinion on behalf of the Balkan Christians, the ever bolder newspapers in the Ottoman Empire raised the banner of Turkish pride. A new phrase, *efkâr-ı umumiye*, 'public opinion', littered the commentaries of the time. In 1872, Namık Kemal, writing in *Ibret*, noted the impact of the spread of ideas among the Muslims of the Ottoman Empire, 'Twenty years ago, the fact that there were Moslems in Kaşgar was not known. Now, public opinion tries to obtain union with them. This inclination resembles an overpowering flood which will not be stopped by any obstacle placed in its way.'[34]

Namık himself learned about this unprecedented populist force in the Empire a year later when his drama, *Vatan yakut Silistra* (Fatherland or Silistria) was staged in Istanbul. The drama was set at the time of the Crimean War and depicted the heroes of the Turkish garrison which repelled the Russian siege of Silistria. In a rousing finale to an unsophisticated piece of theatre, the ensemble belted out:

Blood and sword on our flag are flying
On our hills and plains roams no fear of dying,
A lion in each part of our land is lying,
We rejoice in the fray martyrs' lives to lay down,
We are Ottomans, giving up life for renown.[35]

Namık's rhetorical commitment to *Osmanlılık* could not disguise his references to martyrs, the *jihad* or the electrifying word *vatan*, fatherland. After two performances of the play, Istanbul was overrun by demonstrators calling for a holy war and, more daringly, expressing support for Murad, Abdülaziz's brother and heir to the throne. Pan-Islamic sentiment was now mingling with the Young Ottomans' commitment to a constitution. Abdülaziz acted swiftly by closing down the theatre and exiling Namık to Famagusta in Cyprus. But the words that had been uttered could not be unsaid.

The Bulgarian Uprising in 1876 provoked another upsurge in popular discontent. The rhetorical skills of the Young Ottomans reached new heights, and allies of Midhat Paşa in the bureaucracy had no difficulty in spreading opposition on to the streets. Midhat's agents paid for and organized demonstrations against the Sultan. The signal for revolt was provided by the *softas*, religious students, the *ulema* of the future, who in their thousands downed their copies of the Koran and began purchasing weapons in preparation for an assault on the Porte and the Sultan.

Bereft of public support and unable to mobilize loyal elements in the army, Abdülaziz went quietly when the conspirators came to depose him in the early morning of 30 May 1876. Murad V, a nervous, unstable man, was placed on the throne. Shortly after, however, Abdülaziz died in mysterious circumstances. The official explanation was that the deposed Sultan took his own life. But as one waggish journalist put it, 'Abdülaziz was suicided.'[36] Terrified he might meet a similar fate, Murad V abdicated after just two months as Sultan. Soon afterwards, the Empire's most capable military leader and Midhat's chief co-conspirator, Hüseyin Avni Paşa, and the Foreign Minister, Raşid Paşa, were assassinated. These chaotic events coincided with political change and uncertainty elsewhere, above all in the Bulgarian lands and Serbia.

Cooking the golden goose: Bulgaria, 1876–8

> When the others came up he was still slashing at him almost unconsciously – he was like a wild beast thirsting for blood. The Turk, still living, was reduced to a shapeless and bloody heap of pulp – he had lost all semblance of human form. The blood formed in pools on the melting snow.
>
> Ognianoff turned away in disgust from this butchery and thought to himself: 'It's a savage revenge, but justifiable before God and one's own conscience. It's bloodthirstiness; but it's a good sign. The Bulgarian's been a sheep for five centuries, it'll be well if he becomes a wild beast now. Men respect the wild goat more than the tame sheep, the dog more than the goat, the ferocious tiger more than the wolf or bear, the bird of prey more than the barn-door fowl, which supplies them with excellent food. Why? Because they represent force, which means liberty and justice.
>
> Ivan Vazov ('Chronicler of the Bulgarian Uprising'), *Under the Yoke*[37]

The peasantry in Bosnia and Hercegovina waged a sustained guerrilla campaign for months. Inspired by this example, the Bulgarian Revolutionary Central Committee (BRCC) became convinced that the Empire was tottering and that the suffering Bulgarian masses were now in a position to administer the death blow. From exile in Bucharest, the BRCC divided the Bulgarian lands into four zones and ordered their most able leaders to direct a mass popular rising against the rule of the Sultan.

May 1, 1876 was the date set for the Uprising. But ten days earlier, a villager from Baldevo in the Sredna Gora (Central Forest) betrayed his compatriots to the local Ottoman authorities. Necib Aga, the district governor, responded by trying to arrest the local rebel commander, Todor Kableshkov. Before he could do so, Kableshkov's fellow conspirators attacked the gendarmerie and raised the banner of revolt in the Koprivshtitsa district. In one of the many romantic gestures that marked the Uprising, Kableshkov 'signed a letter with his blood', which was dispatched to the other revolutionary centres appealing for the revolt to be proclaimed everywhere.

The April Uprising of 1876 is ingrained in the Bulgarian imagination as the heroic pinnacle of the *vŭzrazhdane*, the national revival or renaissance. Within two years the first self-governing Bulgarian state since medieval times would be established. Yet the two events are only indirectly linked. The Bulgarians did not seize power in their revolutionary struggle – their rebellion was obliterated within a month. The April Uprising highlighted above all the weakness of Bulgarian nationalism, and the revolutionary leadership's dire misreading of Bulgarians' willingness to confront the might of the imperial state.

For all the planning of the BRCC in Bucharest, the rebels had no clear sense of either tactical or strategic goals. In large areas, the revolutionary committees failed to rouse the population. Where they did, they were unable to provide them with weaponry. Vague messages promising arms proved illusory. The revolutionaries were reduced to fashioning cannon from cherry-tree trunks that frequently blew up. Some of Bulgaria's finest revolutionary leaders were killed in absurd military adventures; and at the first hint of trouble, the majority of peasant warriors often abandoned their positions and fled.

Lack of serious intelligence work also contributed to the catastrophe. The Ottoman army was using the Bulgarian lands as its operational base for the campaign in Bosnia and Hercegovina, and had at its disposal tens of thousands of bored, aggressive irregulars (*başi-bözöks*) who were spoiling for a fight. On hearing the news that the Bulgarian insurgents had been massacring Muslim civilians, they moved quickly to exact revenge.

Trawling through the countryside, the *başi-bözöks* massacred any Bulgarians they encountered and pillaged their settlements. Two months after the events, the American journalist, John MacGahan, sent a series of dispatches on the massacres to the *Daily News* in London. Despite the time lapse, he still found gruesomely compelling evidence of atrocities:

> We . . . all suddenly drew rein with an exclamation of horror, for right before us, almost beneath our horses' feet, was a sight that made us shudder. It was a heap of skulls, intermingled with bones from all parts of the human body, skeletons, nearly entire, rotting, clothing, human hair, and putrid flesh lying there in one foul heap, around which the grass was growing luxuriantly. It emitted a sickening odour, like that of a dead

> horse, and it was the dogs which had been seeking a hasty repast when our untimely approach interrupted them . . .
>
> We looked again at the heap of skulls and skeletons before us, and we observed that they were all small, and that the articles of clothing, intermingled with them and lying about, were all parts of women's apparel. These, then, were all women and girls.[38]

MacGahan was describing the scene in Batak, in which he alleged 8,000 civilians were slaughtered by forces under the command of Ahmet Aga. Discussing the number of victims throughout Bulgaria, MacGahan pointed out that, 'the French and Russian Consuls and the railway officials give much higher figures, and would put the number of villages burned at over a hundred, and the killed at 25,000 to 40,000. There are people who put the number of killed at 100,000. For my own part, once the enormous number of 15,000 killed in four days is admitted, I do not care to inquire further'.[39]

In the following eighteen months, more than 3,000 articles denouncing Batak and other atrocities appeared in some 200 European newspapers. These events played the decisive role in altering perceptions of the Eastern Crisis in the capitals of the great powers, particularly in Britain, whose subsequent actions would result in the establishment of the Bulgarian state.

Most histories of the Balkans accept the evidence of MacGahan, of other correspondents and of the commission organized by the western powers to investigate the atrocities. There is no doubt that the Turkish irregulars were responsible for terrible crimes. However, this testimony also contains inconsistencies. Had 8,000 been killed in Batak, for example, this would have made it a middle-sized town, but by MacGahan's own admission it was an extremely remote rural settlement. The American historian of the Ottomans, Stanford Shaw, is less sympathetic to the Christians. He offers different estimates of the numbers of victims and a different interpretation. Shaw maintains that the Muslim victims outnumbered the Christian dead:

> [N]ow the forces of European propaganda went to work. While no more than 4,000 Bulgarian Christians had been killed (and considerably more Muslims), the British press trumpeted the charge of 'Bulgarian horrors', claiming that thousands of

> defenseless Christian villagers had been slaughtered by fanatical Muslims. American missionaries estimated that as many as 15,000 Christians had been killed, and the Bulgars leaped ahead to estimates of from 30,000 to 100,000! William Gladstone defeated Disraeli by repudiating the latter's Turkophile policies of the previous two decades, accusing the Muslims in Bulgaria and Bosnia of all kinds of atrocities while ignoring the fact that Muslims also had been slaughtered and that the Ottoman troops were acting to restore order. Public opinion in England was so stirred that it was impossible for Disraeli or anyone else to propose British intervention to save the Ottoman Empire if the Russians now intervened.[40]

Shaw protests a little too much, but his is an important corrective. The moment of the Bulgarian massacres was the moment when public opinion assumed a key role in the formulation of policy (in this case in the United Kingdom). Almost every country involved in the Great Eastern Crisis was swayed in one way or another by public reactions to newspaper reports. This added a new dimension to European politics.

Shaw also highlights the *instrumentalization* of massacres, so that external perceptions of the Balkans became polarized. For the bulk of European politicians and newspaper readers, there were no Muslim victims during the Bulgarian uprisings. This was helped, of course, by hostility to Islam in general and the Ottoman oppressors in particular. But the reporting of the Bulgarian massacres triggered a pattern that persists in western attitudes to the Balkans to this day – little sympathy is expressed for the victims of conflict if they belong to the national community which is considered the original aggressor.

The Bulgarian revolutionaries welcomed the sympathy of Gladstone and other liberals in Britain. But as with the activities of the London Greek Committee during the War of Independence, such sympathy had a much greater impact on British politics than on the fate of the Bulgarian Uprising itself.

Serbia succeeded in detaching itself from the Empire through a combination of geographical serendipity, which allowed the development of a guerrilla tradition; proximity to the Habsburg empire; and the adept manoeuvring of Miloš Obrenović. Britain and France had intervened decisively to secure Greek independence and, together with Russia, underwrote the Greek state. Romania had developed its own structures under the aegis of Russia's Balkan policy. In all three cases, great-power politics had a hand in the matter.

The Bulgarians enjoyed no such advantages. Sharing no border with a great power, the Bulgarian lands were not of immediate strategic interest to outsiders. After Austria-Hungary was forced to direct its imperial interests southwards towards Bosnia following its defeat by Prussia in 1866, Russia did turn its attention to the Bulgarians but this was a gradual and cautious process. Above all, the Bulgarian territories were next to the centre of Ottoman power. The implications of this simple fact for Bulgarian nationalism were enormous. As one of the great Balkan historians has observed, 'there are few areas in the world where geography has influenced history as profoundly as in the Balkan Peninsula'.[41] And there are few areas and periods in the Balkans where geography has influenced history as profoundly as in Bulgaria during the nineteenth and early twentieth century.

Proximity to Istanbul meant that the Porte was able to keep the Bulgarian regions on a tighter leash. But from the 1830s onwards, the Bulgarian economy benefited substantially from the independence or autonomy of Serbia, Greece and Romania. Agricultural output boomed while the trade treaty signed by the Empire and Great Britain in 1838 ended the Ottoman state's monopoly on the export of foodstuffs, encouraging competition and the growth of a Bulgarian landed bourgeoisie. Success in agriculture led to the rapid development of Bulgarian towns, craft industries and light manufacturing.

There were dozens of these centres, small by western standards; but when compared to Serbia, which had only one town, Belgrade, with a population larger than 10,000, this Bulgarian urban network was impressive. As early as the 1830s, Bulgaria, which covered one-twelfth of the Empire, accounted for a fifth of all Ottoman exports and this share increased steadily in the following decades.

In contrast to Serbia and to a lesser extent Greece and Romania, Bulgaria was following a more sociologically classical route to national awakening. The new Bulgarian bourgeoisie used its own institutions, notably the craftsmen's guilds, to finance schools, cultural associations and social or municipal amenities of all sorts. And while these schools produced a class of restless romantics who began to express a longing for liberation from the Turkish yoke, a clear majority of the Bulgarian elite turned not to revolutionary activity but instead to a gradualist programme of cooperation with the authorities as a means to extract concessions.

At the beginning of the century, the cultural identity of Bulgarians was the least developed of all Balkan nationalities except the Albanians.* By the time of the April Uprising in 1876, however, Bulgarians could boast the richest network of cultural institutions in the Balkans and probably, together with the Greeks, the most mature national identity. Ironically, the great catalyst for this process was the struggle not against the Turks but against the Greeks, more precisely against the Phanariot hierarchy of the Orthodox Church.

Divine divorce

Modern Bulgarian nationalism owes a great deal to Hellenism and the Greek national revival. While Bulgarians at the turn of the nineteenth century were bereft of a literary language, their children were given opportunities by the growing network of Greek religious and secular schools. Greek was the language of the Orthodox *millet* and of Levantine commerce. Greek culture became an essential element in the expansion of Bulgarian trade into the Levant, the Maghreb and western Europe.

The economic impact of Hellenism on the Bulgarians had helped to define more precisely the Bulgarian equivalent of the Greek notables or the Serbian knezes. For this class, known as the *chorbadjii*, were the keenest Hellenophiles, who despised the peasant culture of their fellow Slavs. In return, they were resented by their social inferiors. Ivan Vazov's 1897 novel, *Under the Yoke*, contributed more than any other work to the romanticization of the April Uprising in the popular imagination of the Bulgarians. But his depiction of a local *chorbadji* was symptomatic:

* Excluding the Slav Macedonians whose emergence is discussed in chapter 4.

> Yordan Diamandieff was now an old man, somewhat feeble, of a morose and nervous disposition: he belonged to that section of the Bulgarian bourgeoisie – the Chorbajis – who have done so much to make the whole class odious. His wealth went on increasing, his numerous family flourished, and he was universally feared, but no one liked him. Certain old stories of iniquitous acts of oppression and wrong, in which the poor had suffered and the connivance of the Turks been obtained by fawning, flattery, or still worse means, kept up his unpopularity, even now that he was unable or unwilling to injure any one.[42]

As was the Ottoman custom, the *chorbadjii* dressed differently from the Bulgarian craftsmen and peasants, spoke Greek at home and sought advantage by securing administrative posts in the Orthodox *millet*. Like much of the Phanariot hierarchy, they were wholehearted supporters of the Empire and opponents of reform. Compared to their fellow Bulgarians, they were often rich.

Yet although the *chorbadjii* reinforced the domination of Greek culture within the Orthodox *millet*, their sons used their educational opportunities to subvert Greek culture. For it was in Greek schools that the new generations learnt of the Enlightenment and rationalism:

> At some point in the education of these young men, a spark appeared to inflame their Bulgarian consciousness. The catalyst might be the reading of Paisius' History;* it might be the arrival of a converted fellow student. Once pushed over the threshold, the young Slav began fervently to apply the lessons so well taught by his Greek teachers. He looked for ways to define and to defend his own nationality in the face of Greek exaggerations and belittlement of other peoples. He searched ancient sources for arguments to use to contradict his teachers. Going further, he instigated his fellow Bulgars to form a stu-

---

* Paissi of Hilendar (a Serbo-Bulgarian monastery on Mount Athos) is considered the father of Bulgarian nationalism for his history of the Bulgarians, written in 1762, which advocated the use of the vernacular for Slavs in the Orthodox Church and attacked Hellenic domination of the hierarchy.

> dent society to look after Slav interests in the now unfriendly confines of a Greek school.[43]

As the manufacturing and handicraft industries evolved, the traders and guild members began to sponsor their own schools and cultural societies. This new bourgeoisie, which acquired influential allies in the Bulgarian diaspora communities in Istanbul, Bucharest, Odessa and Vienna, found in the youthful confidence of Bulgarian culture an instrument to use against the *chorbadjii*.

Reşid Paşa and the *Hatt-ı şerif* of 1839 broadened this struggle considerably by interfering with the *millet* system in the attempt to establish the principle of *Osmanlılık*. As a direct result of the reforms, the Bulgarian community in Istanbul began a campaign for Bulgarian autonomy within the Orthodox Church. This coincided with the emergence of a group of Russophiles within the Bulgarian intelligentsia, anticipating a later shift among Russian nationalists away from pan-Orthodoxy and towards pan-Slavism: brotherhood defined by race, not religion.

The struggle for an autochthonous Bulgarian church is one of the few themes that appears to unite Balkan historians, regardless of nationality: they agree it had nothing to do with religion but was a purely political conflict. What is disputed is the role of the church in the rise of Balkan nationalism. In the four centuries prior to the national awakening, the church had been one of the few repositories of the Christians' cultural identity. As such it assumed a political role in the Ottoman Empire, where it was the centre of the *millet*. Excepting a few anomalies (for example, the Franciscans of western Hercegovina), all the churches were conservative and reluctant to challenge imperial political structures. The hierarchies shuddered at the prospect of social or political change because of their vested interest in the old regime. Yet individual clerics like Proto Matija Nendović in Serbia or Father Paissi in Bulgaria played a key role in the early period of all the national revivals in the Balkans because the church was the only institution in the Orthodox *millet* where reading and writing were taught.

Lay and secular forces played the dominant role in the national awakenings. After the establishment of the Bulgarian Exarchate in 1870, for example, clerical appointments and church finances were controlled by councils in which the laity held a majority. The result, as one of the first western historians of Bulgaria notes, 'was a lay and almost a republican church organization despite the fact that it was set up by the more conservative of the Bulgarian leaders and met with the opposition of the revolutionary elements'.[44] But although the church was politically subordinate to the secular leadership of the national awakening, its residual cultural influence ensured that adherence to a particular rite was central to defining one's national identity. Greek, Serbian and Bulgarian nationalists insist to this day that it is only possible to claim membership of the nation if one adheres to the Orthodox rite. In Transylvania, the Uniate Church* has often come under attack by Romanian nationalists as a fifth column, most comprehensively by the régime of Nicolae Ceauşescu. (This is not an exclusively Orthodox phenomenon – many Croat and Polish nationalists consider membership of the Catholic Church an essential prerequisite of their national identity.)

As objects of political conflict the churches of the Balkans have therefore always been enormously important. This was especially so in the case of the Bulgarians and Greeks. The *tanzimatçılar* supported the movement for an independent Bulgarian church as this would undermine the *millet* system in favour of *Osmanlılık*. Midhat Paşa in particular believed that this policy of divide and rule would weaken the influence of the Orthodox hierarchy on both the Greek and Bulgarian populations, thus strengthening the influence of the administration. He was badly mistaken.

Not surprisingly, the Greek–Bulgarian conflict proved to be most advantageous to the Bulgarians. It culminated with an imperial *firman* in February 1870, proclaiming the establishment of an autonomous Bulgarian Exarchate, separate from the Greek Patriarchate. The independent church led to the creation of political structures, in particular advisory and executive councils within the Bulgarian elite. The church dispute was a valuable training ground for the moderates of the Bulgarian national movement. It also acted as a transmission belt that spread the ideological aspirations of the

* The Uniate Church practises the Eastern Orthodox rite but recognizes the authority of the Pope and not the Patriarch in Constantinople. Its expansion among Bulgarians and Romanians during the nineteenth century was the result of political manoeuvring. Its influence atrophied among the former but survived among the latter.

Bulgarian elite downwards into all the towns and many villages. In 1860, on the most sacred day in the Orthodox calendar, the bishop, Ilarion Makariopolski, omitted the name of the Patriarch, the head of the Church, during the Easter service, intoning instead the name of the Sultan. The Bulgarians' repudiation of the head of both the Church and the *millet* sparked struggles throughout the Bulgarian lands as the Slavs attempted to oust Greek priests in favour of Bulgarians.

The most ominous dimension of this process lay in the regions with mixed populations, above all in Macedonia, where any spiritual aspect of the conflict was swamped by the need to assert future territorial claims. The establishment of the Bulgarian church prepared the ground for one of the most intractable nationalist disputes in Balkan history – the Macedonian Question.* The imperial decree finally granting the right to a Bulgarian church contained the infamous Article X which provided for the holding of plebiscites in disputed areas to ascertain to which branch of Orthodoxy the church would belong.† The Exarchate would be awarded jurisdiction over those regions where two-thirds voted to secede from the Patriarchate. Fyodor Dostoyevsky, apart from being a novelist of genius, was a passionate if deranged supporter of pan-Orthodoxy and pan-Slavism, since both could further the greater glory of the divine mission of imperial Russia. By 1876, Dostoyevsky clearly understood where the rivalry between Bulgarians and Greeks was heading:

> The Greek-Bulgarian 'Church Dispute' we recently witnessed was ultimately nothing more than a national conflict in clerical garb and can to a degree be regarded as an omen for the future. When the ecumenical Patriarch reproached the disobedient Bulgarians and . . . excommunicated them, he stressed that one should sacrifice neither the church's ritual nor the obedience due to the church in favour of the 'new and destructive principle of nationality'. But in fact he himself had made use of precisely this nationality principle when he imposed the ban on the Bulgarians – the only difference being he had made use of it

* See chapter 4.

† Fifteen dioceses were placed under the control of the new Bulgarian Exarchate.

> in favour of the Greeks and to the detriment of the Slavs. In short, one can predict with some certainty that as soon as the 'sick man' [the Ottoman Empire] expires, then unrest and conflict will break out all over the Balkans at the first opportunity.[45]

Of traders and warriors

Despite its strong merchant and artisan class, Bulgarian society remained predominantly agrarian. In 1841 and 1850, Bulgarian-inhabited areas of the Empire had been shaken by peasant rebellions. But discontent receded in the two decades following the Crimean War due to the vigorous economic development of the region and the impact of Midhat Paşa's administrative reforms. The idea of an armed uprising appealed to very few traders and manufacturers. Except along the central mountainous strip running from west to east, there was also a large Muslim population in the Bulgarian lands and a concentration of both regular and irregular units of the Ottoman military.

Writing about the Bulgaria of the 1930s, a noted historian records how

> [f]requently dubbed 'the Prussians of the Balkans' or 'the Slavic world's Japanese', the Bulgarians were considered by outsiders and by themselves to be the most diligent, frugal, sober, orderly, systematic, and correct, as well as practical and alert, people of the peninsula. They prided themselves on sustaining a *robota*-work [drone or drudge] culture, in contrast to the Serbs' *haiduk*-hero culture or the Romanians' and Greeks' alleged mercantile-ingenuity culture . . . While such generalizations about national character may be overdrawn, the Bulgarians are, on balance, rather impressively utilitarian and hard-headed.[46]

This observation applies to most Bulgarians actively involved in the national renaissance – they were cautious, steady and successful at exploiting weaknesses in the Ottoman state to further the national cause. Yet there was an important current of opinion, articulated by young, passionate and highly educated Bulgarians, who were convinced that, as the first great revolutionary, Georgi Rakovski, wrote in 1858, '[t]he Bulgarians lost their freedom by the sword, and now they must regain it by the sword!'[47] Although unrepresentative, their energy and opportunism, not to mention their recklessness, ensured that they would be remembered as the leaders and heroes of the Bulgarian revolution.

These young revolutionaries established their conspiratorial centres abroad, mainly in Bucharest and Odessa. By the early 1860s the Serbian government was cooperating with the Bulgarian revolutionary movement. Their work received a considerable fillip with the appointment of Nikolai Pavlovich Ignatiev to the post of Russian consul in Istanbul. A year after Ignatiev's arrival in 1864, the Russian government disbursed 5,000 silver roubles to educate south Slavs in Russia. While the leading Bulgarian revolutionaries always maintained a certain scepticism towards the ideology of pan-Slavism and Russian great-power aspirations in particular, the growing links with Russia radicalized a number of well-educated, unemployed Bulgarians living in exile. In 1866, the largest group based in Bucharest established the Bulgarian Secret Central Committee which organized armed incursions into Ottoman territory. These ended in failure.

The three main reasons for the defeat of revolutionary violence in the Bulgarian lands were all too evident during these early rehearsals for the April Uprising. Incorrigibly romantic and desperately vain, the rebels made one central miscalculation, which proved fatal for many of them, as a historian of Bulgaria's early modern intelligentsia has pointed out:

> [T]he Bulgarian intelligentsia turned into a class of alienated men who fell far short of developing close and lasting ties with their people as a whole. As nationalists, these activists loved their people – but they loved it as an abstraction. When the people failed to measure up to their image of it, the intellectuals turned on it with disdain. Although such an attitude might serve as a legitimate way to cure societal defects, the social criticism of the Bulgarian intelligentsia had a negativism about it that bespoke something else – the rejection by a cultured elite of what it in its frustration came to regard as the uncouth masses.

In a related way, the intelligentsia established hardly any

> relationship at all with that part of the population which by and large was the people – the peasantry. The nationalists idealized the peasantry as the simple but sturdy backbone of the nation. In practical terms, however, they overlooked the problems of the peasant and they did not train themselves in the things they needed to know. If it largely ignored the peasantry, the intelligentsia came into sharp conflict with the business class, the part of society which gave it birth and with which it most closely lived and worked.[48]

The intelligentsia's intended foot soldiers, the Bulgarian peasantry, had no revolutionary tradition and displayed the classic instinct of the rural fighter – to run at the first hint of impending defeat. Moreover, in contrast to the peasantry of Bosnia-Hercegovina, the Bulgarians had little or no tradition of bearing arms. Supplying weapons to Bulgaria proved immensely difficult, especially as the Ottoman army had so many well-manned garrisons guarding the Danube and the border with Serbia. In addition, the only region where the peasantry and urban population would even consider raising arms against the state was the small strip of mountainous territory, along the Sredna Gora, where very few Muslims lived.

After the formation of the BRCC in 1872, three Bulgarian nationalist intellectuals, Vasil Levski, Lyuben Karavelov and Hristo Botev, began planning the armed assault on Ottoman power. In the thirty years after the April Uprising, the catastrophic culmination of the BRCC's dreams, these men were lionized by the writers, historians and journalists of the new Bulgarian state. To this day, Rakovski, the prophet of revolution, and Levski, Karavelov and Botev remain the central icons of Bulgarian national identity.

Rakovski and Karavelov were impressive political thinkers who reflected on many of the problems that would follow the collapse of Ottoman power in the Balkans. They understood, in theory, the necessity of cooperation with other Balkan nations and the need to secure great-power support for any liberation struggle, even if they failed to make provisions for this in practice. Karavelov even developed the concept of Balkan federalism as a political solution that might neutralize the energy of nationalist conflict between the Christian nations in the Balkans, which many dreaded. Implicit in Karavelov's argument was the belief that the Balkan nations would be swamped by the expanding great powers if they did not act together. 'In these times', he wrote, 'when the European powers range in size of population from fifty to seventy millions, the small peoples must either submit to a large power and surrender their historical existence, or they must unite with other peoples on a most liberal basis (as in the unions of Switzerland and America) and thus form a defensive federation.'[49]

They were all committed patriots and two of them, Levski and Botev, gave their lives to the struggle for the Bulgarian state. But more sober intellects were already warning that the Bulgarians had neither the resources nor the ability to resist Ottoman rule by force of arms. They were dashing, inspiring and brave, but Bulgaria's national heroes also brought untold misery upon tens of thousands of their compatriots victimized by the Ottoman irregulars after the ill-conceived uprising.

Sparta, Piedmont or Prussia? Serbia, 1840–75

In 1839, two weeks before the proclamation of the *Hatt-ı Şerif*, Prince Miloš Obrenović, the man who had secured Serbia's autonomy, was forced ignominiously into exile by the *ustavobranitelji*, or Defenders of the Constitution, as this clique immodestly presented itself. Its members, whose qualities matched those of the despot they so hated, had won great-power support for their *coup*. Indeed, their most enthusiastic backer was the Porte. Miloš's greed and his unwillingness to share power with these disgruntled nobles had been his undoing. He was succeeded first by his sixteen-year-old son, Michael (1839–42, 1860–8), who after three years of intrigue and counter-intrigue was ousted in favour of the Karadjordjević line in the shape of Black George's son, Aleksandar.

Serbian society changed relatively little during the eighteen years of Aleksandar's rule. Urban development was slow while the peasantry remained conservative, wary of technological change that threatened the predictable life of the *zadruga*. However, the constitutional concessions won by the *ustavobranitelji* from Miloš in 1838, with the qualified approval of the great powers, laid the foundations for a system of party politics which enjoyed an erratic life for the rest of the nineteenth century. The system was flawed, not least by the continuing dynastic rivalry between Karadjordjević and

Obrenović which often fanned the flames of factionalism and intrigue. Yet most of the conflicts were over issues of constitutional prerogative. Political discourse in Serbia was slowly becoming modern.

Economic progress was even less rapid. Aside from the livestock traders and a modest number of proprietors of handicraft industries, there was no powerful economic class in Serbia. Social and political advancement involved climbing the ladder of state bureaucracy, and its members were often indistinguishable from the notables and their extended families who vied with one another for political power. Serbia became a state with an elaborate administrative skeleton but not much economic flesh on its bones.

Like Greece, Serbia had built up a modest international profile in the decade since it had loosened its ties with the Porte. Indeed, one of Miloš's final triumphs had been to persuade the government in Istanbul to accept the opening of European consulates in Belgrade. The Principality could credibly claim that it had a foreign policy. Through the offices of Ilija Garašanin, it developed a long-term political strategy for the expansion of the Serbian state and the inclusion of other nationalities in a broader south Slav polity. The *načertanije*, Garašanin's Plan for expansion, remained secret until the early 1900s, but the assumptions underpinning it were soon shared by almost all Serbian politicians until the establishment of the first Yugoslavia in 1918.

Those assumptions contained some devilish contradictions. Garašanin sought both south Slav unity and Serbian hegemony. The Plan was simultaneously federalist and centralist in conception. Serbia's geography and the spread of the Serbian community in neighbouring areas made this contradiction inevitable. It was the only country in the European Balkans that could play the role that Piedmont assumed in the process of Italian unification. The *Megali idea* in Greece, conceived in the same year as the *Načertanije*, in some ways mirrored the Serb strategy. But there was one important difference. As Slavs, the Serbs could claim a racial brotherhood with many neighbouring communities, whereas Greece made no attempt to combat the hostility of its neighbours to the *Megali idea*.

Despite the frequent comparisons made between Piedmont and Serbia after the unification of Italy in 1859, there were important cultural and economic differences between the Slav-inhabited

Balkan regions and the Italian lands. The latter did not suffer the complexity of divisions that separated Serbs, Croats and Bulgarians, not to mention the non-Slav communities in Bosnia, Hercegovina, Macedonia and northern Albania (to which Garašanin also laid claim). Given its vanguard role in challenging Ottoman power, Serbia was now developing its own great-power aspirations.

Perhaps the single most significant force driving this policy was the conviction among Serbs that armed struggle was decisive in establishing and consolidating state power. Alone among the Balkan nations, the Serbs had fought their way, if not yet to statehood, then at least to an autonomy which was virtually indistinguishable from statehood. Greece would have lost its independence had Britain, Russia and France not intervened in its war of independence. Romania's autonomy was a by-product of a Russo-Turkish conflict. But in Serbia, the *hajduk* spirit had smashed the Turkish yoke. There was, of course, a large dose of mythology in this perception of Serbia's military capabilities and recent history. As we have seen, Karadjordjević failed to drive the Turks out of Serbia. In the end, it required the more subtle political skills of Miloš Obrenović. Miloš's real achievement lay in exploiting the political weakness of the Ottoman Empire on its periphery. Serbian military prowess in the nineteenth century was more the product of fertile imaginations than a matter of hard fact.

When Michael Obrenović returned to lead the Principality for a second spell in 1860, he seized upon this domestic perception of the warrior tradition and devised a system of alliances, among Serbia, Greece, Romania and the insurgent Bulgarians, aimed at driving the Ottomans out of the Balkans. The Prince's political career had been resuscitated in 1858 when his father, the ageing Miloš, was invited back to lead Serbia as Prince for a brief spell before his death. During this time, Michael negotiated with Lajos Kossuth, the leader of the Hungarian revolution in 1848, and with the revolutionary Italian leadership, and, indirectly, with Louis Napoleon of France. When France and Italian forces began pressing the Habsburg armies in Italy, Kossuth and the Italians hatched a plan to open a second front in Hungary with the aim of further weakening Austria-Hungary and delivering two simultaneous blows to Vienna. To bolster Hungary's rebellion, Kossuth approached both Michael Obrenović and the leaders of Wallachia and Moldavia. In order to get them to participate in a revolutionary war, he proposed the creation of a Magyar-Serbo-Romanian Danubian Federation, which would also guarantee Croatian autonomy. This might have come to something had the Austrians not conceded the territory occupied by the Franco-Piedmontese forces at Villafranca in 1859. Camillo Cavour, the Prime Minister of Piedmont, was furious at Napoleon's refusal to fight until all of north-eastern Italy had been liberated. Nonetheless, modern Italy was now on the map. The Danubian Federation was dead. France wanted an independent Italy under its influence, but it did not want to weaken Austria further, for fear of antagonizing the other great powers, Britain and Prussia in particular. These events convinced Michael that the Serbian national programme would not be supported by the great powers, unless it happened to suit their interests at a particular moment. The Balkan Christians, he concluded, would have to liberate themselves.

Early in his reign, Michael determined to transform the myth of Serbian militarism into reality. He needed an army. In August 1861, a law was duly passed making all able-bodied men between the ages of twenty and fifty liable for military service. Those between twenty and thirty were to train on Sundays and holidays, while the rest were reservists, obliged to train on a monthly basis. Within ten years, Serbia could field a massive force of some 90,000 men out of a population of one and a quarter million. The construction of an army at lightning speed was accompanied by tremendous patriotic fervour: songs hailing Serbia's great military traditions; articles predicting an imminent revolutionary war which would sweep the Turks out of Europe and keep the Austrians at bay; and endless slogans. 'Educated Serbs even liked to boast of being a modern Sparta, the Piedmont of the South Slavs or, better yet, the Prussia of the Balkans', as a historian of modern Serbia has remarked.[50]

In this respect, the militarization of Serbia, based on the peasantry, fostered a novel nationalist ideology in which the masses, and not just the bureaucratic elite, played a historic role. It also created a dangerous illusion. Sheer numbers did not make an army. Discipline, clothing, medical support, proper logistics and, above all, an abundant supply of weapons and well-trained officers did. The new Serbian military could fulfil none of these requirements, as the country was to learn dramatically during the Serbo-Turkish war of 1876. By the time of his assassination in 1868, Prince Michael was almost certainly aware of these deficiencies, as he had invited foreign delegations to assess his army. Their observations were uniformly dismissive.

Indeed, it was partly these motley legions that persuaded Michael not to launch a war of liberation against the Ottomans in March 1868, a notional date agreed on between Serbia and Greece during their discussions about a military alliance (which was finally signed in 1867). Even if nothing came of the agreement, Serbia, Greece and Romania were at least capable of conducting a foreign policy independent of the great powers (although it should be added that the alliance collapsed quickly amid bitter recriminations).

Serbia was profoundly affected by the defeat of Austria at the hands of Prussia in 1866. Deprived of influence to the north, Austria turned its attentions to Bosnia and Hercegovina. Hungarian nationalism was revitalized in 1867 by the *Ausgleich*, which created the Dual Monarchy and gave considerable autonomy to the Hungarian crown lands. The Hungarians no longer felt the need to cooperate with the Croats or Serbs – they could now risk a little confrontation. And Serbia came under considerable pressure from the north.

But the most persistent problem was that of territorial allocation – who would get what if the Ottoman Empire actually did collapse? The struggle of the Greek and Bulgarian church exacerbated these tensions, especially after the Exarchate was established in 1870. Although the Porte unwittingly strengthened Bulgarian nationalist sentiment by supporting the Exarchate, this also exacerbated the divisions between the Christian communities, burying their alliance system directed against Istanbul.

The role of public opinion in Turkey and Britain during the crisis of 1873–6 has already been noted. A still more sustained and powerful movement, pan-Slavism, had developed in Russia during the 1860s. The Bosnian and Hercegovinian uprisings galvanized Russia's aristocracy and intelligentsia. Throughout the Russian Empire, impassioned supporters of the 'little Slav brothers' established benevolent societies, raising funds to provide for the hundreds of thousands of refugees from Bosnia and Hercegovina who had swamped the border areas of the Habsburg Empire, Montenegro and Serbia. By early January 1876, the benevolent societies combined with the Russian Red Cross and other voluntary organizations to send 360,000 roubles to refugees. Tchaikovsky composed his *marche slave*, based on Serbian folk tunes, to raise money for the cause.

Russia was emerging from the humiliation it had suffered at the hands of the British, French and Ottomans in the Crimean War and pan-Slavism was the vanguard of this revival. Profoundly anti-western, steeped in an obscurantist imperial Orthodoxy, it dreamed of restoring Constantinople as the capital of a Christian empire. This implied, of course, the liberation of the Balkan Slavs under Russian guidance and also gave a mighty impetus to its crusading approach towards Islam, the greatest heresy of all. Pan-Slavism had influenced part of the Russian bureaucracy and it had influential supporters in the Foreign Ministry. However, both Tsar Alexander II and his foreign minister, Prince Alexander Mikhailovich Gorchakov, saw pan-Slavism as a dangerous populist movement that encroached on their policy-making prerogatives. The pan-Slavists were not unified among themselves and they faced some awkward political problems (notably the Bulgarian–Greek church conflict, which highlighted the contradictions between pan-Orthodoxy and pan-Slavism). Nonetheless, after the outbreak of hostilities in the Balkans in 1875, they were able to put considerable pressure on the Tsar and government.

In Serbia, too, the conservativism of the ambitious Milan Obrenović (1868–89) (who succeeded his relative, Michael) was swiftly eroded under pressure from the growing militarist ideology of the Serbian liberals and a new, yet vigorous young force, the socialists. Michael's assassination may have suspended the official policy of expansion through alliances and wars of liberation, but it had not extinguished the idea. On the contrary, in the seven years from 1868 to the outbreak of the revolt in Bosnia and Hercegovina, nationalist passion gripped Serbia.

There were three main schools of thought on the national question. The liberals around Vladimir Jovanović argued for the consolidation and expansion of the state on Enlightenment principles, highlighting France and England as models of constitutional development. Jovan Ristić, who under Milan gradually assumed Garašanin's mantle as Serbia's primary statesman, argued in favour of a Prussian model. He emphasized the importance of a strong bureaucratic state to unify the oppressed Christian Slavs. Finally, a group of young radicals, organized in the *Omladina* (the Union of Serbian Youth), launched an intellectual assault on Milan's government. The writings of the *Omladina* synthesized the principle of national self-determination with the class analysis of the Russian *narodniki*, and advocated uprisings in the Balkans, to be accompanied by a revolutionary transformation to clear out the self-perpetuating bureaucracy of the Serbian state. Typified by the precociously intelligent, humourless Svetozar Marković, the founder of Serbian socialism, this group's glorification of the *zadruga* (the extended rural household) as a uniquely Serbian form of democracy was a conscious attempt to appeal to the peasantry.

Milan clearly underestimated just how attractive such an appeal might be. He was not alone in misinterpreting the vital impact of the Bosnian Uprising. For although many European statesmen were increasingly exercised by the affairs of the Ottoman Empire in the early 1870s, they had no reason to suspect that revolt in Hercegovina in 1875 was anything more than another local disturbance. Returning from Vienna, which he was visiting when the Uprising started, Milan was shocked when he was met in Belgrade 'not only by the usual dignitaries, troops, and public, but also by a contingent of volunteers in full battle dress, who escorted him with cries of "Long live the Serbian King! To battle! At the Turks! Give us war!"'[51]

At first Milan resisted the call to arms. To bolster his position, he requested support from St Petersburg and Vienna. The Three Emperors' League was officially committed to a peaceful solution through negotiations, a position symbolized by the Andrássy Note of December 1875. This demanded that the Porte make further concessions to the Christians of the Balkans. Istanbul reluctantly agreed but was spared embarrassment by the Hercegovinian rebels, who rejected the Andrássy proposal. Nonetheless, both Russia and Austria continued to denounce all warmongering noises emanating from Belgrade. Milan could defend himself from accusations of cowardice in the absence of great-power support for a war of liberation. 'Ce Piémont a besoin d'une France: où est-elle?'[52] was his epigrammatic summary of the Serbian dilemma.

As 1876 dragged on with no solution to the Bosnian conflict, Bulgaria erupted, followed quickly by the punitive massacres carried out by the *başi-bözöks*. At the Porte, Abdülaziz was rudely deposed. The war party in Serbia was now convinced that the Ottoman Empire was so weak that the time had come to liberate Serbs in Bosnia, Hercegovina, the *Sanjak* of Novi Pazar (a special Ottoman zone that separated Serbia and Montenegro) and Macedonia. Prince Milan was convinced that he faced either war or revolution, as he admitted to Prince Carol during a visit to Bucharest in early May in a vain attempt to secure an alliance with the Romanians.

Which France would rescue this Balkan Piedmont?

The shadow of Prussia

The great powers had begun to anticipate the dismemberment of the Ottoman Empire a century before the Great Eastern Crisis. Since the end of the eighteenth century, Paris, London, Vienna and St Petersburg maintained operational plans to deal with convulsions in the East. Prussia was the one power that showed little interest in the region throughout the nineteenth century. France and especially Britain were prepared to use diplomatic and military methods to keep the sick man alive. Russia and Austria-Hungary were open to the idea of dividing his Ottoman spoils. These plans changed as the sands of international relations shifted unpredictably but rarely took account of the aspirations of the people who actually inhabited the region.

By 1875, the balance of power in Europe had undergone a fundamental transformation. The unification of Germany was built upon the devastating defeat inflicted upon the Habsburg Empire in 1866 and then completed with the humiliation of France in 1871. Although he was a little alarmist, Disraeli, speaking in the House of Commons in 1871, was quick to appreciate the implications:

> It is no common war . . . This war represents the German Revolution, a greater political event than the French Revolution of the last century . . . What its social consequences may be are in the future . . . You have a new world, new influences at work, new and unknown objects and dangers with which to cope . . . The balance of power has been entirely destroyed, and the country which suffers most, and feels the effects of this great change most, is England.[53]

Eventually the rest of Europe would feel the effects much more brutally than England. But at the time Disraeli was correct. Britain, Europe's only truly world power, now faced a mighty continental rival whose industrial power was growing rapidly. Bismarck, the architect of a unified Germany, was well aware how the other great powers regarded his country's expansionist potential, and sought to allay their fears by declaring a peaceful strategy. He could afford to. France, whose chief crime in Bismarck's eyes lay in its liberalism, was already in ruins. Britain had no potential allies with which to build an aggressive anti-German alliance. British and Russian disputes in the Balkans and central Asia precluded any agreement, while Austria-Hungary, dependent on Germany's goodwill, was in no position to forge stronger links with London.

At the start of the Great Eastern Crisis, the powers were not remotely interested in revolutionary struggles in the Balkans, let alone in encouraging them. Since 1873, Germany, Russia and Austria-Hungary had been united in the Three Emperors' League whose chief aim was to halt the spread of republican and revolutionary ideology in Europe. Although they were hardly friends of the Ottoman Empire, St Petersburg and Vienna regarded the prospect of an armed rebellion overthrowing an established monarchy with considerable reserve. Germany regarded the Balkans as a necessary conduit for the establishment of its imperial aims in the Middle East. Any further fragmentation of the region would complicate its ambitions and run the risk of provoking a larger conflagration. Britain was still utterly committed to the status quo in order to keep Russian hands off Istanbul; and it did not really matter what defeated France thought.

Two issues threatened this rare unanimity of interests on such a substantial policy issue. Germany was allied formally and ideologically to Russia and Austria-Hungary. But the unification of Italy and Germany had clipped the wings of the Habsburg Empire to the south-west and to the north. Austria-Hungary's aspirations refocused on the south and on Bosnia in particular. This meant that in the event of a crisis, Austria and Russia, Germany's allies, could come into conflict over the Balkans. But Austria's policy was made by the Hungarian noble, Julius Andrássy. Vienna had once hung a price tag on the head of this former Prime Minister in one of Kossuth's revolutionary governments. Now, after the *Ausgleich*, he abhorred the prospect of an expansion of Austrian power into Bosnia and Hercegovina as this would dramatically increase the number of Slavs in the Dual Monarchy. Having won their virtual independence, Andrássy and his fellow Hungarians had no desire to see it undermined. Nor would Austria initiate an assault on the Ottoman Empire. It would almost certainly react, however, if the Russians contemplated such a move.

The influence of pan-Slavism in Russia was much more likely to undermine great-power unity. Alexander II and Gorchakov were implacably opposed to stirring up the Balkans, but others in the Foreign Ministry and the Russian army were pursuing more radical goals in harmony with the pan-Slavists. Nikolai Pavlovich Ignatiev, who became the Russian consul in Istanbul in 1864, is generally regarded as the leader of the pan-Slavists within the Russian bureaucracy. A statement like this assumes that pan-Slavism was a coherent and well-targeted ideology. With over 200 million potential adherents, however, it is no surprise that the movement was an ideological cacophony, conducted by a variety of populist maestros. For all the difficulty in defining pan-Slavism, the elites of Austria-Hungary, Turkey and Britain regarded it as one of the most dangerous phenomena of the 1860s and 1870s. There is no question that it drew support from a broad spectrum of Russian society: industrialists exploited its anti-western tenor to press for higher tariffs; the Russian Orthodox Church embraced it as a way of expressing its hostility to Catholicism and Islam; supporters of the downtrodden peasantry saw in it a road to the redemption of Russia's semi-feudal rural structures; the intellectuals of Moscow used it as a stick with which to beat the Germanized oligarchy in St Petersburg. As the Eastern Crisis deepened, they all came together to voice a baying chorus of Great Russian imperialism.

Until this time, pan-Slavism had been forever contradicting itself. In theory, it should have welcomed all Slavs regardless of creed. But by the end of the 1860s, it had become synonymous with the Orthodox Church. Poles were excluded as rebellious traitors and, worse, the vanguard of Catholicism in the East. Czechs, Slovaks and Croats were acceptable but only if they were prepared to convert to Orthodoxy. When the Greek–Bulgarian church dispute broke out, the pan-Slavist movement was for a time unable to decide where its loyalties lay. After all, the Russian Orthodox Church was spiritually subordinate to the Greek Patriarch in Constantinople. But the romantic vision of Russia restoring Byzantium could hardly be realized with Greek participation.

It took Ignatiev's exceptional political opportunism to resolve such dilemmas. Ignatiev succeeded because, almost uniquely, he knew what he wanted. He was waiting until the constellation of forces in the Balkans allowed Russia to impose a settlement without the interference of other great powers. As the great historian of pan-Slavism noted, he sought 'the revision of the 1856 treaty of Paris (including the suppression of the collective guardianship of Turkey by the powers), the command of Constantinople and the Straits, and some form of common action by the Slavs under the direction of Russia'.[54]

Christian national aspirations in the Balkans were of secondary interest to Ignatiev. On the issue of the Bulgarian Exarchate, Ignatiev came out after careful consideration in favour of the Slavs over the Greeks as the Bulgarian lands were of greater strategic importance to Russia. In consequence, Ignatiev has been hailed by Bulgarian historians as a great friend of their nation. More prosaically, he used his influence at the Porte to persuade the Ottoman government that the establishment of the Exarchate would allow it to divide and rule the Christians.

As Ignatiev explained himself, '[s]ooner or later . . . Russia must fight Austria-Hungary for the first place in the Balkans and for the leadership of Slavdom: only for the attainment of this task should Russia make sacrifices for the Slavs under Austrian and Turkish rule and be solicitous for their freedom and growth in strength. *To aim merely at emancipating the Slavs, to be satisfied with merely humanitarian success, would be foolish and reprehensible* [emphasis added].'[55]

His initial reaction to the Hercegovina Uprising was to try to calm the rebellious tempers of the Christian *raya*. He knew that Russia was not yet ready to launch its attack on the Ottoman Empire, but as the temperature in Serbia rose during 1876 he decided Russia should wait no longer. The arrival in Serbia in May of General Mikhail Gregorovich Chernayev, a swashbuckling Russian nationalist, and 500 volunteers was the final piece in the puzzle. The pacifist policy still adhered to by Tsar Alexander and Gorchakov was being edged out by the parallel strategy of Ignatiev and the pan-Slavists in the bureaucracy. Prince Milan understandably took at face value the assurances of the Russian Consul in Belgrade that St Petersburg would back a Serbian declaration of war. On 2 July 1876, the forces of Serbia and its tiny ally, Montenegro, crossed into Ottoman territory.

Loss of innocence

Few military men knew more about Balkan warfare than the old master, Omer Paša Latas. In the early 1870s, he had the opportunity to observe the new Serbian army on manoeuvres. In the event of war, he observed, this peasant mass would take to its heels after the first bullet had been fired.

The Serbian strategy in the Serbo-Turkish war of 1876 was based on the myth of the peasant warrior tradition and on the conviction that the very act of declaring war would stimulate the oppressed Christian peasantry throughout the Ottoman Empire. It took a matter of days to expose Serbian military philosophy as woefully inadequate. The Belgrade Military Academy, known as the Artillery School, had been turning out at most ten graduates a year since its founding in 1850. When war broke out, the Serbian army could field only 460 poorly trained officers. Together with the 700 Russian officers who had followed Chernayev in the spirit of pan-Slavism, they commanded a total force of 125,000 undisciplined peasants. As a perceptive historian of nineteenth-century Serbia has observed:

> [T]he Serbs were not aware of the enormous changes that had taken place in the technology and tactics of warfare from 1860 to 1875, changes that made an untrained peasant force obsolete, even in the Balkans. Serbian military thinkers had not yet learned the lessons of the Crimean War, the wars of Italian and German unification, and the American Civil War, all of which demonstrated that firepower concentrated in good defensive positions could withstand heavy assaults, and that only very well-trained, highly disciplined troops carrying first-class weapons could have a chance at offensive success.[56]

One of the few areas where the Tanzimat had enjoyed creditable success was in the reorganization of the Ottoman army, which was now well armed with Martini-Henry and Snider rifles and supported by Krupp field guns. The Serbs' Peabody and Martin rifles (which had a disturbing tendency to seize after firing seven or eight rounds) and the homemade guns from the country's one factory in Kragujevac were no match for these weapons.

Just under two months after the outbreak of war, the Serbian army had been smashed. The decision to attack the Ottoman stronghold of Niş with 68,000 men, the bulk of the Serbian force, under General Chernayev's command was disastrous. The Serbian defeat left the road to Belgrade wide open. Suddenly the Serbs contemplated the horrifying prospect of the Ottoman army occupying the capital and reestablishing its rule over the Principality more than seventy years after the First Serbian Uprising. The Russian government prevented the collapse of the Serbian state by warning the Porte that unless it agreed to an armistice the Russians would enter the war. The peace was eventually signed on 17 February 1877. It enforced the status quo ante.

Although Serbia lost no territory, the defeat was disastrous. Some 5,000 were dead and a further 9,500 wounded. Out of a total population of 1,300,000, the conflict left 200,000 homeless. The political consequences were no better. The Russians dismissed the Serbs as contemptible incompetents. Serbia was left without friends or allies. Worse still, the Russians had transferred their affections to the Bulgarians and acknowledged Austria-Hungary's right to occupy Bosnia and Hercegovina.

The conviction of the Serbian elite that it could liberate its compatriots and, indeed, the Christian peasantry throughout the Balkans was exposed as an illusion. When Serbian troops had marched across the Ottoman borders in July 1876, the Bulgarian peasantry watched silently, still digesting the lessons of the Turkish retribution following their own April Uprising. Political power, the Serbs had to learn, did not emanate from the barrel of a jammed gun or from romantic peasant-based movements. The three years of the Great Eastern Crisis revealed a severe disparity between the romantic rhetoric of nationalism in the Balkans and its ability to realize those ambitions.

In the Ottoman Empire Serbia's declaration of war in 1876 generated another surge of pan-Islamic sentiment. Murad V, traumatized by fratricidal blood-letting inside his bureaucracy, handed his throne over to Abdülhamid II (1876–1909). Midhat Paşa had survived and when Abdülhamid II appointed him Grand Vezir, he at last set to work on writing a constitution for the Ottoman Empire. The first three months of Abdülhamid's reign witnessed the crushing of the Serbian army and finally, in December, the promulgation of the Constitution, an event greeted with joy and celebration throughout the Empire. For a very short time, it almost looked as though the Ottoman Empire had survived the transition from feudal absolutism to constitutional monarchy. Any such hopes, however, were dashed when Russia, still fired by pan-Slavism and the smell of Ottoman decay, declared war on the Empire on 24 April 1877. After a heroic Ottoman defence at Plevna south of the Danube in Bulgaria, the Empire was finally forced to capitulate to the Russians in early 1878.

Peace was first concluded at San Stefano, where the Turks were forced to sign a treaty that appeared to fulfil Ignatiev's dreams. It gave Russia, primarily through a vast new Bulgarian state, strategic domination over the Balkans. Had the terms of San Stefano prevailed, then Britain, Austria-Hungary and Russia would have been hard pressed to avoid a large-scale war that would probably also have drawn in Germany and France. Germany was not ready for war, which explains why Bismarck offered his services as 'honest broker', by convening a peace conference in Berlin. That conference would result in a substantial revision of San Stefano. The new Bulgaria would be cut to about half its original size and then divided into two, a Principality and the autonomous region of East Rumelia. The latter was theoretically still part of the Ottoman Empire but actually on the road to unification with the Principality. Russia's influence in Bulgaria was balanced by Austria-Hungary's occupation and strategic control of Bosnia and the Sanjak of Novi Pazar.

Given the geographical diversity and complex demography of the Balkans, any division of the region into new states that neglected to take into account local antagonisms was bound to fail. But as Michael Obrenović, G.S. Rakovski and other Balkan leaders suspected, the great powers would encourage the expansion of nation states where and when it suited their interests to do so, and ignore overlapping national claims.

The 1870s saw another very dangerous development in great-power attitudes to the region. France, Britain and Russia had, in their dealings over Greece in the 1830s, acted in harmony with one another to protect their strategic interests. From the Congress of Berlin onwards, cooperation was replaced by competition; harmony by discord. The peoples of the Balkans would pay dearly for this transformation.

CHAPTER 3

A MAZE OF CONSPIRACY

The southern Balkans, 1878–1914

The pomp: the great powers

The great powers became aware of the military potential of Prussia with its victory over Austria at the battle of Königgrätz in 1866. Four years later, the ease with which the Prussian battering ram smashed through the defences of Paris astonished them. The message was clear: Britain's days as the undisputed master of commerce and industry were numbered. The unification of Germany after the Franco-Prussian War in 1871 signalled a great shift in the balance of power. The long-standing enmity dividing Britain and Russia, for example, would eventually be reversed, and the conservative bonds linking Germany and Austria-Hungary with Russia would snap. The new alignments evolved into two power blocks which went to war in 1914 – the Triple Alliance of Germany, Italy and Austria-Hungary, and the Entente which united Britain, France and Russia. This transformation was most visible on the Balkan peninsula, where it would wreak havoc.

By the summer of 1878, Germany had begun to disrupt Europe's equilibrium. Its industrial output was accelerating at great speed, catching up the economies of all its competitors and overtaking the weaker among them. Berlin was the most obvious symbol of the new Empire's power. Even two decades earlier, the Prussian capital had been a sleepy provincial town. Now, all German railroads led to Berlin. One linked the city to the Junker estates of East Prussia; another to the emerging heavy industries of Leipzig and Cottbus; a third to world markets via Hamburg and the North Sea; a fourth opened up the resources of the Rhine and the great forests of Hesse and Bavaria. The city's population had crossed the threshold of one million and grew by the day as peasants, teachers, bureaucrats and entrepreneurs rushed to this metropolitan Aladdin's cave.

The decision to convene a congress in Berlin to solve the Great Eastern Crisis confirmed the city's precocious status. Indeed, the primary significance of the Berlin Congress lay in its very location. Only Germany, the 'honest broker' in Bismarck's phrase, could claim both the requisite military authority and neutrality in Balkan affairs that would allow it to arbitrate among its querulous peers.

During the Congress, which lasted exactly a month from 13 June to 13 July, German power was invested in Prince Otto von Bismarck. The Congress was held at Bismarck's official residence in the centre of Berlin, the Radziwill Palace. Built in the 1730s, the Palace had been purchased by the German state seven years before the Congress when the imperial offices were established in Berlin. Situated just off Unter den Linden on the Wilhelmstrasse, it was both convenient and magnificent. The Congress meeting room on the first floor was filled by a huge horseshoe-shaped table. The seven delegations were seated around it in French alphabetical order. The Secretary of the Congress, Joseph Maria von Radowitz, had spent days studying the documents of the Congress of Vienna (1815), the Paris Conference (1856) and the Constantinople Conference (1875–6). His most important discovery was that the excellent food provided in Constantinople had served as an antidote to temper tantrums. Radowitz's grand buffet which adjoined the Congress room developed a reputation as the most effective diplomatic influence in Berlin. When tempers were frayed, the delegates would troop into the dining hall to pick at the spread and wash it down with a glass of sherry.

Chairman Bismarck sat at the head of the horseshoe, ever ready to use this position to hurry business along when it threatened to dissolve into fractious tedium. His impatience had a famously low boiling point. Impassioned pleas on behalf of downtrodden nations or digressions on the precise lines of new borders provoked a swift response. The Chancellor would expand his Junker bulk and flick his hand contemptuously as he ruled a speaker out of order or dismissed his contribution as irrelevant.

Not that Bismarck had it all his own way. The Congress of Berlin brought together an extremely powerful group of diplomats and politicians. And though the event was made public barely a week before the opening session, this was long enough for the European and American press to send a battalion of correspondents who were excited at the prospect of a glittering reprise of the Congress of Vienna in 1815. They were disappointed. Bismarck was a diplomatic genius but the antithesis of the flamboyant Metternich, the orchestrator of the Vienna Congress. To the consternation of friend and foe alike, he arrived in Berlin sporting an unaccustomed beard. Radowitz wrote later that 'those of us who knew him better saw how the big beard deprived his physiognomy of its agility, lending it instead something sinister, making it seem older'.[1] Metternich danced down the road to European peace. Bismarck scowled his way there.

The Chancellor's austere cynicism meant poor copy for the correspondents, who turned their attention to the other star attraction – Lord Beaconsfield, the recently ennobled Disraeli. Beaconsfield's intimacy with Queen Victoria and his reputation both as a politician and a novelist ensured that the Prime Minister's daily stroll on Unter den Linden attracted a band of inquisitive onlookers. The *Illustrated London News* tried in vain to add spice to the affair by portraying the Congress as a magisterial battle of wills between 'Bizzy and Dizzy'. In fact, Bismarck had no desire to upset Disraeli and accorded him great respect.*

The German Chancellor's most faithful ally was the Habsburg Foreign Minister, Julius Andrássy, who stood out against the stodgy garb of the other delegates in his dazzling scarlet uniform, sabre at his side. Andrássy found it hard to disguise the strain caused by

---

* An example not followed by one of his staff, the loathsome Hohenlohe, who wrote, 'I really dislike him [Beaconsfield]. A foul Jewface.' ('Ein scheussliches Judengesicht.') Quoted in *Der Berliner Kongress von 1878: Die Politik der Grossmächte und die Probleme der Modernisierung in Südosteuropa in der zweiten Hälfte des 19. Jahrhunderts*, ed. Ralph Melville and Hans-Jürgen Schröder, Wiesbaden, 1982, p. 43, n. 39.

trying to please three constituencies – the Emperor Franz Josef, Bismarck and his unforgiving Hungarian peers. The creeping senility of the Russian Chancellor, Prince Alexander Gorchakov, was such that he had to be transported every day to the Congress Hall in a sedan carriage, as though reflecting Russia's decaying grasp of international affairs.

But despite these characters, the press was deeply disappointed by the Congress of Berlin. Germany's dynamism had brought with it novel problems of social disaffection, with subversive ideologies which challenged the authoritarianism of Bismarck and his Emperor. In the year before the Congress, Wilhelm I had escaped two assassination attempts and had retreated to the countryside, handing over his role as host to his son, the Crown Prince. For all his gravity, Bismarck was a frightened man who feared for his life. In addition to carrying a revolver at all times, he kept his public appearances to a minimum and, with the exception of Disraeli, the other delegates followed his example. The proceedings themselves remained a closed book to most of the correspondents who tired of talking to minor diplomats.

In a way, there was no story because the big four, Germany, Britain, Austria-Hungary and Russia, had already taken the most important decisions of the Congress before it convened. To be sure, disputes at times almost halted the Congress. Under a lesser chairman than Bismarck, it might have failed. But Russia had already agreed that Bulgaria would be dismembered. Having forced the Sultan to accept the creation of this vast new Slavic state in December 1877 in the Treaty of San Stefano, Russia was now compelled to break it up. Rubbing salt into Muscovy's wound, it was also agreed that the Habsburg army might occupy Bosnia-Hercegovina.

The first half of the Congress was devoted almost entirely to mapping the contours of the Bulgarian settlement. Hour upon hour was spent haggling over the precise location and number of troops which the Sultan would be allowed to deploy in Eastern Rumelia. The problem lay not in these devilish details but in the stubborn jousting between Lord Beaconsfield and Gorchakov. Their respective seconds, Salisbury and Petar Shuvalov, were perpetually trying to strike a deal over the heads of their bosses. 'The old man', Shuvalov complained of Gorchakov, 'is full of obscurity and vanity, and would spoil everything.'[2] Similarly exasperated, Salisbury wrote of Beaconsfield that 'he has the dimmest idea of what is going on – understands everything crossways – and imagines a perpetual conspiracy'.[3] But to nobody's real surprise, agree they did. True, Beaconsfield resorted to the theatrical stunt of starting up the ministerial train and threatening an early departure before Russia relented on an obscure point. But it was necessary after all to give the impression to the smaller powers and to the press that the Congress was in the business of real politics.

Count Andrássy faced an awkward dilemma. His Emperor, Franz Josef, and the Austrian military establishment were determined to occupy, if not annex, Bosnia-Hercegovina. Yet, as we have seen the government in Budapest was hostile to the absorption of more Slavs into the Empire. After some skilful backroom dealing, Andrássy persuaded the British to propose that Austria-Hungary occupy Bosnia-Hercegovina to ensure regional stability. Even his Hungarian colleagues understood that it would have been fatally undiplomatic for Andrássy to refuse an offer made by the Ottoman Empire's most resolute defender. So, after Bulgaria, Bosnia, too, was quickly resolved.

Because the major issues concerning the revision of the San Stefano Treaty were settled in advance, personal resentments and foibles came to play a decisive a role at the Congress. Bismarck made no secret of the fact that he wanted the Congress to complete its work as soon as possible. The whole business had forced him to postpone his annual convalescence at his favourite spa resort, and the intense heat in Berlin had aggravated his shingles. By his own admission, the only way he was able to keep the pain at bay was to prepare for every session of the Congress by downing a jug of port. This is reported to have exacerbated his quick temper, and Prince Alexander of Hesse, who met Bismarck in the middle of the conference, observed how 'he had acquired a paunch, and spoke with difficulty among continual hiccups'.[4]

If Bismarck's distemper provoked gossip among the delegates, it was greeted with unease by participants from those 'places of which no one ever heard before this war', as Bismarck referred to the Balkans. The Balkan peninsula was a tangled mess. It had become a laboratory for political change where grand diplomats and impecunious elites tinkered with collapsing authority, local folk traditions, novel nationalist ideologies and, above all, their own short-term interests to create a jagged constitutional and territorial montage. The Congress of Berlin was set against a backdrop of vast movements of refugees, small but vicious territorial disputes and domestic power struggles. All the time the Congress was conducting its business so languidly, Russian soldiers and Bulgarian irregulars joined forces in murderous sprees against Muslim civilians in Bulgaria. Over 150,000 refugees poured into Istanbul that summer, leading to a near collapse of the city's infrastructure. The municipal authorities were already buckling under the strain when an outbreak of typhus and starvation persuaded the government to return the refugees to Edirne (Adrianople) which at the time was under a repressive Russian occupation, run by military commanders content to tolerate atrocities against Muslims. Such features of the Balkan reality were passed over in silence by the Congress.*

When the Turkish delegation, the seventh 'great power' at the horseshoe table, raised these questions for discussion, Bismarck peremptorily slapped it down. The Turks were humiliated at every turn. At one of the Congress's official social engagements, the German orchestra prepared a programme of original music from each of the seven delegate countries. However, the musicians refused to do battle with Turkish music and so offered them Mozart's 'Marcia alla turca' and Donizetti's 'The Sultan's March' instead.[5] This was the gentlest of the insults they had to tolerate.

The head of the Turkish delegation was the intelligent if unlucky Karatodori Paşa who, as a Greek Phanariot, could conveniently be blamed by the Sultan for the disaster that was bound to overtake the Ottoman Empire at the Congress. Bismarck considered insensitive the choice of a Greek to head the delegation, but he regarded as an unforgivable insult the selection of Karatodori's deputy, Mehemed Âli Paşa, who had been a military hero in the Serbo-Turkish war of 1876. Mehemed was born Karl Detroit in Brandenburg a few miles from Berlin. In his late teens, the Prussian youngster had jumped ship in Istanbul to escape a tyrannical captain. Here he became a protégé of Âli Paşa, the great man of the

* Andrássy raised the issue of 200,000 refugees from Bosnia but only because they were placing a strain on the Habsburg authorities in Croatia. He was not interested in the fate of the refugees themselves.

Tanzimat. Detroit converted to Islam and climbed the hierarchy of the Ottoman military in much the same way as the Serbian apostate, Omer Paša Latas, had done thirty years earlier. Mehemed was included in the Turkish delegation because of his thorough geographical and political knowledge of the Balkans, a rare commodity at the Congress. Unfortunately, he was unable to share his wisdom with his fellow delegates as Bismarck persistently snubbed his attempts to contribute to the proceedings.

The Porte and the Sultan made matters worse for the Turkish delegation. Karatodori was given strict orders that he was not to respond to any proposal without first referring it back to Istanbul. Sometimes, he would have to wait days for a response from his purposely indolent government while fudging Bismarck's impatient demands for a Turkish submission. Karatodori suffered his final humiliation by running out of money. Threatened with expulsion from its hotel, the Turkish delegation had to wire its resignation to Istanbul before the Porte finally sent it a miserly *per diem*. For all the tribulations experienced by Karatodori and Mehemed, the outcome of the Congress would have been the same even if the Sultan himself had attended. Despite their formally equal status around the giant horseshoe table, the Ottomans had been summoned to the Congress for one reason alone – to give away large tracts of territory to whomever the other great powers thought appropriate.

The Porte could draw some consolation from the fact that its representatives were present at every session of the Congress. The other Balkan states, hoping to be rewarded either for their valiant efforts on the battlefield or for their scrupulous observation of great-power interests, were lucky if their envoys even received invitations to the social events attended by the minor delegates to the Congress. The single significant intervention of the French Foreign Minister, William H. Waddington,* was to allow the Congress to permit the Greek delegation, led by Theodoros Delyiannis, to put its case for Greece's territorial expansion at a single session. Delyiannis and his deputy, Alexander-Rizos Rangavis, were permitted to enter the hall and expound on the theme of a Greater

* Waddington was English. His father was a businessman with extensive interests in France. Looked down on by some of the British delegates, he was nonetheless the only person in Berlin to have completed an English education.

Greece for half an hour. The urbane secretary of the Congress, Radowitz, observed that during the entire Greek oration, the chief sponsors of Athens – Waddington, Beaconsfield and Salisbury – 'slept the sleep of the just'.

The Romanians fared little better. They were invited to attend the tenth session on 1 July. Their demands, including the key claim to Transylvania, were elegantly formulated and precise. Unfortunately both Kogălniceanu and Brătianu were overawed by the occasion and Salisbury noted that their presentation was utterly inaudible from start to finish. Even if they had made themselves heard, nobody would have taken their opinion into account. As soon as they left the room, the Congress agreed to grant Romania its independence but ignored all of Bucharest's territorial concerns.

The Congress reserved its shabbiest treatment for the Serbs. Bismarck explicitly excluded Jovan Ristić, the Foreign Minister, from access to the Congress. In contrast, the Persians, scarcely central players in the Great Eastern Crisis, were allowed to make a presentation.* Ristić was only allowed to deliver Serbian demands in written form, and the delegates were not obliged to read them. Instead, the Chancellor assured the Congress that the decisions affecting Serbia would be further elucidated by a separate treaty between Vienna and Belgrade. As we shall see, 'treaty' in this instance was a euphemism for 'diktat'.

The Albanians, who sent their two most distinguished intellectuals, Abdyl Frashëri and Jani Vreto, drew a complete blank and left quickly to save money. The Montenegrins were also ignored. The only Balkan nation that might have anticipated the Congress with any hope of success was Bulgaria, which paradoxically did not yet exist as a state. Russia could be relied on to fight the Bulgarian corner because Russia's imperial goals depended on the establishment of a strong Bulgaria. The Bulgarians did not yet know that their fate had already been decided: they were destined to lose

* Bismarck was even prepared personally to receive a petition from the Peace Society for the Congress's attention although, as *The Times* noted, 'the presence of the delegates of the Peace Society at Berlin must have had something of the effect of a Quaker deputation in the midst of the Choctaws or Iroquois accoutred for the warpath'. Quoted in Robert Howard Lord, 'The Congress of Berlin', in *Three Peace Conferences of the Nineteenth Century*, Cambridge, Mass., 1917, p. 58.

Macedonia, in other words almost half of the territory they claimed. So although Bulgaria enjoyed a diplomatic advantage over their future Balkan neighbours at the Berlin meeting, the country's very birth was associated in Bulgarian minds with a grievous sense of territorial loss.

The settlement: the great powers and the Balkans

Bismarck was arrogant but with good reason. His ability to read the motives of the Congress participants, to anticipate discord within individual delegations and to reassure them that he was working in the collective interest of the great powers represent the zenith of nineteenth-century statecraft. And indeed, his claim to be acting as the 'honest broker' was not spurious – unlike the other great powers, Germany had no client among the Balkan peoples. The new Empire had, as yet, none of the foreign and colonial entanglements that were understood to be properly 'imperial' in the late nineteenth-century sense. When Bismarck told the German parliament in December 1876 that the Balkans were not 'worth the bones of a single Pomeranian grenadier', he could equally well have been discussing North Africa, the Caucasus or India. The Balkans merely happened to be the focus of European attention at the time.

The Chancellor had only one foreign-policy goal – to maintain a balance of power which would block the formation of an anti-German alliance. The cornerstone of this strategy was the Three Emperors' League, the informal agreement linking Europe's conservative capitals – Berlin, St Petersburg and Vienna. This stopped short of being a full-blown alliance but encouraged coordination between the three empires. Bismarck reasoned correctly that as long as the arrangement stood, neither Britain nor France, even allied with each other, would ever threaten Germany's fundamental interests.

The Treaty of San Stefano from December 1877 had extended Russia's influence deep into the Balkans and on to the Aegean coast. It enabled the Russians to dominate the Balkans and access to the Black Sea. This was unacceptable to both Austria-Hungary and Britain. In February 1878, Britain had sent warships to the Dardanelles and war had seemed a real possibility. A conflict would have pitched Russia against an alliance of Austria-Hungary and Great Britain. Bismarck, loath as he was to interrupt his vacation, saw no alternative but to convene the Congress of Berlin in order to restore the balance between his two collaborators, the Dual Monarchy and Russia. With the principles of the Three Emperors' League under threat, Bismarck had to offer his services as mediator.

Bismarck's assessment was based on the politics of hard 'interests'. *Realpolitik* was posited on the ability actually to use force. He dismissed as irrelevant both large collapsing empires and small emerging states – if countries could not field and sustain a large army, their opinion was of no value. Instead, these minor players were objects to be shifted around in a game of musical territories: Russia, for example, received southern Bessarabia at the expense of Romania at the Berlin Congress primarily to compensate for the reduction of San Stefano Bulgaria. The cutting and pasting of territories was not a new idea but the steady fragmentation of the Balkans created ever more baffling permutations. The only immutable principle of imperialist cartography was the advancement of great-power interests. It never entered Bismarck's head that other confessional or national groups might have legitimate rights or aspirations.

Although practical, this strategy concealed a serious weakness. Under the guiding hand of Bismarck, the Congress of Berlin subordinated all interests and demands of the Balkan states to three expanding spheres of interest – Austro-Hungarian, Russian and British. As Ottoman influence ebbed from its westerly frontier, the administrations and armies of the other three empires edged ever closer to one another. Yet the proliferating claims and counterclaims of the new Balkan states acted as a knife sharpener, making the lines of intersection between Russia and Austria-Hungary especially jagged and dangerous. Henceforth, relatively obscure disputes between countries in south-eastern Europe could degenerate swiftly into a much larger conflict between their great-power sponsors. After the Congress finished, Radowitz wrote that on balance it had proved a success because it would keep the peace 'for about five years'. In fact, it proved more robust. The dam built in Berlin held back a general European war for over three decades.

Although manipulative and questionable in moral terms, Bismarck's policy did have the virtue of being honest. With no active interests in the Balkans, Germany had no reason to deceive anyone. The other great powers at Berlin, however, could not afford such a luxury. So they lied to each other and they lied to the pathetic Turks,

Greeks, Romanians, Serbs, Montenegrins and Albanians. They were duplicitous and they bullied. Turkey and Britain surprised delegates in the middle of June by announcing Britain's plan to occupy and administer Cyprus. In exchange, Britain committed itself to defending various Turkish territories in Asia against Russian encroachment. It would be wrong to dignify the Cyprus arrangement with the term 'agreement'. Beaconsfield's explanation for the Ottoman evacuation of the eastern Mediterranean was that it allowed the Sultan to 'concentrate and condense' his resources. The Greeks helpfully suggested they might contribute to this ingenious device for reinvigorating Turkey by relieving it of other territorial burdens. Beaconsfield rejected the offer bluntly. The Greeks, he said, 'had utterly mistaken the purpose of the Congress: they seemed to imagine that it was to partition the Ottoman Empire, while nothing was further from the thoughts of the assembly'.[6] Like individuals who have a future, states, lectured Beaconsfield, must learn to wait.

In this instance, Beaconsfield was probably deluding himself rather than lying. However, the Congress marked a turning point in Balkan history. At the denouement of all previous nineteenth-century conflicts, the great powers always strove to return as close to the *status quo ante* as possible in south-eastern Europe; the preferred solution to the Great Eastern Crisis at Berlin was partition and, where necessary, population exchange.

Four centuries of the *millet* system had resulted in complex demographic patterns throughout the Ottoman Empire. This explains the confusing mixture of races, faiths and nationalities which confronted the 'map makers' of Europe when they turned their minds to the Balkans in the second half of the nineteenth century. There were many areas, notably Macedonia, where no amount of careful diplomacy could have obviated the problems caused by rising and competitive nationalisms. But the Congress exacerbated the problems wherever conceivable by wilfully ignoring the local demographic balance. Russia and Austria had originally intervened in the Balkans on the pretext of protecting the Christian communities there, and later in order to lend expression to the political aspirations of the Balkan nations. By the time they reached Berlin, these intentions were forgotten. Andrássy had no difficulty in persuading the British and Russian delegations to stick to pragmatic principles: 'In all delimitations the decisions should in the first instance be based on geographical and strategical considerations, and only on ethnographical grounds if no other basis for decision could be found.'[7]

All the belligerents in the Great Eastern Crisis were aggrieved by the Congress's outcome. Russia and Turkey, the two great powers who had gone to war in 1877–8, were obliged to accept diplomatic defeat: the former had to swallow the huge revisions to the San Stefano Treaty, the latter was effectively kicked out of Europe. Romania and Serbia, who both fought during the crisis, were deeply unhappy with the Berlin Treaty. Austria-Hungary, which had kept well out of the war, appeared to be the winner by gaining control of Bosnia, Hercegovina and the Sanjak of Novi Pazar. However, Vienna's decision to occupy Bosnia proved eventually to be the biggest single foreign-policy error in the history of the Habsburg Empire, leading directly to its collapse in 1918. Britain gained Cyprus and welcomed the blunting of Russia's sword in the region but still feared that St Petersburg had secured too much influence over the Bulgarians.

The *Berliner Tageblatt* (15 July 1878) observed the day after the Congress finished that

> the Peace of Berlin represents a compromise that satisfies nobody and yet guarantees peace in Europe for a short period. Russia demanded too little, England conceded too much. Austria has poked around in a Slav wasp's nest while the little [Balkan] states are unhappy . . . Italy and France go away empty-handed and gripe about it – the honest broker, however, rubs his hands; for the cards have been shuffled in such a way that the planned anti-German coalition looks less likely to emerge than ever. And that is our victory in the Berlin Peace.

There were two distinct aspects to the Berlin treaty. The first was a straightforward territorial settlement. The contours were drawn in Berlin but much of the detailed work was delegated to various boundary commissions or subsidiary negotiations. The second aspect may be described here as the imperialist clauses. These were the diplomatic mechanisms inserted in the Treaty or in related agreements which assured Russian, Austrian and British control of their zones of influence.

After a month of deliberations, the strategic map of the Balkans looked like this: the Treaty restored Macedonia and Thrace to the Ottoman Empire. Serbia, Romania and Montenegro were granted full independence, absolved of any obligations towards the Porte. Serbia, Romania and Montenegro were all granted small portions of territory at the expense of the Ottoman Empire. Greece was also due to receive more land, although in this instance Turkey was given effective leave by the Congress to procrastinate, and they did so for years. Russia would maintain an occupying force in Bulgaria and Eastern Rumelia until May 1879, and beyond that date Russia's influence in both the Principality and the province would still be paramount. Austria-Hungary was permitted to occupy Bosnia, Hercegovina and the Sanjak of Novi Pazar. The Sultan was still the nominal suzerain of the territories (and, needless to say, Vienna made certain that Istanbul remained responsible for Bosnia's debts) but, as with Bulgaria, everybody understood that Bosnia, Hercegovina and the Sanjak were lost to the Ottoman Empire for ever. Even Istanbul's only substantial remaining holdings, Macedonia and Albania, left the Porte with many more problems than advantages.

San Stefano Bulgaria was reduced from 176,000 square kilometres to just 96,000 square kilometres. From being one huge entity, this rump was now split in two along the line of the Balkan mountains while a third portion, Macedonia, was returned to the Ottoman Empire. The Bulgarian Principality was to choose a monarch acceptable to the great powers, although he would still in theory owe fealty to the Sultan. The Congress set the annual tribute by assessing roughly what proportion of the Ottoman debt might be attributed to the Principality. In this way, the Sultan never actually saw the money and it went straight into the pockets of his creditors.

In the south, the province of Eastern Rumelia was supposedly an integral part of the Ottoman Empire. The British had argued long and hard at the Congress that Istanbul should therefore police the province.* In fact, the local militia, trained and advised by the

* Bismarck's response to the problem highlighted how little most delegates knew of the region. On 13 June he said that the Sultan could overcome the difficulty by employing only Christian troops in Rumelia. 'An admirable idea', wrote Salisbury, 'only he has not got any.'

Russian occupying force and staffed solely by Bulgarians, maintained control over Rumelia. The governor-general was a Russian and aside from some discrepancies in the economic régimes of the Principality and Eastern Rumelia, there was little to distinguish between the two.

To compensate for the loss of southern Bessarabia to Russia, Romania was awarded the northern Dobrudja, a valuable wedge of Balkan real estate that encompassed the mouth of the Danube. Unfortunately for Bucharest, part of it was also claimed by the Bulgarians, and under Russian pressure the Berlin settlement gave some of southern Dobrudja to the Bulgarians. This created yet another irredentist sideshow.

The gains for Serbia, the first country to wage war on the Turks, were negligible. It was allotted the towns of Pirot and Niš, an important strategic and commercial stronghold just north of the Macedonian border. But Bosnia, whose Orthodox peasantry had sparked the Great Eastern Crisis, was now strictly off limits because of the impending Habsburg occupation. The Austro-Hungarian Dual Monarchy's control of the Sanjak of Novi Pazar was salt in the wound.

Contemporaries viewed the decay of the Ottoman Empire as a unique phenomenon whose primary cause lay in the irreconcilability of the Christian and Muslim communities. At the time of the Congress, twilight was also dimming the Habsburg sky but so gently that nobody noticed it. The *Ausgleich* of 1867 which granted the Hungarians self-government in lands under their control had already undermined the Empire's cohesion. Now the national aspirations of the Slavic nations had also begun to conflict with the nationalism of the German-speaking population. But in 1878, the occupation of Bosnia looked like a blow against Slav nationalism as it blocked Serbia's westward expansion. So the Serbian state stored its claims to Bosnia for later retrieval and obediently followed the logic of Habsburg policy in the region by turning its expansionist ambitions south in the direction of Macedonia. Russia and Austria-Hungary were goading Bulgaria and Serbia towards expansion in Macedonia. A third source of pressure on this vulnerable territory was of course the Greek aspirations to acquire it.

At San Stefano, the Russians had rewarded their faithful Montenegrin friends with dramatic territorial gains. These were pared down substantially in Berlin although this minuscule country was granted a treasured outlet to the sea at Antivari (now Bar). To compensate for the growing Austrian influence to the north, Montenegro was allowed a modest extension southwards. The further south Montenegro went, of course, the greater became the concentration of Albanians – more trouble in the making. The Albanians received next to nothing in Berlin – except perhaps the merest hint of goodwill from the Austrians.

Beaconsfield and Waddington had given Greece rhetorical support in Berlin but this had brought Athens few tangible benefits. Greece's claim to more land was made dependent on Greek-Turkish negotiations, which Istanbul successfully slowed to a snail's pace. It was three years before the Greeks were finally able to assume control of Thessaly and a small slice of Epirus.

This settlement at Berlin created confusion and resentment in many parts of the Balkans. The first map included some crass constitutional solutions – in effect, a network of mutually exclusive claims, underpinned by historical, demographic or strategic arguments, which primed several bloody future conflicts. The great powers had now linked their imperial interests to the aspirations of emerging Balkan states. This was the great disaster of 1878. The new elites on the Balkan periphery learnt the lesson beaten into them at the Congress: the consolidation and expansion of the state could best be achieved by finding a mighty sponsor, not by cooperating with one's neighbours.

Formally, Serbia, Romania and Montenegro joined Greece as independent states in south-eastern Europe. It was generally assumed that Bulgaria and Eastern Rumelia would soon follow. However, the strictures and conditions attached to this new freedom were so severe that the term 'independence' seems almost risible.

Jovan Ristić, who travelled to Berlin with high hopes for Serbia, was brought down to earth during the second week of the Congress. The Austrians informed him that as a condition of independence, Serbia would have to pay an Austrian contractor, Baron Hirsch, to build a railway from Belgrade to the Ottoman Macedonian border. Further, Serbia would have to cooperate in constructing another line to Bulgaria and Turkey. Serbia was also required to sign a treaty of commerce with Austria after bilateral negotiations. Finally, Serbia must agree to Austria's plans for a navigational regime on the

Danube and afford it immediate 'most favoured nation' trading status. Ristić, accusing Austria-Hungary of holding a knife against Serbia's throat, held out for a few days during which Schwegel from the Austrian delegation cursed the Serbs as a 'shameful rabble' (*Schandgesindel*). Within days, the Serbian Minister had agreed to all these terms. The Austrians were determined to seize control of Serbia's trade and foreign policies, turning Belgrade into an accomplice in their imperialist drive southwards. The strategy culminated in 1881 when Vienna signed a secret defence treaty with Prince Milan.

The Austrians bullied Romania as well on the issues of railroad construction and commercial relations. But above all Romanians resented the 'liberty of conscience' article imposed on them in Berlin. In the single humanitarian gesture included in the Treaty, Romania, Montenegro and Serbia were to insert a clause in their constitutions guaranteeing freedom of religion. In Serbia and Montenegro, this served primarily to protect Muslims. In Romania, it was to protect Jews. Gorchakov tried to block the move, arguing that the Jews of Russia and Romania were a social scourge, not to be confused with the fine merchants of London, Paris, Berlin and Vienna.

Tiny Montenegro was also told by the Congress that it was not allowed to have a fleet and that all its ships must fly the Habsburg flag.

The main focus of the Berlin Congress was the Balkan peninsula. Almost incidentally, however, it also upped the stakes in the 'Great Game', the Anglo-Russian rivalry in the Caucasus and Central Asia. Moreover, France, upset by Britain's surprise occupation of Cyprus, received Bismarck's approval on a nod to occupy Tunisia. The French expansion into the Maghreb sparked 'the scramble for Africa', that extraordinary and fateful burst of colonialist activity – whose consequences the powers are still trying to unscramble.

The modern history of Afghanistan, Bosnia and Sudan, countries the world has recently had to rediscover, all began with the Peace of Berlin. A.H. Layard, the British consul in Constantinople, was one of the first to comment on the implications of the settlement. Nobody else has come up with a more perceptive judgement in over a century:

> Those who think themselves strong enough to support their

aspirations by arms will be ready to rebel against the authority under which they believe they have been placed in violation of justice and of the principle of 'nationality'. Those who cannot recur to force will have recourse to intrigue and conspiracy. Both processes have already begun.[8]

Real life: Albania

As always Albanian and Slav
Were at blood since a tragic fate
Placed fire and gunpowder side by side.
Placed side by side Albania and Montenegro!

Did I not tell you, oh Prince Nikola
That before the fall of night
I would avenge Tringa,
Cutting off three hundred heads,
Taking three hundred slaves,
Making three thousand girls and young brides
Widows before their time.

Gjaku i marrun (Blood avenged)[9]

Three days before the Congress of Berlin opened, a colourful group of men was gathering in Prizren, a town of quiet majesty in the Kosovo vilayet. Prizren's gentle outskirts began on the mountain-side. Across the Bistrica river stood the busy bazaar, the home of the finest silver and gold craftsmen in the Balkans. Nobles from all over the peninsula would buy their brilliantly inlaid guns and sabres in Prizren. But the landowners, priests and chieftains who arrived on that hot June day in 1878 had not come in search of gifts. They had come to organize. Most of the delegates to the League of Prizren were Muslims but there were a few Catholics and one or two members of the Orthodox Church. They were united only by the disaster threatened by the slow collapse of the Ottoman Empire and by their language – Albanian.

Just over three-quarters of a million Albanians lived in the Ottoman Empire. One of the oldest communities on the peninsula, they had adapted remarkably to the Empire's peculiar social environment. The Albanians were concentrated in present-day Albania, Kosovo and Macedonia. But the population extended deep into

Greece, into Montenegro and even into Bulgaria and Thrace. Albanian fighters were the shock troops of the Ottoman army and the region's most effective mercenaries; their trading communities established influential colonies in cities as far apart as Bucharest, Istanbul and Cairo. About 70 per cent adopted Islam as their faith and, uniquely among Ottoman Muslims, they were subject to the *devşirme*. The influence of Albanians who trained as influential bureaucrats to the Sultan was out of all proportion to the numbers culled by the *devşirme*. At least thirty were appointed to the highest office in the Empire, the Grand Vizierate.

There had been cultural cross-fertilization between the Albanians and their neighbours. Turks, Greeks, Montenegrins, Serbs and Vlachs had all borrowed from and contributed to aspects of Albanian folklore, cuisine and social habits. The Albanian mountain warriors of the north shared many customs with their Montenegrin neighbours, most infamously the *gjakmarrje*, the vendetta or blood revenge, which itself was based on the concept of *besa* or honour. To the south, the Greek Orthodox Albanians benefited particularly from the growth of Hellenism. Like the Bulgarians, many Albanians acquired an education in Greek schools. Nonetheless, the Albanians, whose language formed a separate branch of the Indo-European family, remained a mystery to most of their neighbours.

With such a high proportion of Muslims, the Albanians were important allies for the authorities in Istanbul. Geography determined that the Albanians had a crucial role to play in resisting the expansionist urges of Greeks, Montenegrins, Serbs and Bulgarians, provided the Porte could manipulate them with sufficient dexterity. To assist its own survival, the Porte had to prevent the Albanians from following the example of their neighbours and forming their own national movement. The key to Albanian unity was language. Religion, geography and class divided them dramatically, so that during the great Ottoman reform the Men of the Tanzimat insisted that the Albanians stick to their *millet* affiliation. Alone among the Balkan nations, the Albanians were forbidden from teaching in their own tongue.

The League of Prizren sent a message to Beaconsfield on the opening day of the Berlin Congress, urging him to defend Albanian interests at the meeting as 'a bulwark against the Slavs in the Balkans'.[10] The League was not taking any chances. The Treaty of

San Stefano had completely ignored the Albanians and there was no reason to think it would be otherwise in Berlin. Instead, the League busied itself by organizing a huge 'people's army' to resist encroachments on Albanian land. The League was in effect preparing to wage a defensive war against the Montenegrins, Bulgarians and Greeks. But it was also warning Istanbul: the *millet* system was dead and the Albanian national movement was born. In a gesture of profound symbolism, the League invoked the *besa*, whereby all Albanians foreswore blood revenge in order to concentrate their energy on furthering the national struggle.

Within months of the Congress, Albanians were plunged into four very different and difficult armed conflicts. Tens of thousands of men from the north, where a man's gun was his 'best friend',[11] responded to the League's call to form the 'people's army' to defend territories awarded to Montenegro. These forgotten little wars, which were more or less unknown to the world even as they were happening, claimed several thousand lives. Demonstrating courage and tactical skill, the Albanians warded off the equally tough Montenegrin forces in four districts until 1880. They thus achieved the distinction of securing the only revision to the Treaty by force of arms.

The Montenegrins then invoked the Treaty and the great powers awarded them the port of Ulquin (now Ulcinj in Montenegro) in exchange for the four districts. The people's army, several thousand strong, wheeled south to Ulquin and again defeated the Montenegrins. Austria-Hungary and Montenegro pressured Istanbul into sending troops against the Albanians. The great powers reinforced their request by threatening to occupy the Ottoman port of Smyrna (Izmir), which finally forced the Sultan's hand: a Turkish army was sent to deliver Ulquin to Montenegro. And at that moment, with their entry into modern history, the Albanians felt as though the whole world was ranged against them. This sense of national victimhood would haunt them, just as the Bulgarians, too, had begun to curse the Berlin settlement.* The Albanians were particularly disgusted that the Ottoman authorities

* All Balkan nations felt deeply betrayed by the outside world at some point in their modern history, and this has had a lasting impact on the psychology of states and nations throughout the region.

had succumbed to great-power pressure. Âli Paşa Gucija, one of the Albanian tribal leaders, had no hesitation in spitting on the Sultan personally: 'Until this moment I had you in place of a father; but since you have separated me from you, yielding me to Montenegro, I have ceased to be yours any longer . . . Therefore, now that you have abandoned me and you don't have me with you any more, if you come to force me to submit to Montenegro, I will see myself as between two enemies who want to fight against me at any cost.'[12] Muslim Albanians concluded that the protection offered by the Ottoman Empire was worthless. Only an independent state, they reasoned, could save them from being swallowed up by their neighbours.

The Albanians were caught in a nasty trap. On the one hand, tradition and *Realpolitik* taught them to support the Sultan. On the other, the Sultan was clearly trying to maintain his authority by a policy of divide and rule. They had no school system; they were without a properly codified language; communications among them were appalling; and they were divided not just by religion, but by class and regional tradition. Above all, they had attracted no great-power sponsor. By 1881, their 'people's army' was exhausted. Fighting along most of the periphery of the four Albanian vilayets, the army had neither a strategic centre nor the resources to deal with their enemies. A combination of Montenegrins, Serbs and Turks smashed the Albanians' makeshift military structure. Greece, which had been awarded the Arta region of Epirus, was determined eventually to take Ioannina as well, the centre of Albanian culture in Epirus. Surrounded by more powerful neighbours who enjoyed the benefit of statehood, Albanians had no choice but to engage in the politics of conspiracy and guerrilla warfare.

Real life: Macedonia

> It is well-known to all of us that this ill-fated country of ours, Macedonia, owing to the egoistic aims of the Great Powers, was again left to Turkey at the Congress of Berlin. As a result of that, in certain regions of our fatherland many blood-thirsty events occurred. Wanting to throw off the Turkish yoke from our fatherland, each one of us rose up as best we knew to sacrifice himself . . . We rebelled as advocates of freedom. With the blood we shed all over the

> Macedonian fields and forests, we serve freedom, as the Macedonian army of Alexander of Macedon once did, with our slogan, 'Freedom or Death!'
>
> Preamble to 'The Rules of the Macedonian Rebel Committee', 1878[13]

The Congress of Berlin left Macedonia in the sorriest state of all. The shock waves of the previous three years now rolled through this large area of five Ottoman vilayets. From July, thousands of Albanian and Turkish soldiers and *başi-bözök*s streamed into western and northern Macedonia to flee the expansion of Serbia and Montenegro. Whole villages were plundered and put to the torch. Peasants, whether Greeks, Albanians, Turks or Slavs, were expelled from their homes to join a nomadic army seeking shelter in the towns. The Albanian and Slav menfolk swelled the ranks of the *čete*, the small, armed raiding groups. These still survived off the fruits of banditry but were rapidly transforming themselves into the nucleus of guerrilla armies. The Greeks of the region were now caught between the cruelty of the Ottoman Empire's dissipating authority and the frequently merciless behaviour of the Muslim, Albanian and Slav bands. Some months before the Berlin Congress, the Greek government had begun encouraging the Greeks of Macedonia to organize their own guerrilla groups, the *andarte*, and the Vlachs cooperated with the Greeks in these new leagues of self-defence. The vacuum of authority in the countryside destroyed any semblance of stable social relations.

Enmity between Slavs and Turks was most acute close to the demarcation line which separated the new Bulgarian Principality from Ottoman Macedonia. By October 1878, *Edinstvo* (Unity), one of the new nationalist committees which had sprung up in Bulgaria and Eastern Rumelia, was planning an uprising in the Kresna district, 50 kilometres south of the demarcation line. Two local leaders, Pop Georgievski-Berovski, a militant Orthodox priest, and Stoian Karastoilov, together with two of *Edinstvo*'s agents, one a Russian, the other a Pole, began to gather men and weapons. The revolt spread quickly and at its height, the *četa* of the self-declared Macedonian Rebel Committee had 'liberated' some fifty-nine communities, home to about 32,000 people, the overwhelming majority Slavs.

The rebellion held out for just over a month before the Ottoman troops and irregulars crushed the movement and indulged in their mop-up operations. One historian, in dismissing the revolt, maintained that '[t]he only result of the episode was to encourage the Turks to provoke unrest in the Moslem areas of the Rhodope [Mountains] and to put the western powers even more on their guard as to Bulgarian intentions'.[14] It was indeed a largely quixotic affair. Yet the Kresna Uprising posed in a violent way, and for the first time, what is without doubt the most baffling puzzle of modern identity on the entire peninsula: more complicated than Albania, more confusing than Bosnia. To this day scholars have sought to answer the Macedonian Question, the unyielding philosopher's stone of Balkan nationalism.

Although largely unknown outside Bulgaria and Macedonia, several exhaustive studies of the Kresna Uprising have been written, published during the communist period in both Bulgaria and Yugoslav Macedonia. Nobody disputes the basic facts: the Uprising started on 17 October 1878 when 400 insurgents under the leadership of Karastoilov climbed a crag overhanging the river Struma to attack the inn at Kresna where the local Turkish battalion was stationed. Everyone recognizes that Pop Georgievski masterminded the rebellion, and that there was much traffic between the rebels in Macedonia and the 'charitable' committees across the border in Bulgaria.

At first glance, the rival accounts are identical. But a closer examination reveals curious discrepancies in detail. The histories published in Sofia refer always to Pop Georgiev whereas those from Skopje call him Pop Georgievski; one historian will write about the rebels as 'Bulgarians', the next will talk only of 'Macedonians'. Both tell the truth and both, unwittingly, lie.

Macedonia was and is the crossroads of the Balkan peninsula. To travel from Central Europe to the Aegean port of Salonika or from the Adriatic Sea to Istanbul, the trader would always pass through Macedonia to avoid traversing the Balkan mountains. Even Bismarck with his studied contempt for all Balkan affairs conceded its vital strategic location. 'Those who control the valley of the River Vardar', he observed, 'are the masters of the Balkans.'[15]

At the time of the Congress of Berlin, the region was an extraordinary pot-pourri of cultures, faiths and traditions. The four largest populations were Slavs, Greeks, Albanians and Turks, although Macedonia's main port, Salonika (Thessaloniki), was dominated by 50,000 Sephardic Jews and their language, Ladino. There were many other communities too, notably the Aromano Vlachs,* nomadic shepherds and traders who speak a language akin to Romanian. Macedonia also boasted the largest concentration of Roma, or Gypsies, on the Balkan peninsula. The ethnic communities were sometimes divided by religion. There were both Muslim and Greek Orthodox Albanians, not to mention several pockets of Muslim Slavs. Urban Slavs, Jews and Greeks dominated trade in the region, and the last had developed impressive cultural and educational institutions. In many parts of central and western Macedonia, a Slav, a Greek, a Vlach, a Turkish and an Albanian village would exist side by side in docile harmony. Quite simply, Macedonia was Europe's most enduring and complex multicultural region. When the process of fragmentation in the Balkans began, the potential for violence in this region was greater than anywhere else. At some point in the near future, the Ottoman Empire would lose Macedonia. Everybody agreed on that after Berlin. But who would then gain control of the most strategically valuable part of the Balkans?

The Bulgarians were indignant because Macedonia and Eastern Thrace, which the Russians had awarded them at San Stefano, had been taken from them in Berlin. Their claim on Macedonia was based on its Slav population, the largest of all. The Bulgarian elite assumed that these Slavs were Bulgarian. This was not unreasonable. The language they spoke was the same, albeit with great dialectal variation, as the population of the Bulgarian Principality and Eastern Rumelia. The Slavs in Macedonia had also gravitated towards the Bulgarian church after its establishment in 1870. Yet, at the same time, the Slavs of Macedonia referred to themselves as Macedonians. This was not necessarily a denial of their Bulgarian identity. It is merely that they shared with many other inhabitants a sense of belonging to Macedonia. Greeks from the region would call themselves both Greeks and Macedonians.

The question of the origins of the modern Macedonians, who feel themselves categorically to be a Slav people distinct from Serbs

* Also known as the Kutzo-Vlachs, the Macedo-Romanians or the Tsintsars.

or Bulgars, provokes more intellectual fanaticism than any other in the southern Balkans. One scholar, let us say from Skopje, will assume that this nation has existed for over a thousand years; the next, perhaps a well-meaning westerner, will claim the Macedonians first developed a separate identity from Bulgaria about one hundred years ago; a third, for the sake of argument a Serb, will swear that the Macedonians only emerged as a nation at the end of the Second World War; and a fourth, probably a Greek or Bulgarian, will maintain doggedly that they do not exist and have never done so.

Scholars and politicians from Bulgaria, Greece, Serbia and the Republic of Macedonia itself, not to mention their respective apologists from outside the region, regularly work on assumptions about Macedonia and 'the Macedonians' which are irreconcilable. This suggests that nationalism and national identity in the region are built on fragile foundations. Fragile, because such supposedly well-established identities as the Greek, Serb and Bulgarian can feel so threatened by a national community which even now numbers less than two million; and because throughout the region, and especially in contested regions like Macedonia, national identity or identities do not remain stable. They change over a few generations; they mutate during the course of a war; they are reinvented following the break-up of a large empire or state; and they emerge anew during the construction of new states. Balkan nationalism evokes such ferocious passion because, paradoxically, it is so labile.

At the height of the Kresna Uprising in 1878, the rebels produced a document called 'The Rules of the Macedonian Rebel Committee' which codified the aims and conduct of the rebellion. For such an apparently primitive revolt, it is a very detailed text, running to 211 'rules'. These express the paradoxes and contradictions that would afflict the 'Macedonian cause' for decades after the Uprising's collapse. The Committee appeals to 'those people from Macedonia who feels themselves to be Macedonian . . . regardless of faith and nationality' to flock to the rebellion. Yet a few paragraphs later the Committee admits that the aim of the Uprising 'is no secret. It is the liberation of Macedonia, the land of the glorious Slav educators and teachers, SS. Cyril and Methodius'. Thus the Kresna Uprising, and henceforth the movement for the liberation of Macedonia, were simultaneously inclusive of all nations and exclusively Slav.

At the start of the Macedonian struggle, it seems its participants were sure of only one thing – that the Ottomans should leave. But beyond that, the conduct and aims of the Macedonians, of whatever ilk, were changing according to the fluid political conditions. This underlines how swiftly people's identities had begun to change, especially, but not exclusively, in mesmerically complex regions like Bosnia and Macedonia. This has since been particularly true in times of political chaos and violence.

The Balkan Wars of 1912–13 were fought mainly on the territory of Macedonia. From the Congress of Berlin until these terrible events, Macedonia was at its most enigmatic, its most malleable and incomprehensible. The desperate debate between Bulgarian and Macedonian historians about the Kresna rebels' national label is, in an important sense, fruitless and unanswerable. Macedonia was caught between the certainty of the *millet* and the mischievous energy of nationalism. 'Macedonia', wrote the Wanderer in Saki's short story, 'The Cupboards of the Yesterdays', 'is a magical region, with its mountain passes and frozen rivers, with grim battlefields, its drifting snows, and prowling wolves.' Another author detected that Macedonia was melting into a peculiar twilight of imperial decline: 'It was not so much a nonsense world – it was too alarming for that – as a world of nightmare wherein everything was distorted. The spirit of disorder, monstrous, uncouth, terrifying – reigned supreme.'[16]

After the failure of the Kresna Uprising, the Ottomans took three years to re-establish a degree of authority over Macedonia. During this period, the marauding *başi-bözök*s continued to make life miserable, notably in western Macedonia. One Greek agent in the town of Kastoria wrote that 'the Christian inhabitants of these parts have reached such a point, that they would welcome with open arms, not only Russian and Bulgarian bands, but also Indochinese bands, if they would promise them deliverance from the existing yoke'.[17] In response, the activities of the *čete* of all nationalities proliferated dramatically, leading to terrifying chaos in the region until the Ottoman army finally restored order in 1881.

Neither the Albanians, nor the Slavs of Macedonia, had been able to sustain their 'people's armies'. The Ottomans had failed to establish secure conditions in Macedonia, particularly for the peasantry. The revolutionaries created by this state of affairs had no alternative but to resort, as A.H. Layard had correctly predicted, to intrigue and conspiracy. The Macedonians, whomever they may have been, were about to enter the age of the secret society and of revolutionary terror.

Real life: Bosnia and Hercegovina

> July 3rd was a turning point in our uncertain situation which I will never forget as long as I live . . . Count Andrássy had telegraphed from Berlin with the news that the Congress had transferred the administration of Bosnia and the Hercegovina to Austria-Hungary . . . At about 10 o'clock [on 5 July], all the shops in the Čaršija were closed and the Christians and Jews ran home in great fear. For in Turkish lands, the shutting of shops in the Čaršija always meant a huge demonstration if not a rebellion of the Islamic people . . . In the middle of the Mosque's courtyard, someone unfurled a green flag which was greeted with great cheers to be heard far and wide.
>
> Josef Koetschet, the imperial governor's physician[18]

> Many fell victim to the street fighting in Sarajevo. There was shooting from all sides from the small houses and little slits in the wooden roofs. The houses were so low that it was easy to hide . . . The rebels, dispersed and surrounded, found refuge in the nearest house, barricaded the entrance and opened fire on the [Austrian] units who had forced their way through. In this way, the most bloody fights developed on the streets. The rebels who refused to surrender had to be killed. Others retreated towards Pale. At 4 o'clock in the afternoon on August 19th 1878, the commander announced that Sarajevo had been occupied together with its fortresses.
>
> Gustav Ritter von Trauenfest, *Report of the Kärtner Infantry Regiment*[19]

When the Muslim traders closed down the *čaršija* (bazaar) on 5 July, the shutters slammed on four centuries of Ottoman rule in their province. The fury of the demonstrators who swamped the city centre was directed as much at the Sultan as it was at the Berlin Congress. 'You can give away Stambul', they bellowed, 'but not Bosnia.'[20] The Sultan's authority shrivelled as an anarchic government evolved from the angry mob which chanted its way through Sarajevo's streets into the military garrisons and the governor's palace. At the head of this impromptu cabinet stood Hadži Lojo, a charismatic criminal, his huge frame draped in a red cloak edged with gold braid. Under his direction, guns and ammunition were seized from the barracks and distributed among the mob. Hadži Lojo invited some leading Serbs to join his National Committee and urged Muslims and Orthodox alike to resist the invasion of the Austro-Hungarian troops. Of the twenty-three Ottoman battalions in Bosnia, nineteen were made up of recruits from Bosnia who readily came over to the rebel side. Within days, there was no discernible Ottoman structure left for them to serve. The more wealthy Muslim *begs* and *ağas* withdrew from public life, prepared, albeit with heavy hearts, to accept the Habsburg administration as a means of safeguarding their economic interests. In the capital, many ordinary Serbs locked themselves in for the duration of the Lojo rebellion. Leading Croats, regarded as a fifth column, sought temporary protection in the foreign consulates.

The Hadži Lojo rebellion is often portrayed as a wild orgy driven by the fanaticism of the Muslim lower classes. But these were people who had been tossed around and bruised by self-interested external forces, Russian, Austrian, Serb, even Ottoman. Now rumour had proclaimed that their country was to be transferred from one Empire to another. For both Muslim and Serb, the incoming Empire was the enemy incarnate. The Muslims' carefully ordered world and sense of privilege were being torn to shreds. They had reached the limit of their endurance.

The news from Berlin was confirmed almost a month before Austria-Hungary sent its troops to Bosnia. It was inevitable that some force would fill the power vacuum of the intervening period. Although he had lost the territory, the Sultan encouraged the clandestine delivery of arms to the rebels. He hoped that Bosnia could still give the Habsburgs a bloody nose. Indeed, if resistance could be sustained through the autumn, the Austrians would be bogged down in the snow-bound mountains of a Balkan winter, threatening the entire Berlin Treaty.

In the countryside to the south, groups of armed Muslim refugees, who had fled advancing Montenegrin troops, were terrorizing the local population regardless of nationality. In parts of Hercegovina and northern Bosnia, the Serb rebels who had taken up arms against the *begs* three years earlier were continuing their inchoate *jacquerie*.

By the time the first four divisions of the Habsburg army finally crossed the Sava from Croatia into Bosnia, however, many Serbs and Muslims were preparing for a long war against the occupation.

Assuming that resistance would evaporate after a few swift defeats, the Habsburg military commanders assigned 72,000 troops to enter the province in a symbolic show of friendly force – they regarded themselves as liberators. Feldzeugmeister Josef Filipović quickly came to the conclusion that this 'soft strategy' was not going to work and that the aim of occupying Sarajevo would require more manpower and more brutal tactics. The terrain was so bad that in some areas, artillery units needed forty men to move each cannon a few hundred yards. As the 20th Division moved south from Šamac, it lost eleven soldiers on the first day through heat exhaustion. The army began its push towards Sarajevo, but the rebels launched several successful ambushes, driving back the Habsburg columns. Within days Filipović had requested and received reinforcements. It took 268,000 men, a full third of the imperial army, to subdue the Bosnians who were finally crushed only in October. The Bosnians had come close to holding out until winter.

The cooperation between Muslims and Serbs during the resistance contrasted remarkably with the grinding conflict of the three years prior to the Habsburg occupation which set Orthodox *kmet* against Muslim *beg*. It reflected a temporary coincidence of interests between the two groups, rather than a basis for a future alliance. As in the Macedonian case, however, it highlighted how quickly animosity could transmute into unity, and vice versa, in the face of external pressure.

National identity and nationalism remained opaque and unpredictable. Using language as an adhesive, Albanians were overcoming divisions of religion, class and regional identity. The Bosnian communities were also united by language. In their case, though, this was not sufficiently strong to bridge the gulf of class or religion. In contrast to Albania, Bosnia was surrounded by Catholic and Orthodox communities, the Croats of the Triune Kingdom and the Serbs of an independent Serbia, who spoke the same language as their co-confessionals in Bosnia. These neighbours also enjoyed varying degrees of great-power protection, which made cooperation with the Bosnian Muslims less attractive for the Bosnian Serbs and Bosnian Croats, although, as the Austrian occupation demonstrated, circumstances might well conspire to fuse any combination of the three communities into a specifically Bosnian identity. This flexibility of people's identities and interests, in conjunction with great-power interference, meant that the final shape of the Balkan map could only be a matter for pure conjecture – a strong Bosnian state was a possibility, as was a Sloveno-Croat, Serbo-Bulgarian, Yugoslav or any other combination of state formation in the region. The same could, of course, have been said in 1878 about Spain. The difference is, however, that almost 120 years later, the contours of Spain are *relatively* stable, even taking into account recent constitutional changes. In the Balkans, there are several states which may yet melt into air, and doubtless future ones which are still to solidify.

The King *v.* the People: Serbia

In 1883, King Milan Obrenović enjoyed another unforgettable summer. On an extended visit to Austria and Germany, he waltzed with princesses, offered advice to emperors and spent many a convivial evening losing a fortune at the Jockey Club in Vienna. Wherever he turned, he was greeted with the unique gravitas of the Habsburgs and Hohenzollerns. The great father of peoples, Kaiser Franz Josef, bestowed on his new Serbian friend the honorary command of an Austrian regiment. But the highlight of his visit was an invitation extended by crotchety old Wilhelm, probably the most powerful ruler in Europe, to the annual imperial manoeuvres in Homburg. Milan swelled with pride upon reading in the German press that he was the object of 'particular attention', when the Kaiser and a large group of German princes met him at the rail station in Homburg. Seated as guest of honour in the military stand next to the King of Spain, Milan watched enthralled as the Emperor, at the head of a battalion, saluted him at the head of a battalion. He was struck by his conversations with Alphonse XII, admiring in particular his peer's no nonsense approach to dealing with opposition in Spain.

Could a monarch ask for greater confirmation of his exalted status? Milan had finally escaped his shabby origins as the grandson of the illiterate, uncouth pig farmer Miloš Obrenović. True, he could never erase the fact that his success had depended on the cunning of the despotic Miloš, not to mention the vast fortune his grandfather had amassed as Prince of Serbia. But the great courts of Europe would never have admitted Miloš into their midst, regardless of his wealth. The Austrians and Germans now accorded Milan the princely treatment that befitted their man in the Balkans.

Milan remained not a little ashamed of the country he ruled. Belgrade, the capital, was changing but remained in essence an Ottoman trading town of wooden houses cramped in narrow, smelly lanes. At the centre, of course, was the busy *čaršija*, the pivot of Serbia's crucial livestock trade. Pigs and cattle mingled happily with the townsfolk. The hogs were enjoying their last stop in Serbia before crossing the Sava into Austria's outpost, Zemun, on their way to the tables of Vienna, Salzburg, Munich and Berlin. Like most Balkan towns, Belgrade was filthy, lacking a basic sewage system or a programme of garbage collection. The first street lights had started to appear but the few horse-drawn coaches were still so expensive that only the highest-paid bureaucrats could afford to use them. Newer, grander buildings were starting to compete with the old Turkish architecture, and Milan was proud of the royal palace and the new government ministries sprouting in the centre. Kalemegdan, the imposing Turkish fortress which gazed down imperiously at the confluence of the Sava and the Danube, was being transformed into a public park. Such projects underlined the desire of Belgrade's civil servants to emulate the civility of Europe's more established capitals.

Milan and his administrators were imitating King Carol's success in Bucharest, the Paris of the Balkans. The Romanian capital was being transformed by wide boulevards, flanked by stylish architecture and cafés, sweeping away the warren of streets that was the hallmark of Ottoman towns. Bucharest was a beacon to which Belgrade, Sofia and even Athens were drawn. These youthful capitals were purposefully shedding their association with the countryside and with the peasant class – whose labour was paying for the modernization of urban life through increasingly exorbitant taxes.

Milan's ideal was a Serbia of palaces and European manners where his word was nonetheless law. He despised the 85 per cent of his population still living outside the cities – the men, women and children housed together in unhygienic proximity on their smallholdings. 'Don't be fooled by your Bulgarians', Milan wrote to his friend, Alexander von Battenberg (1879–1886), the German Prince of Bulgaria, 'and don't for a minute think that they are good souls but naive. They are Slavs, and that is all you need to know. I can tell you, my Serbs are no better! Do you realize that if anybody wanted to encourage my blessed subjects to make even the minutest progress, he would have to wage a despairing battle against their customs, habits, intentions and wishes?'[21] Milan and his coterie were sophisticated Europeans in their own eyes, his subjects an incorrigible herd of ungrateful Balkan dolts.

Just before the King returned from his triumphant summer tour of 1883, these *canaille* had insulted their monarch in elections to a 'special' parliament. The assembly was due to ratify the final agreement on the railroad system which would link Austria with Bulgaria and the Ottoman Empire through Serbia. The parliament would then be dissolved. Milan, not wanting to upset his patrons in Vienna, expected a smooth passage for the rail agreement. Nonetheless, on 19 September, the local authorities were overwhelmed by the peasants' rush to the polling booths. They had anticipated the usual display of apathy. But as the gap between town and country had grown, so too had the strength of Serbia's Radical Party, as the election results testified.

The Radical leaders included many educated men able to detect and influence the mood of the peasantry. Although some had exchanged the tough simplicity of livestock farming for scholarships in Geneva and Paris, they remained firmly attached to their roots in central and eastern Serbia. They challenged the new state's intellectual and political dependence on Austro-Hungarian Serbs from the Vojvodina, who had influenced the two major parties, the Liberals and the Progressives, in favour of townspeople and to the detriment of the peasantry.

During the previous year, the peasantry had become tired of the tax burden and the arrogant, violent behaviour of the gendarmerie. A few months before the elections of September 1883, the government decided under Austrian pressure to introduce the branding of cattle in areas close to the borders of Romania, Bulgaria and Macedonia to prevent the spread of disease. The peasants considered this a serious breach of trust – they had never had to mark their animals for the Sultan, so it was preposterous that a Serb master should demand it. The Radical Party channelled their discontent into an electoral victory in September. This did not give them a constitutional right to form the next government, but they expected an invitation from King Milan to do so.

Instead, still buoyed by the example of the King of Spain and the authoritarian mood in Germany, the King appointed Nikola Hristić to form a cabinet of non-party 'experts'. As *Samouprava*, the Radical newspaper commented, 'When Nikola Hristić was last in the state administration, there was no constitution. When we finally got a constitution, Hristić disappeared. Now that he has surfaced again, we may take it as a sign that the constitution is about to vanish.'[22] The Radicals feared that the King and his political allies wanted to curb the parliament's constitutional powers. Milan suspected the Radicals of planning an uprising. When Milan decreed that the peasantry should be disarmed, a collision was unavoidable.

The law on disarmament was part of a wholesale reorganization of the Serbian army which had begun in 1881. The wars of the Great Eastern Crisis had demonstrated that the 'people's army', an essential instrument during a war of liberation, was a guarantee of defeat in conventional warfare. King Milan decided to create a professional standing army that would not depend on the fickle morale of the peasant; only then could he brandish his sword as the ultimate sanction of his foreign policy.

A corollary of building a standing army was establishing the state's monopoly on the use of force – the armed peasant might be the laughing stock of enemy generals, but he could still pose a serious threat to domestic order. So when Milan's agents warned him that the Radical Party was planning a rural uprising to prevent a suspension of the constitution, the King struck first by sending his new army units to the countryside to confiscate weapons. Nikola Pašić, the young leader of the Radicals, fulminated in *Samouprava* that the government sought to disarm the people for the same reason as the Turks. But, Pašić wrote, the Serb knows that 'there is no freedom without guns and weapons', so that he would rather 'part with his head and soul than his arms . . . The Turks were always willing to promise much if only the Serbs would hand in their weapons, and the Serb always refused, was always ready to die of torture rather than give up his weapons . . . And why [are they to be confiscated now]? . . . To sell them for a dinar or two to those who laugh and make fun of the Serbian name, Serbian heroes, Serbian freedom.'[23]

Pašić's invocation of Serbian mythology and the implied comparison between Milan and the Turks suggested the increased importance of nationalism in Serbia's domestic political struggle. The two sides had very different ideas of nationalism. Pašić and the Radical leadership still considered the Serbian peasant to be the core of national sovereignty – the armed struggle inspired by free Serbia would eventually liberate the peasantry of Bosnia and Macedonia. Milan believed that the state (by which he understood himself) would define Serbia's national goals and how and when these might be executed. This state, of course, operated within the wider framework of imperialist and regional politics. Pašić recognized that this framework existed but did not consider it legitimate. In aligning himself wholeheartedly with Austria-Hungary, Milan was obliged to forfeit any designs on Bosnian territory, which was under Austrian occupation. So domestic divisions in Serbia did not just have ideological and personal aspects but assumed a geo-political one as well. Austria-Hungary was anathema to the peasants and the Radicals who saw Russia as Serbia's saviour.

On 2 November 1883, peasants in three east Serbian regions refused to hand in their weapons to military units unless they received modern replacements. The Timok rebellion had begun. It did not last very long. The new Serbian military required no more than two weeks to clear up the last pockets of resistance. Yet for a brief period, nearly a quarter of the country was under rebel control and the uncoordinated peasant volunteers almost succeeded in dividing the country along an east–west axis, with the aim of cutting Belgrade from Niš, the main town in the south. Despite its short duration, this was probably the single most important event in Serbian history between independence in 1878 and the outbreak of the Balkan Wars in 1912. The confrontation between an autocratic modernizer and a militant peasantry also established a pattern of militarization which was later repeated in other Balkan states, albeit in slightly different forms.

The defeat of the Timok rebellion dealt a harsh blow to the ideology of rural socialism, inspired by the Russian *narodniki*. In his memoirs, Pera Todorović, a Radical Party leader, noted how the uprising gave vent to the fanatical hatred of the bureaucrats among the peasantry. According to Todorović, at a secret meeting of the Radicals' Executive Committee which preceded the uprising, one activist, Dimitrije Katić, said that it would be necessary to put all bureaucrats 'under the knife'.

For King Milan, the Timok rebellion presented the perfect opportunity to test his new standing army. At first, he hesitated. Would his conscripts and officers, Milan asked himself, 'be willing to fire into the flesh of their own people?'[24] The King had taken precautions by paying his new officer corps twice as much as the most highly paid bureaucrats. He then doubled the pay of all officers and soldiers who participated in the suppression of the rebellion, while the conflict lasted. When put to the test, the gunners did not fail their monarch. They resolutely fired their new French field guns into the peasant crowds. The Austro-Hungarian consul in Belgrade was unable to contain his delight: 'A new page was written in the history of the Serbian people, when the army launched its first shell at the rebels.'

The Prince with the People: Bulgaria

In July 1879, the Bulgarian Principality's Constituent Assembly had conferred the title of Prince on the Hessian aristocrat, Alexander von Battenberg, a handsome twenty-two-year-old officer in the Russian Army. The Assembly had convened in Veliko Tŭrnovo, the medieval capital of the Bulgarian Empire. From here, Alexander's journey to the new capital, Sofia, was like the triumphal return of a war hero. Flowers were strewn at his feet, peasants travelled from all over Bulgaria and Eastern Rumelia to prostrate themselves. As he approached the outskirts of the capital, a huge banner came into view: 'Forward, Prince, the People are with you!'[25] He moved down one of Sofia's crooked, mud-soaked streets where a group of schoolchildren sang the national anthem in their incomprehensible language. He passed under another huge banner: 'Welcome, Prince, we have been expecting you for 500 years.'[26]

The Prince was delighted with his reception in Sofia, but he could not help noticing that the town was an appalling Ottoman backwater. Filthy and crowded, it was also awkwardly located, well away from the Danube and poorly serviced by roads. Under Russian influence, the Bulgarian Assembly had chosen the capital for purely strategic reasons. Its position close to the western border underscored Bulgaria's claim on Macedonia. Sofia was a gesture: it pointed to a future when it would be located at the centre of a Greater Bulgaria.

Through his aunt, the Tsaritsa, wife of Tsar Alexander II, Alexander was linked to the imperial houses of Russia, Germany and Great Britain. But he was the offspring of a morganatic marriage, a circumstance that earned him venomous contempt among the more conservative members of the Russian and German royal families. His personality and his role in European politics earned him the adoration of Queen Victoria and the Crown Princess of Germany, among others, and the enmity of Bismarck and his own cousin, Alexander III, who assumed the Russian throne after his father was assassinated in 1881.

Battenberg had been appointed Prince of a new country that was generally regarded as little more than a Russian fiefdom and whose constitutional and territorial boundaries were exceptionally complicated. His ambition, energy and enthusiasm were offset by an unfortunate tactlessness and a stubborn vanity, which did him no good when he came to deal with Bulgaria's sensitive position in the post-Berlin order.

Despite his rapturous reception in Veliko Tŭrnovo and Sofia, Alexander had immediate difficulties with Bulgaria's young political elite. He stumbled into the first of many disputes, over the critical issue of his own constitutional powers, almost as soon as he arrived in the country. Yet in contrast to King Milan, the greatest threat to Alexander's authority did not come from his own subjects. He was a punchball of the great powers.

Russia resented the dismemberment of the huge San Stefano Bulgaria almost as much as the Bulgarians themselves did. Russia had intended that this short-lived state become the key to its dominance of the Balkan peninsula. The decision of the Berlin Congress to tear up the Treaty of San Stefano meant that to secure its strategic aims Russia felt it needed to have an ever greater say in Bulgaria's domestic affairs. All parties assumed that Bulgaria and Eastern Rumelia would be united at some future point; Russia assumed that this would occur only under the sponsorship of St Petersburg.

The Bulgarian constitution, based on Russian proposals, was among the most liberal in all Europe. Russia's reactionary régime believed this was the best way to support its allies, the Liberals, and hence consolidate its influence in Bulgaria. What neither the Russian

Foreign Ministry nor its agents in Bulgaria wanted was a strong, independent Prince.

Before travelling to Bulgaria, Alexander undertook a grand tour of the imperial capitals, and began to appreciate that although the courts of Europe had little interest in the fortunes of the Bulgarian people, they took a keen interest in Bulgaria's regional position. At his first stop, he travelled to the Tsar's summer residence in Livadia on the Crimea's Black Sea coast. He was regarded with deep suspicion by many of the Tsar's closest advisers, and when he reduced the Tsar – his uncle, Alexander II – to tears by insisting on amendments to the constitution, the incident strengthened their hand and weakened the position of the Tsaritsa, Alexander's aunt. Many at the court of St Petersburg believed Alexander was a German puppet, sent to Bulgaria to rub salt into the humiliating wound that Bismarck had inflicted on them at the Berlin Congress. The great weakness in Bismarck's policy of upholding the alliance of Russia, Germany and Austria-Hungary was that most Russian diplomats and politicians were convinced, quite unfairly, that the German Chancellor was bitterly anti-Russian.* After Livadia, Alexander discovered in Berlin that nothing could have been further from Bismarck's thoughts. The Chancellor was polite but curt, warning Alexander that he, Bismarck, did not wish to be distracted by Bulgarian affairs. He further stressed that Alexander should not tamper with the decisions of the Berlin Congress and that he must avoid offending Russian sensibilities at all costs.

Alexander promptly admitted to Andrássy in Vienna that he would not survive as Prince unless Bulgaria and Eastern Rumelia were united in the near future. He would, if necessary, contradict Bismarck's expressed wishes and ignore the Berlin Treaty. The Prince was quite right – the Bulgarians would not tolerate the separation of the Principality and Eastern Rumelia for long; but he should have exercised more discretion in Vienna. The Habsburg Empire was already beginning to imagine life in the southern Balkans after the Ottomans. Bulgarian claims to Macedonia and its Aegean outlet, Salonika, might threaten Austro-Hungarian plans to make a pliant Serbia its regional client.

---

* An even greater problem was the very real enmity between the courts at Vienna and St Petersburg.

After his tense reception in central Europe, Alexander was greatly cheered when Queen Victoria broke with tradition and received him at Balmoral Castle. The Queen developed quite an affection for the dashing young Prince and resolved to support him wherever she could. The Russians may have been wrong about Bismarck, but they were right to suspect that Britain exerted some influence over Alexander thanks to his relationship with the Queen.

It would require a deftness beyond anything the young Prince possessed to reconcile the various great-power interests, however. Above all, he needed a plan which could reassure the Russians and yet contain their aspirations in Bulgaria. The Russian government expected the Prince to submit to the Tsar as all good Bulgarians were supposed to do. It was no secret that King Milan waltzed to the music of Vienna even though most Serbs despised the Austro-Hungarian Empire. Why then would Prince Alexander not take his place in the imperial Russian ball, especially as he would be in step with virtually the entire Bulgarian population?

Russia sought to control Bulgaria in a variety of ways. After the withdrawal of the imperial Russian army in 1879, its officers dominated all leading ranks in the new Bulgarian army, and ran the Defence Ministry. St Petersburg retained official and unofficial agents in Sofia who tried, not always successfully, to control economic and political life. The Bulgarian Liberals who dominated the Sŭbranie, the parliament, formed a close tactical alliance with the Russians while the Bulgarian peasants believed for several years after the Berlin Congress that their real and deserving master was Alexander II, the Tsar-Liberator, and not the Prince of Bulgaria.

The Tsar could not manipulate his supporters with any precision from distant St Petersburg. Russia's policy relied on the political ambitions of its consuls and generals serving in Bulgaria, most of whom delighted in painting a dark portrait of Prince Alexander. One sent a report claiming that the Prince's inability to find a suitable bride was because he regularly received prostitutes in his residence, and that he had contracted venereal disease. Another insisted that he could not marry because he had 'Turkish tastes', that is, he was a homosexual. The Prince's only consistent allies were the Conservatives, an ineffectual grouping of *chorbadjii* and church elders. Yet everybody overlooked the possibility of political divisions among the Russians in Sofia and between the Russians and the Liberals.

Like the other Balkan states, with independence Bulgaria assumed responsibility for a fistful of unpaid bills, including some uncharitable demands from Russia. As in the cases of Romania and Serbia, the Treaty of Berlin imposed on Bulgaria an obligation to fund various rail-building projects and tender the contracts to specified foreign consortia. The ubiquitous Austrian, Baron Hirsch, was granted the right to extend the Orient Express through Bulgaria to link up with the line he was already building in Eastern Rumelia. The British won a promise that Bulgaria would buy the useless Ruse–Varna line, obsolete since the signing of an international agreement on the navigation of the Danube. The Russians demanded that the Bulgarians pay for a railway line from Ruse on the Danube to Sofia which they knew to be of vital strategic importance. Moreover, the Russians wanted their line built before Baron Hirsch's. Even Russia's allies in Bulgaria, the Liberals, could see that for economic reasons, the Orient Express was a more urgent project. As a consequence, the rail issue became a bone of contention between successive Bulgarian governments and the Russians.

In order to meet the growing demands of public expenditure, both Liberal and Conservative governments had to stiffen the tax régime. This led to unrest among the peasantry. During the election campaign of 1881, one observer came upon a peasant crowd railing against 'priests, officials and teachers' for raising taxes. 'For many peasants their old allies in the intelligentsia were irredeemably compromised for they had joined the small and rapacious clique which was beginning to take control of politics and the nation.'[27] Bulgarian officers also resented Russian domination of all senior military posts even though there was barely a single indigenous soldier with the requisite training for these positions. Bulgarian nationalism was beginning to wean itself from the Russian breast. Both Prince Alexander and the Russians now had to deal with an ever more truculent infant.

Resentments planted by the Treaty of Berlin had a still greater impact on nationalist consciousness. By the early 1880s, Slav refugees from Macedonia had begun to organize themselves into a significant pressure group. Their central demand was an overall revision of the Treaty of Berlin with regard to the Macedonian Question. Obviously, their demands could not be met, but they pushed the Liberals, under the canny leadership of Petŭr Karavelov, into some uncompromising positions on the national question. The Russians, for their part, were unwilling to embark on a crusade on behalf of Macedonia but they were prepared to support the unification of the Principality and Eastern Rumelia.

The Russian officials in Bulgaria believed that such a plan might both rid them of Prince Alexander and further their strategic goals in the Balkans. They set aside their differences with Karavelov and the Liberals on the issue of the Orient Express and began supporting clandestine organizations in Eastern Rumelia which were agitating for unification. If the Bulgarians of Eastern Rumelia were to proclaim unification, Alexander would be placed in an impossible situation. Were he to assume leadership of the movement, he would be tearing up a crucial clause of the Berlin Treaty, invoking the wrath not just of Bismarck but of several other signatory powers; were he to reject unification, he would lose the support of the Bulgarian people. Alexander, whose impulse was in any case to make a grand gesture, needed no reminding that the Bulgarians would be unforgiving if he did not back the nationalist programme. In the summer of 1885, in one of the more unusual encounters between a sovereign and his subjects, he was visited by two men who handed him a piece of paper inscribed with the words, 'Freedom or Death. The Secret Executive Committee'. These two 'delegates' told him plainly that if he opposed unification, he would be 'annihilated' by the committee.[28]

On 18 September 1885, a band of rebels seized control of Philippopolis (now Plovdiv in Bulgaria), the capital of Eastern Rumelia. Thousands of citizens joined in the uprising to proclaim 'North and South Bulgaria' as one country. The *coup* in Philippopolis caught the Prince, who was in the Black Sea resort of Varna at the time, completely off guard. It was greeted in all the European capitals with astonishment. Alexander had reached his Rubicon. After deliberating alone for a short time, he strode into the antechamber of his rooms at Varna to announce 'I am leaving for Philippopolis today', he declared. 'Behold in me the ruler of a united North and South Bulgaria.'[29]

The Prince's decisive action had stolen Alexander III's glory. A German, not a Russian, had presented the gift of unity to the Bulgarian people. Russia immediately withdrew all its officers serving in the Bulgarian army. This move decapitated the defences of the state overnight. It was now vulnerable to attack from the

Ottoman Empire: Istanbul might invoke the Berlin Treaty to re-establish its sovereignty over the region by force of arms. As a conference of the Berlin powers convened in Istanbul to discuss the Bulgarian crisis, Bulgarian forces, enthusiastic but disorganized, surged to defend the borders of Eastern Rumelia.

At Istanbul, the Russians now discovered how they had been outmanoeuvred. Perceiving St Petersburg's discomfort over Alexander's success, the British warmly supported Bulgarian unification while the Austrians were not prepared to make an issue out of it. A compromise was agreed upon whereby the two territories would now be united through the personal union of Prince Alexander, which in theory meant that the Sultan was still sovereign in Eastern Rumelia. In practice, of course, the Ottoman Empire had lost the territory.

The unification of Bulgaria reinforced the widely held belief in Russia that the Berlin Treaty was an Austro-German plot designed to check Russian influence in the Balkans. In fact, it was largely the result of Russia's confused policy towards Bulgaria and the arrogance of the Russian agents there. Yet events in Bulgaria had revealed a severe structural weakness in the Congress system (all the signatories insisted on the Treaty as the fundamental dogma regulating state relations in the Balkans) for Alexander and the Bulgarians had just proved that it was possible to amend and even violate the Treaty in practice, if the divisions between the great powers were exploited with sufficient skill.

The Prince, out of his depth as a diplomat when he first assumed power in Bulgaria, had played his cards well, especially considering unification had taken him unawares. Russia decided to back down from a confrontation with Austria-Hungary and Britain over Bulgarian unification, and a great-power crisis was thus averted. But it was not just the great powers who had a stake in the post-Berlin order. King Milan saw this treaty violation as another opportunity to test the efficacy of his new standing army. For the first time, a new Balkan state prepared to wage war against another in the name of national interests. The Serbo-Bulgarian war of 1885 demonstrated that the Berlin Treaty enabled ambitious states on the Balkan periphery to seduce the great powers themselves into risky adventures.

Strolling to Sofia: Serbia, Bulgaria, 1885

Fear and confusion greeted the mobilization of Serbian reserves in late October 1885. Fear, because Serbia's most recent military efforts against the Turks in 1876 had proved so disastrous. Confusion, because with the exception of King Milan and his closest advisers, nobody knew with whom the Serb army was supposed to do battle. Some dreamt of a war to liberate Bosnia, but only the most innocent believed that Milan would be so suicidal as to attack his Austrian benefactor. Was this perhaps a pre-emptive strike against the weakened Turks in Macedonia? The movement of troops to Niš raised hopes that Serbia was indeed planning to 'liberate' Macedonia. But in the official government newspapers, strident demands for territorial compensation from Bulgaria began to appear.

Belgrade's café society was amazed. Why Bulgaria? Bulgarians were Slav 'brothers' who had fought closely with the Serbs to cast off the Turkish yoke. Surely the unification of Bulgaria was to be welcomed as a further blow against the Sultan's unsteady hold in Europe? This was not idle chat. Despite their defeat in the Timok rebellion two years before, the Radical Party was still the most influential political force in the countryside, from which the bulk of conscripts were drawn. In addition, many Radical leaders, including Nikola Pašić, were living in Bulgaria as political refugees. Neither the peasants, nor much of the urban population of Serbia, could understand a war with Bulgaria. But the Serbian peasants reluctantly mustered in villages and towns in order to accompany Milan, their master and a Serb, on what the King unwisely called his 'stroll to Sofia'.

The King had knowingly locked himself into the logic of the Berlin Treaty. A surrogate conflict between great powers was about to be fought for the first time on the Balkan peninsula. Unification, Milan argued, gave Bulgaria an important strategic edge in the impending struggle for Macedonia. This was no fantasy. The conspirators who had organized the *coup* in Philippopolis had admitted openly to Prince Alexander's secretary, A.F. Golowine, that unification between Bulgaria and Eastern Rumelia was not the ultimate goal: 'We must succeed with the unification of North and South Bulgaria . . . We must bring down the Rumelian government and unite in the interest of Macedonia.'[30]

Milan was playing for even higher stakes than Macedonia. Encouraged by the so-called Military Party in Austria-Hungary, he hoped that his assault on Bulgaria would goad Russia into declaring war on Serbia which, by dint of Milan's secret military pact with Vienna, would have led to war between Austria-Hungary and Russia. In theory, his plan of launching a lightning strike in north-western Bulgaria would allow him to occupy the vulnerable capital, Sofia, on 20 November, his *slava* (name day),* just one week after war was actually declared.

As the main Serbian army crossed the border, it was accompanied by the crowing of a triumphal press. Exhortations were made to the *hajduk* spirit of the Serbs while the Bulgarians were dismissed as docile 'market gardeners'.[31] But the Serbs' progress towards Slivnica, the main defensive bastion between the border and Sofia, was inexplicably slow. The bulk of Bulgarian troops was still in Eastern Rumelia but the first-line defences put up a tenacious struggle. They were outnumbered and outgunned by the oncoming Serbs. But the Bulgarian command, stiffened by the resolve of dozens of Russian officers who had defied their Emperor's order and remained with the Bulgarian army, exploited every tactical error committed by the inexperienced Serbian generals.

Four days into the war, a rumour spread that the Bulgarians had broken through Serbian lines and were now advancing on Caribrod (in Bulgaria), the Serbian field headquarters. King Milan, who was in Caribrod, took fright and scuttled back to the Serbian border, an act of royal cowardice that demoralized his unconvinced troops. Contemporary accounts portray the Serb army as terribly disorientated, hopelessly unaware as to the purpose of the war. Branislav Nušić, who later became Serbia's finest political satirist, was twenty-one when he was drafted to fight the Bulgarians. Nušić's poignant reflections on this war are an antidote to the flatterers of Milan's press corps:

> The traces of the defeated enemy unit are still here on this field. An overturned cooking pot from which a river of military soup has been spilt; extinguished fires; a few pieces of

* Every Serb family celebrates a specific name or saint's day, the *slava*. It is invested with greater significance than birthdays.

> ripped trousers; here a discarded cartridge belt, there a knife; a huge wooden spoon; some dish-cloths; ammunition. Everything was scattered messily, and in the middle of these remains over by the stream there also lay one of the many victims of yesterday's battle – a Bulgarian infantryman on whose epaulettes is written the number 9. The bullet hit him right below the left breast, in his very heart, and it seems he lived for some time after but in the most terrible pain. His left hand had dug in the wound as he probably tried in desperation to pull out the lead which had penetrated deep into his bosom; the right arm was stretched above his head with clenched fist; his blue eyes open; his lips completely bitten off. From the wound, a bloody ribbon trailed across his chest onto the ground where it spread into a little pool of blue blood. Snow and rain, which had fallen that morning, had dampened his sparse hair, and the sockets of his eyes were full of melting snow.
>
> As I approached him two or three ravens with blood-soaked beaks cawed loudly before flying off into the distance.[32]

Where the Serbs were plagued with doubt, the Bulgarians were fired by righteous patriotism. Indeed, as soon as the Serbs declared war, the Turks of Bulgaria, whom Alexander had always treated with respect, immediately announced that they would be sending 6,000 men to fight alongside their fellow Bulgarian citizens. Nothing revealed the depth of Bulgarian popular resolve more than the speed and determination with which the troops were diverted from the Turkish frontier to Slivnica. Using five defective trains, whose engines were held together by old stove pipes, the Bulgarian command transported over 50,000 troops 240 kilometres in six days, to a position within 130 kilometres of the Serbian forces. In appalling weather conditions, the infantry and artillery covered the last stretch on foot. They arrived in time, that is before Slivnica had fallen. Now, their numerical superiority and the discipline instilled by the Russian officers proved decisive. Within days the Serbs were in retreat. The Bulgarian army pushed deep into Serbian territory less than two weeks after the original attack.

Serbia and King Milan were saved by Austria-Hungary who insisted that Bulgaria withdraw its forces back across the border. In the event of non-compliance, Austria-Hungary would enter the war on Serbia's behalf. Milan was fortunate to come away with an agreement for the restoration of the *status quo ante*. Prince Alexander had unified the Bulgarians and then stood firm against external aggression – popular perceptions of the national interest had coincided with the state's interests.

The next two and a half decades would prove decisive in defining the nature of twentieth-century nationalism in the Balkans. The failure of King Milan in the Serbo-Bulgarian war made it clear that in order to prosecute war beyond state boundaries, the ruler had to translate the cultural nationalism of the new Balkan states into a dynamic political force. All parties and states drew similar lessons from the war. First, a strong, disciplined and motivated standing army was an essential prerequisite for a foreign policy based on state interests. Second, a quiescent peasantry was absolutely necessary for domestic order but this in itself was not sufficient for a credible foreign policy – governments would now have to inculcate the peasantry with a sense of commitment to their particular national goals. To achieve this, the governments of Romania, Bulgaria, Greece and Serbia each diverted their energies into creating a strong military and forging a modern, exclusivist and aggressive national identity. The centre of this struggle for the soul of the Balkan peasant was Macedonia.

Freedom or Death: Macedonia

Oh Macedonia, oh dear mother
Oh sacred suffering land
Oh mother, such pain and unhappiness
Have you borne!
We are your children, mother
Weak, without strength
But we know you gave birth to us
As heroes!
Tomorrow we will be brave
And on feathered wings
we will grasp our guns, our bombs
Courageous with strength anew!

Macedonian nursery rhyme, c. 1890s[33]

In 1492, the Christians drove the Sephardim out of Spain. The Great Expulsion from the Iberian peninsula was completed five years later when the Jews of Portugal were also hounded out of their homes. Sultan Bayezid II opened the doors of his Empire and offered refuge and comfort to the victims of both enforced migrations. Of course, the Sephardim were, like the Christians of the Empire, subordinate to the Muslim rulers, forbidden to use 'noble' animals, like the horse, or carry weapons, and were restricted in their forms of dress. At the beginning of the sixteenth century, many Jews were deported against their will to barren parts of the Empire in the hope that they would enliven the local economy. But their treatment at the hands of the Muslims was much better than that meted out to the Jews who remained in Europe's Christian empires. Relations between the Sephardim and Muslims were the most stable among all the *millets* throughout the long history of the Caliphate; mutual respect and cooperation were the norm. And for many centuries, the greatest and safest Jewish city in Europe was Salonika.

Sitting on the north-eastern edge of the Aegean's largest natural harbour, the bay of Thermaïkos, the city was more than a haven for this Jewish community – it practically belonged to them. In the other major cities and ports of European Turkey, the Greeks or the Armenians were the *primi inter pares* of non-Muslim society. But Salonika was a different world, where the Sephardim dominated most aspects of economic, social and cultural life and where, because of their economic clout, they often held decisive political sway over the Turkish governors.

The wealthier Jews lived in villas close to the medieval perimeter walls, cheek by jowl with the Turkish quarter, the upper town. This proximity reflected the close relations binding the elites of both communities.* Away from the frenetic bustle of the harbour, the

* Some 10 per cent of the Salonika Jews professed Islam. Known as the *dönme* (which comes from the Turkish word for 'to turn' – i.e. the turncoats, or converted ones), they were the descendants of the followers of a seventeenth-century charismatic who converted for reasons of political, and indeed physical, survival. The *dönme* lived as a separate community, part of the Muslim *millet* but distinct from both the Muslim and Jewish communities. As Muslims, of course, they were entitled to serve in the Ottoman administration and some governors of Salonika were therefore Jews. They often acted as a link between the Muslims and Jews of Salonika which helped strengthen the bonds between the two *millets*.

upper town had an air of pampered indolence. In the hot summer, rich Turks sat immobile in the shade of the ubiquitous cypress, eyes half-closed, moving only to sip coffee or puff on their *narghiles* (hubble-bubbles). Their spacious two-storey wooden houses were painted bright red, with a thick black band at the bottom to ward off evil spirits. The roofs were covered in verses of the Koran painted in gold. The most renowned Muslim chronicler of Ottoman life, Eliya Çelebi, observed that, 'all of them [the Salonika Turks], even the old men, have the same deep red face and bright vermilion forehead. They attain great ages and enjoy long lives. At the age of seventy, they still happily mount horses, draw their sabres and practise the conjugal act'. These impressive outbursts of energy may be ascribed to the fact that the Turks were under little obligation to work hard. The Muslims' near monopoly on administrative jobs guaranteed the economic prosperity of the Turkish middle class.

Towards the harbour between St Dimitri Street and Zade Yol, the broadest boulevard (the Roman Via Egnatia, which dissected the heart of the town), the luxurious calm of the upper town gave way to the noise of Greek artisans whose front rooms functioned as small workshops or modest trading outlets. Only the Greeks offered serious economic competition to the Jews, and until the end of the nineteenth century, tradition divided their respective spheres of activity with some precision. Most of the pharmacies were Greek-owned, while much of the wholesale food trade with the Macedonian hinterland was in the hands of Jewish middlemen.

The tireless pump engine of the city's trade and industry was the area between the Zade Yol and the harbour. Here the Sephardim lived in tall houses which seemed to climb over one another in a bid to reach the sunlight which never penetrated the dingy, narrow streets.

Since the Jewish colonization of the town in the first two decades of the sixteenth century, Salonika had been the hub of the Sephardic world in the Balkans. Settlers moved along the spokes of a wheel which radiated out overland to Üsküb (Skopje), Sarajevo, Kosovo, Split and Valona (Vlorë) before reaching further to settle in Belgrade, then later in Sofia, Plovdiv and Smyrna (Izmir). The more adventurous traders built new maritime networks across the Aegean to the Near East, the Maghreb and western Europe. Their commercial success was based on the strong bonds which linked the

Salonika community with their co-religionists in the Balkan hinterland and on the establishment of loose but effective trade monopolies in Salonika.

Above all the Sephardim were masters of the cloth trade. Their most important customers were the janissaries. The Salonika Jews enjoyed the exclusive right to supply the vanguard of the Sultan's military power with all their clothes. So when Murad II instigated the bloody destruction of the janissaries in 1826, the consequences for the Salonika Jews were severe, and compounded by the damage done to Jewish merchants by the penetration of cheap mass-manufactured British garments into the Empire.

By the middle of the nineteenth century, the Jewish community was in economic decline. As many businesses collapsed, the Jewish population rose steadily, placing enormous pressure on the infrastructure of the Sephardic common quarter. In this small space between the seafront and Zade Yol, tens of thousands of Jews were packed together, several families to every apartment, in unsanitary conditions. The intense overcrowding meant that Jews were especially vulnerable to epidemics, fires and earthquakes which regularly scourged Salonika. Sickly children played among the garbage which was thrown out of windows into the crowded, narrow streets down which the sewage ran.[34] 'The sight of a population of from 25,000 to 30,000 Jews without adequate resources, and with a prospect of a still worse future, was a truly afflicting picture: crowds of children were allowed to run into the gutter from a tender age, and there they learned to beg for alms without shame. This paved the way to a life of vagrancy for boys and (sad to say) to a life of precocious prostitution for girls.'[35]

At the east end of the quay, on the great sweep of the waterfront, stood the White Tower, which marked the south-eastern edge of the Sephardic living quarters. This cylindrical stone prison had been known more graphically before the nineteenth century as the Tower of Blood, in memory of the countless victims of Ottoman torturers and executioners. It also separated the Jewish quarter from the Muslim and Jewish cemeteries. Once the two largest graveyards in the city, the wars and massacres of the twentieth century have devoured them both. The Jewish cemetery's mounds of collapsing gravestones now lie buried under Thessaloniki's International Trade Fair complex, along with virtually every trace of the largest Jewish settlement in the Balkans, which numbered some 60,000 before the First World War.

Salonika's economic and political rebirth, which began in the 1880s and lasted until the outbreak of the First Balkan War in 1912, was as dramatic as the preceding decline. The Congress of Berlin opened a period of intense western focus on the Empire and on Macedonia in particular. A group of Jewish entrepreneurs, led by the remarkable Allatini brothers, from a family of relatively recent immigrants from Livorno, seized the new opportunities which the French, Italian, Austrian, German and British venture capitalists brought with them. The Allatinis established a brick factory, soon followed by breweries, mills, a huge cigarette-rolling plant and even an unexpected revival of the cloth trade.

Salonika's great outer wall which had defined the city for two millennia crumbled over just two decades in a rush of modernization:

> The ring of stone which for twenty centuries had protected it against the invasions and pillage of peoples and conquerors springing from all points of the compass, was now choking and hampering its growth. The western wall was the first to come down. Next to be demolished was the sea wall, with the rubble of which a broad quay had been built along the water front. Then the eastern wall succumbed under the picks and shovels of the wreckers, to be replaced by the Hamidiye, a wide boulevard bordered with acacia trees.[36]

The Greek community, encouraged by grants and low-interest loans provided by the Greek Kingdom, was also quick to exploit the opportunities presented by this sudden economic growth. Still, the Jews dominated economic life. They were not just the buyers and sellers, the shipping consultants, the insurance agents and the cigarette manufacturers, they dominated all the most important craft guilds; so that, by the end of the nineteenth century, the city was home to a large Sephardic proletariat. The majority of these 10,000 labourers worked at the tobacco factories in appalling conditions which soon bred the Socialist Federation of Salonika, a Mediterranean version of the Polish *Bund*, and which appealed to all communities in Macedonia to cast aside their national differences in the name of social progress. But a large minority of Jewish workers formed a prosperous elite of stevedores, porters and fishermen who were able to keep the Greeks and Slavs out of their industries using a combination of the closed shop and threats of physical intimidation.

Salonika was the only city in the Empire where the Jews employed violence against the Christian population as a means of consolidating their political and economic power. Elsewhere, notably in Izmir and Istanbul, the situation was reversed. Especially after the importation of 'modern anti-Semitism' from western Europe, the Greeks and Armenians would organize pogroms (small-scale affairs compared to those in the Russian Empire) to warn Jews against encroaching on their economic interests. Through most of their history, the Salonika Jews had remained aloof from the tensions which afflicted relations between the other *millets*. Ladino, their language based on Castilian Spanish, underlined this isolation; apart from a few Greek *dragomans*, nobody else in the Empire spoke it.

The *millets* of Salonika lived almost entirely separate lives. Each *millet* had its own fire service, its own urban hygiene programme (or lack of one), its own markets and its own judicial structure. They were joined together in only one activity – every evening a cheerful Babel echoed across the bay when youngsters from all communities strolled up and down the quayside watching the Aegean sun slip behind Mount Olympus.

By the turn of the century, however, the city began to adapt, uniquely in the Ottoman Empire and among other Balkan states, to the pressures of an invasive imperialism. The steady flow of 'Frenks' (the Ottoman name for westerners) and their business into Salonika brought with it material advantages but, as Leon Sciaky later recalled, the people of Salonika felt ambivalent towards this invasion:

> The century was drawing to a close. Stealthily the West was creeping in, trying to lure the East with her wonders. Almost inaudible as yet was her whisper. She dangled before our dazzled eyes the witchery of her science and the miracle of her inventions. We caught a glimpse of her brilliance, and timidly listened to the song of the siren. Like country folk at a banquet, we felt humble and awkward in our ways. But vaguely we sensed the coldness of her glitter and the price of her wooing.

> With uneasiness we gathered tighter the folds of our homespun mantles around our shoulders, enjoying their softness and warmth, and finding them good.[37]

Elsewhere in the Empire, industrialization appeared to encourage the development of nationalism. The urban boom in Salonika was an exception to the rule. The *millet* system here did not show signs of collapse but of mutation. For the Jews of Macedonia, of course, nationalism was anathema – they had no prospect of forming their own state in Turkey and, later, often evinced hostility to the Zionists who periodically turned up to spread the gospel of a Jewish state. Turkish nationalism had barely developed beyond the point of ideological conception in its European exile. The Greeks of Salonika were in close touch with merchants, priests, intellectuals and government agents from the Greek kingdom, but in general showed no desire to sacrifice the economic dynamism offered by Salonika in exchange for a future in a weak kingdom.

The Bulgarians, Salonika's smallest community, found themselves generally excluded from the boom. Living in the crowded north-western corner of the city, most were first-generation arrivals from the Macedonian hinterland. Conditions in the countryside they had escaped stood in marked contrast to the city's dynamism. As Salonika grew, the peasants outside the city limits fought an ever more desperate battle against hardship. In the late 1890s, Macedonia was plagued by a string of bad harvests, at a time when the global market was suffering its greatest ever cereal glut. In 1881, representatives of the five great powers had assumed extraordinary control over the taxation of Ottoman domestic products through an institution known as the Public Debt Administration. Collection of revenue for the tobacco industry, for example, was put into the hands of a French company, known for short as the Régie. Employing its own armed retainers, the Régie acted as a tax farmer on a huge scale, vastly more efficient and merciless than its host of small-time predecessors. It would then distribute the income in favour of the Empire's western creditors, its own shareholders, the Ottoman Empire and finally the producers. The Age of Imperialism turned Salonika into a great city, but it condemned the three vilayets of Macedonia to a terrible future.

Unlike their fellow citizens, the Salonika Bulgarians were acutely aware of the suffering in the countryside, inhabited largely by fellow Slavs. With relatively few employment opportunities, these urban Bulgarians turned their attention to scholarship. Of the 6,000 or so Bulgarians living in the city in the first decade of the twentieth century, almost a third were involved in education either as teachers or students. Their minds focused not on making money but on politics and justice. A chance meeting between three young Slavs marked the start of a gruesome history of bloodletting in Macedonia, which culminated in ruthless wars involving almost all the southern Balkan nations; in the replacement of Sephardic by Greek dominance in Salonika; and in the destruction of the Ottoman Empire.

On the evening of 1 November 1893, Damian ('Dame') Gruev, a student, was walking with a friend on the Salonika quayside when they bumped into an acquaintance, a young school teacher named Ivan Hadzhinikolov. The three men argued at length about the fate of Macedonia and the need to rid the province of Ottoman rule. They finished the evening by forming a revolutionary committee. Not unreasonably, they felt that three men represented too narrow a base for such a task, so a few days later they drafted another three friends into the Macedonian Central Revolutionary Committee (*Makedonski tsentralen revoliutsoneren komitet*).

For the first few months, this was a politburo without a party. Its members designed a seal depicting a gun and dagger crossed under a bomb. Enclosing the three symbols were the words 'Svoboda ili smŭrt' (Freedom or Death). By the time all of sixteen members held the founding congress a year later in August 1894, in the interior town of Resna, they had not yet managed to shoot, stab or blow up anybody. This would soon change.

The two decades of violent chaos in Macedonia that followed the founding of this group, which after several name changes settled in 1905 on the Internal Macedonian Revolutionary Organization (VMRO), form the single most complicated period in modern Balkan history. The exceptional ethnic diversity of Macedonia itself is the primary complication but within each nationality there existed profound social and ideological differences which further muddied the waters. In addition, the relationship of the 'mother ships', Greece, Serbia and Bulgaria, to the Hellenic and Slav populations of the region was liable to change from one day to the next; and then there were the opportunistic aims of the two great powers,

Austria-Hungary and Russia, most closely involved in the Macedonian Question.

This potent mix established violence and intrigue as the two most readily available forms of political discourse in the region, and fixed the Balkans firmly in western minds as 'the powder keg of Europe' and as peopled by congenitally aggressive and intolerant communities. The exceptional brutality of the First and Second Balkan Wars (1912–13) seemed to confirm this perception of the collective psychology of Balkan peoples, and the assassination of Archduke Franz Ferdinand on 28 June 1914 in Sarajevo set it in stone. The British journalist, H.N. Brailsford, writing on the Macedonian Question in 1906, developed a much more persuasive theory as to the origins of political violence in the Balkans. Brailsford was not entirely free from prejudice himself, but he correctly identified the prevailing political and economic conditions in the Macedonian interior, and not their gruesome symptoms as the central problem of the Balkans:

> Fear in Macedonia is more than an emotion. It is a physical disease, the malady of the country, the ailment that comes of tyranny. One enters some hovel which a peasant family calls its home. In the oppressive darkness one becomes gradually aware of a living something which stirs or groans in the gloomiest corner on the floor beneath a filthy blanket. Is it fever, one asks, or smallpox? And the answer comes in the accents of custom and commonplace, 'He is ill with fear.' The word becomes the key to half the circumstances of existence. Fear is the dominant, the ever-present motive. It builds villages. It dictates migrations. It explains deceits. It has created the morals of a country. The Bulgarians are, of all races, the most stolid and enduring; they seem insensible to pain, and proof against panic. It is no common shock which wrings a cry from them or unsteadies their nerves, for their physical organisation has adapted itself to their political conditions. And yet fear is the great fact of their daily lives. Looking back upon my wanderings among them, a procession of ruined minds comes before the memory – an old priest lying beside a burning house speechless with terror and dying slowly; a woman who had barked like a dog since the day her village was burned; a maiden who became an imbecile because her

mother buried her in a hole under the floor to save her from the soldiers; a lad who turned ill with 'fear' from the moment when a soldier put a knife to his throat; children who flee in terror at the sight of a stranger, crying 'Turks! Turks!' These are the human wreckage of the hurricane which usurps the functions of a Government.[38]

Regicide: Serbia, 1903

The Macedonian struggle, as the Greeks named it in the first decade of the twentieth century, not only goaded the governments of Serbia, Greece and above all Bulgaria into interfering in the wider region. The internal stability of all three was rocked in the wash stirred up by that very interference. In this confusion, small conspiratorial groups, centred on disgruntled elements in the military, often proved more effective than the weak forces of parliamentary democracy.

In Serbia, after a short regency following Milan's abdication in 1897, King Aleksandar Obrenović soon began to display his father's arrogance. With the backing of Austria-Hungary and the goodwill of the army, Aleksandar demonstrated he was able to keep his great enemies, the Radical Party, in check both by using force and by manipulating the constitution. However, he had a fatal weakness for Draga Mašin, a lady-in-waiting to his mother, who, ten years the King's senior, exerted a powerful maternal-sexual influence on him. Serbian society was scandalized when news broke in the summer of 1900 that the King intended to marry her against the advice of everybody close to him. A modern historian offers this summary of discussions at the highest level of state:

> Draga Mašin had a shady past as a poor young widow in need of the financial support of gentlemen friends. This was no mere hearsay, though public rumour certainly exaggerated when it made Draga out to be a streetwalker. Nor was the news kept from King Alexander. Not one, but several, men of high position, ministers and generals, told him to his face of Draga's past. One of them even told him that he had had Draga himself for a not excessive sum of money.[39]

To add to Aleksandar's humiliation, it emerged that Queen Draga was unable to bear children – an important political matter because of the succession. There was also the question of her own political ambition and those of her two brothers, universally loathed, who were now next in line to the throne, since Aleksandar was Milan's only child. But Draga's greatest error was to persuade her husband to purge the military. The Obrenovićes could withstand the pressure of the Radical Party, rioting students and, indeed, international contempt but the decision to insult the Serbian officer corps hatched one of the most notorious conspiracies in Balkan history.

At 2 o'clock in the morning of 11 June 1903, Lieutenant Petar Živković pushed open the thick oak door to Belgrade's royal palace from the inside. Dozens of young officers swarmed into the courtyard and were confronted by members of the palace guard still loyal to Aleksandar and Draga. The plotters were inspired by a charismatic if frustrated captain, Dragutin Dimitrijević, who everyone knew by his simple nickname, Apis. School friends had named Dimitrijević after the bull-headed Egyptian deity because of his muscle-bound frame. Leading by example, Apis charged into the royal palace on the night of the *coup*. After a fight, which left several dead, the conspirators searched the palace as a rapidly spreading fire added to the chaos. When they reached the main bedchamber, the sheets were still warm. The royal couple, however, was nowhere to be found. The soldiers had been combing the building for an hour when an officer noticed that behind one set of curtains in the bedchamber there was no window but a wooden panel. With a gun at his head, the King's adjutant called upon his master. 'Can I depend upon the oath of my officers?' his majesty enquired. 'Yes', came the reply in unison. As the secret door opened, the officers opened fire and killed Aleksandar. Queen Draga then collapsed dead on top of him. The soldiers were not yet finished, however. Drawing their swords, they slashed and mutilated the two cadavers before hurling the remains out of the window. Thus was the ignominious end of the Obrenović dynasty. It also opened the way for the return of the Karadjordjević dynasty to the throne after an absence of half a century. The vengeful feud that had begun a hundred years earlier with Karadjordje's death at the hands of his rival Miloš Obrenović was over.

Petar Karadjordjević was regarded as a sober and intelligent successor inside Serbia, in part because he had fought in the Bosnian

Uprising of 1875. At first, he was spurned by the European courts for even if Europe's ruling families had been content to titter at Aleksandar's antics while he was alive they were still shocked by regicide. Gradually, Petar was accepted by them but the conspiracy maintained a hold on him. Until this point, Serbia had paid little attention to the possibility of nationalist expansion in Macedonia. But as Ottoman rule began to disintegrate, a growing number of nationalist intellectuals became convinced that Serbia should resurrect its claims to the medieval kingdom of Tsar Dušan. Such ideas fell on fertile ground in the military among officers like Apis. The regicide dragged Serbia further into the Macedonian imbroglio and ever closer towards war with their Slav neighbours, the Bulgarians.

Stambulovshtina: Bulgaria

Russia never forgave Prince Alexander for unifying Bulgaria without its permission. The year after his victory in the Serbo-Bulgarian war, St Petersburg successfully conspired with its agents and supporters to oust the Prince, replacing him with Prince Ferdinand of Saxe-Coburg (1887–1912) who they believed would be more pliant. He wasn't, and the Russians were soon causing problems for his new régime.

At the beginning of the 1890s, the Bulgarian Prime Minister, Stefan Stambulov, imposed one of the harshest régimes the region had yet seen, stifling opposition with emergency legislation and strong-arm tactics. Like most of the politicians who devoted their youth to the birth of Bulgaria, Stambulov's beginnings were humble, as the son of an innkeeper in the ancient capital, Veliko Tŭrnovo. He emerged after the fiasco of Prince Alexander's departure as the most level-headed and boldest Bulgarian politician. Alexander's successor, Prince Ferdinand of Saxe-Coburg, soon found himself depending on Stambulov's political guile even if the two rarely disguised their mutual dislike.

When Stambulov took over the reins of the country in the wake of Alexander's abdication, Bulgaria was heading for bankruptcy. The country was friendless as the great powers all refused to recognize the legitimacy of Ferdinand, and lack of Russian support, especially, imposed immense strains on the country. Stambulov was confronted with a dilemma which was to become familiar in Balkan politics. To establish a semblance of order in the country, he felt compelled to introduce a range of draconian laws, curtailing the activities of the opposition and capitulating to the predatory economic demands of the great powers. In the face of Russian hostility to Prince Ferdinand and, by extension, the *Stambulovshtina* (as the régime was known), the Prime Minister concluded that a rapprochement with Istanbul was his only viable foreign policy. In exchange, Istanbul demanded that Stambulov curtail the activities of the refugee activists in Bulgaria who were agitating for armed intervention in Macedonia.

For Stambulov as for all Bulgarian politicians, the eventual incorporation of Macedonia into the Principality was an immutable article of faith. However, the army was far too weak for Bulgaria to contemplate war with Turkey, especially without Russian support. Instead, Stambulov preferred to extend Bulgarian influence in Macedonia using gradualist methods, chiefly through the church, the Exarchate and the establishment of Bulgarian schools, and by appealing to Istanbul, usually in vain, to ameliorate the conditions of the Slavs in Macedonia.

In the early 1890s, Sofia and other major cities in western Bulgaria were heaving with embittered Macedonian refugees. As well as being articulate and well organized, they were imbued with revolutionary spirit and very impatient. They devoted verve and energy to infiltrating as many parts of the Bulgarian establishment as they could. The army was not just a prime target for such infiltration, it was a sitting duck, since more than a third of Bulgarian army officers, 15,000 out of 38,000, were actually from Macedonia. The Macedonians hated Stambulov for his perceived collaboration with Turkey and for his role in the murder of key VMRO leaders. They were determined to destroy him.

As Stambulov used his police and intelligence officers to smash conspiracies – sometimes directed from St Petersburg, sometimes from within the army, sometimes by the Macedonian terrorists – the VMRO conspirators replied in kind by assassinating ministers, sending death threats to the Prince and encouraging sporadic peasant disturbances. In 1895, a year after Ferdinand had finally succeeded in manoeuvring Stambulov out of office, the former Prime Minister was attacked by a mob of Macedonians who, quite literally, tore his hands from his arms. Within days, he had died. The jeering Macedonians who attended Stambulov's funeral were only silenced when his distraught widow produced two jars containing Stambulov's pickled hands.

The legacy of Stambulov left Bulgaria stained with blood, and it was a legacy on which the Macedonian refugees and activists were quick to capitalize. In 1895, they had formed in Sofia an organization called the Supremacist Committee which vowed to achieve the liberation of Macedonia and its absorption into Bulgaria. This latter goal placed it at odds with Dame Gruev's party (henceforth the Internal Organization or IO) which, while expecting all manner of aid from Bulgaria, sought to create an autonomous, self-governing Macedonia that would remain independent of Bulgaria. The IO itself later split when the famous *četa* leader, Iane Sandanski, formed a breakaway faction committed to the principles of agrarian socialism.

This sketch of the basic divisions afflicting the Slav Macedonian groups at the end of the last century is necessary to grasp the extent of the violence in the province and its political implications. All three movements, the Supremacists (henceforth the EO or External Organization), the IO and Sandanski's, were committed to the armed struggle inside Macedonia. On occasions, they would cooperate but more often than not their activities and conspiracies were aimed at one another. In addition, the Supremacists contributed to the destabilization of the Bulgarian state by goading the Prince and his government into a war of liberation in Macedonia. At various times, the struggle for Macedonia pitted Slav against Slav (Macedonians/Bulgarians against Serbs, or else Macedonians/Bulgarians against Macedonians/Bulgarians); Slav against Hellene (Macedonian/Bulgarians against Greeks); Slav against Muslim (Macedonians/Bulgarians against Turks or Albanians); Hellene against Muslim (Greeks against Turks or Albanians); and Muslims against Muslims (Turks against Albanians).

After the fall of Stambulov, the Macedonian *četas* roamed around Sofia and other cities with impunity, bribing, intimidating, extorting and shooting. All refugees were expected to contribute a monthly sum of 100 *leva* to the cause. Those who refused could expect a visit at four o'clock in the morning from some burly compatriots.

Attempts by the Bulgarian police to curb Macedonian activities often resulted in violence. In the autumn of 1900, the author, Vojdan

Černodrinski, announced the staging of his play *A Macedonian Blood Wedding* in Sofia. Not wishing to offend Istanbul at a sensitive moment by permitting the performance of this explicitly anti-Turkish drama, the Prime Minister, Todor Ivanchev, slapped a ban on it. As crowds gathered outside the theatre, mounted police blocked the entrance and warned the crowds to disperse. Risking their lives under the horses' feet, the actors attempted to force their way through. Unfortunately for the police, two of the most bullish *četa* leaders in Sofia, Slavko Kovačev and Boris Sarafov, along with thirty of their armed men, had decided to attend the opening. Storming out of the theatre, firing his pistol, Sarafov screamed, 'A Macedonian Blood Wedding will be performed this evening and here is its defender!' The police beat a hasty retreat and under an armed guard *Blood Wedding* did indeed take place.

An end with horrors; horrors without end: Crete, Macedonia, 1903–6

> The eggs had already been eaten, shells and all. Now Captain Michales with a blow from his fist, smashed the pottery eggcups and distributed them to his guests to eat. Bertodulos, terrified, took his piece and clung breathless to a cask. With goggling eyes he watched the Cretans at his feet bite their bits of clay and chew them until they became sand and grit, which they swallowed with a snigger.
>
> There are three sorts of men, Bertodulos slowly explained to himself: those who eat eggs without the shells, those who eat eggs with the shells and those who gobble them up with the shells and the eggcups as well. The third kind are called Cretans.
>
> Nikos Kazantzakis, *Freedom and Death*[40]

By the turn of the century, Serbia, Greece and Bulgaria had suffered indebtedness and political instability, and the manoeuvring of the great powers restricted their foreign-policy options. The governments of all three were committed to schemes of territorial expansion, but the restraining influences of disorganized armies, chaotic public finances and great-power pressure inhibited them. Only through cooperation with one another could they have reinvigorated their expansionist dreams, but the cost of compromise, that is the territorial division of Macedonia, was too high a price to pay – they all wanted to dominate the strategic territory of the southern Balkans. The Macedonian secret societies, which were to play a crucial role in the period leading up to the First World War, spotted this gap between rhetoric and *Realpolitik* and rushed to fill it. In all three countries, military personnel featured prominently in these conspiratorial organizations.

In 1895, a group of sixty Greek army officers sought to revive the traditions of the Philiki Etairia by establishing in Athens a new secret society, the Ethniki Etairia or National Association. Within two years, the Etairia claimed some 3,000 members with branches in 56 Greek cities and among 83 Greek communities abroad. Just as VMRO was preparing to destabilize Bulgaria, so did the Etairia become a virtual state within the Greek state. The Etairia included many Greek Macedonian émigrés in its ranks, but the main focus of its aspirations was Crete.

Since the Greek War of Independence, Crete had been one of the Ottoman Empire's most troublesome provinces. The Great Island, as the Greeks called it, had been the last major conquest of the Ottomans, who wrenched it from Venetian rule in 1699, at a time when their power had already entered its long-term decline. The fall of Crete was not, however, accompanied by a significant influx of Muslims from elsewhere in the Empire. Instead, local Greek notables converted to Islam and continued in their role as chief landowners and administrators so that the Cretan ruling class remained Greek-speaking. But the bulk of the population not only declined to convert, they refused to accept the Sultan's rule, unlike Christians in other parts of the Empire. The politics of Crete was therefore unusually straightforward for an Ottoman Province. The Cretan Christians' propensity for rebellion was born partly of the island's mountainous isolation and partly of the growing realization in the nineteenth century that independence and *enosis* (unification) with Greece was only a matter of time. Barely a decade passed without the Christian villagers and townsfolk abandoning their homes for the mountains, a prelude to a rebellion against the Sultan, or an outbreak of massacre and counter-massacre. In between, the Turks, the Greeks and Jews of the island lived together in uneasy harmony.

Nonetheless, the Christians regarded the apparent indifference not just of the outside world but of mother Greece with scorn, as the celebrated novelist, Nikos Kazantzakis, later described in apocalyptic terms:

> There are peoples and individuals who call to God with prayers and tears or a disciplined, reasonable self-control – or even curse Him. The Cretans called to Him with guns. They stood before God's door and fired rifle shots to make Him hear. 'Insurrection!' bellowed the Sultan, when he first heard the shooting, and in raving fury sent pashas, soldiers and gangs. 'Insolence!' cried the Franks [the great powers], and let loose their warships against the tiny barks that fought, braving death, between Europe, Asia and Africa. 'Be patient, be reasonable, don't drag me into bloodshed!' wailed Hellas, the beggar-mother, shuddering. 'Freedom or death!' answered the Cretans and made a din before God's door.[41]

Aware that they were not capable of defeating the Ottoman army, the Cretans welcomed the formation of the Ethniki Etairia and soon after founded their own revolutionary committee to coordinate their resistance to Istanbul with their sympathizers on the mainland. In the mid-1890s, Turkey once again was the object of intense international pressure because of atrocities committed by its troops against the Armenian population of Eastern Anatolia. The Porte had buckled and agreed to introduce reforms in the region – the Cretans took this as a sign of weakness. With the government and military in Istanbul thus distracted, the Cretans decided to launch another rebellion in May 1896. What the Christians of this island periphery neither knew nor cared was that by pulling Greece, with the aid of the Ethniki Etairia, into an adventure on Crete, they would inflict considerable damage on the cause of Hellenism in Macedonia, a region of much greater strategic significance for Greece.

After the usual unpleasantness on both sides, the Etairia and the Porte both started shipping arms and men on to the island, and eventually the Greek army landed under the leadership of the headstrong Crown Prince Constantine. The great powers, smelling another Eastern Crisis, attempted to mediate between Turkey and Greece by suggesting that Istanbul offer Crete autonomy. By the middle of 1897, the Greeks were still procrastinating and so the Sultan decided to declare war on Greece. Turkish troops massed in Epirus on Greece's northern border and soon put the Greeks to flight. Before long the Ottoman troops were marching on an open road to Athens. Once again the great powers stepped into the breach and imposed a peace deal on the two sides.

The outcome was at first glance advantageous to the Greeks, as Crete was at last given extensive autonomy. But this apparent victory masked hidden dangers. The Greek army had suffered a great setback at Epirus. The Athenian coffers were empty; and the state had incurred an enormous debt. As part of the peace treaty, Athens was forced to hand over control of its budget to a great-power commission. Furthermore, its network of agents in Macedonia had been destroyed.

King George of Greece (1863–1913) had justified the military intervention in Crete by pointing out that 'Britain . . . had seized Cyprus; Germany had taken Schleswig-Holstein; Austria had laid claim to Bosnia and Herzegovina; surely Greece had a better right to Crete!'[42] The argument was not unreasonable, but had the Etairia and King George reasoned more soberly they would have concluded that the Ottoman Empire would be forced to relinquish control of Crete at some future date. By succumbing to the romantic movement for the liberation of Crete and finding itself at war with the Ottoman Empire, Greece was too weak at the end of the nineteenth century to combat the influence of VMRO in Macedonia, and unable to respond when the Ottoman Empire allowed the Bulgarian Exarchate to establish three new bishoprics in Debar, Monastir (Bitola) and Strumitsa. This area extended like a long hand across the middle of Macedonia, marking out the dark shadows of a near future when the Greek Patriarchists and Bulgarian Exarchists would do battle for the souls of the villages. If a community turned to the Exarchate, it would be a victory for Bulgaria; if it retained its allegiance to the Patriarchate, it was a blow in Greece's favour. But the Greek state was in no position to rebuild a network of agents and guerrillas in Macedonia. Meanwhile, the Macedonian refugees in Bulgaria enjoyed unprecedented influence over the government. The time had come for VMRO to strike.

There were two types of VMRO guerrilla band or *četa*. The first was the product of the IO whose primary aim was to expand its membership by means of a combination of persuasion and terror. The IO leadership hoped to raise the consciousness of the peasant masses until an uprising could succeed by sheer weight of numbers. The Macedonian vilayets could be then be transformed into an autonomous Macedonia in the name of all its inhabitants, without regard to faith or perceived nationality.

The EO, operating from inside Bulgaria, preferred more spectacular confrontations with Ottoman power, as a means of provoking retaliation against the Slavs in Macedonia. This would, in theory, engender publicity and sympathy in western Europe, thereby ensuring that the Macedonian Question remained high on the agenda of the great powers. Eventually, the EO believed, the Bulgarian military could justify its intervention, leading to the incorporation of Macedonia into a Greater Bulgaria.

The key to the IO's strategy lay in the villages. There was no shortage of educated but underemployed idealists in the towns of Macedonia to make up the organizational backbone of the IO. But because the projected revolution could not succeed in the cosmopolitan, commercial world of the towns, it had to recruit from the rural hinterland. The only groups competent to act as a transmission belt between the urban intellectuals and the peasantry were the armed *četas*.

Of course, the *četas* were not just revolutionary press-gangs and spreaders of propaganda. They would also seek out and inflict summary punishment and revenge upon the more notorious Turkish notables and gendarmes with a reputation for harshness. These actions were often initially successful, as the *četas* usually enjoyed the advantage of surprise. But a *četa* raid would invariably attract a swift response by the local army garrison, gendarmerie or *başibözöks*. The Ottoman forces could always count on superiority in both numbers and weaponry.

Two institutions held the key to a village's identity – the church and the school. In theory, the IO embraced all the nationalities of Macedonia but in practice most of its activists were Slavs. This meant that soon after the start of its propaganda offensive, the IO ran into hostility from adherents to the Greek Orthodox Church as well as Hellenized Vlachs. A village under the control of a Patriarchate, i.e. Greek Orthodox, cleric would be hostile to the cause of the IO. If, however, it were persuaded to turn its back on the Patriarch and instead embrace the Bulgarian Exarchate, this would also imply its acceptance of the guerrilla movement. If a Bulgarian priest were in control of the village church, this would usually guarantee that the local school would be a Bulgarian and not a Greek or (in the north) Serbian school. The dominance of one branch of the church had an impact on language, and vice versa.

The *četa*, comprising around ten to fifteen men armed with rifles and pistols, would target a particular village, having first carried out some intelligence work to ascertain whether it was Patriarchate or Exarchist, whether it was a mixed village linguistically, whether the local school was Bulgarian or Greek or indeed whether there were two schools. On entering the village, the *četa* would then seek out the priest and the head villager. The guerrillas were an intimidating apparition: they were mostly unshaven, but often had ostentatious, lovingly waxed moustaches; their torsos were criss-crossed with bandoliers; rifles hung behind their shoulders; revolvers and knives and bombs swung menacingly from their belts. If the villagers proved accommodating, they would desist from looting or violence although they expected provisions as a matter of course. The well-defined hierarchy of village life meant that if the guerrillas secured a public pronouncement from either the priest or the head villager or both, then the rest of the villagers would fall in line. Once a village had committed itself to the 'struggle', the IO could consider it a source of both recruits and food. In return, it would offer protection from its own and rival bands.

Less popular were the *četas* from the EO. These were mostly raiding groups from across the Bulgarian border. They would variously rob or murder a few Turks in the name of 'liberating' the toiling peasantry before hightailing it back to safety inside Bulgaria. Behind them, of course, they left villages that were hopelessly vulnerable to Turkish retaliation. The suffering of the men, women and children in whose name the struggle was waged increased dramatically as a consequence. The philosophy behind this politics was grimly encapsulated by Dame Gruev, the student who helped found VMRO in Salonika: 'Better an end with horrors, than horrors without end!'

In November 1897, a group of fifteen bandits, disguised as Ottoman soldiers, slipped into Macedonia from Bulgaria under cover of darkness.* On reaching the village of Vinitsa, they robbed

* Opinions differ as to whether this group was linked to the EO or not. Nonetheless, when they were tried by court martial for the two murders inside Bulgaria, they were eventually acquitted.

the local Turkish noble, Kazim Bey, of 800 *lire* (about $3,600), killing him and his Slav retainer in the process. The bandits escaped with their booty. The dead Slav, however, had been a member of the IO. On hearing of his murder, his wife assumed he had been killed by his colleagues in the local IO and so she informed on them to the local authorities. Calling in military reinforcements, the Turkish governor ordered a sweep through the entire Skopje region, uncovering thousands of guns and illegal funds. Hundreds of IO members and suspected sympathizers were taken in for questioning during which they were 'branded with white-hot iron, squashed in vises, hung upside down, suffocated with the smoke from burning rye and scalded with boiling water'.

The Vinitsa affair revealed how large the IO had grown. The amount of weapons and ammunition seized not only shocked the Porte; even the Bulgarian Government and the EO were staggered by its size. Its leadership, based in Salonika, was determined, if not always blessed with tactical skill. After the Vinitsa affair, its most intelligent leader, Gotse Delchev, ordered the IO to redouble its efforts at harassing the Ottoman authorities to demonstrate that it could not be cowed. Henceforth, violence became Macedonia's common currency.

The execution of traitors and spies was as much part of the *četas*' work as were the attacks on Ottoman soldiery. Well-to-do villagers who refused to contribute to the IO's coffers were advised that the regional committees had the authority to impose death sentences. Contemporary Macedonian historians tend to represent the many traitors who were 'liquidated', to use the IO's euphemistic terminology, as Judases or mercenaries. There were a fair sprinkling of such renegades, but there were also many who objected to the summary justice meted out by the IO. In particular, many adherents to the Patriarchate resisted the enforced conversion of villages to the Exarchate. As the IO grew in strength, so did cooperation between the Greek Patriarchists and the Turks.

The clash between the Greek and the Bulgarian churches did much to foster the idea among western observers that conflict on the Balkan peninsula was essentially religious in nature. In fact, the IO's leadership and activists were fired much more by the secular ideologies of socialism and anarchism. Adherence to one church or the other was simply the most convenient way of labelling the national or political commitment of a village at a time when national or political consciousness in a modern sense barely existed among the peasantry. Conversions of whole villages were common. Sometimes they took place at the end of a gun barrel, sometimes there were compelling economic reasons, as H.N. Brailsford discovered at the time:

> I was talking to a wealthy peasant who came in from a neighbouring village to Monastir market. He spoke Greek well, but hardly like a native. 'Is your village Greek,' I asked him, 'or Bulgarian?' 'Well,' he replied, 'it is Bulgarian now, but four years ago it was Greek.' The answer seemed to him entirely natural and commonplace. 'How,' I asked in some bewilderment, 'did that miracle come about?' 'Why,' said he, 'we are all poor men, but we want to have our own school and a priest who will look after us properly. We used to have a Greek teacher. We paid him £5 a year and his bread, while the Greek consul paid him another £5; but we had no priest of our own. We shared a priest with several other villages, but he was very unpunctual and remiss. We went to the Greek Bishop to complain, but he refused to do anything for us. The Bulgarians heard of this and they came and made us an offer. They said they would give us a priest who would live in the village and a teacher to whom we need pay nothing. Well, sirs, our is a poor village, and so of course we became Bulgarians.'[43]

The steady disintegration of normal life in Macedonia did not appear to worry the great powers unduly. In April 1897, Austria-Hungary and Russia had concluded an agreement to maintain the status quo on the Balkan peninsula. Both had more pressing problems and adventures elsewhere. Austria-Hungary was facing profound domestic upheavals, while Russia had turned its imperialist ambitions to the Far East and China. This effectively closed down the Eastern Question as an area of possible great-power confrontation until 1908 when the Young Turk revolution and the annexation of Bosnia and Hercegovina by Austria led to a dramatic flaring up of the old malady. Yet it was by no means obvious to all the actors on the Balkan stage that the great powers would not tolerate another crisis in their Near East. The governments of Serbia, Greece, Bulgaria and Turkey were almost certainly aware of this. The secret societies and liberation movements, who exercised considerable influence on state policy, were not. In 1902, the External Organization, which had by then escaped all control of the Bulgarian government, felt the time was ripe for a spectacular uprising in Macedonia, in order to provoke the great powers into action against Turkey.

The Ilinden uprising: Macedonia, 1903

In August 1902, Colonel Anastasas Iankoff, the chief agent of the EO outside Bulgaria, suddenly appeared with a hundred armed men in his home village of Zagoritsani in western Macedonia, not far from the largely Greek town of Kastoria. He demanded to see the local IO *četa* leaders, who also arrived with dozens of guerrillas armed to the teeth. Although Iankoff knew several of the local leaders well, the meeting was tense with both *četas* preparing for a shoot out. Iankoff announced that a general uprising was to be proclaimed on 20 September in order to prepare the ground for a full-scale intervention by the Bulgarian army, backed by Russian generals. He also claimed that this had been approved by the central committee of the IO. The local leadership knew nothing of these plans and were entirely unprepared. When it demanded confirmation from the regional IO headquarters in Monastir, they found that their superiors, too, were ignorant of the planned uprising. This was not surprising – by calling the people to arms, the EO wanted to destroy the autonomy of the IO once and for all.

As Iankoff began stirring up western Macedonia, hundreds of EO guerrillas infiltrated a large swathe of Serres county, to the north-east of Salonika near the Bulgarian border. The Ottoman authorities had long been expecting an attempted uprising and had been steadily strengthening their defensive capability in the three Macedonian vilayets. Meanwhile, the leadership of the IO panicked; events outside their control threatened to undermine their strategy of educating the masses before striking for autonomy. Gotse Delchev and Iane Sandanski, much better acquainted with the conditions inside Macedonia than the EO leadership, believed an uprising would be suicidal. Clashes between IO and EO *četas* were recorded before the EO leadership in eastern Macedonia proclaimed the general uprising in the Gorna Dzhumaya region on 23 September 1902.

For a short while, amid exceptionally fierce fighting, the EO guerrillas assumed control of twenty-eight villages near the Bulgarian border. Over 500 Turkish troops and dozens of guerrillas were killed. Within days, the Turkish army had re-established control, driving most of the guerrillas back across the border into Bulgaria. The Turkish authorities then started to hunt down the leadership of the IO, even though these men had done everything in their power to prevent the rebellion.* Those who did not escape to Bulgaria in time were arrested or killed.

Any semblance of authority became eroded in the countryside as the *četas*, bolstered by arms and men from Bulgaria, escaped all control. Tales of misery and violence began to pour into the offices of the European diplomats stationed in Monastir and Salonika:

> The Committee [VMRO] is extorting money from Bulgarians, Greeks, Vlachs, Christians and Muslims, with indescribable arrogance. Christians who don't pay are murdered while the Muslim landowners must reckon with arson attacks on all their property . . .
>
> The longing for order among these unbearable circumstances and for a new, strong administration is becoming ever more intense . . . people do not want reforms, autonomy or whatever – the majority of Macedonians want nothing more than . . . the same fate as Bosnia.†
>
> Punitive executions continue to comprise standard fare of the guerrilla band activities. In the last 14 days alone, there has been a revenge murder of the Greek priest in Zelenic, the death of the teacher from Strebeno, and of a Patriarch supporter

* Most government documents from the period refer to all the various Slav organizations as being Bulgarian – just as all the European consuls in Salonika did. The authorities did not appear to differentiate between the IO and the EO – as far as they were concerned, all were products of the Bulgarian government. The Europeans appeared to have some grasp of the ferociously complicated divisions within VMRO. See *Turski dokumenti za ilindenskoto vostanie*, Skopje, 1993, and *The Events of 1903 in Macedonia as presented in European Diplomatic Correspondence*, ed. Angelos A. Chotzids, Basil C. Gounaris and Anna A. Panayotopoulou, Thessaloniki, 1993.

† I.e. occupation by Austria-Hungary. While life in Bosnia under Habsburg occupation was incomparably preferable to life in Macedonia under collapsing Ottoman rule, the Austrian consul views the ideological complexity through tinted spectacles.

> from Ajtos . . . [then] the Serbian priest from Vrbjani and an Albanian landowner from Lenista . . . whose throat was slit.[44]

The dispatches sent by the consuls assumed an increasingly urgent tone.

When the wake-up call came, it was loud. At about half past ten on a bright spring morning in Salonika, the French commercial vessel, the *Guadalquivir*, was on the point of leaving the harbour when a huge explosion in its engine room ignited a fire which immediately spread throughout the ship. The French consul, Louis Steeg, rushed to the scene. He stopped next to a young man with bright eyes, gaping at the spectacle. M. Steeg asked his secretary whether the ship's engineers had had an accident in the boiler room. 'Absolutely not, M. Steeg . . . There is no doubt that it is the result of an explosion.' This conversation was reported by Pavel Shatev, the bright-eyed boy standing next to the consul. Shatev had planted the bomb.[45]

Shatev was a member of the Gemidzhii, a group of anarchists close to the most radical wing of VMRO. Later that day a bomb derailed a train arriving from Istanbul; after darkness fell the following evening, the town's lighting was extinguished when the gas piping was sabotaged. The frustration and anger this provoked was followed by pandemonium a few minutes later, when the French-controlled *Banque ottomane* was blown to pieces by dynamite. The intensity of the explosion was such that it destroyed the neighbouring Kegelklub and killed many of the German residents of the city who were enjoying a social evening there. Throughout the 'Frankish'* quarter, home-made bombs and Molotov cocktails were hurled at cafés, clubs, hotels and the Eden theatre, causing hysteria throughout the city. The gendarmerie laid siege to a house where a nest of terrorists defended themselves by throwing bombs.[46] The 'military' leader of the Gemidzhii ran on to his balcony and began throwing grenades into the street indiscriminately, before one blew up in his face and killed him.

The chaos of the countryside had now reached Salonika with a vengeance. Infuriated by the attacks, a Muslim mob began lynching the Slav minority in the town, killing about sixty before the

* Citizens of the great powers.

governor imposed martial law, and prevented a worse blood bath. The Gemidzhii had targeted only foreign companies in an attempt, once again, to provoke great-power intervention. British and French warships did indeed steam over the Aegean horizon and drop anchor just outside Salonika, but their mission was to guard 'western' property and lives, not to protect the Christians of Macedonia.

The Balkan peninsula is dotted with obscure towns and villages, high in the mountains or hidden in deep valleys, which emerge from quiet obscurity for a few months to face the furies spawned by a historical process in which they have until then played only a minor role. During the spring of 1903, representatives from Kruševo had requested the Ottoman authorities in the regional capital, Monastir (Bitola), to strengthen the local army garrison – this despite the fact that almost all the 10,000 inhabitants of the town were Christian, divided into three language communities: Vlach, Greek and Slav. The very remoteness of this town afforded it protection, as did the mountains of central-western Macedonia, which formed a natural amphitheatre around it. But the activities of the *četas* in the surrounding villages had begun to worry the town's traders and artisans. Like many others in the Bitola vilayet, the people of Kruševo could sense the approaching storm. By 2 August, the Feast of St Elijah or Ilinden, the authorities had not yet reacted to the townspeople's appeal for more troops.

As twilight descended on the evening of Ilinden, haystacks were set ablaze in villages near Monastir. Soon beacons were burning throughout western Macedonia, as far south as Kastoria and as far north as Debar.[47] Priests began blessing the banners emblazoned with the slogans 'Freedom or Death' and 'Macedonia for the Macedonians' as the *četas* prepared to drive out the Turks from their villages. Throughout the region, hundreds of men began digging, uncovering the buried weapons which had been lying hidden for months and years in anticipation of the event. In a series of strikes, guerrillas cut almost all telegraph lines in the vilayets; bridges were blown up and roads blocked. The biggest disappointment was the failure to seal off the rail link between Monastir (Bitola) and Salonika.

In the single biggest operation of the uprising, 300 guerrillas organized in eight *četas* launched an assault on Kruševo. Most of the guerrillas were Slav but at least one of the *vojvodas* was a local

Vlach. After several hours of intense fighting, they captured the barracks and set fire to it. The entire garrison was either killed or driven out of town, which became the largest settlement to come under rebel control. Kruševo's revolutionary leadership proclaimed the town a republic and set about establishing a new government. This was made up of a 'civilian' commission which drew its members from all communities. Apart from establishing law and order, its only function appears to have been requisitioning material to prepare for the town's defence. Because of Kruševo's size, the Ottoman authorities in Bitola made the town's return a priority. In less than two weeks, a force of 5,000 crack Ottoman troops backed by artillery had been mustered 30 kilometres to the east. In fact, the town was taken without a fight. There were a few minor clashes but most of the insurgents withdrew after some clandestine negotiations with the Turkish commandant, Bachtiar Paşa.

The townspeople were not granted the luxury of talks. Over four days, the Turks first subjected Kruševo to artillery bombardment to 'soften up' the non-existent defences before Bachtiar Paşa allowed his regular troops and paramilitaries to gut the town. After the rapes, the murders and the burnings, the *başi-bözöks* made off with 2,000 cartloads of booty. Remarkably, however, the soldiers restricted their brutality to the Vlach and Greek parts of town. Further up the mountain, the Bulgarian/Slav quarter was left virtually untouched. It has never been established why Bachtiar Paşa threw this cordon around the Slav community although the Greeks and Vlachs both later suggested, quite logically, that he had struck a deal with the retreating insurgents. It is worth noting, however, that the commander was able to set clear limits to the pillaging – a practice which is rarely as uncontrolled as it may appear from a distance.

The precise truth surrounding the Ilinden uprising in Kruševo is probably lost for ever. Like other similar events, however, historians of the various nationalities in the region have milked it in attempts to impute characteristics and intentions to the different communities involved. It has become the central myth underpinning the modern Macedonians' claim to statehood and nationhood. The Greeks use it as yet more proof of the perfidy of the *četas*, who were in their eyes the vicious, willing tools of Bulgarian expansionism. Yugoslav historians stressed its socialist and multiconfessional character as proof of the essentially progressive nature of the Macedonian peasantry.

Indeed, the common assumption uniting these historians, regardless of ideology or nationality, is that the peasant was a conscious actor on the historical stage – a figure who understood his past and had now grasped the hammer of revolution to make his future. H.N. Brailsford took a rather different view, stressing that '[t]he reality behind the whole muddle of racial conflicts, beyond the Chauvinism of the Balkan peoples and the calculations of the greater Powers, is the unregarded figure of the Macedonian peasant, harried, exploited, enslaved, careless of national programmes, and anxious only for a day when he may keep his warm sheepskin coat upon his back, give his daughter in marriage without dishonour, and eat in peace the bread of his own unceasing labour'.[48]

The 'Red Sultan': The Ottoman Empire, 1876–1908

Once more a stubborn mist has swathed your horizons . . .
A dusty, fearsome darkness, which the eye
Takes care not to pierce, for it is afraid.
But for you this deep, dark veil is right and fitting,
This veiling becomes you well, O scene of evil deeds . . .
Yes, veil yourself, O tragedy, veil yourself, O city;
Veil yourself and sleep forever, whore of the world!

'Sis' (Mist), Tevfik Fikret's ode to Sultan Abdülhamid's rule, circa 1897[49]

The photographs of the Macedonian villages that suffered retribution after the Ilinden uprising are shocking even by the standards of the late twentieth century. The *başi-bözöks* and other irregular troops who descended on these settlements often left not a house standing. In addition to the thousands of murdered civilians and rape victims, 119 villages were burnt to the ground, 8,400 houses were destroyed, forcing 50,000 refugees to flee into the mountains, where many more died during the bitter winter that followed. Both the IO and the EO were almost obliterated and, after years of watching the Slav *četas* intimidate Greek villages, the Greek *andartes* swept through western Macedonia forcing the reconversion of Exarchate communities to the Patriarchate.

The *andartes* now administered solace to those Patriarchate villages which had courageously resisted VMRO during the uprising.

However, in the villages genuinely committed to the Exarchate or VMRO, the Greeks behaved like vengeful bullies, executing suspected renegades and holding the Patriarchate version of the Mass at gunpoint if the priest or townspeople were unwilling to perform the service. This Greek backlash was orchestrated by the gun-toting bishop of Kastoria, Germanos Karavangelis. This extraordinary figure, who roamed the countryside in a dark English raincoat with a black scarf wrapped around his priest's hat, 'had a Männlicher slung over one shoulder, a bandolier over the other, a belt round his middle from which hung his holster carrying a large pistol and a knife'.[50] Karavangelis appeared consciously to cultivate an image of threatening romanticism. The bishop considered Bulgarian influence in the region to be the greatest threat to Greek national interests. He therefore advocated close friendship and cooperation between the Greeks and Turks of Macedonia, but only as an expedient. Karavangelis was fully aware that there was no religious aspect to the struggle between the Exarchate and the Patriarchate – he admitted openly that the only issue in Macedonia was the future contours of the Balkan states once the Turks had been thrown out.

As VMRO's influence shrivelled and almost died, Karavangelis and his colleagues began to receive more money, weapons and men from the Greek Kingdom. This renewed Greek activity and the retreat of Bulgarian aspirations hastened a change in Serbian policy, too. Nikola Pašić, the old Radical leader and now Prime Minister, had long given up hope that his ideal of a federal solution for the Macedonian Question might be realized. Serbia would now be fighting for clerical and territorial influence not just against the Greeks and Bulgarians, but also against the Turks and Albanians. Demonstrating again that neither Greeks, Serbs nor Bulgarians have natural allies, Pašić issued an order to Serbia's diplomatic representatives:

> to protect our compatriots from the damaging consequences of the monopoly of Patriarchate organs which have placed themselves in the service of Hellenism to the detriment of the non-Greek adherents to the Patriarchate church; and to counter the activity of Exarchate agents whose Committees are appearing with weapons in those areas of eminent interest to us: Poreč, Kičevo, Drimkol, Dibra, Köprülü.[51]

The suppression of Ilinden had therefore failed to crush the nationalist struggle. On the contrary, it had made it worse. The struggle was spreading, but the balance of forces had changed. Like Bishop Karavangelis, the government in Istanbul considered the Bulgarian insurgency the most threatening. The Greek and Serbian guerrillas concentrated their efforts on expunging Bulgarian or Albanian influence or each other's – they proved less of a nuisance for the Ottoman forces. Indeed, the Christian guerrillas had to an extent assumed the state's role of policing the territory.

However, the violence did prompt increased diplomatic intervention by the great powers, Austria-Hungary and Russia in particular. In September and October 1903, Tsar Nicholas II and the Emperor Franz Josef sat down with their foreign ministers in a Styrian hunting lodge to formulate a policy which could guarantee the status quo in Macedonia while apparently addressing the concerns of the Christian communities. The result was the Mürzsteg Agreement. At the core of Mürzsteg lay a plan to reorganize the Ottoman gendarmerie in Macedonia. Professional policemen dispatched by the great powers were to implement the scheme. This was the first time that an 'international force', comprising members of all the major powers, would be deployed both to quell domestic unrest in the Balkans and to further great-power interests. The mission was half-baked, ill-conceived and poorly executed. It inaugurated a long tradition of bungled interventions.

The presence of foreign bureaucrats on Ottoman territory would undoubtedly serve to remind everyone of the erosion of the Sultan's authority and so the Porte raised a number of objections. But, not for the first time, the government in Istanbul was left with a Hobson's choice: sign up, or else face the anger and discrimination which the concert of great powers seemed ready to inflict. On 25 November 1903, the Sultan duly accepted the Mürzsteg Agreement. In fact the presence of the foreign police had little practical impact. The gendarmes were the least well-paid and most neglected part of the Sultan's repressive apparatus. Nonetheless, they were obliged to police the front line of the Macedonian struggle and to compensate for their poor pay and miserable conditions of employment they turned to corruption. One horrified Austro-Hungarian officer deployed in Macedonia observed in his memoirs that the gendarmerie was a 'privileged gang of extortionists and a rapacious public nuisance . . . Irregularly paid, badly clothed, and indescribably poorly housed, most married with large families, the gendarmes were to look to their own support, and followed the example of their officers by doing so at the expense of the population.'[52]

In addition to the hopeless task of motivating and improving the existing corps of gendarmes, the powers insisted on a fruitless drive to recruit new members from the Christian communities. If there did exist substantial numbers of Christians looking for a new career in the Macedonian gendarmerie, they were soon put off joining by the fate of the first batch. Several of them were murdered, almost certainly by the *četas*; others were warned of their impending fate if they were to stay in post.

The Mürzsteg Agreement did, nevertheless, reaffirm the polite stand-off between Austria-Hungary and Russia in the Balkans, and that was its primary function. It had two awkward side effects, whose significance would become clear a few years later. For the great powers, Mürzsteg was merely an exercise in crisis management, but Greece, Serbia and Bulgaria interpreted it rather differently. Included in the Agreement was a clause allowing for the revision of administrative boundaries 'with a view to a more regular group of the different nationalities'.[53]

The three regional powers understood this clause to be a geopolitical rehearsal for the eventual carve-up of Macedonia. Bulgaria, swamped by demoralized fighters from Macedonia and under threat of war from the Ottoman Empire, could do little more than bleat; but Greece and Serbia saw it as a further excuse to increase their support for terrorist activities in the region – to the degree that they behaved as though the new administrative boundaries marked out the future perimeters of their expanded territories. The arrival of the great-power bureaucrats reinforced the resentment of the Turkish army officers in Macedonia against the rule of Abdülhamid II. Known popularly as the 'Red Sultan' because of his repressive policies, Abdülhamid had now exposed himself as weak in the face of great-power pressure. The Sultan and his vast spy network were universally loathed inside the Empire, but resentment was not enough to provoke coherent opposition to his rule. When discontent was combined with the Sultan's inability to defend the interest of the Empire, however, the result was rather different. Unrest among the Turks of Macedonia was about to assume an organizational form.

Curiously, the events which were really to decide the fate of Macedonia and of the whole Balkans took place many thousands of miles away. In February 1904, the Japanese army rolled back Russia's army in Manchuria, and then the Japanese navy sank a Russian fleet anchored in Port Arthur (Lüshun). Within a year not only had the Russian army surrendered but Russia's Baltic fleet,* exhausted after the long cruise halfway around the globe, had been smashed by Japanese shells and sunk in the Straits of Tsushima, in the Sea of Japan.[54] These humiliating defeats, the first of a western power by an 'oriental' state, astonished public opinion the world over† and marked the end of Russia's Far Eastern adventures and a return to its more traditional concerns in the Balkans. The rivalry between Russia and Austria-Hungary, which had begun to covet the Albanian-inhabited territories in Kosovo and Macedonia, was reignited. After 1905, these two great powers, whilst paying lip service to the language of cooperation in the southern Balkans, once again competed for influence in the region at each other's expense.

At this point, a new and more dangerous element introduced itself into the Macedonian Question – Anglo-German rivalry. Germany was 'a late comer at the feast of vultures', as one contemporary Austrian journalist described Berlin's new imperialist drive.[55] Its aspirations were directed chiefly towards Mesopotamia and Persia, a policy which required the generous assistance of the Ottoman Empire. In no small part, the deep bonds forged between Berlin and Istanbul at the turn of the century were due to the personal understanding between Abdülhamid and Wilhelm II. The Sultan never forgot how the Kaiser had stood by him in the late 1890s when the rest of the world had spurned the Ottoman court in revulsion at a series of massacres of Armenians perpetrated by the mob in 1896. Wilhelm had twice visited Abdülhamid during this period, leading to a significant increase in Turco-German trade – this

* The Black Sea fleet was much nearer but it was, of course, imprisoned behind the Straits with no right in international law to pass through them.

† Nowhere more so than in the Ottoman Empire. Abdülhamid developed an infatuation with Japan after the Russo-Japanese war, seeing in Japan's reviving fortunes a model for Ottoman regeneration. Nothing concrete ever emerged from this infatuation, however, except an intense exchange of priceless gifts between the Sultan and the Emperor.

proved especially profitable for Krupps, the German arms' manufacturer, who monopolized the substantial Turkish artillery market. With Germany's ally, Austria-Hungary, dominating the rail connections throughout the Balkans, if Berlin were to acquire the contract for the completion of the Baghdad railway, then the central powers would boast strategic control of a land mass stretching from the North Sea to the Persian Gulf.

This prospect so alarmed both Russia and Great Britain that the two naval powers entered into much closer collaboration than their interests had hitherto permitted. Their policies towards the Ottoman Empire, which had diverged so sharply throughout the nineteenth century, suddenly appeared to coincide. Germany and Austria-Hungary wished for a stable, peaceful Turkey in order to assist their imperial ambitions. Russia and Britain wanted Turkey weakened in order to sabotage those ambitions. In this way, one of the First World War's main battlelines, both political and military, had been staked out in the Balkans a good seven years before the conflict began.

The contours of this struggle were obvious as early as spring 1907 to Johann, Margrave of Pallavacini, the gifted Austro-Hungarian minister in Istanbul. In a long memorandum prepared for his Foreign Minister, Alois Baron Lexa von Aehrenthal, after arguing that the struggle between imperial interests had shifted since the Russo-Japanese war from the Far East to the Balkans, Pallavacini warned that the British were now determined to aggravate political tensions along a line stretching from Yemen to Albania, making life as difficult as possible for the Ottoman Empire:

> One has the impression that England would like to see the reform programmes [in Macedonia], which we wish to succeed, taken ad absurdum to prevent the establishment of a certain stability in the region . . . On the one side stands Germany, on the other England; these are the two great rivals. But I do not believe that we can stand aside in this struggle . . . We must strive to exploit the economic fertilization of the great Turkish empire together with Germany . . . Indeed this question [of the Bosnian railway] throws its shadows over all other questions relating to Turkey above all on the question of Macedonian reform.[56]

It was not only the Greeks, Serbs, Albanians, Bulgars and Vlachs whose patience had run out at the failure of reforms to bring an end to the chaos. The Turks, above all the Third Army Corps based in Salonika, had also reached the end of their tether. Abdülhamid had deepened his despotic rule from the day he had suspended the Midhat Constitution in 1876. Despite a serious flirtation with pan-Islamic ideas, Abdülhamid was a modernizer who wanted the Ottoman Empire to compete with the West. He was prepared to accept substantial western interference in the Empire's domestic affairs, chiefly through the agency of the Public Debt Administration, as a necessary evil that would nonetheless aid Istanbul's overall financial policing of the Empire. But the bloody circumstances surrounding his ascension to the throne during the turbulent events of 1876* and his naturally suspicious disposition persuaded Abdülhamid that he could trust nobody. And so he began to spy on everybody with influence and on many who wielded none. His network of informers and *agents provocateurs* was seemingly boundless.

In 1896, an Armenian terrorist organization had exploded a series of bombs in Istanbul to draw the outside world's attention to its secessionist aspirations. In response, Abdülhamid's police whipped up the Turkish mob who were permitted to vent their anger on the civilian Armenians of Istanbul. It was after these first Armenian massacres that Abdülhamid's friends in the West began to desert him as evidenced by this account written in 1897:

> A year or so ago, Sultan Abd-ul-Hamid appeared to be earnestly striving against cruel odds, to do what was best for his people. But recent events demand a change of opinion. The good he has done is drowned – drowned in the blood of countless murdered men, women, and children, and, in the lurid light of these scenes of horror, he takes on the semblance of some loathsome spider, caught in the silken web of his own Hareem, and condemned there to re-incarnate the most evil of his ancestors, whose very names conjure up dread memories of murder and rapine.[57]

---

* See chapter 2.

Abdülhamid's unpopularity abroad (with the important exception of Germany, as noted above) contrasted with the warm reception of the Ottoman opposition in exile. This had sprung up in Paris in the 1890s and later spread to the Turkish community in Geneva. Led by the pompous but influential writer and would-be philosopher, Ahmed Riza, these discussion groups blossomed. They produced some excellent, if controversial newspapers and served as an effective irritant to Abdülhamid. The influence of the Young Ottomans inside the Empire, however, was negligible but they sustained an important tradition during dark days, and reopened serious debates about the future of the Ottoman Empire. They were also the first to publicize the nature of Turkey's immediate problem – Abdülhamid himself.

In 1906 small conspiracies arose inside the Empire. Cells loyal to the subversive project began to form inside the army in Salonika and Damascus. These then multiplied, escaping the body of the armed forces to infect parts of the Ottoman administration – officials in the post and telegraph office, in the schools and in the judicial system. In Salonika, many Jews, and a few Armenians, Greeks and Bulgarians were also recruited into this embryonic resistance. The organization in Damascus, *Vatan* (Fatherland), was not remotely as influential as its counterpart in Salonika. But it is worth noting that one of the co-founders of the Damascus conspiracy was Mustafa Kemal, a young, strong-minded officer from Salonika.

In the two years to 1908, the Salonika conspiracy became the most effective of all the underground organizations to have emerged on the Balkan peninsula since the 1880s. This was in spite of the enormous secret-police resources which Abdülhamid had devoted to combating the Ottoman Society of Liberty. (Following the initiative of two émigré opposition groups in Paris and Geneva, the Ottoman Society of Liberty fused with the exiled organizations to become part of the Committee for Union and Progress – the CUP.) However, there was never any question of the Paris groupings exercising influence on the Salonika organization, which specifically rejected any interference in its activities from abroad. In the year before the Young Turk revolution of July 1908, Abdülhamid deployed as many as 40,000 agents in Macedonia in his attempt to throttle the conspiracy.

The CUP succeeded for three reasons. First, the chief organizers drew on a rich tradition of clandestine politics. They employed the cell system of the Carbonari. This meant that an individual member would know at most the identities of four or five of his co-conspirators. If a cell was penetrated by the secret police, adjoining cells could immediately seal themselves from the threat of exposure. But it was the lessons learned from VMRO which proved of particular value to the CUP. Most of the officers in the Committee had spent much time in the struggle against VMRO and had been impressed by the discipline of the Bulgarian and Macedonia guerrillas. VMRO dealt with members or sympathizers considered a security risk, as well as with traitors, by liquidating them. The CUP also admired the mobility and dedication of the insurgent bands and this respect was reflected in its initiation ceremonies, as recorded by a contemporary English journalist:

> The next stage, however, was the most important, and it was invested with every circumstance of awe and solemnity. The man was blindfolded, and led to a secret place whose whereabouts was entirely concealed from him. The bandage was then removed from his eyes, and he found himself in a darkened room, perhaps in a lonely hollow of the hills, in the presence of three strangers wearing black masks. These administered to him the oath which was to become the rule of his life. Swearing on the sword and on the Sacred Book, he bound himself to devote his whole energies to the redemption of his country, to obey every order given to him throughout the channels of the Society, never to reveal its secrets, and to kill any person, however near and dear to him, whom it might condemn to suffer death. His eyes were again covered, and he was led back to the place from which he had started on the mysterious journey.[58]

Second, in contrast to the Christian rebels of Macedonia, the CUP's target did not include other communities in the region, merely the centre of power in Istanbul. Indeed, as it spread throughout the cities and towns of the region, the CUP's local organizations appealed for cooperation from Christian guerrilla networks. This encouraged a tacit recognition that most subversive groups in the province were working towards the same end – the downfall of Abdülhamid's régime and, even more importantly, the restitution of constitutional rule in the Ottoman Empire. The conspiracy was not motivated by Turkish nationalism, an ideology still very much in its infancy. It was fighting for the modernization and strengthening of the Empire under western constitutional principles, and these included the equality of all races.

But the third and most important explanation for the CUP's rapid growth lay in its core constituency – the Third Army Corps headquartered in Salonika. The army was the Achilles' heel of the Hamidian regime.[59] From his accession to the throne, he had depended on the army for the external and internal security of his Empire, especially in Macedonia. But he both resented and feared its power. To clip the military's wings, the Sultan shifted much responsibility over to his loyal Interior Ministry and systematically starved the army of resources.* Yet the one area in which the Tanzimat reforms of the previous century had not only succeeded but prospered was in the advancement of the military education establishment. The Ottoman Empire could not boast a university until 1900, and even then it was subject to the intense scrutiny of the secret police. Under the diligent eyes of Prussian instructors, however, the military schools attracted the brightest minds in Turkey. They knew that here, at least, they could receive the broadest education available, run generally along western lines. The junior officers, like Enver Bey and Niyazi Bey, the two inspirational founders of the CUP, and Mustafa Kemal, were not simply schooled in military strategy. They learned foreign languages and had a genuine interest in western political and literary debates.

Opposition within the army to Abdülhamid was inevitably most intense in Macedonia.[60] As elsewhere, officers' pay was many months in arrears; as in other provinces, promised deliveries of weapons and uniforms never came. But unlike their colleagues, the officers in the Third Army Corps could participate in the relatively relaxed cosmopolitan culture of Salonika, where newspapers were much bolder than in the capital.† Above all, the military in

* He devastated the Ottoman navy, a policy which had severe consequences for Turkey in the Balkan Wars of 1912–13.

† Papers from Salonika were much sought after in Istanbul where deliveries were regularly impounded by the authorities, rather like in postwar Eastern Europe where papers and magazines from Poland, Czechoslovakia and Hungary were eagerly collected by other East Europeans during periods of reform.

Macedonia had been engaged in a tough anti-insurgent campaign for a decade. After the Mürzsteg Agreement of November 1903, they also had to suffer the indignity of police monitors from the great powers.

The Viennese paper, *Die Neue Freie Presse*, reported that in the year preceding the revolution of July 1908 'in all corps-areas, seventeen larger mutinies and revolts of whole troops or garrisons took place, of which most lasted several days, countless smaller mutinies and demonstrations not counted'.[61] In Macedonia, virtually every garrison outside Monastir and Salonika refused to obey orders at some point – some even concluded pacts with the Albanian, Bulgarian and Serbian guerrillas they were meant to be combating. Their officers were actively involved in dozens of assassinations of Hamidian officials and spies during 1907 and 1908. The officers of the Third Army were preparing to assume the mantle of revolutionaries. As the Sultan planned a military assault on the CUP, King Edward VII and Tsar Nicholas II met in Reval to discuss the Macedonian Question, among other topics. Throughout the Ottoman Empire, the meeting was interpreted as a call to wrench the region from the Empire and divide it into new spheres of great-power influence. The CUP decided that the time had come to act.

After the attempted assassination of the special secret-police commissioner sent by the Sultan to root out the conspiracy, both Enver Bey and Niyazi Bey, the leading rebels in the officer corps, took to the hills with several hundred soldiers. At this point, Abdülhamid decided to send the army to deal with the army. One of his most trusted generals, Şemsi Paşa, was dispatched to Macedonia from Istanbul with orders to crush the rebellious military units. On 7 July 1908, he was assassinated in broad daylight. Morale among the Sultan's supporters collapsed almost overnight, as one garrison after another declared themselves in favour of the conspiracy. To the west, the Albanians, upon whose loyalty Abdülhamid had often relied, announced their support for the constitution. The Bulgarian bands operating in central Macedonia, and along the border with Bulgaria proper, refrained from harassing Niyazi's rebels. The headquarters of the Second Army Corps in Edirne (Adrianople), a mere 160 kilometres from Istanbul, also came out in support of the Third Army. On 24 July, less than three weeks after Şemsi Paşa's murder, Abdülhamid, now fearing for his own life, announced that the

Midhat Constitution, which had been temporarily suspended thirty-two years previously, would once again come into force. The power of the Sultan had been fatally weakened.

Challenging history: the Young Turk revolution, 1908

Later cataclysms of the twentieth century have obscured the contemporary impact of the Young Turk revolution. Yet its importance is comparable with the Russian Revolution of 1917 and the collapse of communism in the Soviet Union and Eastern Europe in 1989. The speed with which the Sultan's power crumbled astonished the great powers, and took the revolutionaries themselves unawares.

Within days, however, celebration washed over the entire Empire like an enormous tidal wave. Halide Edib, a future feminist writer, described the human avalanche which poured down from Taksim across the Galata Bridge towards the Yildiz palace in Istanbul as 'radiating something extraordinary, laughing, weeping in such intense emotion that human deficiency and ugliness were for the time completely obliterated'.[62] Muslims joined their Armenian compatriots to attend requiem services for the victims of the 1896 massacres. On 26 July, 'sixty thousand people massed in front of the entrance to Yildiz. They carried banners reading, in French and Ottoman, *Liberty, Equality, Fraternity and Justice* and wore "liberty cockades" in red and white (the colours of the Ottoman flag), aping the tricolour cockade of Paris in 1789.'[63]

But the revelry in Istanbul was muted when set against the spectacular events unfolding in Salonika and Macedonia. Walking in disbelief through the throngs of delirious people on 23 July, Salonika's gendarmerie commander observed how

> [o]n the balcony of the Konak [town hall], Greek and Bulgarian bishops and the mufti shook hands and then in the name of fraternity, they invited their co-religionists to follow suit . . . A cry of joy burst from every lung in the crowd and you could see Muslims, Greeks and Bulgarians, the old mortal enemies, falling into one another's arms. An indescribable delirium ensued as the reconciliation of the races and religions was consecrated underneath an immense flag emblazoned with the words 'Long Live the Constitution' . . .[64]

Beneath the White Tower, a military band struck up the Marseillaise while the squares filled with people from all quarters of the city. For several days, the cafés, the gardens and the squares never emptied as the scenes of fraternization between the different peoples intensified: 'The tigers, the wolves, the foxes and the ewe came to graze on the same pasture', as two poetic French historians put it.[65]

But even more amazing sights were to follow. After embracing the Greek bishop in Serres, Iane Sandanski, VMRO's greatest guerrilla, led his *comitadjis* into Salonika and in an act of momentous symbolism handed his weapons over to the CUP. Acknowledging the sacrifice, the revolutionary authorities returned the guns whereupon Sandanski and his men proceeded to destroy them. In a 'Proclamation to All Nations of the Empire', Sandanski sought to build on this remarkable moment of reconciliation:

> Our fatherland, so sorely tried, is celebrating its rebirth. The revolutionary appeal of our Young Turkish brothers has echoed joyously in the souls of equally sorely-tried people . . .
>
> To my Turkish compatriots!
>
> You represent the great majority of the people and you have therefore carried the greatest weight of our mutual enemy's oppression. In your Turkish empire, you were no less slaves than your Christian counterparts . . .
>
> Dear Christian compatriots!
>
> You were also cruelly deceived in your belief that your suffering at the hands of tyranny was caused by the entire Turkish people . . .
>
> Dear Friends!
>
> Do not allow yourself to be influenced by the criminal agitation which may be used by official Bulgaria to undermine your joint struggle with the Turkish people and the peaceful continuation of this struggle.[66]

The Young Turk revolution was a courageous blow against the despotism of Sultan Abdülhamid; in its early stages, its leaders explicitly rejected the path of nationalism. As the most elegant chronicler of life in Salonika at the turn of the century put it, 'It was to be the end of discrimination and injustice. It was to be the end of internecine struggles and bloodshed, the end of hatreds. They were tired of hating, these people! They wanted to live in peace. Life was something else than constant feud between men speaking different tongues . . . It was time to work hand in hand for the good of all.'[67]

It would, however, be naive to imagine that as late as 1908 a constitutional movement would possess sufficient political and intellectual resources to transform the Ottoman Empire into a modern multinational state. Over three years of counterrevolution and restoration, revolutionary idealism turned into a regime whose brutality surpassed that of Abdülhamid. 'The old espionage had returned, the extortions had never ceased, the oppression against non-Moslems had now acquired a fresher and more sinister vigour, for the measure of freedom that each nationality had once enjoyed was now being ruthlessly crushed by a heretofore unknown chauvinism.'[68] This tragedy had many causes. Of these, three deserve special mention.

The first was the political immaturity of the largest, Turkish, element of the revolutionary movement. The call for the restoration of the Midhat Constitution was a mantra behind which lay no coherent political philosophy. The key debates about the nature of the post-revolutionary Turkish state had taken place among the émigré opposition groups in Paris and Geneva, but these were very far from being resolved. Indeed, the growing bitterness between the two main opposition groups, one led by Ahmed Riza and one by Prince Sabaheddin, indicated just how troublesome these divisions would be. At its core lay the question of identity – were the revolutionaries Turks or Ottomans? And by implication, was the new constitutional empire to emphasize a modernizing centralism, inevitably associated with Turkish nationalism as it refused the privileges sought by the Christian and Arab communities? Or was the new régime to allow a decentralized administration, which would weaken the security of the state? Within a short time, the CUP began drifting towards a radical centralization that alienated the Christian communities.

Their goodwill had in any event been offered subject to extremely onerous conditions. While the Young Turk revolution had temporarily spread the gospel of harmony among the Empire's constituent peoples, it had had no such effect on Macedonia's neighbours in the Balkans – Greece, Bulgaria and Serbia. On the contrary, they saw the success of the revolution as a sign of the Empire's extreme weakness and it galvanized their expansionist ambitions.

The most immediate blow to the movement for reconciliation in the Ottoman Empire was delivered by Bulgaria, Austria-Hungary and Greece. In October, Prince Ferdinand exploited the political chaos in the Ottoman Empire by declaring Bulgaria fully independent – until then it had been nominally under the suzerainty of the Empire. Within days, Austria-Hungary followed suit by announcing the full annexation of the occupied territories of Bosnia and Hercegovina and before long Greece proclaimed *enosis* with Crete. These events, in particular Vienna's annexation of Bosnia, set alarm bells ringing in the Ottoman military barracks, the real power behind the CUP. Henceforth, any Christian demands which smacked of secessionism would be rejected. In response, the guerrillas in Macedonia – Serb, Bulgarian, Greek and, significantly, Albanian – took to the hills once more. The military establishments of Greece, Serbia, Bulgaria and the Ottoman Empire had taken their first steps along the road that ended with the First and Second Balkan Wars of 1912 and 1913.

The maze of conspiracy: the Balkan militaries

> We have become the most militaristic state in the world.
>
> A Bulgarian general, writing in 1910[69]

In the twenty-seven years separating the Serbo-Bulgarian war of 1885 and the outbreak of the First Balkan War in October 1912, the armed forces of the Balkan states underwent a staggering transformation. After the victory over the Serbs in 1885, the Bulgarian parliament declared the creation of a modern mass army with an offensive capability to be the central goal of the state.[70] The loose conspiracy of Macedonian officers in the military badgered the government, especially after the fall of Stambulov in the mid-1890s, to accelerate the reorganization of the army.

The Bulgarian government began acquiring large amounts of artillery from Europe's greatest rivals in arms manufacturing, the French firm, Schneider-Creusot, and Krupps of Germany. The majority of these purchases were financed by loans advanced to Bulgaria from the great powers, a happy relationship for the money lenders and arms dealers. Indeed, after Bulgaria was forced to declare bankruptcy in 1902 and, like Turkey, Serbia and Greece before it, to accept a substantial measure of great-power control over its domestic budget, the powers did not impose any significant restrictions on Bulgarian weapons purchases or the strategic development of the country's railroads. By the middle of the decade, over a third of Bulgaria's total budget, roughly £2,500,000 per annum, was being siphoned off by the army.[71] Universal conscription was introduced, able-bodied men up to forty-six years of age had to do service in the reserves. The growth of the army was so rapid that the new military schools were unable to keep up with the demand for officers. The officer corps, whose rates of pay were the highest in Bulgaria's large civil service, attracted many intellectuals and the sons of small businessmen into its ranks. On the eve of the Balkan Wars, Bulgaria, the most populous young Balkan state, could field some 350,000 men in wartime, almost as many as the Turkish army was able to muster in neighbouring Macedonia and Thrace.

Serbia followed a similar path. Humiliated personally and as head of state after the Bulgarian victory of 1885, Milan Obrenović devoted his energies to constructing a modern Serbian army during the 1890s, after he had abdicated in favour of his son, Aleksandar (1889–1903). Military reconstruction was disrupted by Aleksandar Obrenović's reliance on a small clique in the army leadership, provoking resentment in the officer corps, which eventually led to his assassination in 1903. His successor, Petar Karadjordjević, encouraged weapons purchases and gave the officer corps a growing influence on Serbian foreign and budgetary policy. As in Bulgaria, officers not only received the thickest pay packets, they were respected as the force behind the dreams of national expansion. The army was quite content to see the state fall deeper into debt, while creditor governments also welcomed this growing dependence on great-power capital. In December 1906, when the Serbian debt already stood at over 300 million francs, the French government approved a further loan of 95 million. Serbia committed itself in exchange to an exclusive artillery deal with Schneider-Creusot. Leaving aside the Serbian taxpayer (and soldier-to-be), everybody benefited from these arrangements.

The Macedonian conspiracy helped drive the expansion of the Bulgarian army; Apis's conspiracy played a key role in Serbia's military development. It is a grave mistake to dismiss the work of the conspiracies as the sort of butchery 'typical of backward Asian khanates', as *The Times* did when reacting at the time to the murders of King Aleksandar and Queen Draga. Brutal though they unquestionably were, the conspiracies foreshadowed the nationalist tradition of the modern Balkan state, based on a mythology of military power, which has been alternately vilified and glorified ever since – both in the West and in the region itself. Balkan nationalism and militarism were in fact much more closely related to the practices and morality of great-power imperialism than *The Times* would have liked to admit. The Balkan armies were funded by western loans, western firms supplied them with weapons and other technology, their officers were schooled and organized by Frenchmen, Germans, Russians and Britons. The compulsion of the new states to grab territory, with scant regard to the facts of demography or history, reflected the practices of their great-power neighbours, whose arbitrary decisions at the Congress of Berlin had ensured that there was plenty of territory to dispute.

The first decade of this century witnessed a dramatic increase in the literary activity of Bulgarians, Serbs, Greeks and even the late-starting Albanians, which sought to justify the young nations' claims to as much territory as possible. In Serbia, the eminent geographer, Jovan Cviić, published his study of the ethnography of Macedonian Slavs. While the work remains a valuable piece of scholarship to this day, its primary aim was to dispute Bulgarian claims to the region. Branislav Nušić, who had written so elegantly about the futility of the Serbo-Bulgarian war in 1885, became an enthusiastic supporter of Serbian aims in Macedonia. The clamour of Sofia's newspapers for military action to liberate brother Bulgarians in Macedonia became deafening, while the realization of the *Megali idea* remained an article of faith for most Athenian politicians.

The actual militaries, whether in Bulgaria, Serbia or Greece, were disciplined and willing, at a time of great political uncertainty, to imbibe a simple ideological message – liberate the brethren, expand the national territory. They were hardly sophisticated intellectuals and their work was often hampered by petty jealousies and squabbles. But without the energy with which they consolidated military power and studied tactical manuals, no amount of romantic nationalist demagoguery (and there was plenty of it) could have prepared the young Balkan states for war with the Ottoman Empire.

In contrast to Serbia and Bulgaria, Greece's army remained a shambles until shortly before the First Balkan War. Defeat against Turkey in the war over Crete in 1897 left the Greek army demoralized, without the ability to manipulate civilian governments at which the Serb and Bulgarian military establishments were so adept. International control over Greek finances, severely affected by the war with Turkey, was very strict. In addition, the Greek bureaucracy was hampered by clientelism more than any other young Balkan state. Political parties developed as personal fiefdoms of individual politicians rather than vehicles for ideological debate. In 1900, the Prime Minister, George Theotokis, sponsored an act which conferred the office of commander in chief on Crown Prince Constantine. The Prince then brought clientelism into the army, promoting his followers to senior positions. This led to the slow build-up of resentment among Greek officers, who blamed Constantine, unfairly, for the defeat against the Turks in 1897. By 1908, the British Foreign Office, in its annual report on the country, noted dismissively: 'Greece as a military factor counts far below the other Balkan states.'[72]

Interest among junior officers in the conspiracies that overthrew King Aleksandar in Serbia and Sultan Abdülhamid in the Ottoman Empire combined with the frustration born of Greece's chronic lack of preparedness for war. In August 1909 an army conspiracy, the Military League, launched a successful *coup d'état*. Lacking the guile of the conspirators in Serbia, Bulgaria and even Turkey, the Military League did not form its own cabinet but tried to manipulate the new government from behind the scenes, and soon found it impossible to secure the finances needed to restructure the military. Instead it turned to Eleftherios Venizelos, a Cretan who had successfully used the discontent on his native island to build himself a power base. Venizelos proved to be a masterful politician and broke through Greece's chronic stagnation in time to prepare the country for the Balkan Wars.

The conspiracy in the Ottoman Empire was the exception which proved the rule. The rebels who launched the Young Turk revolution did not intervene in order to bolster an expansionist programme of national liberation. Instead, they were attempting to prop up a ceiling which was fast collapsing. The disaffected army had been drawn into domestic politics against its will and better judgement. Once involved in the labyrinth of the Turkish state, it was extremely difficult to get out again. In the five years prior to the Balkan Wars, the once great Turkish army dissolved into a hopeless, unwieldy mess. Whereas both the Serb and Bulgarian strategists had battle plans and had studied the terrain on which the war would be fought, the Turks had already folded their maps.

'These Balkan troubles might be of some use': the Balkans on the eve of war

The Turkish victory in the war with Greece coincided in 1897 with the *détente* between Austria and Russia. While this obtained (until 1908) there was little prospect of any Balkan state encroaching on the Ottoman Empire's last territories in Europe, chiefly because it would mean opposing the combined power of Austria-Hungary and Russia.[73] This was particularly frustrating for Serbia. The conspiracy to murder King Aleksandar was in part motivated by the Obrenović dynasty's affection for and dependency on Austria-Hungary. For nationalists like Apis, Austria-Hungary was the deadliest opponent of Serbian aspirations. Vienna's occupation of Bosnia-Hercegovina had not only denied several hundred thousand Serbs the right to cohabit with their brothers and sisters in Serbia proper, it also blocked the most direct route between Serbia and its coveted outlet to the Adriatic. Further, by occupying the Sanjak of Novi Pazar, Austria-Hungary had driven a wedge between Serbia and the fraternal kingdom of Montenegro, which offered a second, albeit less desirable, path to the Adriatic. Austrians were showing an unhealthy interest in the Albanian lands and its port of Durrës. Finally, Serbia's economic dependency on Austria and the secret military treaties (with which the late King Milan had sought to bind the two countries) were utterly galling.

After Aleksandar's death, the new king, Peter Karadjordjević, and his Russophile government of Radicals, led by Nikola Pašić, were disappointed to discover that Russia had no intention of disturbing the peace with Austria. In 1903, Russia was preparing to embark on its adventure in Manchuria; St Petersburg needed calm in the Balkans. So Belgrade decided to look elsewhere for allies. Instead of seeking the favour of a great power, Pašić put out feelers to Bulgaria, a country for which he retained some affection since he had found refuge there during the Timok rebellion of 1883. Belgrade and Sofia negotiated a customs union in April 1904. This was the origin of the so-called Second Balkan Alliance system, which after seven tortuous years matured into a network of bilateral agreements that enabled Serbia, Bulgaria, Greece and Montenegro to wage war on Turkey.

At first, however, the plan backfired badly on Serbia. The Austro-Hungarian government reacted furiously as it considered the agreement a disruption of its trading arrangements in the Balkans. The very idea of Balkan states entering into bilateral commercial agreements independent of Austria was preposterous. In response, it imposed a trade embargo on Serbia which lasted for six years and became known as the Pig War.* In the event, the alliance with Bulgaria suffered a setback when Sofia embarked on its own rapprochement with Vienna in 1907. Belgrade and Sofia were also forever at odds over the future territorial division of Macedonia. Nonetheless, the commercial agreements between the two established an important precedent of cooperation between the Balkan states without reference to the great powers.[74]

In 1908, the Russian-Austrian *détente* in the Balkans came to an end when the government in Vienna exploited the confusion caused by the Young Turk revolution by annexing Bosnia-Hercegovina. Austria's borders now penetrated deep into the Balkan interior. There was talk of Russia and Austria drifting towards war. Russia, however, felt itself weak after the disasters of 1905 while Britain and Germany were quietly in agreement that, as Chancellor Bethmann-Hollweg later formulated it, 'these Balkan troubles might be of some use' in promoting Anglo-German cooperation in Europe.[75]

In place of sabre-rattling, Russia now adopted a policy of encouraging all Balkan states, including the Ottoman Empire, to enter into alliances which would function as a system of collective security against further Austrian encroachment. The idea was warmly supported by the Foreign Secretary, Sir Edward Grey, who commented on remarks made by the Russian Foreign Minister in the Duma: 'Izvolsky's speech seems to me very satisfactory . . . I am glad he emphasized the need for community of feeling between the Balkan States and the combination of all three of them with Turkey for

* In the longer term, the embargo proved advantageous to Serbia as the country was forced to find other markets for its pigs and so its economic dependency on Austria-Hungary was broken.

defence of common interests. I am quite in favour of this and will encourage it, whenever I can.'[76]

The enthusiasm emanating from St Petersburg and London suggested that the great powers had not quite grasped the great political and military shift which had taken place in Serbia, Bulgaria and Greece in the previous fifteen years. Their offensive strategies were aimed at grabbing territory from Turkey – in Albania, in Macedonia, in Thrace, in Crete and in the Aegean Islands. Certainly, there were serious differences among the states, especially over Macedonia. And indeed all three occasionally flirted with the idea of improving relations with Turkey for tactical reasons. But what had changed was that Sofia, Athens and Belgrade were no longer prepared to bow to the strategic requirements of the great powers, although they were unlikely to act without some indication of Russian approval. They now understood that if they could agree with one another on military cooperation, then they could expel Turkey from Europe whether the great powers wanted them to or not. A Bulgarian statesman, interviewed by the Russian revolutionary journalist Leon Trotsky, who covered the Balkan Wars, summed up this new-found confidence soon after the First Balkan War had broken out:

> We must, of course, say this, with all politeness, to all the other diplomats of Europe, too, as they labour in the sweat of their brows for our happiness. 'Neither honey nor thorns,' dear sirs! We ourselves will settle with Turkey, without any interference from Europe, and all the more firmly and satisfactorily. Europe puts on an air of being afraid that we shall be excessively demanding. And this from Europe – that is to say, from Austria-Hungary, who annexed Bosnia; from Italy, who seized Tripolitania, from Russia, who never takes her eyes off Constantinople [all former Ottoman possessions] . . . This is the Europe that comes to us preaching moderation and restraint. Truly, a sight for the gods on Olympus! . . . Your diplomats are sulking. They would not be averse to freezing the Balkans for another ten years, in expectation of better days sometime. How is it that they cannot understand that less and less is it possible in our epoch to direct the destinies of the Balkans from the outside? We are growing up, gaining confidence, and becoming independent . . . In the very first years of

> our present phase of existence as a state, we told our would-be guardians: 'Bulgaria will follow her own line.' . . . And so Messrs. Privy Councillors of all the diplomatic chanceries would do well to get used to the idea that the Balkan Peninsula 'will follow its own line' . . .[77]

By 1910, Russia had realized that Bulgaria had no interest in entering into a formal alliance with Turkey, and so instead St Petersburg encouraged Serbia and Bulgaria to bury the hatchet over Macedonia and form an anti-Habsburg axis in the Balkans. The great powers had still not got the message that any such alliance would not be directed against Austria-Hungary. And the consolidation of a Serbo-Bulgarian alliance would almost certainly mean war with Turkey, precisely what Russia wanted to avoid. St Petersburg worried that its military was not ready to act if a war between the Ottoman Empire and the Balkan states were to provoke hostilities between Russia and Austria-Hungary. Until the middle of 1911, however, neither Serbia nor Bulgaria had an incentive to compromise on the Macedonian issue. Two events that year changed this.

In the late summer of 1911, Italy, the final guest to sup at 'the feast of vultures', occupied, as Trotsky's anonymous Bulgarian diplomat noted, the Ottoman province of Tripoli, and in September Turkey declared war, diverting large forces to north Africa to counter the invasion. As the Italian navy threatened some of Turkey's Aegean islands, Russia reversed its policy and stepped up its diplomatic efforts to cement a Balkan alliance including Greece, Bulgaria, Serbia and Montenegro with a view to taking military action against Turkey. Negotiations between Sofia and Belgrade culminated in a treaty provisionally signed on 12 March 1912. This used the 1904 commercial agreement as a starting point, but included a secret military annex. To surmount the disagreements over how Macedonia was to be carved up, the two sides agreed on rough boundaries with a large chunk in the middle whose fate would be decided by the arbitration of Tsar Nicholas II. Equally painful discussions were required to complete the agreements between Greece and Bulgaria, Montenegro and Bulgaria, and Montenegro and Serbia, and the final treaty was settled only two days before the outbreak of the war in October 1912. Collectively these agreements transformed the balance of power in the Balkans. But the foundations were so hastily constructed that, as the leaders of both the Serbian and Bulgarian Social Democrat parties warned, they were bound to lead to conflict among the Balkan states in the event of Turkey's defeat.

Serbia's reluctance to sign an agreement with Bulgaria was overtaken by events in the Albanian-inhabited territories of the Ottoman Empire. The Albanians found themselves in a peculiarly difficult situation after the CUP had defeated a counter-revolution in Istanbul in 1909. The second CUP administration, ruthlessly centralizing and nationalist, adopted the familiar tactics of Abdülhamid. Successive decrees denied the Albanians autonomy and language rights; large military forces were deployed in the region. The attempts by nationalist Albanian leaders like Ismail Qemal Bey to spread the gospel of autonomy also foundered on the tribal fragmentation of Albanian society, particularly in the north and in Kosovo. Qemal and the emerging Albanian intelligentsia knew that cooperation between the other Balkan states spelt disaster for the Albanians. In the event of an Ottoman collapse in Europe, the Serbs, Montenegrins, Greeks and Bulgarians would ignore Albanian territorial claims. These were substantial, as Albanians formed the majority population in the vilayets of Kosovo, Ioannina and Shkoder. There was also a huge concentration in the Monastir vilayet.

Unlike most of their neighbours, the Albanians had no state, the crucial instrument for nurturing a coherent national consciousness; and above all, they had no proper school system. There was even confusion over the Albanian alphabet. These factors combined with tribal divisions and geographical obstacles to render any coordinated response either to the Turkish army or the Balkan alliance exceptionally difficult. The Albanians fiercely resisted any encroachment on their lands, but such valour was undermined by their inability to submit to any central authority. Invoking the *besa*, the commitment to halt the blood feuds, was as close as they came to strategic cooperation amongst themselves.* In the aftermath of the Young Turk revolution, the need for a strong political leadership was paramount but their circumstances precluded it. And yet the

---

* One may almost measure the threat to the Albanian population in any given period by the frequency with which the *besa* was invoked.

Turkish régime had become intolerable – it refused to concede entirely justifiable and moderate demands for autonomy, inevitably pushing the Albanians down the path of separatism.

From 1909 local disturbances developed into open Albanian rebellion against the Empire, encouraged by the Montenegrins who hoped thereby to weaken both the Turks and the Albanians. The elections to the Istanbul parliament in April 1912 were the last straw. The CUP manipulated the results to prevent the return of Albanian deputies. The Kosovo Albanians stormed an arms depot in Djakova and before long controlled the entire vilayet. Hostilities then broke out in the north and the south of Albania, and within weeks several Ottoman army garrisons of Albanian troops mutinied and joined the rebels. The government in Istanbul resigned and the incoming administration promised to address Albanian grievances. There followed a predictable period of foot-dragging. Their patience at an end, the Kosovo Albanians carried out their threat to march on Skopje in Macedonia. The occupation of Skopje in August 1912 by 20,000 Albanian tribesmen was a dramatic demonstration of Ottoman weakness. The Serbs and Bulgarians took it as a signal that the Empire was now uniquely vulnerable. The Albanian rebels even planned to move southwards to Salonika. At this point, the Turkish government finally relented and started to implement plans for autonomy.

This capitulation came too late. Had the CUP conceded earlier and encouraged the Albanians to form a bulwark against the expansionist aims of the Balkan Alliance, the Ottoman Empire might have enjoyed a dignified old age in Europe. But as the exhausted Albanians finally tore their rights from Istanbul, Montenegro, Bulgaria, Serbia and Greece decided to attack.

The First Balkan War: inferno

> Only Dante could properly describe the road from Lozengrad. Only his dark genius could recreate all the horrors of the cold swamps out of which stick the twisted and mutilated bodies of the fallen. Bizarre bulges in the slippery mud. A close look at them and one may identify the features of distorted faces, broken skulls, convulsed hands, shattered teeth . . . Fallen, dead horses and on both sides of the road tens of thousands of shrapnel pieces marked 'Düsseldorf . . . Essen . . .'

Emanuel Skatula, correspondent of the Czech daily, *Právo Lidu*, following the fall of Lozengrad, October 1912[78]

What finally succeeds in bringing armed peace into disrepute, is that today the Great Powers are manifestly unwilling to make war. Each one of them, Germany, England, France and the United States, to name a few, has discovered the obvious truth that the richest country has the most to lose by war, and each country wishes for peace above all things. This is so true that these two Balkan wars have wrought us a new miracle, – we must not forget it, – namely, the active and sincere agreement of the Great Powers who, changing their tactics, have done everything to localize the hostilities in the Balkans and have become the defenders of the peace that they themselves threatened thirty-five years ago, at the time of the Congress of Berlin.

From the Introduction to the *Report of the International Commission to Inquire into the Causes and Conduct of the Balkan Wars*, written five months before the assassination of Archduke Franz Ferdinand in Sarajevo triggered the First World War[79]

The First Balkan War commenced on 8 October 1912 when tiny Montenegro declared war on the mighty Ottoman Empire. It lasted six weeks. The Second Balkan War, ignited by Bulgaria's sudden preventive attack on Serbian forces in late June 1913, was even shorter, barely longer than a month. In these ten weeks of fighting, some 200,000 combatants, excluding civilians, were killed. In addition, tens of thousands fell victim to cholera, typhus and dysentery. The battles were spread out over an area of almost 170,000 square kilometres, stretching from the Albanian coast in the west to a mere 32 kilometres from Istanbul in the east; from the most northerly border of Macedonia down to Thessaly in central Greece. The Ottoman forces were obliged to fight four different wars: against the Bulgarians in Thrace; against the Bulgarians, Serbs and Greeks in Macedonia; against the Serbs and Montenegrins in northern Albania and Kosovo; and against the Greeks in southern Albania. The greatest devastation was inflicted on Macedonia and Thrace.

The vast massacres of the First World War relegated the social and economic impact of the Balkan Wars to the penny place. But those who witnessed or participated in the two wars were given a unique insight into what the twentieth century had in store for the world. Several battles pitted forces against one another which were each larger than Napoleon's largest army, and this at a time when Serbia, for example, had a total population of less than three million. The Bulgarians mobilized a full 25 per cent of their male population, just under 500,000 men. The fighting involved trench warfare and merciless sieges; pitiless artillery assaults on unprotected infantry and civilians; and all sides, except Montenegro and Romania,* deployed aeroplanes against the enemy, mainly for reconnaissance or dropping leaflets but also for the occasional bombing raid. For the first time, technology enabled commanders to fight twenty-four hours a day as huge searchlights illuminated enemy defences.

The atrocities set a pattern of their own. The Russian director, Vladimir Nemirovich-Danchenko, had seen the Russo-Turkish war of 1877–8. During the assignment, he had spent several weeks in a Bulgarian village between Lozengrad and Adrianople, whither he returned in 1912 as a correspondent for *Russkoye Slovo*:

> 'What is that?' I ask our military guide.
> 'A Bulgarian village.'
> 'Karaj-Chiftlik?'
> 'Yes. I know the village well.'
> 'What happened here?'
> 'The Turks came through yesterday.'
>
> The closer we get, the more uneasy my guide and I become. Slaughtered cows. One mooing mournfully while trying to stand . . . We hear a ghastly scream. The guide clutches his rifle . . . It's a little girl. About thirteen years old. The position of her body bears stark witness to what happened. And then cut up with a knife. Around her a puddle of blood . . . She's alive! She screams again. I get down from my horse and peer at her face . . . I will be tortured by that terrible sight through many dreamless nights. Her eyes had been gouged out . . . The dead inhabit every house I enter . . . The church is completely blackened by fire. On the path dead children, little girls with split skulls and legs spread apart. The criminals probably caught the crowd as they were fleeing for sanctuary. The inside

* Calling Romania a belligerent is stretching a point, but Bucharest exploited the massive coalition against Bulgaria in the Second Balkan War to occupy and annex the southern Dobrudja in north-eastern Bulgaria.

of the church is a terrible stage . . . Once my eyes get used to the dark, I see the pile of burnt bodies of people desperate to break down the doors, locked from the outside, as the building went up in flames.[80]

After Montenegrin forces pushed against the open door of Turkish defences in northern Albania, the other countries in the Balkan Alliance waited a week before launching a massive attack on different parts of Ottoman territory. Four large Serb armies swept south. The main force under the command of Crown Prince Aleksandar aimed at the largest concentration of Turkish troops at Kumanovo in northern Macedonia; the second army crossed into Bulgaria and from there into eastern Macedonia to harass the main Turkish army from the rear; Kosovo was the target of the third army, while the fourth took Novi Pazar, linking Montenegro and Serbia across the Sanjak.

In Thrace, the two main Bulgarian armies fell like sledge hammers on the fortresses of Lozengrad (now Kirklareli in north-western Turkey) and Adrianople (Edirne in Turkey), which was the gateway to Istanbul. They were encouraged by patriotic hysteria which had been building up in the press of all the states for months. On the eve of war, banner headlines in the Belgrade papers exhorted Serbs to 'Get ready for war! The joint Serbo-Bulgarian offensive will start any minute now!' News of the Montenegrins' swift progress on the road to Skutari (Shkoder in Albania) was reported ecstatically, while other pages were adorned with fanciful pictures of 'Old Serbia', the medieval kingdom which the new state was determined to win back. Newspapers invited poets to contribute patriotic lines, such as this outburst:

Farewell father! Farewell dear mother!
I can no longer stay with you.
If the King calls me into the battle for vengeance
Do not wait for me, nurture me no more!
God save you! Farewell! God bless you!
And mourn my young life!
Hurrah, comrades! Fall in line!
Under the bloody banner!
Forward! Forward![81]

In Bulgaria, newsboys swarmed through the streets of Sofia, Plovdiv and Stara Zagora, selling *priturki*, special editions of the newspapers bloated with exaggerated accounts of the army's progress. The entire economic life of Serbia and Bulgaria was diverted to the war effort. Belgrade, Leon Trotsky reported,

> has a special air about it – on the alert like a military camp. Everyone and everything is subordinated to the demands of the mobilization . . . The streets are full of mobilized men and men about to be mobilized. The shops are empty . . . Industry is at a standstill, apart from the branch that serves the needs of mobilization and the coming war . . . For ten days already railway travel has been suspended in Serbia: the trains carry only soldiers and war materials . . . If Belgrade is an armed camp, the railway station is the heart of this camp. Military authority reigns there exclusively.[82]

This intense ideological fervour in Bulgaria and Serbia underpinned the crushing military successes of the First Balkan War. All neutral eye-witnesses to the campaigns confirmed the determination and courage of officers, conscripts and reservists alike to realize the simple aim that had been pounded into them over and over again – liberate our Christian brothers; liberate our historical lands. Simplicity was the key, and details were awkward. Nationalist romanticism, based on a dubious mixture of demographic and historical arguments, provided the justification for the war. The real aims were coldly strategic and expansionist.

The Alliance had waited for the right moment before releasing the immense political energy which had built up in their countries. Turkey was compelled to fight a defensive war in a state of exhaustion brought on by political collapse and, on the military level, years of counter-insurgency in its European territories. The apathetic atmosphere in Istanbul in the late summer of 1912 suggests that there was little interest in and certainly no enthusiasm for war, and the lack of popular support was a fatal blow to an already demoralized army. The heterogeneous composition of Ottoman society, especially in and near the theatres of war, prevented the Turkish military from waging a nationalist war, defensive or otherwise. 'On Istanbul's main street, the Rue du

Pera', wrote the French correspondent, Georges Rémond,

> there are impenetrable crowds of this cosmopolitan people, the cinemas are full, cafés where orchestras play are packed – as if there was no war at all! Huge posters inviting people to the film 'Magda, Child of Love.' Of course, the crowds include many Greeks, there are Italians, French, Montenegrins. The Greeks are quite open about what they think. If they see Turks going off to the front, they humiliate them by shouting 'Zoa! Zoa! (Beasts, animals).' Here in Istanbul, three quarters of the population are enemies of the Turks![83]

The First Balkan War: Macedonia, 1912

The battlefields provided still less comfort for the Turks. Nine days after the outbreak of hostilities, the Serbs had routed the main Turkish force at Kumanovo. This victory opened the road to Skopje, which was soon under Serbian control. Hours before the Turks evacuated the town in panic, a twenty-two-year-old official at the railway station described how

> the most terrible events erupted in Kumanovo. Turks began beating Christians and Christians Turks. Most of the Christians hid at home. As the Serb bombardment approached, the earth began to shake and windows started to shatter. The first Turk divisions ran amok through the town in chaotic retreat. They had no guns, open wounds without tourniquet, maimed, blood soaked and barefoot . . . Serbian shrapnel began falling on the station and the railway personnel scattered as if being shot at like sparrows.[84]

The Macedonian campaign was fought in atrocious conditions. Rain and snow created mud-soaked battlefields and trails. The entire region was littered with the corpses of soldiers, civilians and horses. As the Serb soldiery moved to Skopje and beyond, they visited destruction and murder on the local Albanian population. Fired by tales of atrocities committed on Christian peasants during the unrest in the Albanian territories, the Serbs unleashed the full force of nationalist hatred against defenceless villages. A

Serb Social Democrat, serving as a reservist, described how

> the horrors actually began as soon as we crossed the old frontier. By five p.m. we were approaching Kumanovo. The sun had set, it was starting to get dark. But the darker the sky became, the more brightly the fearful illumination of the fires stood out against it. Burning was going on all around us. Entire Albanian villages had been turned into pillars of fire . . . In all its fiery monotony this picture was repeated the whole way to Skopje . . . For two days before my arrival in Skopje the inhabitants had woken up in the morning to the sight, under the principal bridge over the Vardar – that is, in the very centre of the town – of heaps of Albanian corpses with severed heads. Some said that these were local Albanians, killed by the *komitadjis* [*četniks*], others that the corpses had been brought down to the bridge by the waters of the Vardar. What was clear was that these headless men had not been killed in battle.[85]

In Skopje, the chief instigator of the massacres was the Black Hand, which set up its headquarters close to the Russian consulate in a building soon known as the Black House. The Black Hand, with its network of agents, had escaped the control of the military authorities and was increasingly assuming the role of an informal government of 'liberated Old Serbia'. After several weeks, the government in Belgrade started to appoint civilian administrators to these territories, but those who refused to submit to the demands of the Black Hand and the *četniks* were scared. Branislav Nušić, the writer who had welcomed the war with such enthusiasm, resigned as governor of Bitola in fear and disgust at the activities of these units.

Nonetheless, the Serbs marshalled a very effective military force and aside from some criticism of the initial assault on Kumanovo, the general staff had planned an astute campaign which greatly impressed foreign observers. Both the Serbian and the Bulgarian armies were now discussed with respect in Germany, Austria-Hungary, Russia, France and Britain. The myth of both nations as determined and stubborn fighters was born during the Balkan Wars and consolidated (albeit in very different circumstances) during the First World War. Before the emergence of the new Balkan states in the nineteenth century, they had been without military experience for five centuries. The majority of the population were sedentary, listless and extremely unwarlike peasants who occasionally indulged in the brigandage of the *hajduci* – but this hardly amounts to a military tradition. The real warriors among the Balkan peoples were the Albanians. The ability of the Bulgarians and Serbs to create a military tradition out of nothing was due to the success of channelling economic and educational resources into the military in the period between the Serbo-Bulgarian war and the Balkan Wars. Similarly, the decline of the Albanians' reputation as warriors is directly linked to the difficulties the Albanians faced in forging a coherent state out of the ashes of the Ottoman Empire.

The Greek military position lay somewhere between that of the Serbians and the Albanians. Despite facing the weakest opposition in their thrust north to Epirus and east to Salonika, the Greeks were unable to take Ioannina, which was fiercely defended by a Turkish garrison. As they pushed north through Macedonia in the direction of Bitola, which according to the Serb-Greek understanding the Greeks were supposed to occupy, they became the only army in the Balkan Alliance to suffer a serious military reverse at the hands of the Ottomans. For this reason, and much to the irritation of the Serbian command, it was the Serbs who had to push on to confront the Ottoman army at its last stand near Bitola.

The battle for this small town, the inglorious end of Turkish rule in Macedonia, was the largest single confrontation of the Balkan Wars. Some 110,000 Serbs were mustered to the north and west of the town ranged against 80 or 90,000 Turkish soldiers. After three days of fighting, which left 12,000 Serbian and 17,000 Turkish dead, the Ottoman forces finally capitulated on 18 November. Some 45,000 men were taken prisoner by the Serbs; another 30,000 escaped to the mountains of the Macedonian-Albanian border. Turkey-in-Europe was all but finished.

The Greeks were none too perturbed about their failure to fight at Bitola. Five days before the battle commenced, Crown Prince Constantine had made his ceremonial entrance into Salonika, drenched by a cold winter rain. Soon after the Serb offensive against Kumanovo had begun, the telegraphic lines to and from Salonika had ceased working. It was not until large numbers of Turkish and Albanian refugees started arriving in the city that the population began to understand the extent of the military disaster facing the

Empire. Some 20,000 refugees were put up in the local mosques in deplorably unhygienic conditions. They were soon followed by the retreating soldiers, some escaping the Serbs, some the Greeks moving eastwards from Mount Olympus, and others being pushed back by the Bulgarian Rila division racing down the Struma river. The Greek and Bulgarian forces were desperate to reach the city first. Salonika was the single greatest prize of the First Balkan War and there had been no prior agreement about its status. In this case, possession would count for all of the law. Constantine and the troops under his command beat the Rila division by a matter of hours. As he strolled into Salonika, the Greek inhabitants swamped the city in blue and white colours. Accompanying him was Theoktistos, the Patriarch of Athens who joined the Metropolitan of Salonika, Gennadios, in celebrating a special Mass in the Church of St Minas. 'Glory to the triumph of the Hellenes and the venerated diadoque [the Crown Prince]', proclaimed Gennadios. 'Hosannah to the glorious sons of the warriors of Marathon and Salamina, the valiant liberators of our fatherland!'[86]

There was no fanfare and no enthusiasm to greet the belated entrance of the bedraggled Bulgarian troops. Their commanders needed no reminding how serious their failure was to reach the city first. In a noble gesture, the Greeks postponed the restitution of mosques to the Patriarchy so that they could be used by the Muslim refugees. But on 13 November, a platoon of Bulgarian soldiers threw out the refugees in the St Sophia mosque and mounted a cross at its entrance and raised the Bulgarian flag. Not to be outdone, the Greeks did the same in the St Dimitri Church and the Rotonda. The real victims of this hideous little game were, of course, the Muslim refugees, but it also prefigured the divisions among the Balkan states which would soon rip the Alliance apart. The Jews of Salonika, for the moment still the majority population, were hoping that the peace negotiations would award the city to the Bulgarians, the lesser of two evils in their eyes. If Bulgaria controlled the city, it could still maintain its trading connections to the Balkan hinterland. Should the Greeks consolidate their position, Salonika would be cut off from its markets and become an economic backwater. Of all the allies, Greece had suffered the least casualties, human and material, during the First Balkan War and had walked off with the greatest prize. For the Greeks, it was a good war.

The First Balkan War: Thrace

Despite military intelligence to the contrary, and the numerical superiority of the Alliance forces, the great powers all assumed at the outset of war that the Ottoman Empire could not be defeated. In 1895, Sultan Abdülhamid had requested the German field marshal, Colmar von der Goltz Paşa, to reorganize the army. Although von der Goltz was worried about the defensive preparations undertaken by the Defence Ministry, he shared many of his compatriots' illusions about the Ottoman military capability. When in late October 1912 Bulgarian forces surrounded the fortress of Lozengrad, their first tactical target, von der Goltz dismissed the assault. 'Lozengrad is one of the best fortresses in the world', he announced, 'there is no need to strengthen it as it is as unassailable as Gibraltar. It could only be stormed under two conditions. Firstly, it must be besieged for three months. Secondly, the besieging army would have to be Prussian.'[87] Three days later, following a disastrous misunderstanding between two Turkish military commanders, Lozengrad fell to the Bulgarians. The Turkish army began a shambolic retreat, during which it suffered huge losses in the battles of Lüle Burgas and Babaeski. These defeats highlighted the damage which Abdülhamid had inflicted on Turkey's military readiness. Lozengrad, Adrianople, Babaeski and Lüle Burgas formed a quadrilateral of fortress defences intended to block any land advance to Istanbul. In 1882, the military had submitted a plan for the reconstruction and strengthening of all four. Abdülhamid released funds for the reconstruction of Adrianople but not for the other three. After Lozengrad had fallen, the Bulgarians laid siege to Adrianople for a full five months. The city on the Maritsa river was completely cut off from all supplies but the Bulgarians were unable to break the siege. Had the three other fortresses in the quadrilateral been strengthened in the same way, the Turks might not have lost the Thracian war.

Instead, they were forced to evacuate the entire region, except Adrianople. As the Bulgarian army moved forwards the retreating army retaliated against the Christian population. The Carnegie Commission confirmed one incident in which

> a woman of Haskovo described how her little child was thrown up into the air by a Turkish soldier who caught it on

> the point of his bayonet. Other women told how three young girls threw themselves into a well after their fiancés were shot. At Varna about twenty women living together confirmed this story, and added that the Turkish soldiers went down into the well and dragged the girls out. Two of them were dead; the third had a broken leg; despite her agony she was outraged by two Turks. Other women of Varna saw the soldier who had transfixed the baby on his bayonet carrying it in triumph across the village.[88]

Turks who were unable to escape the oncoming army were subject to similar Bulgarian retribution. Mosques, razed to the ground by dynamite or fire, became a familiar sight in the wake of the Bulgarian advance. In the battle for Lozengrad and the battle for the Ervene, as the series of encounters during the Bulgarian push on Istanbul is known, some 25,000 Bulgarians fell, while the Turks lost 45,000 men. The Turkish army, however, was able to regroup 32 kilometres west of Istanbul at the fortress of Çatalca and form a defensive line which stretched north-east as far as the Black Sea. This adroit manoeuvre was carried out despite the terrible spread of disease through the Turkish ranks. Exhaustion was beginning to slow the Bulgarians down as the army's supply lines became overstretched. When the Bulgarians finally reached the Çatalca line, both forces enjoyed a few days respite as the Bulgarians positioned their heavy artillery.

The assault on Çatalca began in the early morning of 17 November. It was the most spectacularly violent event of the Balkan Wars. Some 900 Bulgarian guns let loose their shells on the Turkish defences, creating a dense fog of smoke and explosions on a front of about 50 kilometres, from the Derkos forest on the Black Sea down to Çatalca. Eye-witnesses described the force of the attack as resembling a mighty earthquake. The noise and the smoke was audible and visible 32 kilometres away in Istanbul, where panic seized the inhabitants. Christians and Muslims alike were convinced that the Bulgarians would soon be entering Istanbul to return Constantinople to the Christian world. Both communities were seized by the fear of massacre. The consulates of the great powers were besieged by Christians seeking sanctuary. The powers acted swiftly, agreeing among themselves to send two warships each to the Bosphorus in order to prevent disorder and bloodshed. Sultan Reşid, the puppet ruler installed by the CUP after the 1909 counter-revolution to replace Abdülhamid, fled the capital, the first and last time that an Ottoman sultan had ever left Istanbul under duress.

And yet the Turkish army held out. The commanders had learnt lessons from their crushing errors at the beginning of the campaign. Their artillery defences were well hidden and their tactics seduced the Bulgarians into attempting an advance across the marshy region south of the Derkos forest, where the attackers were literally bogged down. Simultaneously, the well-organized sea-line defence on the Dardanelles rebuffed the Greek navy's attempt to enter the Sea of Marmara. The battle on the Dardanelles was another important lesson for the Turks, which they put to excellent use three years later when Commonwealth forces made their push on Istanbul during the First World War. As the two armies dug in around Çatalca, they both brought in reinforcements. Bulgarian divisions made the long trip via Macedonia with the assistance of the Greek navy, while Turkey's vast reserves of peasant cannon fodder from Anatolia finally started to arrive in Istanbul.

In place of the massive battle which everybody feared, an armistice was arranged. The Bulgarians had made huge territorial gains but their armed forces were stretched to the limit. In addition, growing tension between the Bulgarians and their Serb and Greek allies over the division of spoils in Macedonia had alarmed the government in Sofia.

The First Balkan War: the Skutari stratagem

When the armistice was signed, all that remained of the Ottoman territories in Europe was the small chunk of land between Istanbul and Çatalca; the Gallipoli peninsula; a few patches of central Albania, whither the defeated army from Bitola had fled; and the besieged cities of Adrianople, Ioannina and Skutari. The armistice extended to Adrianople although the Bulgarian siege force was strengthened by the arrival of Serbian troops and the Alliance denied the Turks the right to supply the town with food. However, a state of war remained at both Ioannina and Skutari, the most southerly and northerly fortresses in Albania controlled by joint

Turkish/Albanian forces. The Greeks had refused to sign the armistice so that they could continue the siege of Ioannina, which eventually surrendered to Crown Prince Constantine on 6 March 1913. The commander of the Turkish garrison in Skutari refused the terms of the ceasefire. And so the war continued in little pockets through the winter, the weather restricting fighting to the occasional skirmish.

Although it lay outside the two main theatres of war, the struggle for Albania during the First Balkan War illuminated the intricate web of relationships between the great powers, the emerging states, the haphazard development of national consciousness and, even, personal ambition. It demonstrated how fearfully difficult the transition from an archaic, multinational Empire to modern nation states would be, given the extreme complexity of the Ottoman demographic and social heritage.

After declaring war against Turkey in October 1912, the Montenegrins headed for Skutari in northern Albania – this was to be the great prize for Nikola, King of Montenegro. The Serbs later joined up with Montenegrin forces on their march westwards to the port of Durrës. Serbia and Montenegro wanted to acquire Albanian territory to secure an outlet to the sea. Their actions were dictated by the logic of nascent regional imperialism. At one point during the Albanian campaign, Nikola offered the great powers the limp excuse that he coveted Skutari because one of his ancestors was buried there. Beyond this, however, the Serbs and Montenegrins made little attempt to justify the occupation of the Albanian-inhabited territories. The Serbs had a case to argue with regard to Kosovo, if the validity of ancient 'historical' rights were accepted. But because borders in the Balkans were drawn either according to the arbitrary dictates of the great powers or during war, this meant that the relative merits of historical, demographic or strategic claims to a region were never properly defined. Italy and Austria-Hungary also aimed to extend their influence in Albania. On 12 November 1912, the two great powers issued Belgrade and Cetinje (the old Montenegrin capital) with démarches insisting on a withdrawal from Albania and an end to Montenegro's siege of Skutari. Vienna and Rome both argued quite reasonably that Serbia and Montenegro had no business in the region because it was inhabited almost exclusively by Albanians. Belgrade and Cetinje asked why, since this principle applied neither in Bosnia nor in Tripolitania, territories annexed by Austria-Hungary and Italy respectively, it should apply in Albania.

States or nationalist ideologues could conjure up a territorial claim in an instant. But the key to realizing these claims lay in a mixture of astute politics and naked force. The most effective political weapon the Balkan states could employ was that of divide and rule. Both Serbia and Montenegro incited the Albanians of Kosovo and northern Albania to rebel against the Turks on the eve of the Balkan Wars, thus setting current and future enemies against each other. When Montenegro invaded northern Albania, its armies were initially supported by the Mallasori, a tribe of Albanian Catholics. King Nikola had persuaded the Mallasori that their rights and traditions would be better protected under the wing of a Christian, albeit Orthodox and Slav, ruler than under Muslim Albanians, but it did not take the Mallasori too long to realize they had made a mistake.

As the Balkan states grew in confidence, they began to use the same strategy in their relations with the great powers. During the Albanian events, the Serbs and Montenegrins could emit veiled threats that Russia might be prepared to offer them military guarantees if Austria-Hungary or Italy were to intervene. Translated, this message read: 'Do not interfere with our occupation of Albania as it might spark a European war.' This not only affected Vienna and Rome, it was a matter of the greatest concern to Paris, London and Berlin as well, because Europe was now clearly divided into two hostile camps, the Triple Alliance and the Entente. Of course, for Serbia or Montenegro to toy with the idea of using naked force against a great power involved serious risks for them, because of the awesome disparity of forces.

The Balkan states were also vulnerable to more insidious internal enemies. The extraordinary social mobilization against the Ottoman Empire, fired by a spirit of intense nationalism, could only be sustained for a short period of time. After a few months of war in atrocious conditions, the thoughts of idle soldiers would return to the fields and livestock as spring drew closer, especially after the troops had exhausted the possibilities for plunder. The ferocious version of nationalism considered by many westerners to be endemic in the Balkans has only ever been sustainable for brief periods by governments before it begins to soften, then fragment and finally decay. Its life span is even shorter in times of military defeat, as Bulgaria was to find out to its cost in the summer of 1913. When Serbia and Montenegro raised the stakes in their Skutari stratagem, they were aware that failure or stalemate could have serious consequences. King Nikola, by no means loved by all his subjects, had invested much of his political capital into taking Skutari. His popularity began to be eroded in the early spring of 1913 when the Montenegrin forces sustained enormous losses in failed assaults on the fortress. And as international pressure on Montenegro to withdraw grew, the mood of the besiegers, a quarter of whom had already fallen, became distinctly mutinous. The King was prepared to risk a much bigger conflagration to consolidate his position among the Montenegrins, as he had nothing to lose.

Just before the démarches of 12 November, St Petersburg had warned Belgrade that Russia would not go to war for the sake of Durrës. Nonetheless, Russia began mobilizing. When Vienna issued the démarches, Austria matched Russia's military preparations receiving German backing for its move while France supported Russia. The clouds of European war thickened quickly. Were it not for a deft, conciliatory intervention by the British Foreign Secretary, Sir Edward Grey, Durrës and Skutari would now enjoy the historical notoriety which belongs to Sarajevo. On 20 December 1912, following the Ambassadors' Conference which Grey convened in London to cool tempers, all six powers agreed on the establishment of an autonomous (effectively an independent) Albania and on a guarantee for Serbian access to the Adriatic. The ambassadors at the London Conference could wipe their brows and celebrate Christmas with a clean conscience. Or so they thought.

The Conference deferred the arbitration of the borders of the new Albanian state to a commission. This confounded Austria-Hungary's central aim of ending the Montenegrin siege of Skutari so that Vienna might turn the largely Catholic city into a strategic outpost of Habsburg power in the southern Balkans. The Montenegrins hung on as Russia and Austria-Hungary squabbled diplomatically about borders, and on 23 April 1913, Essad Paşa, the commander of the Turkish garrison defending the city, handed over the keys of Skutari to King Nikola in a shoddy little ceremony on the Neptune, a rickety wooden ship on Lake Skutari. It is widely believed, but never conclusively proven, that Essad pocketed a substantial sum from the Montenegrins. If he did take the money, then he might reasonably have argued that in the absence of aid from the great powers, he was wise to profit from his hopeless situation and facilitate the evacuation of the beleaguered Skutari garrison to fight another day. He left the town with 20,000 men and their light arms in order to link up with another Ottoman army adrift in central Albania.

Skutari was a corpse when the Montenegrins entered it. Civilians were starving and the six months of bombardment had rendered much of the town uninhabitable. This did not prevent Nikola's troops from indulging in the usual spree of violent pillaging. Once Skutari had fallen to Montenegro, the great powers were faced with another serious headache; 'for there was a widespread fear that Russia would not be able to agree to the ejection of the Montenegrins from the city which the Austrians would certainly demand. The British ambassador in St Petersburg thought war inevitable.'[89] A clash between Russia and Austria was again narrowly avoided after mediators succeeded in paying off King Nikola with a loan of 6 million francs, which he used to quell the growing dissatisfaction with his régime. In early May, King Nikola withdrew his bewildered troops from Skutari. The crisis was over. But it was a close call – Germany and Britain had signally failed to cooperate over the second Skutari crisis, preferring instead to stand by their allies in the Triple Alliance and the Entente. The two episodes had demonstrated alarmingly how the idiosyncratic behaviour of the shrewd, if unappealing ruler of the least significant country in the Balkans could lock the great powers on to a course leading to general European war. The great powers seemed to have all but lost their ability to cajole the Balkan states into serving external interests on the peninsula. The Balkans were not the powder keg, as is so often believed: the metaphor is inaccurate. They were merely the powder trail that the great powers themselves had laid. The powder keg was Europe.

The Second Balkan War: Bulgaria's catastrophe, 1913

The Balkan Wars should have finished at the London Conference in January 1913. But the humiliation of the Turkish army reignited the bitter domestic struggle in Istanbul between the Liberals and the

CUP. At the time of the negotiations, the Liberals were in control of the government under the experienced administrator Kiamil Paşa. His negotiating team in London did its best to persuade the Alliance delegates to soften their territorial demands. The chief sticking point was Adrianople – the Alliance insisted that it be handed over to the Bulgarians; the Turks refused to concede it. On 6 January, the conference was suspended and the Bulgarian and Serbian allies surrounding Adrianople prepared to renew their assault on the city. Under intense pressure from the great powers, Kiamil finally conceded Adrianople on 22 January, having extracted a concession that allowed the Turks to protect the grave of sultans in the mosque of Selim II.

The next day saw an ominous gathering of the *softas* in front of the building of the Sublime Porte. These were the religious students whose demonstration had brought down Sultan Abdülaziz in 1876. Their presence in large numbers invariably prefaced major change and the slogan under which they marched in 1913 left nobody in any doubt: 'Death rather than dishonourable peace!' A bloody *coup* led by Enver Bey, the founder of the CUP, followed immediately. The most prominent victim was the Turkish army's commander in chief, Nazim Paşa, who was replaced by the CUP's candidate, Izzet Paşa. The conspiracy tore up the proposed peace agreement and at seven o'clock in the evening of 3 February hostilities resumed in Adrianople – along the Çatalca line and on the Gallipoli peninsula at sea and on land.

These were blood-soaked battles, characterized by a high degree of futility. The battle for Adrianople, which fell to the allies after five months' heroic defence by the Turks on 26 March 1913, was the crowning misery of the Balkan Wars. The figures for those who died during the siege have never been properly collated, and estimates vary between 40,000 and 60,000. Military doctors described how the legs of thousands of Turkish soldiers froze solid in the trenches during the harsh winter; how the thick blanket of snow which fell in January was drenched in red for days after the resumption of hostilities at the beginning of February. When the Turkish commander, Şukri Paşa, evacuated his troops, he gave the order to destroy all stocks of bread in the city. The Bulgarian troops entered a vast mortuary, stepping over the dead bodies which littered the streets, victims of artillery shells, cholera and, above all else, of hunger. A journalist who entered the city with the Bulgarians later wrote,

> The further into this island I go, the more ghastly this theatre of blood. Here are lying those who can no longer move but who nobody on this earth can protect anymore. They are living death on the ground which will claim them maybe tomorrow, maybe the day after . . . The ghastly smiles of the dead and the dying. Everywhere bodies reduced to mere bones, blue hands ripped from their forearms, the bizarre gestures, empty eye-sockets, open mouths as if calling in desperation, the shattered teeth behind the torn and blackened lips.[90]

The Turks held out along Çatalca and in Gallipoli, but nowhere else. In May 1913, all sides, under pressure from the great powers, agreed to the provisions of the Treaty of London. *Enosis* between Crete and Greece was finally realized. Edirne became Adrianople in Bulgaria. Albania's status was promoted from autonomy to full independence. Only one issue remained – the division of Macedonia. The great sabre of Osmanli was sheathed, not quite for the last time, but blunt and rusted.

Bulgaria, whose forces had delivered up the greatest sacrifices to bury the Ottomans, was now a large country – the biggest in the Balkans. Its boundaries looked out on the Black Sea, the Sea of Marmara and the Aegean. But the First Balkan War had drained most of the life blood from this young body. Bulgaria was weak and vulnerable and its allies regarded the new regional power with jealousy and fear.

Serbia had occupied most of the Macedonian territory which was to have been placed before Tsar Nicholas II for arbitration. The Serbian government argued that it now had the primary claim on this territory because it had been forced out of Albania by the great powers and because Bulgaria should be satisfied with its access to the three seas. During the spring, the Romanian government had demanded sovereignty over Bulgaria's north-eastern corner, southern Dobrudja, to ensure a stable balance of power in the region. The Greeks wanted to expel the Bulgarians from the region surrounding Salonika and to press home their claims to the Thracian port of

Kavala. Wherever possible, the Turks encouraged this dissension among the members of the Balkan League whilst continuing to strengthen their forces on the Çatalca line in preparation for retaking Adrianople.

The First Balkan War was characterized by exceptional brutality and an utter disregard for the civilian populations whose misfortune it was to inhabit the combat areas. Wherever any of the Alliance governments spotted an opportunity to grab additional slices of territory, they did so even where there was no historical or demographic justification for it. In the spring and early summer, the Serbs and the Greeks had begun the enforced Serbianization and Hellenization of the parts of Macedonia they now controlled. In the Bulgarian-occupied area, *četniks* victimized Jews and Turks. Civilians who refused to accept the nationality of the incoming administration (if one can call plundering thugs 'administrators') were run out of town, harassed or murdered.

The Balkan Alliance may have been right in its central argument in 1912 that Turkey failed to carry out its commitment to reforms in Macedonia and, indeed, that the position of the Christians throughout European Turkey had deteriorated since the second CUP revolution in 1909. There was no such excuse for the Second Balkan War, which began on 13 June 1913. This was motivated by sheer greed and nothing else. Greece and Serbia simply decided to attack Bulgaria in its moment of maximum weakness, exhausted by its sacrifices the previous winter.

The Bulgarians were by no means blameless. It was the disastrous secret order, sent by General Savov to his front-line troops in Macedonia and Serbia on 28 June, to launch surprise attacks on the Serbs, which triggered the war just as all sides had agreed to hold negotiations under the chairmanship of Tsar Nicholas. The Bulgarian army leadership had been under tremendous strain. A series of mutinies had broken out among the troops in Thrace, who were fed up with war and were demanding to be demobilized. The spirit of Bulgarian nationalism had lost its fire for the time being:

> Harvest time approached and the Bulgarian soldier who, after what he had suffered and endured during the long months of winter and spring at Tchataldja and Boulair, had then, instead of returning home, been compelled to join the army on the

western frontier, had had enough. One thing or the other: it was war or demobilization: but in any case there must be an immediate decision, for uncertainty had become intolerable. This state of mind was general and several officers told Mr. Bouchier what he repeated in the *Times*, 'If the question is not decided in a week, General Savov will no longer have an army.'[91]

The Second Balkan War lasted only a month. Once again, the peasants of Macedonia were the unwilling martyrs. Most instructive, however, is the ease with which those directing this war could manipulate the image of the enemy in the minds of their troops. Less than a month before the outbreak of the war, Serbs and Greeks had been fighting with the Bulgarians. Now, Greeks and Serbs invited local Turks to join them in atrocities against the Bulgarian peasantry. The Greek and Serbian armies swept through the Macedonian and Thracian hinterland, murdering the defenceless. Their hysteria is best summed up, in the words of the Carnegie Commission report, by

> a gaudily colored print, which was seen in the streets of Salonika and Piraeus, eagerly brought by the Greek soldiers returning to their homes, [which] reveals the depth of the brutality to which this race hatred had sunk them. It shows a Greek evzone holding a living Bulgarian soldier with both hands, while he gnaws the face of his victim with his teeth, like some beast of prey. It is entitled the *Bulgarophagos* (Bulgar-eater), and is adorned with the following verses:
>
> *The sea of fire which boils in my breast*
> *And calls for vengeance with the savage waves of my soul*
> *Will be quenched when the monsters of Sofia are still*
> *And their life blood extinguishes my hate.*
>
> Another popular battle picture shows a Greek soldier gouging out the eyes of a living Bulgarian.[92]

Nationalist violence knows no eternal enemy. The current enemy is always eternal.

Under the terms of the Treaty of Bucharest concluded in mid-August 1913, Bulgaria was forced to surrender almost everything for which tens of thousands of its citizens had been required to sacrifice their lives. Adrianople became Edirne again after just three months. The Romanians occupied the southern Dobrudja. Large parts of Macedonia became southern Serbia. Viscount Grey, the British Foreign Secretary during the Balkan Wars, later recalled that the Treaty of Bucharest:

> left Bulgaria sore, injured, and despoiled of what she believed belonged to her. Any future Balkan peace was impossible so long as the treaty of Bucharest remained. Turkey, of course, was also sore and despoiled. Thus when the great war came a year later, there were two Powers, Bulgaria and Turkey, hungering for a revanche and ready to take whichever side would give them a prospect of obtaining it. This naturally was the side of Austria and Germany.[93]

CHAPTER 4

THE EMPIRE OF ILLUSIONS

The northern Balkans, 1878–1914

> The political and cultural backwardness of the Balkan peoples prevented them from seeing the entire political complexity of their situation as it really was. This necessarily led to numerous illusions which assumed the importance of facts and which were then believed to be facts.
>
> Veselin Masleše on *Young Bosnia*, 1945[1]

From Prokuplje to eternity: Serbia and Bosnia

There is a small, drab town in south-western Serbia that I can only ever recall as being bathed in mud, churned up and dirtied by pigs, cattle and fumes from the rattling exhausts of two-stroke engines. Signs on the modest shopfronts that line the main street have letters missing, and the newsstands are covered in yellowing magazines that no one wants to buy. The road leading west out of Prokuplje soon crosses the border separating Serbia proper from Kosovo. This is the region inhabited chiefly by Albanians but claimed by Serbian nationalists as the symbol of an almost supernatural continuity between the medieval Serbian state and modern Serbia.

At the beginning of October 1912, Prokuplje, no doubt as muddy then as now, was a seething military camp. The Serbian army, preparing for the onslaught against the dying Ottoman Empire, looked hungrily not only at Kosovo but beyond the Šar mountains into Albania proper as far as the Adriatic port of Drač (or Durrës as the Albanians, the people who actually lived there, called it). Thousands of Slav volunteers from outside Serbia poured into the region, placing an enormous strain on Prokuplje's fragile infrastructure. But personal discomfort mattered little. These men had mustered to take part in the fulfilment of a dream. After five hundred years, Serbia was ready to avenge itself for the battle of Kosovo in 1389 – the Turks would be run out of old Serbia and the kingdom of Dušan Silni (Dušan the Strong) re-established. They travelled by train, on foot, on mules. They wore tattered uniforms or none at all, brandishing makeshift weapons. Unshaven, straight from the fields or the twilight world of scruffy Belgrade cafés – an army of dream makers, deeply sincere and deeply unaware that their dream, like so many in the sleep of collapsing empires would eventually prove to be a nightmare. Almost a century later, the road to Kosovo from Prokuplje is a geographical and historical cul-de-sac, whether Serbs care to admit it or not. Ninety years ago, it smelt, it felt and it looked like a dream.

From the provinces of Croatia, Slavonia, Dalmatia, Bosnia and Hercegovina in the neighbouring Habsburg Empire, young Serbs but also Croats and Muslims, fired by an emerging, if ill-defined sense of south Slavic brotherhood, offered their services to the Serbian military and the *četnik* irregulars mustering in Prokuplje. Among the students were two teenage Serbs, one from Belgrade, strong and handsome, the other from Bosnia, pale and weak with sunken blue eyes.

Before presenting himself to the recruiting officer, the first young man wrote a postcard to a friend in Sarajevo: 'Look up on the map where Prokuplje is. We have arrived, but where we go from here we do not know. For Freedom and fatherland.' To his brother, he wrote: 'Prokuplje, the road to Kuršumlija. I am heading for the city of Tsar Dušan.* I will be overjoyed if they accept me as a volunteer.' His colleague from Belgrade added: 'If we do not see each other again, please accept our final greetings. I know where we are bound, and if we survive we shall certainly know where we have been. If you are pious, pray to God for us, but if not, ask the young ladies to pray for us.'

Simo Miljuš, the first student, fought for his country in the Balkan Wars and the First World War before falling victim, as a prominent Yugoslav communist in Moscow, to the NKVD when

* Kuršumlija and the city of Tsar Dušan are references to the impending battle for Kosovo (Kuršumlija is the last town in Serbia proper before Kosovo) and Skopje.

Stalin decapitated the leadership of 'fraternal' parties in the 1930s. But Miljuš and his friend were brimming with optimism as they walked into the recruitment centre in Prokuplje. Here they found Major Vojin Tankosić, a gruff senior officer with responsibility for organizing the volunteers, who was also a leading member of the Black Hand. As the two teenagers entered his office, Tankosić was reinterpreting the legend of Wilhelm Tell by firing his pistol at a cigarette packet resting on the head of one of his soldiers. When introduced to the sunken-eyed student from Bosnia, Tankosić dismissed him with a snort. 'You are too small and too weak', he barked, ordering him out of town and threatening to have him beaten up if he did not comply immediately.

Humiliated and in despair at his rejection, Gavrilo Princip returned first to Belgrade and soon after to Sarajevo. By then, he was determined to prove Major Tankosić wrong. Twenty months later, on 28 June 1914, he had his moment when he fired the bullet, supplied, ironically, by Tankosić, which split the jugular vein and then lodged in the neck of Archduke Franz Ferdinand, the nephew of Emperor Franz Joseph I and the heir to the imperial Habsburg throne. 'You must stay alive to take care of the children', he whispered desperately to his wife, the Duchess of Hohenberg, unaware that she was already dead. As he lay dying in the back of his splendid new Gräf & Stift luxury motor car, he gasped repeatedly through blood-spattered lips, 'Es ist nichts. Es ist nichts.'* Although frequently wrong in his lifetime, the Archduke was never quite so wide of the mark as he was in the minutes before his death.

Macedonia was the nemesis of the Ottoman Empire. Bosnia, which Franz Joseph believed held the key to his empire's rejuvenation, was as fatal for the House of Habsburg as Macedonia had been for the House of Osmanli. The Emperor saw Bosnia as the new fortress from which he could dominate the economic and political life of the northern Balkans. If all went well, Vienna would eventually be connected by an unbroken line of Habsburg-owned rail track with Salonika and the Aegean Sea. In this way Franz Joseph sought compensation for the subservient role which Kaiser Wilhelm I and Bismarck had compelled him to play in the German-speaking

---

* 'It is nothing. It is nothing.'

world ever since Prussia defeated the Austrian army at Königgrätz in 1866. Bosnia was a fresh start: the Empire did not intend to follow the Ottoman invalid to its death bed. The occupation of Bosnia, the Emperor thought, would restore the Dual Monarchy's credentials as a great power.

Es wird fortgewurschtelt: Austria, Hungary, Bosnia, Croatia, Serbia

By the time Bosnia-Hercegovina was occupied in 1878, the sharp contours of Franz Joseph's early absolutism had been obscured by the constitutional veil known as 'dualism'. After the defeat of the Hungarian revolutionaries in 1849, the young Emperor had apparently succeeded in establishing a harsh, centralized régime, dependent on his will.* Within twenty years, however, a series of disastrous military and political defeats had forced him to distribute his power widely inside the Empire. Within a year of Königgrätz, the single-minded Hungarian elite had seized on the confusion and helplessness caused by this humiliation to secure the political reforms for which they had fought in 1848–9. It may not have been full independence but it was not far off it.

Hungary's self-government was enshrined in the agreement of 1867, known as the *Ausgleich*. Under the terms of the *Ausgleich*, the Hungarian parliament recognized Franz Joseph as its sovereign but won the right to form its own cabinet which would rule the crown lands of Szent István, St Stephen. The Emperor would still decide matters of war and peace and the Hungarians were obliged to contribute conscripts to the army. But Budapest was permitted to assemble its own, smaller force, the *Honvéd*. The Austrian half of the Empire also now formed its own government. However, Franz Joseph insisted that three joint ministries – Foreign Affairs, Finance and War – would retain jurisdiction throughout the Empire. Despite the unifying role of the three imperial ministries, the Emperor was in effect having to reconcile the aspirations of two empires, locked in a permanent bureaucratic battle to undermine each other. In such circumstances, the execution of foreign policy often had more to do

* See chapter 1.

with chance than intention. Even the most powerful players of the Empire sometimes had not the faintest idea what was actually happening in large parts of it. As for the vast majority of its inhabitants and most outsiders, the entire system was deeply confusing. For one young Irish writer teaching English in Istria (the peninsula now divided between Croatia and Slovenia) at the turn of the century, it was all too much: 'I hate this Catholic country with its hundred races and thousand languages, governed by a parliament which can transact no business and sits for a week at the most and by the most physically corrupt royal house in Europe.'[2]

Both the Austrians and the Hungarians were outnumbered in their respective crown lands by minorities which were systematically excluded from power. With the important exception of the Transylvanian Romanians living under Hungarian rule, the great majority of these were Slavs whose growing political class was ignored by the *Ausgleich* settlement.

The Croats had managed to secure their own agreement, the *nagodba*, with the Hungarians in 1868. This extremely diluted version of the *Ausgleich* was supposed to guarantee the Croats an autonomous administration as well as control over the education system and the courts. In fact, for most of the period leading up to the First World War, the Hungarians ruled the lands of Croatia and Slavonia paying little regard to Croat aspirations or rights.

Until 1878, Vienna and Budapest both appeared to accommodate the awkward provisions of the *Ausgleich* quite well. The occupation of Bosnia disturbed this delicate equilibrium in several ways. Having recently assumed control of their own affairs, the landowners who dominated Hungarian political life were extremely displeased at the prospect of the Empire's absorbing an additional two million Slavs. A large minority of the Bosnian Slavs were Croats whose overall influence in the Empire would rise accordingly, and the Hungarian elite saw them as the greatest threat to its political monopoly.

In addition, the Hungarians feared that Vienna would demand more income from Budapest to fund the administration and defence of Bosnia-Hercegovina, which, though rich in mineral resources, was bereft of anything that might properly be called an industrial and administrative infrastructure.

Some Austrians harboured similar fears about the economic

burden of Bosnia. But Serbia was Austria's greatest problem. Bosnia-Hercegovina was the prize most coveted by the young Serbian state. The Orthodox Serbs of Bosnia had long been awaiting an end to Turkish rule, and Serbia's most direct route to the sea – the economic obsession which was the core of modern Serbian nationalism – lay through the province. Serbia had fought the Ottoman Empire on its own in 1876 and then in alliance with Tsarist Russia in 1877–8, and felt every right to annex Bosnia and Hercegovina. Yet at the Congress of Berlin, Austria-Hungary, which had not fought at all in the Great Eastern Crisis, was granted the right to steal this prized jewel.

There was, of course, nothing Serbia or the Serbs in Bosnia could do about this example of imperial *Realpolitik*. But it had two very serious consequences. The assimilation of just under a million Serbs in Bosnia whose allegiance and territory were claimed by the Serbian state meant that Austro-Hungarian foreign policy and domestic issues of nationality were henceforth impossible to unravel. A parallel existed in Habsburg relations with Romania where the nationalist mood was sharpening and the desire for unification with Transylvania, at that time under Hungarian control, was growing ever stronger. However, the Slav problem was paramount.

The second issue concerned the administration of the occupied provinces. Both Franz Joseph and the so-called Military Party* in Vienna were convinced of the strategic importance of Bosnia and Hercegovina. They would brook no opposition in Hungary to their plans for the two provinces. But where would Bosnia fit in the constitutional puzzle of Franz Joseph's imperial domain? He needed Hungarian participation in the administration so that Budapest would assume some financial liability for Bosnia. The Hungarians disliked the idea of paying for something they had not wanted in the first place. But they were loath to see Vienna dominate Bosnia: the Austrian half of the Dual Monarchy would become much larger and more influential. The solution was to put Bosnia and Hercegovina under the jurisdiction of the Joint Minister of Finance. This placed the burden of administering the territories on both sides

* An influential court faction, centred on senior army officers, and not a formal political party.

of the Dual Monarchy while not upsetting the internal balance of power between them.

In the period between 1878 and the assassination of Archduke Franz Ferdinand in June 1914, the foreign and domestic policies of the Austro-Hungarian Empire were dragged forwards, sideways and back by the nationality question. Beyond the slogan dreamed up by one of his Prime Ministers: *Es wird fortgewurschtelt!* (We must muddle through),* the Emperor had no coherent strategy to deal with the national question.

Franz Joseph's authority was perforce broken up and distributed among a number of constituencies. The central political conflict between Vienna and Budapest was in principle a bureaucratic struggle, anchored as it was in the *Ausgleich*. It was therefore confined within a relatively predictable framework which Franz Joseph, well versed in court politics, undoubtedly welcomed. But the Slav nations and the Romanians, lacking any significant representation, had little choice but to engage in other forms of political activity, legal and illegal. Their actions challenged not only the domestic order, but also periodically disrupted the relationship between Vienna and Budapest. The Hungarians would quietly foster Slav agitation in the Czech lands, which belonged to the Austrian crown, as a way of keeping Vienna off balance. In turn, Vienna would sometimes offer discreet encouragement to Croats who wished to see the creation of a Triple Monarchy. Zagreb would become a third centre of devolved power in the monarchy, free from Hungarian influence. 'Trialism' was of course anathema to Hungary.

A further effect of the occupation of Bosnia-Hercegovina concerned neither Vienna nor Budapest, but was of great moment for future relations between Croats and Serbs, not to mention the prospects of the Bosnian Muslims. After the cooperation of Serbs and Croats, the 'one-blooded nation of two faiths', during the revolutionary years of 1848–9, the intellectual and political perspectives of the two peoples had developed in different directions. With the consolidation of the Serb Principality, which became independent in 1878, Serbia was convinced that it must be the Piedmont of the

* Josip Horvat, *Politička Povijest Hrvatske*, Zagreb, 1989, p. 244. This phrase, including the delightful Austrian neologism, *fortwurschteln*, may best be translated idiomatically by 'We'll just muddle on through'.

south Slavs. Serbia would be the ideologue and executor of the unification process to which all other south Slavs must defer. The Croats, Serb nationalists argued, had no state with which to push forward the programme of unification. The increasingly arrogant tone of Serb intellectuals and politicians grated on sensibilities in Croatia, encouraging the split already evident in Croatian nationalism. Bishop Josip Strossmayer inherited the mantle of Illyrianism, advocating the unity of Serbs and Croats, but two young activists, Ante Starčević and Eugen Kvaternik, argued that Croats should establish their own state, comprising Croatia, Slavonia, Dalmatia and Bosnia-Hercegovina. Two expansionist programmes, one Serb, one Croat, would now be competing with each other for territory, above all for Bosnia and Hercegovina. When the shock of the Austrian occupation of Bosnia died down, Serbian nationalist circles expressed the fear that Bosnia might lose its 'essenzialmente serbo' character, as Senor Ussigli, the Italian consul in Sarajevo put it, and become instead 'croatizzato'.[3]

But if the occupation magnified the possibility for future disputes between Croats and Serbs, the long-term implications for Bosnia's Muslims were still more grave. As Croatia's leading historian of the nineteenth century has pointed out, 'the occupation rendered redundant the argument between Croat and Serb polemicists about the ownership of Bosnia and Hercegovina. Instead, another question took centre stage: were the Muslims Croats or Serbs?'[4]

Swings and roundabouts: Croatia

> Kačić was sensitive in the extreme on the Serbian question. Vuk Karadžić's words 'Serbs all and everywhere' had left a very nasty feeling in his stomach. For a long time this phrase had gnawed away at him as he believed Serbs to be in the ranks of Croatia's eternal enemies . . . he had begun to hate everything associated with the Orthodox population.
>
> Ksaver Šandor Gjalski, *In the Night* (1888)[5]

The last three decades of the nineteenth century were bleak times for Croatia. Hungarian domination of Croatia's political and economic life was made easier by a number of circumstances peculiar to the Croatian lands. The humiliation of Croat national sentiment reached its apotheosis during the long administration of Ban Count Dragutin Karoly Khuen-Héderváry, an influential Hungarian nobleman from Slavonia, who consistently ignored Croatian aspirations in favour of Budapest's interests.

His task was made easy by the tiny size of Croatia's franchised political class, which was restricted to the small nobility and a minority of urban professionals and administrators. Croatia's elite was hopelessly divided. It included many so-called Magyarones or Unionists, who willingly collaborated with the Hungarian overlords. The struggle for Croatian national rights, the Magyarones reasoned, was not worth the candle given the economic benefits that cooperation with the Hungarians brought with it.

Even more debilitating was the division which emerged within Croatian nationalism itself. Neither strand, that of Strossmayer or that of Starčević, could boast a mass following. Yet the mutual hostility between them reached such intensity that together they threatened to inflict severe long-term damage on the interests of the two and a half million Croats in the Austro-Hungarian Empire. Before long this gulf within Croatian nationalism had become unbridgeable. Attitudes to the Serbs of Croatia became a prominent feature of the arguments separating the narrow nationalists in Starčević's Party of Right from the followers of Strossmayer, who saw Croatia's future in a union with the Slovenes and the Serbs. The Serbian question was eagerly exploited by Khuen-Héderváry as one of his most effective tools for dividing and ruling the Croatian lands.

During the early 1870s the enlightened Ban Ivan Mažuranić founded Zagreb University and promoted other Croatian cultural institutions. But the mood of the society in these years was well caught by Ksaver Šandor Gjalski, one of Croatia's most perceptive writers, in his novel, *U Noći* (*In the Night*). First published in 1888, it traces the atrophy of Croatia's national movement through the emotional, political and professional fortunes of a group of students during the early years of the *Khuenovština*, as the twenty years of Héderváry's rule were called. Gjalski's subtle descriptions of Zagreb's baroque elegance contrast with the book's central characters, a band of charmless disciples, misogynist and misanthropic, who preach the gospel according to Starčević. These revolutionaries treat with ascetic contempt those who oppose their vision of an exclusivist Croatian nationalism. Despite his own Yugoslavist inclinations, Gjalski drew an equally withering picture of the intellectuals who supported Strossmayer. Ever ready to abandon their principles to advance their careers, these lawyers, poets and journalists, supposedly wedded to Croatia's destiny, bow and scrape to their Hungarian oppressors as easily and indifferently as they inflict pain on their women. The brief appearances by Serbs in Gjalski's novel illustrate the contempt with which 'the Piedmontese' of the Balkans had begun to treat other south Slavs:

> The Serb actor mimicked the language and accent of Zagreb's barrow-boys . . . to prove that Croats had stolen their language from the Serbs; he denounced the Jesuits; and claimed that all Croats were prisoners of their priests . . . He said that Serbs would rather make a pact with the devil than the Croats . . . The actor claimed that according to the most detailed studies Croats didn't actually exist except for a small bunch on the coast who were in any case dying out . . . and that Croats were aiming to take over Dalmatia, a purely Serbian territory where nobody had even heard of Croats.[6]

There are no heroes in Gjalski's work. This partly reflects the intellectual claustrophobia of Zagreb. And in part it demonstrates the cynicism, apathy and intolerance which unrestrained rule by Hungarian landowners had generated in Croatia and Slavonia.

In the early 1890s, the Héderváry régime stepped up its control of Zagreb's secondary-school and university students. Most who fell foul of the Ban's humourless political police took the well-worn path from Zagreb to Prague in order to finish their studies and, with greater energy, to continue their political activities. The Czech lands, Bohemia and Moravia, suffered similar political indignities in their relations with Vienna as Croatia and Slavonia did with Budapest – Czech and Croat autonomy was, in practice, equally negated by the imperial centre. Conditions in the Austrian half of the Empire, however, were much more favourable for the Czechs than was Hungarian rule for the Croats. The electoral franchise was much larger, and the advanced industrial development of Bohemia and Moravia gave the Czechs a more confident bourgeoisie and a much larger proletariat. In marked contrast to the feeble Croatian movement, Czech demands for reform and autonomy were so widespread and effective that from 1893 Vienna was compelled to impose a virtual state of emergency over the region. As the Austrian administrators panicked in the face of Czech resistance, the Croat intelligentsia could only look on helplessly as German and Hungarian landowners bought ever greater tracts of land, deployed Hungarian-speaking administrators and brought in labour from outside. Croatian emigration from the countryside to the United States increased dramatically. Only Greeks left in greater numbers for America than the Slavs from Croatia, Slavonia and Dalmatia.

Among the students who fled persecution in 1891 was Stjepan Radić, a twenty-year-old student leader. Author of a letter denouncing Hungarian misrule, Radić was the ninth of eleven children born to an illiterate peasant couple near the Croatian town of Sisak. He would become Croatia's most influential political figure before his assassination in 1928.

Radić's round farmer's face was modified by the strong glasses he needed to compensate for his appalling eyesight. His fusion of the peasant with the self-taught intellectual made him a novelty in Croatian politics, hitherto dominated by the nobility and urban professionals. As a young child, Radić had tramped 3 kilometres in each direction to the nearest elementary school where he learned to read and write. His parents could not afford to send him to secondary school but he so impressed the local teachers that they convinced a large charity to fund his further education in Zagreb. As a fifteen-year-old, showing exceptional initiative, Radić decided to use his summer holidays to tramp around Croatia and neighbouring lands.

> I kept a precise record of my travels, taking special note of what ordinary people felt about the nobility and the government and which region boasted what type of rural economy. Even by then, I had decided definitively to devote myself to politics in order to teach and defend the people, as we said at home. My father assented to this by keeping silent but my mother was thrilled despite pointing out that I would spend much of my career behind bars, but who cared . . . at least I was going to be neither pen-pusher nor priest![7]

Instead, the indefatigable young student decided the time had come to break some rules.

In 1895, two years after his return from exile, Radić came to the conclusion that what the Croatian national movement needed was publicity. Budapest's insistence on the sole use of the Hungarian language on the state railway was a perennial irritation to all Croats. Radić picked this issue because the Hungarians were violating the *nagodba* which specifically allowed for the use of Croatian. But even more importantly, Radić sought to highlight how the railways were central to the Hungarian policy of keeping Croatia in an imperialist strait-jacket while sabotaging Austrian commercial interests. The port of Fiume (now Rijeka in Croatia) was under the direct administration of the authorities in Budapest. The Hungarian government blocked the construction of rail links between Zagreb and Vienna so that all goods transported by rail would have to go either via Rijeka or via Budapest.

Over a period of two months, Radić travelled the length and breadth of Croatia by train. Wherever he went, he asked for information in Croatian, demanded that his ticket be printed in Croatian as well as Hungarian and would only speak Croatian to the conductors even though most of them were Hungarians. In a series of articles for the main opposition newspaper, *Obzor* (Horizon), Radić described his adventures on the network and in particular the abuse and threats levelled at him by the staff. His odyssey culminated in a dramatic attempt by Hungarian railway workers to throw him off a speeding train. Most Croatian politicians dismissed Radić's antics as clowning but the reading public loved his articles.

This novel form of direct action was a rehearsal for Radić's most spectacular appearance on the public stage. On 14 October 1895, the Emperor Franz Joseph began a rare visit to Zagreb. The next day Croatian students took to the streets shouting anti-Hungarian and anti-Serbian slogans while professing their loyalty to the Habsburg ruler. The demonstrations dramatically raised the temperature in the normally sluggish Croatian capital. The following morning, 16 October, the fog lifted off the streets to reveal a crisp autumnal day. The Emperor was due to parade through the centre of town which was filling up with inquisitive onlookers. Just before midday, the crowd gasped as a pack of some two hundred boisterous students marched on to Jelačić Square. To commemorate the revolutionary tradition of 1848, some had donned the ceremonial dress of the Illyrian students – black braid jackets, long boots, fur hats adorned by a falcon's feather and a sabre in a silken sash. Another group was marching under the banner of the 'Student Legion', the volunteer fighting unit of 1848. When they reached the statue of Ban Jelačić, a group of five students unfurled the red-white-green Hungarian flag, drenched it in alcoholic spirit and held it aloft on their sabres. 'We have come to the memorial of Ban Jelačić, who fought for the [Habsburg] dynasty against the Hungarians', one student shouted out, 'and we have come to burn the flag of the nation which always fought against the dynasty and by doing so we are expressing our deepest feelings of love for the dynasty.' The flag disappeared in flames as the students cried, 'Long Live the Croatian King; Glory to Jelačić; Hungarians Go Home!' before dispersing.[8] Within hours, the student leaders had been arrested and Radić identified as the ringleader. A month later, fifty-one students were sentenced to short terms of imprisonment – the longest, six months, was imposed on Radić.

Radić had inflicted serious damage on Hungarian rule in Croatia. The imperial visit was covered by many European newspapers and for the first time in half a century the Croatian national movement and its aspirations were discussed in the major capitals. On arrival at Bjelovar prison, the Croatian governor proclaimed Radić a national hero and showered him with privileges. Radić and the student radicals introduced a new militancy into Croatian politics which began slowly to erode the effectiveness of the Héderváry regime. After three decades of treating the Croatian lands like servants' quarters, the government in Budapest found it had a fight on its hands. To defend his fiefdom, Héderváry stirred up tensions between the Croats and the Serbs.

Relations between Serbs and Croats had fluctuated in the fifty years since they had fought the Hungarians side by side in 1848. At times of international tension, that is when future boundaries and new constitutional orders became the subject of dispute, polemics between Serb and Croat nationalists sharpened. These were especially acute during the Great Eastern Crisis of 1875–8 when, for the first time, it became apparent how deeply the issue of Bosnia could divide Croats and Serbs. As the Croatian national movement grew in size and confidence at the turn of the century and the Serbian state strengthened and consolidated itself, discussions about how Serbs and Croats might fashion a common future became more frequent but also more heated.

In the late 1880s, Nikola Pašić, the future Prime Minister of both Serbia and the first Yugoslavia (1918–41), identified succinctly the problem facing those Serbs and Croats who were committed to the creation of a joint state:

> The Serbs strive for the unification of all Serb tribes* on the basis of tradition, memory and the historical past of the Serb race. They have been inspired primarily by the uprising of ordinary people in central Serbia against the Turks and the resulting establishment of the Serb kingdom . . . Croats, on the other hand, wish to see their Triune Kingdom of Croatia, Slavonia and Dalmatia at the centre of unification . . . The road to unification of the Serbo-Croat people under the leadership of Serbia runs in a completely opposite direction to the road of unification under the leadership of the Triune Kingdom.[9]

This difference was complicated by the Starčević tradition in Croatia, which rejected any cooperation with the Serbs. Pašić, of course, went on to argue that only the Serb route to unification could succeed. Notwithstanding Pašić's bias, the riddle he posed was a real one. It was the failure of politicians, not least Pašić himself, to solve this riddle in both the first and the second Yugoslavias which twice led to the demise of the 'united' state at times of revolutionary change in Europe.

'Don't you be frightened of the Croats', Hungary's Prime Minister, Kalman Tisza, told the parliament in Budapest. 'I have an infallible whip to beat them with – the Serbs!'[10] When Radić and the *mladi* (the 'young ones' as the new generation of Croat political activists were called) stepped up their harassment of Hédervár'y's administration, the Hungarian authorities went to ever greater lengths to sow discord between Serbs and Croats. In August 1902 (on this occasion, it seems, in cahoots with Vienna), Budapest

* Pašić uses the word *plemena* which can mean tribe, clan or branch of a family and which in this context intentionally avoids making explicit whether it includes Croats or not.

organized the reprinting of an inflammatory article from a Belgrade magazine in the newspaper of the Zagreb Serbs, entitled, with customary impartiality, *Srbobran* (Defender of the Serbs). The author, Nikola Stojanović, claimed that 'Croats don't have their own language, or any collective customs . . . nor, most important of all, do they have a consciousness of belonging to one another without which people cannot claim a specific nationality'. Croatia's largest-circulation paper, the opposition's *Obzor*, sounded the alarm: 'Everything is absolutely clear. Our Serbs want to wipe us off the face of the earth as a people!' *Obzor* then concluded its commentary by quoting the chilling threat issued by Stojanović in the original article: 'This struggle will end with the extermination of either you or us. One side must go down. We Serbs may rest assured that the Croats will fall because they are the minority, by dint of their geographical position, by dint of the fact that they live everywhere mixed with Serbs and by dint of the evolutionary process which ensures that the idea of Serbdom means progress.'[11]

The vitriol exchanged in *Srbobran* and *Obzor* provoked a mood of hysteria in Zagreb, just as Budapest had hoped it would. After the newspaper polemics, Héderváry's police only had to stoke the fire a little more. Josip Frank, the leader of the Pure Party of Rights and the undisputed leader of exclusive Croatian nationalism, willingly collaborated with the Hungarians by mobilizing his toughs to go on the rampage. The Croat mob in Zagreb took to the streets; barricades sprung up, bonfires were lit. 'Night and day', stated a Serbian doctor in Zagreb, 'this unrestrained rabble looted and destroyed Serb shops . . . flats and houses where Serbs lived were targets as were the Serbian Bank, the Serbian Printers and the like. We were given no protection and I was expecting to be beaten at any time, on the street or in my home . . . I am convinced that had they not declared martial law on the fourth day there would have been a serious massacre.'[12] According to a Croat eye-witness,[13] the rioters had a chant, '*Srbe na vrbe!* – Hang the Serbs on vines',* which became especially infamous under the Croat fascist régime during the Second World War. Josip Frank welcomed the violence, maintaining that his supporters 'had done Croatia a great service', while Stjepan Radić denounced the demonstrations as 'the work of pigs'.

---

* Literally, 'Serbs to the vines', i.e. Hang the Serbs.

The 1902 demonstrations infuriated those Croats like Radić who were in no doubt that the Austrians and Hungarians, not the Serbs, were the greatest obstacle to national progress. But after the initial shock, the disturbances provoked a fruitful debate about Serb-Croat relations, with substantial improvements in relations between the two communities. This led to the formation of a political coalition of Croats and Serbs inside Croatia. Radić, who in contrast to most Croats had spent time in Belgrade discussing these issues with Serb intellectuals, offered a striking observation. In a pamphlet on the crisis, he highlighted the widely held fallacy that the linguistic proximity of Serbs and Croats gave the two nationalities a special insight into each other's mentality. On the contrary, Radić maintained, the linguistic proximity merely allowed both sides to exchange myths and prejudices with greater facility. 'It is high time', he continued, 'that Croats and Serbs . . . began to work with word and with pen in all areas of public life in order to demolish this dam of ignorance and to scatter this fog of prejudice and thereafter to imbue each private and public life with a general national consciousness whereby all of our people can feel at home in Ljubljana and in Zagreb, in Belgrade and in Sofia.'[14]

Behind the scenes, the Croatian opposition and Serb representatives in Croatia were working to formulate a joint political programme. Before this could happen, the influence of the *mladi* finally broke the stuffy conservatism of the old generation of oppositionists in Croatia and succeeded in fusing the two main Croat political parties into what was first known as the United Opposition and later renamed the Croatian Party of Right. Included in the new organization were Croatia's two most artful politicians, Stjepan Radić and Frano Supilo, the editor of the Rijeka newspaper *Novi list*.

On 29 January 1903, the Party of Right (not to be confused with Frank's extremist organization, the Pure Party of Right) released its political programme, which included demands for freedom of the press, freedom of association, universal suffrage and, above all else, the financial independence of Croatia and Slavonia from Budapest. If this new initiative were to be of any political value, the new Party had to organize and mobilize among the people. The Croats needed to break out of the prison of timid, late nineteenth-century coffee-house politics, if they were to mount a serious challenge to

Hungarian imperialism. Croat activists like Supilo and Radić had anticipated that a revolutionary wind was beginning to blow across Europe and the Balkans. As in Macedonia and Serbia, 1903 was to be an important year in Croatia. The Hungarians doggedly refused any concessions but the Croats, emboldened by the militancy of the *mladi*, launched a rebellion which to everybody's surprise (including the Croat rebels) shook Hungarian rule to its foundations.

In March 1903, the opposition held meetings in support of its programme first in Zagreb, then in cities and towns throughout Croatia and Slavonia. The numbers attending grew steadily, for the first time attracting peasants into the towns to express their solidarity, underlining Radić's conviction that the peasantry was *The Strongest Party in Croatia,* as he titled a famous political manifesto in the autumn of 1902. The demonstrations in Croatia and Slavonia coincided with the student protests in Belgrade against the Obrenović dynasty,* a royal house generally regarded as living in the pocket of the Habsburgs. The sense of Slav solidarity (which had all but disintegrated the previous September) cohered once more in opposition to the dual evils of Hungarian nationalism and Austrian imperialism. The remarkable speed with which enmity could dissolve into solidarity and back again became a hallmark of Serb-Croat relations throughout the twentieth century.

The chaos in the region deepened when a bitter dispute between Vienna and Budapest broke out over the Hungarian government's attempt to introduce Hungarian as a language of command among its soldiers in the imperial army. Talk of revolution and monarchical collapse spread around the Empire. On 11 April, peasants from a number of villages surrounding Zaprešić, 5 kilometres west of Zagreb, marched on the town to rip down the Hungarian flag flying over the local government building. They were met by armed Hungarian guards, and in the ensuing riot one peasant was killed and several injured. In consequence, demonstrations and street battles convulsed Zagreb for several days and pressure mounted on Khuen-Hédervary to resign as Ban of Croatia. In early June 1903, Hédervary was attending Mass when he received an urgent telegram informing him of the murder of King Aleksandar Obrenović and his consort Queen Draga in Belgrade. He was ordered to pack immediately for Budapest where, a few days later, he was appointed Prime Minister of Hungary. After twenty years of uncompromising and often brutal rule, Hédervár y's departure from Zagreb was celebrated as a victory by the Croatian national movement. In fact, his recall had more to do with relations between Vienna and Budapest than anything that was happening in Croatia, and the speed with which the unrest then died down in Croatia suggests that the movement of 1903 was less significant than some Croat historians claim.

Nonetheless, a new era of mass participation in public life had dawned in Croatia. It was typified by Radić's new party, the Croatian National Peasant Party, which would later dominate Croatian politics. The euphoric cooperation between Serbs and Croats eventually crystallized, in November 1905, into the Croat-Serb Coalition, the revolutionary development of which its first manifesto proudly boasted:

> Croatian and Serb patriots have joined together in a firm alliance with the task of uniting all forces and with the support of all Croats and Serbs to guide our fatherland Croatia out of the intolerable and deadly situation which it has suffered hitherto . . . We are convinced that our nation, which bears the name of Croat and Serb, can have no brighter future and cannot indeed even survive without both sides of our nation working together in solidarity. We must ensure that we surmount even the smallest obstacle which would deny equality and freedom to the Serbian people.[15]

The programme's tortured language underlined just how hard it was for Serbs and Croats to make common cause. The new Coalition nonetheless represented a significant breakthrough even if its underlying fragility would be exposed in October 1908 when Emperor Franz Joseph I decided to turn the occupation of Bosnia and Hercegovina into an outright annexation of the province. The move led to a deterioration in Serbo-Croat relations, and in relations between Serbia and Austria-Hungary, between Budapest and Vienna, and between Germany and Austria-Hungary. There was nothing good to be said for an annexation which poisoned European politics but had little impact on everyday life in Bosnia and Hercegovina itself.

The Balkan chalk circle: Bosnia

In the spring of 1899, Osman Omanović arranged for his daughter to marry an old friend of his, a common practice in turn-of-the-century Bosnia and Hercegovina. When she learnt of the plan, however, sixteen-year-old Fata Omanović was horrified. She loathed her intended husband and, in despair, this spirited young woman from the mixed village of Kutilivce on the outskirts of Mostar turned for advice to Maria and Ruža Simičić, two Croat teenagers who lived next door to her. They persuaded Fata that drastic measures were needed if she were to escape her patriarchal fate. After night fell on 2 May, the young Muslim crept from her father's house to meet a Croat who acted as her guide on the 32-kilometre journey to the border with Dalmatia, whither the writ of the Bosnian authorities did not extend. When Osman Omanović discovered his daughter's disappearance the following morning, he raised the alarm. Fata was nowhere to be found. Before long, however, the Simičić girls confessed, and a few days later, Omanović's worst fears were confirmed – his daughter had renounced her religion and had been accepted into the Catholic Church.

Within days, the conservative chief mufti of Mostar, Ali Džabić, had transformed the incident into a *cause célèbre*. For the leading Muslims of Hercegovina, Fata's flight epitomized the Catholic Church's exploitation of its privileged position as the imperial faith to seduce young Muslims into rejecting their religion. They demanded that the Austrian authorities find and return Fata and put a stop to conversions.

Despite the mosaic of faiths in Bosnia and Hercegovina, conversions in the two provinces were relatively rare, numbering about twenty-five a year at the turn of the century. The Catholic Church registered the greatest number – gaining 93 new members and losing 118 over a ten-year period. Some 44 people converted to Islam but 65 Muslims became Christians. The Serb Orthodox Church came out best, winning 88 new adherents and losing just 46.[16] Yet although the numbers involved were not great, the hierarchy and laity of all three major religions in Bosnia were especially sensitive on the matter. Conversions provoked more demonstrations, petitions and communal infighting than any other issue in Habsburg-occupied Bosnia.

For the Bosnian Muslims, conversions touched the very heart of their identity. This had little to do with piety and everything to do with politics. Until 1878, the Muslims were the ruling class of Bosnia-Hercegovina, controlling the provinces' feudal economy and sclerotic administration. Their privileges were guaranteed by the primacy of Islam within the Ottoman Empire. Bosnia's feudal structures further emphasized the importance of the churches as arbiters of moral and social questions. So when the Austro-Hungarian occupiers marched into Bosnia to announce that all religious faiths would henceforth be treated as equal, the Muslim landowners, the *ağas*, feared that their power and indeed their cultural world were about to disappear. The *ağas* represented but a tiny minority, 1.5 per cent, of the Muslim population. But their fears were shared by the majority of Muslims, classed as free peasants. They worried that the arrival of the Austro-Hungarians would swiftly be followed by the liberation of the Christian peasants, the last serfs in Europe, who would then be at liberty to compete with their Muslim counterparts for land.

The speed and zeal with which the new rulers set about modernizing the government of Bosnia confirmed these fears. The Muslims, who under Ottoman rules were solely responsible for governing Bosnia, were obliged to yield their grip on the administration straightaway. At the time of occupation in 1878, just 120 Muslims administered Bosnia and Hercegovina. Thirty years later, when Austria turned its occupation into annexation, a grand total of 9,533 bureaucrats were running the two provinces.

Relinquishing control of government was no great loss in itself and the change undoubtedly benefited Bosnia – by 1878 meaningful administrative life had all but expired in the province. But the Double Eagle built its nest in every town and in every village. The sudden invasion of hundreds upon hundreds of Habsburg bureaucrats had a severe psychological impact on the Muslims. Men in neatly cut European uniforms brandished their ink and stamps, demanding endless information about the Empire's new subjects; poking their noses into the private lives and habits of families whose word until a few months earlier had been more powerful in Bosnia than even the Sultan's. Snapping orders in strange tongues, they counted houses and measured roads, or more frequently land upon which roads and railways would soon be built; they put up signs on buildings and signs on streets in foreign languages. They handed out letters telling young men to report for military service; they indulged in futile administrative rituals about which whole novels have been written; and everywhere they hung portraits of His Imperial and Royal Highness, Franz Joseph I. All this contributed to what a distinguished historian of Bosnia has called a 'widespread sense of alienation and fear among the Bosnian Muslims'. The psychological distress occasioned by these changes was 'a major cause of Muslim emigration to Istanbul and other parts of the Ottoman Empire . . . during the era of the Double Eagle'.[17]

A large number of the new clerks, postmen and stationmasters came from neighbouring Croatia. This helped to overcome the language barrier, but it bolstered the Catholic presence in Bosnia. The Habsburg authorities were alert to the importance of religion in Bosnia and, within weeks of the occupation, tried to impose tight political control on the three churches. The Vatican willingly gave its permission for the establishment of an archbishopric in Bosnia, and so in the wake of the bureaucrats there followed a crusading priesthood typified by the leading cleric, Josip Stadler, who became the first Archbishop of Vrhbosna.* Stadler came with the express intention of ending the pastoral monopoly of the Franciscan monks in favour of the more energetic Jesuits; of enlisting the clerical hierarchy in the active service of Vatican policy; and of gathering the souls of apostates. In a number of the more dramatic cases of conversion, Stadler himself gave sanctuary to Muslims fleeing their community, mainly women who wished to marry non-Muslims. When the Habsburg authorities attempted to intervene with the Archbishop on behalf of the Muslims, Stadler remained stubborn. To the Muslims it simply looked as if the government was turning a blind eye to the Catholic Church's proselytizing activities.

The case of Fata Omanović proved one conversion too many. The Muslims of Mostar had watched cultural centres, schools and churches serving the Catholic and Orthodox communities increasing in their city. During the 1890s, a war of words broke out in Hercegovina between the propagandists of Greater Croatia and Greater Serbia. The Croat newspaper *Glas Hercegovca* (Voice of the

* The old Croat name for Sarajevo.

Hercegovinian) claimed Bosnia and Hercegovina as integral parts of Croatia. The Serbs claimed they were exclusively Serb lands. Both wooed the Muslims. The Serbs warned the Muslims that if they made common cause with the Croats, they would face forced conversion to Catholicism and eventually assimilation. The Croats argued the opposite – that the Muslims could only hold on to their faith and traditions in the tolerant embrace of Croatdom.

Neither Serbs nor Croats were in a position to coerce the Muslims. But to become politically effective the Muslim leaders found it necessary to form temporary alliances with one side or the other. The Omanović case saw the Muslim landlords and traders emerge as a serious political force, and marked the beginning of a long spell of cooperation between Muslims and Serbs. An adviser to Benjámin von Kállay, the Habsburg Joint Minister of Finance who ran Bosnia until 1903, noted that 'on June 7th, 1899 members of the Mostar [Muslims] Twelve Committee had explained that the Omanović affair would force them to go through thick and thin with the Eastern Orthodox [Serbs]. The clerk at the High Court, Muhamed effendi Kadić, told our informer on the same day that according to his sources they were working on a programme to demand that Bosnia and Hercegovina be granted a status similar to Crete's . . . Recently one has heard the slogan "Autonomy for Bosnia and Hercegovina" in every coffee house.'[18]

Within weeks of Fata Omanović's flight, the campaign for her return had evolved into something much more serious. The Mostar Muslims travelled across Bosnia and Hercegovina gathering support for their new project of autonomy. A delegation went to Budapest on an expensive and futile excursion to lobby support for their cause. They enlisted support from Serbs who were eager to encourage the movement for autonomy for their own ends, believing that an autonomous Bosnia could be used as a stepping stone to unification with Serbia. The Muslims employed Nikola Djurdjević, a Serb lawyer from Slavonski Brod (now in Croatia across the Sava river from Bosnia), to frame their growing list of political demands for presentation to the Bosnian government. After a campaign lasting over a year, the Movement for Cultural and Religious Autonomy in Bosnia and Hercegovina handed in a petition to Kállay in December 1900. Kállay was quick to calculate the dangers of the movement for the Empire:

> On the one hand, the petition contains specific demands of the Muslims concerning the administration of the *vakufs* and issues concerning the confessional schools; on the other hand, it includes general declarations which go well beyond the bounds of such requests with the apparent intention of creating an autonomous national-political unity among the Muslims, which even includes the establishment of their own administration. In other words, it is a political move, aimed at building a state within a state. This is quite out of the question.[19]

Negotiations over these demands quickly broke down. But the petition is rightly considered a landmark in the development of a modern national consciousness among the Bosnian Muslims. Geographically and demographically weak, the Muslims were destined to shore up their position by forming alliances with either the Serbs or the Croats. But as the Movement for Autonomy spread among Muslims throughout Bosnia, the possibility of their being consumed by either the Croat or Serb national movement began to recede. Their self-confidence was further strengthened in 1906 when the first real party in Bosnia, the Muslim National Organization, was founded. Nonetheless, the Bosnian Muslims had to navigate a peculiar and lonely course on their way to a modern national identity:

> The political awakening of the Bosnian Muslims under Austrian rule was hardly a typical East European nationalist revival. The Muslim movement was not preceded by large-scale social changes such as rapid industrialization, urbanization, or a rise in literacy rates that have frequently been noted as contributing to political nationalism. In addition the Muslims for many years lacked a formally articulated ideology and had no outstanding intellectual spokesmen.[20]

One problem facing the Muslims was that their small class of intellectuals considered religious identification to be reactionary. At first, some accepted the idea propagated by Benjámin von Kállay who tirelessly encouraged all communities to embrace the concept of *bošnjaštvo* or Bosniakdom. His purpose in doing so was to weaken the predatory ideologies of Croat and Serb nationalism. But as it became evident that *bošnjaštvo* had failed to take root (partly because it was so closely associated with Austrian policy), differences emerged among the Muslims. Intellectuals emphasized the need to overthrow Habsburg colonial rule, which led them to embrace Yugoslavism or in some cases Serb or Croat nationalism (in Bosnia the borders between Yugoslavism and Serbian nationalism were often vague). They showed a marked reluctance to defend Muslim sectional interests. In contrast, Muslim landowners, townspeople and peasants regarded themselves as belonging to a distinct community with separate interests. The vanguard of Muslim nationalism was to be found not among the bourgeoisie or the intelligentsia, but among the conservative clerics and landowners.

The railway man: Bosnia

Benjámin von Kállay, a minor Hungarian noble, was a rare bird among Habsburg administrators. Shunning the Viennese traditions of *Schmäh* and *Schlamperei*,* this former consul in Belgrade (who had written *inter alia* a history of the First Serbian Uprising) had an instinct for appeasing the apparently irreconcilable demands of Bosnia's hostile population with Vienna's policy of colonial expansion and pacification. Kállay was appointed Joint Minister of Finance with responsibility for Bosnia in 1882. He realized that the absorption of the province brought with it many dangers for the Austro-Hungarian Empire. To avoid disaster, he reasoned, it was essential for the Empire to win the loyalty of its new citizens in Bosnia, and to win that loyalty it needed a plan. Kállay had just such a plan.

The aim was not a bad one – flesh out the province's economic infrastructure, create jobs and raise the standard of living. In some key branches, Kállay succeeded in laying the foundations of modern industry. Given the paucity of raw material available and the derisory amount of capital at his disposal, this was a real feat. But two circumstances conspired to wreck his vision of a prosperous Austrian Bosnia-Hercegovina. The first of these lay beyond his control in the vindictive minds of the Hungarian Ministry of

* A culture of work in which emphasis is laid on cutting corners, dodging difficult problems and exerting as little effort as possible.

Commerce, who saw it as their business to prevent any development if this conflicted with the narrow economic interests of the Hungarian elite. But Kállay had nobody but himself to blame for the monumental error he committed in refusing, like his Ottoman predecessors, to address the question of agrarian reform.

The Imperial Edict of February 1880, regulating the status of occupied Bosnia and Hercegovina, was admirably honest: this was to be colonialism on the cheap. 'The administration of these lands', it declared, 'must be established in such a manner that their expenses be covered by their own revenues.'[21] A full 95 per cent of the population was employed in agriculture. The entire industrial infrastructure of Bosnia consisted of a single iron factory in Vareš which closed almost as soon as the province was integrated into the Austro-Hungarian tariff system, and of one feeble, narrow-gauge railway line covering the 80 kilometres from Doberlin (now Bosanski Novi in Bosnia and Hercegovina) on the Croatian border to Banja Luka. How Bosnia was expected to pay its own way, especially as it now had to feed and house thousands of bureaucrats, was a complete mystery. Kállay's first projected improvement was the construction of a modest narrow-gauge rail line from Bosanski Brod to Zenica which he could build at a knockdown price because the Habsburg army, convinced of the track's strategic value, was prepared to supply the labour. The estimated cost of this 193-kilometre stretch was just over 8 million florins. To his horror, Kállay discovered that his first annual projected revenue from the province was 6.5 million florins, so that his single investment had eaten up more than his overall budget before he had even considered his ordinary running costs.

Kállay responded by fiddling, cajoling, exploiting loopholes, bribing and evolving his own brand of evasive double-speak when dealing with imperial officials. In 1900, he unveiled his 'grand plan'. This was to ensure that Bosnia's interior would be linked up by rail to Croatia and Hungary to the north, and even more significantly with Dalmatia and the port of Split to the west. Bosnia was and is the economic hinterland of the Dalmatian coast – the two belong together in a natural alliance. Yet whenever the Joint Minister attempted to implement the next stage of his 'grand plan', it was blocked by Hungarian officials. Writing in 1910, R.W. Seton-Watson, the great British scholar of central and south-eastern Europe, noted how 'the Magyars have consistently opposed the building of any railways into Dalmatia, and thus to this day the greater part of the latter province is inaccessible by rail . . . Travellers from Vienna and the West find it easier and quicker to go to Bosnia through Budapest, though that is far from being the shortest route in mere mileage.'[22]

Just as Hungary was wrecking Croatia's transport development, so too was it determined to keep Bosnia a prisoner of its medieval industrial past. Had Kállay succeeded in developing his rail network in Bosnia, linking this up to Dalmatia and through Croatia into Austria itself, the Hungarian overall strategy of undermining Austria would have failed. Budapest's game, which helped to ensure Bosnia's relative backwardness in the Empire, was a largely unnoticed but significant contribution to crisis in Bosnia and the wider Habsburg Empire.

But it was the absence of land reform that ensured the conclusive failure of Kállay's well-intentioned schemes and sealed the fate of Bosnia and Hercegovina. Again the Hungarians indicated their resistance to change whenever the question of land reform in Bosnia was raised. Again the great Magyar landowners refused to look at the long-term implications for Bosnia and Austria but would consider only the short-term impact of reform on their own Hungarian, Croatian, Romanian and Serbian peasants.

Kállay also resisted tampering with the rights of the Muslim landowners for two main reasons. First, the tithe system, although inefficient and punitive, worked after a fashion and certainly guaranteed the occupation régime an income at a time when funds were very short. Second, the Muslims made up 39 per cent of Bosnia-Hercegovina's population at the time of the occupation and they were the most powerful group in the province. Kállay did not wish to attack their most important privilege – land.

Kállay and the Austrians were seeking a political compromise which they hoped would guarantee some internal cohesion in Bosnia: the Christians might welcome the Habsburgs because they were granted political equality with Muslims at a stroke; the Muslims could be persuaded to accept Austrian rule, albeit grudgingly, because their rights as landowners were protected. For many years, this policy was enough to prevent serious political unrest. It did not, however, satisfy either the Christians or the Muslims, nor did it generate much loyalty among them. The Christian peasants were angered that the feudal obligations which they had rebelled against in 1875 remained in place while the Muslims feared that the end of their political dominance would lead to the systematic stripping of their social and class privileges.

Until his death in 1903, Kállay did at least succeed in papering over the cracks. His attempt to create a *bošnjak* consciousness which would unite the Slav inhabitants of the province across the religious divide held little attraction for the overwhelming majority of Bosnians. Beyond this, his public policy on the national question was to deny its existence and threaten to suppress political activity based upon confessional or national identity. This repressive policy started unravelling during his lifetime when the Muslims developed the Movement for Autonomy; both the Serbs and the Croats had long since been organizing politically, using the churches as a cover for what were really national movements.

Kállay and the Austrians assumed that by merely raising living standards, it would be possible to neutralize national tensions in Bosnia and Hercegovina. This classically Marxist assumption failed to take account of the social upheaval for which the Austrian régime of occupation was almost wholly responsible. Unprecedented social mobility between rural areas and the towns (which were growing fast); rural unemployment; competition between indigenous workers and immigrant labour; all this created a volatile situation in both city and countryside. The children of poor peasants could sometimes get a secondary education, during which they were frequently affected by the ideologies of nationalism, Yugoslavism, socialism and anarchism. The increasing bureaucratization of life was considered a burden by almost everybody, and the insistence of the administration on working only in German or Hungarian further alienated the Bosnians. On the eve of the First World War, a perceptive critic of social conditions in Austria-Hungary travelled through Bosnia to report that:

> Nothing has been done for education, nothing to lighten the burden of mortgage, not a sod has been turned for railway building. I have travelled for hours through the countryside without coming across a school. Everywhere agriculture and rural conditions are trammelled by Turkish land law which prevails in Bosnia as at the time of the Turks.[23]

It is small wonder that frustration was simmering among the most restless elements of the local population. Some Croat intellectuals had welcomed the occupation of Bosnia and Hercegovina as an effective insurance against Serbian nationalism, but neither Serbs nor Muslims felt any loyalty towards the occupation régime. When Franz Joseph I and his confidants decided to exploit the uncertainty which followed the Young Turk revolution by proclaiming the annexation of the two provinces, it was like kicking a hornets' nest.

The Citadel of Dreams: Austria

> All in all, how many remarkable things might be said about that vanished Kakania! For instance, it was kaiserlich-königlich (Imperial-Royal) and it was kaiserlich und königlich (Imperial and Royal); one of the two abbreviations, k.k. or k. & k., applied to every thing and person, but esoteric lore was nevertheless required in order to be sure of distinguishing which institutions and persons were to be referred to as k.k. and which as k. & k. On paper it called itself the Austro-Hungarian Monarchy; in speaking, however, one referred to it as Austria, that is to say, it was known by a name that it had, as a State, solemnly renounced by oath, while preserving it in all matters of sentiment, as a sign that feelings are just as important as constitutional law and that regulations are not the really serious things in life . . . Many such things happened in this State, and among them were those national struggles that justifiably aroused Europe's curiosity and are today completely misrepresented.
>
> Robert Musil, *The Man Without Qualities*[24]

Henry Wickham Steed was put out to learn from the Foreign Assistant Editor of *The Times* that he was to transfer from Rome to Vienna in the autumn of 1902. Steed had lived in Rome for six years and he felt he had become 'a child by right of that eternal home'. It was like 'leaving a world of light and warmth for one of the cold, sombre and dusty regions imagined by Dante'.[25] Before the correspondent's final departure, Emilio Visconti Venosta, Italy's veteran Foreign Minister, summoned Steed to his little Alpine château in the Valtellina, east of Lake Como. During Steed's time in Rome, Visconti Venosta had become the journalist's most important mentor. Steed listened intently as the old man foretold bleak times:

> I have seen Europe transformed, and I see forces at work that may transform her again. Of these forces the chief is the growing antagonism between England and Germany. Unless it is checked – and I do not see how it can well be save in the way I shall indicate – England and Germany will come to blows within ten or fifteen years. The aggressive character of German policy will compel England to fight unless she is prepared to forfeit her place in the world.[26]

Visconti Venosta argued that Germany derived its strength from an ability to play off Italy and Austria-Hungary, its two allies, against each other. Germany's ambition could only be checked if Rome and Vienna were to cooperate and transform the Triple Alliance 'into a league of peace'. 'No Italian Ambassador can explain this to the Austrians. It would be too dangerous', Visconti Venosta went on. 'But you might do it . . . I was born an Austrian subject and I know that, at Vienna, the Government is everything. Try to win its confidence and then do what you can to persuade the Austro-Hungarian Foreign Minister, Count Gołuchowski, of the truth of what I have told you . . . Then we may get peace in Europe – but otherwise not.'

Entrusted with the task of saving Europe by an ageing Italian diplomat, Steed set off for Vienna. As befitted the representative of the most influential newspaper in the world, Steed immediately entered Habsburg high society – an 'unreal country', he called it, comprising three strata whose members were only permitted to mix with their own. The high nobility in the top stratum kept their distance from ministers of state, the big financiers and 'baptized Jews together with the majority of diplomatists', who mingled in the middle stratum. Steed explained that 'between these strata there was little communication save when it became desirable to mulct them all for some charitable purpose . . . At the apex of the social structure stood the Emperor, the Imperial family and the Court, so far removed from the common run of mortals and so hedged about by an old Spanish etiquette that they could, on occasion, afford to move as demi-gods among the crowd.'[27]

Perplexed and lost at first, Steed gradually noticed how society folk from the first two strata avoided talk of politics, preferring instead to gossip about the latest goings-on at the Opera. Even parliament, he observed, would prefer to waste time rowing 'over the appointment of some obscure official in Bohemia', than engage in real politics. 'Concerts, theatres and amusements generally, played a far greater part in public life than political issues – as a result . . . of an old system deliberately adopted and carefully applied by the Hapsburgs and their police. Its object was to divert the attention of the people from politics by keeping them constantly "amused". Thus it became a loyal duty to be "merry".'[28]

Amusing oneself and being merry had indeed become a way of life for the ruling classes in Vienna. They would flock to see the latest revival of a play by Grillparzer. Thirty years after his death, Grillparzer was still the top draw at the box office with plays like *Ein Traum, Ein Leben* which succeeded in transforming the Faust legend into a prim Biedermeier tale. Or if Grillparzer were too taxing, the Viennese would watch yet another comic opera by Lehár before dancing the night away to the strains of Strauss, or drinking it away at a *Heuriger** in Grinzing. Politics, by contrast, was a matter for the Emperor and his closest circle of administrators.

Given his acute intelligence, Steed was quick to see through this elaborately constructed citadel of dreams. But Steed was also a snob, often unable to suppress his anti-Semitic reflexes and other prejudices common to members of Britain's ruling class. He was blind to the growing achievements of the third stratum of Vienna society that he had himself identified, but then dismissed, as 'nondescript', comprising 'professors, artists, writers, Jews, journalists, second-rate officials, actors, actresses, singers and politicians'. In the years preceding his arrival, some of these nondescripts had infiltrated the Empire with subversive art and ideas, insinuating fragmentation and distortion into the self-image of Habsburg life. Bad dreams now shadowed the baroque perfection of Prague and Vienna; doctors revealed that behind the frivolous giggles of the Hofrat and the Merry Widow lay oedipal fantasies and schemes of dark revenge.

Behind the inner walls of the citadel, the guardians of Empire exchanged anxious glances as with ever greater clarity they could hear the disturbing din of democracy, nationalism, populism and clericalism outside. Karl Kraus, the torch-bearing tribune of

* From the Austrian German word for 'this year', *heuer*. *Heurigers* are large wine bars selling very young wine which is most refreshing but demands respect.

republicanism, required a mere flick of the pen to rubbish the hypocrisy of the establishment newspapers. The quick-witted populist, Dr Karl Lueger, climbed upon the *fin-de-siècle* insecurity of Vienna's German-speaking petite bourgeoisie to mount an influential platform as Mayor of the city. From here, Lueger issued his prospectus for a future dystopia: 'I warn the Jews most expressly; for the same thing could perhaps happen as in Russia. We in Vienna are anti-Semites, but are certainly not inclined to murder and violence. But if the Jews should threaten our fatherland, then we will show no mercy. I wanted to warn of these sad possibilities.'[29] One young malcontent from the small town of Ried-am-Inn, who listened to Lueger's rhetoric, later recalled his admiration for the Mayor: 'As the enormous funeral procession of the deceased Mayor headed from the Rathaus to the Ringstrasse, I found myself among the many hundreds of thousands who witnessed the solemnities ... If Dr. Lueger had lived in Germany, he would have found his place among the pantheon of our nation's great men. It was the misfortune of his achievement and his personal misfortune that he lived and worked in that impossible state.'[30]*

But corrosive ideologies lapped against the foundations of Franz Joseph's Empire outside Vienna too. With the *Ausgleich* of 1867, a crack appeared, running down the middle of the Dual Monarchy. By the turn of the century, this had widened until a chasm separated its two halves. On both sides of the divide, the calls for greater autonomy and political rights for the Empire's minority peoples, especially the Slavs, suggested that the ancient régime faced a threat to its very existence. From 1903 until the outbreak of war in 1914, Kaiser Franz Joseph's physical condition worsened. And as the man upon whom life and death depended looked ever more fragile, political struggles erupted in several parts of his domain as new and old forces alike raced to fill the deepening void of authority. These conflicts attained a hitherto unprecedented intensity (more dramatic

---

* From Hitler's *Mein Kampf*, quoted in *Der Burgerkaiser: Karl Lueger and seine Zeit* by Johannes Hawlik. Hawlik is one of several historians, mainly Austrian, who have attempted to prove that Lueger's anti-Semitism was of a mild and fundamentally non-threatening nature and that his influence on Hitler had been greatly exaggerated. I would argue that there are few figures in the German-speaking world who did more for the institutionalization of anti-Semitism as a violent, and by implication genocidal, ideology than Lueger.

even than the events of 1848), and they soon wove a dense web of coalitions, understandings, crises, broken promises, false alarms and vendettas both personal and institutional.

Internal contradictions were not, however, the immediate cause of the Empire's collapse in 1918. Instead, the citadel crumbled under the weight of world war. Yet the ten years prior to the outbreak of war led Austria-Hungary to a point where it could only transcend its internal contradictions by going to war – a war that was bound to bring it down. This decade demonstrated just how important the personal authority of Franz Joseph was as a guarantee of stability in the Empire. 'Each time the octogenarian's health waned, tremors about the monarchy's future began anew . . . For the political, military and diplomatic elite of the monarchy and of Europe, the question, "How is the emperor today?" was no rhetorical exercise.'[31] As his grip loosened, Habsburg absolutism found it ever harder to withstand the strains imposed by a fragmenting and modernizing society.

Henry Wickham Steed was in the thick of this. So much so, indeed, that one Austrian scholar claims that 'you would not be wrong in asserting that Steed played a big part in promoting the Empire's collapse'.[32] But neither Steed nor anybody else predicted such a swift end. In puzzling contrast to the widely held conviction that the Ottoman Empire must die, most observers supposed the Austro-Hungarian Empire to be a vigorous great power which, if eccentric in its habits, was quite robust enough to overcome any temporary difficulties. 'There was speed but not too much speed in Kakania, that misunderstood and now extinct country which, although it went unrecognized, was in many ways a model state', Robert Musil reflected. 'It had neither global economic nor political ambitions; it sat in the middle of Europe where the old civilizational axes met; the words colony and overseas sounded strange and distant . . . enormous sums were spent on the army; but only enough to ensure that it remained the second weakest of the great powers.'[33]

When faced with the challenge of imagining what would take its place, the government in Istanbul had proved incapable. It could not disguise the disarray which spread throughout the Ottoman Empire as it attempted to stem the advance of nationalism in the Balkans. In the first decade of the twentieth century, however, Austria-Hungary woke from its dreamy torpor and embarked on a programme of offensive imperialism, setting out to contain the nationalism of the south Slavs and the Romanians. The actual condition of the Empire seemed less important than its ability to behave with imperial swagger as 'a great power had to act like a great power, to show that it had the capacity to determine its own future',[34] in the words of one historian of Habsburg collapse. To prove to the world that it was still a great power, Austria-Hungary focused on Bosnia and Serbia.

The Bosnian annexation: Austria, Serbia, 1908

> This nest of robbers, calling itself the Austrian Empire, was counting on the fact that other such nests of robbers, preoccupied at the present moment in their own affairs, would permit this usurpation [the annexation of Bosnia] without demanding the acknowledgement of the right of each one of them to participate in this robbery. But apparently the leaders of other similar establishments desired to participate in this plunder, and have already for some weeks been discussing in their thieves' jargon, like thieves indeed, all kinds of annexations, compensations, congresses, conferences, declarations, delegations and so forth.
>
> Leo Tolstoy, November 1908[35]

When Austria-Hungary imposed the customs' blockade on Serbia in 1906, triggering the Pig War, it did so for two reasons. Hungarian landowners had encouraged the government in Vienna to ban livestock imports from Serbia. They used the pretext of halting the spread of disease as a means of protecting their industry from cheaper Serbian meat. Vienna was initially sympathetic to these arguments. It wished to send Serbia a forceful message that Austria-Hungary was the decisive economic and political power in the region. The Monarchy's interests had been damaged by Belgrade's decision to sign a trading agreement with Sofia in late 1904. Vienna insisted that Belgrade accept punitive terms during negotiations for a new trade treaty. At the same time, Serbia announced its intention of re-equipping its artillery with heavy guns. Egged on by the Archduke Franz Ferdinand, who had business interests at stake, the Austro-Hungarian government issued blunt threats to Serbia, cajoling Belgrade into placing the armaments order with the Škoda works in Plzeň. The Bohemian firm was in severe financial difficulty, owing some 4 million crowns to the Kreditanstalt in Vienna, and unable to raise any further capital. Austrian government contracts were insufficient to keep the concern afloat and so the Serbian purchase was seen as crucial for its survival. Not only was it an open secret that Škoda guns were inferior to those of Krupp and Schneider-Creusot, competitors for the Serbian contract, but, as one contemporary pointed out, it 'would also involve a still greater danger, namely that Serbia, in arming her military, might then be at the technical mercy of the only power which seriously threatened her independence'.[36]

Serbia's decision to buy Schneider-Creusot guns from France added to Vienna's rage over the Bulgarian trade treaty and led to the imposition of the commercial blockade in January 1906. The Austrian press anticipated an early triumph in the struggle with Serbia. *Zeit* claimed that 'In desiring a customs union with Bulgaria, Serbia will suffocate in her own swine-fat!'[37] It would be a few months, the imperial government assumed, before Serbia, starved of the economic resources which only Austria-Hungary could provide, would be begging for forgiveness and assistance from the Monarchy. Yet by October 1906, Serbia was busy finding new markets and seemed less inclined than ever to request Vienna's help. The Foreign Minister, Gołuchowski, was forced to resign. His ambitious replacement, Aehrenthal, urged an end to the Pig War, telling the Council of Ministers in Vienna that 'our policy of making Serbia economically and politically dependent has failed completely'.[38]

Aehrenthal thought it especially disturbing that the main beneficiary of Serbia's new diverse trading patterns was Germany. The Foreign Minister was pursuing a policy which hoped to lessen Vienna's political dependence on Berlin and create a more equal alliance between the two central powers. His attempt was made difficult by Germany's economic penetration of the Balkans and he was desperate to restore Austrian influence in the region. The economic blockade of Serbia effectively handed commercial domination of the Balkans on a plate to Germany and France. For this reason, Aehrenthal argued in late 1907, Vienna should drop the blockade and find other ways of drawing the south Slav state closer to the Empire.

The Hungarians were reliably on hand to scotch this attempt at reviving Habsburg influence in Serbia. Hungarian farmers had grown accustomed to the lack of competition and were in no mood to see Serbian pigs cross the imperial borders again. On top of this, they were suspicious of a new political coalition, comprising the Archduke Franz Ferdinand, Aehrenthal and Count Franz Conrad von Hötzendorf, the Chief of the General Staff. From late 1906, this peculiar triumvirate began gently expanding its influence at the expense of Franz Joseph and, wherever possible, the Hungarians. All three bore grudges against the Hungarian elite. Aehrenthal accepted the post of Foreign Minister only reluctantly because he felt that his predecessor, Count Gołuchowski, had conceded too many foreign-policy prerogatives to the Hungarians. General Hötzendorf found himself in permanent conflict with the Hungarians over the funding of the armed forces and the vexed issue of Hungarian as a second language of command in the army. He believed, as did Aehrenthal, that if the Hungarians succeeded in establishing two separate chains of command in the armed forces of the Dual Monarchy this would signal the dissolution of the Empire. Hötzendorf frequently vented his frustration with the Hungarians to anybody prepared to listen. But nobody loathed the Hungarians as passionately as Franz Ferdinand. He saw their hand in every political failure, domestic or foreign. 'As I always say and always will say the so-called "upstanding Hungarian" simply does not exist,' he fulminated. 'And every Hungarian, be he minister, prince, cardinal, citizen, farmer, hussar or a servant, is a revolutionary and a whore (alright the cardinal is no whore, but he's a republican nonetheless)!'[39]

Franz Ferdinand, Aehrenthal and Hötzendorf made odd bedfellows. The Archduke had persuaded his uncle, Franz Joseph, to appoint Aehrenthal and Hötzendorf to their posts in the autumn of 1906. Franz Ferdinand now believed that he could control these two key offices of state because the newcomers, he wrote, were 'my men through and through – [we are] a trifolium', as he put it, 'who will get along famously!'[40] But if such a complex plant were to replace the wilting stem of Franz Joseph's authority, its members would need to be united in purpose and complementary in temperament. They were neither.

Archduke Franz Ferdinand von Österreich-Este was not a favourite of Franz Joseph. The Emperor recognized his nephew's loyalty to the Monarchy and to its conservative values, but he thought Franz Ferdinand impetuous. One historian has claimed that their mutual feelings were tainted by 'fear and hatred'.[41] Above all, the heir to the throne had deeply offended his uncle by insisting upon his choice of a Czech commoner, Sophie Chotek, for a wife. In part due to his disapproval of this morganatic match, Franz Joseph blocked the Archduke from holding high office. He did, however, allow his nephew to establish a Military Chancellery at the Belvedere. From this magnificent palace, originally built for Prinz Eugen of Savoy, which stretches grandly from the south-eastern corner of Vienna's Ringstrasse, Franz Ferdinand assembled a network of contacts and friendships which could circumvent the ponderous but deeply rooted 'k. & k.' bureaucracy. Under the direction of a brilliant young general staff officer, Captain Alexander Brosch von Aarenau, who was appointed in January 1906, the Military Chancellery at the Belvedere became the rallying point of influential conservatives, prompting the famous remark that 'not only do we have two parliaments, but two Kaisers as well'. Brosch himself described the Chancellery as 'His Majesty's Most Loyal Opposition'.

As the Archduke sought to extend his influence, his friends and advisers became aware that his personality was his own worst enemy, 'or, more to the point, his most notable feature lay in people's reaction to his personality as he was incredibly unpopular among all classes'.[42] His oblong face, often red with distemper, projected an image which cartoonists seized on with glee. Others were more circumspect – for although Franz Joseph denied his nephew all official functions, the source of Franz Ferdinand's power lay in the knowledge that one day he would be Emperor. Potential opponents thought twice before antagonizing the heir apparent. Often they angered him without knowing why. The shrewd but loyal Brosch, Franz Ferdinand's closest confidant for five years, observed that 'the Archduke suspects that people underestimate him. This results in an understandable jealousy directed against those senior functionaries who boast the greatest reputation in the military or in public life. If these functionaries, like Conrad [Hötzendorf] for example, are unable to hide their feelings of superiority, their action provokes crises which are extremely difficult to overcome.'[43]

Franz Ferdinand's awkward relationship with Hötzendorf was not restricted to matters of personal style. They had serious policy differences as well. The Archduke had a clear but utterly unworkable programme – the restoration of absolutism in anticipation of his own elevation to the throne. Here lay the political explanation for his hostility to the Hungarians, whom he blamed for corrupting both the internal mechanisms and the external image of the Empire. To undermine the Hungarians, Franz Ferdinand cultivated certain leaders of the minorities in the Hungarian lands – Croats, Slovaks and Romanians – with the promise of a 'federalized Empire', which would mean freedom from Hungarian authoritarianism. Such was the hopeless contradiction at the heart of Franz Ferdinand's strategy – he believed he could erect a highly centralized régime on the basis of devolution. These devolutionary principles were not prompted by a belief in the rights of small nations (indeed, he dismissed the south Slavs as a *Gesindel* or rabble) but in an obsessive desire to rub Hungarian noses in the dirt.

His conservative conviction that only a strong monarchy could save the Habsburg Empire also defined his foreign policy, such as it was. He encouraged the revival of the *Dreikaiserbündnis*, the ring binding the three reactionary houses of Hohenzollern, Romanov and Habsburg. The widespread belief that Franz Ferdinand was the leader and inspiration behind the Military Party, the informal group of conservatives committed to offensive military action as the best form of defence, was incorrect. Far from harbouring aggressive imperialist intentions, which he feared might tempt the monarchies into war with one another, the Archduke consistently shied away from the use of force as an instrument of foreign policy since he 'regarded the army primarily as an instrument against "the internal enemy" which he once described as "Jews, Freemasons, Socialists, and Hungarians", and he always considered a revolution far more likely than a foreign war'.[44]

This brought him into regular conflict with his appointee, Hötzendorf. The Archduke sympathized with the Chief of General Staff's never-ending struggle to find extra resources for the modernization of the military. But Hötzendorf's determined attempts to restore the capabilities and prestige of the armed forces could not conceal his addiction to preventive war as the panacea for all ills afflicting the Empire. The mere hint of foreign-policy tension was enough for Hötzendorf to demand a declaration of war on Italy, Serbia or Russia, or even, when at his most excitable, two of the three simultaneously.

As a military leader, Hötzendorf's record was patchy. This was a time of great change in the technology of warfare but, to judge by his military writings prior to the First World War, he had failed to learn the lessons from the Boer and Russo-Japanese wars about the changing relationship between infantry and artillery. Infantry, he declared in 1911, could 'without the support of other arms, even in inferior numbers, gain victory as long as it is tough and brave'.[45] Hötzendorf's anachronistic belief in the values of the parade ground and cold steel later contributed much to the enormous casualties suffered by the Austro-Hungarian forces in the early stages of the First World War.

But to his credit, as a historian of the Habsburg military has pointed out, Hötzendorf did recognize that:

> modern technology and communications had removed the traditional restrictions on the size of armies and he asserted that this was only limited by the willingness and the ability of a state to support its military establishment. But this, of course, was the Achilles' heel of the Dual Monarchy. It was Conrad's [Hötzendorf's] fate to serve a multinational empire where there were deep divisions on military policy . . . Unless Conrad could obtain broad-based support for the military establishment, Austria-Hungary was doomed to fall further and further behind in the armament race. The real question therefore was whether Conrad was indeed the man to overhaul the armed forces of the Dual Monarchy.[46]

Baron von Aehrenthal clearly believed Hötzendorf to be the wrong man. Soon after their appointment, Hötzendorf began to complain that the Foreign Minister was keeping him in the dark on crucial issues, and their diverging opinions 'led to many misunderstandings between myself and some of our diplomats, above all with Baron Ährenthal'.[47]

Of this troika, whose word carried most weight after the Emperor's, Aehrenthal was without question the most competent and dynamic. A series of memoranda which he completed soon after assuming office illustrates his determination to restore the Dual Monarchy's prestige as a great power. He recognized the dangers which Hungarian particularism posed for the Empire. But instead of venting his spleen in public, as Franz Ferdinand did, or, like Hötzendorf, writing a stream of petulant letters complaining about how disrespectfully his colleagues treated him, Aehrenthal devised a plan. It was a complicated plan, it was intellectually rigorous, and it was ambitious. It was based on Benjamin von Kállay's plan for Bosnia, that is, on the wrong one.

Instead of confronting Hungary, Aehrenthal reasoned, it was necessary to coax Budapest back into supporting the imperial interests of the state. So he proposed that Vienna should relinquish direct rule of Dalmatia, which should be restored to its place in the Croatian Triune Kingdom. This would then come under the aegis of Budapest, and bind Hungary into Austria's economic and strategic development of the Adriatic coast. Bosnia and Hercegovina would be annexed, attached to the Triune Kingdom, and the provinces' three Slav communities – Catholic, Muslim and Orthodox – given a degree of political autonomy. The aim was to create a strong south Slav commitment to the Empire. 'If we meet their national aspirations half way, then we would create the *outer framework* of a south Slav group which (in the closest union with the Kingdom of Hungary) would guarantee far into the future the influence of the Monarchy at the gates of the Orient.'[48] The crowning glory of this strategy was that it would neutralize the 'magnetic force' which Serbia exerted over south Slavs in the Empire and elsewhere. Aehrenthal truly believed that if his plan were followed, the relationship between Serbia and the Slavs of Austria-Hungary would be reversed:

> Whereas at the moment, we are forced to defend ourselves in any way we can against greater Serbian greed, the south Slav group created by us under the aegis of the Crown of St Stephen [the Hungarian lands] would *itself* exert such a strong magnetic force that in the long run the Sava Kingdom [Serbia] would not be able to resist.
>
> In economic terms, the magnetic force would manifest itself in Serbia itself being compelled sooner or later to request membership of our customs union.[49]

Later, Aehrenthal would go further, telling Conrad the aim was to dismember Serbia, offering the southern half to an expanded Bulgaria while integrating the north into the Empire. The longer he was in office, the more determined he became to destroy Serbia, that 'nest of revolutionaries'. Yet although the plan was essentially an example of naked imperialist aggression, it actually represented a reduction of Habsburg ambition in the region. Aehrenthal specifically rejected the goal of pushing down towards Salonika* – when Turkey eventually withdrew from Macedonia, he thought, it should be left to the Balkan states (by which he meant Greece, Albania and Bulgaria which would by this time, if everything went according to his plan, be friendly powers). Henceforth, Serbia was to be the central focus of Habsburg foreign policy.

When relations between Great Britain and Russia began to warm during 1907, Aehrenthal became ever more convinced that the status quo in the Balkans could not be sustained and the time for action had come. For the first and last time, all political forces in Vienna could agree on a strategy. Hötzendorf noted in his memoirs that it was only during the annexation crisis that everybody cooperated – Franz Joseph, Aehrenthal, Hötzendorf and later Franz Ferdinand all worked together smoothly, full of mutual congratulation in the erroneous belief that the annexation of Bosnia and Hercegovina would be an unqualified success.

The Young Turk revolution of July 1908 set the ball in motion. Intelligence from the Ottoman Empire suggested that its new masters were preparing to reintroduce the constitution with an expanded franchise. In theory, the occupied provinces were still loyal to the Sultan. Vienna feared that the Young Turks might invite the inhabitants of Bosnia and Hercegovina to send delegates to the assembly in Istanbul, thereby questioning Austria's *de facto* right to administer the two provinces. Throughout September, Aehrenthal cajoled the various domestic constituencies in the Dual Monarchy to agree to the annexation while also encouraging Prince Ferdinand in Bulgaria to exploit the confusion in the Ottoman Empire by declaring Bulgaria's full independence. An independent Bulgaria was an integral part of Aehrenthal's anti-Serbian strategy, and a unilateral declaration of independence by Bulgaria, theoretically a violation of the Congress of Berlin, would deflect great-power attention away from the annexation of Bosnia, another violation. The annexation of

* There is no hard evidence that the Habsburgs sought control of Salonika but it was widely believed both inside and outside the Empire that this was Vienna's intention. There is, however, no question that Vienna sought control over the rail network linking Salonika to Belgrade and the north.

the two provinces implied an end to the status quo as established in Berlin in 1878 while, for Serbia, it meant exclusion from an area which had become by this time a national obsession. If the rumours heard around Vienna were true, and as we have seen, they were, the annexation might also preface an attempt by Austria-Hungary to suck Serbia into its sphere of Balkan influence or even attempt to incorporate the Kingdom into the Dual Monarchy. For the other great powers, the annexation would generate an exceptionally delicate diplomatic situation. But in Serbia, it was perceived as a direct challenge to the country's sovereignty and, indeed, its existence.

The actual announcement on 7 October that Bosnia and Hercegovina had been admitted as a fully fledged inmate to the 'great prison house of nations' was inept. A gaff by the Monarchy's representative in France let the cat out of the bag prematurely. Kaiser Wilhelm II, the rock upon which all Habsburg aspirations ultimately relied, was apoplectic that the Ballplatz in Vienna had not informed him in advance. The Russian Foreign Minister, Alexander Izvolsky, who had supposedly agreed the annexation *a priori* with Aehrenthal, claimed he knew nothing about it.*

But in Austria itself, it was hailed as a great victory. In a letter of 11 October, praising Aehrenthal for his handling of the affair, Franz Ferdinand caught the weird mood of oneiric optimism which was sweeping across both Vienna and Budapest:

> Dear Baron Aehrenthal!
>
> Now that the first days of excitement have passed, I am compelled to offer you my most heartfelt and warmest congratulations on your *superb* execution of the annexation.
>
> It is thanks to *you* that we have shown Europe once again that we are still a great power! Excellent! You yourself must feel genuine joy and satisfaction that your task has met with such success. Carry on as you have done and don't put up with any nonsense from anyone.
>
> Now, however, the *main thing* is to keep the peace in Bosnia with an iron rod. Any attempt at a putsch or an infiltration by

* Izvolsky's claim that the matter had not been agreed upon at his notorious meeting with Aehrenthal at Buchlau seems in part to have reflected the Russian Minister's incompetence and in part the Austrian's cunning.

> the comitadjis [Serbian *četnik* bands] from across the borders must be met with execution by shooting, hanging etc. We have to keep an especially tight rein on the Serbs in Bosnia, keep them frightened . . . And every emissary from Serbia must be thrown out forthwith.[50]

For six months after the annexation, the threat of war hung over Europe. This was when the 'robbers', as Tolstoy called them, began their countless 'discussions in their thieves' jargon' as to who should receive what in compensation. If no agreement were reached, it was assumed, there would be armed conflict. Talks, open and secret, were held, and ultimatums sent. A few weeks after the annexation, the unified front of the Monarchy's leadership again began to crack. Hötzendorf sounded his inevitable call to arms. Austria-Hungary should exploit the moment by attacking Serbia, he argued, thereby ensuring Belgrade's subservience to Vienna's Balkan policy. The Chief of the General Staff pointed out that Serbia had only just begun to re-equip its army and could offer little resistance. But much more significantly, Russia was in no position to offer military support to Serbia in the event of war. Still suffering from the after-effects of the Russo-Japanese war, the imperial Russian forces would not confront Austria-Hungary especially, as Hötzendorf believed with good reason, since the German army would be prepared to back an Austrian attack on Serbia.

Aehrenthal and Franz Ferdinand coordinated their tactics in order to scupper the plans of Hötzendorf and 'his warmongering entourage', as the Archduke liked to dismiss the Military Party. For his part, the Chief of the General Staff tried in vain to persuade Franz Joseph to intervene on his behalf. He was the General who cried wolf: but from the point of view of Habsburg imperialism, Hötzendorf was for once absolutely right – 1908 was indeed the time to strike against Serbia and thereby humiliate Russia when neither England nor France showed any serious inclination to defend a weakened Russia.

Rumours that the Dual Monarchy was on the verge of annexing Bosnia and Hercegovina filtered into Serbia on 5 October. 'The news spread through Belgrade like wildfire and within minutes there was a huge crowd gathered in front of the National Theatre protesting against the annexation.' Branislav Nušić, the author, climbed onto the theatre's balcony and railed against 'the plunder of both these Serbian lands', before demanding the formation of volunteer forces. The Austrian consul in Belgrade reported that all newspapers demanded the immediate mobilization of the Serbian army. Within hours, cavalry units were cantering through the streets of the Serbian capital as the population prepared for a massive demonstration on 6 October. Day in, day out, the crowds screamed for vengeance and called for Bosnia and Hercegovina to be saved 'from the clutches of the loathsome Black Eagle'. Politician after intellectual after diplomat after journalist denounced the annexation in ever more violent and emotive terms. The Habsburg flag was burnt in public. No less a figure than the young Crown Prince Djordje assumed the role of standard-bearer of anti-Austrian sentiment, and was to be seen daily leading demonstrations to protest the sudden violation of the Berlin Treaty.

The Serbian government first requested that the remaining signatory states of the Berlin Treaty compel Austria to rescind the annexation; 'if, however, this is not deemed possible then the Royal Government, appealing to the just sentiments of the Signatory Powers of the Berlin Treaty, demands that Serbia be awarded appropriate compensation'.[51] To underscore its demands for compensation and, at the very least, autonomy for Bosnia's population, the Serbian cabinet sent leading politicians to all great-power capitals, with the exception of Vienna. They soon learnt that the Russians were not prepared to back any Serbian action and that ultimately Serbia would have to accept the annexation. For several months, the Serbian government continued to agitate for some form of compensation, acting under immense popular pressure. The National Theatre was packed every day as patriotic works by Nušić and the Bosnian playwright, Petar Kočić, were staged. These were followed by demonstrations, torch-lit processions and appeals for volunteers to form *četnik* bands. But eventually, after the Russian government (itself under enormous pressure from Germany) warned Serbia in March 1909 to accept the Dual Monarchy's incorporation of the two provinces, the government reluctantly accepted the new status quo in Europe.

A few days before Serbia's humiliating recognition of the annexation, Milovan Milovanović, the Serbian Foreign Minister, appeared after midnight at the Hotel Moskva on Terazija, Belgrade's main thoroughfare. Sitting with some friends, he remained quiet for some time. Then, suddenly, he drew breath to speak:

> The situation for us Serbs is unfortunately very difficult. We must bow to the inevitable. Europe wants quiet, nothing but quiet. We are told that we are in the right but that being in the right is of no use to us. Things are also bad in Europe. Violence will be avenged, must, indeed, be avenged. Europe will not remain as she is now for long. On my travels through the European capitals, I could see that much is rotten. How the change will come is impossible to know. Perhaps some social upheaval; I believe that a revolution in Russia seems most probable. But I may be mistaken. But, dear friends, one thing I know for certain, I can feel it – that Bosnia and Hercegovina will not remain in Austria's possession for long. I can't tell whether it will last another two or three years. But I will put my life on it that Bosnia will be free by 1920. Who knows whether any of us will witness it . . . and who knows how it will all come about?[52]

Around the time that Milovanović was reflecting on a dark future, Serb nationalists founded two organizations which would play an important role in answering the Foreign Minister's question as to how change would come about. The first, *Narodna Odbrana* (National Defence), was established with the specific aim of 'protecting and promoting our interests in the annexed provinces'. The second, *Ujedinjenje ili Smrt* (Unification or Death), was the creation of Apis, the leader of the 1903 regicide. Apis's decision to form Unification or Death was, in Vladimir Dedijer's words,

> a direct product of the climate of despair provoked in Belgrade by the annexation . . . Up to that time the regicides . . . had been concerned primarily with military affairs, leaving foreign and internal political issues to the political parties . . . After the 1908–9 crisis they turned toward a so-called 'national propaganda' and through that to the realm of foreign policy, in which they no longer saw eye to eye with the political parties. This change in Colonel Apis's political course coincided with the growing importance of the army in both the external and internal relations of Serbia.[53]

The annexation crisis had ended but the Bosnian crisis was far from over, despite Baron Aehrenthal's serene optimism. The gun had not yet been placed in young Princip's hand, but the final elements of catastrophe were coming together.

Vukojebinje: Bosnia

Several months after the outbreak of the Great War, the usual émigrés were to be found in the Café à la Rotonde in Paris: the small Russian sculptor whose dog was more popular on the Left Bank than his sculptures; the Spaniard, whiskers trimmed to perfection, who never took off that coat with the distinctive red and green lining; and two Romanians wearing large gold rings who, like everyone else except the Italian engaged in seducing a young model, were discussing politics. Through the curtain of cigarette smoke, it was possible to detect 'one of those figures who looks as if he were created just to induce a sense of unease in decent folk. Tall, thin but strong, coal-brown with an expression of unrest and energy in his eyes, he glares sharply at everything and everyone, greedy for new impressions of a strange world but sufficiently capable to avoid losing himself in it.'[54]

Few worlds could have been more distant from the louche cosmopolitanism of wartime Paris than the dusty plateaux around Rudina in Hercegovina, the place where the disturbing man, Vladimir Gaćinović, had been born in 1890. This landscape was as tough as any on the Balkan peninsula. The very name, Rudina, was taken from the type of soil which can only sustain the hardiest grass. Although only 40 kilometres north-east of Dubrovnik, any memory of the Adriatic's Venetian masterpiece was erased by the grim landscape around the tiny village of Kačanj. This was the quintessential *vukojebinje** of south Slavic lore. The thinly scattered population lived in primitive dwellings of stone, timber and mud. The soil's infertility meant that the peasantry were mainly sheep and goat farmers. Most families would leave during the winter, unable to tolerate the hardships it brought. Gaćinović's elders 'could still remember the times when they had to make bread from the bark of the maple-tree'.[55]

The Gaćinović family, who were Serbs, had always enjoyed the

* The land where wolves fuck.

privilege of appointing the local knez or chief. It was thanks to this position as the senior family of the clan that Vladimir became only the second boy ever from Rudina to attend primary school in Bileća before going to the *Gymnasium* in Mostar. Gaćinović demonstrated astonishing aptitude and was soon reading fiction and political literature, most of it Russian, above all Herzen, Bakunin and his special mentor, the anarchist Prince Petr Alexandreyevich Kropotkin. The Muslim Movement for Autonomy and the political and cultural organizations of Serbs and Croats had turned Mostar into a lively intellectual centre – no school in Bosnia and Hercegovina produced more political activists of all denominations than the *Gymnasium* in Hercegovina's capital. In his late teens, Gaćinović visited Belgrade for the first time and, under the influence of nationalist circles in the Serbian capital, began organizing underground cells, so-called *kružoks*, throughout Bosnia and Hercegovina but also in Zagreb, the Croatian capital, and among the Serbs of western Slavonia. In 1911, he became a member of Unification or Death, Api's secret society committed to liberating Bosnia from Habsburg rule, the only leading figure from *Mlada Bosna* (Young Bosnia)* to do so.

Gaćinović's friends and followers were mostly like him – quiet, young, undernourished, intense, swinging furiously between moods of sentimentality and ruthless revolutionary aggression. For many, the single most formative experience in their lives was to be introduced into urban life after a childhood of rural isolation. The majority of those who formed Young Bosnia after 1908 came from extremely poor rural backgrounds, and most of them hailed from eastern Hercegovina or from Bosanska Krajina, in the north-west of the country. One of them was Gavrilo Princip, the humiliated volunteer of 1912. His modest family dwelling in the Krajina was built in a style described by one visitor as 'Bosnian Gothic':

* The name *Mlada Bosna* was first used in the nationalist newspaper of Bosnian Serbs, *Otadžbina*, in 1907 and then popularized in an article by Gaćinović in 1911. However, both understood Young Bosnia to be a broad movement of intellectual activity against Austrian rule in Bosnia, particularly among students. Gaćinović's two models were Young Italy and Young Russia. After the First World War, Young Bosnia soon came to mean the narrow conspiracy which succeeded in the assassination of Franz Ferdinand. Although not an active participant of the conspiracy, Gaćinović was considered this Young Bosnia's chief ideologue.

> In the old house the doors are small, and so very low that you can enter the house only by bowing your head. Inside it is dark. The house has no windows; instead of floor only beaten earth. To the left from the door is a stone bench on which a wooden barrel for water was standing; behind this, on a shelf, some cooking utensils, earthernware pots; a big round low table was hanging against the wall . . . Smoke went through a *badza*, a hole in the roof above the open fireplace. The only light in the house came through it.[56]

Young Princip knew nothing else until his teens – rocks, windswept shrub, poverty worsened by the annual cash tribute to the absentee landlord, and a rigid patriarchal system inverted fortuitously by his own parents' unusual relationship. His strong-willed mother encouraged Princip's reading and he, like Gaćinović, was able to break out of this crushing environment. When Gavrilo was still a young teenager, his father accompanied him on the three-day trek to Sarajevo where he hoped to attend secondary school. In the Bosnian capital, Princip was confronted with a world of unimaginable colour and drama. The *čaršija* (market) was

> buzzing with peoples of every faith and every station. Each street boasted its own craft – the leather guild, the copper smiths, locksmiths, gunsmiths, taverns . . . Old nags being led through the streets by peasants in makeshift shirts with short open sleeves and shoulders swelled up. Around their heads they had wide towelling in contrast to the green sashes worn by Muslims . . . Hubo, Pipi-Rafo, Nazif and other clowns were always trying to brighten the general mood, and one would always play the tambura and sing . . . At dusk you could meet a veiled woman offering herself. Often these were not Muslim women but Christians who thought they were more alluring by dressing as forbidden fruit.[57]

The decades following the Habsburg occupation of Bosnia had seen a sharp rise in prostitution in the capital. The authorities allowed a red-light district to flourish behind the *čaršija*. Women from across the Austro-Hungarian Empire and the Balkans travelled to Sarajevo to work there as tens of thousands of German- and

Hungarian-speaking soldiers, bureaucrats and businessmen visited the city. For the young Bosnian idealists arriving from the countryside, this decadence represented most of the things they despised – colonialists who not only brought their sabres but their corruption as well. The young nationalists speculated bitterly that the colonizers had established these brothels in a conscious attempt to demoralize Bosnians by introducing venereal disease into a hitherto chaste population, attacking Bosnia's very soul – the strong family bonds so integral to rural life. Princip and his friends were rigid ascetics – they abjured alcohol and considered physical love impure, an insult to women, whose role in their world should be restricted to that of mother or sister.

These rebellious offspring of the peasantry came to despise the towns and cities where they received an education. Austro-Hungarian rule had of course brought not only prostitution, but architectural innovation and the first signs of affluence to Sarajevo. None of this, however, filtered down to the penniless students like Gavrilo Princip, dependent on the charity of relatives earning modest livings in business, or on stipends from religious organizations dedicated to improving the cultural life of Catholics, Orthodox Christians or Muslims. Their contact with people outside their own peer group was minimal. Instead, they sat in particular coffee houses and held endless awkward discussions about the relationship between social and national revolution, about romanticism and realism in literature, and about their dreams of national liberation.

Despite their confused adolescent yearnings, they did represent the peasantry's first authentic political voice, and 'could see that the population from the villages, ignorant and lacking organization, had been left to fend for themselves'.[58] Until 1908, these new intellectuals remained relatively passive, following the orthodox line of evolutionary struggle which south Slav students had imbibed from the Czech philosopher and politician, Tomáš Garrigue Masaryk, who by this time wielded substantial influence in Croatia and Bosnia. Then, when the annexation of Bosnia and Hercegovina in October that year led to a swift radicalization of school students and young intellectuals in the two provinces, they remained isolated in Bosnian society. The annexation may have excited a nationalist fever in Serbia, fed by intellectuals, soldiers and politicians; in Bosnia itself much of the population accepted it without a murmur.

Bosnia had a reputation for violence. 'It was always our Spain', lamented Jovan Skerlić, Serbia's leading turn-of-the-century literary critic and a significant influence on the Young Bosnians, 'the Spain which was torn apart by Moors, Jews and papists.' Yet this pessimistic vision of a province traumatized by relentless, irrational violence was as inaccurate at the beginning of the twentieth century as it would be at the end. It assumed the three Bosnian faiths were engaged in a Hobbesian struggle with one another. There were in fact two distinct causes of violence in Bosnia from the mid-nineteenth century onwards – the peasant revolt, and the resistance of the elite to imperial centralization, Ottoman or Habsburg. In 1908, neither the peasantry nor the landowners and the merchants of Bosnia were sufficiently disadvantaged by the annexation (very little was changed by it *inside* the provinces) to risk their livelihoods for a futile adventure. Indeed, among the strongest backers of annexation was the increasingly influential elite of Serbian traders in the towns, especially in Sarajevo, but also in Banja Luka and Mostar. Evgenije Letica, the Metropolitan of the Serbian Orthodox Church in Sarajevo, even held a special service to celebrate the event, and asked 'all the worshippers to kneel down and pray for divine blessings for the Emperor Franz Josef and the Habsburg dynasty. All went down except a group of boys from the high school. They stood firmly upright among their kneeling elders.'[59]

This was the first public protest of the young intellectuals, although the event was equally striking as a manifestation of *support* for the annexation among the Serb elite. The Young Bosnians denounced their elders as collaborators bought off by the colonial power. One student, Nedeljko Čabrinović, was in a peculiarly awkward position as his father was a professional spy for the Austro-Hungarian police. Čabrinović's need to cleanse the stain of his compromised father was his primary motive for participating in the assassination of Franz Ferdinand. During his interrogation after the assassination, Čabrinović revealed that his group had not intended to stop with the murders of Franz Ferdinand and General Oskar Potiorek, the military governor of Bosnia. The conspiracy had also sentenced to death Metropolitan Letica and three leading Serb businessmen and politicians from Sarajevo.

The Black Hand and Young Bosnia: Bosnia, Croatia and Serbia

Baron von Aehrenthal, the Austrian Foreign Minister, justified his decision to annex Bosnia and Hercegovina with the claim that Serbia was already using its network of secret agents and conspiratorial cells to destabilize the provinces. On the day in August 1908 that Aehrenthal announced in cabinet his intention to annex Bosnia and Hercegovina, Hungarian police arrested leading Serbs in Croatia who stood accused of being in the pay of *Slovenski Jug* (Slav South), a nationalist organization founded in Belgrade in 1903. Relying on the testimony of an experienced police agent, the state prosecutor demanded death by hanging for fifty-three men accused of committing high treason.

The evidence was ripped to shreds by the brilliant Zagreb lawyer, Dr Hinković, aided by an invaluable intervention from T.G. Masaryk. 'So scandalous were the proceedings', Wickham Steed reported, 'that an outcry arose throughout Europe . . . The judges, who had been chosen for their subservience to the Magyar political authorities, eventually feared to pronounce any death sentence, and inflicted only long terms of penal servitude.'[60] The Serbs were eventually released. Then, as if the Habsburg authorities had not yet sufficiently humiliated themselves, in December 1909, Aehrenthal persuaded a historian attached to the Foreign Ministry, Dr Heinrich Friedjung, to publish a series of documents which demonstrated that several politicians in Croatia, including Frano Supilo, had been in receipt of large sums of money from the Serbian government. When the Serb-Croat Coalition sued for libel, Dr Friedjung was forced to retract the allegations. It emerged that the documents had been forged by members of the Habsburg consular mission in Belgrade.

Apart from leaving a poor impression on international public opinion, the collapse of the two trials proved beyond doubt that, contrary to Aehrenthal's claims, there was no Serbian-backed conspiracy in either Croatia or Bosnia. Aehrenthal justified the annexation of Bosnia as a means to throttle embryonic terrorism. In fact, it created the problem. Immediately after the annexation, nationalists in Belgrade founded *Narodna Odbrana* (NO; National Defence) to tremendous public acclaim. And although the leading Serbs, Muslims and Croats of Bosnia rather welcomed annexation, it turned the dreamy students of Sarajevo into a group of self-sacrificing fanatics.

The humiliating ultimatum, which the Serbian government was forced to accept under Russian pressure in March 1909, included a paragraph insisting that the NO be transformed into a harmless cultural organization, which must cut its links to Serbs in Macedonia, Bosnia and Croatia. True to its word, the Serbian government had soon all but extinguished the fire which the NO had generated in the early days of its existence. The volunteer brigades were disbanded, and planned *četnik* raids into Bosnia cancelled. Nationalist rhetoric clamouring for war with Austria disappeared from most newspapers. But some of the NO's members, especially a small but influential group of officers in the military, deeply resented what they regarded as the government's cowardice. Nonetheless, it would be another two years before these men decided to take policy into their own hands.

On 3 March 1911, the seven founding members of Unification or Death, known as the Black Hand, met at an apartment located appropriately on Bosnia Street (since renamed Gavrilo Princip Street) in the centre of Belgrade. The May 1903 conspirators, the murderers of King Aleksandar Obrenović and Queen Draga, made up the core of the Black Hand. Their organization was treasonable, as its oath contradicted their duty as military officers to serve their king. It was imperative to maintain secrecy, for the May Coup of 1903 had ensured that the authorities were sensitive to the merest whiff of conspiracy inside the army. The reigning Karadjordjević dynasty enjoyed no special protection from any future regicide.

The existence of the Black Hand was revealed within months of its foundation, but by then its influence extended into most branches of the military and into many government departments, notably the Foreign Ministry. So, although its mission was compromised, the Black Hand's leadership was able to exert pressure through its high-placed sympathizers, thereby maintaining a certain mystery about its nature and aims. Colonel Dragutin Dimitrijević – Apis – had agreed reluctantly to join the Central Executive Committee of the Black Hand, and it was not long before he had become the motor of the whole operation. 'His reasoning was always exhaustive and convincing. He could demonstrate how the most insurmountable task was in reality a small detail, how the most dangerous undertaking was innocent and harmless', explained Stanoje Stanojević, one of Apis's boldest critics inside the conspiracy. But the key to his mastery of conspiracy and political influence was his ability 'to hold everything in his hands while allowing even his most intimate friends to be informed only of that which affected them directly'.[61]

Apis and his friends were either politicians or army commanders. Intellectuals, however, they were not – patriotism for them meant the expansion and consolidation of the Serbian state through the agency of militarism. They relied on one man, Ljubomir Čupa-Jovanović, an ardent nationalist and co-founder of the Black Hand, to articulate any more literary version of their ideas. Gaćinović, who was usually sparing in his praise of others, held Čupa in the highest esteem. Emphasizing Čupa's exemplary sense of self-sacrifice, he called him 'the Mazzini of Young Serbia. Extremely tall, thin, with a high forehead, he [was] a tireless worker and a resolute ascetic . . . Čupa-Jovanović travelled throughout all Serbian lands, often on foot, to learn more about the regions and their people.'[62]

Čupa's most important role was as editor of the Black Hand's *Pijemont*, whose name underlined the ideological debt the organization owed to Italian nationalism. Another model its members extolled was German militarism. The German army had played the crucial role in the 'regeneration of the German nation', as *Pijemont*'s Berlin correspondent put it. He advised that Serbia follow Germany's example in creating the League of German Youth (*Jung Deutschland Bund*), founded, ironically, by General von der Goltz, the man who would prepare the Turkish Army for its war against the Balkan Alliance in 1912–13. The correspondent even went so far as to advocate, as Apis's biographer says, 'that Serbia adopt the League's racist and militarist approach, redolent of the later Hitler Youth, to achieve its goal of national unification'.[63] From a practical point of view, however, the Black Hand could hardly woo Germany as a potential ally because of Berlin's relationship with Vienna, the scourge of Belgrade. Since Serbian national interests coincided with Russian imperial interests after 1908, Apis forged close links with Russian consular staff, in particular the military attachés.

Although Čupa and Gaćinović together formed a rickety bridge between the Black Hand and Young Bosnia, the motives, methods and members of the two organizations were very different. The Black Hand had the resources and the ability to meddle in high politics. Its nationalism was free from ideological baggage, wedded instead to a militaristic concept of the state. Its members were disciplined, untroubled by questions of morality, and many were ruthless, accomplished soldiers. Its ultimate goal was the creation of a greater Serbia, which would include Macedonia, Bosnia and Croatia and all the Slavs who lived there. Although Young Bosnia's membership was predominantly Serb, it also attracted an important minority of Croats and some Muslims. And while the Young Bosnians regarded Serbia as the pillar which held up their aspirations, they recognized the contribution which Croat students and Muslim sympathizers in Bosnia could make to the movement for national liberation. The Young Bosnians were, however, less successful in specifying what the relationship between Serbia, Serbs and other south Slavs should be if Bosnia and Croatia were able to detach themselves from the Habsburg Empire. Emotionally bound to the peasantry, the Young Bosnians considered social revolution a necessary corollary of national liberation.

In 1910, a peasant revolt in a Croat village of the Bosanska Krajina spread throughout most of the Serb villages of the region. An Austrian force confronted the disorganized peasant rebels near the town of Doboj as they fled towards the Serbian border. The army then launched retaliatory raids throughout the region. This short uprising in the Krajina occurred just before the opening of the new Bosnian Sabor in Sarajevo, an institution which for the first time would allow Muslims, Serbs and Croats some influence on the decision-making process in Bosnia. The Austrian authorities under the relatively liberal Finance Minister, von Burián, had observed the growing loyalty of the merchant class and townsfolk towards the Empire. Von Burián regarded modest democratic reform as a way of integrating and embracing the Serb and Muslim elites. General Marijan Varešanin, the Military Governor of Bosnia, was given the honour of opening the new Sabor on 15 June. As he headed across the Kaiser's bridge in Sarajevo on the way back to his official residence, Bogdan Žerajić, a twenty-four-year-old Serb, fired five shots at him (all of them wide of their target) before turning his gun on himself.

Žerajić became the cult figure for all Young Bosnians. As a

student in Switzerland, he had come under the influence of Russian Social Revolutionaries who had encouraged his obsession with individual terror and martyrdom as political instruments. He too was raised in a Serb peasant family in Eastern Hercegovina and had studied in the Mostar *Gymnasium*. Gaćinović, who knew him well, wrote a famous obituary of the assassin, *Smrt jednog heroja* (Death of the Hero). He described Žerajić as 'young, lithe and primitive. He had dreamy eyes which stared far into the distance. His look was fiery, nervous . . . but he was quiet and melancholic, alone and free of personal caprice . . . He was divorced from us, living contentedly in his own world . . . Life haunted him, bringing fog into his warm, sunny soul.'[64] The assassination attempt, Gaćinović concluded ominously, was a harbinger of 'new people, new Serbs who will arise after the great sins of their fathers'.[65] In death, Žerajić inspired would-be assassins in Croatia, Bosnia and Serbia. Gavrilo Princip was a regular visitor at his grave to lay flowers. He, along with Čabrinović, Mehmed Mehmedbašić, Danilo Ilić, Gaćinović and others who were involved in the assassination of Franz Ferdinand in 1914, all committed themselves at different times to avenging Žerajić's death.

When war broke out between the Balkan Alliance and Turkey in October 1912, the community of Young Bosnians streamed into Serbia to volunteer their services to the Serbian army and *četnik* bands. Some like Gaćinović, who participated in the Montenegrin siege of Skutari, saw sustained military action. But most, like Princip, were rejected as being too young or puny. Several came into contact with the Black Hand for the first time and two members of its central executive committee, Vojin Tankosić, the guerrilla leader, and Rade Malobabić, Apis's personal spy in Croatia, Bosnia and Montenegro, cultivated friendships with these enthusiastic revolutionaries from 'the occupied Serbian lands'. These tenuous links were renewed over a year later when Trifko Grabež, a young Serb from Pale near Sarajevo, visited Tankosić and asked him to supply some bombs and guns for a secret operation in the Bosnian capital. After clearing the matter with Apis, Tankosić handed over four Browning revolvers and six bombs to the Young Bosnian conspirators.

Es ist nichts!: Sarajevo, 1914

> These events have been arranged by the same elements who, as early as 1914, brought untold suffering upon the world when they organized the assassination in Sarajevo. (Berlin, 6 April 1941)
>
> Adolf Hitler's appeal to the German people on the occasion of the attack on Yugoslavia[66]

In the final fourteen years of the nineteenth century, assassins around the world claimed the lives of major public figures at an average rate of one a year. The victims included the President of France, the Mayor of Chicago, the Prime Minister of Bulgaria and the Empress of Austria. At the turn of the century, however, successful political murders suddenly increased, heralding the age of the assassin. From 1900 to 1913, forty heads of state, politicians and diplomats fell victim to the terrorist's bullet or bomb. Among the victims were four kings (two from the Balkans, two from the Latin Mediterranean), six prime ministers, three presidents (all from the American continent, including William McKinley of the United States), and a host of ministers, military governors and senior policemen. Twenty-eight of the killings were carried out in Europe. 'The entire series of assassinations and terrorist acts', reflected one Yugoslav communist during the interwar period, 'formed a part, albeit an inevitable one, of the political reaction to the imperialist policies of great powers in the colonies.'[67] With a mildly exaggerated reputation as the capital of political murder (Russia was in fact the most dangerous place to be a police or government leader), the Balkans recorded eight successful assassinations; including two kings, one queen, two prime ministers and the commander in chief of the Turkish Army. Successful murders were dwarfed by the number of attempted assassinations.

In retrospect, each individual act of terrorism seems to take its place in the pattern of political violence leading up to Franz Ferdinand's assassination, a kind of crescendo. No other murder in history is perceived to have triggered such calamitous events – world war, imperial collapse, socialist revolution. In the interwar years alone, one Serbian historian claimed, some 3,000 works were published around the globe debating the issue of war guilt, starting with the assassination.[68] Just under thirty years later, Adolf Hitler and the German government used the events of 28 June 1914 as a justification for the *Wehrmacht*'s attack on Belgrade. Yet, despite all the scholarship and considerable detective work, the words of Edward Grey, the British Foreign Secretary in 1914, still hold true: 'The world will presumably never be told all that was behind the murder of the Archduke Franz Ferdinand. Probably there is not, and never was, any one person who knew all there was to know.'[69]

It is known, however, that the six conspirators who were lined up* along Sarajevo's Appel Quay by the Miljacka river on 28 June 1914 formed one of the most disorganized and inexperienced squadrons of assassins ever assembled. The most enduring mystery surrounding the assassination is not who did it or why, but how they ever succeeded. The Balkans had registered an astonishing number of assassinations which failed because the perpetrators either lost their nerve, or proved to be poor shots. The morning which culminated in Franz Ferdinand's death was littered with mishaps. The six conspirators were excitable teenagers with no practical experience of handling arms. Four of the assassins were either too scared or too incompetent to use their weapons. One, Čabrinović, threw a bomb which missed its target, bouncing off the back of Franz Ferdinand's car and wounding a member of the entourage and passers-by. Princip himself had a clear shot at the Archduke only because Franz Ferdinand's Czech chauffeur, who had never been to Sarajevo before, missed the turning from Appel Quay and had to stop and reverse, making the Archduke a sitting target for twenty seconds. That Princip actually succeeded in shooting Franz Ferdinand dead was nothing short of a miracle. After firing that shot, Princip let off a second, which fatally wounded the Archduke's wife. He had been aiming at the Military Governor, General Oskar Potiorek, but a bystander had tried to knock the gun out of his hand and the bullet hit the Duchess instead. Both Čabrinović and Princip swallowed the cyanide they had been given by Major Tankosić in Belgrade, but the poison had oxidized, causing them both excruciating pain but leaving them alive and fully conscious for the relentless beatings they received at the hands of the soldiers and policemen who arrested them.

In 1917, enemies of Apis in Serbia's government in exile in

* Mehmedbašić, Čubrilović, Čabrinović, Cvjetko Popović, Princip and Grabež, in that order.

Salonika put him on trial for murder and treason. During the proceedings, he said he had approved the Young Bosnians' plan because he believed Franz Ferdinand to be the moving spirit behind the Military Party in Vienna. Franz Ferdinand's death, Apis argued, would have reduced the risk of Austria declaring war on Serbia. Of course the assassination had precisely the opposite effect from that which Apis intended as 'alive, Franz Ferdinand had acted as a brake upon the pressures [in Austria] for military action; dead, he became the pretext for war. In his absence, Conrad [Hötzendorf], Krobatin [Minister of War], and even Franz Joseph could give full rein to their conservative realism.'[70] By killing Franz Ferdinand, the Young Bosnians signed Serbia's death warrant. Gavrilo Princip was also horrified by the outcome of his deed. The Habsburg Empire did collapse, although Princip did not live to see it as his pain-wrenched, fettered body finally expired in Theresienstadt (now Terezín in northern Bohemia) a year before the event. But according to the psychiatrist, Dr Martin Pappenheim, who interviewed him a number of times in 1916, he was stricken with guilt about the retribution unleashed on the Serbs during the First World War. 'The news about the Golgotha which his people were experiencing destroyed him utterly. He comforted himself that the World War would have broken out even without the assassination.'[71]

Princip was right. It was not the immediate cause of the Great War; hostilities did not break out until a month after the assassination. These followed Serbia's rejection of Vienna's demand for a full investigation into the Archduke's death, to be carried out by Austrian agencies in Serbia. Most European foreign ministries agreed that the Austrians had formulated the ultimatum in terms so harsh that the Serbs would be unable to accept it. It was also felt that Belgrade was given very little time (a mere forty-eight hours) to formulate its response.

With the exception of Count Leopold von Berchtold, Aehrenthal's successor as Foreign Minister and a close friend of Franz Ferdinand, few figures at the Viennese court mourned the death of the Archduke. The Emperor displayed little grief on learning the news of his nephew's death. He and Count Berchtold were now convinced by Hötzendorf's arguments in favour of war with Serbia, which they believed could easily be subjugated. This was their most glaring, but not their most serious miscalculation. The assumption made in Vienna that Germany and Austria were powerful enough to pacify Russia indicated that the Austro-Hungarian court had not fully understood Germany's war aims. Berlin was preparing to send troops not to the east but westwards to France. Hötzendorf had clearly misinterpreted Germany's intentions, although to his credit he no longer believed that Austria-Hungary could occupy Serbia without provoking a much wider war. He was also sceptical about the ability of the Habsburg military to win such a war (and this without taking into account his own serious shortcomings as a strategist). Nonetheless, over the next two weeks of that warm July in 1914, the most influential figures in Vienna's establishment agreed that Serbia must either abase itself and deny its sovereignty or face war.

CHAPTER 5

A HOUSE OF WARS

War and peace, 1914–24

Ein Verwundeter
tastet sich kriechend vorwärts

Fluch, Kaiser, dir! Ich spüre deine Hand,
an ihr ist Gift und Nacht und Vaterland!
Sie riecht nach Pest und allem Untergang.
Dein Blick ist Galgen und dein Bart der Strang!
Dein Lachen Lüge und dein Hochmut Haß,
dein Zorn ist deiner Kleinheit Übermaß,
der alle Grenze, alles Maß verrückt,
um groß zu sein, wenn er die Welt zerstückt.

Laß deinen Kanzler, deine Diplomaten
durch dieses Meer von Blut und Tränen waten!
Fluch, Kaiser, dir und Fluch auch deiner Brut,
hinreichend Blut, ertränk sie in der Flut!

A wounded soldier
groping forwards on all fours

I curse you, Emperor! I feel your hand,
In which you hold poison and night and Fatherland!
It smells of plague and the end of hope.
Your look is the gallows, your whiskers the rope.
Your laughter is the lie, your arrogance hate,
As your girth is small, so is your wrath great,
Exceeding all measure and breaching all limit,
To gorge on the world when you plunge in your knife.

Let your Chancellor, and let your diplomats,
Wade through this sea of blood and tears!
I curse you, Emperor, and curse your brood,
Let all this blood, drown them in the flood![1]

The Great European War

In 1914, imperialist rivalry celebrated its zenith by persuading all the Eurasian empires to divert their enormous economic and technological resources into one vast industrial conglomerate of death. During the five months of the battle of Verdun in 1916, for example, 'more than twenty-three million shells were fired by the two contending armies [French and German] . . . on average more than a hundred shells a minute'.[2] This was war beyond all comprehension or recognition. The generals who marshalled gigantic armies had never conceived of military action on this scale; hundreds of thousands of young men paid for the inexperience of their military chiefs.

Reducing the events of the First World War to an inevitable consequence of imperialist competition is neither original nor especially revealing. Not only, 'is this insufficient', as one Yugoslav historian has noted, 'it is a truism which offers no clues as to why peasants, belonging to different churches, were fighting one another many miles from the front line on some Balkan hills as though it was their war'.[3] It is an explanation that has masked the complex web of relationships between and within the two blocs, the Entente and the Central Powers. Most Balkan countries, especially Serbia, Turkey, Bulgaria and Romania, were hopelessly tangled in the web.

Kaiser Wilhelm II's enthusiasm for war was fired by a highly charged nationalism and facilitated by an immense economic potential. Germany belonged, with Italy, to the so-called *verspätete Nationen* (late-coming nations), which sought to compensate for their delayed arrival in the game of imperialism. From the 1890s, Germany developed its *Weltpolitik*, a determined attempt to establish itself at the very least as an imperial power and, if possible, the leading great power. The population of 'the young German Empire . . . grows annually by 800,000–900,000 people', argued Kurt Riezler, Chancellor Bethmann-Hollweg's senior adviser, 'and for these new masses food must be found, or, what amounts to the same, work . . . The demands of the German nation for power and prestige, not only in Europe, but throughout the world, have increased rapidly.'[4] It was this push for global influence which turned Bismarck's cautious foreign policy on its head. By 1914 the German Reich was prepared to sacrifice the bones of any number of Pomeranian grenadiers for its Macedonian and Turkish policies.

Germany's *Weltpolitik* was an implicit threat to the hegemony of Great Britain, which at the turn of the century was still the pre-eminent imperial power. Such was the danger posed by Germany's growing ambition that London eventually concluded agreements with France and Russia, its traditional imperialist enemy, despite the fact that Britain was still involved in serious disputes with the two (especially Russia) in various parts of the world. Speaking with the American ambassador to London at the very beginning of the war, Sir Edward Grey, the Foreign Secretary, spelt out the challenge that Germany posed: 'The issue for us is that, if Germany wins, she will dominate France; the independence of Belgium, Holland, Denmark, and perhaps of Norway and Sweden, will be a mere shadow; their separate existence as nations will be a fiction; all their harbours will be at Germany's disposal; she will dominate the whole of western Europe, and this will make our position quite impossible. We could not exist as a first class State under such circumstances.'[5]

The First World War went on so long because of this central contest between Britain and Germany. Whether Britain bears greater responsibility for the conflict because it attempted to exclude Germany systematically from all imperial spoils, or whether the cause of war lay primarily with Germany's brutish ambition, remains open to dispute. But that the Anglo-German conflict was at the heart of the First World War is no longer an issue. The other great powers who went to war in 1914 did so for very different reasons: Austria-Hungary believed it necessary in order to survive as a great power; France went to war because it was attacked by Germany (once at war, France naturally hoped to avenge its defeat at German hands in 1870 and restore the territories of Alsace-Lorraine, but Paris would never have initiated a war for this); Russia went to war primarily in the hope of extending its influence in the Balkans by smashing Austria-Hungary and taking Istanbul.

Strategic issues everywhere took precedence over ideological affinities in defining the relationships between the other major combatants and Britain and Germany. Wilhelm II and Franz Joseph I were, it is true, both deeply conservative and hostile to democracy, but as a zealous nationalist Wilhelm looked upon Austria-Hungary's cosmopolitan mix of peoples with disdain. And yet the survival of the Habsburg Empire was crucial for Germany's

Weltpolitik because it was the strategic stepping stone to Berlin's primary imperialist goals, Turkey, Mesopotamia and Baghdad. Tsar Nicholas II was united with Wilhelm and Franz Joseph in his love of autocracy and his loathing of parliaments. Yet Russia allied itself with republican France and liberal Britain without hesitation. St Petersburg's need to control the Straits directly contradicted Germany's aim of dominating Turkey. The mistrust of democracy shared by Hohenzollern and Romanov was not sufficient to overcome the conflict of interest over the Straits.

Initially, both the Entente and the Central Powers appeared reluctant to open a new front in the southern Balkans. But by late October 1914, the German military had decided that provoking Russia in the south would cause Russia logistical problems on the Eastern Front where, after early losses, the Tsarist forces were now driving the Habsburg army deep into Austrian territory. Sailing under a Turkish flag but commanded by Germans, the battle cruiser *Goeben* and the light cruiser *Breslau* received the order from Enver Paşa, the pro-German Minister of Defence, to bombard Russian ships harboured in the Crimea. The Southern Front had opened.

Istanbul and the Straits held the key to domination of the Middle East, the region full of oil fields and strategic waterways, but the course of the war in the Balkans was dictated by the great powers' much narrower struggle for control of the Straits. The Entente and the Central Powers insisted that their respective allies in the Balkans would have to tailor their local war aims to these imperial goals. The fate of the south Slavs, the relationship between Transylvania and Romania, the ultimate size of Bulgaria, the Macedonian Question and finally Greek–Turkish relations were all profoundly influenced by the need of Britain, Germany and Russia to control access to the Black Sea from the Mediterranean.

Serbia was the only hostile territory blocking the Germans' rail route from Berlin to Baghdad. The Austrian attack on Serbia in late July 1914 served two purposes. The Habsburgs intended to eliminate Serbia as a destabilizing influence on the Slavs of the Empire while Germany was keen to see the country subdued for strategic reasons. Romania and Bulgaria allowed the passage of German war materials for Turkey at the beginning of the conflict. Nonetheless, control of the rail route through Serbia was of exceptional importance to the German military. This was underlined in September 1914 when the Romanian government emphasized its neutral status by blocking German transports across its territory. The road to Turkey was blocked; the German high command now devoted considerable attention to the establishment of a land link with Turkey.

The Turkish relationship with Germany, which Wilhelm II had diligently nurtured in the 1890s, had been furthered by the cooperation between senior *Reichswehr* officers and the Turkish general staff during the Balkan Wars. In late 1913 and early 1914, however, the leadership in the Ottoman Empire sent several clear signals to Britain and France that it was eager to cooperate and hoped to avoid closer ties with the Central Powers. But at the outbreak of war, Britain did not consider the Balkans or the Straits to be a theatre of war and, in any case, its commitment in that part of the world was to Russia, presumed to be Turkey's implacable foe. France was at this stage too preoccupied with defending its own territory to worry unduly about a theatre of war which had not opened as yet.

To begin with, Bulgaria, Romania and Greece were content to sit on the fence and observe the fortunes of war before deciding whether to declare their sympathies. The issue of the Straits did not feature prominently in the diplomacy which led to the war, but as soon as the fighting had begun in Belgium, France and Poland the strategic focus of the struggle in southern Europe shifted quickly to Istanbul and the Straits and hence the Balkans as a whole. Both the Entente and the Central Powers began to exert pressure on Sofia, Bucharest and Athens to enter the war.

Mesopotamia, the Arab region of the crumbling Ottoman Empire, was the only main battlefront in the First World War which was geographically clearly outside Europe. The chief combatants here, however, fought under European flags – British, Turkish and German. Within Europe troops of different nationalities fighting under the flags of multinational empires sometimes camouflaged the force of nationalism which lay behind much of the fighting. Large numbers of Serbs and Italians served under the Habsburg colours against the armies of Serbia and Italy, while Romanians from Transylvania participated in the joint German-Austro-Hungarian offensive against Romania. The Russian military was not as cosmopolitan as the Austrian but it included large numbers of non-Russians from Europe, the Caucasus and Asia.

It may not have been the first *world* war, despite the presence of colonials in the British and French armies; and indeed, at the start, when Austria bombarded Belgrade and launched its invasion of Serbia, it was known briefly as the Third Balkan War. This conflict was soon swallowed by the wider war on the Western and Eastern Fronts but the war in the Balkans remained an awkward anomaly. As the crisis deepened, both the Entente and the Central Powers diverted ever greater resources to persuading the young Balkan powers to join their alliances. With the exception of Serbia, whose very existence was threatened by Germany and Austria, no Balkan country had an obvious ally. Joining either of the great-power systems had its disadvantages, and fortunes on the battlefield meant that the gravitational force of both blocs changed daily. The attraction for a small Balkan country in declaring war lay in the possibility of furthering its regional goals, not in the fact that it particularly sympathized with its ally. These regional goals, however, often clashed with the overarching tactics of a great-power ally. Serbia was the first to discover this, as soon as war had broken out; Turkey, Bulgaria and Romania were to learn the same lesson.

The Entente's first victory: Serbia, Austria-Hungary

In the opening minutes of 29 July 1914, the first shell of the Great War was fired on Belgrade from the Austro-Hungarian town of Semlin (now Zemun in Serbia) across the river Sava. In the eight hours before the first bomb fell, the men and women of Belgrade were in the grip of a controlled frenzy. As the tradesmen in the central market began rolling down the shutters on their stalls, people rushed around town buying as much food and other essential items as possible before scurrying home to prepare their cellars, or even to bed down in large caves in the hills outside Belgrade. After the bombardment began, families in the districts closest to the Sava and Danube huddled together in makeshift shelters as the Austro-Hungarian artillery pounded away at the Serbian forward defences. That first night was terrifying: 'All of a sudden, between one and two in the morning, an almighty explosion shook Belgrade's houses to their very foundations so that every window in every house from

Dorćol to Čubura* was completely obliterated', one young man recalled twenty years later. 'A terrible panic gripped the civilians of Belgrade who had no idea what had happened.'[6] The big bang was, it turned out, the work of Major Vojin Tankosić, Black Hand member and supplier of weapons to Gavrilo Princip and his friends. Tankosić had sent one of his units to blow up the railway bridge separating Belgrade from Semlin, Austria-Hungary's eastern outpost across the Sava from Belgrade. Now the Austro-Hungarian army would have to land troops by boat or build pontoon bridges to launch an infantry assault on the city.

Austria used Krupp and Škoda heavy artillery to bombard Serbian towns on the Danube, Sava and Drina rivers along a front line of 225 kilometres. The two main targets were Šabac in the north-west and Belgrade itself. After a week of softening up, the Austrians launched a massive, concentrated artillery attack on the centre of Belgrade and all the key industrial installations. A Serb soldier, returning to the capital from service in Macedonia, recalled 'how much of our old city deserved the name the Turks had given her, *Derul el Džihad* – The House of Wars. Shells fired from all sides were crisscrossing above her. As well as the fixed cannon positioned behind Zemun [Serbo-Croat for Semlin] on the horizon, they had other peculiar weapons: the so-called monitors, little boats armed with heavy guns circled Belgrade like rabid dogs and firing from every direction.'[7] At night almost every street in Belgrade was lit up either by the huge network of floodlights constructed by the Austrian army or by the fires raging out of control at the cigarette factory, saw mill and oil depot. Early on, the waterworks was destroyed, leading to a rapid deterioration in sanitary conditions. Drinking water was soon in short supply, and swarms of mosquitoes tormented the flesh of the hundreds of homeless people who had been forced to abandon their homes to seek shelter in a huge cave in Topčider.

In the 110 years of Serbia's modern history, the military threat to the country had always come from the south† – from the Ottoman

---

* Dorćol is a district in north-western Belgrade close to the confluence of the Sava and Danube rivers. Čubura is south-east of the centre.

† The one exception was the threat posed by the fighting in Vojvodina and Srijem during 1848–9 but this was never a serious problem for Serbia proper.

army or the Bulgarians. Southern Serbia was the front line whose industrial and economic potential had always been subordinated to the country's security concerns. Conversely, the bulk of Serbia's industry had developed in the north either along the Danube and Sava or a short distance from the border – mainly along the line that over 300,000 Habsburg soldiers were now attacking. The Serbian government and military were thus faced with two grave problems. First, the planned invasion threatened the bulk of the country's industrial capacity and by implication the army's ability to fight. But a much more immediate problem for that army was its location – facing the traditional enemies in the south, thanks to Serbia's military occupation of Macedonia and the occupation of large areas of Albania. In his memoirs, a school teacher from central Serbia remembered how 'the general situation . . . was very difficult at the point of mobilization. Many of the units were down in the newly liberated territories [Macedonia] while at first they couldn't use the railway for mobilization because they were evacuating the government and civil service from Belgrade . . . There was a terrible lack of weapons and ammunition, for the artillery in particular . . . All they had for the camp facilities and uniforms were the remains from the campaigns in the Balkan Wars.'[8]

The Serbian army was exhausted. For the two years prior to the outbreak of war, the military establishment in Austria-Hungary had finally succeeded in increasing the defence budget. Policy makers throughout Europe (above all in Vienna and St Petersburg) assumed that Austria-Hungary's 'punitive expedition' against Serbia led by General Oskar Potiorek, the Military Governor of Bosnia and survivor of Princip's attack on Franz Ferdinand, would last a matter of days, thus eliminating the Balkan front. Yet the Austrians inexplicably kept up their artillery attack for a full two weeks, and although they were able to exploit the bombardment to construct a system of pontoon bridges across the Sava and Drina, the Serbian high command grasped the precious breathing space to bring 250,000 soldiers north to face the invaders. Many were extremely poorly armed, wielding pitchforks and axes they had brought from their farms. But the Serb fighters were highly motivated, which compensated in part for their lack of weaponry. Nonetheless, when the Austrian infantry offensive began on 12 August, their forces quickly crossed the Sava and entered the fortress town of Šabac, occupying the large salient in north-western Serbia, the Mačva plain, and then linking up with their colleagues who had crossed the Drina to the south-west. It looked as if General Potiorek would indeed march into Belgrade within a week.

On 15 August, the Chief of the Serbian General Staff, General Radomir Putnik, ordered a counter-offensive, the battle of Cer Mountain. Mačva, which juts out of Serbia to the confluence of the Drina and the Sava, is the point where Bosnia, Croatia and Serbia meet. By the second week in August, the Serbs had successfully established a defensive arc which ran from the southern edge of Šabac to Krupanj, just east of the Drina. In the middle of the Serb lines was Cer Mountain. To hold the line, the army had to establish itself on two key peaks and one strategic village. On the night of 16 August, Captain Ješa Topalović was deployed in the assault on Kosanin, the village at the very top of Cer.

> The forward battalion had advanced during the night towards the Troyan peak and when we made it to Parlog, the shower began, followed by volcanic thunder and sheet lightning. Water was drenching us from all sides . . . Suddenly another soldier, out of breath and excited, screamed:
>
> 'Major, Sir, the Krauts!'
>
> That's how the night-time clash between our Combined Division and the enemy's 21st Landwehr Division started and with it the battle of Cer Mountain.[9]

Three days of ruthless fighting ensued in which neither side made any ground, before the Austrian lines suddenly collapsed and the soldiers retreated in a panic across the Drina and Sava. Numerous Habsburg soldiers were lost in the rivers. It was an astonishing victory but one which heralded the tremendous cost in human lives of the following four years. 'The area between Cer and the River Jadar where this tremendous battle took place was nothing but mass graves and putrefying flesh', reported the French journalist Henry Barby. 'From the shadow of the woods emerged a stench so foul that it rendered the approach to the summit of Cer impossible. The number of corpses there was so enormous that the Second Army was constrained to abandon their burial due to a lack of time.'[10] Further on in the towns and villages, the Serb army uncovered evidence of massacres. Hundreds of men had been summarily executed, women and children raped, then shot. Many would have been victims of fellow Slavs, Serbs, Croats or Muslims, serving in the Austro-Hungarian army, although most Serbian history books refer to the criminals as 'Germans' or 'Krauts'.

Several 'firsts' were recorded during the battle of Cer. The first dog fight of the Great War took place when one of Serbia's three aeroplanes encountered a Habsburg plane while undertaking a reconnaissance mission over Austrian army positions. The enemy aviator waved at his Serbian counterpart who returned the compliment. Aviator Tomić, whose plane looked like a box kite on perambulator wheels, watched as the Austrian pilot took out a revolver and started firing at him. Tomić ducked and wove and made it back home. From then on, all pilots were armed with handguns. Within a matter of weeks, machine guns had been fitted on all Austrian and Serbian planes.

Both sides suffered heavy casualties in this opening battle. Almost 30,000 Austrians were wounded and 6–10,000 killed. The Serbs lost some 3–5,000 men with over 15,000 wounded. But above all the battle of Cer was significant as the first military success for the Entente. As the Austro-Hungarian army was retreating, the Germans were steamrollering through Belgium. Liège had been taken three days before the battle of Cer Mountain and Brussels fell two days after the Serbian victory. Less than two weeks later, the Germans won their mighty victory against the imperial Russian army at Tannenberg. 'The history of Austria-Hungary has been studded with a remarkable collection of defeats and the reign of Franz Joseph has been particularly fecund in military disasters', Barby commented on 19 August from the front line, 'but until today, the old monarch was able to claim that he had only ever been beaten by the great powers, by France in 1850, and by Prussia in 1866. Today, it is Serbia, a tenth of the size of Austria, with a tenth of the population, which has inflicted a first and resounding defeat.'[11]

In the first three months of the war, the Serbs mounted an astonishing military operation. The Habsburg forces successfully invaded Serbia in the middle of September. In November, the final struggle of the campaign, the battle of Kolubara, began soon after

Austro-Hungarian troops occupied Belgrade. Less than a month later, however, the Serbian army inflicted a second humiliating defeat on the Austrians, pushing them out of Belgrade and following them into Bosnia and Croatia. For a short period, the Serbs even threatened to conquer Sarajevo. Serbia's victories, combined with the growing tension around the Straits and the entrance of the Ottoman Empire into the war on the side of the Central Powers, focused German and British attention on the Balkans. By this time, the armies on the Western Front had already become bogged down in a gory quagmire which would hold them fast for almost four years. A victory for either side in the Balkans could undermine the enemy's campaign on the Eastern Front, and by extension on the Western Front. Suddenly the great powers were competing with one another to broaden the Balkan war.

Deutschland über Allah!: Turkey

> Without warning a shot is fired. There is no lively crackle but a dull, muffled thud which echoes on the flat surface of the sea and the walls of far-off mountains. Before I can focus my spy glass, the silhouette of an armoured cruiser slowly breaks out of its hiding place behind the northern hill and glides in front of the smoking coast of Kum Kale. A second shot, a second ship! This one sails into the centre of the entrance of these narrow Straits, these Dardanelles . . .
>
> Suddenly, I feel associations as never before in this war. I am resting on Priam's wall protected by a hill covered with flowers. The burial mound of Achilles rises before me down by the sea. To the west of Ajax's grave, I see a twisting river which gleams then disappears – Skamandros. Far in the distance, I can feel the power of the Mountain of the Gods . . . Hector's father stood here. And from within the dark tower, he looked down through the tiny opening at the ships of the hated Greeks who had hacked son after son from him – all for the sake of a woman's beauty . . .
>
> The ring is sealed. From the metal lips of an English cannon is spoken the magic word – and everything that appeared long dead is alive in an instant.
>
> Emil Ludwig, Troy, March 1915[12]

As the German essayist Emil Ludwig gazed down on the Aegean from Priam's palace, neither he nor his many compatriots stationed in Istanbul as diplomats, writers, military advisers or businessmen held out much hope that the Ottoman defences could resist the British fleet's drive through the Dardanelles into the Sea of Marmara. Ammunition would last for a fortnight, perhaps three weeks at most; the battle for the Dardanelles could not match the bloody heroism of the Trojan wars. After the terrible battles in the main theatres of European war, the failed attempt by British, French and Anzac (Australian and New Zealand) forces to break down the Turkish defences on the Dardanelles was to be the most intensely violent campaign of the war.

Six months before Ludwig visited Troy, in September 1914, the German government had, after some hesitation, signed a treaty of alliance with the Ottoman Empire. Responding to enquiries made by Chancellor Bethmann-Hollweg, the German ambassador to the Porte, Baron Hans von Wangenheim, warned that Berlin must consider carefully whether this new partnership would prove an asset to Germany's war effort or a liability. He was finally persuaded, however, that the Turkish alliance was a risk which Germany had to take.

As in all Balkan countries except Serbia, the leadership in Turkey, already riven by intrigue and factionalism, was divided in its sympathies as between the Central Powers and the Entente. The two main groupings in the Committee of Union and Progress (CUP) opened secret talks with the Entente and the Central Powers respectively in the hope of foisting a military and political alliance on their domestic opponents as a *fait accompli*. A third, weaker faction argued for a policy of neutrality. All three factions were united, however, in the need to rid Turkey of the Capitulations and reduce the country's economic dependency on the great powers.

The appeals of the pro-Entente forces were rebutted. The British and French were slow in understanding the potential importance of the Straits issue. In his detailed history of the war in Turkey, Commandant M. Larcher noted that Britain, France and Russia slighted Turkish sensibilities unnecessarily. 'Negotiating actively with the Slav states in the Balkans, they [the Entente powers] protested solemnly [to the Turks] about the violation of time-honoured international conventions, threatening the Turks with reprisals and withholding from them any real favours. Furthermore, unaware of the gravity of having Turkey enter the World War, they took no military measures, either of intimidation or security.'[13]

Indeed, the efforts of the pro-Entente lobby were regularly undermined by an imperious British policy towards the Ottoman Empire. In August 1914, a Turkish naval delegation arrived in Britain to take possession of two dreadnoughts which Turkey had already paid for, in part by popular subscription. On the eve of the handover, however, the War Office ordered the requisition of the two ships without compensation. Turkish public opinion turned sharply in favour of Germany.

Above all, the Entente faced a serious problem coordinating its strategic aims. France was simply not very interested in the Straits while Russia prevaricated on the Turkish issue, unsure whether it might not actually prefer a neutral Turkey to the liberation of the Straits by the British. Throughout the Dardanelles campaign, Russia remained suspicious of British aims in the region. Even though Britain's expressed goal was to force open the Straits to supply Russia with munitions, the Russians were evidently unable to shake off memories of a century of rivalry with the British.

The German ambassador, von Wangenheim, played a crucial role in accelerating the formation of a Berlin–Istanbul axis. His word carried almost as much weight at the Porte as had once the word of Stratford Canning or of Count Ignatief. The Baron's diplomacy evolved through a series of negotiations undertaken at the behest of the Defence and Interior Ministers, Enver Paşa and Talât Paşa. Much of the Turkish Cabinet, however, was kept in the dark about these talks. From late July 1914 onwards, although Turkey was still uncommitted, Enver felt sufficiently confident to take the law into his own hands. He assured the Germans that Turkey would provide Germany with active military support. He did warn, however, that he needed a little more time both to outmanoeuvre the pro-Entente forces in the Cabinet and to prepare for the defence of the Dardanelles.

At the outbreak of the Great War, the Ottoman Empire was in a state of chaotic contraction. It was still recovering from the impact of defeat in the Balkan Wars. Its government appeared unstable and prone to violent change. Turkish nationalism and the drive towards modernization of the state competed against pan-Islamism; regional governors or non-Turkic communities fought the centralizing impulse. Reform was still hampered by the Empire's chronic indebtedness which together with the Capitulations allowed British,

French, Austrian and German imperial interests to keep the economy in a state of neo-colonial dependency. The Balkan Wars had exposed how feeble the proud Ottoman military had become. Yet the extraordinary Enver Paşa had used the intervening period to carry out a purge of the officer corps on the advice of the German Military Mission established in 1913 under General Liman von Sanders.

Germany had tactical and strategic considerations in mind. The opening of a new front in the Caucasus would quickly draw Russian troops away from the Eastern Front, allowing the German high command to release more troops for the Western Front. If Turkey could hold out, Russia would be denied access to Istanbul, and the Russian Black Sea fleet would remain confined and impotent.

In the longer term, the Ottoman Empire might become the stepping stone for Germany's imperial ambitions. Just under half of the route of the Berlin–Baghdad railway lay in Ottoman territory, including, of course, the Straits. The Germans were also convinced that if the Muslim hierarchy were to proclaim the conflict a *jihad*, or holy war, then the Muslims of Africa, the Middle East and the Indian sub-continent would rise against the British Empire. The obsession of German policy makers with the potential of a pan-Islamic crusade found its way into the proclamation that the *Şeyülislam* (the chief Muslim cleric) wrote for the Sultan, who announced Turkey's entry into the war in November 1914:

> Russia, for centuries so cruel and infuriate an enemy of human happiness, has now dragged the Governments of Great Britain and France into the World War. The national pride of these countries delights immoderately in enslaving thousands of Mohammedans . . .
>
> The oppressive group known as the Triple Entente has not only robbed, during the last century, the Mohammedans of India, Central Asia, and most of the African countries, of their political independence, of their governments and even of their liberty; but it has also, owing to the mutual help extended by its members, caused us to lose the most precious parts of the Ottoman Empire. In addition, in a more recent day, almost yesterday, it has been morally and materially responsible for the annihilation of hundreds of thousands of innocent

> Mohammedans, for the rape of thousands of Mohammedan virgins, and for the fanatical profanation of the sacred things of Islam during the Balkan War, which it provoked by encouraging and protecting our neighbours . . .
>
> Oh Mohammedans, true servants of God! Those who will share in the Holy War and come back alive will enjoy a great felicity; those who will find in it their death will have the honour of martyrdom.[14]

The inner circle of the CUP viewed this visionary rhetoric with amused scepticism. And if the Muslim hierarchy had been fully apprised of the war aims of Enver, Talât and their supporters in the CUP, it would have thought twice about endorsing the German alliance. Within two years of Turkey's entrance into the war, the CUP exploited the exceptional wartime circumstances to destroy the power of the clerics. Like most contemporary observers, the American chargé d'affaires in Istanbul was especially impressed by the zeal of Enver Paşa. In August 1914, he recorded in his diary that Enver was 'no longer the modest young officer fresh from Macedonia I knew in 1908, who blushed professionally when praised as a "hero of liberty". The Bulgarian Minister calls him "the Prophet of the Prophet", and on either side of his desk at the War Office hang portraits of Napoleon and Frederick the Great!'[15] Soon after Russia declared war on Turkey in October 1914, Enver underlined his ambition by proclaiming himself 'vice-generalissimo' (the 'vice' was used in deference to the Sultan who was theoretically commander in chief of Ottoman forces although he was merely a figurehead). He now assumed operational charge of all Turkish land and sea forces. Only thirty-two years old at the beginning of the war, Enver soon became the prototype for any number of nationalist military leaders in the next two decades. Bright, dynamic and self-regarding, he also suffered from a physical inferiority complex due to his modest height. His affection for Germany, which he developed during a two-year stint as the Ottoman military attaché in Berlin, was well known. But it had limits, as he explained to von Wangenheim with disarming openness. Turkey entered into the alliance with Germany not for sentimental reasons but because it needed 'the support of one of the groups of Great Powers' to secure her borders 'against attacks from abroad',[16] in order for the government to concentrate on the radical reform of the Empire.

Domestic reform was the primary war aim of the Turkish leadership. Within the turmoil produced by the Great War, the profound change experienced by the Ottoman Empire between 1914 and 1923, when the Turkish Republic was finally constituted, has often been overlooked. Yet in this short space of time, the triumvirate of Enver, Talât and Cemal Paşa, and then later Mustafa Kemal Atatürk, ripped up all remaining structures of the Ottoman Empire and replaced them with a modernizing, secular state underpinned by militarism and nationalism. It was an extremely violent transformation.

But the immediate significance of Turkey's declaration of war against Russia in October 1914 lay to the north in the Balkans. In December 1914, General Colmar von der Goltz, who had directed Ottoman strategy during the Balkan Wars, returned to assist the Turkish military in the new campaign. He spelt out his conviction that, in strategic terms, the Balkans had suddenly become the centre of the First World War. After the stalemate on the Western Front, he averred, the war would be largely decided

> by the small Balkan powers, however peculiar this may sound. For the deployment of their not insignificant armed forces will secure military superiority for either one or the other side. This is why the Entente has now begun to use all available means to create a Balkan League which could provoke a collapse of Austria-Hungary if it were to attack from the south. If, on the other hand, we were able to win over the remaining Balkan states by swiftly defeating Serbia, this would finally guarantee our superiority over Russia.[17]

Victory in the Balkans would lead almost certainly to victory for the Central Powers on the Eastern Front. The combined forces of the Balkan states amounted to more than one and a half million men. If the Central Powers held sway not just in Turkey but in Romania, Bulgaria and Greece as well, then Austria-Hungary could also free up the hundreds of thousands of troops it was forced to devote to its southern flanks. The Russian imperial armies, progressively starved of munitions and supplies, would not be in a position to counter such a mighty force. The German leadership assumed, not unreasonably, that a successful Austro-Hungarian offensive against Serbia would soon bring its supply lines within 320 kilometres of Turkey. Surrounded by the jubilant Central Power allies, neither Bulgaria nor Romania would be so foolish as to resist the offer to join the winning side.

Lord Kitchener, the British War Minister, appeared to concur with von der Goltz's assessment. On 5 January, he told the War Council that 'the Dardanelles appeared to be the most suitable objective, as an attack here could be made in co-operation with the Fleet'.[18] Kitchener went on to suggest that a successful campaign in the Straits would 're-establish communication with Russia; settle the Near Eastern question; draw in Greece and, perhaps, Bulgaria and Roumania; and release wheat and shipping now locked up in the Black Sea'.[19]

It was at this point in the winter of 1914–15 that Serbia's successful counter-offensive against Austria-Hungary effectively saved the Entente from disaster in the Balkans, and opened up the possibility of an Entente victory in the Dardanelles. After Turkey had declared for the Central Powers, Romania announced that in keeping with its neutrality it would not permit the transit of German war materials across its territory. Turkey, beset by economic chaos and with a very limited supply of ammunition, could no longer expect to receive the war materials promised by Germany. This presented the Entente with a perfect opportunity to seize the Dardanelles and Istanbul, and even bring the Great War to an end.

Beyond the Dardanelles: Turkey

The surprising failure of the Allies to seize the Straits and the even more remarkable ability of the Ottoman forces to defend them made for one of the most tragic and bloody episodes of the war. From the opening bombardment by the British fleet in March 1915, the Turkish government and inhabitants of Istanbul were planning their retreat into the Anatolian interior. 'The Turkish army is absolutely worthless', General von Moltke told his Austrian counterpart, Hötzendorf, two and a half weeks after the first Allied landing on the Dardanelles began on 25 April 1915. 'It has neither weapons, nor ammunition, not even uniforms. The officers' wives even beg along the roadside.'[20]

After the British imposed a blockade on Turkey's Aegean coast, the country's economic infrastructure crumbled. Famine struck the capital in 1915, not at first because food supplies had dried up but because the entire transportation system had buckled and collapsed under the weight of military mobilization. The failure of the transport system then did indeed begin to affect agriculture. One Turkish writer recorded that 'the loss in overloaded animals on the bad roads was very great. Bubonic plague and other contagious diseases were frequent among the draft animals. The veterinary staff numbered only 250 [in the entire empire]. New animals had to be constantly requisitioned, which gravely hindered the carrying on of any agricultural work. Finally, the peasants had to be supplied with a certain necessary number of animals to prevent a general famine.'[21]

Military communications were equally found wanting. In contrast to the other great armies, the Ottoman forces were unable to use telephone communications except between a few positions on the Dardanelles. The Turkish Cabinet could talk to its opposite numbers in Berlin, Vienna and Sofia on the telephone, but not with its commanders in the field. And Turkey was not only fighting on the Dardanelles. It was waging war on two other major fronts – the Transcaucasia and Mesopotamia. Enver Paşa opened the proceedings disastrously in the Armenian mountains to the east with a winter campaign against the Russians, in which all but 10 per cent of his Third Army had died of frostbite and starvation by January 1915. In Mesopotamia, the Ottoman army could not supply its forces because the Baghdad railway between Istanbul and Adana, 725 kilometres south-east of the capital, was still interrupted in two places due to unfinished tunnels.

On the Dardanelles, the Turks lacked fuel, ammunition, food and uniforms. 'The Germans, however, have charge of all the technical departments, which fortunately for the Turks run smoothly. "Deutschland über Allah" they say here!'[22] But the German commanders were well aware that if the Entente powers knew the real state of the Turkish military, then Allied forces could have stormed the Dardanelles very quickly. As late as June 1915, after Liman von Sanders and Enver Paşa had successfully toughened the fortress defences of the peninsula, General von der Goltz could still remark, 'the Allies can force their way through whenever they want'.[23]

It is a story which has been told many times elsewhere, although the tenacity of Turkish defences is often overlooked in Commonwealth histories. Between the Gallipoli landings begun on 25 April 1915 and the Allied pull-out in November, 70,000 Turks were killed, roughly twice as many fatalities as the Allies sustained. What was unique about the Gallipoli war was the concentration of so many deaths in such tiny areas, minute bays and ridges in which tens of thousands of troops were packed on either side of the front line. It was here in early August at Chunuk Bair, the ridge overlooking the beach of Ari Burnu on the Aegean coast of the peninsula, that the courage of Mustafa Kemal became a legend. (On more than one occasion, Kemal ignored the orders of both his German and Turkish superiors. While at Gallipoli his suspicion of the German–Turkish alliance and of Enver's power grew, and following the Allied withdrawal he began to use his increasing authority to criticize government policies, which he believed were driving Turkey into Germany's colonial embrace.)

The authorities in Istanbul at first tried to conceal the losses on the peninsula from the public. But soon the capital became clogged with the ceaseless flow of dying and wounded. Schools, monasteries and hospitals were requisitioned to accommodate the casualties while the streetcar networks and the trans-Bosphorus ferry service choked to a halt. When the larger institutions were full, the mayor of Istanbul sanctioned the persecution and expulsion of the Christian population of the city to find space for the wounded soldiers. For behind the shield of the Dardanelles, the traditions and values of the Ottoman Empire were disappearing as if in quicksand. The most significant entry in the diary of the American diplomat, Lewis Einstein, on 25 April 1915, did not concern the Allied landings begun that day (of which he knew nothing) but the confirmation of a rumour: 'There have been wholesale arrests of Armenians – several hundreds are being deported to Angora and Konia.'[24]

Unknown to Lewis Einstein or anyone else in Istanbul (with the exception probably of Talât, Enver and senior members of Talât's murderous paramilitary force, the *Teşkılat-i Mahsusa*), the slaughter of Armenian civilians had begun in Van province on the eastern edge of the Empire. It took just weeks and in some cases days for this purge to rip communities from the lands which their people had inhabited for thousands of years. The Armenian tragedy lies outside the scope of the present work, except as it reflects on the nature of

Turkish nationalism. It is worth remembering the words which the Armenian lyric poet Avetik Ishakian wrote in February 1916: 'So great is the anguish and suffering of the Armenians, so hideous and unprecedented, that the infinity and fathomlessness of the universe must be considerate in gauging it; there are no words in the dictionaries to qualify the hideousness of the terrors. Not a single poet can find words . . .'[25] Ishakian was not the last poet to concede the failure of language in the twentieth century.

To the diplomatic corps in Istanbul, including von Wangenheim's successor, Wolff-Metternich, who energetically protested the genocide, the CUP leadership raised their hands in fake helplessness. It put down the rapes, murders, forced marches, torture and infanticide to the excessive passion of indignant Turkish citizens who suspected the Armenians of collaborating with the Russians. The evidence, however, points to the instigation by and collaboration of several leading members of the Cabinet, above all Talât. Armenian terrorist organizations had, it is true, been cooperating with the Russians for some time, representing a genuine security problem for the Turks; and the role of Armenian nationalist aspirations in stirring up tension between the two communities is often overlooked. Apologists for the Turks, in turn, play down the extraordinarily violent response of paramilitary forces against Armenian civilians.

This pattern, whereby those members of a minority least able to protect themselves attracted the full force of the majority's wrath, would repeat itself many times in Europe and elsewhere in the course of the century. The relatively high incidence of such persecutions and massacres in the Balkans is the legacy of the Austro-Hungarian and Ottoman empires. They left a complex demographic patchwork within which 'ethnic' violence became lethal. The Armenian case was soon followed by violence between Greeks and Turks: the Greco-Turkish war and the Great Population Exchange between the Greek Orthodox and Muslim populations of Greece and Turkey. Henceforth, murder and expulsion became the two most overused instruments in dealing with nationality questions in the Balkans.

The role of the elite and the political environment in which such disgusting phenomena occur have often been underappreciated in favour of a more emotive response, which accuses a particular nation or community of being especially prone to bloodthirsty behaviour. This lay behind Talât's cynical argument that the government in Istanbul could not tame the tribal passions of its wilder compatriots. The mob always has the effect of minimizing or obscuring the role of those who bear political responsibility for its direction. All Balkan massacres this century have enjoyed the specific approval of state organs, whose agents have usually been the instigators as well. This is not merely a case of an army commander winking to his troops surrounding defenceless women. In Turkey during the Great War, in Croatia during the Second World War and in the Republika Srpska during the Bosnian war of 1992–5, the legal system was turned on its head – murder was encouraged and approved by the state and its propaganda apparatus. Not participating in murder, conversely, was regarded if not as 'illegal' then certainly as hostile behaviour. Such events are invariably accompanied by a historical justification which can usually be boiled down to the simple formula of 'eternal enmity' between two communities. The construction of this justification by historians, newspapers and other media under state influence, however, tends to mask the real intentions of the elite.

In Turkey, the massacre of the Armenians and the growing hostility towards Greeks and even Jews were driven primarily by an economic nationalism, militaristic and dynamic, but also disastrously shortsighted. Armenians and Greeks dominated trade and small-scale industry in the Ottoman Empire. Larger enterprises were usually in the hands of foreigners so that at the outbreak of war only 54 major businesses out of 244 were Turkish-owned. When still divided over the choice of partner in war, the Turkish Cabinet agreed to abolish the Capitulations and suspend payment on the national debt. The Germans opposed these decisions and spent much of the war trying to have them rescinded; but the Turkish government was determined throughout to assert its economic sovereignty. Having eventually worn down the Germans, it

> sought to build a strong national bourgeoisie by forming entrepreneurial cadres, candidates for which they sought among Muslim traders in the provincial towns, the guilds and even among bureaucrats. They encouraged the members of this embryonic bourgeoisie to accumulate capital by making

use of the exceptional market conditions during the war, which made profiteering possible.

The victims of these policies were the consumers in the cities and above all the Greek and Armenian entrepreneurs, who were not only obliged to use Turkish in their administration and on their shop windows and to take Turks onto the boards of their companies, but were also subjected to a terror campaign by the *Teskilat-i Mahsusa* which drove many of them into exile. 130,000 Greeks from the Western coastal regions alone left for Greece. Their companies were given to the new Muslim entrepreneurs, who in many cases proved incapable of making a go of them, deprived as they were of overseas contact, markets and management skills.[26]

Turkish national identity which had been held back by the persistence of the Ottoman régime began to assert itself with a vengeance. The Turkish language invaded Jewish, Bulgarian, Greek, Armenian and foreign-sponsored schools, where the teaching of Turkish and Turkish history and geography was made compulsory in March 1916. Across the Empire, branches of *Türk Ocaği* (The Turkish Hearth) sprang up to offer lectures, discussions, theatrical and musical performances and exhibitions spreading Turkish nationalist ideology. Its journal *Türk Yurdu* (Turkish Homeland) was widely read. One historian has noted how 'it is remarkable that, like the CUP itself, which had its origins in the ethnically mixed region of Macedonia, most of the important thinkers and writers who took part in the debates, were from peripheral or mixed areas. Apart from those who came from the Turkic areas of the Russian Empire, the most ardent Turkish nationalist Tekin Alp was a Jew from Seres, the Westernizer Abdullah Cevdet a Kurd from Arapkir, Zia Gökalp half Kurdish and from Diyarbakir.'[27] This observation about the origin of nationalist writers and thinkers is certainly striking, but remarkable it is not. Throughout modern Balkan history and especially after the consolidation of the new states around the time of the Great War, the more extreme nationalist leaders have emerged from the geographical periphery of communities with such frequency that coincidence can be safely ruled out and a psycho-political pattern ruled in.

The rise of Turkish nationalism was reflected by the ascendancy of Zia Gökalp in the leading circles of the CUP. This western-educated sociologist became the intellectual prophet of the Turkish national state, urging the destruction of Ottoman backwardness in favour of the modern, secular nation state. 'Turkish society cannot escape the effects of the social evolution which Europe has been submitted to', he warned. 'It must entirely separate its national institutions from those religious institutions that are common to the whole brotherhood of Mohammedanism.'[28] The Muslim hierarchy could no longer avert its gaze from the writing on the wall. Church and state were divorced with immediate effect. All citizens would now submit to a civil code of law which replaced the *şeria*. Civil marriages without distinction of religion were introduced and polygamy severely restricted. After the victory of Gallipoli, when it appeared for a while that Turkey had backed the winning alliance in the war, the secular authorities were able to push through exceptionally far-reaching reforms whose passage would have been much more difficult in peacetime.

The impact on life in both the towns and cities was enormous. The battered Muslim clerics warned of spiritual corruption as alcohol consumption leapt astonishingly from 2,130,192 litres of *raki*, the local aniseed spirit, in 1915 to 5,243,358 litres in 1916.[29] Prostitution, which before the war had been tolerated only among non-Muslim women, although their clients were drawn from all denominations, was now taken up by some Muslim women as well. Combined with the devastation wrought by war, the extremity of these political and social changes set the Ottoman Empire on the path to oblivion. In a letter written in 1917, Mustafa Kemal despairingly observed the descent of his commander, Enver, into megalomania and by late 1917 was all but accusing the vice-generalissimo of treason:

> There are no bonds left between the Government and the people. What we call the people are composed now of women, disabled men, and children. For all alike the Government is the power which insistently drives them to hunger and death. The administrative machinery is devoid of authority. Public life is in full anarchy. Every new step taken by the Government increases the general hatred the people feel for it. All officials accept bribes, and are capable of every sort of corruption and abuse. The machinery of justice has entirely stopped. The

> police forces do not function. Economic life is breaking down with formidable speed. Neither people nor government employees have any confidence in the future. The determination to live rids even the best and the most honest of every sort of sacred feeling. If the War lasts much longer, the whole structure of Government and dynasty, decrepit in all its parts, may suddenly fall to pieces.[30]

But as Kemal wrote this everything pointed to victory for the Central Powers in the war, and as long as success appeared imminent, the position of Enver, Talât and their friends was impregnable.

The impact of Turkish military success was felt not only in the Empire. The rest of the Balkans scrutinized the campaign in the Dardanelles in great detail. Tsar Ferdinand and the government in Sofia interpreted the Turkish victory as a sign to board the German train before it left the station. 'The most important development is now awaited from Bulgaria', the American chargé in Istanbul noted in June. 'Kouloucheff [the Bulgarian ambassador] called to say he was leaving at once for Sofia, the reason being his wife's confinement, though it is her third child. The news here is that Adrianople is completely evacuated, even the railway archives having been removed, and report has it that the Bulgars are to occupy the place within a few days.'[31]

German diplomats were working furiously to persuade Bulgaria to declare for the Central Powers. Not only would this bring the prospect of victory on the Eastern Front much closer, but it would surely herald the final demise of Serbia's army and indeed the destruction of Serbia itself. Just as Turkey had skilfully negotiated an end to the Capitulations and for large territorial concessions in Thrace to secure its entry into the war, so too was Bulgaria responding to the highest bidder. The Bulgarian government was set on avenging itself against the coalition which had ravaged it during the Second Balkan War. The Germans had to promise Bulgaria not only Serbian-controlled Macedonia, but also the southern Dobrudja from Romania and from Turkey, Adrianople and eastern Thrace. This was a hard pill for the Turks to swallow, but they did it.

Sixteen years later, Winston Churchill was still unable to forgive those who had ruined the Allies' chances at the Dardanelles and opened the way for the Central Powers' mastery of the Balkans:

I marvelled much in those sad days at the standard of values and sense of proportion which prevailed among our politicians and naval and military authorities. The generals were so confident of breaking the line in France that they gathered masses of cavalry behind the assaulting troops to ride through the huge gaps they expected to open on the hostile front. To sacrifice a quarter of a million men in such an affair seemed to them the highest military wisdom. That was the orthodox doctrine of war; even if it did not succeed, no error or breach of the rules would have been committed. But to lose one hundredth part as many sailors and a dozen old ships, all of which were in any case to be put on the Mother Bank in a few months' time, with the possibility of gaining an inestimable prize – there was a risk before which the boldest uniformed greyhead stood appalled. The Admiralty and Generals had their way. The fleet continued idle at the Dardanelles. The armies shattered themselves against the German defence in France. The Bulgarians carried an army of 300,000 men to join our enemies; and Serbia as a factor in the war was obliterated.[32]

Golgotha: Bulgaria and Serbia, 1915–16

We slowly creep towards the sheer cliffs of Mount Čakor, step by step on the compacted snow. This is the mountain of death. Yesterday we saw the dead, frozen and sticking out of the snow. Here, on the edge of the mountain of death, the sights are still worse.

On either side of the ice road, refugees are resting. Immobilized by the snow, their heads are glued to their breasts. The white snowflakes dance around them while the alpine winds whistle their songs of death. The heads of horses and oxen which have fallen off the path protrude from the snow . . .

Somehow we make it over Čakor although we are still in the empire of mountains . . . On a plateau below Čakor's peak we see a mound of human bodies. Barefoot, without coats, uniforms in shreds. Nothing covers their heads. These are the remains of the Austrian POWs who have been left there in their thousands. Their bodies are just skeletons, their faces despair. Those still living sway about aimlessly in the deep snow – a vain attempt at saving themselves.

A bunch of these miserable creatures come across a frozen horse in

> the snow. They throw themselves like hungry wolves on it, stripping away its body piece by piece . . . Oh, poor wretches, brother Czechs and other Slavs who never wanted to be dragooned into another Austrian fight. Now you too must carry the Cross of Golgotha together with the Serbian people!
>
> From the diary of Josip Jeras, a Slovene volunteer in the Serbian army who survived the retreat across the Albanian mountains in the winter of 1915–16[33]

Winston Churchill was wrong about only one thing. The Bulgarians fielded an army of 800,000 men, half a million more than he had estimated. Indeed, by 1918, almost 40 per cent of Bulgaria's male population, around 900,000 soldiers, were with the colours. The Bulgarian intervention, sealed by secret treaty with the Germans in September 1915, had an enormous impact on the course of the conflict. The country straddled the Aegean and the Black Sea and blocked free passage of war materials from Germany to Turkey. Throughout 1915, the two alliances competed to expand hostilities across the Balkans, and Bulgaria was the main focus of this rivalry.

At first it appeared likely that Istanbul would fall to the Entente. But as the land assaults on Gallipoli were repulsed, in the summer of 1915, the confidence of the Ottoman leadership was restored, only to be deflated again when Italy announced in May that it had joined up to the Entente, opening once more the prospect of a defeat for the Central Powers. With each twist and turn, the Bulgarian government of Prime Minister Vasil Radoslavov, and Tsar Ferdinand, whose influence over foreign policy was paramount, were able to increase the price of their entry into the conflict.

Tsar and Prime Minister strongly favoured joining the Central Powers; Radoslavov was instinctively pro-German, Ferdinand more calculating. It is often assumed that as a Saxe-Coburg with close ties to Germany, he was bound to favour his original compatriots. But Ferdinand's mother was a member of the House of Orléans and he was happy to receive distant maternal relations in Sofia at the beginning of 1915 as part of a French effort to persuade him to choose the Allies. Ferdinand was an ambitious realist who wished only to advance Bulgarian interests and, by extension, his own. He was highly intelligent, well educated and a shrewd investor of money. For the Tsar, Bulgaria's eventual entry into the war was much too important a transaction to be influenced by sentimentality. Bulgaria wanted to inflict deep wounds on all its neighbours in retaliation for its own dismemberment and humiliation in the Second Balkan War. Ferdinand was interested in giving up neutrality to the bloc which could both guarantee the return of those territorial losses and which looked like winning. Until the Second Balkan War in 1913, Ferdinand had been a very popular monarch. But Bulgaria's defeat had seriously damaged his standing. He worried, and as it turned out with good reason, that another defeat in the pursuit of territorial aggrandizement would mean the loss of his throne.

There was no mistaking Bulgaria's least favourite neighbour. 'The purpose of my life', Ferdinand commented on the eve of war, 'is the destruction of Serbia.'[34] It was easier for Germany and Austria-Hungary to meet the conditions for Bulgarian entry because the Central Powers were already at war with Serbia. In May 1915, the Serbian leadership discovered the details of the secret Treaty of London by which Italy agreed to join the Entente: London and Paris had promised Italy most of the Adriatic coast, which Serbia viewed as central to her war aims. To the Serbian government, whose army had already made a significant contribution to the Entente's war effort, this smacked of treachery. Attempting to persuade Serbia to hand over northern Macedonia to Bulgaria (the only way in which the Entente could have secured Sofia's support) would have been near impossible. Nonetheless, Churchill considered Bulgarian intervention so important that he wrote to Lloyd George in late June that 'I am all for playing the game right out to get Bulgaria. She is the real prize, & it is only if and when we know she will not come that we should consider Greek & Serbian interests.'[35]

No Balkan nation joined in the Great War because of any special sympathy for either of the two power blocs (although Serbia had a marked aversion to the Central Powers). Bulgaria's entry, however, had the effect of transforming the conflict in the region from an extension of Anglo-German or Austro-Russian rivalry into a Third Balkan War whose participants cared not one iota whether the Germans or British won the global struggle, except as it impacted on them. Bulgaria attacked Serbia not to open up supply lines from Berlin to Istanbul, but to regain Macedonia. The Great War in the Balkans served chiefly to underline and deepen the deadly competition which had developed since the Congress of Berlin between Bulgaria and Serbia, who were now the two main competitors in a bitter struggle for regional hegemony. In October 1915, the Bulgarians prepared to avenge themselves for the perceived betrayal by the Serbs during the Second Balkan War.

Although Bulgaria was thus inclined to alliance with Germany, Berlin had to expend considerable diplomatic effort to secure the agreement. But once Sofia was persuaded, the German High Command was determined that Austria's military incompetence would not foul up their plans again. To ensure that Serbian defences could be breached, the Germans placed one of their ablest commanders, Field Marshal August von Mackensen, in command of an expanded German and Austro-Hungarian force which renewed the bombardment of Belgrade on 6 October 1915. Within three days, Belgrade was taken and the Serbian army was streaming southwards towards Kragujevac and Niš. Five days later, the Bulgarian army crossed into Macedonia and southern Serbia while Austrian troops started marching from Dalmatia. In early November, the Serbian army successfully retreated to Kosovo. Prince Regent Aleksandar had to decide upon a course of action in consultation with a trio of septuagenarians – his father ex-King Petar who had fought in the Bosnian Uprising of 1875, Radomir Putnik, the desperately ill commander in chief, and the Prime Minister, Nikola Pašić. Should the Serbian army establish a modern historical myth by making a last stand against the enemy coalition on Kosovo Polje, the Field of Blackbirds, where the Serbian medieval kingdom had collapsed in 1389 in the central event of Serbian national mythology? Recognizing this as a gesture of poetic futility, the four Serb leaders ordered hundreds of thousands of soldiers and refugees to destroy all heavy weaponry and munitions, gather up thousands of Austrian prisoners, and hundreds of horse and oxen, before setting off on a terrible trek across *Prokletije*, the Accursed Mountains, that separate Kosovo and Albania, as the snow began to fall.

Heroism and fortitude are cheap words in the Balkans and the Serbs are prone to excessive usage of both. But the soldiers who attempted to reach the island refuge of Corfu from Kosovo deserve great respect, even in this century of suffering. Besides the ferocity of the weather, the Serbs faced harassment from Albanian raiders. This frozen 'army of wraiths', as one of its soldiers dubbed it, was of course easy prey for the Albanian villagers who paradoxically enjoyed one of their most comfortable winters that year. But the

Albanians were also taking their revenge on the Serbs for the atrocities committed against the Kosovar and Macedonian Albanians during the First Balkan War. Fratricidal war between the offspring states of the Ottoman Empire had begun in earnest only three years prior to these ghastly events. Yet it had set in motion a series of disturbing conflicts between Bulgar, Serb, Albanian, Greek and Turk in which demographic, historical, confessional, racist and economic claims were mercilessly pitted against one another.

The Germans were to learn to their cost that Bulgaria was interested only in its narrow war aims. Once the Bulgarians had occupied southern Serbia and northern Macedonia and helped the Germans and Austro-Hungarians drive the Serbian army south-west through Kosovo and Albania, their commitment to the Central Powers faded. 'They were short of food, they had caught typhus from the Serbs and . . . they had lost interest in the whole affair. A Bulgarian general had blandly informed his German liaison officer, "For us Bulgars the war is really over. We have all we want."'[36] The Bulgarians not only refused to launch an offensive against the British and French troops who had landed in Salonika after the defeat at Gallipoli, they extended their occupation west of Macedonia into lands claimed by their supposed ally, Austria-Hungary.

In the spring of 1916, the sideshow of Kosovo and Albania very nearly resulted in armed conflict between Bulgarian and Austrian forces. In February, Austrian troops were sent into a number of towns in Kosovo and Albania already garrisoned by Bulgarian troops. The Bulgarian military commander in Macedonia, Racho Petrov, issued an ultimatum to the Austrians to evacuate Kačanik, on the border with Macedonia. 'I beg your Excellency to offer assistance as soon as possible', General Hötzendorf, the commander of Austrian, forces telegraphed the Foreign Minister, von Burián, in Vienna, 'because I must disclaim all responsibility for the consequences of the Bulgarians' approach which is heading inexorably towards a military conflict.'[37]

In a state of panic, General von Falkenhayn, the German commander in chief, ordered von Mackensen to mediate between the two allies immediately, and after Austrian territorial concessions the tension receded. Hötzendorf had admitted in confidential correspondence with Vienna that his army was too weak to beat the

Bulgarians – an astonishing reflection of Austro-Hungarian decline.

There were two reasons for Ferdinand's readiness to wage war on his Austro-Hungarian partner in 1916. The first was his proven audacity, which during the First Balkan War had inspired the attempted march on Istanbul so that Ferdinand might enter the city as liberator. Having failed in his hopes to revive Byzantium, the Tsar was now gripped by a vision of Bulgaria stretching from the Black Sea to the Adriatic, dominating all communications on the Balkan peninsula and even striving for great-power status.

The second reason was fear. Ferdinand was afraid of being deposed, afraid of revolution, in short afraid of the backbone of Bulgarian society – the peasant. The government's decision to side with Germany in the war was not popular – the majority of Bulgarians were still sentimentally attached to Russia. And after the fiasco of the Second Balkan War, Bulgarians were loath to go to war at all. The memory of the destruction and the disruption to daily life was very fresh in the minds of the Bulgarian peasant who was, of course, the mainstay of the Bulgarian infantry. In the period between the Balkan Wars and Bulgaria's entry into the Great War, two parliamentary elections were held and both registered the growing influence of the peasantry.

The Bulgarian Agrarian National Union (BANU) was the beneficiary of this new peasant consciousness. As its influence grew, so did the reputation of its young chairman, Alexander Stamboliiski, a barrel-chested farmer who possessed a rare ability to translate sharp rural wit into the language of political struggle. One of Stamboliiski's election manifestos took the form of a vernacular conversation between him and a fictional elderly peasant, Bai Koliu (Grandpa Kolyu), whose pithy folk wisdom exposed the gulf between the urban elite and the toiling peasantry. 'Never elect for mayor a man who lets chickens climb on his head', he once told an audience during an election campaign. He denounced one opponent in parliament as 'an old hen who can neither lay an egg nor cluck properly'.[38] When translated from Bulgarian rustica, Stamboliiski argued that the expansionist adventures of Ferdinand, the professional classes and the military had poisoned the minds of Bulgarians towards all the country's neighbours. The new elite had done this, he claimed, to distract the rural masses from its enormous wealth and power. 'If the Bulgarian government has already allied itself with the side that urges Bulgaria on to adventurism', Stamboliiski warned the government and the Tsar in a parliamentary session on the eve of Bulgaria's entry into the Great War, 'with the side that seeks the occupation of Macedonia by Bulgaria . . . it is our deep conviction that this adventurism will lead Bulgaria to the grave. We can assure you that . . . before you can complete that adventure you will have to pass over our dead bodies.'[39]

When Bulgaria embarked on its 'adventure' Stamboliiski commanded almost a quarter of the votes in Bulgaria (and given the institutionalized rigging of election results, real support for the BANU was almost certainly greater) while the Narrow and Broad Socialists (the respective equivalents of the Bolsheviks and Mensheviks in Russia) had each won some 10 per cent of the vote, so that parties with explicit anti-war and anti-expansionist programmes were supported by a good half of the electorate. Stamboliiski himself was arrested just before Bulgarian troops crossed into Serbia. Found guilty of high treason and *lèse-majesté*, he was incarcerated for the duration of the war.

Opposition to Bulgarian militarism was strengthened by the fact that a full third of the annual budget was devoted to the military, the highest figure of any Balkan country in relative terms. Ferdinand's programme of expansion was driven by the military, above all by the Macedonian officers, the energetic young bourgeoisie and the country's countless professionals and civil servants. To refinance the army after the Second Balkan War, the Bulgarian government desperately needed to negotiate a loan. As the Entente powers dithered, imposing unnecessarily humiliating conditions, Germany willingly provided the cash in February 1915 as a further inducement to join the Central Powers' war effort.

Under the conditions of the loan, the country began to resemble a German colony, as a British historian of Bulgaria has described:

> The Bulgarians were required to place orders with Austro-Hungarian firms for the purchase of arms and railway equipment, the contract for the construction of the railway to Porto Lagos was to be given to a German company and all the materials used, as well as all replacement orders for the next fifty years, were to come from Germany and Austria-Hungary. This was a clear breach of the 1884 Railway Act.

> Even more galling was the stipulation that the Pernik and Bobov Dol coal-mining complexes, owned by the Bulgarian government, were to be handed over to a German company with the Sofia administration guaranteeing to buy at least 150,000 tons of coal per year. This was done on the pretext that only a German company would have the necessary experience, equipment and expertise to sink the deeper shafts that were now needed but the agreement gave the German company complete control over Bulgaria's major coalfield and over the prime source of fuel for the state's rail network.[40]

From late 1915 onwards, the German presence in Sofia and other Bulgarian towns became ever more noticeable. German troops passing through Bulgarian territory were permitted to send home 5 kilograms of food per week. Due to the relative strength of the German and Austrian currencies, which were legal tender in Bulgaria during the war, these troops began sending massive amounts of food back to Germany, exacerbating the shortages that the war effort had created throughout Bulgaria. Although the might of Germany genuinely impressed many Balkan politicians, the Germans failed to endear themselves even to friendly peoples, a pattern which would repeat itself in the Second World War. Imperious and greedy, the behaviour of the Germans in Bulgaria was a significant factor in the erosion of support for the war inside Bulgaria. As the conflict dragged on, more and more Bulgarians were unable to tolerate the deprivations. With most farm labourers at the front, women, children and the infirm were required to bring in the harvest, leading to a 50 per cent drop in yield over the three years from 1915 to the end of the war. By 1917, women around the country organized and took part in a series of riots demanding an end to the war and an equitable distribution of food. Tsar Ferdinand was well aware of the revolutionary spirit stirring in Bulgaria: the only way out was through the territorial expansion of the state. For the Tsar to survive, Bulgaria had to win the war; for his own grandiose self-image, it had to emerge as the undisputed master of the Balkans.

'My Old Kentucky Home': Romania, Macedonia

As many predicted at the time, the treaty of Bucharest in 1913, ending the Second Balkan War, was bound to stir future conflict. Among other provocations, it sanctioned the Romanian seizure of the Dobrudja, the unusually fertile parcel of land which lies south of the Danube delta and east of the great river as it flows north from the present Bulgarian border. Some apologists in Bucharest dreamed up historical and demographic justification for this transparent larceny. The facts, however, contradicted Romanian claims so stubbornly that even the most silken-tongued propagandist could not disguise that the annexation was a question of economic and strategic expediency.

When war broke out, the Romanians knew they would probably have to pay for their gains in 1913. They faced a bleak choice. Just as the acquisition of Bosnia and Macedonia had become an obsession with the elites of Serbia and Bulgaria, the Romanians dreamed of creating a Greater Romania by absorbing the mixed Hungarian-Romanian region of Transylvania, and eastern Moldavia (or Bessarabia). The former territory was part of the Austro-Hungarian Empire while the latter belonged to imperial Russia. An alliance with the Central Powers would mean forsaking Transylvania, while joining the Entente implied giving up Bessarabia. Of the two, Transylvania occupied a more prominent place in Romanian national psychology, which explains in part why there was little popular support for the Central Powers. The perceived cultural affinities with France were also important in pulling Romania in the direction of the Entente. But the entry of Turkey and Bulgaria into the war, followed by the defeat of Serbia, placed Romania in an awkward position.

With the Straits closed to shipping, Romania was hemmed in on all but one side by the Central Powers. Before the war, 80 per cent of its trade sailed out of the Danube and through the Dardanelles to the markets of western Europe and the United States. The war had closed down that route, and now the only exit through an Entente country was to the north across the war-ravaged dirt tracks of Russia. Traditionally, Romania's relations with Russia were poor, and, of course, it wanted a chunk of Russian territory for itself (with considerably greater justification than its claim on the southern

Dobrudja). After Bulgaria's declaration for the Central Powers, Romania was forced in a matter of weeks to restructure completely the pattern of her foreign trade. This led to a deepening recession, which did not hurt Romania's powerful landowners unduly. With wheat prices enjoying a revival on the global market, the landowners were able to maintain high profits at the expense of the rural workers who were again showing signs of restlessness. Peasants smuggled livestock over the Habsburg border to sell to the Hungarians. Mindful of future wartime needs, the government imposed heavy penalties on people found guilty of trafficking in cattle. The ferocious suppression of a peasant uprising in 1907 ensured that relations between the peasantry and landowners were worse in Romania than anywhere else in the Balkans. The threat of war acted as a brake on large-scale disturbances but there was a steady increase in localized *jacqueries*.

In Bucharest, tension grew between supporters of the Entente and of the Central Powers, occasionally leading to violence at the university. And all over the city diplomats from Britain, France, Austria-Hungary, Russia, the United States and Germany were engaged in persuading or cajoling influential Romanians, spying on one another and the Romanian government, and monitoring the Romanian army as it expanded and re-equipped itself. Bucharest was the European capital of suspicion: 'Each national group has its favourite haunt and no-one ever crosses into anyone else's domain', noted the American ambassador, Charles Vopicka.

> The Germans strut in their Teutonic fashion around the Palace Athena which is full of gold and elaborate ornaments creating a suitable frame for the Prussian officer. The French feel more relaxed in the soft bohemian atmosphere of the Moderna; two or three Englishmen, prune-faced but comfortable, guard their spot in the refuge known as the Capsis. Nowhere on the front line which stretches from the Baltic to Bukovina are the enemy armies so precisely compartmentalised as in this neutral city – the centre of the political vortex in the Balkans.[41]

The last thing Romania wanted was war, but no Romanian could find the magic formula needed to avoid it. As with Bulgaria, the government in Bucharest and the inexperienced Romanian king, also called Ferdinand (1914–27), were soon subject to what a Romanian politician called 'a veritable campaign to intimidate our country: a swarm of Allied publicists descended on Bucharest. The journals which espoused the Allied cause launched a furious campaign to push Romania into war. In turn, Romanian politicians, friends of the Allies, organized an ardent campaign of public meetings in order to force Romania's hand.'[42] In contrast with Bulgaria, the Germans expended less effort on securing Romania's support, as they assumed that Bucharest was geographically too isolated to risk declaring for the Entente.

Yet the Romanian government, headed by Ion Brătianu, feared that failure to declare war against someone would leave Romania empty-handed when peace finally came, a view that underlay the surge of pro-Entente sentiment that swept the country in the summer of 1916. Its more immediate cause was the breathtaking success of the Brusilov offensive. From the Pripet Marshes in Byelorussia to the Bukovina, the nearly 2,000 guns of General Alexei Brusilov's army shelled Austrian positions, and within hours, the Austrians had begun a chaotic retreat. Throughout June, the Romanian government watched the Russian advances with amazement. From the vantage point of Bucharest, it looked as if the turning point of the war had come. A collapse of the Central Powers' defences in Transylvania, should the Romanians attack there, seemed very probable. The government in Bucharest approached the Entente and opened negotiations.

The Allies, especially the French General Joseph Joffre, made extravagant promises to the Romanians, who were not to know that these were hot air, based on exaggerated assessments of the Entente's military capability in the region. The French assured Bucharest that the Franco-British expeditionary force based in Salonika would launch a major offensive northwards to pin down the Bulgarian forces in Macedonia. The Romanians believed them, and on 27 August 1916, Bucharest declared war on Austria-Hungary. Germany reciprocated the next day and within three days both Turkey and Bulgaria had followed suit. Romania had acquired powerful enemies; her friends were less potent.

French and British troops had landed in Salonika and then commandeered the harbour city in the autumn of 1915. They were under the command of the maverick French general, Maurice Sarrail, who cherished the fanciful notion that his force could link up with the Serbs in Niš and Kragujevac before piercing Hungary, the soft underbelly of the Central Powers, and then driving on triumphantly to Berlin. The first troops arrived in Salonika almost simultaneously with the beginning of the Austro-German-Bulgarian offensive against the battered Serb army. By the time the expeditionary force in Salonika had found its bearings, there was no friendly army left to link up with because the Serbs were already preparing to cross the Albanian mountains on their retreat to Corfu. Once the Bulgarians had established their forward defences some 80 kilometres north of Salonika, the Allied force there, which had grown to 300,000 by May 1916, found it impossible to break them down.[43]*

These circumstances did not persuade Sarrail that his plans were unrealizable. 'What was the point of the occupation of Salonika? What was the mission of the troops of the Orient beyond the defence of Salonika? What was the concept behind this force?' one military historian later asked. 'In truth, the allies had no single concept, just so many contradictory ideas of the individual coalition states.'[44] In fact, the British, French, and later the Serb, Yugoslav and Russian, troops in Salonika would have a distinct impact on the course of the war both in the Balkans, especially within Greece, and in the wider European arena.† But this was certainly not by design. As Commandant Larcher pointed out, each power had its own idea about what the troops at Salonika should be doing. The British argued for a complete pull-out. The Russians, seeking to relieve the pressure on the Eastern Front, wanted to land ten army corps on the coast of Bosnia and Hercegovina and to attack Austria-Hungary there. The Italians watched the squabbles and contributed little to the regional operation, but consolidated their domination of the southern Albanian coast. And the fate of Romania's intervention rested on the sands of her allies' fine words.

For ten days after declaring war on Austria-Hungary, Romanians revelled in illusory success as almost half a million soldiers poured into Transylvania, securing the six passes in the southern rim of the

---

* The Macedonean Front has been ill served by historians, although a single volume, Alan Palmer's riveting study, *The Gardeners of Salonika*, has gone a long way to redress the balance.

† The contribution of the other two allies, Greece and Italy, was less decisive.

Carpathians that controlled the western approaches to their capital. But in the second week of September, a joint Bulgar-German offensive in the Dobrudja smashed through Romanian defences 5 kilometres south-east of the main front and began driving northwards to the Danube delta. The Romanian nightmare of a war on two fronts had come to pass. For two months, the Romanian army leadership juggled its forces back and forth between the fronts, but on 11 November, General Falkenhayn launched a new offensive from Transylvania which broke the Romanian lines in the Jiu valley, to the west of Bucharest. A general retreat north-eastwards towards Iaşi was sounded, and amid scenes of tremendous chaos king and government left the Romanian capital, the wheat plains of Wallachia and the oil fields of Ploeşti to the Germans.

Romanian losses in the war were staggering. By December 1916, some 250,000 soldiers had been killed, almost a third of those mobilized just three months before. Field Marshal von Mackensen's martial régime, which replaced the civilian government, was especially harsh as the Germans considered the occupied territory's economic resources legitimate plunder. Immediately on arrival in Bucharest, Mackensen ordered citizens to hand over two-thirds of their food supplies to the military authorities. Failure to do so was punished by imprisonment or death. Those able to leave Bucharest did so. Thousands flocked to the American Embassy in the city begging for passports. The Entente diplomats had left Bucharest, leaving US Ambassador Vopicka looking after the interests of eight countries (during the first phase of the war he looked after German interests as well) in addition to his own work. Vopicka recorded that among the Romanians besieging the embassy were groups of American 'black vaudeville artists who worked the Balkans throughout the war. In groups of between four and ten, they would pitch up at the Embassy asking for financial support to make their way to Russia where the earnings were supposed to be good.' Suspicious of their story, Vopicka demanded that the artists prove they were who they claimed, and so in front of the astonished Romanians and German guards, 'two of them changed like lightning to reappear as a convincing camel while another group, who had applied for passports, gave an impromptu performance of *My Old Kentucky Home*. They sang so beautifully that not only did I give them all the documents, but I advanced them all the money they needed for their travel costs as well.'[45]

Few if any Romanians succeeded in fleeing to America, of course, but many did make it to Iaşi in the north-east. This became the temporary capital, its population swelling from 90,000 to 400,000. Ion Brătianu formed a Government of National Unity which pleaded with the Allies for help. The latter had promised to deliver 300 tons of war material a day to the Romanians, but these goods proved as imaginary as the promised Allied offensives. The French and British did actually send supplies, but they had to be routed via Archangel in Russia's far north and Vladivostok, 7,400 kilometres to the east of Iaşi as the crow flies. By the time the shipments arrived in Romania, they had been stripped of anything useful.

The Romanians were besides themselves with fury. One parliamentarian accused the Entente of breaking every promise they had made:

> The Allies suspended all of their offensives: Brusilov's army just ground to a halt; the Franco-English offensive on the Somme ended while Sarrail made not one single step forward; Italy concluded a tactical armistice with the winter and her enemies. Everybody jostled for space on the balcony to watch little Romania, attacked from the north and from the south, defend her borders doggedly along more than 1,500 kilometres against an enemy ten times more numerous and a thousand times better equipped than her for three months.[46]

A less passionate commentator pointed out that 'the Rumanians had temporized too long. Had they intervened at the height of the Russian offensive, the impact could have been immense.'[47] And to give Sarrail his due, a combined French, British and Serbian offensive in October suffered heavy losses but also saw Monastir (Bitola) in Macedonia fall to the Entente, which alleviated Romania's position slightly. But it was too little and, as the bitter winter gripped Macedonia's mountainous terrain and halted the Allied offensive, too late for Romania. Despite having lost over half their territory, most of their industry, all their oil and their most fertile land, the Romanians fought on, inspired by the prospect of gains at the peace conference in the event of an Allied victory. Yet it was not

Romanian exhaustion or cowardice which led to the government's finally suing for peace. In December 1917, newly Bolshevik Russia agreed to an armistice with the Central Powers at Brest-Litovsk. This sealed Romania's fate. Brătianu succeeded in drawing out negotiations over the conditions of Romania's surrender until well into February 1918. But von Mackensen then lost his patience and gave the government five days to capitulate or face a new onslaught. The Romanians went to Paris for the peace conference as a vanquished member of the Entente. It seemed almost half a million Romanians had died in vain.

The winter of 1916–17 saw millions of people all over the Balkans homeless, diseased, wounded, avoiding shelling or genocidal assaults, undernourished and frozen. Many were living under foreign occupation. The Great War had splintered into a myriad of local conflicts – latent civil war in Greece; a revival in Serbia of the bandit heroes, the *hajduci*, who harassed the Bulgarian occupiers; anarchic patterns of warfare in Albania and Kosovo, where several aspirants for control battled it out with one another and makeshift indigenous forces; genocide in Turkey; the rout of the Romanians. Some conflicts saw Balkan armies pitted against one another; some were exclusive battles of the great powers; others were an incomprehensible mixture of the two; some battles were fought according to the rules of warfare; others were mere displays of barbarism. Most Balkan leaders had no clear idea as to their war aims; all were almost as suspicious of their great-power allies as they were of their enemies. For the growing urban population and for the peasantry, who still made up over three-quarters of the population in most countries, life since the outbreak of the First Balkan War in 1912 had oscillated between terror and deprivation. Dragooned into fighting far from their fields for a national cause about which they understood very little, the peasants of some countries were now showing signs of angry exhaustion. As the war ground on, the impact of the two Russian revolutions on the Balkans was predictably huge. The resourceful, corrupted elites in the Balkans now braced themselves for revolutionary revenge by workers and peasants; and, worse still, for the Paris Peace Conference.

Digging for victory: Macedonia, Greece

British and French critics heaped scorn on the 'Army of the Orient' from the moment the first troops landed in Salonika in autumn 1915. Georges Clemenceau had led the charge. 'What were Sarrail's men doing? Digging! Then let them be known to France and Europe as "The gardeners of Salonika".'[48] His particular target was General Sarrail, commander of the Army, and when news filtered through to Paris of the General's public and melodramatic wooing of a much younger woman in Salonika, Clemenceau humiliated him by writing that Sarrail was to be especially commended for fighting a war on two fronts – one in Macedonia, the other in the bedroom. In Britain, the Macedonian Front became a popular music-hall joke in 1917 as the favoured destination for skivers in search of a holiday.

There is no doubt that Salonika itself was probably the most vibrant and diverting front-line city in all Europe. If the commanders had not laid special emphasis on entertainment for the troops, mutiny would have followed. The weather was either humid and stifling, or cold and miserable. With the exception of Sunday, never a day went by during the occupation of Salonika without the performance of at least one play or variety show by the British. Football tournaments were organized under the watchful eye of Bulgarian artillery units, who obligingly held their fire when a game was scheduled. The French fraternized with the locals, taking their lead from General Sarrail himself, establishing particularly warm personal and commercial relations with the Salonika Jews. Again Sarrail was central in this as in addition to commanding the Army of the Orient he doubled as France's most energetic trade representative in Greece.

But the image of the Macedonian Front as one enormous holiday camp could not have been further from the truth. Not only was Macedonia a much tougher posting than the journalists and comedians of France and Britain appreciated, it was on this front and not in France that the military breakthrough essential for the defeat of the Central Powers was made in the autumn of 1918. But the combined troops (British, French, Serb and later Italian, Russian and Greek) spent most of the war hemmed in by Bulgarian and German artillery, restricted to the defensive arc protecting Salonika and its environs. When either side launched an offensive, the opposing armies sustained numerous and futile casualties. But the worst enemy facing the Entente troops, who were surrounded by the marshes of the Vardar delta, was the mosquito. By 1917 over one-fifth of the total British contingent of just under 100,000 was laid up in hospital with malaria.

The consequences of another disaster were even greater. As most of Salonika's 150,000 inhabitants were enjoying their siesta on 18 August 1917, a fire started in the old Turkish quarter above the Via Egnatia:

> After four rainless months, every balcony was tinder dry and with a fierce north-west wind blowing, the city had as little hope of escaping destruction as Chicago in 1871 or London in 1666 . . .
>
> It was becoming clear that the fire was a grievous blow to the poorer people; but still nobody believed that it would cross the Via Egnatia, the old Roman road which formed a social as well as a geographical division through the city. They were mistaken: around ten o'clock that night the fire swept over this barrier. By midnight it stretched in a mile-long arch across the night sky, with the minarets of mosques burning like candles on the altar of destruction.[49]

Some 300 acres of tightly packed wooden housing were totally destroyed by the fire. But just days after the massive operation of clearing the debris had begun, Eleftherios Venizelos's liberal Cabinet dumbfounded many of Salonika's inhabitants by announcing that it would be expropriating all the gutted areas from the 4,100 people who had lost their property in the fire. Some three-quarters of these were Jewish landlords as the fire had razed nearly the entire area inhabited by the Sephardim. Venizelos decreed the formation of three committees to supervise Salonika's reconstruction. The second body was named the International Commission of the Salonika Plan. It was chaired by Ernest Hébrard, a well-known architect serving with the French army and an enthusiastic modernist. He was charged by the Greek government with rebuilding the city centre, taking into account the latest theories of urban planning while also emphasizing neo-classical and Byzantine (i.e. Greek) styles. The projected population of the resurrected Salonika, he was told, would number some 350,000, an increase of 130 per cent on the population before the great conflagration.

Hébrard was thus presented with an architect's dream – the chance to mould an entire city. The population in the city centre had been forcibly uprooted by the fire; the government had seized the land; and so there was no one to interfere with Hébrard's grandiose plans. Where there had been a maze of higgledy-piggledy houses, accommodating dozens of families and tiny little workshops and stores, there grew up row upon row of uniform angular structures. Monuments and statues representing the highlights of Greek history and architectural style were erected in squares linked by broad boulevards and streets crossing at right angles which were dissected by diagonals. Detailed instructions about the design of façades in the centre were issued to prevent the rebirth of the uneven, colourful and unpredictable patterns of Ottoman Salonika. Trams trundled back and forth along straight new roads, shuttling tens of thousands from their workplaces in the centre to the suburbs which were developed rapidly to accommodate the growing number of Greeks who were encouraged to settle in the city. This development of housing estates on the outskirts was central to the 'unified concept and organization of the urban space which focused on a sole civic and cultural centre . . . the imposition of a uniform architectural style by means of strictly regulating what could and could not be built; bestowing the city's memory upon "noble" buildings, Roman or Byzantine, which alone were considered sufficiently dignified to represent its past and ennoble its present.'[50]

It dawned on the leadership of the Jewish community that its people were being uprooted from traditional residential areas in the city centre and dispersed into various outlying districts. Jewish and Zionist organizations in Europe applied significant pressure on the British and French governments, who were, after all, still occupying Salonika, to halt this dual programme of modernization and Hellenization.

Of course, Venizelos's ambition stretched well beyond his stated aim of modernizing Salonika. Just before his resignation in early 1917, the French Prime Minister, Aristide Briand, had developed a deep suspicion of the Greek leader, 'because I fear that Venizelos may have very long teeth when peace negotiations open. He has not renounced his dream to recreate the Byzantine Empire . . . Now, a large scale expansion of Greece would be a threat to the peace of the world. I have for a long time desired the cooperation of the Greeks but not under these conditions.'[51]

Venizelos considered the transformation of Salonika crucial to his expansionist plans. His ardent desire for Greece to fight with the Entente during the war was fired by his plans for the realization of the *Megali idea*, the Great Idea of a Greece on 'two continents and five seas'. As an ally of the Entente, Greece would be in an excellent position to drive home its territorial claims against Bulgaria, Turkey and even Albania. The starting point for this adventure had to be Salonika, the largest community on Greece's front line. Yet although the city lay in such an important strategic position, Greeks were only the third largest population in Salonika after the Jews and Turks, whose loyalty to the Greek state was open to question. In the event of an untoward outcome to the war, it lay exposed, especially to Bulgaria whose military made no secret of its desire to absorb the port. For Venizelos's grandiose dreams, the Salonika fire could hardly have happened at a better time.

Throughout the second decade of the century, Venizelos demonstrated diplomatic skills and a political intelligence which exceeded those of any other Balkan statesman. But his sophisticated charm and agile wit were deceptive. He was a brilliant, narrow technician of power – maintaining and consolidating his political position and, above all, convincing his great-power allies, especially Britain, that he should play the key role in their strategy for dealing with Ottoman collapse. Even here, he occasionally misread developments, in particular his standing with the Greek electorate. The reconstruction of Salonika proved to be only one of several gigantic errors which not only led to his political demise but contributed to the deepening of the National Schism – the polarization of Greeks into two violently resentful camps.

Greece had entered the Great War flushed with its successes in the Balkan Wars, which had been won at relatively little cost to itself. The country was united and optimistic. Yet just over two years after the outbreak of the war, the country had been torn down the middle both geographically and politically. In the north, Venizelos had established the so-called Government of National Defence with its capital in Salonika and under the patronage of the Entente's Army of the Orient. Venizelos had fled there to join rebel army commanders when it became clear that Athens could not accommodate two men intent on running the country's foreign affairs – especially since the Prime Minister wanted at all costs to join the Entente and his chief rival, King Constantine (1913–17, 1920–2), did not. A foreign-policy dispute provoked political crisis in Greece in 1915–16 because of the country's peculiar constitutional development since independence. As one Greek historian noted as early as 1940, 'for a century the course of Greek politics was determined by the exigencies of foreign policy rather than by the correlation and clash of forces within the nation. The fact that the anti-monarchy movement originated in a conflict over foreign policy . . . is a striking demonstration of the influence of international factors and the protecting powers – the third party to the constitutional development of modern Greece.'[52]

In Athens, the Germanophile monarch had built up considerable public support for his policy of neutrality. But his most important power base was the officer corps of the army. Constantine's resistance to the Entente's perpetual interference in Greece's affairs, notably the Allies' attempt to seize control of the country's postal and transport systems during the war, won him support. There is only circumstantial evidence that Constantine ever considered actually joining the Central Powers. He may have been influenced to a degree by his wife, Sophie, Kaiser Wilhelm's sister, but the Greek King was no fool. He could see perfectly well that the Entente controlled the Mediterranean and had 300,000 troops in Salonika backing Venizelos's insurrection (although the same troops also prevented the hotter heads in the Venizelist military leadership from attacking the areas loyal to the King). To declare for the Central Powers would have provoked a massive assault from the Entente and plunged the country into a violent civil conflict.

Yet the French diplomatic mission in Athens bombarded the Quai d'Orsay and the Prime Minister, Aristide Briand, with fanciful reports of conspiracies directed by German agents in Athens. The French government trusted neither Constantine nor Venizelos. Throughout 1916, a powerful lobby comprising General Sarrail and the senior Embassy officials in Athens urged on Paris the policy of establishing a protectorate over Greece, humiliating Constantine with ultimatums whose conditions he could not possibly fulfil without provoking his own army. This diplomatic pressure culminated in the events of 1 December 1916, when French and British troops under the command of the French Admiral Dartige du Fournet landed at Piraeus and marched on Athens. The army resisted the Allied assault. Dartige had assumed that his display of superior force would be a stroll. He was wrong. Within hours of entering Athens, fifty-seven French and five British soldiers had been killed and many more wounded. The Allies beat a hasty retreat. The monarchist soldiers were enraged at this violation of Greek sovereignty. Even before the Entente troops had departed, members of the paramilitary League of Reservists had begun to daub red paint on certain houses, shops and businesses in the Greek capital:

> When the British and French withdrew to their ships, this strange contest seemed ended; but there was no peace within Athens. That night and all the following day the Athenian Chorus, which had witnessed these events with traditional submissiveness, became actors in the play. The shops of leading liberals were looted, the offices of the Venizelist press were ransacked, the homes of known sympathizers with the Entente attacked. The purpose of those sinister red paint marks became all too clear. Opponents of the army leaders were murdered or cast into prison. And while murder and arson filled the streets, King Constantine himself issued an order of the day congratulating his troops on their forbearance, loyalty and spirit of self-sacrifice.[53]

Within two days this prologue to the National Schism had played itself out, although the Schism proper would bedevil Greek politics and progress for decades to come, and some historians argue that its effects may still be seen in contemporary Greek public life. Its opening scene took place in the spring of 1917 when the French finally succeeded in forcing Constantine's abdication and exile. Venizelos returned to Athens in triumph to govern the reunited country. He began by purging the armed forces and civil service of known monarchists. 'The mass dismissals', one historian has noted, 'created an unfortunate precedent in Greek politics. The country entered a vicious circle as every *coup* was followed by widespread purges of opponents and undesirables in the armed forces and the state apparatus. The 1916 military meddling in politics was one step further in making the soldiers the ultimate arbiters of Greek policy-making.'[54]

But Venizelos could at last sign up to the Entente; and the presence of Greek troops on the Macedonian Front meant that Greece would attend the peace conference as a victor with claims on the spoils.

The French had bullied Constantine; now they placed political and military obstacles in the way of Venizelos. But Briand and later Clemenceau were frustrated by the British and especially by Lloyd George, who enjoyed a close friendship with Venizelos. Why did the French assume such a consistently hostile attitude towards Greek interests during the war, and why did Britain seek to defend Greek policy ever more energetically as the war neared its end? Greece had become a crystal ball in which it was possible to see the future of relations between the two major Entente powers, as one contemporary writer observed:

> France was playing for infinitely higher stakes [than political influence in Greece]. Greece was merely the strategic stepping stone to the Balkans and the Ottoman Empire where France hoped to preserve her immense pre-war economic interests, especially in Istanbul, and if possible to win additional concessions after the war in Syria and Asia Minor. To achieve these goals France considered it as important to win the diplomatic war against Britain and Russia as it was to win the military struggle against Germany.[55]

War's end: The Macedonian Front

> On the evening of September 13th, 1918, Duke Živojin Mišić, Chief-of-Staff in the [Serbian] Supreme Command, clambered up to the observation post on Mount Floka. He wanted to spend the night here so he might judge the situation first thing in the morning. If there was fog, as was often the case at this time of year, the mountains would be covered and the rain clouds would hover above Veternik. In that case the guns hidden around and under the observation post would remain silent; they would not yet start to spew their fire. But on this occasion the old veteran was in luck. At five in the morning, September 14th, the eastern peaks of Veternik began to twinkle with the rays of the rising sun. The weather conditions for starting the offensive were ideal, so Duke Mišić did not waste any time. Immediately, he sent a curious message to all troops, Serbian and Allied who were deployed from Bitola to the banks of the Vardar:

> '*Mettez en route quatorze officiers et huit soldats.*' The message meant that at 8 o'clock on that morning, the 14th, the artillery should commence firing.
>
> From the official history of the Serbian National Defence Ministry[56]

Rising over 2,130 metres above sea level, the highest peaks of Macedonia's central mountain range had been left undisturbed since time immemorial by all but a few shepherds. When General Mišić gave the order to fire on 14 September 1918, that peace was obliterated in spectacular fashion. An 'iron storm' soon developed 'into a hurricane', wrote one of the German commanders on the Macedonian Front. With French and Serbian planes buzzing above the Bulgarian trenches, directing fire and reporting back on the effect of Serb artillery fire, the guns 'shake the Crvena Stena and Peak 1248 [m], they hammer at the crags of Peak 1050 and crash with immense force against the stone walls of Sokol, Dobro-Polje, Kravica, Veternik and Kukuruz . . . Trees come crashing down, branches and stones fall like hail, and the [Bulgarian] positions are drowned in smoke and debris.'[57] The sound of the largest artillery assault the Balkans had ever seen, comprising just under 1,800 Allied guns, was magnified many times by the mountain acoustics. For two months, French and Serbian engineers had been transporting their guns, using tractors and winches, up many hundred metres of mountain. This operation could only be undertaken at night, to avoid detection by the German and Bulgarian forces, and before sunrise each day the guns and their transport were camouflaged. Some 105 kilometres north-west of Salonika, the mountain peak of Dobro Polje was the last point in the German/Bulgarian defences at which the German commander, General von Scholtz, anticipated coming under attack because the terrain was so difficult. But twenty-four hours after the artillery attack had fatally damaged the Bulgarian front line, Serb and French troops poured into Bulgaria's forward trench system and immediately set about storming the second line of defence.

Four years and one month after the Serbs had sustained the first casualties of the Great War in the Austro-Hungarian attack on Belgrade, the Allied Army of the Orient was engaged in a military operation, conceived by Serb military commanders, which would trigger Germany's defeat. It took General von Scholtz three days to realize that the Allies were slicing through Bulgarian defences on a rapid push towards Gradsko, the communications' junction that coordinated the activities of the German troops in western Macedonia with the Bulgarian armies in the centre and east of the region. Hindenburg had described the town as 'the most important centre of all communications in the Macedonian theatre of war',[58] and if Gradsko were to fall, the entire defensive system would collapse. The General was in desperate need of reinforcements. General Ludendorff, the commander in chief of all German forces, had been systematically depriving von Scholtz of men for twelve months, transferring troops to the Western Front for the great spring offensive planned for 1918. When von Scholtz's urgent request for reinforcements reached the German chief of staff, it was dismissed and passed on to Austro-Hungarian headquarters. In retrospect, Ludendorff bitterly regretted his neglect of the Macedonian Front. He later wrote, 'August 8th [the start of the Allied offensive in France] was the black day of the German army in the history of this war. This was the worst experience that I had to go through, except for the events that, from September 15th onwards, took place on the Bulgarian front and sealed the fate of the Quadruple Alliance.'[59]

Quite apart from the shortage of German troops, the morale of the Bulgarians, whose soldiers made up the vast majority of von Scholtz's forces, was dissipating rapidly. The harvests of 1917 and 1918 had yielded much less grain than usual and hunger had begun to stalk the Bulgarian army: 'One of the German officers highlighted just how bad things had become. During a visit to the front line, Bulgarian soldiers presented themselves in their underwear because they were too ashamed to present themselves for inspection in their miserable rags.'[60] Within days of the mountain offensive at Dobro Polje and Sokol, almost the entire Bulgarian army was in full flight, pursued by the Army of the Orient. As the soldiers struggled to make their way home through narrow mountain passes, British aviators opened a new chapter in the history of modern warfare. They caused havoc by carpet-bombing and machine-gunning the narrow files of undernourished and ill-clad Bulgarians. Air power meant that a hasty retreat would no longer guarantee the safety of a defeated army.

Two weeks after the offensive had begun, reports from the front line reaching the German headquarters in Skopje were still confused and distorted. On the night of 28 September, Lieutenant Ahrendt, whose machine-gunners were protecting the southern approaches of Skopje, was unnerved by the rumour that 500 Bulgarians from the Reserve Battalion had fled. Ahrendt was ordered to move closer to Vodno, the long hill which forms a doleful backdrop to Skopje. He was relieved to find that German troops were in full control of the situation, holding the ground from the eastern flank of Vodno to the railway station at the edge of town. Suddenly at 5 o'clock in the morning some exotically dressed horsemen appeared from nowhere. Ahrendt gave the order to fire and the mysterious cavalry brigade faded back into the early morning darkness.

Three hours later, hundreds of these horsemen reappeared – the Chasseurs d'Afrique, comprising 'a section of armoured cars and six squadrons of Spahis from Morocco, natural horsemen with proud traditions of their own. Mounted on Barb stallions as sure-footed as any mountain goat and with long hair streaming out from beneath light blue turbans, the Spahis made a terrifyingly impressive mobile column.'[61] Skopje, the centre of Serbia's medieval kingdom, was being liberated from the Germans by Muslims from Africa, commanded, incidentally, by General Jouinot-Gambetta, the nephew of Léon Gambetta, hero of the Paris Commune. Lieutenant Ahrendt ordered the armoured trains at the railway station to open fire while troop carriers and hospital coaches were hurriedly shunted northwards. Finding his retreat cut off by the Spahis now swarming into the city, Ahrendt and his men had to fight their way through old Skopje to the bridge across the Vardar which they blew up once they were safely across it. The Lieutenant and his troops 'succeeded in setting up their machine-gun positions on the old Turkish citadel in the north of the city. Spreading out beneath him was the colourful jumble of houses with their mosques and minarets glowing in the dazzling sun seemingly as tranquil as in times of peace.'[62] Within hours, Ahrendt had joined his compatriots scrambling back to central Europe almost as fast as the Bulgarian troops were heading towards Sofia and Plovdiv. Germans and Bulgarians alike were met by chaos, defeat and revolution. On 3 October 1918, Hindenburg wrote, 'As a result of the collapse of the Macedonian Front and the weakening of our western reserves which this has brought about, and now that it is impossible to make good the very considerable losses which have been incurred in the battles of the last few days, there is, so far as can be foreseen, no longer a prospect of forcing peace on the enemy.'[63] Two days later, the Germans appealed to President Woodrow Wilson to arrange an armistice. The war was effectively over.

The Radomir rebellion: Bulgaria

> At the time I was only 18 years old, a student on work experience at Radomir station. I was also a sympathizer of the Agrarian movement and the honour fell to me (well, actually I was given an order) to transmit the Proclamation of the Radomir Republic to our government in Sofia. Just as I was about to read out the Proclamation, I was interrupted:
>
> 'Hello, who's that?' It was the Minister of War, General Savov, himself!
>
> 'This is Apprentice Dŭngŭrski!'
>
> 'What's the situation in Radomir? Is the unrest spreading?'
>
> 'A Republic has been proclaimed, General! And you are no longer either general or minister.' You can imagine how excited I was, me just a teenager being able to talk to a general like that. 'The people have stripped you of power. The army will soon be in Sofia! Think hard, you blood-sucker, about who was responsible for driving Bulgaria headlong into catastrophe.'[64]

With the Chasseurs d'Afrique marching on Skopje, Alexander Stamboliiski, the leader of BANU, the Bulgarian Agrarian National Union, was finally released from prison on 25 September 1918. In what has become a familiar transition in twentieth-century central and eastern Europe, he went straight from prison to a meeting with the head of state, Tsar Ferdinand. The country's infrastructure was crumbling and hundreds of thousands of disillusioned, angry soldiers were returning from the front. Ferdinand was unconcerned whether the rioting, looting and mutiny were inspired by the Agrarians, the Bolsheviks, or sheer anarchic frustration. He was looking Nemesis in the eye and he would accept help from any quarter.

Bulgaria's participation in the war had never commanded the support of more than half the population. In the final twelve months of war, any remaining enthusiasm for the alliance with Germany had evaporated. There were many reasons for this. First and foremost was the casualty toll. According to official statistics, 101,224 Bulgarians were killed and 144,026 wounded. This was the highest per capita toll of any country in the war. Agriculture, the core of the country's economy, had been devastated by the mobilization of such a huge proportion of the peasantry, by two years of bad harvests and the increase in fallow land, and by a requisitioning régime which ensured that by June 1918 'horses and oxen had virtually disappeared from the countryside, where the old and the infirm were often to be seen dragging their own carts'.[65]

German influence over the Bulgarian economy (and food purchases in particular) was also extremely unpopular. Disgruntlement turned to revulsion when in May 1918 the German government announced after Romania's capitulation that its forces would be occupying the southern Dobrudja, as Berlin considered it strategically and economically vital. For Bulgaria, its economic value was obvious because although it included 'only eight percent of the agricultural land [of Bulgaria] and six percent of the farming population, it produced 230 to 250 million kilograms of grain or almost a fifth of the country's total production'.[66]

As sympathy for Germany drained away, the Bulgarians began to invest their hopes in a distant and somehow magical great power, the United States of America. Although President Woodrow Wilson had committed America to the Allies' cause in 1917, the United States did not declare war on Bulgaria.

In February 1918, President Wilson added Four Principles of America's approach to peace to the Fourteen Points he had outlined the month before. The Fourth Principle proposed that 'all well defined national aspirations shall be accorded the utmost satisfaction that can be accorded them without introducing new or perpetuating old elements of discord and antagonism that would be likely in time to break the peace of Europe and consequently the world'.[67] Bulgarians naturally considered that national aspirations were 'well defined', and indeed much of Wilson's rhetoric was peppered with the concept of 'self-determination'. This was good news for the Bulgarians, it seemed, on the issues of the southern Dobrudja and, above all, of Macedonia. Wilson's academic advisers, whom the President had convoked in his so-called Commission of Inquiry, were clearly sympathetic towards Bulgaria's aspirations. The

American ambassador in Sofia arranged for the translation of almost all Wilson's speeches on the impending postwar settlement and for their distribution among the troops and mutineers. They all understood the message to mean that Macedonia would finally be theirs. Only a few Bulgarians, however, understood the implications of the final version of the eleventh of Wilson's Fourteen Points:

> Romania, Serbia, and Montenegro should be evacuated; occupied territories restored; Serbia accorded free and secured access to the sea; and the relations of the several Balkan states to one another determined by friendly counsel along historically established lines of allegiance and nationality; and national guarantees of the political and economic independence and territorial integrity of the several Balkan states should be entered into.[68]

Here, the pragmatic claims of three Balkan states which had joined the winning side clearly took precedence over principles of ethnically defined self-determination. A substantial and troublesome conflict was in the making between the aims of what became known as the 'old diplomacy' of Europe's imperial powers and the 'new diplomacy' of Wilson. The former conjured up a world of skulduggery, secret treaties and imperialist bullying, masked by the stylized language of protocol. The latter presented itself as principled and open, although sceptics labelled it naive. The American attitude to Bulgaria also suggested that Wilson's principles contradicted themselves in several important respects. In the Balkans, however, almost every nation had begun to view Wilson and his Fourteen Points as its good friend. Bulgarians, traumatized and in despair, foolishly believed that America would not perpetrate the inequities of the 1913 Treaty of Bucharest.

In September 1918, when the Bulgarian army was being driven out of Macedonia, economic hardship joined with anti-German sentiment and the effects of military collapse to produce rebellion. On Stamboliiski's release from prison, Tsar Ferdinand did indeed try to enlist his help to stop the soldiers' rebellion from turning into a revolution. A year later, Stamboliiski argued that he had decided to assume leadership of the revolt centred on the town of Radomir, some 40 kilometres south-west of Sofia, because he did not trust the

Tsar. Ferdinand later claimed he had promised to seek an armistice with the Allies in exchange for Stamboliiski's cooperation in dampening the rebel passions at Radomir. In fact, the true story of the rebellion and of Stamboliiski's attitude towards it remains obscure, in part because the Bulgarian Communist Party loathed Stamboliiski with such intensity that no serious research into his seminal role in Bulgarian politics was ever undertaken in the postwar period. The rebellion, in fact, seriously divided the leadership of BANU. By 27 September, Stamboliiski had left Radomir and travelled on to the headquarters of the Bulgarian army at Kiustendil, another 40 kilometres to the south-west. In Radomir, he had appealed to the rebellious masses not to storm Sofia in accordance with the deal he had struck with Ferdinand. While discussing the armistice issue with the generals in Kiustendil, he was called to the phone. His deputy, Raiko Daskalov, announced breathlessly, and to Stamboliiski's considerable consternation, that he had issued the following proclamation in the name of Daskalov, commander in chief of the Bulgarian armed forces, and Stamboliiski, President of the Radomir Republic:

> Today, September 27, 1918, the Bulgarian people break the chains of slavery, throw down the despotic regime of Ferdinand and his henchmen, proclaim them enemies of the people, proclaim themselves a free people with a republic form of government, and hold out the hand of peace and understanding to the peoples of Europe. From this day Tsar Ferdinand and his dynasty and the former government are fallen. All provincial administrators, district officials, police commandants, mayors, and military officers will carry out the orders of the provisional government of the republic.[69]

In Sofia, the rest of BANU's leadership denounced the proclamation of the Republic, possibly influenced by their location in Ferdinand's stronghold and possibly influenced by common sense. Suddenly Stamboliiski found himself riding the tiger of 15,000 very unhappy soldiers who were demanding that decisive action be taken against the government and Tsar in Sofia, notwithstanding the approach of large numbers of German troops. In desperation, he sought the support of Dimitŭr Blagoev, promising the leader of the 'Narrow'

(Tesnyaki or Bolshevik) socialists extensive powers in the new government. Blagoev, now relishing the prospect of a full-blown Bolshevik revolution for which the Radomir rebellion would be a mere prologue, dismissed Stamboliiski's appeal. Here lay the origins of the Bulgarian communist movement's intense myopia – the 'Narrows' demonstrated almost as much disdain for the peasantry and its political representative, BANU, as did Ferdinand. Instead, Blagoev and his supporters placed their trust on a proletariat that barely existed.

To the outside world, however, obscure doctrinal differences between the two revolutionary forces, the Agrarians and the Narrows, were irrelevant. As far as both the Entente and the Central Powers were concerned, communism was on the rise in Bulgaria – and that was in nobody's interest. Daskalov did bring his force to the edge of Sofia but proved an incompetent commander when he led the charge on 30 September. Fiercely patriotic Bulgarian troops from Macedonia were bolstered by German reinforcements. Within two days, the rebellion was crushed and Daskalov, badly wounded in the fighting, was forced into hiding. In a serious misjudgement, Stamboliiski decided to continue the revolutionary struggle and suggested to the brilliant young leader of the Narrows in Sofia, Georgi Dimitrov, that they cooperate. Just as his mentor, Blagoev, had dismissed such cooperation, so too did Dimitrov. Stamboliiski, despondent and isolated, became a fugitive from justice.

Although it proved a shambles, the defeated Radomir rebellion did achieve two things – it made Ferdinand's position untenable and, on 3 October, he abdicated in favour of his son who became Tsar Boris III (1918–43). It also laid down a blueprint for future lack of cooperation between the Agrarians and the Communists. The Bulgarian army, utterly defeated, signed a humiliating armistice. After three months, Stamboliiski was granted an amnesty and he gradually regained his pre-eminent position in the BANU. In 1919, he was appointed to the Bulgarian delegation at the Paris Peace Conference and by the end of the year he was Prime Minister. As a Bulgarian representative at Paris, Stamboliiski, who had spent three years in prison for his vigorous and principled opposition to Bulgaria's participation in the war, was shunned and reviled by the delegations of the victorious Allies. But this was par for the course: Paris was the Looking-Glass Peace Conference. To succeed, a proposition there had to be either unjust, absurd, plain unworkable or better still all three.

The peace to end all peace

Paris had few redeeming qualities at the beginning of January 1919. The cold, damp snow and the disasters of the war had erased any traces of the glittering *fin-de-siècle* culture that had made the city so seductive. Instead, delegates to the Peace Conference saw the squalor of Paris, its narrow, grasping petite bourgeoisie, its brutal police and its oppressive government. As they arrived from all corners of the world, they were obliged to make their way through hundreds of field guns parked in the centre of the French capital.

The first war to mobilize Europe's masses, unleashing an unprecedented quantity of military and economic energy, was capped by a 'mass' peace. No previous peace negotiations could begin to match the sheer industry of the Paris Conference. These tireless efforts had a malignant impact on the affairs of the world although most of what went on was inherently valueless except as a means of justifying the presence of the huge delegations lumbering into town. The British Prime Minister, David Lloyd George, alone brought 400 people with him. These included domestic staff to work at the Hotel Majestic where the British were based. The French employees they replaced were considered a security threat and possible carriers of disease (government chaperones were on hand to attend all women attached to the delegation should they wish to leave the premises). Woodrow Wilson brought with him more than 200 men and women, including the Inquiry, an entire academic think-tank which had been working on all aspects of the impending peace treaty for over a year. The President made use of the personnel and administrative facilities at the American military headquarters in France. Most Americans stayed at the Hotel Crillon, overlooking the Place de la Concorde which housed the densest concentration of artillery in the city. The French government, of course, used its entire civil service as its delegation.

Dozens of other countries and political movements were represented. Neither the French organizers nor the major participants had the faintest idea what role, if any, these minor delegations would play but in the meantime they were occupied in finding accommodation and establishing offices before launching their diplomatic crusades. The Greeks, led most ably by Venizelos, had invested so much in the outcome of the negotiations that they hired the entire eighty-bed Hotel Mercator for their sixteen-strong delegation. After four years geared to war, the hoteliers and café owners of Paris reasoned not unnaturally that with demand for space and food at an absolute premium, 1919 would be a year to make hay from foreign taxpayers. And so it proved. Prices in the French capital went through the roof. For some of the Balkan delegations, this presented serious problems (although clearly not for the Greeks). But for tenacious freelancers like Ho Chi Minh, who spoke up at the Conference for the rights of the population in French Indo-China, participation also necessitated moonlighting at some of the hotels where fellow participants were staying!

There were also some noticeable absentees. In a dramatic break from tradition, the vanquished powers were not invited to the Conference. They would only be summoned once the various treaties affecting them had been drawn up – to be presented with *faits accomplis*. Somewhere on the hazardous road from the Congress of Berlin, the precious right of defeated parties to negotiate a peace settlement had been lost. They were given no right either to offer factual advice or to contest the final provisions of the Peace. More than any other procedural issue, this decision would ensure the short-term failure of the Peace with Turkey and its long-term failure, with dire consequences, in Germany, Austria, Hungary and Bulgaria. Woodrow Wilson insisted that he would only negotiate on the basis of a 'new, open diplomacy'. He also demanded that this diplomacy be in harmony with his Fourteen Points, Four Principles and Five Particulars. Even if these elements of the Wilsonian credo of self-determination had been internally consistent with one another, adjusting them to the confusing demographic structures of Europe and the Middle East would have tested the most agile minds. But in fact, Wilsonism was applied haphazardly, incapable of smoothing the workings of a vindictive postwar order.

The President himself was not averse on occasions to bending his principles. In his zeal to promote American influence in Brazil, he recommended that the Brazilians be honoured with three delegates to the Peace Conference, despite having contributed just two torpedo boats to the war. But Belgium and Serbia, countries that were all but obliterated, were expected to make do with two delegates.

Wilson's acolytes in Europe, like Harold Nicolson, who was among the most gifted and enlightened British negotiators in Paris, were also guilty of double standards. Nicolson never ceased warning how myopic the French were in wanting to anchor their loathing of Germany in the Treaty by means of 'many hypocritical devices' and 'petty punishments of Germany by which resentment is perpetuated and revenge rendered inevitable'.[70] The intervention of such level heads as Nicolson's proved crucial in reining in French attempts to humiliate the Germans. Yet he himself sought to apply precisely those 'hypocritical devices and petty punishments' to Bulgaria, for whose people he admitted to cherishing 'feelings of contempt'. For a man who had served in the Embassy at Istanbul and was well acquainted with the southern Balkans, he failed miserably to understand the regional dimension to the war in southern Europe, allowing himself to be influenced by fatuous notions of Slavic brotherhood: 'Their traditions, their history, their actual obligations', he wrote of the Bulgarians, 'should have bound them to the cause of Russia and the Entente. They had behaved treacherously in 1913 and in the Great War they had repeated this act of perfidy. Inspired by the most material motives of acquisition they had joined with Germany, and by so doing lengthened the War by two whole years.' With the exception of Serbia, all countries who engaged in war were inspired by the same motives – Britain had, indeed, attempted to lure Bulgaria into the Entente by promising to rip Macedonia from its ally, Serbia. Nor did Nicolson acquaint himself with Bulgaria's domestic situation. He was apparently astonished that a man like Stamboliiski, who had spent the war behind bars, would endeavour 'to cast upon King Ferdinand the blame for what had in fact been a movement of national egoism. I did not feel that Bulgaria deserved more mercy than she would have herself been prepared, in similar circumstances, to accord.'[71]

Lloyd George angrily dismissed the Turks as 'a human cancer, a creeping agony in the flesh of the lands which they misgovern, rotting away every fibre of life'.[72] This blind conviction that all Germany's allies had not so much made an error of judgement, as were somehow intrinsically evil, goes some way to explaining Lloyd George's role in one of the most catastrophic episodes of the Peace deliberations, the encouragement of Greek expansionism in Anatolia at Turkey's expense.

When he made them public in January 1918, Woodrow Wilson's Fourteen Points shook the complacency of great-power diplomacy. They gave both a voice and a hitherto unimaginable legitimacy to the claims of small nations who could never win the argument against imperial hegemony, expressed as it was in the language of military power. They immediately changed the balance of political forces in central and eastern Europe, emboldening dozens of political movements, especially inside Austria-Hungary, to put forward maximalist demands for statehood. One Croatian writer recorded this as a messianic turning point for Europe, old and new:

> Like Christ, Wilson brings the good news first and foremost to the small and the weak; to the humiliated and the insulted, he delivers the idea of equality. The European Cabinets are none too enthusiastic about Wilsonism; he upsets many of their calculations and undermines old assumptions; they receive him with deep reservations and, recognizing the dynamism of this path-breaking force, are already trying to establish how they could exploit his ideas for their own purposes. But the ordinary masses, disregarding front lines and borders, believe in Wilson and his power one hundred percent; they see in him their chief ally.[73]

Despite the power of his message, Wilson was as yet no match for the prejudice, still less for the diplomatic cunning, of the traditional great powers. Even when stiffened by his legions of academic specialists on central and eastern Europe, Russia, the Balkans and the Middle East, the American President was a dilettante with regard to the geo-politics of the old continent. In addition, he had to deal with opposition from the Republican-controlled Congress. The Republicans distrusted Wilson's policies in Paris and were determined to veto American membership of his most treasured project, the League of Nations. Like every other at Paris, the American delegation's position was systematically undermined by political opponents at home.

Russia was a conspicuous absentee in Paris. More Russians had been killed during the war than all other Allied soldiers combined, but this was not sufficient to secure Russia a place at the table. The Allies excluded them because, they said, no Russian government had the confidence of all the Russian people. The truth was, they did not approve of the government. Indeed, they were engaged in extensive military operations in an attempt to bring it down, at a time when Europe and the world needed a secure peace that would include a dangerously volatile Russian Empire.

Another cardinal error perpetrated by the Big Four (the United States, France, Britain and Italy)* was the decision to consider the issue of peace with Germany at the same time as resolving every other issue, from the status of Albania to the future of the Shantung peninsula in China. Germany, starving and defeated, was to be humiliated. The conditions in Germany for murderous revolutionary activity from both Left and Right, but chiefly the latter, had already matured before the Peace Conference. Neglect of the German question at Paris allowed such conditions to ripen.

The Balkans presented delegates with a tangled mess of constitutional and territorial issues which demanded more time and work at the Conference than any other question. For not only were the Balkan states once again competing over territory, as a result of the collapse of two empires, the Austro-Hungarian and the Ottoman, they were also having to accommodate or, more accurately, combat the aspirations of the new regional great power, Italy. Of the four main territorial questions under review at Paris, Italy claimed a vital and acquisitive interest in three of them – the future borders of Yugoslavia, Albania and the intended carve-up of Turkey. Luckily for Romania, whose territorial aims formed the fourth big question, Italy was indifferent to Transylvania and Bessarabia. Italy's chief opponents were Yugoslavia and Greece, and the Italian delegates did not lose an opportunity to trick or bully the former, in particular, out of territory and influence upon which Rome had only the most tenuous claim.

The new Yugoslav state was not just in dispute with Italy about the fate of the eastern Adriatic littoral. It had to negotiate disputed

* After Italy's highly theatrical break with Woodrow Wilson in late April 1919, the Big Four became the Big Three.

borders with six of its seven new neighbours (Italy, Austria, Hungary, Romania, Bulgaria and Albania), the only exception being Greece. At the time of the armistice in November 1918, Yugoslavia did not exist as a country. It was constituted as the Kingdom of Serbs, Croats and Slovenes a few days later on 1 December. But it was established without clear borders and with no clear constitutional order. Had the Kingdom of Serbia merely absorbed the south Slav regions of the Habsburg Empire and the Kingdom of Montenegro? Or was the country a novel entity in which Croatia, Slovenia, Dalmatia, Bosnia-Hercegovina and Montenegro would assume equal constitutional weight with Serbia?

The Serbian government, and naturally the Serbian army, insisted on imposing its concept of a centralized state on Croatia, Slovenia and other incorporated regions, which, they argued, had no modern tradition of state-building and had depended on Serbian sacrifices for their liberation from the Austro-Hungarian enemy. Politicians from Croatia, Bosnia and Slovenia (mainly Croats but also Slovenes and Serbs) had organized themselves during the war in the Yugoslav Committee which lobbied the Entente capitals indefatigably to further the cause of a Yugoslav state. They intended to balance the economic and political domination of Serbia by creating a federal or regionalized state, which would prevent the accumulation of power in Belgrade.

This was no idle debate but a passionate, bitter struggle which eventually consigned Yugoslavia to ashes. The failure of Yugoslavia's founders, in particular Serbia's monarchists, to work out an equitable solution to the national question ensured the victory of a royal dictatorship over parliamentary democracy within a decade of the country's birth, and the entire state's violent collapse when the European constitutional order buckled under the weight of Nazism in the late 1930s.

Fascist futures: Italy, Yugoslavia

From the Hotel de Beau-Site on the rue de Presbourg, members of the Yugoslav delegation could look out onto the Étoile and the Arc de Triomphe. The names must have struck some of the ninety-three-strong delegation, the largest from any Balkan country, as an ironic commentary on their situation. In contrast to the Entente's other

Balkan allies, the Romanians and the Greeks, the south Slavs were anything but sanguine about their prospects at the Peace Conference. Depressed and fractious, the delegates from the Kingdom of Serbs, Croats and Slovenes (known to the Conference by the acronym SCS) were compelled, despite profound internal hostilities, to maintain a united front during the proceedings.

Not a single great power had given official recognition to the country. Bewitched by the patriotism and virtuosity of the concert pianist, Ignace Paderewski, President Wilson lavished diplomatic favour upon the resurrected Polish state. Under the masterful leadership of Tomáš Garrigue Masaryk, the Czechs and Slovaks formed a new hybrid state with international blessing. But nobody, not even the author of the Fourteen Points, was willing to concede the existence of the Yugoslav state. The Kingdom of Serbia had been invited to the Paris Peace Conference, but following the proclamation of the SCS on 1 December 1918, the old kingdom no longer existed and, as a state of the Serbs, could not in any case properly represent the millions of Croats, Slovenes, Dalmatians, Bosnians, Hercegovinans, Hungarians, Germans, Montenegrins and Italians who had now joined it. But the main reason why the great powers would not recognize the country was because they were scared of upsetting Italy's ambitious politicians.

If the country's anomalous diplomatic position was depressing, Yugoslav domestic affairs appeared even more so. Insurgency had gripped large parts of Kosovo, Montenegro and Macedonia where the Serbian army and assorted vigilantes were imposing a centralized régime in the teeth of dogged resistance by the non-Serb populations. Peasants in Croatia and Dalmatia, and workers in the towns of Austria-Hungary, had taken to the streets to express their despair and anger at the chronic inadequacy of food supplies; to resist the rapacious Italian army; and to protest against the police forces dispatched from Serbia. As the Yugoslav delegation made its way to the Paris Peace Conference, the former Habsburg regions were still recovering from the 'period of "great rebellions and terrible days"', when 'stores were looted; landed estates and estate manors plundered and often burned; furniture, clothes, and farm animals were removed; and the forbidden solitude of estate forests was disturbed by the peasants and armed bands . . . who could finally completely satisfy their yearning for game and firewood. Disorder was rampant.

As one leader of a Slavonian local council reported to Zagreb, he was powerless to do anything: "He cannot introduce a court martial, because he would have to hang the whole locality."'[74]

The stress which these circumstances caused for the south Slav delegation in Paris was immense. Yet still more ominous was the absence of any agreement between the elites of the SCS's main constituents, the Serbs and the Croats, with respect to the political order of the new state. Their mutual suspicion was typified by the relationship between Nikola Pašić, the head of the delegation and leader of the Radical Party in Serbia, and his *de facto* deputy, the Croat, Dr Ante Trumbić, formerly the President of the Yugoslav Committee and Foreign Minister of the new state. During the war, both had attempted to map the future Yugoslav state according to very different cartographical principles.

As head of the Yugoslav Committee, Trumbić had developed close friendships in London and Paris. His two most notable supporters abroad were the Slavicist, R.W. Seton-Watson, and the former *Times* correspondent in Rome and Vienna, Henry Wickham Steed, who was now the newspaper's editor. The opinions of both men were to have an important impact on the detailed deliberations in Paris on the south Slav question. Both were convinced that for a Yugoslav state to work, the Serbs must concede regional autonomy to the Slovenes and Croats. Even before the conference had begun, Seton-Watson had fired a warning shot across Nikola Pašić's bows in an article, 'Serbia's Choice', which amounted to a sustained assault on the then Serbian Prime Minister. Seton-Watson accused Pašić of 'ruling by illegal methods . . . of suppressing all political opposition'. He then honoured his patriotism and role as Serbia's wartime leader but finished by claiming that Pašić's 'outlook and standards are those of a vanishing era, and he is too old to shake off altogether the semi-Turkish traditions of his youth'.[75]

Ever since the Timok rebellion of 1883, Nikola Pašić had dominated Serbian politics. Serbs and non-Serbs alike often assumed that his long flowing white beard was matched by a sagacious mind. In fact, his noble forehead hid nothing of the kind. Pašić, seventy-four years old at the time of Paris, was a politician without vision, beyond his unoriginal aim of maximizing Serbia's territory and influence in the region. Over the years, he had forgotten his youthful conviction that Serbia's peasantry deserved better education and improved economic conditions. Now, his energy was expended in keeping himself in power and warding off his many enemies. In this endeavour (later labelled 'the technology of power' by critics of Marshal Tito), he really was a past master, setting a precedent which has been imitated repeatedly in Balkan politics ever since, but which has been especially noticeable in Yugoslavia where the national question has made political survival so challenging. Pašić demonstrated a remarkable ability to conserve his energy and emotion. 'He was able to hate', commented Serbia's finest modern historian, 'but he never allowed himself to be blinded by hatred. He would only persecute those who really were a danger and then only the necessary minimum. This economy of hatred was because he had, along with a large number of political enemies, few personal friends.'[76]

He certainly did not count Trumbić among those few personal friends. And he was determined not to allow Trumbić's influential friends at foreign courts to undermine his belief that the new state would be an extension of the Kingdom of Serbia, and that the Croats, Slovenes and other nationalities must play a subordinate role to a centralizing government in Belgrade dominated by his own Radical Party. To achieve these aims, Pašić was prepared to sacrifice the legitimate territorial aspirations of the Croats and Slovenes in the north-west of the country in order to obtain satisfaction in Albania and Macedonia, that is in those areas which mattered to him as a Serb nationalist. Trumbić had already noted during the discussions about the armistice in November 1918 that the Radical Party representative 'agreed to the Italian occupation of the areas in the London Agreement; agreed that the Allies, specifically Italy, could seize the entire commercial fleet sailing under the Austro-Hungarian flag, including of course Yugoslav ships; agreed that the naval fleet which was already under Yugoslav control, should be handed over to the Allies [i.e. Italy] who should be granted the right to occupy at their convenience railways and other strategic points on Yugoslav territory – by which of course Rijeka was directly threatened'.[77]

As soon as the armistice with Austria-Hungary was signed on 3 November 1918, Italian troops had poured into Istria, Dalmatia and the Dalmatian islands – those regions assigned to Italy by the Treaty of London. But in the meantime Italy's appetite had grown: it now wanted Fiume (Rijeka)* as well, and so Italian diplomacy launched its campaign to prevent the great powers recognizing the Kingdom of Serbs, Slovenes and Croats. Had recognition been granted, the Italians would not have been able to justify their occupation of Fiume on 19 November. The occupation was personally authorized by the Italian Prime Minister, Vittorio Orlando, even though his government had not even claimed it during the London Treaty negotiations. But now, Orlando told his colleagues, the situation had radically changed. Fiume must be Italian. Yugoslavia possessed hundreds of kilometres of magnificent coastline, he argued, and would scarcely miss the town.

With the dissolution of the Austro-Hungarian Empire, Italy could have realized Mazzini's dream of national integration. It was already at peace with France and Switzerland, and Yugoslavia wanted to be at peace. Italy could have been the sole continental power without enemy neighbours but Orlando threw this all away, for the sake of Fiume.

It is hard to identify exactly when Vittorio Emanuele Orlando discarded his credentials as a humane democratic liberal in favour of his new persona as grasping imperialist. During one discussion between the Big Four in Paris, somebody remarked that the Covenant of the League of Nations insisted on the 'consent and wishes of the people concerned' when mandates were being dished out. Orlando laughed uncontrollably at the preposterous idea that the indigenous folk should be asked their opinion. Nicolson, disgusted, watched 'Orlando's cheeks wobble with laughter and his puffy eyes fill with tears of mirth'.[78] The Italian Prime Minister had taught constitutional law at the University of Palermo and was once considered as altruistic as Wilson. In the past, he had worked hard to foster good relations between Italy and its Slavic neighbours. But now he had to justify 500,000 war dead and a ruinous national debt. So great a price could not have been paid for less than a transcendent object. The Italian government declared that object was the redemption of Fiume, of which few Italians had previously heard, but without which most Italians were now convinced they could not live.

---

* The town's name means 'river' in both Italian and Croatian.

Italy sought to control the eastern Adriatic littoral for two strategic regions. First, it gave it a foothold in the Balkan peninsula. Second, it gave it complete control of the Adriatic, especially since Italy also controlled the Albanian port of Valona (Vlorë) and its offshore island, Saseno (Sazan) from which its fleet could dominate the Otranto straits. Nothing could now enter or leave the Adriatic without Italy's approval. But to achieve all this, Italy did not need Fiume. No historian has yet given a convincing explanation for Orlando's motives in adding Fiume to the imperial shopping list. Nonetheless, he and his Foreign Minister, Baron Sidney Sonnino, used Fiume to whip up domestic support for their political programme, especially after Woodrow Wilson made public his dramatic ultimatum to Italy about Fiume in April 1919.

For President Wilson the secret Treaty of London, by which Britain and France persuaded Italy to join the Entente in 1915, symbolized all that was perfidious in European diplomacy. It assigned to Italy extensive territories on the eastern Adriatic and in the Aegean Sea in the event of an Entente victory. Italy argued for a victor's justice in those areas which it claimed but which were inhabited mainly by Slovenes, Germans or Croats. The formation of the Kingdom of Serbs, Croats and Slovenes did not invalidate those claims, the Italians argued, because the bulk of Croats and Slovenes had fought willingly on behalf of the Austro-Hungarian empire and should therefore be punished. While there were doubtless Italians who genuinely believed their country deserved territorial compensation for the half-million Italian casualties in the war, Orlando and Sonnino instrumentalized these sentiments as a means of weakening the south Slav state. Were a strong Yugoslavia to emerge as the dominant Balkan power in alliance with an invigorated Greece, Italy's imperial expansion into the Balkans and further east might be frustrated. It was obvious to all inside the Yugoslav lands that were Italy to succeed in taking Fiume it would deliberately damage Croatia's economic prospects. As an unintended consequence, Croatia's standing in the SCS would be weakened and the Serbian concept of a centralized state much strengthened.

In an effort to lessen the rivalry between Italy and the SCS, President Wilson had countless meetings in Paris with Orlando and Sonnino. He found the pair insufferably arrogant and querulous. Before long the President reacted to any mention of Sonnino with an involuntary grimace. In contrast, the President was delighted with Trumbić to whom he granted a couple of audiences. Trumbić was suitably deferential and his expositions mercifully crisp and free of overwrought sentimentality. It did not take long for the President to conclude that Italy was guilty of imperialist bullying. It followed that he had a moral duty to make a stand on behalf of the Yugoslavs. Defenders of the Italian claims have suggested that 'the America of Woodrow Wilson was the America of the Sacco and Vanzetti trial',[79] implying that the President regarded Orlando and Sonnino as nothing more than a pair of Latin subversives. They also argue that were Wilson to have applied the self-determination principle rigorously then he would have supported Italy's claim to Fiume because Italians were a majority in the city. In fact that majority was the result of a conscious policy of the Hungarian government, who controlled Fiume after the *Ausgleich* of 1867. In order to dilute the concentration of Croats in the port, Budapest encouraged thousands of Italians to settle in the city during the later decades of the nineteenth century. Further, the Italians could only boast a majority if the working-class (i.e. Croat) suburb of Sušak, an integral part of the city, were discounted. In short, the claim to Fiume was tenuous at best, artificial and disingenuous at worst. Wilson was determined to defy both the Treaty of London and the claim on Fiume.

But the Italians played one of the toughest games of old-style great-power diplomacy – stick it out until your opponents get bored and lose interest. No matter how much Wilson declaimed, no matter what compromises the British and French proposed, the Italians clung to their mantra – the Treaty of London *and* Fiume. Exhausted and infuriated by this game, the President appealed to the Italian people and issued a statement, explaining why the Italians should reject the intemperate counsel of their government and forgo unjust territorial claims. Pompous references to the Fourteen Points, 'these sacred obligations', and a patronizing rhetoric did not play well at the Hippodrome. The following day, Rome was engulfed by a tidal wave of anti-Americanism. 'Why does he want to impose what he considers absolute justice on the Italian people alone . . . Why does he not send a message to the American people that the Monroe Doctrine cannot be reconciled with a League of Nations?' enquired *Unità*. *Epoca*, Orlando's mouthpiece, asked, 'How could he for a moment think that at his bidding the Italian people would rise against their government and force it to accept a program dictated by a foreigner shut up in an ivory tower of his own abstractions?'[80]

When Orlando and Sonnino returned to Rome to extract as much political capital out of their nationalist posturing as possible, they discovered a country crackling with discontent and revolutionary spirit. Wilson's bold populist diplomacy had not only blocked any way out of the Italian-Yugoslav dispute, it had emboldened the forces of extreme Italian nationalism.

Three days after Wilson's letter was published in the Rome press, Romania ignored the appeals of the great powers and invaded Bela Kun's collapsing Hungarian Soviet Republic. It had been a bad week for the President – four months into the Peace Conference Europe appeared to be disintegrating. It did not, of course, disintegrate and within two months, a peace treaty with Germany was signed, five years to the day that Gavrilo Princip had assassinated Franz Ferdinand. But Europe's peripheral problems continued to block the restoration of order and for many months the most difficult question remained Fiume.

Gabriele D'Annunzio now made his brief, theatrical appearance in Balkan history. He had long fascinated and delighted *fin-de-siècle* Italy. His prose and poetry, setting Nietzschean sentiment in a florid Romantic diction, had brought him acclaim and sponsors whose wealth slipped through his fingers like sand. In other European countries, his ostentatious love affairs might have resulted in social exclusion. But in Italy, an invitation to one of D'Annunzio's risqué parties was a sign of social elevation. His string of young and beautiful female conquests were regarded not as a sign of insecurity and immaturity but of virility. When his fellow Futurist and subsequent rival, Filippo Marinetti, proclaimed war to be the 'the only hygiene' capable of cleansing the sins of the modern world, D'Annunzio applauded enthusiastically. Despite his advanced years – he was fifty-three when Italy entered the Great War – the poet joined up to fight.

As a warrior, Lieutenant Colonel D'Annunzio demonstrated exceptional courage on the battlefield, gilding his legend with a number of breathtaking stunts: 'Whether it was bombing Trieste from the air twice in one day (first with pamphlets, then with bombs), charging Austrian trenches in the middle of the night with pistols and knives, dressed in a flowing cape, or sailing torpedo boats into the middle of the Austrian fleet at anchor and blowing up a torpedo-boat in the Bay of Buccari, D'Annunzio achieved a reputation as the great poet-warrior of the war.'[81]

D'Annunzio, a fervent advocate of the Entente, had expected Italy's territorial wish list to be fulfilled as soon as the war was over. His disappointment was all the keener for having witnessed at first hand the sacrifices made by Italian soldiers on the mountain front with Austria-Hungary. D'Annunzio was demobilized almost immediately after the armistice, but some 300,000 Italian volunteers were obliged to remain on active service pending the outcome of the Paris Peace Conference. By the end of November 1918, many were being deployed to secure Italy's new acquisitions from the London Treaty, as well as Fiume. But following Woodrow Wilson's appeal to the Italians to soften their territorial demands in April 1919, rumours spread through the army that the government in Rome was preparing to sell the Adriatic pass. The spirit of irredentism among Italy's officer corps was strengthened further when Saverio Nitti replaced Orlando as Prime Minister in June 1920.

Nitti was considered a moderate and his appointment was especially welcomed by the other great-power delegations at Paris, who had had their fill of Orlando and Sonnino. But despite his reputation, Nitti did not alter his government's position on Fiume, fearing the reaction of Italian nationalists were he to give up the claim. But he was also quite firm in pursuing an imperialist agenda. Italy's nationalist hotheads failed to see this because the Prime Minister forswore histrionics. They cast him instead in the role of corrupt stooge of the Big Three who were preparing to sabotage Italy's rightful claims. The time had come to take matters into their own hands.

Several conspiracies were hatched in 1919. But D'Annunzio was initially reluctant to become involved with any revolutionary plans, though he did keep in touch with former colleagues in the armed forces. Many of his comrades belonged to the *Arditi*, Italy's elite units trained for special operations during the Great War. When the Paris Peace Conference ordered the evacuation of the Italian military from Fiume in August 1919, seven junior officers appealed to D'Annunzio to join them in the small town of Ronchi in preparation for a march on Fiume. The poet-condottiere finally agreed to lay down a challenge to the European order.

In the early morning of 11 September, D'Annunzio set off from Ronchi, 80 kilometres north-west of Fiume. He led a column of just under two hundred Sardinian grenadiers, hardly a force to threaten the Allied garrisons of Fiume. But news of the poet's heroic gesture spread fast among the *Arditi*, and by the time he reached the gates of the city, he commanded some 2,500 men, backed by an assortment of armoured cars and tanks. D'Annunzio's rhetoric and symbolism were striking. He was marching to 'liberate' what he called 'the city of the Holocaust', which, he claimed, would be the start of a fire that would burn throughout Italy, destroying the dead wood of the old regime. To highlight the cleansing nature of his new movement, he adopted the black flame, the symbol of the *Arditi*, as his own. There could be no greater contrast to D'Annunzio's zeal than the nervous disposition of General Vittorio Pittaluga, the commander of the Italian garrison in Fiume, appointed less than a month before, and loyal servant of the Rome government.

In early autumn, the eastern Adriatic coast is usually suffused by a warm, yellow sunlight. The distinctive slate of Croatia's port towns soaks up the mellow light in an elegant glow. The buildings are gently shaded by palm trees. Human exertion drifts to a halt, people sit over long lunches, or walk aimlessly, eyes half-closed, and the trace of a smile on their faces. This was not General Pittaluga's state of mind on the morning of 11 September. In a state of 'considerable agitation', he visited one of the British officers stationed in the town. He refused to discuss the operational issues at hand and, 'pressed for an explanation, he replied vaguely that he was always expecting some disturbance in the town'.[82] He then disappeared, leaving the skeleton force of British, French and American soldiers quite baffled. Unknown to the Allied officers, the General had been summoned urgently to the road leading north from the city. He had received intelligence that D'Annunzio had set out from Ronchi. Earlier in the day, Pittaluga had followed instructions received from Rome by ordering his men to stop the march on Fiume. If necessary D'Annunzio was to be shot. He later learned that the officer with whom he had entrusted this mission had gone over with his men to D'Annunzio. Now, with the walls of Fiume receding in the distance, General Pittaluga was suddenly faced with a force of 2,500 jubilant Sardinian Grenadiers, assorted *Arditi* and an intimidating phalange of tanks and armoured cars. At its head stood Gabriele D'Annunzio.

When General Pittaluga ordered him and his troops to turn back, D'Annunzio swept his coat open to reveal his row of wartime medals: 'All you have to do is order the troops to shoot me, General!'[83] With the briefest hesitation, Pittaluga capitulated. At that moment, Italy's first Duce and European fascism were born in the Balkans.

Over the next eighteen months, theatre and politics merged into an astonishing spectacle. The set pieces were D'Annunzio's impassioned speeches from the balcony of the Governor's Palace overlooking Piazza Dante in the centre of Fiume. He drove his audience into frenzies of patriotism, worshipping huge blood-bespattered flags as the central icons of the new politics. As a Dutch historian has noted,

> virtually the entire ritual of Fascism came from the 'Free State of Fiume': the balcony address, the Roman salute, the cries of 'aia, aia, alala,' the dramatic dialogues with the crowd, the use of religious symbols in a new secular setting, the eulogies to the 'martyrs' of the cause and the employment of these relicts in political ceremonies. Moreover, quite aside from the poet's contribution to the form and style of Fascist politics, Mussolini's movement first started to attract great strength when the future dictator supported D'Annunzio's occupation of Fiume.[84]

Throughout the fourteen-month existence of the Free State of Fiume, the government in Rome denounced D'Annunzio's adventure but never felt compelled to remove the municipal dictator by force. Fiume attracted thousands upon thousands of mutinous Italian soldiers, so that within five months of having proclaimed his city state, he had to appeal to the troops to stop signing up for his militia. Fiume could no longer accommodate or feed them. On a number of occasions, the Italian government was deeply concerned that D'Annunzio understood Fiume as the prologue to an assault on Rome itself. Yet despite the animosity between D'Annunzio and

Nitti, the régime in Fiume bolstered the Italian delegation's position in Paris. The Italian government also did nothing to prevent D'Annunzio's attempts to spread his irredentist message into Dalmatia, and when, in the summer of 1920, Italians embarked on a violent spree against Croats and Slovenes inside Italian-occupied areas, Rome was slow to respond.

Gradually Yugoslav resistance to Italy's expansionist programme was worn down. In the middle of January 1920, Clemenceau called in Trumbić and Pašić and told them to give up Fiume or else the entire London Treaty would be implemented while Fiume was still up for discussion. The Yugoslav delegation held out for another nine months with commendable, if progressively less effective, support from Washington. But in November 1920, its representatives were finally forced to sign the Treaty of Rapallo. This created an independent Fiumean state under the control of neither Italy nor the SCS. But the Yugoslavs had to make substantial concessions in Istria and the Dalmatian islands. Fiume/Rijeka had been denied the SCS and would inevitably be dependent on Italy. The only consolation for the Yugoslavs was that the Rome government managed to oust D'Annunzio, installing a more moderate administration. In March 1922, a fascist *coup* overthrew this government in a dress rehearsal for Mussolini's seizure of power later that year. Italy then exerted immense pressure on Yugoslavia to concede Italian sovereignty over Fiume, and in January 1924, old Nikola Pašić, in his last spell as Prime Minister, travelled to Rome to sign away the city. The Kingdom of Serbs, Croats and Slovenes had been mutilated at birth. As Rijeka, Zadar, most of Istria and the islands of Lošinj, Cres and Lastovo slipped from Yugoslavia's grasp into the bosom of revolutionary Italy, tensions between Serbs and Croats deepened. The 'Vidovdan' (St Vitus' Day) constitution, promulgated in 1921 on the sacred Serbian date of 28 June, which commemorated Kosovo Polje and, more recently, Sarajevo, was regarded by all Yugoslavs as a victory for the centralizing aims of the Serbs. In Croatia, it greatly compounded the profound sense of loss and alienation that Croats, and especially Dalmatians, had felt at Italy's irredentist programme.

The great catastrophe: Greece, Turkey

> Personally I have always thought that the right policy was to turn the Turks out of Istanbul and confine them to Asia . . . But the idea that Greece, France and Italy were to gallop about all over Asia Minor, I confess, never entered my head. From such knowledge of the East as I possess, I cannot help thinking that this great pack of cards which is being reared, will, almost at the first blow, tumble into fragments to the ground.
>
> Private letter from Curzon to Balfour, 20 March 1919[85]

The dreams of a new Roman Empire did not fade at Fiume. The Italians, frustrated in their African colonial ambitions in 1898, cast their eyes eastwards to the fertile coast of Anatolia. It seemed to promise a solution to the chronic problem of rural unemployment in Italy. The Ministry of Agriculture in Rome was preparing to ship hundreds, perhaps thousands of impoverished peasants from the *mezzogiorno* across the Mediterranean once the Italian army had established its control over the coast around Antalya.* A week after Lord Curzon expressed his fears to the British Foreign Secretary, Arthur Balfour, Italy surprised everyone by landing its troops in the port of Adalia, as it persisted in calling Antalya. Smyrna (Izmir) was the real prize. Yet to claim this, the main port in western Anatolia, would have meant a confrontation between Italy and its allies, Britain, France and the United States, whose warships were patrolling the entrance to Smyrna.

The delegations at the Paris Peace Conference saw the Ottoman Empire in one key respect just as they saw the Austro-Hungarian Empire – as a 'prison of nations'; and now the inmates deserved recompense in the form of their own states. In another respect, however, the Ottoman Empire was very different – it contained large reserves of oil, especially in the Mosul region (now in northern Iraq), and much territory which both the British and French considered strategically vital. So significant were parts of the Empire that it could not, unlike the territories of the Austro-Hungarian

* In retrospect, the Italians should probably be very grateful for the failure of this project which would doubtless have mired them in some ghastly long-term colonial commitment, not to mention into conflict with some west Anatolian liberation army or other.

Empire, be handed over to the locals (who were also, of course, Asiatic and therefore presumed less able to look after themselves than the peoples of central and south-eastern Europe). In order to guide these unschooled regions, the South African Prime Minister, Jan Smuts, helpfully conceived the idea of 'mandates', whereby the League of Nations would assume sovereignty over a territory on behalf of its people and a specified great power would administer the region. When the Italians seized Adalia, the League of Nations had not yet been constituted, although the principle of mandates had been accepted by the Supreme Council at the Peace Conference. Rome did not consult its allies over its Anatolian expedition, but simply assumed control of what it believed it would fairly receive in any case.

It did not seem fair to Woodrow Wilson, however. When the Italians moved into Adalia, the President had just returned from a most upsetting trip to the United States where he had felt the cold wind of isolationism blowing up Pennsylvania Avenue from the direction of Capitol Hill. The Republican-controlled Congress had taken against the intellectual southerner. Many Congressmen were suspicious that Wilson was getting carried away in Paris and involving America far too deeply in Europe and Asia. Discussions on the future of Turkey at the Peace Conference assumed that the United States would be willing to accept the mandate either for Istanbul or for the embryonic Armenian state or even for the whole of Turkey. Wilson returned to France, knowing that Congress would never ratify an American mandate in Turkey. Indeed, Wilson found the whole idea of mandates in Turkey disturbing as it appeared to reduce the United States to the level of a grasping European great power. As if his Turkish dilemma was not sufficiently worrying, the Italian landing at Adalia seemed to preface a 'scramble for Turkey'. He was already livid with Orlando and Sonnino for their obtuse behaviour over Fiume. Should the opportunity arise, he would happily punish the Italians.

He did not have to wait long. The Big Three exploited the absence of Orlando and Sonnino at the beginning of May 1919 by holding talks on the issue of Turkey. Lloyd George suggested that in order to block Italy's expansion into Turkey, the Big Three should authorize another of the Allies, Greece, to occupy Smyrna. To the Prime Minister's surprise, Wilson readily agreed. Two hours later,

Lloyd George summoned Venizelos to tell him and to prepare detailed plans for the landing at Smyrna. Lloyd George assured his Greek counterpart that this was no holding operation. The request for the Greeks to take Smyrna, he continued, was a tacit recognition that the Conference would without question allot the port to Greece. Lloyd George's verbal commitment was explicit. Venizelos had every reason to believe that Greece enjoyed the unqualified support of the British government in this matter. But both he and Lloyd George brushed aside Field Marshal Henry Wilson, also present at this *tête-à-tête*, when Wilson blurted out angrily that the decision was madness and that it would result in war. General Wilson did secure a guarantee that this was a Greek operation, under Greek command – which implied, of course, that the British military would bear no responsibility if it went wrong.

If Venizelos had not yet smelt a rat, he should have when Wilson issued this warning. The Greek leader had first conceived the idea of joining the Entente in exchange for extensive territorial gains in Anatolia in early 1915. He had immediately consulted Colonel Ioannis Metaxas, a military hero of the Balkan Wars, who had studied the strategic implications of a future Greek presence in Asia Minor. The two memoranda that Metaxas prepared for Venizelos are uncanny in their accuracy. The Colonel pointed out that as the Greeks almost all lived on the coastal periphery of Anatolia and since a large proportion worked as merchants or professionals, they offered a very poor social and geographic base from which to wage a war of expansion. 'The Moslems, numbering about 7,000,000', he explained, 'not only occupied the whole of the Central Anatolian plateau in a compact mass, but also outnumbered the Greeks in most of the coastal districts . . . The bulk of the Moslem population – Turks, Circassians, Kurds, Yuruks and other warlike races – was composed of peasants, inured to the use of arms, whereas the contrary was the case with the Greeks and Armenians.'[86] Above all, Metaxas stressed, the military challenge could never be met as the Turkish army would always be able to lure the Greek forces into the interior, an operation which the Greek army could not sustain: 'In other words, Napoleon's experience of 1812, when he invaded Russia, would be repeated over again.' An Anatolian expedition could be mounted only if two conditions were met. 'Firstly, that, when it came to actually occupying Asia Minor,

the Allies should bind themselves to participate in the campaign with forces sufficient to enable the operation to be brought to a successful conclusion. Secondly, that the whole of Anatolia should be partitioned among the Allied Powers or, failing this, that the portion left under Turkish sovereignty be reduced to such small proportions as no longer to constitute a serious menace to the Greek possessions around Smyrna.'[87]

The Greek Prime Minister should have pulled out then and there as soon as Wilson had spoken. Yet it is perhaps difficult to resist temptation when over a celebratory dinner the British Prime Minister appears to be promising you the earth:

> Greece has *great possibilities* in the Near East and you must be as powerful as possible in the military sense in order to take advantage of them. We are trying to get America to take the mandate for Istanbul, and her presence there will in no way prevent Istanbul from coming under Greek sovereignty in the fullness of time. President Wilson is not against the idea, but he doubts whether American public opinion and therefore the Senate will approve it. If they don't approve it the only solution which England will accept for Istanbul is for it to go to Greece.[88]

Byzantium reborn! How painful this memory must have been to Venizelos when the final curtain fell on the Anatolian tragedy three years later. By then the Pontic Greeks, with their indescribable wealth of cultural tradition stretching back to Homeric times, had been ripped almost literally overnight from their homelands; old Greece had been reduced to economic rubble and suffered political and social dislocations whose effects would be felt for decades; thousands upon thousands of Turkish, Greek and Armenian civilians were dead, and had been subjected to barbarous cruelty. Yet the tragedy was prolonged still further by the diplomatic negotiations at Lausanne which finally brought an end to the Great War for Greece and Turkey as late as 1923. Here, all parties, with the solemn blessing of Lord Curzon whose wish to become Foreign Secretary had finally been granted, agreed to the compulsory exchange of almost two million Greek and Turkish people. In the Balkans, one of the most pernicious improvisations of the great powers was brought to

an end by the massive transfer of populations. Although this 'occasioned a great deal of human misery', one historian of Greek has commented, 'it did largely remove what would have undoubtedly remained a permanent and potent source of tension between Greece and Turkey and it did ensure that Greece itself became an ethnically homogenous society.'[89] Ever since the Treaty of Lausanne, diplomats have readily succumbed to the temptation of partition, population exchange and the harmony that nationally homogenous communities supposedly promise.

Responsibility for the Anatolian catastrophe must rest squarely on the shoulders of two men – David Lloyd George and Eleftherios Venizelos, although President Woodrow Wilson and Prime Minister Georges Clemenceau were unswerving in their support for the doomed land-grab. There were many in Britain, including Curzon himself, General Wilson, and Churchill, most eloquently of all, who considered Lloyd George's patronage of Greek expansionism a grave error, and they frequently said so. But the Prime Minister was possessed of an unshakeable conviction that Greece must dominate the Mediterranean as a regional great power. It was essential that Britain should encourage Greece to establish total control over western Anatolia. Together, London and Athens would then control the Near East.

From Ankara to Smyrna: Turkey, Greece

As dawn broke on 15 May 1919, many thousands of Greeks waited expectantly on Smyrna's quayside. The town was alive with blue-and-white flags. Slowly the liner *Patris* approached the harbour, its fog horn bellowing, its sailors cheering and waving at the crowds on shore. 'As the Greek troops began to land, Metropolitan Chrystomos came forward to bless them. The first men off the ships stacked arms and did a little dance on the shore. The crowds cheered and wept. By about nine thirty, all three regiments of the 1st Division composing the army of occupation had landed.'[90]

It only took another half an hour, as the crack Evzone border units were passing by the Turkish barracks, before trouble broke out. A shot was fired near the main square and the Greek troops reacted within minutes by storming the barracks where a small Turkish detachment was billeted. The Turkish soldiers were dragged

out as prisoners after which 'they were made to go through no end of humiliation',[91] as Donald Whittal, a British businessman watching the events, noted. One Turkish officer being force-marched down the quay stumbled out of line. He was struck repeatedly on the head, before being bayoneted and finally having his head blown off. The Greeks of Smyrna took their cue from the behaviour of these soldiers, and began a riot in the Turkish quarter, killing, maiming, looting and raping.

When news of the atrocities filtered through to Paris, the French, American and British delegations were beside themselves with anger. 'I admit', concluded a trusted lieutenant of Venizelos in his report, 'that I could not have imagined a more unfortunate execution of the Greek occupation.'[92] Venizelos had devoted particular care since the Balkan Wars to creating an image of a Greece simultaneously young and vital, yet in possession of a wisdom nurtured by the people's long historical memory. The Great Idea was presented as an act of long overdue national resurrection. Venizelos seems genuinely to have been appalled by the violence in Smyrna, which was followed by a steady stream of crimes committed by Greek soldiers against Turkish civilians. 'The events of Smyrna', noted one Allied general monitoring the Greek occupation, 'have undoubtedly cheapened every Christian life in Turkey, the landing of the Greeks there being looked upon by the Turks as deliberate violation by the Allies of the terms of their armistice and the probable forerunner of further unwarranted aggression. The moral responsibility for present unrest throughout Turkey is very heavy on foreign Powers.'[93]

Responding to the atrocities, Venizelos dispatched his friend, Aristeidis Stergiadis, as civilian High Commissioner of the occupied Smyrna region. Over the next three years, Stergiadis would dispense commendable justice, despite a temperament that may best be described as paranoiac. Small, dapper and given to astonishing outbursts of temper, Stergiadis was one of the very few Greek officials who treated Muslims and Muslim traditions with respect. Venizelos regarded him as a model representative of the reborn Greece. But not even a second Pericles could have guided the new Hellenic lands to prosperity and security.

Elsewhere in Anatolia, a second rebirth was under way. Almost simultaneously with the Smyrna landings, Mustafa Kemal had arrived by boat from Istanbul at the Black Sea port of Samsun. The government in the capital, which from March 1920 came under Allied military occupation, had appointed Kemal as army inspector in eastern Turkey as a way of removing this self-willed young war hero from the centre of affairs. By the time he arrived in northern Anatolia, Kemal and his friends were certain that Turkey was being crucified by the Allies at Paris. For the Turkish nation to survive, they argued, it would have to fight before the country was dismembered. The arrival of Greek troops in Smyrna, and the humiliation of occupation, galvanized such malcontents into action. Kemal convinced himself that he would have to act as Turkey's saviour.

But on arrival in Samsun, Kemal was little more than an exile, effectively stripped of his power and unsure of how matters stood in Anatolia. Initially, he was under constant surveillance by British officers engaged in confiscating weapons from what remained of the Turkish army, and spied on by agents of the government in Istanbul. In order to create a political movement, Kemal decided to resign his commission in the army. This was a leap in the dark for a man who had been with the military since his school days, but it worked. As a politician, he forged and strengthened links with old comrades who now commanded the remnants of the Ottoman army in eastern and northern Anatolia. But Kemal also mobilized the Turkish peasants. Before long the despondent military of a fallen Empire had been stiffened by a new spirit of patriotism and resistance.

Mustafa Kemal cut a curious figure in the bare, windswept landscape of eastern Anatolia. When he arrived there, he barely knew the region; for although he had fought at the Dardanelles and in Mesopotamia during the Great War, he had grown up in Salonika, then the most sophisticated city in the Ottoman Empire. He had much to learn about the Anatolian peasant and made a point of visiting farms and villages, carefully cultivating the image of warrior with the common touch. Yet despite his soldierly bearing, he had delicate hands and feet, 'and a voice that had a suggestion of femininity'.[94] In contrast to most Turks, he had fair hair and bright, intensely blue eyes. It was said one could never look directly into those eyes as they reflected the light too sharply. This is one of the many myths about Atatürk, who remains at the end of the twentieth century the object of profound secular adulation in Turkey. But even when the myths are discarded, one is still left with a quite exceptional leader. Despite mood swings exacerbated by his drink problem, Kemal had a rare ability to temper and manage the jealousies and ambitions of his entourage. He did not tolerate failure. He was not vindictive, but had no time for sentimentality in politics beyond his own mystical belief in the sanctity and purity of the Turkish nation. It is no exaggeration to say that without Kemal's audacity, Turkey might not exist today and certainly not within its current borders. Instead, it would have been carved up in accordance with the Treaty of Sèvres, which was finally signed on 10 August 1920, just south of Paris.

The Istanbul government's capitulation to Sèvres bolstered the Turkish nationalists around Kemal who had by then established their capital in Ankara, a small, undeveloped town of just 20,000 inhabitants. Kemal's forces and the Greek army in the Smyrna zone were already in a state of low-level war. If Greece were to destroy the Kemalist threat once and for all, it would have to send its forces deep into Anatolia across inhospitable terrain, stretching supply lines to the limit. At this point, Kemal demonstrated his ability to exploit the military and diplomatic weakness of the Greek position. Turkish irregular forces cooperated with Italian troops in Adalia, just south of the Greek zone of occupation. Kemal also made clandestine contact with the French, who were growing ever more suspicious of Britain's pretensions in the region and who were looking for a way out of their mandated military commitment in the south-east of Turkey. Even more important, Kemal had established close links with the revolutionary government in Russia, from which he began to receive weapons and ammunition.

But the greatest problem facing the Greeks was internal. Above all, morale in the army was miserably low. By 1920, it had been fighting for eight years. The state coffers were empty, and maintaining the occupation in Anatolia was contributing to severe hardship in the Old Greece of the Peloponnese, Attica and Thessaly. Venizelos's energies went into the diplomatic struggle in Paris. Now that he had secured the Great Idea, he decided to hold elections in November 1920 in the expectation that he would be swept back to power on a wave of nationalist euphoria.

Five weeks before those elections were due, fate intervened in a curious way on the sunny morning of 30 September: 'King

Alexander took a walk in the grounds of the palace at Tatoi with his wolfhound, Fritz. During the walk, the dog jumped suddenly into a clump of bushes. Hearing barks and the sounds of a scuffle, Alexander followed, and found him vigorously shaking a pet Spanish monkey in his teeth. While he was trying to free the monkey, the King was attacked by its mate, the male of the pair, and severely bitten in the calf. The wounds were cleaned and dressed, but two days later severe fever set in. After a three-week struggle for life, Alexander died of blood-poisoning on 25 October.'[95] Churchill wrote, 'It is perhaps no exaggeration to remark that a quarter of a million persons died of this monkey's bite.'

Churchill made his startling retrospective claim because Alexander's death opened the vexed issue of the royal succession just as elections were approaching. The Venizelos régime had systematically persecuted supporters of ex-King Constantine since Venizelos forced the King's abdication in 1917. Royalist sentiment now combined with the legacy of eight years of war and deprivation to smash Venizelos's Liberal Party at the ballot box. The impact of this defeat was enormous. King Constantine returned, to the displeasure of the Allies who still believed that he had worked with the Germans during the war. The King's followers were bent on revenge: Venizelos was forced to retire from politics, and the new masters in Greece replaced most of the key army commanders. The curse of the National Schism struck Greece at a moment of extreme crisis. But Churchill's theory (that essentially Constantine's inexperienced generals wrecked the strategy of the Venizelist general staff) does not stand up to scrutiny. Venizelos had already committed almost every blunder Colonel Metaxas had warned him against.

Indeed, there was even a faint chance that the change of government might limit the scale of the impending catastrophe by pulling out of Smyrna in an orderly fashion and giving up the *Megali idea* with reluctant grace. After all, the royalist victory had been fuelled in part by opposition to the foreign adventure. Once again, Lloyd George was on hand to cajole the Greeks into continuing the great adventure, declaring in the House of Commons in March 1921 that 'the best thing to do [is] to use the force at the disposal of the Greek Government for the purpose of clearing up the situation'. He added that the 'British Government has no objection whatsoever to any military operations that Greece deems expedient to undertake against Mustapha Kemal'. As Lloyd George issued this appeal just six months after the Treaty of Sèvres, one has to agree with Churchill who remarked: 'At last peace with Turkey: and to ratify it, War with Turkey! However, so far as the Great Allies were concerned the war was to be fought by proxy. Wars when fought this way by great nations are often very dangerous for the proxy.'[96] The Greeks were about to learn this hard lesson.

The great powers made a final attempt to avert full-scale war between the Greek army and Kemal's nationalist forces at the London Conference in March 1921. Five days after it ended in failure, the Greeks attacked. Until this point, Sterghiadis had protected the Turkish population in the occupied zone as best he could. Discrimination and intimidation were rife but did not degenerate into slaughter. With the start of the summer offensive in 1921, he lost control as the army spread north and east over hundreds of kilometres. Atrocities were committed in village after village. A Commission of Enquiry dispatched by the Allies to observe the Greek offensive reported that

> there is a systematic plan of destruction of Turkish villages and extinction of the Moslem population. This plan is being carried out by Greek and Armenian bands, which appear to operate under Greek instructions and sometimes even with the assistance of detachments of regular troops. This destruction of villages and the disappearance of the Moslem population consequent thereon doubtless has as its object to guard the flanks and rear of the Greek army against any possible attack by the population in the event of an early offensive, and perhaps even to create in this region a political situation favourable to the Greek Government.[97]

Time and again since the Greco-Turkish war, military expediency has been used as a justification for the perpetration of atrocities. As the Commission was watching the razing of Muslim villages on the Izmit peninsula, Kemalists on the Black Sea were unleashing their fury on the Pontic Greeks.

The Greek Anatolian expedition had to succeed during the summer offensive in 1921. At first the Greeks registered some impressive military successes. But as Kemal lured his enemy into the

Anatolian interior, the Greek army begin to tire. All supplies, even water, had to be brought up to the front line by soldiers in trucks which were for ever breaking down on rocky tracks. The further east the army progressed, the colder it became at night, the hotter during the day. The Greeks soon controlled large tracts of territory but they had no means of delivering the fatal blow to Kemal. By October, the two sides were digging in for the winter.

That same month, the government in Paris struck a deal with Kemal whereby the French would withdraw their occupation force in Cicilia, south-east Anatolia. This would release many thousands of Turkish soldiers to fight the Greeks. But the political message was still more grim for Athens – there was no longer any coherent Allied policy in the Near East. Britain still supported Greece verbally, although it refused both military and financial assistance. France and Italy were now inclined to favour Turkey. As 1922 dawned, disaster loomed for Greece. As Kemal prepared for his summer offensive, 'the Greek army was like an apple eaten out inside by insects or disease, superficially whole and apparently firm, but ready to disintegrate at the first sharp blow. Not even the enemy knew how near it had come to dissolution.'[98] Kemal's rejuvenated army attacked on 26 August 1922. Within two days, 50,000 Greeks, a quarter of the occupation forces, had surrendered to the Turkish army while the Greek supply lines were cut like ribbon. Several divisions evaporated. The commanders did not need to give the order to retreat – the Greeks dropped everything and ran. Across 650 kilometres, the retreating soldiers razed every village to the ground in order to slow the Turkish army's pursuit: a final outburst of barbarism.

On 9 September, the inhabitants of Smyrna woke to the news that the Greek army was streaming towards the coast and that Kemalist forces were bearing down on the port at great speed.

Inferno: Turkey, Greece

> The entire city was ablaze and the harbour as light as day. Thousands of homeless were surging back and forth along the blistering quay, panic-stricken to the point of insanity. The shrieks of women and children were painful to hear. In a frenzy they would throw themselves into the water, and some of them would reach the ship. The

> crowds along the quay were so thick and tried so desperately to close in abreast of the men-of-war anchorage, that the masses in the stifling center had nowhere to go but the sea. Fortunately, the quay wall never got actually hot enough to roast these unfortunate people alive but the heat must have been terrific there to have been felt on the ship two hundred yards away . . . The US headquarters at Smyrna theatre appeared like a large ball of fire. So hot was it in the street in front of this building that the four automobiles and two trucks parked at the door were burnt to cinders. Some of us saw a grim humour in the sign over the arched door in black letters two feet high. It was the name of the last movie show: 'Le Tango de la Mort'.
>
> From the Diary of Lieutenant A.S. Merrill, US Intelligence Officer in Smyrna[99]

Tucked into a well-camouflaged inlet, the harbour of Smyrna was shaped like a graceful crescent. Until 31 August 1922, it was a vibrant cosmopolitan city, its opera house packed with Greek, Armenian, Levantine, French, British, American, Dutch, Czech and Italian patrons. The cinema was especially popular with the American sailors who manned the three US destroyers anchored at the port. As the chronicler of the Smyrna catastrophe has written, the city was surrounded by a garland of 'almond trees, laurel, mimosa, and oleander bordering the banks of streams with luxuriant clusters of delicate pink flowers, and the rich-scented jasmine'.[100] The harvest of 1922 was a bumper one, and the city's optimism was secured by the presence of a massive Allied fleet in the harbour: twenty-one military vessels, including two British battleships, and dozens of smaller civilian boats. The Armenian and Greek inhabitants of Smyrna were greatly reassured by the presence of this fleet. Yet few were able to disguise their alarm when the trickle of wounded, exhausted soldiers arriving in the city from 1 September became a torrent. All but the most incapacitated were not stopping in Smyrna. They were continuing their retreat as far as the coastal village of Çeşme from where they would be evacuated to safety 16 kilometres across the bay to the island of Chios.

Alarm soon turned to panic. In the wake of the military came the civilians. By 3 September, 30,000 terrified refugees were arriving in the city every day, seeking shelter, food and above all else the reassurance that they could escape the hardened, unforgiving Turkish army now racing towards Smyrna. What neither the refugees nor the inhabitants knew was that the British, French, American and Italian commanders on their ships had not the slightest intention of interfering with the Turkish conquest of Smyrna, regardless of what it might entail. They were under strict instructions to maintain their neutrality.

George Horton, who had worked for several years as the American consul in Smyrna, understood only too well that the Allied forces in the harbour would remain passive over the next few days. Barely sleeping or eating, he spent a week trying to evacuate as many people as possible despite the American commander's placing endless obstacles in his way. The American quarter, known as 'Paradise', was stormed by thousands of Armenians and Greeks. On the 9th, Turkish patrols began distributing leaflets around the city, printed in Turkish and Greek, which read: 'Mustafa Kemal has given strict orders to the soldiers to harm no one. Those who disobey these orders will be punished by death. Let people be assured of safety.'[101]

Looting began sporadically and unsystematically that Saturday afternoon. The Turkish quarter was of course untouched and the Italians, who enjoyed a privileged status because of the military assistance they had rendered the Turks during the campaign, ensured that the Jewish quarter also remained unharmed. In the early afternoon, Smyrna's new military commander, Nureddin Paşa, sent for Archbishop Chrystomos. Nureddin explained calmly that a military tribunal had already sentenced the Greek Metropolitan to death:

> The Prelate was walking slowly down the steps of the *Konak* when the General [Nureddin] appeared on the balcony and cried out to the waiting mob, 'Treat him as he deserves!' The crowd fell upon Chrystomos with guttural shrieks and dragged him down the street until they reached a barber's shop where Ismael, the Jewish proprietor, was peering nervously from his doorway. Someone pushed the barber aside, grabbed a white sheet, and tied it around Chrystomos's neck, shouting, 'Give him a shave!'
>
> They tore out the Prelate's beard, gouged out his eyes with knives, cut off his ears, his nose, and his hands.[102]

That evening, the Turkish troops sealed off the Armenian quarter. Kemal had informed the Allies that he would not prevent the evacuation of the Greeks, provided that they were transported by the beginning of October. But the Armenians had nowhere to go. That night not a single house in the Armenian quarter was spared. Three days after this gross atrocity began, a French officer recorded that 'The Armenian quarter is a charnel house. In three days this rich quarter is entirely ravaged. The streets are heaped with mattresses, broken furniture, glass, torn paintings. Some young women and girls, especially pretty ones, have been taken away and put into a house that is guarded by Turkish sentries. They must submit to the whims of the patrols. One sees cadavers in front of the houses. They are swollen and some have exposed entrails. The smell is unbearable and swarms of flies cover them.'[103]

As Smyrna sank in the blood of Armenians and Greeks, and the crazed people begged any non-Turk for refuge or a passage out, Mrs Minnie Mills, dean of the American Collegiate Institute in Paradise, watched as Turks started dousing the entire Armenian quarter with petrol and paraffin. Within hours, 300,000 men, women and children in a state of total panic were packed on the quayside. A huge wall of fire pushed them ever closer to the water. Hundreds took their chances and jumped, hoping, in most cases in vain, that the Allied ships would rescue them. Many of them were used as target practice by Turkish troops. Somewhere in the chaos, sixteen-year-old Aristotle Onassis was buying his father out of custody and his family out of danger. From the safety of one of the British ships, a disbelieving Ward Price, reporting for the *Daily Mail*, described the mayhem:

> What I see as I stand on the deck of the *Iron Guard* is an unbroken wall of fire, two miles long, in which twenty distinct volcanoes of raging flames are throwing up jagged, writhing tongues to a height of a hundred feet. Against this curtain of fire, which blocks out the sky, are silhouetted the towers of the Greek churches, the domes of the mosques, and the flat square roofs of the houses . . .
>
> The sea glows a deep copper-red, and, worst of all, from the densely packed mob of thousands of refugees huddled on the narrow quay, between the advancing fiery death behind and the deep water in front, comes continuously such frantic screaming of sheer terror as can be heard miles away.[104]

Such was the finale to the Balkan Wars, which had begun eleven years earlier in the autumn of 1912. The postscript the following year was much less dramatic but even more destructive in the long term. At the peace negotiations in Lausanne, chaired by Lord Curzon, the Greek delegation, led by Venizelos, and the Turkish delegation, led by Ismet Inönü, agreed that peace would be underwritten by the Great Population Exchange. Some 1.3 million adherents of the Orthodox faith would be expelled from Turkey to Greece, while nearly 800,000 Muslims would travel the other way. The Muslims of western Thrace and the Greeks of Istanbul were to be spared this fate. Under the eye of Britain's senior diplomat, two Balkan nations agreed to end a conflict that British diplomacy had inspired, by setting a terrible precedent. It would be decades before the Greeks would properly recover from the Great Population Exchange; but the principle of partition and forced removal would be imitated again and again.

CHAPTER 6

THE PALACES OF DECEIT

The royal dictatorships, 1923–41

> They were packed like sardines upon the deck, a squirming writhing mass of human misery. They had been at sea for four days. There had not been a space to permit them to lie down to sleep; there had been no food to eat; there was not any access to toilet facilities.
>
> For these four days and nights many had stood upon the open desk, drenched by an autumn rain, pierced by the cold night wind, and blistered by the noonday sun. They came ashore in rags, hungry, sick, covered with vermin, hollow-eyed, exhaling the horrible odour of human filth – bowed with despair.
>
> Henry Morgenthau, the American chairman of the Red Cross Refugee Commission, watching 7,000 men, women and children being disgorged in Thessaloniki from a ship whose normal capacity was 2,000[1]

New dawn: Greece, Turkey

During a two-week period in early 1923, some 750,000 Greek refugees were dumped like cattle from all manner of vessels at the harbours at Piraeus and Thessaloniki. From eastern Thrace tens of thousands more streamed westwards, their heads bowed under sacks containing their belongings or pulling the remains of a life on rickety carts.

Greece, the mother country, was bankrupt. Its diplomats were encountering rigid hostility at the Lausanne Conference and later at the League of Nations in their efforts to secure loans to feed and clothe the refugees. 'When I appeared . . . to request the support of the League for a Greek loan to be devoted to the 1,300,000 refugees from Asia Minor and Thrace', reported M. Kaklamanos, the Greek ambassador to London, 'I faced a rebuke from M. Hanotaux, the French delegate: "Address yourselves to bankers," he said, "We are not financiers here."'[2] With the great powers so indifferent to the plight of this refugee army they had done so much to muster, it was left to the Red Cross, in particular its American Committee, to establish a Refugee Commission and organize relief. The Commission's aid workers toiled for eight months, managing shipments of food, clothing and tents. They contained cholera and typhus epidemics which threatened to spread out of control and fed over half a million people every day until June 1923 when they closed down the operation. The total cost to the Red Cross was $2,605,696.09, raised almost entirely from voluntary contributions.

In the postwar years of the mid-1920s, the Greek economy was so severely disrupted that it was largely dependent on foreign loans and on remittances from Greek immigrants in the United States. The chaos of the Anatolian and Thracian exodus caused untold social problems. The Red Cross reported that, 'the refugees, coming from different parts of Asia Minor and the shores of the Black Sea, exhibited . . . a variety of characteristics and attitudes'. The Refugee Commission soon realized that it was dealing with a plethora of varied cultures. The hundreds of different communities had very little in common save their Christian religion and a vague affinity to Greece. Among those who had lived in towns and large urban centres, such differences were naturally less pronounced. The peasant refugees, however, reflected very strongly the environment of their origin. It was found that those who came 'from inner Anatolia, living in the midst of Turks and Kurds, had the characteristics of Asiatic peoples, being "backward, submissive and timid."'[3]

A majority of newcomers, however, were traders, doctors, lawyers and teachers. In order to survive, these Pontic and Anatolian Greeks had to turn their quick brains and delicate hands to the cultivation of semi-barren land which the Greek authorities had hastily divided into tiny plots. The region around Salonika became the centre of an ambitious plan to transform large tracts of fallow and swampy ground into farmland. The first few years of exodus for the refugees were miserable, exceptional even by Balkan standards, and exacerbated by resentment at the newcomers' presence in Salonika (even though many of the Salonikans had themselves arrived as immigrants after the Greek occupation of the city in 1913).

Meanwhile the new Turkey, basking in its military victories, had different economic problems. The departure of the Greeks and the Armenians deprived the Turkish economy of its vital organs – of commerce, finance and small business. In Istanbul, Turkish war profiteers had no intention of returning the booty they had garnered during the war to the economy: they had yet to grasp the advantages of systematic investment. Western firms and banks quickly appreciated that local capital was not exploiting the vacuum created by the flight of the Christian traders and industrialists, and western companies found it easy to maintain a tight grip on manufacturing industry. The Treaty of Lausanne may have recognized Turkish control over Constantinople, Smyrna/Izmir and eastern Thrace, but the British and French diplomats, who were its authors, carefully denied the Ankara government the right to raise import tariffs for six years. Under such economic pressure, President Kemal and Ismet Inönü, who had established himself as the President's favourite, consolidated the political links with the Russians established during the War of Independence by adopting some of the novel economic theories emanating from the Soviet Union. As long as the issue of the Ottoman debt remained unresolved, Turkey had difficulty securing capital investment. Early in Kemal's dictatorship, the country's leading economists concluded that large-scale state intervention was essential. In 1923, the government held the First Turkish Economic Congress, one of the earliest attempts this century to claim a 'third way' which would be neither capitalist nor socialist. In fact, what this amounted to (quite sensibly if not always successfully) was an economy based on private ownership and enterprise but underwritten by massive state intervention.

Throughout the Balkans, peculiar geographic and political circumstances added to the material devastation caused by the war. With the exception of Greece and Turkey, all Balkan countries were worried that their access to the sea was conditional on the whims of others. Italy's control of the Otranto Straits hemmed in Yugoslavia's fleet, while Romania and Bulgaria were dependent on the precarious régime of the Black Sea Straits. The most stubborn infrastructural difficulty facing all Balkan countries was the mismatching of railway lines – in every country, rail track headed in directions which satisfied the economic and strategic needs of the old empires, not the requirements of the new states. Even to this day, it is impossible to travel the 160 kilometres from Skopje to Sofia by train.

The primary industry of all Balkan countries remained agriculture, on which roughly 75 per cent of the population was dependent. Civil servants and government, however, systematically ignored the needs of the rural population. Many city dwellers, even recent migrants, looked down on the countryside with disdain. Meanwhile, staring at the city from the 'neglected village' was, in Joseph Rothschild's words, a 'vegetating, unemployable, undernourished, disease-ridden, semiliterate, surplus population, [which] presented a more refractory and a more explosive problem than did the urban slum'.[4]

In Yugoslavia, a minuscule 1 per cent of the annual budget was allotted to agriculture. The bulk of the state's revenue was diverted into defence spending. Between 34 and 50 per cent of national budgets were spent on the military throughout the Balkans, except in Bulgaria, which under the Treaty of Neuilly was permitted only a token defence force. This neglect of the rural population did not escape the notice of the more shrewd populist politicians, who saw in the peasantry an inexhaustible source of recruits, and could pick up rural votes by denouncing urban centres as so many Sodoms and Gomorrahs devouring the fruits of the peasant's honest toil.

Red dawn: Bulgaria

In Bulgaria, the violence latent in this postwar situation burst through the surface, establishing a pattern of political terror and counter-terror. Nowhere was the peasantry better organized or more politically aware than in Bulgaria, and its rural population did not suffer exceptional levels of poverty by regional standards. Bulgarian peasants were also the most literate in the region.

As the war ended, support for Stamboliiski and his Bulgarian Agrarian National Union (BANU)* grew rapidly. Ferdinand's abdication in favour of his son Boris was the first sign of a profound shift in the political mood of the country. In the elections of August 1919, BANU won 28 per cent of the vote, the Communists 18 per

---

* See chapter 5.

cent and the Socialists 13 per cent. BANU became the first mass peasant party in the Balkans to form a government. At first, the urban bourgeoisie welcomed Stamboliiski and the BANU as agents of order. One of the peasant leader's first acts was to mobilize tens of thousands of his paramilitary Orange Guard to break a general strike backed by the Bulgarian Communist Party, centred on the mines of Pernik, 32 kilometres south-west of Sofia. With pitchforks, shovels and their hallmark clubs (*tsepinitsa*), the Orange Guardists stormed the Pernik complex, expelling the miners from the shafts. It was clear to the city elite that here was a possible ally in the battle against Bolshevism. But once Stamboliiski had succeeded in winning an overall majority for the first time (with 'administrative' adjustments to the results) in the elections of March 1920, he turned his attention away from his working-class opponents and towards those he dismissed contemptuously as 'the generals, the professors, the journalists and the lawyers'. Stamboliiski saw himself as the sole representative of the downtrodden 'agriculturist, long despised by the cities, [but who] is now king in Bulgaria. None of the people-eaters feels secure anymore. The tyrants are worried. The cities are upside down . . . Little by little, the peasant who used to be ridiculed and pressured, who was the eternal slave, raises the banner of emancipation. Soon he'll cease to carry the heavy load that the city-dwellers, the bourgeois, and the intellectuals have placed on his shoulders!'[5]

Over the next two years, Stamboliiski's heavy-handed treatment of his opponents – harassment, censorship, bans – inspired some unlikely coalitions. Socialists, nationalists, businessmen, intellectuals and army officers came to agree that something would have to be done about this new dictatorship of the peasantry. The opposition was jealous of BANU's political monopoly but it also felt threatened by the radical agrarian reforms which the Agrarian government was implementing. Stamboliiski's dirigiste economic programme mobilized tens of thousands of young men on public reconstruction projects, which was, in many respects, just what Bulgaria required to overcome the economic trauma of war. Yet power intoxicated BANU – the more influence Stamboliiski and his colleagues wielded, the more insecure and aggressive they became. In the late summer of 1922, rumours began to circulate around Sofia that opposition leaders were conspiring to unseat Stamboliiski, counting on troops commanded by the White Russian General Wrangel, who, following his expulsion from Crimea at the end of the Russian Civil War, was offering his services to the highest Balkan bidder. As the leaders of the anti-Stamboliiski parliamentary front, known as the Bloc, were heading for a rally in Bulgaria's ancient capital, Tŭrnovo, they were set upon by members of the Orange Guard, dragged from their railway coaches and badly beaten, only narrowly escaping with their lives.

The peasant militants attempted to dispense this rough justice to two groups which they should have treated with greater caution – the officer corps and VMRO (the Internal Macedonian Revolutionary Organization). In accordance with the diktat of the Entente powers, the Treaty of Neuilly, Bulgaria had reduced the size of its army from 700,000 to 33,000 men. Indeed, one reason why Stamboliiski had expanded the Orange Guard was because the Treaty of Neuilly had so depleted the forces of law and order. The Orange Guard was, however, no refuge for unemployed young officers. These men were out of favour with the Stamboliiski régime. A group of disaffected officers established a conspiratorial group, the Military League, which carefully built up contacts with opposition politicians and with VMRO.

Because the Paris Peace Conference had given Yugoslavia the bulk of Macedonia, Petrich in south-western Bulgaria (that small part of Macedonia still belonging to Bulgaria) was teeming with angry armed men. Since Stamboliiski had put his signature to the Treaty of Neuilly, it had become the sacred duty of every VMRO activist literally to sever the Prime Minister's treacherous hand from his body. In turn, Stamboliiski made no secret of his hostility to VMRO: 'Since you've taken Macedonia', he told a group of Yugoslav journalists with characteristic bluntness at the end of 1922, 'why don't you also take all Macedonians still in Bulgaria? You can have them – good riddance! . . . Take them all, and make them into human beings . . . I would never wage war with you [Yugoslavs] for the Macedonians!'[6] Stamboliiski's nationalism was not motivated by the desire to recover lost Bulgarian territory: what drove him was a passion to improve the living standards of the peasant majority of the actual Bulgarian state. But his vision of national progress was not shared by all Bulgarians, many of whom backed VMRO's revisionist struggle for the return of Macedonia, not to mention the southern Dobrudja, and the Thracian outlet to the Aegean and Adrianople.

In the early hours of 9 June 1923, the *coup* against Stamboliiski was launched. Within three days, the seemingly omnipotent BANU was smashed and the entire country was under the control of the army or of VMRO. Stamboliiski himself was not in Sofia, as the conspirators believed, but in his home village, Slavovitsa, in central Bulgaria. On hearing of the *coup*, he attempted to organize resistance in the nearest town, Pazardzhik, but he was too late. He was captured by VMRO, then dismembered. His head was sent to Sofia in a tin.

During the *coup*, the Bulgarian Communist Party (BCP) sat back and applauded the actions of the Military League. The BCP had not forgotten Stamboliiski's role in smashing the general strike of 1919/20, nor could its leaders abide the Prime Minister's claim to be the authentic voice of Bulgarian socialism. However, in the previous three years, the communists had enjoyed an unprecedented degree of freedom under Stamboliiski's régime, its membership rising to 40,000 and the Party establishing branches throughout the country. The BCP had never been stronger. Despite filling state offices with BANU placemen, Stamboliiski had never prevented other political parties from organizing. Soon after the *coup*, the BCP Central Committee issued a manifesto, explaining that it was indifferent to the military takeover as it amounted to nothing more than 'a fight of the cliques of the rural and urban bourgeoisie for power', adding that 'the toiling masses in town and country will not participate in this fight . . . because such a participation would mean that the exploited fight the battles of the exploiters'.[7]

When Grigory Zinoviev, the President of the Communist International (Comintern) in Moscow, learned of the BCP's decision to remain neutral during the *coup*, he was enraged. How could the BCP sit back and watch the forces of reaction crush the revolutionary potential of the Bulgarian peasantry? The inaction of the local communists, the Comintern argued, had allowed the forces of 'monarcho-fascism' to ride roughshod over workers and peasants. Zinoviev ordered a special investigation as to why the BCP had acted as handmaiden to the putsch. The BCP initially put up a spirited defence of its position but, under pressure from Moscow, it had no choice in the end but to concede that it had erred seriously. To repair the damage, the Bulgarian communists agreed to a plan which, even by the standards of the Comintern, was breathtaking in its stupidity. They were to mount an insurrection against the new, military-backed government in Sofia. The communist uprising was planned for September 1923, by which time support for the Agrarians, bereft of Stamboliiski's charisma, had all but disappeared. The Moscow-inspired insurrection was an abject failure and the consequence was several years of 'white terror', orchestrated by General Ivan Vŭlkov, the fascist strongman behind the new régime who earned the epithet 'the butcher' and who unleashed the bored *čete* of VMRO on to a defenceless population.

In the first few weeks after the failed insurrection, the régime admitted to killing 1,500 people although the opposition claimed 15,000 murdered. Diplomats put the figure at 10,000. What was perfectly clear, however, was that the Vŭlkov terror was a bloody business which far exceeded any repressive measures dreamed up by Stamboliiski and BANU. The BCP had learned the first of many hard lessons: there was a world of difference between the cliques of the urban and the rural bourgeoisies.

In February 1925, Marko Friedman, smoking one cigarette after another, paced up and down a darkened room known grandly as the Headquarters of the Military Centre. Friedman had just been told that the body of his close friend, the popular communist leader Valcho Ivanov, had been found under the Eagle Bridge which spans the river Perlovez in Sofia. Bent on revenge, Friedman began work on a project which climaxed on 16 April 1925 in what remains one of the most spectacular, bloody and self-defeating acts of terrorism in the history of the twentieth century. First, the communists assassinated a retired general, who was highly respected and not a controversial political figure. King Boris agreed to a funeral for the general with full state honours at Sofia's Sveta Nedelya Cathedral. Since the New Year, communist activists had been blackmailing a sexton at the Cathedral into storing 45 kg of explosives in the roof. On 16 April, the entire Cabinet filed into Sveta Nedelya for the general's funeral. Tsar Boris (who was still recovering from an assassination attempt earlier in the week) had been required to attend the funeral of another murdered friend earlier in the day and so had not yet arrived. As he motored towards Sveta Nedelya, the Archbishop was preaching from the Gospel of St John: 'Verily, verily, I say unto you', he intoned, 'he that heareth my word, and believeth in Him that sent me, hath everlasting life, and shall not come into condemnation. But he is passed from death unto life.'[8] These words were followed by an explosion which shook like thunder around the capital. It ripped off the main cupola of the Cathedral; 160 people died, and hundreds more were badly injured, but not a single member of the government, nor the late-running Tsar, was killed. After a swift police investigation, three men were hanged in public (Boris suspended his opposition to the death penalty for the occasion) although one of the accused had only the most tenuous connection to the crime. But worse was to come. The 'white terror' now entered its most intense phase.

> All the latent sadism in monsters common in Bulgaria had now an unprecedented opportunity for indulgence . . . Ferdinand and Berkovitza [two towns north of Sofia] were bombarded and sacked; villages burnt; girls raped; the wounded bayoneted; prisoners mutilated. Untried men, women, priests, teachers, schoolboys and girls, even babies were slaughtered by the hundred for days after the revolt ended. The towns were purged of Left sympathisers, lorries rumbling through the streets by night to take victims from their houses. From every village people 'disappeared' and their dogs grew fat.[9]

Bulgaria's bloody entry into the postwar period was not mirrored elsewhere; but with the exception of Greece and Albania the most serious conflicts in the Balkans arose from tensions between urban and rural communities. The lack of diversification in the economies, and the persistent problem of rural underemployment, ensured that the Balkans were especially susceptible to the adverse effects of downturns in the world economy. In the 1930s, these two problems intensified. Local politicians were inspired by the aggressively seductive theatricality of the Italian fascists and the Nazis. One after the other, Balkan democracies expired after brief, sickly lives, to be replaced by royalist dictatorships. Yet although these régimes borrowed some of the paraphernalia and rhetoric developed by Mussolini and Hitler, none was consistently harsh enough to warrant the epithet 'monarcho-fascism', as the communists initially described them. Indeed, King Carol of Romania considered the Iron

Guard, the only powerful indigenous fascist movement in the Balkans, to be a threat to his régime. In addition, the characteristics of the Balkan autocracies varied from country to country, often quite markedly – there was no generic Balkan dictatorship.

All Balkan countries during the interwar period had to deal with complicated national questions which severely hampered their political stability. The one exception was Albania whose people faced difficulties of a more fundamental nature. Greece began its postwar life in the midst of a national catastrophe. Turkey believed that, with the Treaty of Lausanne and the Armenian killings and expulsions, it had solved the national question. It was wrong. Having once been united in their hostility towards the Armenians, the Turks and the Kurds now discovered that the establishment of an explicitly Turkish national state made their own relationship problematic. Romania's small political elite basked in its success at the Paris Peace Conference, where it had been awarded large chunks of territory, including all of Transylvania. Greater Romania now included millions of non-Romanians, forming 30 per cent of the population. The government soon realized that this could lead to severe political complications in both domestic and foreign policy.

In Romania, and Greece, dictatorships were only imposed after the Great Depression caused by the Wall Street Crash in 1929 had ripped through their agrarian economies. But in one country, the national question disturbed every heartbeat of the infant state. In Yugoslavia, the apparently irreconcilable aspirations of the 'one-blooded nation of two faiths', the Serbs and the Croats, persuaded King Aleksandar Karadjordjević (1921–34) to dispense with democracy well before the global crash.

The impossible country: Yugoslavia

Few European states have faced such perplexing difficulties as the Kingdom of the Serbs, Croats and Slovenes after it emerged from the ashes of the Habsburg and Ottoman Empires. Its Constitution was promulgated on 28 June 1921, or Vidovdan. This date warmed Serbian hearts because it commemorated the battle of Kosovo in 1389, and the assassination of Archduke Franz Ferdinand in 1914. It did not, however, impress many Croats, Slovenes, Muslims or Albanians. The Constitution's legality was questionable as it was passed by a simple majority and not the 60 per cent required by the Corfu Declaration, the agreement reached in 1917 by the Serbs and Croats on the establishment of a Yugoslav state. Worse still, the two most powerful opposition parties did not participate in the vote of the Constituent Assembly. The interim government had declared the Communist Party illegal several months earlier, while Stjepan Radić's Croat Republican Peasant Party (HRSS), by far the largest political force in Croatia, absented itself in protest at what it considered an assembly rigged in favour of 'centralizers' and 'Greater Serbianists'. By boycotting parliament and concentrating on its extraparliamentary struggle for a Croatian republic, the HRSS ensured that its voice would not be heard in Belgrade. Its obstructionist tactics and Radić's romantic nationalist rhetoric meant that in Yugoslavia's crucial first five years, Croat grievances did not receive the airing they deserved. Indeed, Radić's stubbornness helped to confirm the ingrained Serbian prejudice that these grievances were nothing more than covert separatism.

The dispute between 'centralizers' and 'federalists', terms not always but usually synonymous with Serbs and Croats, had its roots in two different perceptions of statehood. When Croat politicians pointed to their state traditions, such as the Sabor, the Croat parliament, and their established legal system, the cry would go up from the Serbs, 'Ali mi smo ratovali!' – 'But we fought the war!' Convinced that their heroic contribution to the First World War earned them privileges in the new state, the Serbs also believed that the experience of a century of *de facto* independence should give them automatic seniority. 'If your lot imagine that we are all going to be on an equal footing', Milenko Vesnić, the Serb Radical Prime Minister, warned the Croat sculptor Ivan Meštrović* in 1920, 'then you haven't yet grasped the reality. Certainly for the next few years, it's a practical impossibility', he continued. 'Serbia was a state in its own right with its own state apparatus which you cannot just dismantle overnight. And I'll tell you something else . . . If the Germans and Austrians had by chance won the war, we would all be sitting in Zagreb discussing this. And even though there are more of us Serbs, we would have had to lump the fact that you Croats would have had the most powerful voice.'[10]

* Meštrović was in fact well known as a supporter of a Yugoslav state.

Radić's party dominated Croat political life after it defeated all opponents in Croatia and Slavonia during the elections to the Constituent Assembly in 1920. He at first called for a Croatian republic, which ensured that he was never trusted by the Karadjordjević monarchy. He provoked a hysterical campaign against himself and brought on charges of treason by signing up to the Soviet Peasant International, the Krestintern. This was a serious mistake which assisted the imposition of a Greater Serbian state, not just in Croatia but in Bosnia and Macedonia as well. Pašić and his Radical Party had degenerated into little more than a machine for the enrichment of its members. But by staying inside parliament and other democratic institutions, they could at least make a case for their claim to be a pillar of responsible statehood. The mismanagement of the economy, the chronic inequality in the tax system which saw Croatia, Slovenia and other areas pay much more than their fair share, all these abuses continued barely noticed because Radić was too proud to join in the political process. His fabled 'instability', as his friends delicately referred to his unpredictable outbursts, left the Croats high and dry. Although he only ever advocated the establishment of a Croat republic through agreement with the Serbs, his language often raised the political temperature, for example, when on 14 July 1923 he famously likened Yugoslavia to a 'Serbian Bastille'. Radić himself believed both in the establishment of Croatia's sovereignty *and* agreement with the Serbs. But the effect of his politics was to convince both Serbs and supporters of Yugoslav unity among the Croats that he was a subversive and a revolutionary. The perception of Radić was considerably more significant than his actual politics.

Pašić and the Greater Serb lobby did not have everything their own way. As Pašić approached his eightieth birthday, he could no longer prevent his own party from splintering. Between the intransigent federalism of Radić and the Greater Serbian arrogance of Pašić and the Radicals lay the middle way of the genuine believers in a Yugoslav polity. Supporters of the 'united' state, however, came in all shapes and sizes, none of which fitted together especially comfortably. King Aleksandar's resistance to Greater Serbian pressure was not born of hostility to the ideology – he was in essence a 'Greater Serb', even if he genuinely wished to reach an amicable agreement with other peoples in Yugoslavia – but arose because he saw the ambition of all parliamentary parties as a threat to his own power.

During the 1920s, the contrasting cultural and political traditions of the Ottoman and the Austro-Hungarian empires were channelled into a dispute about the nature of Yugoslavia's constitution. The vicious disputes over the Vidovdan Constitution led directly to the butchery that accompanied the break-up of both the first Yugoslavia in 1941 and its second manifestation in 1991. On both occasions, these catastrophes were triggered by tectonic shifts in European politics. But the domestic causes of the Yugoslav tragedy were firmly rooted in the years separating the formation of the Yugoslav state in 1918 and the assassination of King Aleksandar in 1934.

Notwithstanding his impetuous behaviour, Stjepan Radić made a serious attempt to repair the damage in 1925, when after half a decade in the wilderness he announced a *volte-face* that left other Yugoslav politicians quite stupefied. Radić himself was in jail as his nephew announced to a disbelieving Skupština (parliament) that, 'the Vidovdan Constitution exists here today *de facto*, this is a political fact of life, with the Karadjordjević dynasty as the head of state. This is a fact which we accept unconditionally and with which we agree . . . Although it may look as though we have made concessions to our brothers, those brothers are the Serbian people and represent our joint future together (*stormy applause from the opposition and from the other side Janjić and several other Serb Radicals applaud*).'[11]

This sudden transformation of the Croat Peasant Party from proud republican outsiders to loyal monarchists was the result of the King's intervention. Through an intermediary, Aleksander had approached Radić in prison, offering the Croat exploratory talks with Pašić and the Radicals. The King calculated that agreement between the biggest parties in Serbia and Croatia might overcome the political instability of the past few years. By July the Cabinet was formed and immediately dubbed the R-R, Radical-Radić, government. The following day, Stjepan Radić was released from prison and travelled to Belgrade to negotiate with Pašić. Radić himself accepted the Ministry of Education and, in a magnanimous gesture, dropped the word 'Republican' from his Party's name.

The creation of a Radical/Peasant Party government caused a political sensation. A number of senior Croat politicians who until now had maintained a cautious dialogue with Belgrade were unable to accept what almost smacked of betrayal. As always, Radić could rely on the support of the peasantry. But he also now convinced urban Croats, shrewdly observing that people were concerned about more than interminable debates over Yugoslavia's constitution. Political stability would enable them to enjoy the cultural influences filtering into Croatia from Austria and Germany and from across the Atlantic. For the first time in decades, Zagreb and other cities were beginning to prosper and, as the leading Croat journalist of the time remembered, 'the urban population had been gripped by a new morality – American civilization with its outrageously short skirts and black dance music, the cult of sport and the exciting search for new sensations'.[12] The artists and literati of Belgrade and Zagreb entered into a good-natured competition in an attempt to prove which city was the more cosmopolitan and creative. The presence of 30,000 White Russian refugees in Belgrade revived its theatre and opera while the work of Otto Wagner, the great architect of the Viennese *Sezession*, inspired the Zagreb school, headed by Viktor Kovačić, lending the Croatian capital a more graceful modern appearance than Belgrade (which had sustained heavy damage during the war). As the politics of the new kingdom became ever more vitriolic and unstable, some elements of Slovene, Serb, Croat, Bosnian and Montenegrin culture began to mix well, laying the foundations of a genuine 'Yugoslav' social and national identity. Cooperation in government also led to a relaxation of the five-year repression in the Croat regions; and Croatian cultural nationalism was no longer regarded as the Trojan Horse of separatism.

This gentle renaissance reached a climax in the middle of August 1925 when the royal couple, King Aleksandar and Queen Mignon, visited Zagreb to join in the celebrations marking 1,000 years since the establishment of a Croatian medieval monarchy. The centrepiece of the festivities was the annual convocation of the Croatian Sokol, the pan-Slav gymnastics movement founded by the Czech, Miroslav Tyrš, which specialized in spectacular mass displays of young gymnasts. The Sokol was the Slav equivalent of the teutonic *Turnvereine*, though less aggressively nationalistic. The new spirit of fraternal understanding so inspired Radić that he composed a special hymn for the occasion. Except for artistic merit, it had everything:

Hrvatski sokol sad k Tebi leti	*The Croatian hawk is flying towards you*
Zvijezdo Karadjordjeva doma	*Star of Karadjordje's house*
Iznad oblaka, munja i zvona	*Above the clouds, lightning and bells,*
Pozdrav će Tebi donijeti	*It will bring you greetings*
Pozdrav od roda Hrvata	*Greetings from the family of Croats*
Roda seljaka, ribara,	*Family of peasants and fishing folk,*
koji nauk povijesti shvata	*Who understand the lesson of history*
I seljačku državu stvara.	*And are building the peasant state.*
Stvara ju sa srpskim džinom	*They build it jointly with the Serbian giant*
Slavenskog uma dubinom,	*Of profound Slavic wisdom*
Slavenskog srca širinom,	*Of broad Slavic heart*
Sokolskog lijeta visinom.	*With the height of a hawk's flight.*[13]

Despite Radić's eulogy, this grand edifice of unity between Serbs, Croats and Slovenes had been built on quicksand. It was not long before the R-R government started to splinter. The octogenarian Pašić could no longer discipline his troops and some of his more senior colleagues, with their eyes firmly fixed on the post-Pašić era, were organizing their own factions in the Radical Party. Radić, although in government, could not resist echoing the accusations levelled by the opposition Democrats that Pašić's son, Rade, was up to his neck in corruption and that the old man himself may have been implicated. In December 1926, the King, also aware of Pašić's waning influence, turned down the Radical leader's request that he form yet another government. The old man stormed out of the palace in a fury and later that evening suffered a massive stroke from which he never recovered. The Radicals were broken, leaving three enfeebled factions who were as hostile to one another as to the opposition.

At this point, a remarkable reconciliation took place between Radić and the acknowledged leader of the Croatian Serbs, Svetozar Pribičević, who, as one of the Kingdom's earliest Interior and

Education ministers, had earned the reputation of a spiteful centralizer. During the first half of the 1920s, it gradually dawned on Pribičević that the Radicals were using him as a stooge. He underwrote their governments by delivering the votes and support of the Serbs in Croatia but was always made to feel subordinate to the Belgrade Radicals. Ambition and grudges drove Pribičević. As an enemy, he was dangerous. In 1927, after a decade of mutual antipathy, Radić and Pribičević joined forces to curb, as they saw it, the unlimited pretensions of Belgrade. In fact, the effect of their alliance was not so much to curb power as to obstruct meaningful government. As parliamentarians, the two men specialized in carping, in irony, in insults and in demagogy. They were both splendid performers, especially Radić, but in the toxic atmosphere of the Skupština such behaviour carried serious risks.

In one sense, the alliance between Radić and Pribičević was born of opportunism. But it also highlights an aspect of Yugoslav politics in the interwar period that is often overlooked. Political conflicts were not necessarily always national or religious in character; regional conflicts were often as virulent. By the time of the imposition of the royal dictatorship in January 1929, Pribičević and his Serb followers were as embittered opponents of Belgrade centralism as were Radić and his Croat supporters. Even political parties in Slovenia rarely expressed solidarity with their fellow Catholics, the Croats. Throughout the 1920s, the Slovene People's Party, and in Bosnia, the Yugoslav Muslim Organization, preferred to back Belgrade in its conflicts with first the Croatian People's Party and later the Serb-Croat coalition in Zagreb.

Death of a lawmaker: Yugoslavia

June 19, 1928 'was one of the worst nights of my life', Sekula Drljević recalled two months later. 'I didn't fall asleep until some time after two o'clock but was wide awake again by five so I got up with no further ado.' Impatient and agitated, he took the first boat across the Sava from Zemun to Belgrade and hurried to the apartment of Pavle Radić, the nephew of Stjepan. Radić senior was sitting quietly in the small reception area next to the dining room, drinking tea and reading that morning's *Politika*, Belgrade's most influential daily. Ignoring Drljević's excitement, Radić gently told his colleague to wait until he had finished reading the paper. But Drljević* was unable contain himself:

> 'Don't bother to read it. I'll tell you what's in it – the justification for your murder. Have a look at the report on yesterday's session of the Skupština under the headline, *Are you the speaker of parliament or a cowherd?* And then underneath, *Mr Radić addressing Dr N. Perić yesterday afternoon*. You said no such thing and even if you had, the only reason they would print it would be to justify your murder.'[14]

Try as he might, Drljević could not dissuade Radić from leaving the apartment when the local church bell chimed 9 o'clock. Bringing the conversation to a close, Radić said, 'Pavle warned me about my possible murder yesterday as well and even I can sense something fishy is going on. But, Sekula, understand this – I am like a soldier in a trench from where I am fighting a war for the rights of the Croatian people. Either I will emerge from my trench as victor or the Croatian people will have to bring out my dead body.' And with that, off they all went to the Skupština, the two Radićes and Drljević. Having arrived safely, Drljević managed at least to extract a promise from Stjepan that the Croat Peasant Party leader would keep his mouth firmly shut during that day's session.

A little later that morning, Puniša Račić, a member for the Radicals, the largest parliamentary party from Serbia, strode purposefully out of King Aleksandar's chambers. Nobody knows what he discussed with the King, but he left the palace an angry man and with a revolver in his pocket. Along with other Radicals, he had been obliged at recent sessions of the Skupština to listen to intolerable accusations of corruption hurled at him from the Croats and from their leader, Radić, whom he considered especially loathsome. As a sixteen-year-old in 1902, Račić had entered the employ of Nikola Pašić, the master of Serbian politics. Pašić came to look on Račić as a son, encouraging his political ambition. The young man then embarked on a sinister career in the name of Serbia, claiming later that he had organized assassination attempts

* Drljević was actually a member of the Montenegrin Federalists.

against Kings Ferdinand of Bulgaria and Constantine of Greece as well as against Wilhelm II, Emperor of Germany. When Serbia regained much of Macedonia after the First World War, Račić earned a fearsome reputation as one of the main pacifiers of 'pro-Bulgarian groups' (i.e. ordinary villagers) in the region. As the Kingdom of Serbs, Croats and Slovenes began its awkward experiment with democracy, the Radical Party, overburdened with geriatric politicians, sought fresh cadres among the *četniks*, military commanders and successful traders of 'Southern Serbia', as northern Macedonia had by now been renamed. They were expected to bid goodbye to the assassin's bomb and the jackboot, and reinvent themselves as democratic politicians. For many, including Račić, the transition was a stiff challenge. For his part, the Croat, Stjepan Radić, had also encountered difficulties in graduating from his role as scourge of the Austro-Hungarians to coalition partner in the new democracy. The Skupština was an ill-tempered, fractious debating chamber, a cacophonous chorus as the main actors in government engaged in a ceaseless game of musical Cabinet chairs. Governments rose and fell but the squawking and bickering in the Skupština never stopped.

Radić's supporters were especially nervous on 20 June 1928 because the previous day Puniša Račić and his fellow Serbian Radical, Toma Popović, had screamed out during one of the Skupština's habitual slanging matches: 'Heads are going to roll here and until someone kills Stjepan Radić there can be no peace.' But when Radić took his seat that morning, he kept his promise to Drljević. He remained serene, not rising to any bait cast from the dispatch box. The atmosphere was tense but quiet until Ivan Pernar, a member for Radić's Croat Peasant Party, suddenly hurled an insult at a *četnik* Serb member. 'Oh yes, what a hero! He slaughtered defenceless people in cold blood. You're real Robin Hoods, you are [*To su šumski junaci*]! . . . You've slaughtered people, you've eaten people and you know it. And after such heroic deeds, you proclaim yourselves Dukes!' According to the report in *Politika*, Pernar then targeted another Serb member. 'Oh we know about Comrade Kosta Pećanac! He massacred two hundred Muslim children and pensioners! He slaughtered them like sheep. You killed them like chickens . . . Is it not true that Vojvoda [Duke] Pećanac killed 200 Muslims in 1921? Just tell us it's not true!'[15]

The mood in the Skupština now turned extremely nasty, even by its own standards. When Popović repeated his warning that he would murder Radić, there was uproar on the opposition benches. Insults were bawled across the floor, tables were banged and death threats hurled around with abandon. Ninko Perić, the Radical who presided over this undignified assembly as Speaker, refused to cancel the session and instead ordered a recess of five minutes. Having spoken with Puniša Račić in his private chamber, Perić then invited the Radical member to take the floor. At one point, Pernar interjected that Račić had looted Muslim houses in Macedonia ['Opljačkao si begove!']. The correspondent of the Zagreb newspaper, *Novosti*, reported what happened next:

> Račić, expecting Dr Pernar to be called to order, turns towards the Speaker while slipping his hand into his right pocket where his revolver is hidden. At this time, the most indescribable commotion is going on. At exactly 11:25, seeing that the Speaker does not intend to enforce the satisfaction he had demanded of Dr Pernar, Puniša Račić takes the gun from his pocket. The Justice Minister, Vujičić, who is sitting behind the podium, grabs Račić's back. The former Minister of Religion, Obradović, seizes his right shoulder.
>
> Puniša Račić shrugs them off, throwing Vujičić against the ministerial bench while Obradović is sent flying several metres. Rude Bacinić runs to the Speaker screaming, 'Stop this, blood is going to be spilled!' Everything happened so quickly and the whole House was so shocked that nobody was able to prevent the catastrophe.[16]

Pernar was the first to be hit, followed by another member of the Croat Peasant Party. Throughout the chaos, Stjepan Radić sat as if oblivious to it all, not moving an inch. Račić next turned on Radić, aimed the gun at his stomach and fired. Pavle Radić was racing down from the back of the hall just as his uncle groaned and slumped on to his desk. On seeing Pavle, Račić growled, 'I've been waiting for you.' Pavle was shot at point-blank range and died on arrival in hospital.

Stjepan Radić was operated on straight away and the surgeon's prognosis was optimistic. The bullet had not torn his gut and there was every chance that he would pull through. Within less than a month, he was well enough to return to Zagreb. But his condition deteriorated unexpectedly and he died on 8 August. Thus ended the life of a remarkable politician and with it the first phase of Yugoslavia's short and tragic history.

A month after the assassination attempt on Radić, and while he was still alive, a compromise coalition was formed. It was the first and only government not led by a Serb, but by the leader of the Slovene People's Party, Anton Korošec. But Radić's unexpected death two weeks after the Cabinet had been sworn in made life very difficult. The mood in Croatia deteriorated. On the evening of 1 December, Zagreb celebrated the anniversary of the foundation of the Kingdom of Serbs, Croats and Slovenes. During the official ceremonies marking the occasion, students unfurled three black flags. One mourned the foundation of Yugoslavia, the second mourned a demonstration when Serbian troops had killed fourteen people, the third mourned the death of Radić. Three students were killed in the ensuing battles between police and demonstrators.

The Croats and Pribičević, the leader of the local Serbs, froze all cooperation with the government in Belgrade, and Serbian parties now also presented Korošec with lists of impossible demands. In despair, the Prime Minister handed in his resignation. On 6 January 1929, Aleksandar announced that he was seizing power, suspending the constitution, and transforming the Kingdom of Serbs, Croats and Slovenes into the Kingdom of Yugoslavia. 'Blind political passions', the King explained in the proclamation of his dictatorship, 'have started to abuse parliamentary democracy . . . to such a degree that it has obstructed all fruitful endeavour in this state.'

Sisyphus in Tirana: Albania

> Tell the king . . . I despise [him] for the following reasons: Having watched him since he was eighteen, I never caught him telling a truth. He has never kept his pledged word. He has no sense of responsibility. He is greedy, selfish, callous, dishonest. He hates all those who have something, – be it culture, birth, wealth, a capacity in any field, or simply a rugged and honest patriotism. He ignores fundamental things, and gives a grotesque importance to trifles. Albania had always been noted as a nation with a certain tragic dignity; he has

lowered Albania to the level of a cheap musical farce.

Faik Konitza, Albanian ambassador to Washington, asked by an envoy from Tirana if he had any message for his monarch in 1938[17]

As soon as Ahmed Zogu* stubbed out a cigarette, he would reach for the next one from his little silver case. The windows of his office in the presidential palace remained firmly shut. The thick fog that filled the room would swirl towards the ceiling on the hot air emitted by radiators which remained on throughout the day. Ascetic not by choice but by necessity, Zogu slept at most four hours a night and took no exercise. When he was just thirty-four years old, he collapsed with a severe pulmonary and circulatory condition.

The paradox was that he remained indoors and stayed away from windows precisely in order to avoid being killed. Zogu's mother, who lived in a villa across the street, was the only person permitted to prepare his meals. After cooking them, she would place them in a locked container. This would then be escorted under armed guard to the presidential cabinet. Zogu had to leave the palace only infrequently, as the building was connected by a covered passage to his actual residence. On those rare occasions when he could not avoid venturing on to the open street, his mother would act as his chaperone. According to the strict code of the *gjakmarrje*, the blood feud, a marked man could not be killed if accompanied in public by a woman. Towering well over 6 feet with unusually conspicuous red hair, Zogu was a tempting target in a country where most people were dark-haired and stood at under five and a half feet.

Zogu had recently accepted the title 'Saviour of the Nation', which he had offered himself, on behalf of a grateful people, as an adornment to his constitutional position. Yet it has been estimated that by 1928 'Zogu had as many as 600 blood feuds on his hands, more than a few with extremely important families. The lengthy list of his victims included six clan chieftains of Mirdite, numerous priests, and many prominent politicians.'[18]

Most of these vendettas were indeed Zogu's responsibility, the

* Born Ahmed Zogolli, he changed his name to Zogu (meaning 'the bird') in the early 1920s as a sign of modernization and then changed this for the last time to Zog I when he became King in 1928.

result of his five-year struggle to become the undisputed political master of Albania. He resorted to assassination, torture, blackmail and bribery on a scale never before seen in the history of the Albanians. The *besa*, the word of honour which had the power to postpone or abrogate the blood revenge, was only applicable to feuds relating to personal matters. Zogu's trail of murder and revenge was caused by political and financial ambition. According to the code of honour, nothing could stop political vendettas before they were carried through.

Zogu's violent methods were not exceptional. Bishop Fan Noli, a Harvard graduate, the founder of the Albanian Orthodox Church in the United States, and an avowed admirer of the American constitution, raised a rebel army which overthrew Zogu briefly in June 1924. Noli then ruled by decree, handing out death penalties and gagging his opponents. Six months later, when Fan Noli's naive and poorly executed programme of autocratic liberalism had alienated almost all core constituencies of Albania's tiny political class, Zogu stormed his way back into power. He had mustered a hybrid military force comprising warriors from his own people, the Mati, and other northern Albanian tribes; soldiers from the Yugoslav army; and a mercenary force commanded by General Wrangel, the White Russian leader who arrived fresh from his Bulgarian adventure.

In Albania, six years of chaos followed the Great War. Zogu finally brought this to an end with the *coup* against Fan Noli in December 1924. The President was pursuing an ambitious goal: he sought to create a united and stable Albanian state, a quest fraught with danger both for the country and for Zogu himself, and quite unattainable from the outset. He suffered from paranoia; his behaviour was unpredictably vicious; he chose his counsellors unwisely; he found himself caught between the Italian rock and a Yugoslav hard place; European financial institutions scorned him; and he was the object of an estimated fifty-five assassination attempts. Yet for about four years after his return to power in 1924, Zogu played a creditable, cunning game which it is hard not to admire. In 1928, he anointed himself King Zog I of the Albanians and became intoxicated by delusions of grandeur.

One could barely describe Albania as a state in the early 1920s. Its borders were not properly regulated until 1924. Italy coveted it as a colonial springboard in the Balkans. The Kingdom of Serbs, Croats and Slovenes hatched plans to partition the country with Greece and Italy. Above all else, Albania was dreadfully poor and riven by the most fragmented social structure in Europe, the product of extreme underdevelopment and manifold internal rivalries exacerbated by the divide-and-rule policy of the late Ottoman sultans and the Young Turks. The northern tribes had their clan system and primitive agricultural methods, relied on brigandage and, of course, were crippled by the blood feud that ensured the persistence of pre- and early modern social structures. The great landowning *beys* of central and southern Albania held the majority of the population in merciless bondage. Whenever anybody – Sultan, colonial occupier or self-proclaimed president – attempted to impose order on the economy or society, the landowners would gather their retinues in preparation for revolt. In the far south, Albanians were tempted to exchange their Albanian identity for a good Greek education. There were many Greek schools in southern Albania and northern Greece, but virtually no Albanian schools. Being Albanian meant staying poor. Becoming Greek offered a possible escape.

The Albanian intelligentsia was dispersed and lacked resources. Yet in 1912 its efforts at last succeeded in bringing the Albanian cause to the attention of the great powers. At the London Conference, the first Albanian state was founded, to the chagrin of the Serbs and Greeks who had intended carving up the territory after the First Balkan War. The great powers appointed the minor German aristocrat, Prince Wilhem von Wied, as the new state's ruler but this inexperienced and weak man never succeeded in establishing his authority in the country, which slid into anarchy during the First World War. Zogu's father, Xhemal Pasha, had subdued the entire territory of his tribe, the Mati, and was recognized as the ruler of lands which stretched from Krujë to the border of the other great warrior tribe of the north, the Catholic Mirdite. Upon Xhemal's premature death in 1908, Zogu was sent to Istanbul where he came under the influence of the Young Turks. He went to the officers' school in Monastir, also a Young Turk stronghold. He returned to the Mati an ambitious military man who had been exposed to modernizing ideas. His skills as a commander and organizer led to a rapid rise up the political ladder after he participated in the Congress of Lushnjë in 1920. This historic gathering reasserted Albanian sovereignty, particularly against Italian attempts to establish a colonial protectorate in the country. Later that year, the Italians evacuated the port of Valona and gave up their goal of seizing Albania – for the moment.

Zogu was quick to appreciate the expulsion of the Italians in 1920 and realized that divisions among Albanians were often healed by external threat. Albania's isolation in the world had produced a proud xenophobia, especially among the northerners, which proved a real asset when President Zogu began building his centralized state from 1925 onwards. But the President understood that this patriotism had drawbacks as well. Permanent resistance to his rule came from the Albanians of Kosovo, whose paramilitary forces were organized by two of the most determined fighters, Bajram Curri and Hasan Bey Prishtina. After Zogu was defeated by Fan Noli in the *coup* of June 1924, he fled to Yugoslavia where the government supported his military build-up in the hope of securing influence in Albania after Zogu's return to power. To ensure this support, Zogu had no choice but to deny the Kosovo Albanians their aspirations.

On his return to power, the hostility between the Kosovars and Zogu continued. But the President's political motivation for opposing the Kosovars had changed. Indeed, to the dismay of the Yugoslavs, Zogu was flirting with Rome. Zogu repudiated the Kosovars because he found it difficult enough to establish a stable state within Albania's borders, and the notion of an irredentist struggle in Kosovo, Montenegro, Macedonia or northern Greece was simply indefensible. The President barely had sufficient resources to keep Albania together let alone attempt to expand his power at the expense of states with much more effective armies. Instead, he played off his neighbours one against another whenever he could.

In one of the most dramatic blood feuds of his reign, an insult to family honour, thwarted political ambition and Italy's imperialist machinations in Albania became tangled in a knot of intrigue and murder. In October 1927, the President dispatched his brother-in-law, Ceno Bey, to Prague as the first Albanian minister to Czechoslovakia. Ceno Bey was assassinated within days of his arrival, and during the trial in the Czechoslovak capital the assassin was himself assassinated. Ceno was a vocal sympathizer of Belgrade and Zogu surmised that the Italians were in fact behind his murder. At the time, the Italians were attempting to exert pressure on Zogu to force him to bow to their demands for ever greater control over Albania's army. Ceno's death was a warning. The President suspected that Rome had instigated this latest round of feuding in collaboration with the clan chief from the Elbasan region, south-east of Tirana, Shefqet Bey Vërlaci. Vërlaci was an influential former Prime Minister. He was also Zogu's prospective father-in-law. Despite this, the President was convinced that Vërlaci was out to kill him. So Zogu decided to pre-empt the whole issue by sending an infantry unit to eliminate Vërlaci. In this way, Ceno's murder would be avenged; the Italians would lose their stooge; the marriage would be off (he had been looking for a way out); and his strong-man image would be greatly enhanced. Unfortunately, although two of Vërlaci's retainers were killed, Vërlaci himself survived, thus adding yet another unforgiving member to the long list of people who wanted Zogu dead.

But despite repeated attempts to unseat Zogu, by 1928, when he was finally able to persuade a sceptical international community that he should be enthroned as King Zog I, the President could legitimately claim that he had brought a semblance of political and even some economic coherence to the country. Under his rule, there was a steady decline in brigandage; and a measure of law and order as well as functioning administrative structures were introduced. Modest economic stability persuaded villagers to return to farming in preference to living off robbery. But the cost of maintaining this system and of extinguishing the merest flicker of opposition to Zogu's rule was very high.

The rocks of Caesar: Albania

> I am opposed to the policy in Albania since I do not see the point in risking such a venture in order to grab a few rocks.
>
> King Victor Emmanuel on learning of Count Ciano's plan to invade Albania in 1939[19]

Benito Mussolini was not especially bothered by foreign affairs during his rise to power. In contrast to the Nazis who were obsessed with the Versailles Treaty as the *Dolchstoß*, or 'knife-in-the-back', Italian fascism did not feed on any real or supposed conspiracies hatched by Jews, Bolsheviks, or the French and British establishments. Instead, it focused on the chaotic degeneration of Italian politics and society.

Mussolini's interest in foreign policy was first stimulated by a group of nationalist intellectuals who joined the great circus of sycophants surrounding the fascist leader after he came to power in 1922. They persuaded him that for Italy to be truly great it was not sufficient to purge Italian society. The revolutionary credo of fascism, they argued, needed to find an external expression so that Italy's status as a great power would no longer be in doubt. The establishment of Empire would not only allow fascism to glow in the resurrected light of Caesar's dominions, it would restore the Mediterranean to its rightful place as *mare nostrum*. Hitler's plans for expansion and conquest in the East were the fruit of unbridled racism and a perverted social Darwinist ideology. Italy's empire was born of fatuous vanity.

Mussolini's imperial ambitions focused on Albania and Ethiopia. Italy's erratic army had been humiliated in both countries. In 1896, the Italians were defeated by the Abyssinians at Adowa; and in 1920 a few thousand disorganized but fiercely patriotic Albanians had driven Italy out of Valona (Vlorë). If there was a single thread running through the fabric of Mussolini's imperial ambitions it was the need to restore Italy's honour. What they lacked, however, was any systematic planning, strategic or tactical. Had the government in Rome restricted its penetration of the Balkans to Albania, dominating all access to the Adriatic, such a policy could conceivably have furthered Rome's more extravagant goals. These included establishing control over the Mediterranean and 'civilizing the dark continent' (the widespread use of mustard gas and the roasting alive of Ethiopians became an integral part of this mission to civilize) by creating an Italian imperial belt in north Africa from the Horn to the Atlantic coast.

But Mussolini was not satisfied simply to dominate the Albanian coast and seal the Otranto Straits – he was determined to become the arbiter of the Balkans. He planned to squeeze Yugoslavia by forging pacts with its neighbours, most importantly Albania, Bulgaria and Hungary; then, in the late 1920s and early 1930s, by sponsoring terrorist training camps for VMRO (the Internal Macedonian Revolutionary Organization) and the extreme Croat nationalists, the Ustaše (Rebels) formed by the lawyer Ante Pavelić, who fled Yugoslavia after Aleksandar imposed his royal dictatorship in 1929. But no country excited Mussolini's competitive imperial spirit more than Germany. After the Nazi seizure of power in 1933, the Italian dictator's feelings towards Hitler and Germany's reawakening ambition were a complicated mix of fear, admiration and jealousy, and found expression in Mussolini's patronizing behaviour towards the Führer. Hitler's refusal to defer to Mussolini as fascism's elder statesman intensified the Italian's jealousy. His pride wounded, il Duce made his displeasure known by guaranteeing Austria against *Anschluß* by the Nazis, and trying to ensure that south-eastern Europe remained an Italian domain. The Balkans, Mussolini insisted, were now irrevocably Italian and must not be allowed to fall under German influence.

In the 1920s, Albania had been an ideal starting point for Mussolini's Balkan adventure. It was close at hand; the Italian army actually knew the terrain. The locals were divided and their many factions easily bribed. Mussolini decided he could buy Albania and its oil and mineral reserves, before expelling the Albanian peasantry from the fertile regions of the country in the centre, the south and along the coast and replacing them with Italian colonists. President Zogu, however, posed something of a problem. For although on regaining power in December 1924 he had expressed a desire for friendly relations with all his neighbours, he owed his success in bringing down the Fan Noli régime entirely to military backing provided by the Yugoslavs. Mussolini had to assume that Zogu was in hock to Belgrade, but he also knew that the Albanian President could appeal to the British for diplomatic support when under pressure from the Italians, the Yugoslavs or the Greeks.

In September 1926, Austen Chamberlain was cruising the Mediterranean in a luxury yacht accompanied by his wife and son. Mussolini invited the British Foreign Secretary to join him for a few days in the Tuscan port of Livorno. Chamberlain hoped to thrash out various diplomatic problems, including Mussolini's concern that Sir Harry Eyres, the British consul in Tirana, exercised undue influence over Zogu and that he was undermining Italy's natural primacy in Albania. Chamberlain had, in fact, recently admitted to finding tiresome the increasingly byzantine telegram traffic from his man in Tirana, warning specifically of Italy's growing military presence in the country. Now Chamberlain could lay the matter to rest. He assured Mussolini that Britain had only economic interests in Albania and these had been correctly regulated by the

Italian–English Petroleum Agreement. 'Should the need arise to discuss any other matters [regarding Albania]', Chamberlain wrote in a clear snub to Harry Eyres just before his encounter with Mussolini, 'then I wish to speak directly with Rome without having to go through Durazzo.'[20] Evidently, Chamberlain's advisers had neglected to inform him that Albania's capital had long been transferred from Durazzo (Durrës) to Tirana. But in light of the Foreign Secretary's decision to allow Rome to represent Albania's interests (without, of course, consulting the Albanians), this oversight was rendered unimportant.

Chamberlain, who had just been honoured with the Nobel Peace Prize, got on well with his host in Livorno. 'In his heart of hearts', Mussolini noted in his diary, 'Chamberlain is something of a fascist sympathizer.'[21] Like several leading Conservative politicians, including Winston Churchill, Chamberlain approved of Mussolini's authoritarian political programme as a bulwark against bolshevism in southern Europe. After several pleasant days together, Mussolini waved goodbye to his visitors. He noted with especial pleasure that Chamberlain's wife and son were sporting the fascist insignia they had received as gifts. As their boat pulled out of the harbour, they raised their arms in the fascist salute. Mussolini had made some influential friends and been given a free hand in Albania by the British.

Military action in Albania was not necessary. Zogu's Achilles' heel was money. Creating a state was proving an expensive business, especially since the President diverted over 50 per cent of the country's paltry income into the police and army. There were other expenses – the loyalty of Zogu's entourage was won almost exclusively by bribes. For three years, as Zogu expanded his power over the Albanian state, he registered some impressive achievements. To establish the authority of the police, he gathered in tens of thousands of guns from villagers, quite remarkable in a society where for most men weapons were an essential part of daily life. He also founded primary schools throughout the country, a task made difficult not merely because of a shortage of funds but because Albania suffered a chronic lack of teachers. The contours of a state began to take shape. Yet this could not compensate for the appalling economic difficulties facing the country: 'Even by Balkan criteria', one Albanian historian has written,

> the Albanian people had very low living standards: poor hygiene and nutrition and the total lack of preventive medicine left the door open to the ravages of epidemics and disease, particularly malaria in the lowland and marshy areas. There was no such thing as social security. Between 1927 and 1932 the budget of the General Directorate for Public Health varied between 519,000 and 592,000 gold francs a year. There were no medical schools, and the number of doctors, forty-four dentists, twenty-nine pharmacists and twenty-nine midwives, with a total of eleven hospitals, only three of which had modern equipment. The standard of living remained woefully inadequate.[22]

In 1927, the per capita national income stood at a mere $40 which was half the average of all other Balkan countries. It did not take much taxation to try the patience of the Albanian peasant, and he would feel particularly inclined to resist the state if he was protected by a strong regional tribe. Zogu's investment in government buildings in Tirana gave the capital a certain neo-classical grandeur, but the extravagance aggravated Albanians in other regions who harboured economic or tribal grievances against the President. In November 1926, a serious anti-Zogu uprising broke out in the north of the country at a time when the President was approaching bankruptcy. He was obliged to turn to Rome for help.

The Italian government had won control of Albania's fiscal policy two and a half years earlier, in 1924, when the Società per lo Svillupo Economico dell'Albania (SVEA) was founded in Rome. This became Albania's currency-issuing bank, and the Albanian government was supposed to hold the controlling interest; because Tirana did not have sufficient funds, the Italians swept in and provided enough initial capital to take a 53 per cent holding. The bank was located in Rome and was run by a board consisting of three Italians and two Albanians. All of Albania's gold reserves were transferred to the Italian capital. The SVEA issued loans for infrastructural projects in Albania and significant sums were paid out for bridge and road construction, land reclamation (like Greece, Albania suffered from a chronic incidence of malaria) and public buildings:

> On the surface these [projects] seem to indicate that the Italians might have done some good with their money, but on closer

> examination it becomes clear that Albanian priorities were rarely considered. The roads were constructed not according to the needs of Albanian transportation and communications. As with the bridges, they were built for Italian military purposes, primarily in the direction of the Greek and Yugoslav borders.[23]

With Italy's grip on Albania's money supply now firm, Mussolini exploited Zogu's plight in November 1926, when he had to face rebellion in the north, by taking control of Albanian foreign policy. The initial price for Zogu's servitude was around 20 million lire, of which three-quarters went into the President's pocket. Large areas of the national economy had seemingly merged with the President's personal budget. In exchange, Italy persuaded Zogu to sign the friendship and cooperation treaty known as the First Pact of Tirana. Article 2 effectively signed away all Tirana's rights to an independent foreign policy: 'To safeguard the above-mentioned interest, the High Contracting Parties undertake to give their mutual support and cordial collaboration. They likewise undertake not to conclude with other powers political or military agreements prejudicial to the interests of the other Party as defined in the present Pact.'[24]

Momcilo Ninčić, at the time Foreign Minister in Belgrade and one of the few outstandingly competent interwar politicians in Yugoslavia, handed in his resignation as soon as he read the treaty. His admirable efforts to resist the emergence of axes binding great powers to local Balkan countries were ruined with this one step. It was apparent to Ninčić that this was the beginning of an Italian campaign to assert Rome's authority over the region. For his part, Mussolini was satisfied that Article 2 gave him an absolute right of veto over Albania's actions on the world stage – the country was now effectively a protectorate. He had not, it should be noted, calculated the long-term cost of propping up Zogu (Article 1 had stipulated that 'any disturbance directed against the political, judicial and territorial *status quo* of Albania is opposed to their reciprocal political interest'). In the following years, Italy would pour millions of dollars down the black hole of Zogu's greed. This was money which Rome could ill afford: as expensive protectorates go, Albania had precious little of economic interest to offer in return. It did have real strategic advantages, however, and for this reason

Mussolini persisted. In November 1927, exactly a year after the First Pact of Tirana was concluded, he seized on Zogu's renewed financial difficulties by insisting on the Second Pact of Tirana. Italian officers and military supplies began streaming into the country. All key units of the Albanian army now fell under direct Italian command. The offices of the Chief of Staff became no more than a regional headquarters of the Italian army, while the Albanian government was 'persuaded' to purchase large amounts of Italian weaponry. In exchange for handing over the keys to the guard room, the Italians approved Zogu's transformation into Zog I, *Mbret të Shquiptarvet* – King Zog I of the Albanians (1928–39).

It was perhaps fortunate for Zog that his decision to sell out Albanian sovereignty occurred just before the Wall Street Crash of 1929. Responsibility for the stability of Albania now rested as much with Rome as it did with the King. Henceforth, Zog steadily discarded what idealism he had cherished in the 1920s and permitted the Italians to do more or less what they wished with the country. Within tight confines, he asserted Albanian independence where he could but was always prepared to be bought off for further gifts of cash. For their part, the Italians ensured that Zog was no longer seriously threatened by the many unhappy Albanians living under his rule.

The scissors of Wall Street

If I had a little shop in Struga

'A craft is golden . . .'
Macedonian proverb

1.
Burning, our strength is burning,
Burning and ashes are forming!
Just don't awaken the pain
Of our good, old craftsmen.

The hard times have come,
Even harder ones await,
Every day souls are dying
Or ageing before their time.

The markets are dying out,
The shops now stand empty –
All is collapsed, all is ruins,
Craft, so golden, is rusting!

Kočo Racin,
Macedonian poet, 1939[25]

During the Great War, with the grain-growing fields of the old continent otherwise engaged, wheat producers in the United States, Canada, Australia and Argentina stepped in to fill the gap. When the peasants of eastern Europe and the Balkans were finally able to start harvesting properly again in the early 1920s, they were faced with a problem whose causes they could not immediately grasp: the world was awash with wheat and other agricultural goods and, try as they might, they could not secure decent prices for their crops or livestock. Some peasants in Yugoslavia, Bulgaria and Greece diversified into tobacco and soft fruit, for example, though these, too, suffered from declining prices in the second half of the decade. The impact of this shift in global agricultural patterns on the Balkans can scarcely be overestimated. In the interwar period, agriculture accounted for 90 per cent of exports from the region. Yet because of the hugely expanded production elsewhere in the world, the Balkan states found that their exports generated substantially less income than they had before the war.

In the three and a half decades which separated the Berlin Congress of 1878 and the Balkan Wars, the regional elites failed to lay the foundations of a sustainable industrial base. Investment was channelled into the military, a bloated civil service, and into the construction of architectural white elephants, usually in the capital city, in order to project an image of modernization. Amongst the palaces and barracks were marks of real progress – street lighting, municipal transport, sewage systems, not to mention new cinemas and shops that brightened Athens, Belgrade, Bucharest and Sofia. But the cost of these blossoming cities was borne by the peasantry which, overtaxed and underemployed, rarely benefited from them. Nonetheless, peasant culture played an important role in the economy of urban areas. The strong family ties that people maintained when they emigrated from the countryside had an impact on economic culture which is still very noticeable today in most Balkan countries (especially in Greece and Turkey, which did not suffer the distortion of Soviet planned economies): Balkan businessmen often shy away from large enterprises, preferring the unambitious security a small shop offers them. In the 1920s, small businesses competed against one another. In western Europe and the United States, however, ever larger conglomerates were producing industrial goods ever more cheaply with ever more sophisticated technology. During the boom from 1925 to 1928 which preceded the Wall Street Crash of October 1929, the relative backwardness of the Balkan economies was actually increasing.

In an attempt to offset the decline in national income, Balkan states turned to the international money markets and started to borrow, often recklessly, less to support the development of industry than to keep their modest current accounts from going too far into the red. By the end of the 1920s, one economic historian has claimed that 'foreign capital accounted for 50–70 per cent of the financing of the economies . . . Foreign participation was even higher in Bulgaria and Yugoslavia: in the former case 72.3 per cent of the national debt and 48 per cent of equity capital was owned by foreigners, while for Yugoslavia the respective shares were 82.5 and 44 per cent.'[26]

Before the war, the bulk of trade in eastern Europe and the Balkans had taken place within the large empires. But after the collapse of these empires and the Revolution in Russia, many of the old markets simply disappeared. The new states found they were competing with one another. As a consequence, they were compelled to reroute their trading relations westwards. They began servicing the agricultural and, increasingly, the mineral requirements of Germany, France, Britain and Italy. In return, they imported manufactured goods whose quality and relatively low prices inhibited the development of industry in the Balkans. After the war, the Balkans were much more tightly integrated into the global economy, without possessing the skills or resources needed to survive it. The peninsula soon found itself caught between the blades of the price scissors – a collapse in the value of its chief agricultural exports as the cost of industrial imports remained relatively high.

Black Thursday, 24 October 1929, hit the economies of the United States and western Europe like a gale-force wind. The stock market could no longer attract enough capital from new investors to underwrite the spectacular profits made by earlier investors, and the crash signalled the most devastating depression ever to affect the global economy. But the negative effects of the crash were not evenly distributed. Of the four largest capitalist economies, Britain, France, the United States and Germany, the first two fared notably better than the latter. In 1932, industrial production in France and Britain stood at 75.6 and 88.5 per cent respectively, set against the 1928 figure. In the United States, it was as low as 57.7 per cent while in Germany it had dipped to 54 per cent. Germany's vulnerability to economic collapse, Dieter Petzina writes, arose 'from the war and its consequences . . . The great inflation of 1920–23, coming after a wartime financial policy that had speculated on eventually loading the cost of the war onto defeated opponents, undermined the capacity and the will to save and limited the domestic accumulation of capital . . . [so] public and private undertakings resorted more and more to foreign capital after 1920.'[27] Most of that foreign capital, upon which the good name of Germany's banks rested, came from the United States. After Wall Street went down, American capital fled Germany, leading to an insolvency crisis in the German banking system. When the vote for Hitler's NSDAP (*Nationalsozialistische Deutsche Arbeiter Partei*) leapt tenfold in the elections of September 1930, most remaining holders of capital took fright and withdrew their funds.

The upturn in the Nazis' electoral fortunes was clearly the least desirable consequence of Germany's inability to cope with the Great Depression. But for the Balkans, the immediate consequences of the German banking crisis were also very grave. Most Balkan banks were funded and underwritten by German and Austrian banks (the Austrian banking collapse was even more shattering than the German). Germany was the most important trading partner in the region. When the Balkan economies began to buckle under the pressure of German failure, France, Britain and the United States made matters worse by blocking all capital credits to the area. It was thus left hopelessly indebted and with no means of paying from dwindling agricultural sales. The value of exports dropped by over 50 per cent everywhere so that the percentage of export revenue which had to be diverted to debt-servicing grew dramatically, reaching 36 per cent in Romania and Yugoslavia by 1931. Starvation stalked less fertile regions like Hercegovina and Dalmatia in Yugoslavia, Epirus in north-western Greece and parts of Moldavia and Wallachia in Romania. Belgrade received regular demands for assistance from local government officers in Bosnia and southern Croatia. These regions also issued repeated warnings that peasants were defaulting massively on their debts. Debt moratoria and exchange controls were eventually introduced to stop the worst effects but for three or four years, the Balkan countries became subsistence economies.

As we have seen, by the onset of the Great Depression two Balkan countries, Yugoslavia and Albania, had dispensed with parliamentary democracy in favour of royal dictatorships for peculiar political reasons. Electoral politics in Romania, Bulgaria and Greece during the 1920s had been crudely corrupted, occasionally suspended, punctuated by violence and often completely ineffective. But despite this and the grim economic outlook, democracy had survived. The impact of the Wall Street Crash on the Balkans via Germany proved a challenge too far for democracy. In quick succession, the landowners, civil servants and generals throughout the Balkans backed dictators, royal and republican, to ensure stability against the rising danger of peasant radicalism. Democracy would be barred from large swathes of the Balkans for the next six decades. More immediately, the Balkan countries had to seek help in order to restore some form of economic order. France, Britain and the United States withdrew into their shells. Germany, however, adopted a very different course. Hitler began to court the Balkans:

> Economic despair [in the Balkans] . . . prompted political radicalization . . . The political-economic myopia of the West, which had already been foreshadowed by France's earlier and persistent refusal to support her alliances in the area with adequate trade relations, virtually invited Nazi German penetration. Germany, in turn, did not intend to integrate East Central Europe into the world economy, but the reverse: she wished to tie it to her own and thus create a large and autarkic *Großraumwirtschaft* supplementing and facilitating her projected political and military conquest of Europe.[28]

In the 1930s, Germany identified the Balkans – or as they more often referred to it, *Südosteuropa* – as the cornerstone in a policy of economic expansion, the *Ergänzungswirtschaft*, which Hitler considered an essential prerequisite to his programme of European domination. In implementing this policy, the 'bloodless invasion', as one contemporary identified it, the Nazi leadership was confronted by a series of intricate political and economic puzzles which it needed to solve in order to gain access to the considerable agricultural and mineral resources of the region. From an initial position of weakness, Germany gained a little more strength and confidence each time it cracked one of these puzzles. Each German success inhibited the diplomatic freedom of movement of the Balkan countries, but some of the royal dictators were willing victims of Nazi statecraft.

King Aleksandar of Yugoslavia

On 6 January 1929, Aleksandar seized power in Yugoslavia with the grudging blessing of most leading political figures in Slovenia, Croatia, Bosnia and Serbia. To his subjects, he presented the dictatorship as a necessary evil, unwillingly imposed. It was, he explained, a selfless act to prevent the tension provoked by Stjepan Radić's death from tearing the country apart. However, the King's first act as dictator was to rewrite the Law on the Protection of the State, which was draconian enough already. Undeniably, Aleksandar felt comfortable ruling with an iron rod. But he did not anticipate, or perhaps chose not to anticipate, just how forcefully the police would use the new law against political opponents.

Of the Balkan monarchs, Aleksandar and Zog were the only two indigenous rulers. Aleksandar was able to trace his lineage back to the Karadjordje who instigated the First Serbian Uprising in 1804. For a man who played such an important role in Serbian and Yugoslav history, it is surprising that he has never found a serious and impartial biographer. He spent a large part of his childhood in Swiss exile during the last years of the Obrenović dynasty, yet he often seemed in tune with ordinary people, with his penchant for earthy language. But King Aleksander unquestionably regarded himself as an aristocrat. Unfortunately, the thin-rimmed spectacles he always wore highlighted the contours of his sharply chiselled nose to give the impression of a calculating, scheming character. He was gifted with real political intelligence, but his psychological insecurity guaranteed the regular commission of errors.

Aleksandar had seen active service during the Balkan Wars and the Great War although he did not display any exceptional courage on the battlefront. He fancied himself as a behind-the-scenes strategist, a political soldier among the powerful, ambitious officer cliques. Early in his career, he came to rely upon one officer, Petar Živković, to such an extent that it was rumoured among Belgrade's *čaršija* (chattering classes, gossip-mongers) that the two men were lovers. As a young lieutenant, Živković had opened the oak gates to Belgrade's royal residence on the night in May 1903 when Apis and his co-conspirators stormed the palace and murdered King Aleksandar Obrenović and Queen Draga.* Later, Živković turned on Apis, and formed a counter-conspiracy to the Black Hand called the White Hand, which exerted considerable influence on the young Prince. Aleksandar participated in the conspiracy hatched against Apis at Salonika during the Great War which led to the trial and execution of the Black Hand's leader in 1917.

By the time he came to rule the Serbs, Croats and Slovenes in 1918, Aleksandar was an experienced politician. Unfortunately, his ungovernable cynicism was tempered only by sentimental ties to close friends like Živković who knew how to exploit the King's weaknesses. Živković's appointment as Prime Minister in January 1929 was greeted with undisguised dismay not only in Croatia but also in Serbia, Slovenia, Bosnia and Montenegro. Many said openly that if men like Živković were to administer the dictatorship there was little prospect of the King solving Yugoslavia's political crisis.

Aleksandar was well able to understand the profundity of the gap which separated Serbs and Croats – the central problem facing the state. He also understood that the great powers regarded Yugoslavia as the key to the geo-politics of the Balkans and that an intimate connection existed between domestic and foreign policy – when Yugoslavia appeared unstable, it invariably provoked diplomatic flurries in and between Paris, London, Rome and Berlin. The source of the King's personal frustration, which manifested itself in temper tantrums and rash decisions, lay in the realization that he did

* See chapter 3.

not have the political skills to solve the Serbo-Croat conflict, and therefore the instability of the state.

Yugoslavia, he was convinced, owed its existence to the heroism of the Serbian army in the Balkan Wars, during its retreat across Albania in the winter of 1915, and throughout the Macedonian campaign of the Great War. But in contrast to the shallow Greater Serbian counsellors who surrounded him, Aleksandar to his credit developed an appreciation and even an admiration for the Croats and Slovenes during the late 1920s and early 1930s. Two men played a particular role in his gradual awakening to the subtleties of the Croat question. One was Stjepan Radić, who Aleksandar grew to like and respect in the months before the Croat leader's death. The second was Ivan Meštrović, the internationally respected Croat sculptor, a fascinating man who moved gracefully and discreetly among artists, thinkers and politicians in Belgrade and Zagreb.

After the establishment of the royal dictatorship in 1929, Aleksandar came increasingly to rely on Meštrović as a patient listener. He also used the artist as a messenger and as a wise counsellor who gently nudged the King's political thought in the direction of a Yugoslavism based on the equality of its constituent nationalities and away from his assumption of Serbian superiority based on the mythology of military sacrifice. Meštrović never hid his conviction from the King that the dictatorship was a dangerous, blunt instrument and that Aleksandar should restore parliamentary democracy at the earliest opportunity. 'This close contact I had with the King', Meštrović noted in his memoirs, 'strengthened my belief that whatever his other character traits the King was a patriot such that he would have fought for his country like an ordinary soldier if somebody had deposed him . . . However I could see that he was not sure of his foundations, that he was anxious, nervous and perhaps overtired of continually thinking about the same thing.'[29]

That 'same thing' was the Croat question. After the imposition of the royal dictatorship, the Croat question became ever more intimately and ever more dangerously related to the issue of Italian–Yugoslav relations. In the two years prior to the dictatorship, Croat political parties had cooperated in an attempt to persuade the international community to pressurize Belgrade into giving Croatia much greater autonomy. A busy émigré network had developed, centred chiefly on former Habsburg officers based in Vienna. But

Mussolini and the Italian foreign ministry had begun to take a close interest in Croat affairs, especially when Italy's penetration of Albania and aggressive strategic interest in the eastern Adriatic littoral led to a deterioration in relations between Belgrade and Rome.

Several leading Croat politicians fled Yugoslavia in 1929 and sought refuge in neighbouring countries. Among these was Ante Pavelić, a successful lawyer, thirty-nine years old at the time, who, as the leading light of the Hrvatska Stranka Prava (Croatian Party of Rights), sat in Yugoslavia's parliament from 1921 as one of Zagreb's two members. He visited Bulgaria, where he made several public appearances with leading members of Vanche Mihailov's VMRO, the wing of the Internal Macedonian Revolutionary Organization which was committed to the violent overthrow of Yugoslav rule in Macedonia: 'We cannot fight against those forest bandits [Serbs/Yugoslavs] with a prayer book in our hands', Pavelić told large crowds of VMRO supporters in Vidin and Sofia. 'After the World War many believed that we would have peace . . . But what sort of peace is it when Croats and Macedonians are imprisoned? These two peoples were enslaved on the basis of a great lie – that Serbs live in Macedonia and Croatia and that the Macedonian people is Serbian . . . If we tie our hands and wait until the civilized world helps us, our grandchildren will die in slavery. If we wish to see our homeland free, we must unbind our hands and go into battle.'[30]

Pavelić's appeal for the violent overthrow of Yugoslavia and the secession of Croat lands led to a Belgrade court sentencing him to death *in absentia* on a charge of high treason. *Persona non grata* in Austria, Pavelić chose Italy as his place of exile. With the financial assistance of the Italian government, Pavelić set about the construction of two main training camps, one in Hungary, one in Italy, for his new organization, the UHRO (Ustaše – *Hrvatska Revolucionarna Organizacija*; Rebels – Croatian Revolutionary Organization). The Ustaše began to attract members from the émigré community in the Americas and from across western and central Europe, as well as disgruntled Croats from inside Yugoslavia.

On 23 March 1929, at around 8 o'clock in the evening, Toni Schlegel, the Croat editor of the pro-Yugoslav newspaper *Novosti*, and a personal friend of King Aleksandar, left his office in Zagreb's Masaryk Street. Walking past the elegant shop fronts on one of the city's most charming streets, Schlegel took a cab from the stand outside Zagreb's most popular meeting point, the Theatre Café. Marko Hranilović, a member of the recently formed *Hrvatski domobran* (Croatian Home Guard), jumped into the next taxi and followed him home. When Schlegel reached his front door at Prilaz No. 86, Hranilović leaped out of the taxi and drew his revolver. Before he could fire, however, one of his two co-conspirators who had been waiting at the flat gunned Schlegel down. The hit team succeeded in killing two policemen before Hranilović was finally taken into custody. His two co-conspirators escaped but, under interrogation, he revealed their names and Pavelić's role in the killing.

The Ustaše thus opened a bombing and shooting campaign which met with a ferocious response from the régime. The Croat writer, Josip Horvat, has vividly described the cruelties that followed:

> The death of Schlegel became a pretext for [state] terror in all forms. Politics was soon indistinguishable from gangsterism. Legal authority was regularly pushed aside while in its place came the secret police, the military police, the court police, the police of influential individuals with their own gang of informers, agent provocateurs – all with teams of torturers versed in the practices of the Spanish Inquisition and the methods of the tsarist Ochrana . . . Bedković [the chief of the Zagreb police] was himself a clinically pathological sadist . . . He would personally torture victims, above all women, at night and then, having changed his blood-bespattered clothes for a clean dinner jacket, would attend high society dinners until dawn when he would find a church and confess his sins as a torturer (he would, of course, receive absolution) and then start the whole process again the next afternoon.[31]

Aleksandar's police also began arresting leading members of most political parties in Croatia, including the local Serb leader, Svetozar Pribičević, and Radić's successor as head of the Croatian Peasant Party, Vladko Maček. The Communist Party of Yugoslavia was especially badly hit and sank still deeper into conspiracy. The atmosphere of terror, perpetrated both by the state and by the Ustaše, once again cast a long shadow over Zagreb. Far from cleansing the bad air in Yugoslavia, the dictatorship had poisoned relations between Serbs and Croats.

Mussolini continued to back the Ustaše camps. He told a French diplomat in Rome that 'Yugoslavia does not exist. It is a heterogeneous conglomerate which you cobbled together in Paris.'[32] The country, he was fond of repeating, teetered on the verge of collapse. The violence that stained the first three years of the royal dictatorship convinced him that it was only a matter of time before Yugoslavia ceased to exist. And when that happened, Mussolini wanted to be sure that he would exercise control over Greater Croatia which he felt certain would emerge from the ashes.

In the early years, the Ustaše was an extremely small organization. It was not conceived as a mass movement but as a cadre organization whose central goal was to provoke instability through violence. Those who joined the camps were supposedly members of an elite fighting force, numbering some 600 by the beginning of 1934. Dressed in a grey uniform, they sported caps which ironically resembled the *šajkača*, the Serb military cap. The cap had, however, been specially designed so that it could cover the soldier's face. Sewn on to each cap was a metal 'U' for Ustaše.

Many of the Ustaše leadership came from the petty-bourgeois milieu of Zagreb and the Zagorje hinterland. But its foot soldiers were more likely to be students or workers and peasants from the poorer areas of Croatia, especially the Dalmatian hinterland, Kordun, Banija, Lika and western Hercegovina. The peasantry was central to the extreme nationalist/fascist philosophy of the Ustaše. Paragraph 12 of the *Principles of the Ustaše Movement*, published by Pavelić in June 1933, asserted that:

> The peasantry is not just the base and source of our life but alone contains the essence of the Croatian people and is, as such, the executive of all state power in the Croatian state. In the final analysis, all estates of the Croatian people make up a single national whole since the members of all estates boasting Croatian blood not only have their roots and origin in the village but permanent familial relations there. Ninety out of one hundred of those in Croatia who do not hail from the village are neither of Croatian origin nor blood but foreign immigrants.[33]

Pavelić's obsession with the peasant is only partly explained by the romanticism that underpinned Ustaše ideology. It was also necessary for recruitment purposes, reflecting the revolutionary potential of the impoverished peasantry. Lika and western Hercegovina proved to be the strongholds of the Ustaše because these were the areas where the poorest and most desperate Croat peasants lived. These were also the only areas (together with Macedonia) where Aleksandar's police acted with no restraining authority whatsoever. This state violence, usually executed by Serb policemen, ensured that these regions became hotbeds of Croat separatism, with many armed incidents between the police and Ustaše supporters during the early 1930s. The Communist Party of Yugoslavia was convinced at first that the Ustaše movement was progressive and should be cultivated as a political ally. 'The Communists cited economic reasons for the rebellions: hunger, poverty, and terror of the régime', observed one Yugoslav historian, adding, however, that 'the Party recognized that national oppression was a contributing cause. The *Proleter* [Communist Party newspaper] announced in December 1932:

> The Communist Party salutes the Ustasha movement of the peasants of Lika and Dalmatia and fully backs them. It is the duty of all Communist organizations and of every Communist to help this movement, to organize it and to lead it. At the same time the Communist party points out this movement's present shortcomings and mistakes, which can be explained by the fact that a considerable role is played by Croatian fascist elements . . . who have no interest in developing a broad mass movement against Serbian dictatorship; they fear that such a movement might turn out to be not only against the Yugoslav dictatorship, but also against their own Italian masters.'[34]

What neither the Communist Party nor the Ustaše knew was that the 'Italian masters' were holding secret talks in the early 1930s with Aleksandar. The King was extremely keen to mend his fences with Mussolini as the impact of the Great Depression worsened national and social unrest in the country. Aleksandar needed Mussolini's help in order to throttle Ustaše activity, in order to revive Yugoslavia's foreign trade, and because France, Belgrade's long-standing ally, had initiated a rapprochement with Italy and was pressurizing Aleksandar to do the same. When, however, in

December 1933, a plot was uncovered to assassinate the King in Zagreb on his birthday, Aleksandar broke off all negotiations with the Italians. 'Yesterday, I received a letter from Mussolini', he screamed in a great fury to Meštrović, 'in which he assured me of his best intentions for the establishment of friendly relations, so now on the one hand he sends me a letter, and on the other, at the same time, he sends assassins to kill me!'[35] Less than a year later, in October 1934, on his arrival in Marseilles for a state visit, Aleksandar was indeed assassinated. The operation, which also killed the French Foreign Minister, Louis Barthou, was the most sensational and unsettling event that year in Europe. The murders were organized by Vanche Mihailov's VMRO (the actual assassin was Mihailov's chauffeur) and Pavelić's Ustaše. While there is no conclusive evidence of Italian government involvement in Aleksandar's murder, Rome had made no attempt to curb Ustaše terrorism.

Yet the two years prior to Aleksandar's death had witnessed a remarkable development. Mussolini's main international rival was now not France but Nazi Germany. Soon after Hitler came to power in January 1933, the German Foreign Ministry elaborated a plan for the expansion of German influence into south-eastern Europe. Two countries, Yugoslavia and Romania, were identified as key to the success of Germany's strategy. The policy had both a political and an economic purpose.

On the political front, Hitler was disturbed by the defence pact signed by the leaders of the Little Entente, Czechoslovakia, Yugoslavia and Romania, in February 1933. By improving Germany's relations with Belgrade and Bucharest, he hoped to drive a wedge between them, on the one hand, and Prague, on the other, which would help to isolate Czechoslovakia, a country on which Hitler had lethal designs.

On the economic front, closer ties with Yugoslavia and Romania (and, indeed, Bulgaria, Greece and Turkey) would provide Germany with the agricultural and mineral resources it needed for rearmament and, ultimately, a policy of imperialist expansion in Europe. In order to succeed, Germany had to combat Mussolini's policy of encouraging the destruction of Yugoslavia, which the German Foreign Ministry and Chancellery believed was essentially healthy. Aleksandar responded positively to German overtures and, in the summer of 1933, Berlin sent a team of agricultural experts to

Yugoslavia to discuss the possibility of shifting agricultural production away from crops like wheat, which Germany did not need, to rapeseed, soya and other oil-producing plants. Over the next year, the Yugoslavs agreed to offer Germany exclusive access to key mineral products – primarily copper, lead, zinc and bauxite, all useful in the armaments industry. In exchange, Germany agreed to supply Yugoslavia with finished industrial products on a clearing system, a form of barter. In this way, the Yugoslavs (who were encountering tremendous difficulty raising loans in Britain, France and the United States) would not have to find large amounts of capital in order to revitalize their exports.

Germany also offered Yugoslavia diplomatic support. At Aleksandar's funeral in Belgrade, Germany was represented by Hermann Göring who, together with another leading Nazi, Alfred Rosenberg, was responsible for coordinating the German push into south-eastern Europe. 'Germany will never support any activity', Göring announced, 'that aims at the break-up of Yugoslavia.'[36] And, indeed, as Germany grew in strength, attaining first equality with Italy and then superiority over it, the Nazis successfully pressurized Rome into withdrawing its support for the Ustaše and, further, into shifting its attention away from the Balkans and towards Africa instead. Under the regency of Prince Pavle and his proto-fascist Prime Minister, Milan Stojadinović, the ties binding Serb-dominated Yugoslavia and Germany would grow even stronger. The Nazi penetration of the Balkans had begun.

Tsar Boris of Bulgaria

On 18 September 1933, the Orient Express pulled into Belgrade. Out stepped Tsar Boris III of Bulgaria to be greeted rather coldly by Aleksandar who, in diplomatic language, was 'by chance' strolling around the railway station. Queen Giovanna, Boris's wife and the daughter of the King of Italy, then leapt out from behind her husband and hugged the Yugoslav King warmly. 'Sandro!' she cried warmly, greeting her cousin, and for once Aleksandar's public aloofness yielded to a moment of genuine personal affection.

It was just as well that Giovanna broke the top layer of ice, as the two monarchs had a thick sheet to penetrate. Relations between Belgrade and Sofia had been cool from the Serbo-Bulgarian war of

1885* onwards, but the epic military confrontation between the two countries in the Second Balkan War and the Great War had left deep and unhealed scars. The Bulgarians felt greatly aggrieved by the Treaty of Neuilly which had confirmed Serbia's control of northern Macedonia (whose official title was now southern Serbia). The Treaty also forced Bulgaria to pay hefty reparations to its Slav neighbour in the form of annual coal deliveries. Boris's decision to initiate personal contact with Aleksandar was all the more courageous as it coincided with an attempt by the leaders of Romania, Turkey, Greece and Yugoslavia to forge an alliance, the Balkan Pact, which they eventually signed in February 1934. The Pact was clearly aimed at Bulgarian revisionism. Bulgaria had never officially repudiated its claims against all four neighbours – the southern Dobrudja (Romania), eastern Thrace (Turkey), western Thrace (Greece) and northern Macedonia (Yugoslavia).

For Belgrade, Bulgaria was home to the most persistently violent terrorist organization in the Balkans, VMRO, whose avowed aim was to seize control of Macedonia. Serb suspicions of Bulgaria had become even more acute since VMRO had extended the hand of friendship to Ante Pavelić and his Ustaše movement. Bulgaria had also established warm relations with Italy, where the Duce hoped to squeeze Yugoslavia by fashioning a pincer out of alliances with Bulgaria, Hungary and Albania.

Any thaw in the relationship between the two countries was almost certain to provoke rumblings of discontent in Serbia and Bulgaria; and so both Boris and Aleksandar approached their 'chance' meeting at Belgrade station with some trepidation. There was, however, a third party encouraging this rapprochement – Nazi Germany. Konstantin von Neurath, the German Foreign Minister, and Hitler himself pointed out in meetings with Boris that the Tsar and Aleksandar should cooperate as they faced common difficulties: both were fearful of Soviet intentions in the Balkans; there was growing political violence in their countries and a revival of agrarian and communist opposition to the established order as a consequence of the Great Depression. Yugoslavia and Bulgaria had both suffered from the scaling down of British and French economic interest in

* See chapter 3.

the Balkans. Where Aleksandar faced the problem of Croatian separatism, Boris had to contend with the murderous activities of VMRO and a rising political force, known as Zveno (The Link), which, although led by civilians, maintained close ties with influential figures in the illegal Military League. Boris was not greatly concerned about Zveno's corporatist authoritarian tendencies (which were, in any case, not too distant from his own political thinking); but he did fear the strongly republican sentiment of Zveno's membership.

Boris was pleased with the outcome of the meeting with Aleksandar, although it raised the spectre of confrontation with VMRO. In the previous three years, VMRO violence had spiralled out of control. Sofia witnessed hundreds of cold-blooded murders, bombings and shoot-outs. The worst culprit was Vlado Tchernozemski (aka Vlado the Chauffeur, who would become famous throughout the world a year later when he murdered Aleksandar). Most of these killings were fratricidal, for the two main VMRO groups, the Supremicists and the Federalists, were engaged in a war of mutual extermination. The first group, run by Vanche Mihailov, a young militant from Štip in Yugoslavia (now in the Republic of Macedonia), was reactionary and revisionist. Its programme aimed at seizing northern Macedonia from Yugoslavia and establishing a Greater Bulgaria. The second, weaker group, the Federalists, agitated for autonomy for Macedonia inside Yugoslavia. The Supremicists controlled Petrich, an entire region in south-western Bulgaria, levying taxes, running the administration and meting out 'punishment' to anybody whose face did not fit.

Balkan history and politics are often easier to understand than they might appear at first sight. But in the late 1920s and early 1930s, all political organisms in Bulgaria split into countless and bewildering factions. By 1933, some forty-four parties and splinters were operating inside the Sŭbranie, the national parliament. This coincided with the worst effects of the Great Depression and the most chaotic VMRO violence yet witnessed in Sofia. If it is legitimate to be baffled by just one historical episode in the Balkans, Bulgaria in the late 1920s and early 1930s must be one of the strongest contenders. But matters were about to become a little easier to grasp.

Until 1934, most parties had dismissed Tsar Boris as politically impotent. He was laughed off as 'The Man in the Fedora', an awkward, uncharismatic figure who was happier studying Alpine flowers or indulging his hobby of driving trains than attempting to run the country. The only task Boris consistently refused to carry out was signing death penalties as required by the constitution. His principled opposition to the death penalty was one of his most admirable and humane qualities.

He had to cope for a long time with an inferiority complex caused by his overbearing father, Tsar Ferdinand. Throughout Boris's reign, Ferdinand, who had been forced to abdicate at the end of the Great War, tried to interfere from his exile in Germany. The young Tsar was physically unprepossessing: he went prematurely bald and had a thin face whose perceptive grey-blue eyes were its only saving grace. Yet Boris had real intellectual gifts. He had a photographic memory, was fluent in French, German and Bulgarian and conversant in English, Albanian, Italian and Russian. On Saturday evenings, he would lay down the rhythm on drums accompanied by his sister, Princess Evdokia, on the piano and three aides-de-camp on violins and flugelhorn in the palace jazz combo. In contrast to Aleksander and King Carol II of Romania (1930–40), his charm and diplomatic skills left an excellent impression on political leaders throughout Europe. When the Tsar finally worked out how to apply his impressive wit to Bulgaria's conspiratorial political process, he proved himself an adroit and successful player. During the Great Depression, which affected Bulgaria later than other states in the Balkans, the Tsar began to develop real ambitions.

The breakthrough came in 1934. The government and the political parties in the Sŭbranie could not maintain order in the country. Zveno and its allies in the Military League decided that the time had come to dispense with parliamentary rule and to stage a showdown with VMRO. On 19 May 1934, they executed a bloodless political *coup*. The new power behind the throne was Damian Velchev, a Zvenarist who, as a colonel stationed in Sofia, had been sacked from the military for daring to criticize the 'butcher', General Vŭlkov, leader of the White Terror during the mid-1920s. Significantly, Velchev was anti-revisionist, a determined opponent of Mihailov's VMRO and an advocate of strengthened relations with Yugoslavia. For pragmatic reasons, Boris, too, did not consider revisionism a practical policy in the mid-1930s, but he was loath to spell out his policy in public: he still feared the strength of the revisionist camp, and almost certainly recognized that he himself might need to adopt revisionist policies in the future. His equivocal attitude to the question of borders left both camps, revisionist and anti-revisionist, suspecting that Boris opposed them.

Boris's objection to the Zveno régime was rooted not just in his fear of republicanism but in the fact that Zveno drew its key political support from the army. He was convinced that as long as the army felt able to intervene in Bulgarian politics at will, then the country would be unable to develop any coherent political structures. The Tsar's distrust of the military contrasted with King Aleksandar's belief that the army was the very essence of his power and of Yugoslav identity. But given the *fait accompli* of the February 1934 *coup*, Boris reluctantly accepted the new Zveno government as legitimate. Velchev declined any position in the Cabinet, preferring to run things behind the scenes, and his close associate, Kimon Georgiev, was appointed Prime Minister.

The Georgiev government offered a precious gift not just to Bulgaria but to the rest of the Balkans when, soon after taking office, it confronted Mihailov's VMRO. Within a matter of weeks, VMRO had been wiped out (although it was still capable of mounting a brief revival some years later). Petrich in south-western Bulgaria was liberated from VMRO control and Sofia's authority reestablished throughout the country. The Zveno régime was far from liberal: political parties were banned and corporatist organizations and structures fashioned to replace them; but while the régime was authoritarian, it was not vindictive. And catching the wind of the global economic revival, it started putting food back on the Bulgar table.

Before the year was out, however, Velchev was engaged in a complex struggle within Zveno and the Military League and, for the first time in his life, Boris took control of the state. After a transitional period, he appointed a prime minister in April 1935, dismissing any opposition to his choice. Zveno had done the dirty work of dismantling parliamentary rule and Boris was the one stable source of power left in the country. Significantly, the Tsar insisted that the Minister of War report to the monarch alone. He still did not trust the military, but at least he could now subject it to the closest scrutiny. In a dramatic departure from his constitutional role, he now made all Cabinet appointments and directed policy through his own prime ministers.

By the time Boris had become the unostentatious dictator of Bulgaria, Italian pressure on Bulgaria to subvert Yugoslavia had ceased. After the assassination of King Aleksandar, Hitler had successfully redirected the Duce's imperial urges away from the Balkans and towards his atrocious adventure in Abyssinia. Apart from its outpost in Albania, Italy had begun to lose interest in the Balkans. Hitler, on the other hand, maintained the most lively interest in the peninsula. The victory of non-revisionist forces in Bulgaria encouraged friendship between Yugoslavia and Bulgaria, which in turn greatly assisted communications within the Balkans and between the Balkans and the Third Reich.

In the mid-1930s, Hitler tested the strength of the Versailles order to destruction. In October 1933, Germany withdrew from the Conference on Disarmament and then from the League of Nations. In March 1935, Hitler signed the Law on Compulsory Military Service in Germany, thereby tearing up the Treaty of Versailles and preparing the way for the reoccupation and remilitarization of the Rhineland in 1936. The diffident response of Britain and France to German treaty violations was carefully monitored in south-eastern Europe.

Tsar Boris was fully aware of Bulgaria's expanding economic dependence on Germany when he took up the reins of power. Over 50 per cent of the goods imported into Bulgaria now originated in Germany, while just under half of Bulgaria's exports were sent to Germany in return. Boris personally intervened in London and Paris in the hope of persuading Britain and France to revitalize their economic contacts with Bulgaria. His pleas fell on deaf ears. American cultural influence led smokers in Britain away from the tobacco of the Balkans and the Near East to Virginia blends. As a result, the British minister in Sofia, George Rendel, recorded, 'the British tobacco companies lost interest in the Balkans . . . and were not prepared to risk the interest of their shareholders for political reasons'. As late as 1938, Rendel was desperately urging London to assist the Bulgarians in their attempts 'to escape from the steadily tightening German economic fetters'.[37] His appeals, like those of his colleagues in Belgrade and Bucharest, were ignored.

Boris was anxious to avoid a reprise of the German–Bulgarian relationship during the First World War when Berlin and the *Reichswehr* treated Bulgaria like a colony. Under the provisions of the Treaty of Neuilly, Bulgaria was all but defenceless, and the Tsar wished to build up the offensive capability of his army. As early as April 1935, Boris made a personal appeal to Germany to sell war materials to Bulgaria. This was forbidden under the Versailles Treaty. Hitler refused but added his regrets, explaining that the international situation was not yet propitious for the sale. Within just over a year, however, he had started selling weapons not only to Bulgaria, but also to the newly installed dictator of Greece, General Ioannis Metaxas, and to Yugoslavia and Turkey as well.

> Under the influence of German Nazis from the Reich and with the full support of Nazis and militarists from the [Balkan] countries, the discrepancy in trade between them and Germany was being gradually resolved by the supply of war material to south-eastern Europe. This poor-quality weaponry was accompanied by an army of advisers and instructors whose considerable influence revealed what role these military-industrial transactions played in the preparation of the political and military subordination of the region to the Third Reich.[38]

On 20 October 1936, Count Galeazzo Ciano, Mussolini's new Foreign Minister, opened discussions with senior German representatives about future cooperation between their two countries. On the 25th, an agreement between Italy and Germany was signed which Mussolini referred to in a speech a week later as the 'axis of the new Europe'. The Balkans were now hemmed in to the north and west by the Axis powers and, to the east, by Soviet Russia. In three years, south-eastern Europe had become massively dependent on the German economy. France and Britain seemed uninterested in the political and strategic implications of these changes. One country, however, was still energetically fighting off the Nazi embrace. In economic terms, Romania was Germany's biggest regional prize for one overwhelming reason – oil.

Carol II of Romania

If in Yugoslavia the monarch's spare time was occupied by pondering the insoluble problems of state and nationality, and in Bulgaria the unassuming Boris relaxed by playing drums or driving trains, the royal family in Romania liked to indulge in recreational sex. King Ferdinand, submissive husband to Queen Marie and hopeless father of an indeterminate number of children, was a master of what one diplomat referred to as 'indiscriminate fornication'.[39] Marie herself, granddaughter of both Queen Victoria and the Russian Tsar Alexander II, used her lovers as counsellors, bankers, intermediaries and confidants. Their son, Carol II, developed a similar appetite for sex as a teenager but he lacked his parents' discretion.

Before finally ascending the throne in June 1930 at the age of twenty-seven, Carol had twice renounced his right to it in perpetuity. In 1918, he eloped to Odessa with a young dancer, Zizi Lambrino, although his parents persuaded him both to annul the marriage and to retract his renunciation of the throne. Before his second gesture of princely denial, he married Princess Helen of Greece and sired an heir, Crown Prince Michael, and then, in 1926, ran off with Elena Lupescu, a glamorous *femme fatale* with innocent eyes and Titian hair.

Carol's lifelong relationship with Lupescu would mire the future King's career in tabloid farce. For four years before his return to Romania, the couple were hounded by newspaper journalists. When the story broke in 1926 that Carol was holed up in a 'love nest' in Milan, hacks and photographers from all over Europe and America camped outside his hotel, hoping for a snap or an interview. On more than one occasion, Carol and Elena left in disguise from the back of the hotel before speeding off in a car to avoid the photographers (who had yet to add the motorcycle to the tools of their trade). After moving to Paris, they embarked on an increasingly impecunious bourgeois existence in the fashionable suburb of Neuilly. Their affair was still generating cheap novels (the most successful was called *Au Pied du Trône*) and endless gossip-column inches.

After the death of his father, King Ferdinand, in 1927, Carol became restless. He started plotting his return to Romania and to the throne he had so hastily renounced. Although a Hohenzollern,

Carol's extravagant behaviour was more in keeping with the long-standing tradition of Romania's elite. Unlike Serbia, Bulgaria and Greece, where over the previous century most of the ruling class had emerged from the peasantry and the small merchant communities, Romania had its own aristocracy, the boyars, which had existed since Ottoman times. The boyars had fought hard to maintain their privileges and life style at the expense of the country's downtrodden peasantry. Their sons were usually educated in Germany and France and gravitated towards Bucharest and other cities where, together with the industrious sons of the Sephardic Jewry of Wallachia, they developed the foundations of Romanian industry and capitalism.

From France, Romania's elite imported a taste for good food and chic clothes. Two western writers, Olivia Manning and R.G. Waldeck (the pseudonym of the American journalist, Goldi Horowitz), have left minutely detailed descriptions of Bucharest's decadent atmosphere, the 'Paris of the East', on the eve of the Second World War. Harriet Pringle, Manning's autobiographical heroine, is stunned by her first visit to a garden restaurant:

> The heart of the display was a rosy bouquet of roasts, chops, steaks and fillets frilled round with a froth of cauliflowers. Heaped extravagantly about the centre were aubergines as big as melons, baskets of artichokes, small coral carrots, mushrooms, mountain raspberries, apricots, peaches, apples and grapes. On the one side there were French cheese; on the other tins of caviare, grey river fish in powdered ice, and lobsters and crayfish groping in dark waters. The poultry and game lay unsorted on the ground.
>
> 'Choose,' said Guy.

Women writers played an important part in fashioning western perceptions of the Balkans, particularly in the twentieth century. On her arrival in Bucharest in 1940, Waldeck immediately identified that women were treated much like food:

> I learned which cabinet minister was having an affair with what lady, what was the *specialité* of which cabinet minister, and what was the price of what lady. That every lady had a price was a foregone conclusion with the wicked old men, but only

> from 20,000 leis up did they consider her a lady. It was the same with the politicians; they also had a price, and if they were expensive enough they could be considered statesmen.[40]

Nowhere in the Balkans was the discrepancy between wealth and poverty so visible as in Romania. Four-fifths of the population were peasants eking out miserable lives from pitiful resources, suffering from chronic pellagra and skin disease due to monotonous diets and insanitary conditions, and sagging under the weight of indebtedness. The Liberal Party, which dominated politics until the late 1920s, was cynical in its treatment of the peasantry. 'The unhappy condition of the peasantry', argued their ideologue Stefan Zeletin, '[is] a necessary price to be paid for the building of capitalism in Rumania.'[41] Millions of Romanians did not share these economic values. The cornerstone of Liberal economic policy was a protectionism which provoked Romania's trading partners to impose tariffs on the country's agricultural produce. Pursuing an economic programme which ran counter to the material interests of an overwhelming majority of the population made for some awkward difficulties at election time. To tackle this, the Liberals devised a two-pronged system of gerrymandering – first, they introduced a law automatically conferring a parliamentary majority on any party which won 40 per cent of the vote; second, the Interior Minister used his police forces to guarantee the return of the party.

The elite was astonished when, in 1928, the Liberals did lose an election. Even their core supporters deserted them. For the first time, power was transferred to the National Peasant Party. The NPP was an amalgam of the old Peasant Party and the National Party of Transylvania, a coalition that fused the two great romantic symbols of Romania, the peasant and Transylvania, the territory won by Romania from the Hungarians at the Paris Peace Conference. In its leader, Iuliu Maniu, the NPP possessed another great electoral asset. Maniu's courageous opposition to Hungarian rule before 1919 had elevated him in the eyes of ordinary Romanians above the sordid self-serving cliques which ran the other parties. Above all else, Maniu was honest. He neither slept with young women, nor did he supplement his income with kickbacks. And for this reason, the Liberals found it extremely difficult to discredit him.

Carol II returned to Romania in 1930 as the Great Depression was beginning to destroy what little security the Romanian peasant had enjoyed. The NPP was finding the task of governing under such circumstances uncommonly difficult and most of its members now yearned for the return of the King. Here was a man, they believed, who could unify Romanians and put an end to their squabbling, rising above the squalid deals of Romanian politics. His arrival on 7 June 1930 caused a sensation in Bucharest.

Carol found considerably more political capital and goodwill at his disposal than he or anybody else had expected. Maniu himself had been apprehensive about the return of the King, and set but one condition: Elena Lupescu was to be banished from Romania. The King solemnly agreed to abide by his Prime Minister's demand. But Carol was not one to allow a promise to a politician to thwart his appetites, and Lupescu emerged from his luggage almost as soon as he had arrived.

The King installed his favourites at court and in key positions in the civil service. He also exploited the unstable political atmosphere of the Great Depression to encourage discord in the ranks of the political parties. The Liberals had opposed Carol's return and the King regarded them as his most dogged opponents. He began wooing influential figures in the Party and soon the leadership was riven with mistrust. This internecine battle also benefited the King by provoking the political break-up of the Brătianu family. The Brătianus had been the most powerful political dynasty in Romania for over half a century. But the godfather of the clan, Ion Brătianu, had died in 1927, leaving brothers and sons vying for influence inside the Liberal Party. Now convinced that Carol was a permanent fixture, Gheorghe Brătianu, Ion's son, broke ranks with his relations in early 1934, declaring his support for the King. By 1934 Carol had also successfully prised open an unbridgeable gap in the NPP, weakening Maniu as a national political figure. Within a short space of time, Carol had broken the tradition which saw powerful, charismatic individuals controlling entire political parties. Instead, all Carol's potential opponents were hindered by indecisive and fractious collective leaderships. Using his right to appoint the Prime Minister, Carol gradually detached the executive from the parliament. The Cabinet became ever more dependent on the King and less dependent on the electorate.

One leader and his movement refused to participate in the king's new system: Corneliu Zelea Codreanu, who both fascinated and repelled Carol. As the glamorous Codreanu's power grew, the King's own popularity began to wane; within months of his accepting the throne public hostility to Elena Lupescu and his inner circle, the camarilla began to make itself felt.

God's executioner: Romania

> The most beautiful aspect of Legionary life is death. The Legionary death has nothing in common with ordinary death. Through his death the Legionary becomes one with Eternity; through his death the Legionary becomes the earthly incarnation of history. He becomes a legend. The Legionary must not hesitate before death. Legionary death is dear to his heart; a goal is achieved through it; it becomes a symbol. The death of the Legionary is a symbol, a cult.
>
> Iron Guard newspaper[42]

An eight-year-old Hungarian Jewish lad, Miklós Nagy, was holidaying with relatives in a small village deep in the Apuşeni, the very heart of Transylvania's mountains. Miklós sat open-mouthed as he listened to local Hungarians talk of a man whom they described as the devil's envoy, sent to spread terror among the Hungarians 'of both the Christian and Mosaic' faiths. And now this fallen angel was due to arrive at the very village where he was staying. Miklós's best friend was a Romanian boy, four years older than him, and he agreed to supply Miklós with Romanian peasant garb so the two could sneak off the next morning to the local Orthodox church where the *Căptanul* (Captain) was due. The churchyard was packed when they arrived. The local prefect had banned Codreanu from speaking but, fearful of the peasants' reaction, had not actually forbidden the gathering. Suddenly, a hush gripped the company. Astride a giant white horse, wrapped in the traditional white costume of the Romanian peasant, 'a tall, darkly handsome man', appeared. 'Charisma is an inadequate word to define the strange force that emanated from this man', Nagy-Talavera later wrote. 'He was more aptly, simply part of the forests, of the mountains, of the storms on the snow-covered peaks of the Carpathians, and of the lakes and rivers. And so he stood amid the crowd, silently. He had no need to speak. His silence was eloquent; it seemed to be stronger than we, stronger than the order of the prefect who denied him speech. An old, white-haired peasant woman made the sign of the cross on her breast and whispered to us, "The emissary of the Archangel Michael!"'[43]

Codreanu was born into a mixed Romanian-Ukrainian-German family at the very end of the nineteenth century in Huşi, a small town south-west of Iaşi. His father, a secondary-school teacher, had romanized his name to Zelea from the Slav Zelinski and then added the name Codreanu (from the Romanian *codru* meaning 'forest') in honour of his father and grandfather who had been foresters. Throughout his life, Codreanu would seek the comfort of Romania's mountains and woods, sometimes withdrawing for weeks on end to a remote shepherd's hut. He grafted this near-pagan devotion to the soil on to an obsessive reverence for the Orthodox Church. After he had founded his tightly knit cadre organization, the Legion of the Archangel Michael, in 1927, he travelled to the fields where Romanians had once fallen in battle. Here he gathered earth, stained with the sacred blood of the Dacians. Each new member of the League would be presented with a small leather pouch filled with this soil, and swear to wear it next to his heart.

Two figures defined Codreanu's Manichean perception of the world – the Romanian peasant and the Jew. The one embodied all natural wisdom and held the key to salvation; the other was the agent of Satan. 'The Jews, the Jews, they are our curse', Codreanu told a British journalist. 'They poison our state, our life, our people. They demoralize our nation. They destroy our youth. They are the arch enemies . . . The Jews scheme and plot and plan to ruin our national life. We shall not allow this to happen. We, the Iron Guard, will stand in the way of such devilry. We shall destroy the Jews before they can destroy us.'[44]

Interwar Romania was home to Europe's most diverse Jewish population. While never accepted as Romanians, the Sephardic Jews of Wallachia were relatively well integrated, by dint of their concentration in towns and their established positions among the urban elite. They held pre-eminent positions in banking and heavy industry and made up a significant part of the proletariat, especially in textiles. They were traditionally well connected with the Jews of Germany, Austria and France – countries which together with Great Britain used international treaties in an attempt to compel Romania to guarantee equality for Jews. Although anti-Semitism was a peripheral phenomenon in Bucharest compared to other parts of the country, the Romanian state systematically denied citizenship to Jews on racial grounds, classifying them instead as 'foreigners'. Regardless of how long Jews had lived in Romania, they were denied certain basic rights and often had to battle for years to gain entrance to higher education.

The situation in Moldavia was very different. In the second half of the nineteenth century, tens of thousands of Ashkenazi peasants had fled there to escape Russian persecution. They were joined by a second massive influx when Bessarabia was incorporated at the end of the First World War. These Jews were triply disadvantaged. They lived in closed communities, many of them were Hasidic, and they spoke either Russian or Yiddish. They rarely learned Romanian. In this region, they also regularly filled the class gap, in their capacity as estate managers, between the landowners and the peasantry. For the peasants, they were the symbols of injustice; for the landowners, they were dispensable tools. These Russophone Bessarabian Jews were suspected of sympathy for the Soviet Union; and Romanian nationalists looked darkly on the high incidence of Jews in the Romanian Communist Party.

Romanians rightly suspected that the Jews of Transylvania were pro-Hungarian. Until the interwar period, the Hungarian Jews were usually well assimilated, obeying the logic of Hungarian nationalism which accepted most nationalities into its ranks as long as they recognized the superiority of Hungarian language and culture. The Jews of Transylvania, together with the Hungarian elite, were discriminated against after the area was transferred to Romania under the Treaty of Trianon at the end of the Great War.

Over 30 per cent of Iaşi's population was Jewish. In this city one of Europe's most virulent strains of anti-Semitism found a fertile culture in which to develop. The leading anti-Semite was Professor Alexandru Cuza, whose lectures inspired Codreanu as a young law student. Codreanu specialized in dramatic gestures, challenging authority over symbolic issues and organizing peasants and workers to engage communists and Jews in street fights. Early in his political career, Codreanu convinced himself that violence was a legitimate political instrument.

In 1930, Codreanu announced that the Legion of Archangel

Michael was to give birth to a new mass movement – the Garda de Fier or Iron Guard. In contrast to the Legion, which remained a conspiratorial cell-based network, the Iron Guard was to be a mass movement. To symbolize their peasant roots, members wore green shirts with a leather belt slashed diagonally across the front and embossed with a white cross on a black background. In the Great Depression, unemployed students and desperate peasants flocked to the ranks of the Iron Guard. Codreanu organized work brigades throughout Romania to build bridges and roads and help peasants to bring in the harvest. As Bucharest's politicians enriched themselves, the Iron Guard had by 1933 accumulated considerable support in the countryside of Moldavia and Transylvania, less for its anti-Semitism (although this was very important) than for the practical assistance it offered peasant communities.

Carol was rather attracted to the Iron Guard, although jealous of Codreanu's popularity. The King shared Codreanu's belief that Romanian democracy was rotten to the core. From 1932, however, his Foreign Minister, Nicolae Titulescu, and other leading Liberals urged him to see the Iron Guard as a mortal enemy. Carol allowed the arrest of several thousand members of the Guard.* Normally, such an exceptional act required a royal decree, but Carol would not sign it, hoping perhaps that Codreanu might remember this gesture gratefully in the future. But he did permit a ban on the Iron Guard by Cabinet decree. Three weeks later, the Prime Minister, Ion Duca, left the King's country retreat in a snowstorm to catch the train back to Bucharest. 'It was ten after he finally arrived at the station. With the exception of the Prime Minister's party the little station was practically deserted. As Duca bid his colleagues farewell, four shots from a revolver reverberated through the cold, crisp December air. One hit Duca in the base of his skull. He slumped to the ground, mortally wounded.' An Iron Guardist had assassinated the Prime Minster, the opening act in a bloody decade of Romanian history. And by this time, Adolf Hitler had become very interested in the squabble between King and *Căptanul*.

* According to official figures, it was 1,700, while Codreanu himself claimed it was 18,000. The truth almost certainly lies somewhere in between.

A rock and a hard place: Romania

Two German organizations were busy monitoring Romania's domestic, foreign and economic policies in the mid-1930s. One was the *Außenamt* (Foreign Office) in the Wilhelmstraße in Berlin, which had been partly subjected to the process of *Gleichschaltung** but the majority of whose officers remained bureaucratic civil servants. The second was the NSDAP's own Foreign Policy department headed by Alfred Rosenberg. Rosenberg exhibited great zeal in his mission as the bearer of the Nazi gospel around southern Europe. His agents had identified Alexandru Cuza, the old professor from Iaşi who had since broken with his protégé Codreanu, as Romania's most effective preacher of anti-Semitism and fascism. Another Rosenberg favourite was Octavian Goga, considered one of Romania's finest lyric poets and a vicious anti-Semite. Codreanu's activities were also closely observed, but after the Iron Guard was driven underground following Duca's murder, even the Nazis considered it politic to maintain their distance from Romania's most militant fascist group.

Rosenberg's most urgent desire was to see the Romanian Foreign Minister, Titulescu, removed from the Cabinet. Titulescu, who became Foreign Minister in 1932, was a curious man. Historians have variously described him as 'asiatic', 'ugly' and 'stubbornly peculiar'. Corrupt, vain and abnormally tall, Titulescu was nonetheless the Balkans' outstanding diplomat of the interwar period, a man who valued the preservation of peace above all else. Had he represented one of the great powers, he would be remembered as a progressive statesman. The minister travelled around Europe in his own custom-built railway carriage. A stream of orders to his subordinates and proposals to his counterparts issued from his train, all in the hope of securing maximum advantage from Romania's delicate position in the European order. Here the limitations were many and the possibilities few: Germany's primary strategic interest in Romania lay in its location as Russia's gateway to the Balkans – for Germany the country was thus the front-line defence against Russian penetration of south-eastern

* The fusing of NSDAP (*Nazionalsozialistische Deutsche Arbeiterpartei* – National Socialist German Workers' Party, the Nazis) functions with state functions.

Europe. Its location between Germany and Russia was Romania's great geographic misfortune, and although Bucharest tried to break out of it by developing strong cultural and commercial ties with France, in the circumstances of the 1930s the French could offer little protection.

Romania was also one of the three members of the Little Entente, together with Yugoslavia and Czechoslovakia. The Nazis had first wooed Yugoslavia's King Aleksandar and then, after his assassination, the Prince Regent, Pavle, and the Prime Minister, Milan Stojadinović, in order to isolate Czechoslovakia. They also attempted to undermine Romania's commitment to the Entente. Titulescu would have none of it. While not wishing to alienate the Nazis unnecessarily, he was a committed believer in Romania's traditional cultural, economic and security ties to France. He expressed vocal support for Czechoslovakia and the Little Entente whenever he could, and was also the most energetic mover behind the Balkan Pact of 1934 which sought to curb the revisionist demands of Bulgaria and Hungary. These East European alliances were prominent features of the security landscape between the wars, and were similarly flawed. The Little Entente (Czechoslovakia, Yugoslavia and Romania) was developed to block Hungary's determination to tear up the Treaty of Trianon, while the Balkan Pact (Yugoslavia, Romania, Greece and Turkey) was designed to thwart Bulgaria's revisionist demands. As a consequence, these pacts also locked Romania into the certainty of armed conflict should a revisionist great power (Germany, Italy or even the Soviet Union) decide to back Hungary or Bulgaria. Hence, both the Little Entente and the Balkan Pact suffered from the same defect: they were strong alliances against the weak and weak alliances against the strong.

Concerning the great powers, Titulescu most controversially established diplomatic ties with the Soviet Union. Hostility to both Russia and communism ran deep in Romania but, to feel secure, it needed to remain on good terms with Moscow (which refused to recognize Romanian sovereignty over Bessarabia and which also coveted Bukovina). At the same time, Titulescu also had to reassure Germany (which was vigilant against the emergence of a Franco–Russo–Little Entente alliance and sympathized with the revisionist dreams of Hungary and Bulgaria) as well as remind France that it had vital security interests in south-eastern Europe, centred on

Romania. Between 1932 and 1936, when Titulescu enjoyed the full support of Carol and his cabinets, Romania succeeded in balancing these difficult options.

In contrast to Alfred Rosenberg's ambitious operation to destabilize Titulescu's position in the Romanian government, the *Außenamt* was more sober in its assessment, especially given the very deep-rooted Francophilia of the Romanian elite. The Foreign Office was interested in political realities and possibilities, not Rosenberg's Nazi fantasies. So although Romania was clearly very important to German strategic pretensions, the Foreign Office knew that asserting its influence required subtlety and patience. 'There's not much in it for us politically down there', Foreign Minister, Freiherr Konstantin von Neurath, advised his new envoy to Bucharest, Dr Wilhelm Fabricius, so 'the main task' was the regulation of economic relations.[45] As elsewhere in eastern Europe, Germany enjoyed considerable success in penetrating the Romanian economy. Happy to absorb much of the country's agricultural surplus, the German government also persuaded Romania to enter into a long-term agreement with IG Farben* which put several hundred thousand hectares of wheatfields under soya beans and other oleaginous plants.

But the one industry that remained out of bounds for the Germans was the most important of all – the petroleum fields of southern Romania. The fifth-largest oil producer in the world at the time, Romania could sell oil at premium prices on the open market. Throughout the 1930s, successive Romanian governments not only restricted the amount of oil they were prepared to sell to Germany, they also prevented German enterprises from establishing a foothold in the industry, allowing British, French and American companies to maintain their dominance in partnership with the government.

Of all the south-east European countries, Romania put up the stiffest resistance to Germany's gradual monopolization of regional trade.* It was still notably less dependent on Germany than Yugoslavia, Bulgaria or even Greece in 1936 when Titulescu was

---

* A company later distinguished by its manufacture of Zyklon B of Auschwitz fame.

finally forced out of the government. His resignation was overshadowed by two much more significant events – the Wehrmacht's reoccupation of the Rhineland in March and the formation of the Axis pact in November. The era of Titulescu's Francophile balancing act was coming to an end.*

By now, Carol's political sights were set firmly on imposing a personal dictatorship, controlling both foreign and domestic policy without the irritation of a parliament. His ambition was stoked daily by the camarilla, which was now led by Lupescu and Carol's factotum, Colonel Ernest Urdăreanu. This officer, who was once responsible for the care of Carol's fleet of automobiles, fused in himself the character of Middleton's de Flores with that of Shakespeare's Iago. He suffered from chronic acne and wore a mask of powder and rouge over his pitted face. A short man with a silver plate in his head, he had, despite his bizarre physiognomy, a seductive charm and used it to bed countless women. In 1934, Lupescu became one of his easier conquests and, besotted with the man, she secured him a position as Carol's chief gatekeeper. He became the single most powerful man in Romania. Nobody could get close to the King without being approved by Urdăreanu, and the Colonel's services did not come cheap. 'Young [Crown Prince] Michael detested him and behind his father's back called him "Murdareanu,"' a play on the Romanian for 'shit'.[46]

The camarilla included industrialists, like Max Auşnit, Romania's iron and steel magnate, and bankers, like the country's richest, Aristide Blank, or the fabulously wealthy Nicolae Malaxa. These men were happy to bankroll the extravagance of the court, for in exchange they could control economic policy. Carol's drift towards dictatorship was determined as much by these individuals' economic interests as it was by a desire to adopt the paraphernalia of fascism which was so *en vogue* in Europe at the time. His intimates privileged industry over agriculture. 'Clearly such a policy was exposed to opposition from an electorate consisting largely of peasants – if the representative parliamentary system functioned', noted one of

* The clearing system of barter trade, which the Balkan countries had welcomed as a means of hauling themselves out of the Great Depression, had one significant economic drawback: Germany was only interested in importing agricultural and mineral products from the region. It had no interest in acquiring industrial goods.

the most perceptive commentators on interwar Romania. 'The economic policy of these years by its very nature implied an extension of control over political activity.'[47] If Carol and his cronies wished to continue the rapid industrialization of an agrarian state, they would have to dispense with democracy.

Corneliu Zelea Codreanu and his Iron Guard, now revived under the name All for the Country (Totul pentru Ţara – TPŢ), acted as the catalyst. Emboldened by Germany's growing might, flattered by the attention paid him by Nazi agents active in Romania and augmented by more peasant recruits, the Captain went on to the offensive. The main focus of his attack was the camarilla, for him the incarnation of evil in Romania.

Elena Lupescu's father was born Grünberg. He had changed his name to the less obviously Jewish Wolff, which Elena had then romanized into Lupescu. But to most people in Romania she was known as 'the Jewess'. For this reason, King Carol was, in Codreanu's eyes, the lowest form of humanity: he had violated the vows of his Orthodox marriage to Princess Helen by committing adultery with a Jew. He was also close friends with Jews like Blank and Auşnit, and held up to 30 per cent of the shares in some of the largest Romanian companies. According to one contemporary, 'four of the largest sugar mills were in Carol's hands, as well as a beer factory. He had important shares in the gold mines and the telephone company and a large control of Banca de Credit Român.'[48] Carol was more than just a dissolute adulterer, Codreanu believed, he was the very instrument of 'foreign', i.e. Jewish, interests, which were enslaving the Romanian peasant through forced industrialization.

In 1936, the Guard began to focus its verbal attacks on the camarilla. Jews and Hungarians fell victim to Codreanu's mobs. In the same year, at the Guard's Youth Conference in Tărgu Mureş, the leadership announced the formation of a new elite detachment, the Death Commandos (*Echipa Morţii*). After a group of these Commandos murdered their most prominent victim, the renegade Nicolae Stelescu, 'they chopped his body with an axe, danced around the pieces of flesh, prayed, kissed each other and cried with joy'.[49] (All this, incidentally, at a hospital where Stelescu was recovering from an appendectomy.) If Carol needed any further warning about the danger posed by the Iron Guard, it came in the elections of November 1937. TPŢ won 16.5 per cent of the vote, becoming the third largest parliamentary force in Romania with sixty-six seats. Some 9 per cent had voted for the Goga–Cuza alliance, meaning that a quarter of the electorate had voted for rabidly anti-Semitic parties. The Liberals, through whom Carol had been ruling, had sunk below the 40 per cent mark and so were unable to form a government. Instead, Carol turned to Goga and Cuza. Carol convinced himself that an extremely reactionary government would take the sting out of Codreanu's tail.

Yet as soon as the two racist geriatrics felt the reins of power in their hands, they chose to realize the fantasies which they had been nurturing in institutions of learning for several decades. Far from discouraging the Iron Guard, as Carol had planned, Codreanu and his accomplices – the Death Commandos, the Lancieri, and the Green Shirts – indulged in a bacchanalia of murder, rape and looting. As Nagy-Talavera recalled, 'in the realm of the arts, the "Rumanian classic," *Bloodsucker of the Village*, a century-old play depicting Jewish activities in the villages, was dusted off for the cultural enlightenment of the Rumanian public. As Goga explained in an interview, "I keep the poet and the politician in two separate rooms." He continued that the door between these two rooms was closed. In politics, he was a realist, and if the Jews were the salt of mankind, he found the Rumanian dish too salty.'[50]

The Goga–Cuza government was in power for less than two months. They were the most shameful two months in Romania's modern history up to that time, and a foretaste of what was to come when the Iron Guard was finally permitted to transform the country into the Legionary State in 1940. Carol's wish for discord between the anti-Semites and the fascists eventually came true at the beginning of 1938 when the rival mobs turned on each other during the election campaign occasioned by the fall of the Goga–Cuza Cabinet. The country was sinking into bloody anarchy and Carol took the opportunity to seize control. On 12 February, he announced a blanket ban on political activity, and the promulgation of a new, authoritarian constitution. Faced with the choice of a revolutionary fascist Iron Guard future, or a conservative Caroline autocracy, the grandees of the Liberals and the National Peasant Party chose the latter and bowed out of the political process with a minimum of fuss. The King celebrated his dictatorship by arresting the entire leadership of the Iron Guard, accusing them of being in

the pay of the Nazis (a public accusation to which Hitler did not take kindly). In November 1938, Codreanu and thirteen other Iron Guard leaders were garrotted and acid was poured over their bodies. It was announced that they had been shot 'while trying to escape'.

Peace in our time

The Balkan states wanted war neither in 1914 nor in 1939. Yet at the start of the Second World War, they found an unlikely ally in their deep desire for peace – Adolf Hitler. When Germany invaded Poland in September 1939, the German leader may still have been pressing for greater political influence in the Balkan capitals, but he was confident that in principle he had them where he wanted them. The Balkans did not form part of Germany's designated *Lebensraum*. The *Siedlungsgebiete*, or settlement areas, lay to the east of the Reich in Poland and, later, in the Ukraine. The philosophers of *völkisch* expansion believed that the German minorities in Romania and Yugoslavia should enjoy privileged positions. But, with the exception of a large chunk of Slovenia, Nazi theorists did not wish to incorporate the Romanian and Yugoslav German minorities into the Reich. As we have seen, south-eastern Europe's allotted role was to be Germany's mineral bank and agricultural hinterland.

Naturally, Hitler hoped that as many Balkan countries as possible would commit themselves to his vision of a New Order in Europe, but this should if possible be brought about as the result of systematic economic and diplomatic pressure, not of violence and occupation. Of course, the efficacy of German pressure relied ultimately on the threat of force but peace, tranquillity and order were what was needed for the Balkan peninsula so that supplies for Germany's war industry would not be disrupted.

A year after war broke out, the Balkans were still at peace. Hitler's economic and political control over the area was now almost complete. Although not a single government wished to be too closely aligned to Berlin, they had become resigned to the idea as the events of 1938 and 1939 unfolded. They watched as Hitler absorbed Austria in March 1938. They then observed the preparations for Czechoslovakia's destruction at Munich six months later. As members of the Little Entente, Romania and Yugoslavia should

in theory have rushed to Czechoslovakia's rescue when Hitler ordered the actual dismemberment of the country in March 1939. But faced with an aggressive, resurgent Germany, both Belgrade and Bucharest looked at the floor, shuffled their feet and decided that the Little Entente had never been conceived to protect Czechoslovakia from Germany but from Hungary, and so they had no contractual obligations to Prague.

In truth, there was not much Romania and Yugoslavia could have done once Britain and France had given Germany the green light in Czechoslovakia. Hungarian designs on Transylvania hung over Romania's head like Damocles' sword – one wrong step and Germany would have cut the thread in Budapest. And if Britain and France were indifferent to the fate of Czechoslovakia, why would they risk defending Romania? The Balkan states were coming to terms with the fact that France's elaborate security policy, which sought to hem in Germany in both east and west, was not working. In August 1939, the policy evaporated with the announcement of the Molotov–Ribbentrop Agreement. The countries of central and south-eastern Europe were now left to fend for themselves. The only way to escape German or Russian aggression was to ask for protection from one against the other. In Romania's case, this was especially difficult since in the secret addendum to the Molotov–Ribbentrop Agreement Germany had conceded to the Soviet Union the right to snatch Bessarabia and northern Bukovina.

The western powers barely reacted to the precarious position of the south-east European states despite repeated appeals from Yugoslavia, Romania, Bulgaria and Greece for increased commercial ties. London and Paris parried these advances by sending second-rate trade delegations to the area or, in the spirit of Munich, by arguing that a trade drive would be interpreted as a provocation by Hitler. Only with the outbreak of war in September 1939 did Britain and France act by attempting to assert control over the most important mineral resource in the region, Romania's oil.

Germany was now subject to Allied blockade. The grandiose schemes of Hitler's engineers, of producing synthetic oil in boundless quantities, had come to nothing. Russian petroleum supplies were erratic and of poor quality. The nearest and cheapest reserves were in the Ploeşti fields of Romania. Berlin needed to increase the

monthly delivery of 120,000 tons a month which Bucharest was obliged to sell to Germany. The French, aware of this, bought or rented the bulk of the lower Danube's barge fleet to block the transport of oil to Germany. British agents also mined large parts of the Ploeşti fields in the hope of persuading the Romanians to blow them up in the event of a German invasion. More immediately, Britain began to pay over the odds for Romanian oil. This economic manipulation sent the price rocketing. Because Germany suffered from a serious shortage of foreign-currency reserves, it could no longer afford to buy even its allotted quota.

Imaginative though this Allied action was, it came much too late. The Soviet Union had annexed the Baltic states and in late November 1940 fired the opening shots in the Russo-Finnish war. Germany sent a clear diplomatic signal to Bucharest that, if the government were not prepared to resist British and French interference in the oil trade, Germany would consider Romania to have violated its neutrality. Affixing a carrot to the stick, Germany offered armaments for oil. In March 1940, Romania finally agreed to sell Germany 200,000 tons of oil a month, at well below world prices, in exchange for weapons captured from the Polish army. Needless to say, German arms were superior, so that Germany could be confident that Romania's military posed no threat to the *Wehrmacht*. The oil deal 'deprived the British of one of their most effective weapons in their economic warfare against the Reich'.[51]

In June, the Soviet Union decided the time had come to occupy Bessarabia and northern Bukovina. Carol II, having by now sold out most of Romania's economic interests to Germany, begged Hitler to intervene in Moscow on Romania's behalf. As the American journalist, R.G. Waldeck, reported, Hitler was displeased with Russia's decision to seize these territories 'for in the two provinces to be ceded were 20 per cent of Rumania's corn, 20 per cent of her wheat and 32 per cent of her sugar beets, 42 per cent of her industrial plants, and all her caracul sheep, her main export article to America . . . and . . . the Germans had 100,000 out of their 140,000 soya-planted hectares in Bessarabia'.[52] But Hitler was in no position to block the Soviet move, and curtly informed Carol that Romania must accept the situation.

Carol's acceptance of the Russian occupation led to his immediate downfall and flight from Romania with Lupescu and Urdăreanu.

The new dictator was General Ion Antonescu, a military man sober only by comparison with the fascist Iron Guard with which he was obliged to share power. Ironically, this new régime was forced by Hitler later in the year to accept the loss of four-fifths of Transylvania to Hungary. By then they were so deeply in the Nazis' pocket that these extreme Romanian nationalists had to preside meekly over the death of Greater Romania.

By the autumn of 1940, Germany dominated a Balkan peninsula which was at least nominally at peace. Hitler had his wheat, his soya, his minerals, his oil. And since May, France had been an occupied country, the most important victim of *Totalkrieg*. Hitler had no need for war in the Balkans. Yet six months later, over two dozen divisions of the *Wehrmacht* were marauding across the region. Belgrade had been bombed to ruins; Yugoslavia cut to ribbons; and German soldiers were patrolling territory as far south as the Peloponnese and Crete. This was a vast military operation that threatened to consume resources needed for Operation Barbarossa, the attack on Russia originally planned for May 1940 and which had to be postponed because of Balkan operations.* Why did Hitler tear the Balkans apart?

The road to hell, 1940–1: Greece

Andremo nell'Egeo	*We'll go to the Aegean*
Prenderemo pure il Pireo	*And then we'll take Piraeus*
E – se tutto va bene –	*And if all goes as it should*
Prenderemo anche Atene!	*We'll take Athens too!*

Marching song of the Italian army, popular in early autumn 1940[53]

Signor Emanuele Grazzi was tired and worried. Motoring along the empty road from Athens to Kifissia with the military attaché, Colonel Luigi Mondini, he was briefly cheered by the clear sky, which was, remembers Mondini, 'dotted with the myriads of stars that make the sky of Attica so marvellous'. It was a quarter to three in the morning on 28 October 1940, in southern Greece's Indian

* Or so Hitler claimed. For several decades, historians took him at his word on this. In the 1970s, however, one historian made a convincing case that the Balkan campaign did not actually interfere with the planning for Barbarossa.

summer. The piece of paper Grazzi was about to deliver to the Greek dictator, General Ioannis Metaxas, would bring that late summer mood to an end. The sentry at Metaxas's modest two-storey house mistook the Italian flag on Grazzi's car for the tricolour. Metaxas had been told that the French consul wished to see him urgently and so, half-asleep, he was baffled to see the Italian minister instead. Still somewhat bemused, Metaxas ushered Grazzi into a sitting room furnished in the dictator's unassuming lower-middle-class style. He offered his visitor a seat on the green divan in front of a large desk, and apologized for the fact that he had not yet changed out of his nightshirt and dressing gown. Outside the door, Metaxas's wife, Lela, listened quietly. 'Their conversation began calmly', she wrote later, 'but soon I heard an animated exchange, and an angry tone in my husband's voice followed by a loud bang of the palm of his hand on top of the desk. This was the exact moment of the Οχι! [No!] which was followed by Grazzi's departure.'[54] In his memoirs, the Italian does not recall Metaxas's becoming overexcited, nor does he remember the Prime Minister banging the table and shouting 'No!' Whether true or not, the rumour became fact throughout Greece within a matter of days – the Οχι War had begun.

Grazzi's embarrassment was genuine. A hard worker and an admirer of Greece, his attempts to calm the troubled waters of Greco–Italian relations made no impact whatsoever on his boss, Count Galeazzo Ciano, Italy's whimsically irresponsible Foreign Minister. Even if Metaxas had so desired, the ultimatum had been worded so as to preclude Greece's capitulation to the Italians. Benito Mussolini was set on invading and occupying Greece, not because this might be of any strategic value to Italy but, as Ciano reported, because the Italian dictator was furious with Hitler. Without telling Mussolini before the event (not for the first time), the Führer announced on 11 October that the Luftwaffe had assumed control of the Ploeşti oil fields 'in accordance with the Romanian request'. Ciano saw a blustering Mussolini that day: 'He says that this has impressed Italian public opinion very deeply', Ciano wrote, quoting Mussolini as saying, '"Hitler always faces me with a *fait accompli*. This time I am going to pay him back in his own coin. He will find out from the papers that I have occupied Greece. In this way the equilibrium will be re-established."'[55]

Hitler's consistent refusal to inform Mussolini of any major operations he was planning wounded the Italian's excessive pride, and it was thus in a fit of pique that Mussolini decided on the invasion of Greece, allowing a mere two weeks for preparations. Ciano backed his leader enthusiastically although he was alarmed to note that the

> three heads of the General Staff have unanimously pronounced themselves against it. The present forces are insufficient, and the Navy does not feel that it can carry out a landing at Prevesa [in northern Greece] because the water is too shallow . . . Badoglio foresees the prolongation of the war, and with it the exhaustion of our already-meagre resources. I listen, and do not argue. I insist that, from a political point of view, the moment is good. Greece is isolated. Turkey will not move. Neither will Yugoslavia. If the Bulgarians enter the war it will be on our side. From the military point of view I express no opinion. Badoglio must, without any hesitation, repeat to Mussolini what he has told me.[56]

Notwithstanding his habitual tendency to equivocate, Marshal Pietro Badoglio, chief of the general staff, was trying to indicate the sheer lunacy of an assault from southern Albania through the Pindus massif without adequate preparations. A year earlier, the general staff had ordered General Alfredo Guzzoni to formulate a detailed plan for an invasion of Greece. Guzzoni concluded that it would require eighteen to twenty divisions and that the operation would take three months. Now, Mussolini was expecting nine divisions (including one useless cavalry division) to do the same job with advance notice of a fortnight.

Ciano pretended not to listen to the military objections. He certainly understood the implications of what the Chief of Staff was saying. But had he acknowledged them then he would have been obliged to relay such serious misgivings to his father-in-law, il Duce. And Ciano never questioned Mussolini's political wisdom.

Mussolini's contribution to the Axis war effort stood in inverse proportion to the damage he visited on his own new order. His régime is surely one of the most powerful historical arguments against autocracy, dictatorship and the adulation of 'strongmen'.

No wartime episode demonstrates this better than the Greco-Italian war of 1940–1, which caused tens of thousands of unnecessary Greek and Italian casualties. In April 1939, Britain had extended a security guarantee to Romania and Greece in the wake of Czechoslovakia's dismemberment. Metaxas did not discourage British protection but he kept London at arm's length in order to stress Greece's essential neutrality. Germany was now soaking up the bulk of Greek exports, and was able to apply economic pressure. Metaxas was balanced delicately between the two camps. Italy's attack put an end to all that, placing Greece unequivocally on the side of the Allies. In theory, Metaxas might now place Greek territory at the disposal of British armed forces.

Metaxas was deeply troubled by the realization that Greece was at war with Italy. He had received much of his military training in Germany, and nurtured fond memories too of many years spent in Siena. To be sure, Metaxas was pragmatic; he saw Germany and Italy as greater threats to Greece's independence than Britain. But his dictatorship resembled other Mediterranean régimes. The last thing he wanted was for Greece to be at war with anyone. Despite this, he showed great resolve, convinced that, as his wife recalled, 'they [the Italians] can come, we are ready. We will defeat them.'[57]

Metaxas's road to power had been smoothed by the self-destructive actions of the pro-Venizelos officers in the Greek military during the first half of the decade. The National Schism, the battle between monarchists and republicans which was fought out primarily and catastrophically within the army, had negated all attempts to establish a coherent democracy during the interwar years. While in private Metaxas, a monarchist, had been inclined for a long time towards dictatorship, it did not follow that the republican, Venizelist forces were therefore principled supporters of democracy. Indeed, as Venizelos neared his death, his contempt for the democratic process deepened. The republican officers made a final attempt to secure a monopoly on power in March 1935 when they mounted a disorganized *coup*, which quickly collapsed. The monarchists then exploited the widespread popular disaffection with Venizelos by holding a referendum on the monarchy. King George II (1922–4, 1935–47) returned in triumph. After an interim period, Metaxas proclaimed himself Prime Minister in August 1936 and assumed dictatorial powers, all in alliance with the King, who retained a considerable, if discreet influence on the military strongman.

The centrepiece of Metaxas's attempt to build popular legitimacy on corporatist lines was the National Youth Organization (EON), whose members took centre stage in many large parades glorifying Metaxas's role as 'the first peasant', 'the first worker', and so on. Squat, with a round face and circular glasses, Metaxas was probably the least charismatic of all Balkan dictators. He employed a brutish chief of the secret police and kept his opponents in shocking conditions on island prisons. But in contrast to many of his peers, he stopped short of murder and systematic torture.

The August 4th Régime was careful to soothe the peasantry by lowering its excessive tax burden. The key to the stability of Metaxas's régime, however, lay with the military. When Metaxas took over, the overwhelming majority of the 5,000 officers were at least passively pro-monarchist. Like most other European leaders from the mid-1930s onwards, Metaxas identified his primary task as the overhaul and modernization of the armed forces. This gave him a distinct advantage in suppressing the resurgence of republican sentiment in the military. Soldiers were given new guns and accelerated promotion.

Greece was anti-revisionist. The national catastrophe of 1923 had actually led to the collapse of the *Megali idea*, of a Greater Greece. None of the major political forces wished Greece to make significant claims against any neighbour and in the interwar period Greece had established good political relations with its old enemy, Turkey. The threat of Bulgarian revisionism in western Thrace and Macedonia led Greece into the Balkan Pact and, at the beginning of the Second World War, all Greek leaders recognized Bulgaria as the major threat to their country's security (although they remained wary of Yugoslav intentions regarding Salonika). But Metaxas began planning for a possible Italian invasion from Albania soon after he assumed power. If for nothing else, Metaxas deserves credit for this foresight.

The mountains of Epirus (Chamuria, as the Albanians know it) are carved into spectacular, craggy canyons that appear unexpectedly in the walls of stone. They are crisscrossed with small rivers which usually pose only a minor obstacle to the serious walker. But as often happens in autumn and spring, the mountains in the early morning of 28 October were covered in grey, threatening clouds. As Italian troops entered the first passes of the mountain range, these clouds released a torrent of rain. Italian bomber command was forced to ground all its planes, denying the military the use of the one arm in which they enjoyed a clear superiority over the Greeks. The Italians moved forwards in appalling visibility as the earth turned to thick mud. Within hours the little streams became unfordable rapids. The Italian force was divided into two main sections. The first, comprising some 55,000 men, was to drive down through Epirus. The second army group of 30,000 men was to strike out from Korçe south-east into Macedonia before moving westwards to link up with the larger force. This would then cut Greece in two, leaving Thessaloniki hanging ready 'to drop into Mussolini's hands like a ripe fruit'.[58] That, at least, was the general idea; but on Day 2 the navy had to call off its planned occupation of Corfu because of rough seas.

The troops on the Epirot front became bogged down even before they had encountered the enemy, and in the first two days several thousand men became hopelessly lost. Spearheading the assault was the Alpine Julia division, comprising 10,800 men and twenty guns. The advance units pushed forward doggedly after crossing the river Sarandaporos, which had burst its banks. They struggled on as far as the pretty hillside village of Konitsa. The Greeks had gained enough time to organize a robust welcome. The Julia Division withdrew under fire, but in good order. Unlike il Duce and Ciano, who were celebrating in Rome, the soldiers of this crack unit already knew that the invasion was a débâcle.

Back inside Albania, supply lines broke down. A special envoy for the War Ministry reported on the eve of war that 1,750 lorries would be required for the invasion force. Three weeks later, the operational commander, General Count Sebastiano Visconti Prasca, complained that 'only 107 lorries had been landed in Albania'. The majority of these had fallen foul of Albania's dirt tracks. Small wonder that Visconti Prasca was so impatient. After all, this aristocratic general had incautiously promised Mussolini that he would deliver a 'colpo di mano in grande' in northern Greece from which the enemy would not recover. This, he argued, would leave open the road to Athens; within a matter of weeks, the Italian flag would fly over the Acropolis. In fact, within ten days,

Visconti Prasca had absolutely no idea what was happening to his troops over the border. This did not dissuade him from sending messages back to Rome claiming they were advancing rapidly on a wide front. Inspired by such mendacity, Ciano, a qualified pilot, dropped in on Tirana to make his contribution to the war effort. 'The sun has finally come out', the Foreign Minister enthused in his diary entry for 1 November. 'I take advantage of it to carry out a spectacular bombardment of Salonika. On my return I am attacked by Greek planes. All goes well. Two of theirs fell, but I must confess that it is the first time that I had them on my tail. It is an ugly sensation.'[59] Ciano's raid destroyed the building next to the hall where the Italians of Thessaloniki were being mustered, pending their deportation.

Visconti Prasca could dissemble no longer as news filtered through that the Italian forward divisions were dispersed, lost and suffering severe casualties. Having allowed the Italians to stretch their supply lines, the Greek army had co-opted the enthusiastic local villagers to help transport their weaponry and supplies across the difficult terrain. The men took up arms, creating their own units or joining the main army. The women volunteered to act as bearers, scaling mountains with cannon parts and ammunition roped to their back. 'We tie thick ropes around their waists', explained Warrant Officer Simetzis, 'and policemen standing on higher levels pull them up . . . And these women, heavily loaded as they are, climb up like goats, now clinging to a rock, now grasping at stray roots, buckling under the weight of their load and always in danger of falling into the precipice which opens below them. They climb up and down continuously and often throw rocks at the enemy below who have advanced as far as the huts of Tservatiotika.'[60]

The Italians dodging the rocks thrown by the mountain women were from the Julia Division, the toughest group of soldiers on the front line. After five days, with no supplies forthcoming, their advance units were living on dry biscuits. Sensing the enemy's weakness, the Greek Commander General Papagos wheeled round on the right flank, pushing back the division covering the Julia's left flank and cutting their communications completely. Within a fortnight, the Italian army was in general retreat. A week later, Papagos was able to lead his troops into Korçe, the main town in south-eastern Albania, and a week after that the Italians were driven from Pogradec in central-eastern Albania. The Greeks knew that if they were to push the Italians back into the sea this would snap their own supply lines and so instead they decided to keep the enemy tied up in central Albania. A third of the country was now under Greek control.

That winter, Mussolini could not contain his delight when it snowed in Rome. In a jovial mood that Christmas Eve, he told Ciano: 'This snow and cold are very good.' Perhaps inspired by the central heating in the Palazzo Venezia, Mussolini warmed to his theme. 'In this way our good-for-nothing men and this mediocre race will be improved. One of the principal reasons I have desired the reforestation of the Apennines has been to make Italy colder and more snowy.'[61] As he spoke, thousands of Italians across the Otranto straits were putting his theory about climate and the Mediterranean character to the test, as the Italian writer, Mario Cervi, has documented:

> Frostbite worked havoc among the men of the Ninth Army, who spent months at the highest altitudes, sleeping in the open without proper winter clothing, often living in undrained trenches amid the mud and snow . . . Among these long-suffering troops, fighting for reasons unknown to them an enemy they did not hate, the dreaded 'dry gangrene' or 'white death' started insidiously to spread. Its onset was painless. Legs swelled above the ankle, all feeling disappeared from the foot, the flesh changed colour, turned purple and then blackish. Then there was the agonizing journey to overcrowded field hospitals of men who often had to be carried bodily by their comrades because of the lack of stretchers, and were then loaded on to lorries that caused agony at every jolt on the appalling roads to Valona or Durazzo or Tirana, where they awaited transport to Apulia.[62]

The Balkans and Barbarossa

As the Germans had feared, the British began landing soldiers and aircraft in southern Greece as early as November 1940. Had Mussolini delivered on his claim that he would stroll into Athens within a month, then the Balkans (with the exception of Greece) would probably have remained an island of peace for most of the war. But with the planned invasion of the Soviet Union, Hitler could not afford to have his rear threatened by British forces. Mussolini's failure to subjugate Greece provoked the Nazi military sweep through the Balkans.

Mussolini was able to pay Hitler back 'in his own coin' at their summit meeting in Florence on 28 October, the day of the attack on Greece. Far from admonishing Mussolini, as il Duce had expected, Hitler congratulated him briefly and advised him to concentrate on grabbing Crete. Mussolini ignored the advice. Although he did not know it, his casual announcement of the invasion had not taken Hitler by surprise. The Führer's information-gathering network was too good for that. On receiving the same intelligence, Ernst von Weizsäcker, Undersecretary of State at the *Außenamt*, 'set about making a very clear demarche. I drew up an unambiguous instruction to Rome that we should not allow our ally, who was weak enough in any case, to bring new countries into the war without our advice and consent as allies. Ribbentrop approved this, but Hitler said he did not want to cross Mussolini. Hitler's silence meant indirectly giving Italy the sign to go ahead with her . . . step in the Balkans.'[63]

Hitler even offered Mussolini paratroop support for an operation against Crete. 'People are too prone to think of the Mediterranean as an east–west channel for shipping', observed 'Wild Bill' Donovan, the head of America's intelligence service, the OSS, in a memo to Roosevelt sent from the Balkans a month after the Italian offensive had begun. 'It should be thought of primarily as a no-man's land between Europe and Africa, with two great forces facing each other from the north and the south. Germany controls, either directly or indirectly, most of the northern battle-line on the continent of Europe. It is imperative for the British – or the British and the Americans – to control the southern front along the Mediterranean shore of Africa.'[64] Donovan had not quite read Hitler's mind, but it was a passable summary of what the Führer was thinking.

Hitler could have blocked the Italian invasion of Greece but did not. First, he wanted to prevent Britain from establishing an airbase in Thessaloniki from which British bombers could reach the oil fields in Ploeşti. But he had a still grander reason. Operation 'Seelöwe', the invasion of Britain, had failed, and Hitler had dropped the idea of a second attempt. He had switched instead to the so-called 'peripheral strategy' which involved cutting communications between Great Britain and its imperial outposts. At the time of the Italian invasion, Hitler was planning an assault on Gibraltar and a push, with the Italians, towards Suez. If Germany and Italy could seize Crete, then they would control the main naval and aerial staging post in the Mediterranean. They could monitor and regulate traffic along an east–west and a north–south axis. Hitler accepted and even supported Italy's Greek operation within the context of the 'peripheral strategy' against England. But his modest enthusiasm for the offensive soon soured when he realized it had been planned and executed by a clown. The British occupied Crete on 6 November while the Italians were still bogged down in the mud of Epirus just 24 kilometres from their base camp. 'A matchless dilettantism', fulminated Goebbels in December when the extent of Italy's failure became clear.

> The Italians have ruined the military prestige of the Axis. This is why the Balkans have become such a stubborn problem . . . So we must now intervene. Not to help them but to run the English out of Crete where they have installed themselves. They must get out of there. The Führer would prefer to see a peace deal between Rome and Athens but it is a difficult policy to sell. Mussolini has really messed this one up . . . If only he had occupied Crete straight away as the Führer had advised. But Rome is incorrigible.[65]

By this time, Germany's need to intervene in the Balkans had become still more pressing. Vyacheslav Molotov, the Soviet Foreign Minister, arrived in Berlin on the afternoon of 12 November 1940 for two days of talks. Hitler wished to invite the Soviet Union to join Germany, Italy and Japan in the Tripartite Pact. Were Stalin to accept the offer to join the Axis, this would create the mightiest political alliance in history, stretching from the Atlantic and Mediterranean to the Pacific. Hitler had hit upon the idea of incorporating the Soviet Union into his scheme partly to pre-empt a future alliance of the Soviet Union, Britain and, possibly, the United States, and partly because he had become anxious about the gradual westward expansion of the Soviet Union through

Finland, the Baltics, Bessarabia and northern Bukovina. In the Molotov–Ribbentrop accord of August 1939, Hitler had effectively recognized the Balkans as a Russian sphere of interest. Meanwhile, however, Germany's interest in the region had become more urgent. By persuading the Soviet Union to sign up to the Tripartite Pact, Hitler hoped, among other things, to extinguish Soviet influence in the Balkans. Berlin offered to compensate Moscow by supporting Soviet expansion in what Hitler termed the '*Großasiatischer Raum*' (greater Asian space). When Molotov asked what '*Großasiatischer Raum*' actually meant, the Germans were unable to give him a concrete answer; it has been assumed that it meant India, Central Asia and Iran.

As Hitler unveiled his vision of the new order, covering half the globe, Molotov sat impassively and, having heard the Führer out, stated he agreed 'in principle' to the idea. He then proceeded to raise difficulties about all the individual issues that Hitler had hoped to resolve in Germany's favour. The Foreign Minister mentioned Finland, Poland and Romania but he also raised for the first time the question of Bulgaria. Molotov claimed that Britain was threatening the security of the Black Sea Straits, which had prompted the Soviet Union to consider an offer 'of a Russian guarantee to Bulgaria'.[66]

Molotov's intervention threatened *Wehrmacht* plans to invade Greece, which included sending its divisions through Bulgaria. Stalin's response to the Tripartite proposal arrived by letter two weeks after Molotov's visit. The Soviet leader was adamant on the issue of Bulgaria: '2. Provided that within the next few months the security of the Soviet Union in the Straits is assured by the conclusion of a mutual assistance pact between the Soviet Union and Bulgaria . . . and by the establishment of a base for land and naval forces of the USSR within range of the Bosphorus and Dardanelles by means of a long-term lease.'[67]

Hitler needed the Balkans for economic reasons. He could not tolerate Soviet interference in the region, and certainly not a Soviet military presence there. Persuaded that Stalin was becoming too conceited and dangerous as an ally, Hitler decided to destroy the Soviet Union once and for all. The great gamble was begun.

> This momentous decision . . . had immediate and far-reaching consequences. Firstly, the war against Britain now turned into

a secondary matter, and the 'peripheral strategy' was therefore eliminated at a stroke. Secondly, the mess created by Italy's failure in Greece turned from a secondary nuisance within the framework of the 'peripheral strategy' (and not wholly unqualified, as it had presented the Germans with the opportunity to install themselves in the eastern Mediterranean while circumventing Italian objections) into a first-class blunder from the point of view of the future war against Russia.[68]

After Greece's seizure of Korçe, an optimistic editorial in the *New York Times* suggested that 'it probably needs only a comparatively small number of British divisions with accompanying artillery, tanks and airplanes to bring it [victory over the Italians and control of the northern Mediterranean] to fulfillment. But where are the divisions and whence are they coming? Is British land armament and trained man power yet sufficient to spare enough for this providential chance? If the answer is affirmative, this may prove to be a turning point of the war.'[69] The answer was negative; it was a turning point nonetheless.

Bulgaria and Yugoslavia

> Early this morning the Yugoslav nation found its soul. A revolution has taken place in Belgrade, and the Ministers who but yesterday signed away the honour and freedom of the country are reported to be under arrest. This patriotic movement arises from the wrath of a valiant and warlike race at the betrayal of their country by the weakness of their rulers and the foul intrigues of the Axis Powers . . .
>
> The British Empire and its Allies will make common cause with the Yugoslav nation, and we shall continue to march and strive together until complete victory is won.
>
> Winston Churchill, addressing the Conservative Central Council for the first time as party leader on 27 March 1941[70]

Everywhere on the evening of 27 February 1941, German military teleprinters spat out one word – *Heerestraße*, Army Road. The starting gun for the Balkan campaign had been fired.

Within hours, pontoon bridges appeared across the Danube, linking Romania with Bulgaria. Infantrymen squeezed themselves into transporters and trains. On 1 March, an unending phalanx of armoured cars, tanks, gun carriages, anti-aircraft equipment and horses began to roll past the Bulgarian peasants in their fields as the most ruthlessly efficient and best-equipped army in history crunched its way across the Balkan mountain range towards the Greek–Bulgarian border and the fortified defences of the Metaxas line.

Bulgaria had held out against German, Russian, British and American pressure as long as possible. Ribbentrop had threatened that if Bulgaria did not sign the Tripartite Pact and allow the passage of German troops through the country, then the *Wehrmacht* would simply invade and treat Bulgaria as occupied territory. The Russians had demanded that Bulgaria sign a mutual-assistance pact, which would allow the deployment of the Red Army in Bulgaria. Turkey had moved thirty-seven divisions to Bulgaria's south-eastern border. The British warned that they would attack Bulgaria in conjunction with the Turks if Sofia cooperated with Berlin. In a last-ditch attempt to stiffen Bulgarian resolve against the Germans, Bill Donovan, Roosevelt's personal envoy, urged Tsar Boris and leading members of the Cabinet to follow Greece's example and proclaim their determination to resist Nazism. Donovan admired Ivan Popov, the pro-Allies Foreign Minister, and could appreciate the dilemma Bulgaria faced. Popov tried to explain to the OSS chief what lay behind Bulgaria's policy of procrastination: 'I'll tell you an anecdote. A criminal, sentenced to death, begged the sultan to postpone his execution for a year while he taught his camel to talk. To his friends, at a loss to understand how he was going to do this, he explained: I have a whole year at my disposal; God knows what may happen in one year – the camel, or the sultan, or I may die.'[71]

Unfortunately, Hitler was in no mood to watch Bulgaria teach the camel to talk. The invasion of Russia was scheduled to begin at the end of May. It was essential that Operation Marita, the invasion of Greece, be completed in good time. With thirteen German divisions on their northern borders, the Bulgarians agreed to join the Tripartite Pact on condition that it was not signed until the very day that Operation Marita was to begin, 1 March.

Important though Bulgaria was to the *Wehrmacht*'s plans, the military engineers and transport officers who had been sent there at the end of 1940 reported immediately that the road and rail facilities in Bulgaria were atrocious. The preparation for the assault was itself a triumph of logistics and planning over the obstacles of a terrible winter and rough mountains. In order not to jeopardize the timing of Barbarossa, the Chief of Staff insisted that the *Wehrmacht* would have to send war materials through Yugoslavia as well.

As Bulgaria was pulled closer towards the Axis and hundreds of thousands of German soldiers poured into Romania through Hungary, Yugoslavia felt the 'ring of steel' tighten around its neck as winter gave way to spring. Hitler and Ribbentrop mixed threats and inducements to persuade the so-called Cvetković–Maček government and the Regent Prince Pavle to sign up to the Tripartite Pact and allow the country to be used in the invasion of Greece. The inducements included 'the ripe fruit' of Mussolini's dreams, Salonika. Dragiša Cvetković, the Prime Minister, was especially tempted by the idea of Yugoslavia's gaining this prized outlet to the Aegean. German support of Yugoslavia's seizure of Salonika implied that Hitler would not reward Bulgaria with Macedonia for having signed up to the Tripartite Pact. And if the prospect of retaining Macedonia and adding Salonika was not sufficiently rich to hook the Yugoslavs, the implicit threats were menacing enough.

Bill Donovan's offer from Roosevelt, by contrast, must have looked unconvincing. Making a final attempt to whip up armed opposition to Hitler in the Balkans, Donovan delivered a personal message to Prince Pavle from the President, warning the Yugoslav Regent that 'the US is looking not merely to the present but to the future, and any nation which tamely submits on the grounds of being quickly overrun would receive less sympathy from the world than a nation which resists, even if this resistance can be continued for only a few weeks'.[72] The Prince replied laconically that the Prime Minister, Cvetković, and the Foreign Minister, Aleksandar Cincar-Marković, were on their way to Berchtesgaden and that the decision to make common, if limited, cause with Germany had already been taken.

In fact, the text regulating Yugoslavia's entry into the Tripartite Pact as negotiated by Cincar-Marković in Vienna was a diplomatic triumph. The only real concession made to the Germans in the secret clauses attached to the published agreement concerned the transport of war materials through Yugoslavia. The Germans were not permitted to send troops across the country; nor did the agreement burden Yugoslavia with any other military obligations towards the Axis powers. Although a member of the Tripartite Pact, Yugoslavia would keep her neutrality virtually intact.

Before leaving Belgrade, Donovan crossed the Sava to visit the head of the Yugoslav Air Force, General Dušan Simović, in Zemun. 'Detailing the dangers of our situation and the unsatisfactory state of our forces and materials to put up a determined defence', Simović wrote later, 'I insisted that America send us technical and weapons assistance as soon as possible, especially for the airforce and for our anti-tank and anti-aircraft defences.'[73] At the time, the United States arms industries were producing at full capacity for the British and American armies. Under no circumstances could any of this arsenal be diverted to Yugoslavia. Nonetheless, Donovan promised moral support to Simović and his fellow officers, if they resisted the Germans. The OSS chief's biographer has pointed out that 'Churchill stated later that Donovan's visit with Simović delayed Hitler's attack on Russia by a fatal five weeks, and as a result he could not carry out his campaign [against Russia] within the first year, a failure which led to Hitler's ultimate downfall'.[74]

Churchill did indeed make this claim but it is untrue for all that. Without question, the *coup d'état*, planned and executed by Simović on 27 March 1941, reflected the deep indignation felt by many Yugoslavs, most particularly the Serbs, on hearing that the government had signed up to the Tripartite Pact. In the heated atmosphere of the time, it was difficult to understand the diplomatic brilliance of the Vienna Agreement with the Nazis. The day before the *coup*, on 26 March, students had poured into the streets of Belgrade, chanting '*Bolje rat nego pakt*' (Better war than the Pact) and '*Bolje grob nego rob*' (Better the grave than a slave).

Most of Belgrade slept through Simović's chaotically organized *coup* in the small hours of the 27th. It was bloodless largely because forces loyal to the Prince Regent Pavle and the government saw no point in resisting. Crown Prince Petar, completely oblivious to the events, woke that morning 'utterly astonished' to hear himself reading out a proclamation:

> SERBS, CROATS AND SLOVENES
> In this difficult moment for our people, I have decided to take power into my own hands. The regents, who have understood the justification for this act, immediately offered their resignation.

> My loyal army and navy immediately offered their services and are already carrying out my orders.
>
> I appeal to all Serbs, Croats and Slovenes to gather behind the throne. This is the safest way to maintain order inside and outside the country in these difficult moments.
>
> I have entrusted General Dušan T. Simović with a mandate to form a government. With a belief in God and in the future, I appeal to all citizens and authorities in the country to carry out their duties towards king and country.[75]

Simović and the conspirators had been unable to find the Prince and so they had ordered Lieutenant Jakov Jovović to imitate him over the radio. Everybody was fooled except, of course, Prince Petar himself.

In a BBC radio broadcast some time later, the journalist and translator Lovett Edwards described his feelings as he watched hundreds of thousands of people express their support for Simović's action later that day on the streets of Belgrade:

> There are few events in history which can be said in all truth to have occurred because of the spontaneous, lively and popular enthusiasm. The Yugoslav *coup d'état* was one such event. Those lacking a generosity of spirit claim that the conspiracy chose a bad time to strike. Maybe they are right. Germany was at that time the strongest military power in the world and fell upon Yugoslavia with all its might at a time when the country was unprepared and left to its own devices. But what is most important of all is that this was one of the most magnificent gestures of this age.[76]

But Simović and his co-conspirators behaved with criminal irresponsibility. The Yugoslavia whose government they seized was no longer the centralized state of King Aleksandar's time. In August 1939, Cvetković, the Prime Minister, had come to an understanding with Vladko Maček, the man who had assumed the leadership of the Croatian Peasant Party after the murder of Stjepan Radić. The Cvetković–Maček *Sporazum* (Agreement) had effectively split the country in two, creating an autonomous area of Croatia which included roughly half of Bosnia and Hercegovina.

Most Serb opposition parties deeply resented the *Sporazum* and the authoritarian rule of Prince Regent Pavle. But although the *Sporazum* posed problems for the future (especially with regard to Bosnia), it was on the whole a radical and successful means of preventing civil war between Serbs and Croats in the troubled international atmosphere of the late 1930s.

Simović was not in a position to establish control throughout the country unless he could come to an agreement with the Croats, and with Maček, in particular. He secured this agreement, but only under certain conditions. The most important of these was a declaration to stand by the Vienna Agreement, committing Yugoslavia to the Tripartite Pact. Belatedly recognizing that the Yugoslav Army could not possibly resist a German onslaught, Simović and the new government consented to Maček's condition. So the very reason for organizing the *coup* in the first place – resistance to the Tripartite Pact – was thrown out by the new government almost as soon as it was formed.

Yet before Simović persuaded the Croats to back his government, Hitler had undergone a dramatic change in mood. Irritated by the intricacies of Balkan politics, the Führer exploded in fury on receipt of the news from Belgrade. Almost immediately, he tore up the Tripartite Agreement with Yugoslavia, and ordered the *Wehrmacht* to invade the country. As Maček appeared to be cooperating with Simović, Ribbentrop was persuaded by Mussolini to switch German backing in Croatia to Ante Pavelić and his small gang of fascist thugs, who numbered no more than 360 when they seized control of the government in Zagreb in early April. They were brought to power solely by German guns and Italian politicians, and not by popular sentiment in Croatia, which overwhelmingly backed Maček. The installation of Pavelić's brutal fascist régime resulted in the single most disastrous episode in Yugoslav history, whose consequences were still being felt in the 1990s.

At a quarter past five on the morning of 6 April, German bombers began the assault on Belgrade. A few hours later, they left a pile of ruins and 17,000 dead. The *Wehrmacht*, crossing from Austria, Hungary, Romania and Bulgaria, smashed the Yugoslav army within a matter of days. The most perceptive Croat historian of this period has observed that 'the masses whose slogan had been "*Bolje rat nego pakt*" assumed the burden of this new situation and stayed in the country to fight while the politicians who had taken over the slogan "*Bolje rat nego pakt*" fled the country. From the very beginning, March 27th had followed this double standard.'[77]

Greece collapsed with equal rapidity. The Balkans faced four years of occupation, resistance, fratricide and genocide.

CHAPTER 7

CITY OF THE DEAD

Occupation, genocide, liberation, civil war, 1941–9

Hunger – Greece

The Nazis' objectives in the Balkans from 1941 onwards were simply 'defensive'. Hitler needed to protect his oil supplies from Romania to secure his southern flank for Operation Barbarossa, the invasion of the Soviet Union. The dismemberment of Yugoslavia and the occupation of Greece were by-products of Germany's strategic requirements. Once the *Wehrmacht* had defeated the Greek army and expelled the British from Greece, however, Hitler proclaimed an additional aim: Germany was to reassert the 'economic privileges which it had enjoyed' in Greece before the war.

Hitler's euphemism hid a policy which was part old-fashioned plunder and part *Vergeltungsmaßnahme* – 'retaliation measures' against Greece for having found itself on the wrong side. German officials at first assured Greece of their friendly intent. Germany had not waged war against Greece, the *Wehrmacht* propagandists insisted, but against the British on Greek soil.

Hitler's euphemism did not, however, seek to disguise what his occupying force was now preparing to inflict on the Greeks. He wanted merely to hide his real purpose from his Italian allies. The Führer had already conceded Italy's *preponderanza* in Greece. For compelling strategic reasons, the *Wehrmacht* insisted on retaining control of Salonika and the Macedonian hinterland, the border zone with Turkey, Piraeus (the Athenian harbour), most of Crete and three islands in the eastern Aegean. Bulgaria, too, at last got its outlet to the Aegean by occupying western Thrace. Hitler was resigned to handing over the rest of Greece to Mussolini in due course, but before he did so, he could not resist exploiting the material and ideological opportunities afforded by the *Wehrmacht*'s temporary control of the country.

In the wake of the *Wehrmacht*'s march south to the Peloponnese came a second army of specialist units. The *Sonderkommando* Rosenberg, for example, named after the chief of the Nazis' Foreign Policy unit, was to trawl the country in search of information on the Greek Jews and any opposition to Nazism among the local German community. Rosenberg had issued special orders to attach five 'scholars' to his *Sonderkommando* to investigate matters archeological, artistic and religious and to draw up an inventory of treasures from antiquity and the Byzantine period with a view to taking them under Nazi 'protection'. The *Sicherheitsdienst* (SD – the Security Service) had its own *Sonderkommando*, with a vague brief of arrest and torture, while the *Sonderkommando* Künsberg gutted the Greek government's archives, uncovering espionage networks and embryonic resistance organizations.

Then came the economic advisers, businessmen, engineers and factory managers whose task it was to seize anything of economic value. This was not a united team but included men from the military, from the Economics Ministry, from Ribbentrop's *Auswärtiges Amt* (Foreign Office) and from newly organized hybrids, like the Southeastern Europe Society, presided over from his province in Vienna by the former head of the Hitler Youth, Baldur von Schirach. The German plunderers were not only racing to pluck the choicest economic fruits before the Italians, they were frequently in competition amongst themselves. The Greek mining industry was of special interest to the Economics Ministry. Krupp's representative, Hans-Günther Sohl, reported enthusiastically to Berlin that 'between 1 and 10 May 1941, the entire Greek mining production of pyrites, iron, chrome and nickel ore, magnesite, manganese dioxide and gold had been safeguarded for the long term interest of Germany'.[1] (Herr Sohl's diligence in such affairs earned him the presidency of West Germany's club of industrialists, the

Industrieverein, after the war.) Entire factories, like the Bodosakis armaments factory, were dismantled and dispatched to the Reich.

The *Wehrmacht*'s primary interest was in finding food and accommodation to sustain the occupying force. The invading troops arrived in Greece empty-handed, intending to live off the land. Even before the Germans had established overall control, they began requisitioning supplies of wheat, oil, fish, fruit, cigarettes and sugar. Some foodstuffs, it is true, were exported to Germany and paid for through the trade clearing system. But this was of scant value to ordinary Greeks as most basic goods rapidly disappeared from the shops and into *Wehrmacht* warehouses.

Medicine, clothes, all forms of transportation, fuel and, of course, military materials were also subject to immediate confiscation – anything which could further the war machine was targeted. For, soon after its occupation in May 1941, Greece assumed a new strategic role as a logistical bridgehead for Rommel's campaign in North Africa. The Germans countered their cash-flow difficulties by introducing the *Reichskreditkassenschein*, a sort of Occupation Mark. They immediately embarked on an inflationary printing campaign, which devalued the *drachma*. If no *Reichskreditkassenschein* was to hand, the Germans simply appropriated the goods. During the first days of the occupation of Salonika, the Special Marine Commando 620 was tipped off that a tunnel system in the hills behind the town led to hidden supplies of clothing and military equipment. The unit's job was to load the booty on to lorries and send it back to Germany. 'The marine artillerist Kirchsteig together with his mate Hollerbusch hide a load of blue work overalls. They'll come in handy for him after the war as he's a farmer . . . I can see the lust of possession flashing out of his greedy eyes; this becomes standard practice wherever we go.'[2]

The response of the peasant farmers to all this larceny was predictable – they hid their produce. At first they sought to protect their goods. But as food became ever more scarce in the towns and cities, the value of their produce rose at staggering rates. Here, many peasants reasoned, was an opportunity to take revenge on the cities and the evil fiscal policies which had kept country folk poor for so long: to pay off their debts with the sale of a barrel of olives. Large numbers of peasant farmers did solve their indebtedness in this way, but as it involved withholding large amounts of produce from the market, their economic rationality implied disaster for the urban population.

The German forces in the First World War had ignored local sensibilities in the Balkans; the behaviour of the *Wehrmacht* twenty-five years later was far worse. In Greece, restaurants had to reserve the best food for German officers. During high summer when water is a most valuable commodity in a Mediterranean climate like that of Athens, the *Wehrmacht* permitted unrestricted use of water by officers, even for obsessive car-washing.

Economic disruption was exacerbated by Allied naval blockade. In contrast to other Balkan countries, Greece was not self-sufficient in food. It depended on imports for about 50 per cent of its wheat consumption which came chiefly from western Europe and the New World. Its external supply constricted, Greece's dismemberment into three occupation zones then cut the country's internal commercial and transport links.

Hitler had sanctioned Bulgaria's occupation of western Thrace, not its annexation. The Bulgarians disregarded this fine point. They had just re-emerged as the most powerful country in the Balkans and saw that possession was nine-tenths of the law. The Bulgarian administration in western Thrace was arguably one of the harshest occupational régimes in all Europe. Up to 100,000 Greeks were expelled from the region, and many thousands imprisoned on the island of Thasos. The smallest manifestation of Greek culture was persecuted. The Bulgarians also seized Greek-owned land and distributed it to tens of thousands of Bulgarian peasant colonists. The panicked Greeks fleeing western Thrace were drawn to Salonika and, above all, Athens, which they believed to be centres of work, security and food.

The effects of these policies were immediate and drastic. Just over a month after the German occupation began, the philhellene German envoy to Athens wired to Berlin in desperation at the 'catastrophic supply situation'[3] in the country. By the beginning of July, Greek smugglers and refugees arriving in Turkey had brought 'the first reliable reports since the capitulation of the Greek army', giving 'a terrifying picture of the situation in a sorely-tested Greece. After the defeat came hunger, disease and epidemics . . . In the past two months food supplies have dried up as the fertile wheatfields of Macedonia and Thrace have been lost to Bulgaria. In the impoverished suburbs of

Athens, the number of starvation victims is beginning to grow. Undernourished women who queue in front of empty shops break down on the streets with exhaustion.'[4]

The Germans and Italians ordered the government of Greece's hopelessly impotent and incompetent quisling, General George Tsalakoglu, to establish a rationing system. The government, however, had no means of imposing its authority on the anarchic black market which was by now the main regulator of food supply. Several ministers and local security chiefs played pivotal roles in the black markets, as did Tsalakoglu's wife.

By October 1941, deliveries of basic foods to Athens had dried up. Long lines of apathetic women and children with the trance-like gaze of the starving formed in front of makeshift tables from which thin, tasteless soup was distributed. The National Catastrophe of 1923, when over a million Greeks had been expelled from Turkey, had created huge suburbs in Salonika and Athens which had never overcome their chronic infrastructural weakness. In the summer of 1941, disease-carrying rats began multiplying in these districts where large families were obliged to share a single room. Running a volunteer canteen for impoverished mothers and their offspring, Ioanna Tsatsou dreamt of huge children's parties with food overflowing the tables. She would then wake 'with the feeling that I had just left Paradise, and, fully awake, I sank slowly into the familiar nightmare. My room is freezing cold. I am hungry. I never get up from the table satisfied. Around me gather all the little faces of Plaka, but as they really are, skeletons, all eyes. Eyes full of bewilderment, eyes that do not understand.'[5]

The famine, which affected millions of Greeks (although conditions were nowhere as bad as in Athens, except on some of the islands), also encouraged infectious disease, above all tuberculosis. 'Vitamin deficiency caused tumours and boils to appear on their hands and feet, and, unless cured, these spread on to the body and the face', Mark Mazower has recorded. 'Around half the families in the poor quarters showed these symptoms by the beginning of 1942.'[6]

From the summer of 1941 the death toll from starvation or related illness rose every day. Hundreds simply dropped dead from exhaustion in the street. Often their bodies were left to rot before the overworked collectors slung them on to carts already piled with corpses. Thousands of these were taken to the outskirts of Athens and buried in mass graves. There is compelling evidence that the number of deaths ran into the hundreds of thousands and, in the Greek consciousness, the famine understandably holds as powerful a position as the Catastrophe of 1923.

In October 1941, the Foreign and Food Ministries in Berlin successfully blocked the diversion of any wheat supplies from the *Reich* to Greece, arguing that every last ear would be required for German domestic and military consumption because of the Russian offensive. The International Red Cross advised the British government that the only way to prevent millions of deaths would be to lift the blockade on Greece and allow emergency food supplies through. 'How much do we value the good will of the Greeks', Edward Warner asked cold-bloodedly in a Foreign Office investigation into the problem of food shortages. 'Is it more important for us to have a healthy population of 7½ million Greeks in order to bolster our postwar position in the Eastern Mediterranean? Or can we accommodate the reduction of Greece's population through hunger ~~being reduced to five million through starvation~~ ?* We have to consider the pros and cons very carefully before we decide whether the Greeks should starve or not.'[7] Mercifully, humanitarian considerations prevailed, although the Allies and Axis powers only came to an agreement allowing shipments of Canadian wheat for the Greek population a year after Warner's report. The first deliveries were made in August 1942, after which the threat of famine receded.

For a century, Germanophilia in Greece had vied with affection for Britain and France. It vanished during the famine. Indifference soon turned into resentment, and then resistance. At first it was small-scale. Throughout the winter of 1941–2 graffiti appeared on the walls of Athens and Piraeus, prophesying an Allied victory and vengeance on the Germans, Italians and Bulgarians for the suffering they had inflicted on Greece. Resistance took many passive forms. In schools children refused to learn the new compulsory languages of Italian and German; soldiers found it especially hard to woo the local women. But it was young people who proved the most imaginative. It was their particular pleasure to sabotage German cars and

* Crossed out in the original.

lorries by throwing sand into petrol tanks and by slashing tyres. 'The *saltadori* achieved particular notoriety by jumping on to moving lorries carrying food and throwing large amounts of produce to their pals who were strategically placed along the route.'[8] Small beer it may have been, but it was a signal of the infinitely greater violence to come.

In late May 1942, a few men gathered around a barn near Sperkiades, just below the southern tip of the Pindus mountain range in the interior of Thessaly. The numbers were not as impressive as Anathasias Klaras had hoped. Nonetheless, the men were armed and willing, and so the group headed off to the mountains. These new *andarte*, the descendants of the *klepht* guerrillas of the Liberation War,* left their names and identities behind them. Klaras, the quiet communist functionary, was buried that day and resurrected immediately as Aris Velouchiotis, the *Archigos* (leader) of the first unit of ELAS, Ellenikos Laikos Apeleutherotikos Stratos (Greek National Liberation Army). It was an inauspicious start. To avoid the attention of the real *klephts*, bandits whose numbers had increased dramatically since the food shortages began, and in order to win the affection of the peasantry, Aris banned his men from plundering: 'Thus the "People's Liberation Guerrillas" concealed themselves during the day and gathered berries and roots at night. The discovery of a tortoise is considered a rare piece of fortune. Hunger, cold and depression reduced the band to five men.'[9]

Aris improvised a new strategy. He led his tiny band of men to the village of Domnista, deep in the mountains of central Greece, and called a meeting of the locals. 'Patriots! I am Aris Velouchiotis, Colonel of Artillery. Starting today, I am raising the banner of revolt against the forces occupying our beloved country. The handful of men you see before you will soon become an army of thousands. We are just a nucleus.'[10] Notwithstanding his militant atheism, Velouchiotis bent to kiss the hand of the priest and swore allegiance to the elders. In return for protecting the village, the ELAS men were guaranteed food and accommodation. Greece had taken a first step on the road to civil war. This movement was destined to

* See chapter 1.

become an army of thousands, as Aris had predicted. To the north in Yugoslavia, it was by then already possible to see how a complex mixture of resistance, civil war, ethnic and class conflict could provoke utter mayhem in a Balkan country.

Bloody Fairy Tale: Serbia and Bosnia

> Henceforth one hundred prisoners or hostages are to be shot for every soldier killed and fifty for every one wounded. Every regional garrison to arrest as many communists, nationalists, democrats and Jews as possible without endangering combat capability thereby. Announcement in public of operation aims and to arrested and their relatives.
>
> Order telexed on Monday, 13 October 1941 from the German High Command to the 718 Infantry Division of the *Wehrmacht*, detailing new measures to be taken in response to the widespread guerrilla activity in Serbia[11]

Nothing on the Balkan peninsula was as shocking during the war as the fate of Yugoslavia and its peoples after the Germans and Italians sent in their troops to prise open the route to the Aegean in April 1941. What had been a single country was now chopped up into at least nine units (although few of these were stable). Slovenia was split in two; Italy annexing the south-west, including Ljubljana, and Germany grabbing the plum industrial areas in the north-east. As part of the deal which saw the Ustaše come to power in Croatia with Italian help, Italy seized Dalmatia, the Adriatic islands and a large part of Istria. The Independent State of Croatia (*Nezavisna država Hrvatska – NDH*) included all of Croatia, Slavonia, Bosnia and Hercegovina, but it was also divided into Italian and German military zones. Montenegro lost part of its territory to Albania and became an 'independent' province under Italian protection. The Italians also used the Albanians to annex part of Kosovo and western Macedonia. The Germans occupied the Banat; the Hungarians took Vojvodina while Bulgaria reclaimed Macedonia and small areas of southern Serbia. Serbia itself was under direct German military rule, although in August 1941 a puppet government under General Milan Nedić was established, which drew support from Serbia's fascist movement, the Zbor.

In almost every part of the country, the establishment of a new authority was accompanied by the settling of old accounts and the opening of new ones. Governance was replaced by state terror on a horrifying scale. The Ustaše turned their territory into one great slaughterhouse. The Germans in Belgrade lost no time in drawing up their lists of Jews, Gypsies and subversives while in northern Macedonia, Bulgarian soldiers and secret policemen were torturing suspected Serb sympathizers and hanging their mutilated bodies from street lamps. Those who found themselves in Italian occupied zones were the least unfortunate. Yet uniquely in occupied and fascist Europe, armed resistance organizations mounted a challenge to the Nazis' New Order from the very beginning. There were several reasons why this happened in Yugoslavia and why Serbia and the Serbs were the focus of this resistance.

The speed with which the Royal Yugoslav Army had been defeated and dispersed surprised everybody – the Yugoslavs themselves, the Axis powers and the Allies. Large numbers of officers and soldiers evaded capture, however. They withdrew with their weapons into the mountains and forests, chiefly in Bosnia and Montenegro but also in Serbia. These men would make up the core of the Chetnik resistance loyal to Colonel Dragoljub ('Draža') Mihailović and the London-based government in exile.

At their headquarters in Belgrade, a rival resistance inspired by a very different ideology was taking shape. Members of the Politburo of the Yugoslav Communist Party (KPJ) under the leadership of the energetic Josip Broz Tito decided to spread out across the country. Their task was to activate the KPJ's highly disciplined underground network (a fortunate by-product of many years of illegality) and develop a strategy for guerrilla warfare. These men and women were the first Partisans.

In Croatia, the terror unleashed by the Ustaše against the Serbian villages of Croatia, Bosnia and Hercegovina drove Serbs into the arms of the Chetniks and the Partisans. These peasants had a choice – to be incinerated or butchered in their homes by the Ustaše, or to fight. Many of them had family traditions of military prowess as they inhabited what had been the *vojna krajina*,* or Military

---

* See chapter 1.

District, of the Habsburg Empire. The Ustaše created so many and such troublesome enemies that the German military and civilian authorities in Zagreb repeatedly attempted to bring Pavelić's genocidal campaign against the Serbs to a halt. They were not moved by the victims' plight,* but were concerned that the terror was forcing tens of thousands of Serbs to flee to Serbia, Montenegro and contested areas of Bosnia where they often took up arms. Relatively large numbers of Serbian and Croatian Jews also joined the Partisans.

The Germans had not expected any resistance in Yugoslavia. As soon as the army surrendered, Germany redeployed most of its own troops in Serbia to the Russian Front. Hitler retained a minimal force to keep open the main north–south trunk route from Belgrade to Bulgarian-occupied Macedonia, but this left large areas of eastern, central, western and north-western Serbia exposed to Partisans and Chetniks.

In September 1941, Tito established his headquarters in Užice in western Serbia. Wherever they went (and they developed into an extremely mobile fighting force), the Partisans first set about building an administration and trying to ensure an adequate local economy and a varied social life. Hampered too often by a sectarian devotion to Leninism and Stalin, the Yugoslav Communists nonetheless recognized that an unhappy warrior was an unreliable one. In contrast to the Chetniks, the KPJ leadership devoted much energy to propaganda and to ensuring that morale remained as high as possible in often catastrophic conditions. In the Užice Republic, as their first base became known, the Communists set up a functioning postal system and a railway over 145 kilometres long. Schools were open normally, as were cinemas and the dance halls. The newly founded newspaper, *Borba* (*The Struggle*), appeared every other day. A weapons factory in the vaults of Užice's bank turned out 400 guns a day and valuable quantities of ammunition.

Cheek by jowl with the Užice Republic was Ravna Gora, Draža Mihailović's mountainous operational centre. Mihailović did not

---

* Germany's military representative in Zagreb, General Edmund Glaise von Horstenau regularly expressed his disgust at the gruesome behaviour of the Ustaše, although as a pre-*Anschluß* Austrian Nazi, he could hardly claim to be morally spotless himself.

preside over a community as the Partisans did in Užice, but support for the Chetniks among the peasantry of central Serbia was much greater than it was for the communists. The two groups watched each other uneasily but, for two months at least, they were content to live as neighbours with distant but correct relations, according to the slogan, *Једна земља а два господара* – ONE COUNTRY, TWO MASTERS.

Aside from the occasional territorial skirmish, neither side was inclined to force the central issues dividing them: leadership, tactics and ideology.

The leadership question was straightforward: who would head the resistance to the Germans? The two men met to discuss their differences on 19 September and Tito offered Mihailović the post of Chief of Staff of all resistance forces in Yugoslavia. Smelling a rat, the Chetnik leader turned this down, aware that Tito was happy to sacrifice military control if the KPJ retained political control. So they remained as divided on the leadership question as they did on the matter of military strategy.

The Partisans were proving more effective as a fighting machine than the Chetniks because they used better tactics. They aimed to liberate broad swathes of territory and place them under the political supervision of the KPJ. Partisan troops were not attached to any specific region and would obediently go wherever the leadership told them to. This meant that in the event of the Germans reoccupying territory, the Partisans would effect a tactical retreat and attempt to establish new liberated territory elsewhere in the country.

The bulk of Chetnik forces, on the other hand, were attached not just to specific districts but to individual villages. Their tactics were defensive, aimed at maintaining local freedom of action. As such, the Chetniks were not highly organized or flexible; although most played lip service to Mihailović as their leader, they did not consider themselves bound to him: if they did not feel like leaving their villages on a mission, they would not do so.

The KPJ orchestrated the Partisans according to the Leninist principle of 'democratic centralism'. Tito and the Politburo arrived at decisions which the rank and file were supposed to carry out unquestioningly. To disobey orders was to risk one's life. In contrast, there was no single Chetnik organization. Not only did village units wield considerable operational autonomy, but the Chetniks were drawn from a large spectrum of pre-war political parties – they were not driven by a single ideology. One group of Chetniks were known from the start as the 'legal' Chetniks, who cooperated openly with the Germans, Italians and the quisling régimes in Serbia and Montenegro. Some of Mihailović's officers were implacably anti-German and demanded that the Chetnik movement cooperate with the Partisans. Others regarded the Partisans with contempt, and were bent on wiping them out as agents of Moscow. Broadly, however, the Chetniks fought on behalf of the old royal régime, which put them at odds with the Partisans, whose aim was to replace a discredited bourgeois system with a socialist order based on the Soviet model.

Ideological divisions between the Chetniks and Partisans were often hard to untangle from their differences in military tactics. Tito approved guerrilla hit-and-run tactics as a means of provoking retaliation against local civilians. The more cruelly the Germans acted, reasoned the KPJ, the more new recruits for the Partisans. Resistance was only one part of the Partisans' programme. The second part was the preparation for socialist revolution.

Mihailović's main war aim, by contrast, was the 'biological survival' of the Serbian people and the creation of a homogeneous Greater Serbia. In the most widely distributed Chetnik manifesto of 1941, one of Mihailović's supporters argued that 'transfers and exchanges of population, especially of Croats from the Serbian and of Serbs from the Croatian areas, is the only way to arrive at their separation and to create better relations between them, and thereby remove the possibility of a repetition of the terrible crimes that occurred even in the First World War, but especially during this war, in the entire area in which the Serbs and Croats live intermixed, and where the Croats and Moslems have undertaken in a calculated way the extermination of the Serbs'.[12] The Chetniks' conviction that they were fighting for the survival of the Serb race was, of course, an exaggeration. But in the light of Serb experiences during the Great War; in light of the Ustaše's genocidal policy against Serbs in Croatia, Bosnia and Hercegovina; and in light of the ruthless behaviour of the Nazis, the Chetniks may be forgiven for thinking that there did exist a plan to liquidate all Serbs. For this reason, Mihailović and his commanders were most reluctant to provoke the Germans for fear of reprisals against civilians.

The Chetniks were rooted to areas where Serbs lived; the Partisans appealed to all Yugoslav nationalities. Croats and Muslims could not join the Chetniks, but they were welcome in the Partisans. When Chetnik bands came into contact with Croats and Muslims, one side usually ended up being massacred. Chetnik leaders who supported the old order of royal Yugoslavia suspected that the KPJ's policy of equality for all Yugoslav nations was a way of subordinating Serbian interests to those of Croats, Slovenes and Muslims.

During the early autumn of 1941, tension between the Chetniks and Partisans in western Serbia grew as the communists attempted to expand their 'liberated territory', often at the expense of their rivals and by using force against the Germans. Mistrust between Chetniks and Partisans spilled over into serious armed conflict in October. By this time, even Hitler realized the uprising in Serbia was serious, because it was disrupting his north–south communications. He redeployed an infantry regiment from Greece to Serbia and an entire division from France to Serbia in early September. He now had four and a half divisions in the country. A month later, he issued his notorious order that one hundred Serbs would be killed for the death of a single German and fifty if a German was wounded.

German intelligence failed to identify the growing rift between Partisan and Chetnik. The *Wehrmacht* was even convinced that Mihailović and Tito were deepening their collaboration. General Franz Böhme, the German commander in Serbia, prepared to meet the uprising in Serbia with decisive force.

In the middle of October, a joint Partisan–Chetnik force laid siege to the 2,200-strong German garrison in the small town of Kraljevo. During the course of the fighting on 17 October, the Germans were shot at from inside the town. The commandant issued orders for the arrest and summary execution of 300 Serbs. But he did not stop there. Over the next few days, eye-witnesses reported how *Wehrmacht* patrols went from house to house, seizing all men from the ages of fourteen to sixty, and herding them into a makeshift camp at the local rolling-stock factory. Their papers were checked and their names entered into a ledger. When the camp was full, the Germans took a group of one hundred, and placed them in front of open graves and machine-gunned them. The soldiers then examined the bodies. If a victim showed any signs of life, he was finished off with a bullet to the temple. After the first group had been exterminated, the Germans went back to the camp for the next 100.[13] And so it went on, until all the men were dead.

According to the official records of the 717 Infantry Division, 'altogether 1736 men and 19 communist women',[14] were killed that day, which also saw twenty Iron Crosses, 2nd Class, conferred upon members of the units responsible for the massacre.

The killing went on for another seven days as the *Wehrmacht* fanned out around Kraljevo, burning all the neighbouring villages and killing indiscriminately; but there was worse to come. At the very end of September, the Partisans launched an attack on Gornji Milanovac, a town of some 3,000 people, situated in a verdant central Serbian valley. Milanovac had barely existed at the turn of the century and had grown by attracting disparate, isolated outsiders from other villages and towns. There was little sense of a local patriotism and its inhabitants adopted a cautious attitude towards the Chetniks, Partisans and Germans alike. Without informing the Chetniks, Tito's headquarters in Užice dispatched a Partisan unit to attack the small German detachment stationed in Milanovac's newly built school. The Partisans stood little chance of actually taking the German garrison which was heavily defended. But this was not the point: the Partisans anticipated that the disruption and fighting would generate new recruits. Zvonimir Vučković, the twenty-four-year-old district Chetnik commander, learnt of the Partisans' intentions and hastened to Milanovac to join in the operation, even though he thought it suicidal. 'There was no doubt that we Chetniks would have suffered a significant loss of prestige at that time if we had just washed our hands of the operation and stood to one side', he later wrote. 'The powerful propaganda machine of the Partisans would have had no difficulty persuading the locals that they were the only real fighters for freedom.'[15] As so often, competition between Chetniks and Partisans led to the use of reckless tactics. Vučković worried that once the joint resistance force had seized the town, it would not be able to hold on to it. Instead, it would become a battleground where civilians would become the main victims.

At three o'clock one morning, the Partisans led the charge against the Germans holed up in the school. Although the attackers succeeded in disabling the German sentry posts, the occupiers' modern weaponry, particularly their heavy machine guns, soon neutralized the assault. In the first hour and a half of fighting, ten Germans were killed and twenty-six wounded, relatively small losses. Yet this was a demoralized unit on the very edge of German-controlled territory. A week earlier, the German garrison commander had radioed regional headquarters in a vain request for food and ammunition. Vučković, the Chetnik leader, and his Partisan counterpart judged that flushing out the Germans would cost too many casualties and too much precious ammunition, so Vučković suggested negotiating with the Germans instead. To everyone's surprise, the German commander agreed to surrender almost immediately. Vučković took the men into custody and handed them over to the Chetnik command at Ravna Gora. Franz Egger, an officer with the company, escaped and reported to Belgrade all that had happened at Milanovac and that the German prisoners in captivity 'were being decently treated'. When General Böhme heard of the case, however, he decided it warranted retaliation.

Kragujevac, a town of 10,000, lay 37 kilometres to the east of Gornji Milanovac and was the regional headquarters of the *Wehrmacht*. On instructions from Böhme, the district commander, Baron von Bischofshausen, ordered the arrest of all suspected communists and male Jews on 18 October 1941. They were held for two days without food. Then, without warning, on the evening of the 20th, German troops entered the barracks and courtyard where they were being held and started firing at random. The prisoners scattered and ran but were all eventually picked off like fleeing animals, the first victims of the Kragujevac massacre. At the same time, *Wehrmacht* units entered the town's main secondary school, removing entire classes of schoolchildren aged fourteen and upwards. Workers from the local factories (including hundreds of men engaged in vital military industries) were also brought to the Stanovija Field, the barracks of a former motorized battalion. Troops seized priests and monks from Kragujevac's churches. Every single man was then registered and his belongings noted meticulously.

At precisely 7 o'clock the next morning, the pattern established at Kraljevo was repeated. Fifty men were taken from the barracks and made to stand in two rows in front of the small river which ran behind the barracks. They were then mown down with a heavy machine gun. For seven hours, groups of between 50 and 120 men and boys were led to the same spot. After the war, at least thirty-one mass graves were discovered. According to German statistics, the *Wehrmacht* (which concluded the day's work by organizing a celebratory parade through the town centre) killed 2,324 men in retaliation for the ten dead and twenty-six wounded in the attack on Milanovac. One hundred and forty-four secondary-school students were killed, often in groups comprising an entire class with their teacher standing at their head. 'It was in a land of peasants', wrote Desanka Maksimović, one of Serbia's greatest postwar poets in *Krvava bajka*, 'Bloody Fairy Tale', 'In the mountainous Balkans / Where a little class of students, learned their lesson of death'.[16] The murdered children included five twelve-year-olds.

Four days after the Kragujevac massacre, Colonel Bill Hudson, the first SOE operative to reach Yugoslavia, arrived at Mihailović's headquarters after a tiring journey made by submarine, donkey, truck and on foot. In his baggage he carried confirmation that the British government was prepared to extend recognition to the Chetnik leader as the only legitimate resistance force in Yugoslavia. In a matter of months, the Allied press had mythologized Mihailović as an invincible hero, defying the Nazis in the face of incredible odds. On the other hand, the role of the Partisans, who had done most of the fighting against the Germans, was barely recognized. One American journalist claimed that Tito was not a person but an acronym for a shadowy, ineffective conspiracy – the Third International Terrorist Organization!

Hudson's news of Allied recognition for Mihailović soured still further the relations between Chetniks and Partisans. The atmosphere was already thick with mutual recriminations about moral responsibility for the Kraljevo and Kragujevac massacres. Mihailović resolved to address the Partisan question once and for all. 'This attack which I am going to launch on the partisans, and my relations with them', he warned Bill Hudson, 'is entirely a Yugoslav affair and I am the legitimate representative of my government.'[17]

Vicious clashes between Partisans and Chetniks broke out in November 1941 just as the *Wehrmacht* finished preparations for a massive air and infantry assault on both the Partisans' Užice Republic and the Chetnik headquarters at Ravna Gora. The plan for destroying the Chetnik base went ahead despite an offer of cooperation from Mihailović to the Germans. The Chetnik leader had suggested a truce in exchange for arms, which he would use against the Partisans. These brief negotiations failed. Nonetheless, Mihailović had taken a first step on the treacherous road to collaboration.

By early December, the Partisan army found itself in disorganized retreat from Užice into the Sanjak and south-eastern Bosnia. The sedentary Chetniks, in contrast, melted back into their villages. Mihailović escaped the German assault on Ravna Gora and continued to direct offensive operations, but mainly in eastern Bosnia.

The outbreak of civil war between the Serb Chetniks and the predominantly Serb Partisans completed the panorama of murderous chaos that now filled the Yugoslav canvas. When the Partisans arrived at their new base in Foča in eastern Bosnia, they discovered that the violence had already reached a terrible pitch of intensity. According to the Nazi carve-up, Bosnia was now a part of Pavelić's Independent State of Croatia (NDH), a Croatia, as the saying went, *sve do Drine* (all the way to the Drina). However, the government in Zagreb did not have the forces to control such a large territory. Pavelić adopted the Croat nationalist theory that regarded the Muslims of Bosnia and Hercegovina as 'Croats of the Muslim faith', brothers in the struggle against the Serbs who were subject to the same rights and responsibilities as Catholic Croats. The new state was always able to find a group of Muslims, usually influential traders and landowners, willing to work with the Ustaše. The first task of the new administration in Bosnian towns was the rounding-up and execution of the most important local Serbs. In just one incident, the Ustaše slit the throats of Serbs over a large vat until the vessel was overflowing with blood. Very quickly, as the rumours spread, the Serbs in Hercegovina and eastern Bosnia began to organize themselves into Chetnik units to take revenge against the civilian population, most of whom were Muslims not Croats. In early December 1941, Chetniks from Pale, Rogatica and Višegrad, led by a white Russian émigré, Sergei Mihailovich, stormed Foča, and the reprisals began:

> When they took us to the railway bridge one of the thugs shouted: 'How come you've brought so few?' The second answered that these 16 were merely a taster for the next 84 they had rounded up. After this they began the slaughter. They killed like this. One Chetnik fell to his knees, holding a huge knife in his left hand. Every victim had to lie down under the

> knife and if he refused to do so, he was hit with the butt of a gun until he collapsed on the ground. Another Chetnik would then drag him until he was in position under the knife. After each killing, they would search the victim and take anything of even the slightest value. They would then disembowel the body and throw it in the river. This went on until it came to my turn. I can still see all the others who were killed in front of my eyes like this. But just before I was due to die, my Chetnik guard turned away and I was able to escape . . . Despite being shot at I reached the Drina river. As I swam for my life, the body of my brother Jusuf floated by me.[18]

Between two and three thousand Muslims were killed in the town of Foča alone, including children and women, many of whom were routinely raped beforehand. When the Partisan army finally entered Foča, Milovan Djilas noted that those who had survived, regardless of their nationality, were so traumatized by the events in the town that they exhibited 'no ray of warmth or curiosity in their expressions, which remained apathetic, dull, inhuman. They were emaciated and yellowed, and dressed in rags.'[19] This pattern of slaughter, counter-slaughter and trauma could be found in most corners of Bosnia and Hercegovina, and several regions of Croatia, from the summer of 1941.

Genocide – the Balkan camps: Romania, Croatia, Bosnia and Serbia

A year after the establishment of Jasenovac, independent Croatia's largest concentration camp, one government-controlled newspaper wrote that 'Jasenovac is no sanatorium, but neither is it a torture chamber. It is a work camp.' Jasenovac offered its inmates the opportunity to integrate into Croatian society by using their skills in building 'the great industrial complex' on the Sava river 97 kilometres south-east of Zagreb. 'Jasenovac is at the same time a college which genuinely seeks to cure the "political internees" of their poisonous views and ideology so that they might return to public life as useful members of society and proud sons of the fatherland.' Jews would regrettably need to stay in the camp until the war's end in order to prevent them from fraternizing further with the enemies of

Croatia. Thanks to Jasenovac, however, they would 'be afforded the opportunity to work for the benefit of Croats and Croatdom for the first time ever'. The camp had even 'given the Gypsies a chance at last to work for the good of society – for the first time in their legendary nomadic history'.[20]

Milko Riffer found this article about Jasenovac on the floor of the train which was transferring him from a prison in Zagreb to the camp. His suspicions were confirmed when his group of detainees reached the camp's entrance at the end of a dusty track beside the Sava. Riffer noticed a heap of discarded rail sleepers by the side of the road. On one sleeper somebody had used a piece of coal to scrawl the words '*Lasciate ogni speranza voi ch'entrate*'.* As the camp gates shut behind him, Riffer and his four friends were struck on the head with rifle butts. Through a cloud of thick dust, they then saw an Ustaše guard riding towards them in a cart. Standing with a whip in his right hand, the guard was lashing the backs of the four Jewish men in rags who were harnessed to the front of the cart and pulling it.

The programme to exterminate one and a half million Balkan Jews was implemented in many different ways. From the *Wehrmacht*'s meticulously recorded deportation of Salonika's 50,000 Jews to the random hell created by the Ustaše in the Croatian camps, the Final Solution in the Balkans was improvised according to local conditions. It had started in Romania in 1940. Initially, the country's new military dictator, General Antonescu, was obliged to share power with the Iron Guard and its leader, Horia Sima. In November 1940, Sima gave the green light to his mob. 'Two hundred squads of six men each were turned loose in Bucharest every night for raids on Jewish houses. Officially the purpose was to search for hidden money, but in reality these Guardists looted, terrorized, and blackmailed the Jews into giving up silver, jewels, money, whatever was in reach. The leather-clad figures of these boys with their high fur caps and their motor-cycles became a nightly feature of Bucharest, the symbol of Guardist terror.'[21] The killings began almost immediately, reaching a terrifying intensity in Moldavia and its capital Iaşi, the intellectual home of Romanian

* 'Abandon hope all ye who enter here' – from Dante's *Inferno*.

anti-Semitism. Eventually, in one of the bloodiest pogroms, 4,000 Jews were killed in a three-day spell in Iaşi. Emboldened by the bullying and murder of Jews, the Guardists extended their persecution to their other enemies – Gypsies, political opponents, even some remaining British and French citizens. The chaos these death squads caused interfered with economic and administrative life to such a degree that Antonescu felt compelled to move against the Guard with force. 'Still no clear picture in Romania', Goebbels noted on 24 January 1941. 'The Legionaries [Guardists] are now in open rebellion and Antonescu has opened fire on them. The Führer is on his side. He wants a contract with a state, not with a *Weltanschauung!*'[22]

Antonescu was not a pronounced anti-Semite, and in Wallachia – in contrast to Moldavia – anti-Jewish measures were implemented in a dilatory fashion. The Marshal did not save all the Romanian Jews from the Polish death camps and their fate in Moldavia and Bessarabia was gruesome. But he probably did save tens of thousands in Wallachia. In general, Jews in Balkan countries which had joined the Axis powers fared much better than in those occupied by the Nazis, regardless of traditional attitudes towards the Jews among the local populations. The most remarkable record is that of Bulgaria where 'more Jews were living . . . after World War II than before'.[23]

Some Yugoslav Jews found temporary safety and a possible escape route in the Italian-occupied areas of the Balkans – Dalmatia, Montenegro, parts of Bosnia-Hercegovina, Albania and western Greece. After the attack on Yugoslavia, the Jewish population of Split, the Adriatic port under Italian control, swelled from 300 to 3,000. Most of the newcomers arrived from the German zones of Bosnia. Split was the centre of the so-called Zone I of Italian military operations in Croatia and Dalmatia. The Croatian government exercised no authority here – Italians ran both the civilian and military administration. The Italian civil commander in Split did sanction some anti-Semitic measures, but no lives were threatened. After the capitulation of Italy in the summer of 1943, most of the Jews of Split were either evacuated to southern Italy, where they survived the war, or they joined the Partisans. Roughly 250 remained in Split to await a joint Ustaše–*Wehrmacht* force after the Italian withdrawal. They all died either in Jasenovac, in the Sajmište camp in Zemun or in Auschwitz.

In Italy's military Zone II, where 3,400 Jews found refuge after April 1941, the Ustaše formed the civil administration and sought permission from the Italian military to start rounding up the Jews as a prelude to deportation. Mussolini actually approved this measure, but the commander of Italy's army in Yugoslavia, General Mario Roatta, refused to hand them over to the Ustaše, arguing that such an act would damage the prestige of the Italian military. Instead, he ordered their internment under Italian protection. Some historians have doubted Italian motives. They have suggested plausibly that the Italians hoped by saving the Jews to be treated leniently should the Allies win the war. Yet whatever their reasoning, Italian military leaders provided vital assistance to Yugoslavia's Jews until the collapse of Mussolini's regime in 1943.

Matters were very different in those areas, Serbia, Bosnia and Croatia, where the Germans set the agenda. Here the registration, collection and extermination of the Jewish population began within days of Yugoslavia's dismemberment. Towns like Sarajevo which came under joint Ustaše-*Wehrmacht* control had the worst of both worlds – unfettered violence and Teutonic efficiency. On 16 April, the day after the Germans walked into Sarajevo, they were joined by local mobs who raised their right hand and displayed their four fingers and thumb to identify themselves as 'fifth columnists'. The primary targets for violence were synagogues. The *Wehrmacht* marched into the temples 'shooting down the chandeliers with machine guns and hurling grenades at the altars. German officers laughed and smiled as the mob plundered and destroyed for two days, removing rugs, chandeliers, pews, windows, doors. They even removed sheet-copper plating from the synagogue's cupola and the linoleum from the floor.'[24] The Jewish library was completely destroyed; holy scripts were set alight on the streets of Sarajevo.

The terror in Croatia (which now included Bosnia and Hercegovina) was directed against the usual targets of a fascist party – Jews, Gypsies, homosexuals, and political opponents of the Ustaše. But Pavelić was also determined to 'solve' the Serb question in Croatia: a third of the two million Serbs in the NDH would be expelled; a third would be assimilated through conversion from Orthodoxy to Catholicism; and a third would be killed. With such a range of potential victims, the Ustaše leadership tried to simplify its policy of mass extermination wherever possible. As early as 17

April 1941, the Legal Decree for the Defence of the People and State was published. The first clause proclaimed: 'Whosoever in whatever manner offends or has offended against the honour and vital interests of the Croat nation, or in whatever manner threatens the existence of the Independent State of Croatia or the state authorities, whether in deed or whether in mere intent, this person has committed the crime of high treason.'[25] The decree allowed for retroactive prosecution and made no attempt to define the 'honour' or 'vital interests' of the Croats; it was a formula that allowed the Ustaše to fashion a case of high treason against anyone. The Decree on the Protection of Aryan Blood and the Honour of the Croat Nation, in defiance of Hitlerian racial theories but with the Führer's implicit approval, redefined Croats, who, according to all ethnic criteria, were Slavs, as Aryan. Mixed marriages between 'Aryans' and 'non-Aryans' were henceforth forbidden, while sexual relations between male Jews and female Croats were criminalized, and Jews were not allowed to employ as domestic staff any Croat female younger than forty-five.

The Ustaše had more difficulty defining Serbs, who were indistinguishable from Croats in racial terms. Serbs were stigmatized instead on grounds of culture and confession. They were defined as 'Eastern-Greek' in the Decree on Conversion from One Faith to Another which came into force on 3 May 1941, and warned Catholic clerics to take great care if 'Greek-Eastern teachers, priests, traders, rich industrialists and rich peasants and the intelligentsia in general' asked to convert. The leadership wanted to ensure that Serbs with money and education did not survive the planned genocide. Like the Jews and Gypsies, Croatia's Serbs were denied citizenship in the NDH, a measure designed to speed up the sequestration of the victims' assets. The proceeds were used in part to pay for the physical liquidation of the original owner.

Armed with these various decrees, the Ustaše established a series of kangaroo courts to deal with the tens of thousands of NDH inhabitants who had been transformed overnight into traitors. The only penalty for high treason was death. Throughout the NDH, the judges presiding over the *ad hoc* courts became willing bureaucrats entering countless urban Serbs, Jews, Gypsies and Croat communists into a ledger of summary execution. In the countryside, the Ustaše were less legalistic. Villages and small towns were stormed and peasants butchered or dispatched to the burgeoning network of 'collection' and concentration camps around the country. In July 1941, for example, some 500 Serbs, including women and children, from Glina, a small town 65 kilometres south-east of Zagreb, were arrested and shot dead. As a consequence, the peasants from the surrounding villages hid themselves in the woods. The Nuremburg Tribunal described what happened next:

> The Ustaše offered an amnesty if they would convert to Roman Catholicism. A majority of peasants agreed and returned to their villages. The mass conversion was organized and the peasants duly arrived at the Serbian Orthodox church in Glina. 250 people turned up for the event. They were greeted by six members of the Ustaše. When all were inside, the church doors were locked shut. The peasants were forced to lie on the ground and the six Ustaše began hitting them with spiked clubs. More Ustaše appeared and one after another every single peasant was murdered in this fashion.[26]

For two and a half months, the Ustaše concentrated on the Serbs. In this brief period, some Jews were able to escape either to join the Partisans or to find sanctuary in the Italian-occupied areas. For a few thousand Croatian Jews, there was also the long shot of applying for 'honorary Aryan' status. This peculiar loophole in the Croat decrees on race was prompted by the high incidence of Jewish spouses among members of Pavelić's Cabinet. But for the great majority of Croatian Jews, it proved an irrelevant anomaly.

Of the 40,000 Jews who lived in Croatia, Slavonia, Srijem (eastern Croatia), Bosnia and Hercegovina, between 20,000 and 31,000 were killed. The question of the total losses sustained by Yugoslavia during the war, especially at the hands of the Ustaše and the Chetniks in Croatia, Bosnia and Serbia, was answered by Marshal Tito in 1945. He claimed that 1,700,000 people had died as a result of the conflict. After the war, Yugoslav schoolchildren cited like a mantra the figure of one million dead in Jasenovac alone. The numbers were exaggerated at first to ensure maximum reparations for the country in the postwar settlement. Later, the claim helped to underline the authority of the Partisans and the KPJ. Because Tito himself had made the original statement, '1,700,000 dead' became an article of faith in communist Yugoslavia. To deny this figure was to question Tito's omnipotence, and so historical research into the issue was distorted for several decades. The number of Jews killed is uncontroversial. Not so the question of Croat, Serb and Muslim victims. Fifty years later, in the prelude to the wars of Yugoslav succession in the 1990s, heated debates about the losses in the Second World War played a significant part in the propaganda battle fought out between Zagreb and Belgrade.

The Croatian terror was not, however, distinguished by its extent (even though the NDH authorities marked a greater percentage of their population for extermination than any other Axis régime). Its uniqueness lay in its brutality. The Ustaše lacked significant popular support, although they were able to rely on seemingly limitless passive acceptance of their activities by most Croats. To staff his genocidal machine, Pavelić and his two chief henchmen, Dido Kvaternik and Andrija Artuković, turned to Croatia's lumpen class. The collection and concentration camps of the NDH were poorly built, atrociously run and extremely unhygienic. Jasenovac was the most notorious camp. Most of Croatia's Gypsies perished there as well as a sizeable proportion of the Jewish population, and a large number of Serbs. Death was due to disease (typhus in the main), starvation and industrial accidents (particularly on the Sava dyke construction project which accounted for many Gypsy deaths as early as summer 1942). Finally, inmates feared the trip across the Sava from the main camp at Jasenovac to the village of Gradina, which became a slaughterhouse for much of the war. Hammers were used to beat victims to death in night-long orgies of mass murder. Photographic and eye-witness evidence demonstrates forms of humiliation, torture and liquidation so obscene that it would be pornographic to detail them here. But it should be remembered that Jasenovac was one camp among many. Some 1,500 Jewish women were held at Loborgrad to the north-west of Zagreb, where the camp commanders and staff were responsible for the routine rape of inmates as young as fourteen. The most notorious Ustaše administrator of all, Vjekoslav Luburić, dispatched hundreds of typhus-ridden internees from one camp at Stara Gradiška to another near Djakovo (at the time disease-free) specifically in order to spread the infection. The sheer incompetence of the Ustaše probably saved a few thousand people from death during the four years of Pavelić's rule. But those who were caught in his web of camps experienced unrivalled barbarity.

In Serbia, three German institutions – the *Wehrmacht*, the *Sicherheitsdienst* and the Gestapo – at first claimed credit for and then later denied knowledge of the destruction of the local Jewish population within a year of their arrival in April 1941 – the most comprehensive campaign of annihilation throughout Axis-occupied Europe. The Nazis were assisted by several thousand ethnic Germans in Belgrade as well as by supporters of Dimitrije Ljotić's Serbian fascist movement, Zbor, and General Milan Nedić's quisling administration. But the main engine of extermination was the regular army. The destruction of the Serbian Jews gives the lie to *Wehrmacht* claims that it took no part in the genocidal programmes of the Nazis. Indeed, General Böhme and his men in Serbia planned and carried out the murder of over 20,000 Jews and Gypsies without any prompting from Berlin. Its warped sense of honour was shown when, after gunning down over 10,000 Jewish men, the *Wehrmacht* in Belgrade refused to execute the women and children on the grounds that this was 'dishonourable'.

The largest Jewish communities were in Belgrade, the Banat (north-east of Belgrade) and Šabac. Many of the latter became members of the so-called Kladovo transport, a group of some 1,300 Austrian, Czech, German and Polish Jews who attempted in 1939 to flee down the Danube en route to Palestine. Before reaching the Black Sea, however, their boat was refused entry into Romania. Instead they were held in the Yugoslav port of Kladovo before being sent to Šabac in the Mačva valley, the region where the first major battle of the Great War had taken place. Early in the Second World War, the Mačva valley became one of the main areas of Partisan resistance. In response to this challenge, the Germans decided to make an example of the (defenceless) local Jewish population. During the night of 20–21 August 1941, several Jews were hauled out of their apartments in Šabac by German soldiers and shot in the street. After daybreak, 'the bodies were gathered in the town square. Jewish refugees from the Kladovo transport were brought up from the internment camp . . . The refugees were forced to carry the dead men through the town and then hang the bodies from electricity poles.'[27]

This marked the beginning of a two-month-long frenzy which

resulted in several thousand deaths. In late September, Milorad Jelesić, a Serbian peasant interned in the nearby camp at Sremska Mitrovica, was taken to a field near the Sava river, close to where it passes Šabac. Jelesić assumed he was going to be shot but 'a German who spoke Serbian told us we were not going to be killed but [were there] as workers'. After the *Wehrmacht* soldiers had lunched,

> a group of fifty people who I could see were Jews were led from behind a field of corn . . . An officer gave the command and then the Germans would aim at the back of the head – two soldiers for each Jew. We then had to run to the open grave and throw the dead into it. Then the Germans ordered us to go through all their pockets and take out any items of value . . . If we couldn't get the rings off, the Germans gave us a little knife and we had to cut off their fingers and give them the rings like that . . . After the first group had been dealt with, we were ordered back behind the guns and the next group of fifty were brought out and the process repeated. The next day we were taken back to the same place at Zasavica and the shooting began again. On the first day, it was only Jews, on the second day there were more of our Gypsies than Jews.[28]

In two and a half days, the Germans shot dead all the male Jews and Gypsies of Šabac.

General Böhme soon began shooting thousands of the Belgrade and Banat Jews as well. He later argued that this did not constitute collaboration in genocide because these men were shot as hostages in retaliation for the killing of German soldiers by Partisan and Chetnik units. Felix Benzler, the German minister in Belgrade, realized that the executions were driving greater numbers into the arms of the Partisans. He wired Berlin asking for the remaining Serbian Jews to be deported, rather than shot. Reinhard Heydrich, Himmler's deputy, had just begun the massive operation of deporting the German and Low Country Jews to collection centres in Poland and the Baltic region. To stop Benzler pestering him about 2,000 Serbian Jews, he dispatched a team to Belgrade 'to sort out the problem on the spot'.[29] Benzler's objections were dismissed and Böhme was asked to finish off the Jews. The General did not hesitate, despite reports from his unit commanders that the men carrying out the executions had begun to develop serious symptoms of psychological damage. By 20 October 1941, Heydrich was told 'the male Jews will be shot by the end of the week'.[30]

By December 1941, only the women and children of Serbia's Jewish community remained alive. They had been corralled into the camp at Sajmište, the site of the Industrial Fair in Zemun, the Croatian town across the Sava from Belgrade. Over 6,000 women and children were penned in there, as ever in the most appalling conditions. By the beginning of 1942, the military demanded that the camp be cleared of Jews to accommodate the growing number of prisoners taken in the war with the Partisans. Once again the civilian authorities requested permission from Berlin to deport them and once again this was denied.

Work on a solution had begun several months earlier after Himmler had ordered German engineers and chemists to come up with a 'more humane' way of killing than execution by firing squad. The head of the SS had witnessed one of his *Einsatzgruppen* in action, shooting Jews in Poland. Badly shaken by the event, Himmler was determined to reduce the psychological suffering which mass murder inflicted on his executioners. As a direct consequence of Himmler's visit, Friedrich Pradel, head of the *Sicherheitspolizei*'s 4,000-strong vehicle pool, asked his chief mechanic, Harry Wentritt, whether it would be feasible to divert the exhaust from the engine of a Saurer truck into a sealed compartment behind the cab. The mechanic built a switch into the exhaust of the Saurer, which the driver worked simply by capping the exhaust pipe. The fumes would be diverted via a T-bone joint to a perforated U-shaped joint which was then positioned in a hole cut into the floor of the truck. A local engineering firm, Gaubschat, soon diverted most of its staff to converting Saurers, Opels and even two Dodge trucks into gas vans. They were dispatched to eastern Poland to assist with the annihilation of Russian and Ukrainian Jews.

It is unclear whether the German administration in Belgrade requested a 'delousing truck', as one official referred to it, or whether Berlin made the decision to dispatch it. But by late February 1942, a converted Saurer with its two drivers, Messrs Götz and Meyer, was heading for the Serbian capital.

A few days later, Herbert Andorfer, the camp commandant at Sajmište, was told by his superiors that all the inmates were going to be 'put to sleep', in a special truck. Andorfer was further instructed to accompany the van from the camp to the site of the mass grave to ensure the mission's secrecy. Andorfer baulked at the idea. Over the past few months, he had developed good relations with the 'camp administration', the Jewish volunteers who distributed food and attempted to maintain basic standards of hygiene. By Andorfer's own account, 'he had even drunk coffee and played cards with some of the prisoners in the camp administration after they had learned not to fear him'.[31] Stricken with guilt that he would now play a central role in the mass execution of these people, Andorfer requested a transfer. This was denied. He then constructed an elaborate fiction, convincing the women that they were being transferred to another camp in Serbia. He drew up a set of rules and regulations for the fictitious camp and insisted that a Jewish doctor or nurse travel with each van. Under the impression that the 'new' camp would be more comfortable, several hundred women and their children volunteered for the first transport. They were permitted to take their most valuable personal belongings and to pack a small case of essentials.

On the morning of the first transfer, a large truck and a big grey car drew up into the camp. The SS personnel in the car loaded up the truck with luggage before helping 100 women and children into a second truck (designed to accommodate 50) which was parked outside the camp. Hedvige Schönfein, a Swiss woman married to a Yugoslav Jew, recalled that the drivers, Götz and Meyer, 'often came into the camp, gathered the children together, kissed and hugged them and then distributed sweets to them all'.[32] Ten minutes later, after the van had crossed from Zemun to Belgrade, one of the two drivers would be underneath the truck, capping the pipe and diverting the exhaust into the compartment packed with children chewing their sweets. Instead of accompanying the truck from the camp itself as instructed, Andorfer waited a few hundred metres down the road, unable to look his charges in the eye before their final journey. From late March to mid-May, every day except Sundays and holidays, the grisly convoy drove through the centre of Belgrade to Avala, a few miles outside the city. On arrival, seven Serbian prisoners were required to unload the god-forsaken cargo. After almost the entire camp had been murdered, the seven Serbs were shot but the gravedigger, Vladimir Milutinović, survived: '81 or 82 trenches were prepared and I helped dig all of them. At least 100 people fitted into each trench . . . These ones were only for those who were suffocated in the truck. We dug a different set for those who were shot.'[33] Of the 8,000 women and children who passed through Sajmište, only six – foreign citizens married to Serbian Jews – remained alive at the end of the war. By the summer of 1942, a mere handful of Jews remained in hiding or had escaped to join the Partisans. The German military authorities were close to the truth when they proudly informed Berlin that Serbia was now *Judenfrei*.

The eleventh hour: Bulgaria, Macedonia and Thrace

The refusal of Bulgaria to hand over a single Jew for deportation to Poland is a little-noted episode which confounds the Balkan stereotype. If the Balkans are inhabited by congenitally xenophobic peoples, why did the Bulgarians stop the Nazis getting their hands on Bulgarian Jews? Bulgarian and Jewish historians have attempted to popularize this apparently remarkable act of defiance. Yet admiration for Bulgaria's record should be tempered. Opportunism, not idealism, played the key role in the attitude of the Bulgarian government towards the Jews. During the first two years of the war in the Balkans, Bulgaria was eager to accommodate Berlin in this matter. The first group of Bulgarian Jews earmarked for deportation only escaped death at the eleventh hour. Moreover, the switch in policy came too late to save the Jews of Macedonia and Thrace.

In September 1942, less than a month after the Bulgarian government had passed a decree approving the deportations, Petŭr Gabrovski, Bulgaria's Interior Minister, appointed Alexandŭr Belev as chief of the newly created Commissariat for Jewish Questions (*Komisarstvo za evreiskite vŭprosi* – KEV). A lawyer by training (like so many leading figures in European fascism) and a protégé of the Interior Minister, Commissar Belev was a professional anti-Semite. He drew his authority both from his position as the head of KEV and from the Law on the Defence of the Nation (*Zakon za zashtitata na natsiiata* – ZZN), among the most draconian pieces of anti-Semitic legislation in Axis Europe. Belev had himself drafted the paragraphs relating to Bulgaria's Jews after a summer spent in Germany studying the Nazis' institutionalization of anti-Semitism. After his appointment to the KEV, Belev lost no time in sending his agents to the major towns and cities in 'old' Bulgaria as well as in Macedonia and Thrace, the so-called 'newly liberated territories'. These agents were charged with drawing up registers of Jews as a prelude to internment and deportation to Poland.

Although endowed with sweeping powers, Belev was hampered by resistance from several quarters. His most persistent critic was the head of the Bulgarian Orthodox Church, Metropolitan Stefan, known for his pro-Allied sympathies. Stefan succeeded in badgering the Prime Minister, Bogdan Filov, to cancel orders forcing Bulgaria's Jews to wear the Star of David in the autumn of 1941. When Belev managed to restore the order after a knotty bureaucratic battle, he encountered further problems: an absence of popular anti-Semitism, and defiance among the Jews. Many of the latter simply refused to wear the yellow patches while some who did were ostentatiously greeted in public by ordinary Bulgarian citizens, determined to invert the Star's ostracizing intent. 'Some Jews even disregarded the regulation stars of the commissariat and devised their own, which contained pictures of the king and queen.'[34] On occasions, Tsar Boris himself would publicly acknowledge the Jewish community and its achievements, a habit which irritated German representatives in Sofia. The combined hostility of influential Bulgarians and the populace at large to Belev's anti-Jewish measures proved critical in blocking the mass deportation of Bulgaria's Jews in March 1943.

Notwithstanding this resistance, Belev was confident that his plans would be carried through. The government had passed all the necessary laws and the authorities had zealously stripped the Jewish community of its financial assets; the Cabinet was highly susceptible to German pressure. Tsar Boris and the government had been reluctant, it is true, to join the Tripartite Pact in March 1941. But they lost no time in taking up Hitler's offer of Macedonia and western Thrace. Berlin naturally expected concrete expressions of gratitude for restoring these territories. By the beginning of 1943, the government had signed an agreement on deportation with Germany, written by Belev and SS *Oberstürmführer* Theodor Dannecker, Eichmann's special envoy to Bulgaria. At the beginning of March and in great secrecy, Belev began the final preparations for the round-up of all Jews from western Thrace and Macedonia (in all about 14,000 people) and 6,000 'undesirables' (i.e. the wealthy, influential or politically active) from 'old' Bulgaria's community of

51,000 Jews. The first round-up was in Drama, Kavala, Serres and other towns in western Thrace whence 3,000 Jews were taken to collection points in Gorna Dzhumaya (now Blagoevgrad) and Dupnitsa (now Stanke Dimitrov) in 'old' Bulgaria. After Thrace came the larger operation in Vardar Macedonia.

In the early hours of 11 March 1943, Skopje's cold night air was pierced by the incessant howl of a lone dog. Heskija Pijade listened as the animal's cry was underscored by the dull, muffled thudding of the hundreds of pairs of heavy boots of Bulgarian gendarmes and soldiers taking up their positions. Two policemen with three dogs charged into the Pijade home, ordering the family to take with them 'all gold, jewellery, watches, and cash'.[35] Heskija, his wife and his grandmother soon found themselves naked, shivering and being strip-searched by men in the warehouses of the State Tobacco Monopoly in Skopje. For ten days, 7,318 Macedonian Jews, drawn from three main centres, Skopje, Bitola and Štip, were crowded together in the suffocating atmosphere of drying tobacco. They were terrorized by the guards who performed mock executions and raped the teenage girls. The camp's lieutenant commander strode around with a bullwhip and a cylinder of thick, hard rubber, beating Jews senseless – men, women and children. 'That is how we spent ten days', Albert Sarfati later testified. 'Everyone was ill. They gave us food once a day, and then not regularly. We received nothing for breakfast or dinner. Life was unbearable.'[36]

The transports to Poland began on 18 March from Gorna Dzhumaya via Bulgaria's Danubian port, Lom, where the Jews were transferred on to barges bound for Vienna. Here, the Bulgarian guards handed them over to the German authorities who sent them on by train to the death camp at Treblinka. In Skopje, Alexandŭr Belev arrived to oversee in person the departure of the first train on the tortuous route to Treblinka. Another spectator was Albert Sarfati:

> Until that moment, we had hoped that we might be sent to Bulgaria, but now we realized what lay ahead. As soon as we saw the Germans, men and women alike understood that we had been sentenced to death. Everyone was crying. Early in the morning, the train was loaded with its 'livestock'. Each wagon carried between 60 and 70 people with all their baggage . . . As

> soon as the 'livestock' had been loaded into a car, it was locked and sealed. Only heads were visible through the small windows . . . Hands were waving good-bye from the small wagon windows and all of us in the building were shedding tears . . . The last coach had no windows and from inside one could hear voices calling 'help, help'. The people were suffocating . . . Two days later, my destiny was decided. I was to be on the final transport. Life or death. I preferred death over being taken to Poland.[37]

Sarfati, one of only two men to escape from the Skopje camp, survived the war.

The number of 'undesirables' to be deported from old Bulgaria had increased by two and a half thousand to 8,500 on explicit instructions from Belev. He even made the final selection of victims. The KEV Commissar also brought forward the round-up by twenty-four hours, fearing that moves were afoot to intervene on behalf of the Jews. His instinct was correct. What he did not know was that there was a traitor in his own office. In late February, Belev's personal secretary, Liliana Panitsa, leaked the entire deportation plan to some leading Sofia Jews.* The information made its way to the town of Kiustendil where members of the Jewish community organized a campaign to try and block the deportation. The Kiustendil Jews alerted Dimitŭr Peshev, a vice-chairman of the Sŭbranie and hence a government supporter. Despite these ties, Peshev was a passionate critic of the government's anti-Jewish policy. On the evening of 9 March, just hours before the round-up was due to start, Peshev saw Gabrovski in Sofia. The Interior Minister at first denied the impending deportations but, when confronted with incontrovertible evidence, agreed to talk to the Prime Minister, Filov. Filov and Gabrovski insisted the Cabinet decision could not be rescinded but that they would order a postponement of the deportations from old Bulgaria. Peshev and his colleagues immediately sent messages to the major cities ordering a halt to the operation.

---

* This was not the first nor the last time that Liliana Panitsa risked her life for Bulgaria's Jews. She was rewarded by being acquitted of complicity in Belev's crimes at her trial in 1945.

The next day, protests spread across the country. Most dramatically, Kiril, the bishop of Plovdiv, sent a telegram to Tsar Boris, demanding an end to all deportations. If they went ahead, Kiril warned, he would personally lie across the tracks to block the first rail transport from leaving Plovdiv. A stream of Bulgarian dignitaries visited the Tsar and the Prime Minister, urging an immediate change of policy. The communist-backed Partisan movement had opened a campaign of hit-and-run sabotage operations across the country. The leadership vehemently denounced the deportations and helped organize demonstrations and petitions against Belev's plans.

The battle was not yet won, however. Nobody was protesting against the round-up in the 'newly liberated' territories which was well under way, and Filov had insisted that he had only postponed the operation in old Bulgaria, not cancelled it. Boris remained enigmatic. The Nazis resented his gestures of solidarity with Jews, and yet surviving documents suggest that until the late spring of 1943 he raised no major objections to the planned genocide in his discussions with Filov and Belev. The event which seems to have changed Boris's mind was the German defeat at Stalingrad in January 1943 – he could no longer be confident of a German victory. When the Chief Rabbi, Asher Hananel, tried to protest against the deportation programme as late as February 1943, and Belev had him arrested and then brought to his office, the Commissar was furious that Hananel had appealed directly to the King and Metropolitan Stefan: 'Don't you know . . . that we don't do anything without the crown?'[38] Until the dramatic halt to the round-up of Bulgaria's Jews in March 1943, Tsar Boris was not prepared to stick his neck out for them.

The Jews were not a humanitarian passion for the Tsar; he saw them as crucial pieces in a four-way game of chess played by himself, the Bulgarian elite, the Germans and the Allies. The Russians made the winning move in forcing the Germans to surrender at Stalingrad in January 1943. Boris had long realized that a German defeat would enable the Soviet Union to extend its influence in eastern Europe and the Balkans. Boris dropped his strategy of flattering the Germans while keeping Bulgaria far removed from actual combat (in stark contrast to the Romanians, who enthusiastically joined the Germans in the Russian campaign, Bulgaria refused to send a single man to the Eastern Front). After Stalingrad, he sought to ingratiate himself with the western Allies to ward off the prospect of Soviet domination. The easiest way to show willing was to save Bulgaria's Jews. On a visit to Hitler in Berlin in April 1943, he mentioned to Ribbentrop that only the Macedonian and Thracian Jews ought to be deported (they already had been transported, as Boris well knew). After this, Boris and his allies in government systematically frustrated Belev's attempt to revive the deportation process for 'old' Bulgaria. Several thousand Jews suffered the indignity of expulsion from Sofia to the rural interior and 2,000 were interned in the small Danubian port of Samovit. From there, they could see the barges which Belev had chartered for their journey to the north. The boats stayed at their moorings.

Block 25: Greece

Girls – Greeks – who listen to me,
I say everything by singing, so you will understand.
Here the chimneys you see are the biggest factory of death.
Thousands of Jews, old, young, children
Fall into the arms of the flames.
I know they will burn me too.
After a while, I will not be around
To describe what my tired eyes have seen.
Do you hear me? Believe me.
It's true, horrible, I live it every day.
Girls – Greeks – I beg you,
If you get out of here alive,
Tell the entire world the story I sing to you.

Song of an unknown Greek Jew from the
Crematorium 4 work detachment in Auschwitz[39]

In early April 1941, the Greek army evacuated Salonika. Before the retreat, soldiers set fire to as many warehouses and depots as possible to prevent supplies of oil, munitions and food from falling into the hands of the advancing *Wehrmacht*. The population was encouraged to stock up on any goods it could find in preparation for the hard times ahead. As the panzers and armoured cars rolled down the Via Egnatia, Salonikans stayed indoors waiting for the eye of the storm to pass. Before it did, Greek anti-Semites began posting warnings at shops and restaurants – 'Jews Not Welcome Here'. Several leading members of the Jewish community were arrested and some property was confiscated. After a few days, a big car with a swastika fluttering on its bonnet pulled up in front of the seafront house of Salvator Kounio in Koromilas Street. 'Two German giants with metal plates on their chests asked where our father was', remembered Salvator's daughter, Erika, who had just turned fourteen. 'He came down, pale and frightened. Without saying much, they showed him to the car and drove off.'[40]

For several hours, Erika, her brother, her grandparents and her mother waited in a state of near panic before Salvator returned with a simple explanation. The Germans needed cameras and film, and since Kounio owned a big photographic shop on Venizelos St, they had come to him first. 'I told you so', scoffed Ernst Löwy, Erika's maternal grandfather, 'the Germans are incapable of behaving badly – they are a civilized and educated people! A nation which has produced Beethoven, Goethe and Heine has no capacity for evil!'[41] The grandfather was a Jew from Karlsbad (now Karlovy Vary in the Czech Republic) and a veteran of the First World War. Convinced that the reputation of Hitlerism was traditional English propaganda, he and his wife had been reluctant to leave Karlsbad in 1939 to join their daughter and son-in-law in Salonika.

During the first year of the German occupation of Salonika, it seemed that Löwy was right. No particular measures were taken against the 50,000 Jews. The entire city suffered from hunger during the winter of 1941–2 but the situation was never as desperate as it was in Athens. In the Kounio household, there was even a hint of optimism. Erika would catch snatches of her parents' conversation. 'You see, they are leaving the Jews alone! . . . They haven't applied the Nuremberg Laws! What they did, they did in Germany.'[42]

The Salonika Jews were different from their counterparts in central Europe. They spoke a different language, nor had they encountered anything remotely as sinister as north European anti-Semitism. The twentieth century had witnessed the rise of anti-Jewish sentiment among Greeks, born of economic rivalry, but it attracted an insignificant minority. So the Salonika Jews were not prepared for the fate about to befall them. They were certainly unaware that German agents had been taking a systematic inventory of Greece's Jewish community – its population, its treasures, its assets – since 1937. This was when Hans Reegler, whose mother was Greek, arrived in Athens posing as a British Jew named William

Lions. Reegler's network of thirty agents built up such a comprehensive picture of Greek Jewry that when the *Sonderkommando* Rosenberg arrived in Salonika in September 1942 it knew where to find the priceless collections of books, documents and holy scriptures for which this learned community was renowned. Salonika's Jewish culture was a unique blend of Ottoman, Balkan and Hispanic influences and therefore of especial interest to Alfred Rosenberg for his museum of Jewish history and culture.

One hot morning in July 1942, Dr Max Merten, Salonika's corrupt chief administrator, ordered all Jews between the ages of eighteen and forty-five to report to Eleftherios Square in the centre of town at eight o'clock in the morning. This was the spot where in 1908 the Young Turks had issued their manifesto celebrating brotherhood and equality in ten languages.* The Germans wished to select several thousand men for forced-labour brigades, but this was also an exercise in ritual humiliation. In extreme heat and fully clothed, 9,000 men were compelled to take part in a gymnastics drill lasting six and a half hours. Under the threat of being beaten, whipped, shot or set upon by dogs, they had to 'gaze fixedly at the hot July sun for minutes at a time, without being allowed to make the slightest movement, either of eyes or body. If anyone lowered his eyes or turned his gaze aside through sheer physical necessity, he was whipped until the blood ran . . . the SS ordered their victims to go back to their homes and required them to run the first 150 meters or to go on all fours, turning somersaults or rolling in the dust.'[43] In the following days, several men died of brain haemorrhages or meningitis.

These 'games' and the forced-labour programme were designed to soften up the Jews, not yet for deportation, but to rob them. The twenty-eight-year-old Merten was above all an extortionist. He allowed thousands of Jews drafted into forced labour to purchase an exemption for the equivalent of £12,000 in gold. At his trial after the war, victims of his avarice testified that bribes and ransoms were paid in cash, stuffed in sacks which were brought to his office by wheelbarrow. Merten found a naive partner in Salonika's Chief Rabbi, Zevi Koretz, who bowed to every demand made of him.

---

* See chapter 3.

Koretz believed that by acquiescing the Jews would be saved from extermination. The Rabbi acted in good faith, but he undoubtedly made life easier for the German authorities.

When Erika Kounio returned to school in the autumn of 1942, the atmosphere had changed. Her Jewish friends exchanged stories of uncles and fathers who had returned from forced labour in terrible condition. Quiet rumours about sabotage and resistance mixed with dreamy adolescent talk about boys and the future. In the evening, Erika and her family would lock the front door and gather around the radio to listen to the latest news from the BBC. In November, they heard that two Polish Jews claimed to have fled 'from something called a "Lager" named "Lublin." In this place – the news reader added in his clipped, neutral voice – Jews had been killed *en masse*.'[44]

Each passing month brought with it some new sinister development. Merten's office announced that Jews wishing to disinter their relatives should do so immediately as the authorities were taking possession of the Jewish cemeteries, which dated from the time of the migration in 1492. The marble headstones were all confiscated and laid down as pavement which, to the shame of democratic Greece, the public walks over to this day. Others were used to build public baths and an open-air swimming pool for the Germans.

'A Sonderkommando of the SS has arrived', Erika overheard her father say in February 1943, 'it's led by a certain Brunner and a Wisliceny. I don't like it one little bit.'[45] Another lawyer, Dieter Wisliceny, a thirty-year-old from East Prussia, had already distinguished himself in the eyes of Adolf Eichmann, for his swift dispatch of Slovakia's Jewish community in 1942. (He was executed in Slovakia for this crime after the war.) His collaborator, the twenty-three-year-old Austrian Alois Brunner, was less the fastidious bureaucrat and more the violent sadist (at the time of writing, it is believed that he still enjoys the hospitality of the Syrian government).

Wisliceny lost no time in issuing the anti-Jewish decrees, familiar from the rest of Europe and the Balkans – the patches, restrictions on movement, confiscation of property and goods, and, finally, ghettoization. As the Jews made up almost half the city's population, this latter process required some improvisation. Several non-contiguous ghettos were established, including one in Kalamaria, today a fashionable district on the eastern outskirts of Thessaloniki. The most crowded quarter was called Baron Hirsch after the great Jewish railroad builder of the Austro-Hungarian empire.

The camp at Baron Hirsch was surrounded by a high wooden fence and barbed wire. Signs written in German, Greek and Ladino hung from the three entrances, warning Jews not to exit the camp and non-Jews not to enter on pain of death. By early March, 2,500 people were squeezed into 593 cramped rooms in Baron Hirsch. Pandemonium ruled as the inmates moved through the tiny streets with their possessions piled on carts and wheelbarrows. They looked for extra room for their children; they hoped to swap goods for food or warm clothing; a few plotted their escape. In the evenings the SS guards swivelled their searchlights on to the square near the main entrance and compelled the terrified inhabitants to entertain them with traditional dances and songs as the cameras of Goebbels' Propaganda Ministry whirred.

The first 2,500 people incarcerated in this ghetto were working-class Jews from the poorer districts, with the exception of two well-to-do families, the Salems and the Kounios. When Wisliceny arrived, Erika and her family had been forced to move out of their seafront house to a much smaller dwelling in one of the outlying ghettos. On 10 March 1943, an SS officer turned up and ordered the Kounio family to pack their bags and go to Baron Hirsch within two hours. Erika's father had secretly transferred his business to a Greek friend in an attempt to save his assets but somebody had denounced him to the SS – the relocation was their punishment. 'Men, women, children, babies, on the move, ceaselessly and senselessly', noted Erika, as the Kounio family searched desperately for a place to sleep. 'At last we found a café with broken windows. Water was coming through the roof and had begun to form puddles in some places . . . We were freezing and hungry and couldn't sleep at night for the cold and despair.'[46]

Salvator queued up with everyone else at the 'bank', as the Germans had told them to exchange all their *drachmas* for *złotys*. The money would be issued by cheque, they were told, on arrival in Poland. So the Kounios learnt where they were bound. Out of the main gate, Erika and her family could see Salonika's railway station on the opposite side of the Via Egnatia. After Baron Hirsch had brought the railway to Salonika at the turn of the century, he built a hospice opposite the station to accommodate the victims of pogroms in Russia. Once a place of rescue and convalescence for Hirsch's fellow Jews, the district had been transformed into the final point of departure on the road to Auschwitz. 'The misery went on', remembered Erika. 'In shock and, even more, in amazement we drifted through the second day. On the day after, everyone was talking about the goods carriages which had been made ready in the station . . . Forty carriages! An endless line just waiting to be loaded!'[47]

Hirsch's great enterprise had created a dense web of railway lines which linked all parts of central and eastern Europe with the Balkans. It had brought commerce and prosperity to Salonika. Half a century later, the Sephardim of the city were taken by these same tracks from their southern tip to the northern terminus of Kraków. As the wailing mass was shoved into the carriages, orchestrated by the 'barbaric, wild screaming of the Germans', Erika gripped on tightly to her mother, father and younger brother, Heinz. '"Bamm, bamm!" the doors were slammed shut, one after the other and we finally climbed in. Our carriage was bursting at the seams . . . Men, women, children, old people talking, crying, moaning, all at the same time! At the end of the carriage was a bag with ship's biscuits, worm-ridden figs and olives. In the middle stood a bucket.'[48]

Seven or eight days later, the trucks disgorged the panicked mass into the bitter cold of a Polish winter, 'the coldest night of our lives'. SS personnel ran here and there, brandishing pistols and whips. 'Los! Los! – Raus! Raus! – Schnell! Schnell!' Dogs barked wildly, baring their teeth as they strained against their leads. 'Which are more wild', wondered Erika in her terror, 'the SS or their dogs?'[49] The Kounio family was an anomaly – they all spoke German, a rarity among the Salonika Jews. As the bulk of the first transport was channelled towards the gas chambers, Erika, Heinz and their parents were told to wait. They were needed as translators and interpreters.

Erika was, of course, separated from her brother and father but managed to stick with her mother. She worked in the Political Department (*Politische Abteilung* – PA), the crucial office in the camp. This afforded her certain 'privileges', the most important being work indoors. But she still had to pass muster at reveille; she was still required to march in time to the Auschwitz orchestra as Dr

Rohde and the SS women, Drechsler and Mandel, 'selected' the weak or ill for transfer to Block 25, the ante-chamber of the gas room. She slept tormented by lice, suffered extensive blistering, chronic malnutrition and frostbite, and a debilitating attack of spotted typhus. And she had to hide this from the SS – a hint of infirmity meant death.

In the PA, she chronicled the names of Auschwitz's dead. Soon after she started, she saw the name of her dear friend, Sarika, on the list of transfers to Block 25: 'It was the first time I cried since our deportation had begun and was the last time for many years.'[50] Erika herself had no prospect of survival. As the cataloguers of genocide, she and her colleagues knew more about the operation of Auschwitz than any other inmates. Such important witnesses would not be permitted to live. So her work detachment was known as the Ascension to Heaven Commando (*Himmelfahrtskommando*). 'The only way you'll get out of here', the SS overseer sneered at her, 'is through the gas chambers and up the chimney!'[51]

Meanwhile, the Greek Jews poured into the camp in their thousands. The transport of 46,000 men, women and children from Salonika was completed with unprecedented speed. The majority was immediately dispatched to the gas chambers where 96 per cent of the Salonika Jews were killed. Erika's grandfather, Ernst Löwy, was among those who made the journey. In hiding for many months, Löwy remained convinced nonetheless that the Germans had no dishonourable intentions. Alone and miserable, he decided 'one Sunday morning to report to the Gestapo in Salonika, taking all the medals he won as a captain in the German military . . . "I am Dr. Ernst Löwy and here are my papers . . . Will you please send me to wherever my daughter and family are?"'[52] Received with respect by the desk officer, he was told that he would see his daughter again after a train journey lasting several days. He was last sighted by an acquaintance in the back of a lorry heading for the gas chamber.

The Greek Jews in Auschwitz looked out for their compatriots from Salonika, and later from Ioannina, Corfu, Athens and the islands. The Nazis attempted to erase individuality through uniforms, shaved heads and terror. Yet although Erika experienced the solidarity of Jews and Christians from various nations in Auschwitz, she felt herself to be a Greek and a Salonikan as much as a Jew. In October 1944, the astonishing resistance organization in Auschwitz succeeded in sabotaging Crematorium No. 4 with explosive devices. Erika felt pride rising in her breast when she heard that Greek Jews had played a major role in the attack. 'Greeks!' she exclaimed to herself. 'Our people had held their heads up high. I could hardly believe it and yet it was true! I was so proud of them: they obviously wouldn't make it but what a beautiful death! They chose the death that they wanted.'[53]

Erika Kounio was spared only one horror at Auschwitz – Block 25 and the gas chambers. In January 1945, she took part in the Death March when tens of thousands were forced to transfer to other camps in Germany by foot. After that she and her mother survived weeks of misery at the women's camp at Ravensbrück. Despite losing twenty-two relations in Auschwitz, all of Erika's immediate family survived – the only Jewish family from Salonika to return from Auschwitz with all its members alive.

Liberation: death of the peasantry – Romania

In September 1943, Italy capitulated to US and British forces. The two Allies were obliged to consult the Soviet leadership on all decisions relating to the Italian occupation but in the event they systematically excluded Moscow. Two years before the war's end, the western Allies had thus marked out the first 'sphere of influence' in Europe, a policy which would have an early and substantial impact on the Balkan peninsula. At this stage, the United States and Britain were not yet working together to counter a perceived threat of Soviet expansionism; the relationship between Roosevelt, Stalin and Churchill was more complicated. On occasion, Roosevelt would confide his dislike of British imperialism to Stalin. The Soviet dictator sometimes sought Churchill's advice on dealing with the Americans if they were behaving inflexibly. None of the Big Three had a clear idea of its own country's war aims and only the fuzziest picture of what the other two were thinking. In an effort to prepare for an Allied victory, they formed the European Advisory Council in 1943. The EAC was charged with developing a strategy of cooperation which could be implemented as soon as the Germans signed an armistice. The resourceful American diplomat, George F. Kennan, was appointed as American delegate to the EAC. 'So far as I could learn from my superiors in the department', he later wrote, 'their attitude toward the commission was dominated primarily by a lively concern lest the new body actually do something.' The State Department was particularly nervous 'lest the American delegation, through overeagerness or inadvertence, contribute to so unfortunate an occurrence'.[54] Although the need for strategic coordination was pressing, the tactical requirements of the battlefield rendered futile any attempt to establish a coherent vision of Europe's future. The Red Army liberated the Balkans before it reached central Europe. As a result, this is where first Britain and later the United States began dividing up Europe with the Soviet Union.

Soon after Italy's surrender, an argument broke out between Britain and the United States about a possible invasion of the Balkans. Britain was keen to move swiftly into the western Balkans with the aim of pushing the Nazis back behind the Alps. Despite encouraging intelligence reports, the Americans stalled, insisting instead on driving up through difficult Italian terrain in preparation for Operation Dragoon, the seaborne assault on southern and western France. 'I still don't understand', noted General Rendulić, the man coordinating the *Wehrmacht*'s struggle against Tito, 'why the Allies gave up their drive across the Balkans after they had taken Sicily in August [1943]. Instead, they sustained many losses over a period of months as they squeezed their way through the narrow roads of the Italian peninsula before finally landing on the West coast of France, far away from all the strategic theatres of war. I am convinced that by giving up an assault on the Balkans in 1943, the Allies have postponed the end of the war by a year.'[55]

Eden attributed this American strategy to a reluctance to become involved in the Balkans. The Foreign Secretary concluded that 'the President shared a widespread American suspicion of the British Empire'. In consequence, 'he was always anxious to make it plain to Stalin that the US was not "ganging up" with Britain against Russia . . . The outcome of this was some confusion in Anglo-American relations which profited the Soviets.' During the war, the Americans treated the British obsession with the Balkans as an example of London's anachronistic imperialist urge. After the Yalta Conference in February 1945, and Harry Truman's accession to the presidency in April that year, the United States hastily borrowed the mantle of chief warrior against Stalinist expansion in Europe and Asia from Britain. The fate of the Balkans had long since been decided by the overwhelming presence of the Red Army, a reality which the Americans had been unable to grasp in 1943. When Eisenhower dismissed Britain's plan for intervention in the Balkans, he inadvertently guaranteed Russia's dominance over much of the peninsula. The Red Army was the source of political authority in Romania and Bulgaria just as the British army, and later the American military, was the arbiter of power in Greece.

For the Balkan peoples, this was merely part of a familiar pattern whereby their political orientation was decided in the distant capitals of great powers. The Allies would argue that they had earned the right to interfere in the Balkans by dint of sacrifices made on the battlefield. (This was also the reasoning employed by Soviet generals to justify their soldiers' pillaging of central Europe and the Balkans.) It is true that people in the Balkans contributed little to their own liberation. The impact of the Chetniks in Serbia on Germany's military capability has never been properly assessed. Chetnik units controlled most of the Serbian countryside by 1944 but it would seem that the Germans were not unduly troubled by them. In Bosnia and Croatia, the Partisans kept up to thirteen Axis divisions (not all German) busy, but they spent most of the war fleeing and evading pitched battles with the *Wehrmacht*. Tito's men were heroic, but not necessarily effective.

One Balkan political drama certainly had a big impact on the course of the war in Europe. On 20 August 1944, Red Army troops stationed north of Iaşi in western Moldavia and south-west of Tiraspol launched their major push into the Balkans against joint German-Romanian forces. Three days later, Marshal Antonescu visited King Michael (1940–47) to recommend that Romania seek an armistice immediately. In response, the King announced he was sacking the government. He promptly arrested the Marshal. Michael and his advisers had discovered that Antonescu's agents had been holding talks with the Soviet ambassador to Stockholm, the old Bolshevik feminist, Alexandra Kollontai, about armistice terms. The new rulers in Romania wanted to hold armistice talks with the British in the hope of securing more favourable terms. Russians still inspired warmth in some Slav hearts, especially the Bulgarians and the Serbs, but the Romanians viewed their imminent arrival with despair. The armistice negotiations opened in Cairo but as the nearest British troops were almost 1,600 kilometres from Romania and the Red Army was already inside the country, the talks soon transferred to Moscow. Despite all this, had Romania not decided to switch sides and seek an armistice, 'the losses of the Western armies in France would have been higher and so would those among the civilian population in Great Britain and the Netherlands from V-bombs. To the whole of Europe and to Rumania, as well, the final defeat of Germany would have brought greater destruction.'[56]

Unfortunately for the Romanians, the Red Army intended to extract the maximum concessions from the surrender. The deeper Soviet troops penetrated Romania, the more complete Moscow's control would be over the territory. In the event, King Michael's offer of an armistice to the Soviets was not actually taken up. Nor had Hitler finished with Romania. He felt personally betrayed by the *coup* against Antonescu, and issued orders to crush the conspirators and restore the Marshal to power. A day after the *coup*, Romania was attacked simultaneously by German and Soviet troops. At 11 o'clock in the morning of 24 August, 150 Luftwaffe bombers and dive bombers appeared in perfect formation over the Romanian capital, which had already suffered devastation in Allied air raids since April. To the east, Soviet forces were taking tens of thousands of Romanian prisoners. They were also ripping up all rolling stock, requisitioning every motor car and, in some cases, dismantling entire factories for export to the Soviet Union. It was not long before the Germans were expelled. In September 1944, the armistice was finally signed and the looting came to an end. Romania was now obliged to start paying reparations of $300 million.

In the baggage of the Red Army came the hitherto insignificant Romanian Communist Party (RCP). Returning from her exile in Moscow, Ana Pauker, the future Foreign Minister and show-trial victim, admitted frankly that the RCP had about 1,000 members in the entire country. Within less than three years, it had over 200,000. In the north-east and in Transylvania (which the Soviets restored to Romanian sovereignty), the communists swiftly filled the power vacuum. In these regions, the Party was dominated by Jews and Hungarians, which made it still less attractive to Romanians. In Wallachia and southern Romania, the old parties were still strong. The tens of thousands now streaming to join the RCP included some who were disaffected by the old parties but the majority were not signing up out of ideological conviction, and the RCP was not choosy: 'Though themselves willing to admit former Iron Guardists to their ranks, they raised a storm when other parties did the same.'[57] The converts felt the powerful new wind blowing from Moscow and regarded the RCP as the best place to find shelter. Gradually, RCP members began filling local councils and the police force throughout the country. However, Russophobia and the peasantry's stubborn resistance to change meant that communism encountered more difficulty establishing itself in Romania than anywhere else in the Balkans.

King Michael struggled to keep a non-communist national government afloat, in the hope that the Americans and the British would put pressure on the Russians. Had the King and his adviser, Ion Maniu, been apprised of discussions in Moscow during October 1944, they might have spared themselves the effort. In an attempt to solve the Polish and Balkan problems, Churchill had visited Stalin:

> 'Let us settle about our affairs in the Balkans. Your armies are in Rumania and Bulgaria. We have interests, missions, and agents there. Don't let us get at cross-purposes in small ways. So far as Britain and Russia are concerned, how would it do for you to have ninety per cent predominance in Rumania, for us to have ninety per cent of the say in Greece, and go about fifty-fifty about Yugoslavia?' While this was being translated I wrote out on a half-sheet of paper:

Rumania	
Russia	90%
The others	10%
Greece	
Great Britain (in accord with U.S.A.)	90%
Russia	10%
Yugoslavia	50–50%
Hungary	50–50%
Bulgaria	
Russia	75%
The others	25%

> I pushed this across to Stalin, who by then had heard the translation. There was a slight pause. Then he took his blue pencil

and made a large tick upon it, and passed it back to us. It was all settled in no more time than it takes to set down.[58]

Europe was divided at Yalta at February 1945. But by then the postwar fate of the Balkans had long been sealed. As relations between the Soviet Union and the West steadily deteriorated in the mid-1940s, the division of Europe became inevitable as Moscow sought to strengthen its *cordon sanitaire* in eastern Europe and the Balkans. The British and the Americans disapproved of Russia's political monopoly in Romania and they issued sporadic protests. But as practitioners of great-power *Realpolitik*, they understood the logic of Stalin's actions. 'The Russians have been in undisputed control from the beginning', Roosevelt observed to Churchill in March 1945, 'and with Rumania lying athwart the Russian lines of communications it is moreover difficult to contest the plea of military necessity and security which they are using to justify their action.'[59] The alternative was war between the Soviet Union and the West which neither side was willing to risk. In the Balkans, there were still adjustments to come in Yugoslavia and Hungary (largely in Stalin's favour), but after the Moscow summit Romania and Bulgaria fell under exclusive Soviet influence, while Britain would have a free hand in Greece.

In both Romania and Bulgaria, the communist parties were committed to fashioning a state based on the revolutionary potential of the working class. But the proletariat was scarce in both countries, overwhelmed in a sea of peasants, most of whom favoured private ownership of land, and for whom the idea of 'collectivization' was anathema. The CP leaderships understood the need to woo the peasantry whilst neutralizing its popular leaders. Their attempts to do so were alternately comical and vicious. Romania's first communist-dominated government was led by Petru Groza who headed the Ploughman's Front, a tiny organization of rural fellow travellers. Groza's cabinet ordered several thousand tractors from the Soviet Union which would be sent to the 320 newly established Agricultural Machine Centres. The order was duly submitted but the tractors never arrived. Romania and Bulgaria found themselves in the company of a powerful ally whose economy was in shreds. The revival of industry and agriculture in both countries proved exceptionally difficult, particularly in Romania where the Soviet

Union imposed punitive demands. Not only were Bessarabia and northern Bukovina annexed to the Soviet Union, but Romania's entire oil production, a unique economic asset in the Balkans, was turned over to the Soviets.

There was little cooperation between the opposition and the communists in Romania and regular outbursts of violence. The future First Secretary, Gheorghe Gheorghiu-Dej, commanded the loyalty of the country's largest group of workers, the railway men, and organized them into paramilitary bands, which were frequently called upon to 'restore order'. During 1945 and 1946, Britain and the United States attempted to pressurize the Soviet Union into allowing broader participation in the Romanian government. This coincided with western measures to exclude the communist parties of Italy and France from government, leaving Stalin with a watertight excuse to behave in a similar fashion in the Balkans. On 19 November 1946, 'the Rumanian people went to the polls in an election in which every fraudulent, violent, and unscrupulous device ever used in the Balkans was brought into full play'.[60] The communists were now in total control.

Liberation: Death of a peasant – Bulgaria

The Soviet occupation was initially more tolerable in Bulgaria than in Romania. Americans, Britons and Bulgarians all agreed that the Red Army behaved with some discretion and deference. Russian officers did not stay 'in the best hotels and . . . were seldom in the best restaurants or the best shops. They looked like strangers from a long way off.' Elizabeth Barker, the perceptive Reuters correspondent in the Balkans, contrasted this behaviour with the situation in Greece where 'the British occupation . . . was far more conspicuous and outwardly irritating. The British had all the best hotels in every town where there was a garrison . . . They walked the streets as though they were patrons or colonisers; their clean khaki drill uniforms and white belts and pink faces stood out loudly against the Greek background.'[61] Bulgaria had resisted Hitler's demand to declare war on the Soviet Union. True, Moscow did declare war on Bulgaria just before crossing from Romania in September 1944; but it was Europe's shortest war – the hostilities only lasted a few hours before the Bulgarian surrender was accepted.

There was much less looting, rape and expropriation in Bulgaria than elsewhere. In general, Bulgarians welcomed the liberating troops with polite enthusiasm. The Soviets found the local Communist Party larger and better-organized than its Romanian counterpart.

The communists lost no time in settling old scores by establishing special tribunals, known as People's Courts. Throughout 1945, thousands associated with the wartime régime were summarily tried. In the space of six months, 2,138 people were executed and as many again received life sentences. The accused included opponents of the communists who had refused to collaborate with the pro-German régime. The most prominent victim of this first wave of postwar repression was the leading figure of the left-wing Agrarians, G.M. Dimitrov, who was known either as 'The Doctor' or plain GM, to distinguish him from his namesake, Georgi Dimitrov, the undisputed leader of the Communist Party who was still directing operations from his exile in Moscow. The persecution of G.M. Dimitrov, who had returned from exile during 1945, revealed that while promising a new dawn, the Communist Party also drew on an important tradition from the interwar years – that of state terror. People quickly learnt to fear the People's Militia, whose officers patrolled the towns and villages in their distinct uniforms of khaki with magenta piping. A lawyer who defended the Agrarians, when asked the difference between the new People's Militia and the prewar police, remarked, 'on the whole they are just the same, except that they take less trouble. In the old days, the police held the prisoners until the prison doctors had managed to heal the scars so that they didn't show much. Now the Militia turn them out without bothering about that sort of thing.'[62]

Such carelessness led the Militia to return the body of Mara Racheva, GM's secretary, to her mother after days of interrogation in early 1945. Officially, she had committed suicide by throwing herself out of a fourth-storey window. In an embassy memo, the American military attaché, Colonel S.W. Bailey, reported his conversation with the doctor who examined the corpse at the mother's request. '[T]he following injuries – difficult to explain by the effect of a fall even from the fourth floor window – were established, in addition to the bullet and knife wounds. 1. All the nails on both feet had been torn out. 2. Three fingers of the left hand had been hacked off at the second joint. 3. Both ears cut off. 4. Right breast excised. 5. Tongue torn out and all teeth extracted. 6. Flaying of a strip of skin about two inches wide through one quadrant of the waist. Demands for the preparation of a protocol setting out these facts were, somewhat understandably, refused.'[63]

GM fled the country with American assistance and Nikola Petkov assumed the leadership of the Agrarians. Petkov was no stranger to political violence. In 1907, his father, Dimitri, then Prime Minister of Bulgaria, was assassinated minutes after emerging from a Cabinet meeting at the parliament, the Sŭbranie. His brother, Petko Petkov, Stamboliiski's most effective lieutenant, was shot dead in 1924 by one of the fascist General Vŭlkov's agents.* Until his brother's death, Nikola Petkov had been studying law in Paris, a *bon vivant* with no interest in politics. But after this second tragedy, he resolved to rebuild the Agrarians, working closely with GM in the 1930s. Unlike GM, who went into exile in 1941, Petkov stayed in Bulgaria throughout the war to organize the Agrarian underground resistance. This led to two spells of imprisonment. Talented and charming, Petkov's political record and courage were unimpeachable.

In the summer of 1945, the Agrarians and the Social Democrats fell victim to the communists' celebrated salami tactics. To weaken opponents, the Communist Party would entice key members of rival parties to split off from the main leadership and establish a competing organization. These communist-backed groupings remained in the Fatherland Front while the old Agrarians and Social Democrats left the coalition. Over the next two years, they fought a losing battle to prevent a communist dictatorship. But Petkov, the most popular politician in Bulgaria, refused to give up without a fight.

The Agrarian leader proved adept at drawing American and British representatives on the Allied Control Commission into domestic Bulgarian politics. He also maintained friendly contacts with elements in the Fatherland Front leadership who were open to political compromise. In August 1945, his persistent manoeuvring paid off: the communist Interior Ministry had sanctioned such blatant intimidation against the opposition during the campaign that

---

* See chapter 6.

the British and Americans dug their heels in, demanding a postponement. Irritated by Petkov's success, Moscow ordered the deployment of its most powerful political weapon – Georgi Dimitrov.

Dimitrov was born into a family of working-class revolutionaries. He became a political organizer as a thirteen-year-old print worker. Within two decades, he had risen through the hierarchy of the 'Narrows', Bulgaria's equivalent of the Bolsheviks, to become one of the two most influential communists in the country. His siblings died in the Balkan Wars or at the hands of the police forces of Russia and Bulgaria. During Vŭlkov's White Terror in the 1920s, Dimitrov chose exile. He found himself in Germany when Hitler came to power. Arrested by the Nazis for suspected involvement in the Reichstag fire, Dimitrov seized the imagination of a world audience at his trial in Leipzig. His verbal demolition of Göring, acting as prosecutor, earned him deserved renown. After his acquittal he took out Soviet citizenship, and Stalin rewarded him for his Leipzig performance by placing him in charge of the Communist International (the Comintern).

When the Fatherland Front assumed power in Bulgaria, Dimitrov remained in Russia. Nonetheless, he hovered

> over Sofia in his absence. A twice-life-size statue of him in rough plaster, wearing a long-frock coat, carrying a scroll in one hand and looking noble in the style of Beethoven, towered before the gateway of the disused royal palace . . . Photographs of him, with a flowing Edwardian moustache, and books about him were in the main shops. Portraits of him and banners hailing him as founder of the Fatherland Front were carried in all processions . . . It was impossible to be in Sofia for forty-eight hours without feeling his brooding presence.[64]

On the evening of 8 November 1945, Dimitrov returned to Bulgaria for the first time in two decades. The National Theatre was packed with dignitaries who were joined by a throng outside in the rhythmic chant 'Di-Mi-Trov'. But the Lion of Leipzig was old, living by all accounts a joyless life since his only son had been killed in the war. Instead of enjoying this triumphant reception, he gave a speech replete with personal bitterness. He angrily attacked the pre-war régime for having refused to invite him back to Bulgaria during the Reichstag trial and spoke of how his homecoming had been blighted when he saw 'the filthy rags of the opposition' on sale in Sofia. Dimitrov was not carrying a brief of reconciliation.

Immediately, the newspapers of the Fatherland Front began accusing Petkov of enriching himself and building a large house on the proceeds. In fact, the Agrarian leader lived in a small house in the centre of Sofia which was frequently crowded with peasants from the countryside who had travelled to the capital to ask the great man's advice. Dimitrov in contrast appropriated a villa, surrounded by a huge wall topped with barbed wire. At night four searchlights lit up the building, giving it the appearance of a prison. Haughty and distant from ordinary people, Dimitrov was always surrounded by bodyguards and rarely made public appearances. He was the first Balkan member of the New Class that the Yugoslav dissident, Milovan Djilas, was to anatomize a decade later.

In 1946 and the first half of 1947, leading members of all opposition parties who refused to collaborate were tortured, put on trial and, in some cases, executed. But it was not until the British and American governments finally recognized the postwar Bulgarian state in early summer 1947 that Dimitrov felt sufficiently confident to move against Petkov. On 5 June, People's Militiamen walked into the debating chamber of the Sŭbranie. They forced their way through dozens of opposition MPs and dragged Petkov off. He was charged with treason in a show trial which included features soon to become familiar throughout the Balkan 'people's democracies' – forced confessions, counterfeit documents and a preordained sentence of death, which was carried out in his case on 23 September 1947. Mass demonstrations demanding the death penalty were held throughout the country. The Sofia mineworkers' union, a backbone of the Communist Party, declared that the death sentence would give its members 'an incentive for harder work and greater achievements in the production field'.[65]

In his last remarks to the court, Petkov, who had signed no confession, declared, 'I am not afraid of whatever fate awaits me, nor am I perturbed by shouts of "traitor." For both my father and my brother were murdered in the streets of Sofia, denounced as traitors, only to be recognized as heroes by the Bulgarian nation afterwards.'[66] (Fifty-three years later, I witnessed a mass demonstration in front of a plinth where a statue of Dimitrov had stood until the previous year. The crowd had gathered to honour the memory of Nikola Petkov.)

In 1933, the Bulgarian Section of the League of Human Rights had organized a campaign in protest against the trial of Dimitrov in Leipzig. After his acquittal, Dimitrov sent his personal thanks to the President of the Bulgarian Section, Nikola Petkov. A year after Petkov's trial, Dimitrov admitted that he had directed the judge to pass the death sentence. 'Of course, if they had not intervened from abroad, and if some had not ultimately attempted to dictate to our sovereign court, Petkov's head could have been saved. The death sentence could have been commuted to some other punishment. But when I came to the question of blackmailing the Bulgarian nation and infringing on the right of our sovereign people's court, the death sentence had to be executed.'

'The sentencing of Petkov', commented the French weekly, *Une Semaine dans le monde*, 'is yet another episode in the general offensive launched against the peasant parties of central Europe and the Balkans, the offensive of the Red International against the Green International.'[67]

Liberation: the black sheep – Yugoslavia

From 1943 onwards, revolutionary movements were gaining momentum in two other Balkan countries, Yugoslavia and Greece. Both movements had matured in the harsh environment of Nazi occupation, and both were engaged in fighting ruthless civil wars against supporters of the interwar monarchies and local fascists. Their aim was to combine liberation with the establishment of a new socialist order. The source of their authority was not the Red Army but their struggle against the occupier. This lent them both mass support and an unrivalled militancy that did not fit well into the Allied plans for 'spheres of influence'.

In their percentage agreement of October 1944, Churchill and Stalin divided influence equally in Yugoslavia. Yet although Tito had persuaded Churchill to switch his support from Draža Mihailović and the Chetniks to the Partisans, he had no intention of allowing the British into the country after the war. Tito told Stalin that if the British landed on the Dalmatian coast, the

Partisans would attack them. But far from encouraging the Partisans' anti-British stance, Stalin ordered Tito to tone down his revolutionary zeal. The West, the Soviet leader warned, would assume that Tito was operating on Moscow's explicit instructions. Stalin sincerely wanted to cooperate with the West and to avoid any impression that he was undermining the delicate negotiations of the Big Three. The revolutionary paraphernalia of Tito and the Yugoslav communists, which had played such an important role in the Partisan struggle, was little more than a provocation as far as Stalin was concerned. 'What's all this nonsense I hear about you wearing red stars on your caps?' he demanded angrily, 'Form isn't important. What you actually achieve is important. And you prance around with – red stars! My God, the last thing we need is red stars!'[68]

The leadership of the new Yugoslavia made some formal concessions to the Big Three. They invited Ivan Šubašić, Prime Minister in the royal government in exile, to become Foreign Minister, to show that the new régime enjoyed a broad democratic base. On the ground, however, they imposed a harsh revolutionary justice. As German troops streamed out of Yugoslavia, the Croat fascist leader, Ante Pavelić, and 1–200,000 Ustaša troops and civilians set off for the Austrian border on 7 May 1945, with Partisan forces in hot pursuit. They got as far as Bleiburg, a small Austrian border town, before being surrounded by British troops to the north and Partisans to the south. With RAF Spitfires buzzing overhead, about 30–40,000 soldiers, including Pavelić, managed to disappear into the surrounding woods and then deep into Austria. But the remainder were taken prisoner by Partisan forces amid scenes of carnage. Some 30,000 Ustaše were killed on the four-day march towards the Slovene town of Maribor. On 20 May, near the village of Tezna, '50,000 Croat soldiers and about 30,000 refugees, mainly women and children, were executed over a five-day period . . . A macabre end to the "Independent State of Croatia."'[69]

In Serbia, the Chetniks fared little better even though many had fought bravely against the Germans. Mihailović, the Chetnik leader, led a small band of fighters into the mountains of eastern Bosnia. He was eventually caught, tried and executed in 1946 as an alleged war criminal. But thousands of Chetniks became fugitives in a twilight world. Many were secondary-school pupils when they joined the resistance. Now, they were hunted in villages and towns throughout Serbia. Thousands hid from the secret police in Belgrade, moving at dusk from one safe place to the next. Occasionally, they would risk capture by visiting their families. In place of the bright adolescent who had left three or four years before, mothers and fathers now saw a 'tall, grim-looking young man . . . who appeared . . . on their doorstep with one hand always clutching something in the pocket of his raincoat and whose eyes were ringed with dark circles'.[70]

Arrested by the Gestapo during the war, Dimitrije Djordjević, a young Chetnik leader, survived Mauthausen only to fall into the hands of the Gestapo's communist successor when he returned to Belgrade. 'Both [organizations] had in common the violence with which they imposed their authority. The Gestapo destroyed the body; Ozna raped the soul. The Gestapo killed by shooting and by imprisonment in death camps; Ozna engaged in brainwashing, demanding repentance for sins not committed and self-abnegation. The difference was one of physical as opposed to spiritual annihilation.'[71]

OZNa, *Odsek za zaštitu naroda* (Department for the Protection of the People), modelled itself on the Soviet secret police, the NKVD. But during the war, under the dour leadership of Aleksandar Ranković, the Communist Minister of the Interior, it matured independent of Soviet control. Ranković built a network of informers and a devoted political police whose efficiency gave birth to the popular Orwellian rhyme, *Ozna sve dozna* (Ozna finds out everything).* He aimed to make OZNa omnipresent, recruiting 'in every block of flats, in every street, in every village and in every barrack room'.[72] The Nazi and Ustaše camps throughout Yugoslavia were turned over for use by the communists. Tens of thousands of people were executed in 1946–7 while hundreds of thousands were interned. In 1947, there were so many men in camps or prisons that the penal system started to buckle under the strain. The mass arrests had removed so many young men from the labour market that the economy was being disrupted. Against Ranković's better judgement, the Party was forced to declare amnesty for tens of thousands.

* OZNa's name was soon changed to UDBa – *Uprava državne bezbednosti* (Office of State Security) which also had its own phrase *UDBa – tvoja sudba* (UDBa – your fate).

Thanks chiefly to OZNa, the Communist Party of Yugoslavia (*Komunistička Partija Jugoslavije* – KPJ) was able to neutralize all political opposition soon after the elections of November 1945, which were comprehensively rigged. The communist monopoly on power took hold in Yugoslavia much earlier than anywhere else in eastern Europe. But OZNa had another significant historical role beyond the imposition of domestic order through terror. Notwithstanding the Yugoslav leadership's unrivalled devotion to Stalin, problems between Moscow and Belgrade cropped up early in the postwar relationship. Even before the war had ended, Milovan Djilas, Tito's lieutenant in charge of propaganda and the press, had protested to the Soviet military command in Belgrade about the behaviour of the Red Army: 'There were so many serious incidents perpetrated by individuals and groups of Red Army soldiers on civilians and members of the Yugoslav military that this became a political problem for the Communist Party . . . There were 1219 rapes including 111 murders and 1204 cases of looting – figures which are not so insignificant given that the Red Army only operated in the north-eastern part of Yugoslavia.'[73]

Stalin personally upbraided Djilas for daring to question the honour of the Red Army and further accused the KPJ of spying on Soviet representatives in Belgrade. OZNa and the NKVD were indeed becoming rivals. Both gathered material not only on the opposition in Yugoslavia but on each other as well. OZNa's investigations during 1946 and 1947 revealed how industrious the Soviet secret police had been in penetrating the Yugoslav Party and military: NKVD agents were present in the highest organs of the Yugoslav state apparatus.

Tensions between Moscow and Belgrade were further exacerbated by difficulties in economic relations. Yugoslavia turned down the Soviet offer to establish joint-stock companies. These companies were the Russians' preferred way of extracting as many resources as possible from its satellite countries in order to revive the Soviet economy. The Yugoslavs rejected the joint-stock system, but also unveiled an ambitious five-year plan for economic development, well before any other east European country. Such bold behaviour might have been mistaken for impudence: a five-year plan implied ideological parity with the Soviet Union. Stalin was disturbed by the Yugoslavs' militant zeal. The KPJ accepted communist dogma at face value and had not yet grasped that it was a mere tool used by Stalin to legitimize his personal power and the new Russian imperialism.

As Soviet influence spread through eastern Europe, Stalin took care not to alarm Britain and America. But the Balkans presented some strategic problems both for Stalin and for the Yugoslavs. 'The mountain barriers of the Balkans', observed one contemporary historian, 'form a natural obstacle which separates Russia and north-eastern Europe from the Mediterranean. Existing communications provide only three important gaps in the barrier – the north-east corner of the Adriatic and Fiume, the Vardar valley leading down to Salonika, and the Black Sea Straits passing Constantinople. It is no accident that Trieste, the Straits and Macedonia are the three danger-spots of south-east Europe.'[74]

In April 1945, Yugoslav forces raced to Trieste ahead of New Zealand troops advancing from the Po under overall British command. The port had an Italian majority and a Slovene minority although the surrounding countryside was predominantly Slovene. The Yugoslavs desperately wanted to annex the town to give them easy access to the Adriatic. But under western pressure, the army reluctantly evacuated the city and fell back to an agreed line, leaving Trieste under Allied occupation. Britain had insisted on the Yugoslav withdrawal in part because it feared that the Yugoslav claim was really a Soviet attempt to establish a warm-water naval base. In fact, true to his policy of cooperation with the West on strategic issues, Stalin pointedly refused to back Yugoslav claims to Trieste.

In Macedonia, the Yugoslavs hoped to gain access to Salonika by supporting the revolutionary war being waged by the Greek communists, EAM/ELAS, against the Athens government and British forces. But Stalin had granted Britain a free hand in Greece in exchange for his control over Romania and Bulgaria. The Soviet dictator had no intention of going back on his word, and so the Yugoslavs and Soviets pursued diametrically opposed policies towards Greece.

The perception in the West that Stalin would expand his empire wherever he could obscured the tensions between Moscow and Belgrade. Indeed, Yugoslavia's uncompromising line on Trieste and the Greek civil war strengthened the belief that Belgrade was

Moscow's most faithful ally. Yet it was its very militancy which made Stalin suspicious of the Yugoslav leadership. He found it impossible to corrupt an indigenous Yugoslav Stalinism whose leaders placed both revolutionary purity and Yugoslav national interests above Soviet strategic requirements.

In March 1947, President Truman outlined his celebrated 'doctrine' to the US Congress. The President promised support to both Greece and Turkey against communist encroachment. The United States assumed the role of chief imperial backer of the Greek government against the insurgents of EAM/ELAS. In the case of Turkey, Washington was prepared to use its military might against Soviet attempts to establish a presence in the Straits or annex parts of eastern Turkey to which Moscow had recently laid claim.

In the wake of the Truman doctrine, Stalin increased pressures on the people's democracies to obliterate opposition to communist rule. As a consequence, Yugoslavia's ideological purity appeared to gain in importance. Amongst the other East European parties and the French and Italian communist parties, the largest in the West, the Yugoslav leadership was seen as a hammer wielded by Stalin to smash opposition. At the founding meeting of the Communist Information Bureau (Cominform), held in the south-western Polish town of Szklarska Poręda in September 1947, Milovan Djilas led the charge against Togliatti and Thorez for their 'rightest' deviation from the general line.

Stalin's East European and Balkan policy in 1947 and 1948 was thus two-pronged: there was to be no provocation of the West by going beyond the boundaries of Yalta; and the East European allies were expected to subordinate their domestic and foreign policies to Soviet interests. Djilas repeatedly assured the Soviet leader of the Yugoslav leadership's loyalty and good intentions. 'And what greeted those good intentions?' he later reflected. 'The arrogance and rejection typical of a great power towards a small power – the strong towards the weak.'[75] There was little to distinguish the Stalinist and Tsarist attitudes to the Balkans.

It was not intransigence in foreign policy which finally provoked Yugoslavia's excommunication from the Church of Moscow. The heresy began with the idea of a Balkan federation or confederation, a project promoted by both Tito and the Bulgarian leader, Georgi Dimitrov, albeit in different forms.

In 1947, the Albanian leaders, Koçi Xoxe and Enver Hoxha, agreed that their country would be absorbed as a seventh republic into Yugoslavia. Tito then planned to invite Bulgaria into the Yugoslav federation as an eighth constituent republic. But while Dimitrov supported the idea of federation, he preferred Bulgaria to preserve its own state identity and join Yugoslavia in a confederation.

To outmanoeuvre the Yugoslavs, in January 1948 Dimitrov announced his ambitious plan for a Balkan/Danubian confederation. This would not only include all the people's democracies but Greece as well. The Bulgarian leader had neglected to consult Moscow before dropping this bombshell which, by including Greece, directly contradicted Stalin's policy of avoiding confrontation with the Americans in southern Europe. Dimitrov probably believed that as the former chief of the Comintern, and hence the most authoritative figure in the people's democracies, he was still in a position to take foreign-policy initiatives. On 29 January, *Pravda* disabused him of any such notion: 'The editors of *Pravda* believe that these countries have no need of any sort of more or less dubious or artificial federation, confederation or customs union.'[76] Stalin immediately interpreted the confederation plan as an attempt by his allies to organize independently of Moscow.

Summoned to Moscow with the Yugoslav leadership, Dimitrov mounted a feeble defence of his actions before publicly criticizing the whole idea. The Yugoslavs, however, were not so willing to renounce their right to an independent regional policy. In a series of letters, Stalin accused Tito and his 'clique' of heresy, demanding immediate obeisance. In February 1948, *Le Figaro* reported that Tito's portraits had been removed from public places throughout Bucharest. But nobody in the West or the East appreciated how serious the issue was until a meeting of the Cominform, which the Yugoslavs refused to attend, published its famous Resolution on 28 June 1948 (the date was chosen because of its historical resonance for Serbs and Yugoslavs, being the anniversary of the battle of Kosovo in 1389, the assassination of Archduke Franz Ferdinand and the promulgation of the first Yugoslav constitution). The Yugoslav Party stood accused of slandering the Soviet Union. It was denounced as having 'abandoned the Marxist theory of classes and the class struggle', an especial irony, as the victims of Yugoslavia's class terror could testify. Finally, the Yugoslavs were solemnly accused of constructing a bureaucratic system which left the Party bereft of 'inner party democracy . . . elections . . . criticism and self-criticism'. In a clumsy racialist reference to Balkan history, the Resolution described OZNa as having imposed a 'disgraceful, purely Turkish terrorist' régime in Yugoslavia.

The Soviet Union and the people's democracies froze all cooperation with Yugoslavia. Stalin was convinced that he could bring the country to its knees in a matter of days. According to Khrushchev, he mocked that he only had 'to lift [his] little finger' and the Yugoslavs would be begging for mercy. The disruption caused by Stalin's economic blockade was indeed severe. The Soviet Union and people's democracies supplied Yugoslavia with most of its raw materials, including almost all its oil. Truman and the Americans were alert to Yugoslavia's dilemma and devised a policy 'to keep Tito afloat', as a potential ally in the global war against Soviet communism.

Yugoslavia did establish trade links with the West but in domestic affairs the KPJ remained true to its Stalinist practices. Denunciation and political persecution, never far from the surface, were revived: this time, however, it was the supporters of the Soviet Union who were on the receiving end. Up to 50,000 so-called 'Inform Bureauists' were locked away in camps. With the aid of UDBa (formerly OZNa), Tito resisted Stalin's bullying by mobilizing a new spirit of Yugoslav nationalism (the first and last time that Yugoslavism was warmly embraced by the masses as a unifying ideology). The Yugoslav Communist Party and the Titoist leadership survived expulsion from the Soviet fold – but the Cominform Resolution delivered a fatal blow to another revolution.

Liberation: the Greek Civil War

The *Wehrmacht* began its hurried retreat from Athens towards the end of September 1944. When the last troops left, the Greek capital bubbled in 'a ferment of Dionysiac joy . . . Demonstrations and counter-demonstrations, slogans and counter-slogans in red and blue paint, political songs of all complexions, often set to the same tunes, propaganda and counter-propaganda through megaphones at street corners, all these had violently broken out.'[77] Grigori Popov, the chief of the Russian Military Mission, was driving through the centre of town when the joyous crowd physically lifted his car and marched it to the centre, shouting 'Long Live the Soviet Union! Long Live Stalin!' Popov, who held Greece's popular movement in contempt, remained stony-faced. For several days and nights, the people of Athens impatiently awaited the triumphant entry of the communist army, ELAS. Churchill and his network of agents inside Greece admitted that if ELAS and its two political sponsors, the Popular Front (EAM) and the Communist Party (KKE), had wanted to take over Athens and thereby assume absolute control of Greece nothing could have stopped them. EAM/ELAS was already master of four-fifths of the country.

Streaming down from the peaks of the Pindus range in anticipation of the event were thousands of ELAS warriors, known collectively as 'the Mountain'. The power and mystique of ELAS lay in a fusion of the *klephtic* traditions of the mountainous interior and more recent communist-organizing techniques. 'It was not the easy-going peasants who started the resistance to the Germans', remarked Monty Woodhouse, the most perceptive SOE agent in Greece. 'That was the last thing they wanted: they had hardly seen a German, or noticed the slightest difference in their way of life, until the talkers from the towns arrived with exhortations to take arms against the invader . . . He was obliged to choose between the alternative leaderships offered to him: to become either a collaborator or a Communist or a republican or whatever it might be, unaware that these alternatives were not exhaustive; often only dimly aware that they were mutually exclusive.'[78] The KKE's strength lay in urban areas, especially in Athens and the towns of Thessaly. But many of the men and women who were sent to organize the peasantry were themselves first- or second-generation immigrants from the countryside. They carried with them a Romantic notion of struggle that was often reflected in the pseudonyms they adopted – Ares (the God of War), Orestes, Hermes or Pericles. Moreover, they understood how to mould rural codes of honour with the iron discipline of their Stalinist training.

The successful recruitment of this peasant army may be ascribed to the KKE's organizing ability. Discipline was maintained by the systematic use of terror both by ELAS commanders and, more ominously, by OPLA, the nascent communist secret police whose acronym spelt out the Greek word for 'weaponry'. But, like the Partisans in Yugoslavia, EAM/ELAS invested money and effort into alleviating the considerable hardships which ordinary Greeks had suffered since the German occupation. In a society notoriously divided by wealth and run by fractious elites for their own benefit, the impoverished population of towns and villages supported the resistance in great numbers. By the end of 1944, membership of EAM has been estimated at about two million, an astonishing figure in a country of seven million. They had been drawn to the movement because it established rudimentary health and education facilities, food supplies where necessary and, above all, a sense that for the first time the peasantry actually mattered to the men and women of the cities. The stage was set for victory in Athens where the KKE held enormous popular appeal. But the order to march on the city was never issued.

For reasons not yet comprehensible to the *kapetanoi*, ELAS commanders, the leadership of the KKE had signed the Caserta Agreement in Italy on 26 September with the British, with representatives of the royalist government in exile and with General Napoleon Zervas, the commander of EDES. The latter was the only remaining non-communist resistance movement loyal to King George II. It established its stronghold in the north-western province Epirus. A settlement in February 1944 had ended a struggle between EDES and ELAS which bore similarities to the Partisan/Chetnik fighting in Yugoslavia. Now, the Caserta Agreement effectively placed under British control all military units in Greece.

Since his arrival in Greece at the end of July 1944, Colonel Popov had impressed on the KKE leadership the importance of cooperation with the British. The Party was to join a government of national unity, sponsored by the British and including all manner of politicians. On Molotov's instructions, Popov warned the KKE that the Soviet Union did not support an armed takeover, nor would it be sending any weaponry to ELAS. As the British were prepared to sell out Romania, the one country in the Balkans where there was absolutely no support for a communist régime, the Soviet Union was quite happy to reciprocate in Greece where the communists enjoyed overwhelming popular backing. The deal was then enshrined in the Churchill/Stalin percentage agreement of October 1944.

But when General Ronald Scobie, the commander of British

forces in Greece, installed himself in Athens with the vaguest comprehension of conditions inside Greece, he overplayed his hand. With Churchill's explicit support, he demanded a demobilization of ELAS on conditions which proved too humiliating for its commanders and provoked a split in the KKE Politburo. Negotiations between the KKE and the British-backed Prime Minister, Giorgios Papandreou, broke down at the beginning of December before the British had established a major military presence in southern Greece. When the KKE called a mass demonstration in Constitution Square in the centre of Athens on 3 December the stage was set for what is known as the Second Phase of the Greek Civil War.

On that freezing Sunday morning, a bright low sun lit endless columns of people heading towards the centre of Athens from all directions. The mood was jubilant as thousands upon thousands jammed into Constitution Square in front of the Tomb of the Unknown Soldier. Encouraged by the boisterous crowd, a young man 'surged from the front ranks and . . . began a wild dance. He leapt high in the air once, twice. Suddenly, he doubled up and fell to the ground, his chest covered with blood.'[79] From atop the official buildings in the square, the police, many of whom had worked throughout the Axis occupation, began firing machine guns indiscriminately into the crowd. Twenty-eight were killed and over a hundred injured as foreign journalists looked on in horror from the safety of General Scobie's headquarters, the Hotel Grande Bretagne.

The following day a general strike was proclaimed throughout the country. ELAS units descended upon Athens, laying siege to all police stations although careful not to provoke the few thousand British troops in the capital. Within days all but one of Greater Athens' 130 square kilometres were in the hands of ELAS. Only the very centre, which was referred to as 'Scobia', was held by the British and loyalist forces. In the wake of ELAS came the OPLA units, scouring every district for suspected collaborators and class enemies, not to mention class traitors, who fell victim to OPLA's 'revolutionary justice' along with hundreds of innocent refugees and hostages caught up in the fighting.

By mid-December, Greece lay at the feet of the KKE and ELAS as it had done two and a half months earlier. Once again, the KKE leadership hesitated, torn between the parliamentary tactics recommended by Moscow and the revolutionary movement represented by ELAS. Markos Vafiadis, the gritty *kapetanios* directing the resistance in Aegean Macedonia, was ordered with three divisions to join Aris Velouchiotis in a final assault on General Zervas's EDES forces in Epirus. Both *kapetanoi* were astonished at the directive. Until it came, Vafiadis had hemmed in the British army's India Division at their quarters in Salonika. When the ELAS troops left for the offensive against Zervas, the India Division took ship for Piraeus to relieve Scobie's embattled forces in the capital. This crucial military error later came to symbolize the KKE's failure.

The collusion of the British and the Russians during the battle for Athens presented ELAS with difficult obstacles. Yet this in itself was probably not sufficient to prevent the communists from seizing power. American public opinion was clearly sympathetic to EAM/ELAS and, in Britain, Churchill's bitter determination to defeat EAM/ELAS came under sustained assault in the pages of *The Times* and the Manchester *Guardian*; the House of Commons, too, rang with criticism. Indeed, Churchill's government came close to collapse because of the Prime Minister's desire to restore George II to the Greek throne. Had the KKE acted decisively by seizing Athens and proclaiming a government, the British could only have restored the monarchy by mounting a full-scale invasion of Greece, calling on much greater political and material resources than they could easily have mustered.

Instead, the British were able to prise open the harbour at Piraeus and divert troops from both the Ardennes and Italy to Greece. After holding out in Athens for another three weeks, the understrength ELAS units agreed to an armistice in early January 1945 and withdrew 150 kilometres north and west of the capital.

Athens was in a state of shock. Thousands had been killed in a month of revolution and civil war. Whole districts had been strafed by RAF fighters; there was no electricity, and food supplies had dried up. Bodies littered the streets, most of them victims of the fighting; but in the weeks that followed ELAS's and OPLA's withdrawal, the cost of bloody retribution emerged: mass graves containing up to seven or eight thousand corpses, including women and children.

The Varkiza Agreement, signed on 9 February, led to the disarming of ELAS. In exchange, the transitional government headed by

General Plastiras promised an amnesty for political crimes and the disbanding of the right-wing formations that had collaborated with the Nazis. EAM/ELAS continued to control the Greek interior and much of Macedonia. Plastiras's government enjoyed little support and the General was unable to administer the entire country; yet in Attica and the Peloponnese, the Government was at least the nominal power. As the communists receded, the brutal killers of χ, a right-wing paramilitary organization, and other anti-communist groups, roamed the Athenian walkways and the mountains and coasts of the Peloponnese. White Terror was eager to prove that it was more than a match for Red Terror.

Popular support for the communists waned after the Varkiza Agreement. Their behaviour during the December uprising had alienated many ordinary Greeks, not only because of the murder of hostages. In Aegean Macedonia, they had fought with the SNOF, the Titoist Liberation Front representing tens of thousands of Slav Macedonians still living in Greece. EAM had permitted the publication of Slav newspapers and encouraged cultural autonomy for the Slavs which many Greeks considered a real threat to the country's sovereignty. The economy, ravaged by inflation and shortages, had taken a further hammering during the rebellion.

The Right was in contrast bolstered by the Varkiza Agreement. Over the next twelve months, the National Guard, the police and the army expanded rapidly to a strength of almost 200,000 well-armed men. In areas like the Peloponnese and Epirus, where monarchists and rightists drew their traditional strength, these forces were swift to exact revenge on the communists. The authorities were unable to prevent the lumpen fascists of χ from infiltrating the security forces. Inside the Army's officer corps a new conspiracy, the Sacred Bond of Greek Officers (IDEA), disseminated its anti-communist and expansionist philosophy. With their allies in the government, IDEA members weeded out suspected liberal or left-wing sympathizers from the officer corps.

The absence of war improved the material circumstances of most Greeks, who benefited from a heroic effort made by United Nations Refugee and Rehabilitation Agency (UNRRA). The British presence curbed the more extreme political violence in the major towns and introduced a greater professionalism into the police force. But as one bumbling administration after another fell, it was hard to disguise the fact that the British troops were propping up a sordid coalition of unforgiving nationalists and businessmen intent on reviving the hugely exploitative interwar economy. The elections called under American and British pressure in March 1946 were boycotted by the KKE, who rightly objected to the atmosphere of violence and intimidation created by the police and army. In retrospect, it is tempting to draw parallels between the electoral process in Greece and those in Bulgaria, Romania and Yugoslavia. The populist administration which was swept into office redoubled the repression against communists and their sympathizers. Pressure for action mounted in the ranks of ELAS, emboldened by the return of veteran fighters from Yugoslav camps. When King George was welcomed back in September 1946 after a dubious plebiscite restoring the monarchy, chaos was come again.

The winter of 1946–7 was particularly severe in Britain. The country was threatened with a fuel crisis and its people had grown tired of privation. Hugh Dalton, the Labour government's Chancellor of the Exchequer, resented having to devote a large chunk of his budget to the operation in Greece. 'Nor, even if we *had* the money, was I satisfied that we *ought* to spend it in this way', he complained to his Prime Minister, Clement Atlee. After two months of badgering the Cabinet to 'put an end to our endless dribble of British taxpayers money to the Greeks',[80] Dalton won his argument. At the end of February, the British told the Americans that their support for the Greek government would come to an end.

The atmosphere in the State Department in early 1947 had changed dramatically in the two years since its officers had deprecated the British intervention during the December uprising. There was a growing realization that the Middle East was of enormous strategic value to the United States in the postwar period. Washington had clashed bitterly with Moscow over the communist takeover in Poland and in 1946 it detected a Soviet attempt to expand southwards into Turkey and Iran. In the opinion of George Marshall, the Secretary of State, and his energetic team of crusading advisers, the days of cosy chats between the President and Stalin were long gone. It was necessary to confront and contain Soviet expansionism. The news that Britain was pulling out from Greece came not as a shock but as the call to action for which they longed. Truman needed little convincing. But Republican leaders of

Congress, who had won the 1946 elections on an isolationist programme, would need persuading if they were to sanction a military adventure to prop up a tottering Balkan régime. Truman called on an aide he later dubbed his 'top brain man', Dean Acheson, Undersecretary at the State Department, to launch the offensive. 'Like apples in a barrel infected by the corruption of one rotten one', Acheson warned, 'the corruption of Greece would infect Iran and all to the East . . . Africa . . . Italy and France . . . Not since Rome and Carthage had there been such a polarization of power on this earth.'[81] By the time Truman presented his 'doctrine' in March, he had understood exactly how to embarrass the parsimonious Republicans into giving him the money he wanted for Greece and Turkey. 'The world is essentially divided in two. On one side are totalitarian and the enslaved peoples. On the other side are the free peoples.' He looked at the Republicans and said, 'Which side are you on? If you are on the side of the free peoples, give me the $400 million dollars.' The money was granted within weeks. The Cold War was destined to start in the Balkans.

The Americans had not fully appreciated what they had committed themselves to doing. In October 1946, ELAS had reformed itself into the Democratic Army of Greece (DSE) under the leadership of Markos Vafiadis. As British support for the monarchists faltered, the DSE began successfully mobilizing its support in villages throughout the country. Government forces were in steady retreat throughout 1947 although the DSE did not possess sufficient fire power to sustain assaults on well-fortified towns even in areas like Thessaly where they controlled most of the countryside. Despite numerous appeals to the 'fraternal states' for arms, Stalin blocked all supplies. In February 1948, when the power of the DSE was at its peak, Stalin was categorical in a conversation with Edvard Kardelj, a member of Tito's politburo:

> 'The rebellion in Greece must be crushed. Do you believe in the victory of the Greek rebellion?' he said, turning to Kardelj.
>
> Kardelj answered: 'Yes, provided that foreign intervention isn't stepped up and they don't make any crass political or military mistakes.'
>
> Stalin continued: 'No. They have not the slightest chance of winning. Do you really imagine that Britain and the United

> States – the strongest countries in the world – that they will tolerate any disruption to their communications artery in the Mediterranean! What rubbish. And we don't have a fleet. No – the rebellion in Greece must be crushed and the sooner, the better.[82]

Stalin was right. The Soviet Union could hardly have avoided war with the United States if it had responded to the programme of American military aid by sending large amounts of weaponry to the DSE. The Soviet dictator was, of course, playing the game of great-power politics in the Balkans, a tradition familiar to Russian statecraft. The United States, on the other hand, was becoming involved in the Balkans for the first time. Washington stopped short of sending troops, aside from 250 military advisers. Instead, the British granted a US request to leave a few troops in Greece. But Washington was liberal with its weapons. 'By the end of 1949, military aid alone amounted to $353.6 million, and included 159,922 small arms weapons and 4,130 mortar and artillery pieces . . . Even the participants in the DSE, insulated as they were from the outside world, saw that for every mule load of foreign aid reaching themselves, a ship load reached their opponents.'[83]

Ferocious fighting raged throughout the second half of 1948 and the first half of 1949 as the DSE were slowly but surely pushed northwards. Riven by factional disputes, the 13,000 soldiers of the DSE nonetheless mounted a heroic but futile last stand on the mountains of Vitsi and Grammos just south of the Albanian border. To this day, Grammos sports a bald patch on its forested head where the royalist army used napalm, the first time the American military was able to gauge the effects of this material. The fighters who withdrew into Albania and the refugees who followed them were subsequently scattered throughout eastern Europe and Russia where many still live, the youngest branch of the Greek diaspora. As they went, they closed the door on the Second World War.

The Balkan peninsula was now divided by ideology, one Russian, one American. Crushing repression awaited one half, chaotic democracy and military dictatorship the other.

CHAPTER 8

PRISONS OF HISTORY

Communism and militarism, 1949–89

The Cazin rebellion: Yugoslavia

In March 1950, a Serb farmer, Milan Božić, set out from his hamlet in north-western Bosnia to visit his friend, Ale Čović, a Muslim who lived in a village 5 kilometres away. The two had met during the war, fighting in the same Partisan unit around Bihać. After the war, their friendship helped build bridges between the Serbs and the Muslims of Cazin District, where relations between the two communities were strained. Fratricidal conflict among Serbs, Croats and Muslims had been intense in north-western Bosnia and the neighbouring Croatian districts, Kordun and Banija. Božić and Čović, however, used their influence to encourage reconciliation. Both were respected by their peers as successful farmers, and Božić even joined the Communist Party of Yugoslavia (*Komunistička Partija Jugoslavije* – KPJ). But the optimism which the two men shared had dissipated when the spirit of Partisan resistance made way for communist reconstruction. Six years after Tito had taken power in Yugoslavia, Božić called on his old comrade, Čović, to persuade him to take up arms once more.

Both men belonged to the peasant farmer class which made up three-quarters of Yugoslavia's population. The countryside had contributed the majority of recruits to Partisans, Ustaše and

Chetniks alike. They suffered much more than their cousins in the cities. After liberation, however, the orthodox Marxists of the KPJ proved no better at accommodating the peasantry than the liberals of nineteenth-century Serbia or the Yugoslav autocrats of the 1930s. Instead, the new communist leadership diverted political and economic resources into ambitious industrial projects while neglecting rural investment. The aim was to strengthen the country's small working class at the expense of the peasantry, the symbol of backwardness in communist eyes. Rural labourers were expected to embrace their subordinate position in the socialist order. Their job was to produce enough food to satisfy the needs of a growing proletariat.

This rule applied throughout the communist Balkans, and party leaders were quick to curb independent political activity in the countryside. First they ordered the destruction of the peninsula's influential peasant movements, the most serious threat to the communists' monopoly on power.* They then turned their attention to the peasants' economic interests. Collectivization promised an eventual end to private holdings, large or small. The scheme would leave control of the production and distribution of food in communist hands. Yet the leaderships faltered. They were so apprehensive about the peasant's reaction to collectivization that even in Albania, Europe's most ruthless police state, the communists hesitated to implement the policy. Only Yugoslavia defied the trend and began collectivization immediately.

There were several reasons for this. Until the summer of 1948, Yugoslavia was considered the Soviets' most faithful East European satellite. It announced the start of collectivization as early as 1947 to underline its Stalinist credentials. Then, in June 1948, the country was expelled from the Cominform (the Communist Information Bureau). Stalin accused Tito of deviating from socialism in the direction of both Trotskyism and capitalism. Central to its betrayal was Yugoslavia's alleged soft treatment of the peasants. Soviet communists denounced the KPJ as a 'Party of *kulaks*', a transparent nonsense as the Yugoslav Party's behaviour towards its peasantry was worse than that of most of its counterparts. To disprove the claim of revisionism, the leadership in Belgrade decided instead to

---

* See chapter 7.

speed up collectivization, demonstrating that it was not Yugoslavia but the Soviet Union and its allies that had strayed from the path of Stalinist orthodoxy.

The Yugoslavs were able to justify the temporary imposition of strict state controls over agriculture on economic grounds. The Soviet Union and its East European allies imposed a comprehensive trade ban on Yugoslavia after the split while ties with the West were still non-existent. There was a genuine threat of invasion from Eastern Europe and tension with the West over the Trieste dispute remained high.* After years of devastation caused by occupation and civil war, agricultural production was down by more than half over pre-war figures. In Cazin District, for example, '56% of the agricultural inventory had been destroyed, 20.7% of all houses . . . the number of horses had fallen by 60%, sheep by 63.2%, cattle by 55.6%, swine by 58.7%. The herds were exhausted, undernourished, ill.'[1] Despite its significant potential, Yugoslavia was unable to feed itself in the immediate postwar period. The state had to intervene to provide the necessary investment and incentives to stimulate production. It forced peasants to hand over their holdings to unwieldy agricultural conglomerates, the collective farms. Those who refused to join were subject to a harsh régime of requisition.

The number of collective farms rose in 1949 from 1,318 to almost 7,000. The Party increased the requisitions to unrealistic levels, often demanding more from peasants than they could produce in a year. Some farmers had to use their savings in order to buy produce on the black market which they would then hand over to the requisitioning agent. The consequences of this policy were dramatic. Peasants unable to fulfil their quotas risked losing everything (the so-called 'total confiscation' régime). Failure could also result in a spell at a work camp, where they would join political prisoners and students on construction or mining projects. Some resorted to the age-old resistance tactics of hoarding their produce and slaughtering their livestock rather than hand it over to inspectors. Instead of stimulating agricultural production, the policy led to a drop in output. In the countryside, some communities began to go hungry. Protest assumed ingenious forms. A farmer in the Bijeljina region of eastern Bosnia led his cow to the steps of his local government

* See chapter 7.

office. At the top of his voice, he then invited the bureaucrats to impregnate his animal themselves as this was the only way he could meet his quota. By 1950, however, others, like Milan Božić and Ale Čović, were considering more radical forms of resistance.

The gentle green hills of north-western Bosnia are reminiscent of England's South Downs, in contrast to the forbidding rocks of the nearby Dinaric mountains. Cazin District, or the Bihać Pocket as it is also known, is unique not just for its verdant landscape. For most of the Ottoman period, the area was the Empire's furthest European outpost. It was a restricted military zone similar to the Habsburg Vojna Krajina, or Military District, which lay at the other side of the narrow Korane river. Because of its strategic importance, the sultans secured Cazin District's loyalty by encouraging the settlement of Muslims and the conversion of the local population to Islam. As a result, Cazin still boasts the highest concentration of Muslims in Europe. Like their counterparts in the Military District, the menfolk of Cazin were trained to take up arms in defence of the Empire whenever so ordered. This helped develop an identity distinct from the Muslims of Sarajevo, not to mention Istanbul. Throughout the nineteenth century, the Muslims of north-western Bosnia resisted by force the imposition of reforms by the imperial centre. During the Bosnian uprising of 1850–2, they offered the most stubborn challenge to the military dictator sent by the Sultan, Omer Paša Latas.*

Cazin's independent traditions re-emerged during the Second World War when a local guerrilla commander, Huska Miljković, formed an army that at its peak numbered 3,000 fighters. Miljković was a remarkable opportunist who cooperated alternately with the fascist Ustaše and communist Partisans in order to protect the inhabitants of *Huskina država* (Huska's state). Relations between Miljković and the Serbs were generally good but some Muslims joined the Croat Ustaše and joined in atrocities against the local Serb population. Some Muslim fascists formed small groups, the Green Cadres, who took to the forests at the end of the war. In the six years following the communist takeover in 1944, they killed several dozen people in Cazin, and the last group of outlaws evaded capture until 1950. The communists found Cazin more difficult to control than most parts of the country.

* See chapter 2.

The Cazin Muslims were conservative and devout. Polygamy survived well into the Titoist period, and the patriarchal social system was underlined by the highest rate of female illiteracy among Bosnia's Muslims. The communist authorities were deeply suspicious of Cazin's autonomist tendencies. After the war, they cracked down on all religious hierarchies, Muslim, Orthodox and Catholic, provoking much ill-feeling. Tensions were exacerbated by the requisition policy. The inspectors who demanded that peasants hand over their produce bore an unmistakable resemblance to the tax farmers of the Ottoman Empire,* except that in the 1940s and 1950s they had the authority of a repressive communist state behind them.

A drought in 1949 had led to a sharp drop in production and by January 1950 the Cazin District inspectors had collected 800,000 kilos less than their annual quota. The figures were worse for cattle and swine. In response, the communists mounted a renewed confiscation drive. This was too much for Milan Božić and his friend, Mile Devrnja, a Serb who lived over the Korane river in the Slunj district of Croatia. They met secretly at Božić's home in mid-March to lay the groundwork for an armed rebellion against the Yugoslav state. For this to have any prospect of success in Cazin, the Serbs would have to persuade the Muslim peasantry to join in: hence Božić's visit to his old comrade, Ale Čović.

The Muslim did not hesitate. 'Popular dissatisfaction with the requisitions was rising everywhere and more and more were going hungry', Bejza Čović, Ale's wife, remembered later. 'My husband couldn't sleep at night for worry and he became ever more withdrawn . . . There had been a terrible drought that year and the shortages meant the cattle were weak and scrawny.'[2]

The economic conditions were sufficient to overcome resentments which had lingered since the war between Muslim and Serb peasants. Both communities were keen to make common cause. Over the next six weeks, the peasant army attracted hundreds of recruits from their friends and extended families in both Cazin and the neighbouring Croat districts. Some of the leaders were so-called *prvoborci* (founding fighters) of the Partisans who recognized the need to instil discipline and organization. However, in three critical

* See chapter 2.

respects the men of the Cazin rebellion belonged to a long tradition of Balkan *jacqueries*: they were gullible; they were poorly armed; and their tactical ability was restricted to a single manoeuvre – the panicked retreat.

Their naivety manifested itself in wild exaggerations about the movement's strength. At the first planning meeting, Božić's son, Nikola, announced that an influential sympathizer 'somewhere in the district', was in radio contact with exiled royalist forces. With the backing of Great Britain, monarchist troops were massing on Greece's border with Yugoslavia, Nikola reported, ready for invasion. Meanwhile, others claimed that peasants in Vojvodina were also preparing to rise. As the date set for the uprising approached, many peasants believed they were the vanguard of a great rebellion which would engulf all Bosnia, if not Yugoslavia. In this unreal atmosphere, unit leaders vied for primacy by overestimating the numbers of their units and the quality of their weaponry.

Despite these boasts, the local UDBa (secret police) failed to notice that plans for an uprising were afoot. This was an astonishing indictment of a ruthless secret police force, which can be explained by the fact that all UDBa officers in Cazin were Serbs while almost 90 per cent of the rebels were Muslims. UDBa's network simply did not penetrate the closed society of local Muslims. The day before the uprising, a rumour of trouble finally reached UDBa's regional headquarters in Banja Luka, where it was dismissed as nonsense – the police simply could not believe that the peasantry would be so bold, or stupid, as to rebel.

The uprising itself was a disaster. The rebels succeeded in cutting most of the telephone lines between the major towns in the district but news of the disturbances soon reached Banja Luka. Aleksandar Ranković, the Interior Minister in Belgrade, immediately ordered an overwhelming counter-attack. After a few skirmishes with the army and special police, the peasants retreated while some of the leaders fled into the forests. Over a hundred held out for several weeks and it was not until the army was sent in that they were eventually rounded up. The leaders were executed and a reign of terror imposed on the district.

Despite the ignominious outcome, the rising was significant. Over 1,000 peasants heeded the call to arms, prepared to risk everything in order to make their protest known. For fifteen hours, they took their revenge against the most important symbol of the new order – the collective farm. They trawled through farms and agricultural warehouses, looting everything they found before distributing the foodstuffs and tobacco among their families and villages.

What they could not have known is that during 1949 and 1950, several other attempted uprisings took place, mainly in Bosnia and Hercegovina but also in Croatia and Macedonia, all detailed in UDBa's archives. Some of these were provoked by Chetnik and Ustaše outlaws but there was usually a high incidence of *prvoborci* and active Party members in their ranks.

> Overnight, it was forgotten that all of us leaders were from villages, no further removed than the second generation, if not the first. It was forgotten that without the peasant – who lived in poverty and backwardness, suffering and sacrifice – we Communists could not have overthrown the old order and seized power. All of a sudden, interest in the peasants was reduced to herding them together for meetings; pressuring them into selling to the state at set prices and donating their 'voluntary' labour; or, at best, sympathizing with individual cases of hardship and talking with peasant relatives and former village neighbours on holiday visits home.[3]

In the long term, the rash of armed peasant resistance forced the leadership to rethink its agricultural policy, slowing and eventually reversing collectivization.

Western interest in the Balkans subsided soon after the imposition of communist rule. It was not long before the heroic stands of East Germans and Czechs in 1953 and of Poles and Hungarians in 1956 overshadowed the fate of Romania, Bulgaria, Yugoslavia and Albania. Having asserted for decades that the Balkans were inherently violent, journalists and writers now dismissed the nations of the region as docile people who lacked the initiative and courage of their north-eastern neighbours. Yet the resistance to Stalinism in the Balkans went largely unnoticed because it lacked coordination and was centred on the countryside and not in cities like Berlin and Budapest. Furthermore, since the collapse of communism in 1989, the archives have revealed that Stalinism in the Balkans was applied with much greater brutality than even western scholars have previously assumed.

The iron fist: Romania and Bulgaria

The notoriety of Romania's last communist dictator, Nicolae Ceauşescu, has obscured the role of his predecessor, Gheorghe Gheorghiu-Dej, in constructing a state based on fear and coercion. Among the 'little Stalins', Dej was the worst thug of all. Even before the Soviets had installed communism in Romania, Dej was murdering his party comrades to clear a path to power. Born in the Moldavian town of Bîrlad on 8 November 1901, Gheorghe Gheorghiu (as he was born – he added the Dej later) was already working at Galaţi docks as an eleven-year-old. He completed an apprenticeship as an electrician and became a working-class party activist, a genuine rarity in Romania. In the 1930s and 1940s he experienced strikes, prison and internecine warfare in the Party. The leadership was divided between the 'home communists', of whom Dej was the most prominent and the 'Muscovites', whose leading representative was Romania's first communist Foreign Minister, Ana Pauker.

In the wake of the Soviet–Yugoslav split, bitter struggles broke out in the leaderships of the East European parties as Stalin ordered a witch hunt to root out potential Titos, so-called 'national communists' like Władysław Gomułka who spoke of a 'Polish road' to socialism. Dej was victorious in the Romanian Party over the country's best-known communists, Lucreţiu Pătrăşcanu, Ana Pauker and Vasile Luca. For a long time, most western scholars interpreted this as an exceptional case. They argued that in Romania it was the home communists (cadres like Dej who had spent the war in Romania) who had won at the expense of people like Ana Pauker who had spent many years exiled in the Soviet Union and were regarded as Stalin's agents. The apparent success of Dej and the home communists was seen as the beginning of Romania's defiance of Soviet dictates, which matured two decades later when Dej's successor, Nicolae Ceauşescu, was courted by both China and the West while implementing the most repressive domestic policy in the Warsaw Pact.

In fact, Dej sought to flatter Stalin with as much zeal as his counterparts like the Bulgarian dictator, Vŭlko Chervenkov. His immediate entourage was full of NKVD agents or communists with close links to the Ukrainian and Russian parties. His opponent in the early years, Pătrăşcanu, was not a Moscow communist. Indeed, Pătrăşcanu had long since condemned himself in Soviet eyes by his attempts to establish better relations with the British and French. By the time Dej engaged Ana Pauker in a second round of the power struggle, she was already isolated in the party. The attack on Pauker, who was Jewish, coincided with Stalin's manufacture of Jewish conspiracies. Far from distancing Romania from the Soviet Union, Dej flattered the Soviet leadership by the most meticulous imitation. The process of separation between the Romanian and Soviet parties did not begin until the late 1950s when Khrushchev finally crushed Stalinist opposition in the CPSU (Communist Party of the Soviet Union). Khrushchev's revisionism implicitly threatened Romania's economic interests and Dej's political position. The new leader wanted Balkan communists to concentrate their efforts on developing the agriculture sector to help feed the Soviet Union. Dej wanted the prestige and wealth that a strong industry promised. The Romanian leader exploited the Sino-Soviet split to carve out an autonomous niche for Romania while remaining inside Comecon (the Council for Mutual Economic Assistance – the communist trading block) and the Warsaw Pact.

Dej's fanatical Stalinism entailed harsh consequences for one class above all, the peasantry, many of which made up the largest subset of a miserable social group, the political prisoners. But the countless victims of Romanian Stalinism hailed from all backgrounds and professions. The prison and camp system in Romania had no rivals in the people's democracies. The first inmates were pre-war politicians and businessmen. Then came the religious leaders. From 1949 to 1952, 'in the name of the struggle against the kulaks', Dej reported to the Central Committee in late 1961, 'more than 80,000 peasants, most of them working peasants, were sent for trial; more than 30,000 of these peasants were tried in public which provoked great concern among the peasant masses brought to attend these infamous frame-ups'.[4] Dej used the opportunity of the Central Committee meeting in 1961 to shift his own responsibility for the assault on the peasantry from his shoulders on to Ana Pauker's. In fact, she had tried to slow down collectivization and, in

January 1951, she had demanded that the Central Committee arrest the Party members who had forced peasants into collectives, declaring that 'those who acted in this fashion are not humans'.[5]

As in Yugoslavia, there was resistance in the countryside. Spontaneous unarmed uprisings were reported from all over Romania. The militia responded by shooting rebels, burning villages and confiscating livestock and grain. Throughout the late 1940s and 1950s, armed resistance groups took to the forests and mountains in northern and central Romania. Many evaded capture for years, engaging in occasional shoot-outs with special Securitate units and, in one case, escaping arrest until 1976. No single protest reached the scale of the Cazin uprising in Yugoslavia, but the resistance lasted much longer.

These fugitives were heroic exceptions to the rule. For most Romanian citizens, the 1950s were bleak years of state terror. At the apex of this régime stood the Danube–Black Sea Canal, the cutting of a huge channel south of the Danube delta from Constanţa on the Black Sea coast 56 kilometres inland to Cernavodă on the river. This would have spared boats from the final 290 kilometres and allowed larger vessels on to the Danube. The scheme was reminiscent of the vast construction programmes of the Soviet Union in the 1930s. Decreed in May 1949, it was one of the first projects backed by Comecon. Romania's communists proclaimed it the dawn of modern industry; western commentators believed it was inspired by the Red Army's strategic requirements; Soviet diplomats praised it as the embodiment of socialist internationalism and cooperation. In fact, its most significant role was to create a giant camp for forced labour. During the most intense phase of construction in 1952, the fourteen camps scattered around the marshlands of Dobrudja housed 19,000 political prisoners (or 'Labour Resources of the Ministry of the Interior' as they were officially known), 20,000 'voluntary' civilian workers and 18,000 conscripts from the army. 'The inmates had to work 12 hours daily, seven days a week', one Transylvanian Hungarian writer recorded. 'The work they performed was heavy manual labour digging ditches, carting soil by wheelbarrow, loading trucks. The scene was similar to the Egyptian or Roman Empires of the past, when slaves were used to build pyramids or roads.'[6] Underfed, maltreated and working in appalling conditions, men died at a rate that reached a hundred a month.

In 1951, the Interior Ministry extended the 'Re-education Programme' to the Danube–Black Sea Canal labour camps. This complicated form of institutionalized torture was the Romanian Communist Party's unique contribution to Stalinist terror. Devised by the Deputy Interior Minister, Alexandru Nicolski, 're-education' involved prisoners agreeing to betray their friends and then to torture them on behalf of the Securitate:

> It progressed in four stages. The first was known as 'external unmasking' by which the prisoner had to show his loyalty . . . by revealing everything he had hidden from the *Securitate* interrogators . . . In the second phase, called 'internal unmasking', the tortured student had to reveal the names of those who had behaved more kindly or leniently towards him in prison, be it a fellow inmate or a member of staff. The third and fourth stages had another purpose: the destruction of the prisoner's personality and moral fibre . . . Only when his moral collapse seemed . . . complete . . . was the student subjected to the final stage, the one which guaranteed no return: the re-educated figure was forced to conduct the process of re-education on his best friend, torturing him with his own hands.[7]

Each 're-educated' prisoner was allotted a number of prisoners to 're-educate', using the techniques of extreme physical and psychological violence which he had acquired during his own ordeal. In this way, the Interior Ministry was able to impose a reign of terror throughout the prison and labour camp network, using minimal resources. The imprisoned were victims and perpetrators simultaneously. In 1951, a former medical student from Cluj was administering 're-education' to a prominent doctor at the Danube–Black Sea Canal network, provoking the victim to hurl himself on to the barbed-wire perimeter fence where he was shot by camp guards. The incident was reported by the BBC and other foreign stations. 'Their reports prompted a Ministry of Interior inquiry at the peninsular camp. Here is a vivid illustration of the iniquity of the communist régime's machinery of repression: the very body which, in the person of Nicolski, implemented the programme, on realising that its details could no longer be kept secret, set up an enquiry to absolve itself of responsibility.'[8]

Stalin's death in March 1953 unnerved both Dej and his counterpart in Bulgaria, Vŭlko Chervenkov. The latter was another slavish imitator of the Soviet Union; Stalin had been the only source of his political legitimacy. Having spent over twenty years of exile in the Soviet Union following his involvement in the Sveta Nedelya bomb plot of 1925,* he enjoyed a narrow band of support inside Bulgaria itself. Chervenkov did more damage to the agrarian sector than any other East European dictator. In a matter of three years, he destroyed the system of smallholdings that had fed Bulgarian towns and villages without serious interruption since Ottoman times: 'The greatest paradox was the lack of popular Bulgarian produce on the market', remembered the journalist, Georgy Markov, from his exile in London (where he was eventually killed by a poison-tipped umbrella). 'Bulgaria was a country famous for its vegetables and fruit, but in the markets there was a constant shortage of them . . . Chervenkov's régime reduced the villages to penury. Those years [1950–6] will be remembered as the most wretched in the existence of our peasants. The enforced collectivization, which caused the disappearance of male labour from the fields, plus the abolition of personal smallholdings, inevitably brought famine to the country . . . Thus we townspeople no longer had the reserves of the countryside behind us.'[9]

Industrialization went hand in hand with collectivization. Without sufficient resources of their own, Romania and Bulgaria became highly dependent on the Soviet Union for raw materials and plant machinery. Stalin's demise and the emergence of the collective leadership in the Soviet Union posed serious problems for Bucharest and Sofia. Faced with an economic crisis of its own, the Soviet Union slowed down or ceased deliveries of vital supplies to her Balkan allies. The most spectacular victim of Soviet belt-tightening was the Danube–Black Sea Canal. Tired of pouring resources into this white elephant, the Soviet leadership withdrew its engineers after Stalin's death, leaving an unusable basin left empty for over a decade, until Nicolae Ceauşescu resurrected the idea both as a symbol of Romania's industrial prowess and as a forced labour camp.

The Bulgarian and Romanian leaderships responded differently

* See chapter 6.

to the reformist wind blowing from Moscow and to the East European economic crisis. Dej played tough. He offered lip service to the criticism of Stalinist practice that culminated in Khrushchev's attack on Stalin in the Secret Speech given to the 20th Congress of the Communist Party of the Soviet Union (CPSU) in February 1956. But he refused to relinquish any power to a collective leadership, as happened everywhere else. Chervenkov, by contrast, went quietly, handing over the post of First Secretary to a young war hero, Todor Zhivkov, who for a short while threatened to breathe some life into Bulgaria's moribund Communist Party. The limits of Zhivkov's liberalism were demonstrated in 1956 when the BCP joined the Romanian Party as the only communist organization in Eastern Europe not to publish the Secret Speech. The Bulgarian leadership did at least release a large number of political prisoners. The Romanians stalled on the issue.

On the economic front, Dej pushed successfully for the dissolution of the Sovroms, the joint stock companies used by Moscow as an instrument of colonialist control over the Romanian economy. The two most important joint enterprises – responsible for oil and uranium extraction – were finally dissolved by November 1956. Here lay the beginnings of Bucharest's dispute with Moscow in the late 1950s and early 1960s, concerning Romania's role in the international 'socialist division of labour'. When the Hungarian Revolution exploded in October 1956, Dej discovered he could exchange unswerving support for the Soviet Union's broad strategic interests in Eastern Europe for a certain flexibility in domestic policy. He gave the Soviet Politburo ideological and practical support in its crushing of the Hungarian uprising. In return, he was exempted from introducing reformist practices – Stalinism remained the Romanian norm. Neither Khrushchev nor Dej could tolerate the spread of the Hungarian revolution into Romania via the Hungarians of Transylvania. Nonetheless, students throughout Romania, and not just the Hungarian minority, added their voices to the protests and resistance which had engulfed Poland and Hungary in the autumn of 1956. This was an unwelcome development for Dej, and the Securitate responded zealously, breaking up demonstrations in towns as far apart as Iaşi and Timişoara. The Romanian leadership did, however, make one concession to the students – Russian was abolished as a compulsory subject in Romanian universities and was replaced by the more traditional languages, French and German. This was a small but significant step towards a more independent policy.

Although the Bulgarian Party leadership considered it unwise to publish the Secret Speech, it did respond to Khrushchev's attack on Stalin with a Central Committee Plenum in April 1956 that promised all manner of reform and liberalization. The April Plenum was in fact a prophylactic, designed to dissipate the rising pressure of popular and intellectual discontent in Bulgaria. But it did finally bury Chervenkov. Associates of Traicho Kostov, the main victim of the Stalinist show trials of 1949, were rehabilitated and the Bulgarians had a genuinely collective leadership for a short period with Zhivkov as *primus inter pares*. The thaw lasted less than two years but writers and journalists exploited the atmosphere of tolerance to the full. Nikola Lankov, a hitherto uninspiring communist writer, shocked Sofia by composing an indictment of Chervenkov which summed up the contempt in which most Bulgarians held their 'Little Stalin':

Did I live through this night
of cult oppression?
Did I live?
Oh, no!

I dare not admit that
a certain person, who some called '9,'
in a disgusting epoch
shot Communists
to clear his own path
to a throne and personal power . . .

The door opens
the investigator enters
and begins to rail:

– What are you talking to?

My head shakes
My sleep is broken

and on this late evening
I hear again:

– To interrogation,
to interrogation![10]

In July 1957, Khrushchev succeeded in ousting the 'anti-Party group', Malenkov, Kaganovich, Molotov and Shepilov. The period of collective leadership came to an abrupt end. Both Dej and Zhivkov used this opportunity to carry through purges in the Romanian and Bulgarian parties to shore up their positions. While Khrushchev still intended to pursue a reform programme in the Soviet Union, Zhivkov now decided to put an end to Bulgaria's literary thaw. Journalists were expelled, controversial writers no longer published and tedium descended once again on Bulgarian society. Khrushchev was too distracted to care unduly about Bulgaria's return to neo-Stalinist orthodoxy while Dej remained confident of his power in Romania. One small group of Balkan communists, however, were becoming ever more unhappy about Khrushchev's apparent deviation from the path of righteousness.

A world of his own: Albania

I first heard those five dear letters at the dawn of my life.
Ever since, your name became as dear to me as my paternal home,
As precious as socialism,
As lofty as the mountains,
As vital as light . . .
We shout ENVER!
And the sky seems to us loftier than ever,
The space around us vaster,
The sun bigger,
And our perspectives ever more magnificent.
We shout ENVER!
And our days take on colour and meaning
As they fall in like soldiers
Into the great ranks of the revolution.

From Sulejman Mato's poem 'Enver', published in the literary monthly, *Nëndori*, September 1979[11]

Communism, like nationalism, came belatedly to Albania. When the Communist Party (ACP) was finally established on 8 November 1941, it was under the guidance of two Yugoslav agents, Miladin Popović and Dušan Mugoša, who united three small groups – one pro-Italian from Shkoder, one pro-Soviet from Tirana, and the third pro-Greek from Korçe. This vanguard of Albania's phantom working class boasted seventy members and a few hundred sympathizers at most. Yet within a decade the tiny organization had transformed the country into one of the most inflexible totalitarian edifices of the century. Until the communist-led Partisan victory in November 1944, Albania's modern history had been one of chaos and instability. Although King Zog had forged a semblance of order for a decade, this crumbled quickly under the pressure of Italian expansionism. The legacy of the fascists and the Nazis meant that the communists were obliged to draw on indigenous traditions much more powerful than the alien ideology of Marxism-Leninism to attract sympathizers. Enver Hoxha, the strongest of communist strongmen, admitted this freely, quoting the nineteenth-century Albanian poet, Pashko Vase Shkodrani: 'The religion of the Albanian is Albanianism.' With the exception of Stalin and Hoxha himself, the icons of socialism in the country were drawn almost exclusively from Albania's national struggle – the medieval king Skënderbeu, the brothers Frashëri and Ismail Qemal.

Hoxha underpinned his vision of Albanian unity with a formidable xenophobia. The warmth with which he embraced foreign powers was outdone only by the ferocity with which he subsequently rejected them. Hoxha wooed, then spurned the British, the Americans, the Yugoslavs, the Russians and the Chinese, turning the full force of a defensive nationalism on the perceived heretic. Fear of invasion inspired outlandish policies that became a focus of fascinated disbelief outside the country. Here was a Balkan régime that seemed stranger than the fiction of Bram Stoker. Its very isolation gave rise to a kind of cultish logging of craziness: the construction of pill-boxes every few yards along the entire length of its borders; the ban on private car ownership; the compulsory shaving of beards; and, above all, the deification of two men – Josef Stalin and Enver Hoxha – whose memory remained sacred until 1990 when Albania was torn apart by half a century of pent-up popular anger.

Hoxha's xenophobia had a sound historical footing – the Ottoman Empire, the European great powers and Albania's neighbours, Serbia and Greece, had sought to deny the country its independence ever since the League of Prizren first raised the idea in 1878.* And after Hoxha came to power, foreign states did indeed try to bring him down. In 1948, Stalin had told Milovan Djilas that Yugoslavia should swallow up Albania. A year later, the British and American intelligence services concocted a plan to destabilize Albania by infiltrating supporters of King Zog into the country. This preposterous scheme failed in part because Kim Philby leaked the details to Soviet agents. When the Soviets themselves were spurned by Hoxha in the 1960s, the Khrushchevites (Hoxha's greatest *bêtes noires*) tried to topple the Albanian dictator.

The foreign threat was genuine but exaggerated. The embellishment of external foes had an additional purpose – to expose the internal enemy. No ruling communist party thrived on a diet of purges like the Albanian Party of Labour. Rising to a position of influence under the scrutiny of Hoxha brought great risks. Official sources concede that after the first great purge, which followed the break with Yugoslavia, a quarter of Party members were expelled or arrested. Politburo and Central Committee members were periodically arrested or shot. Nikita Khrushchev claimed that one Politburo member, Liri Gega, was pregnant when executed as a Titoist agent in 1956. During Hoxha's forty-one years in power, the seven interior ministers directly responsible for the carrying out of purges were all themselves purged. Founded in 1941, the ACP's first major purge was instigated in 1942, a year after its founding, establishing a pattern which continued unbroken for over four decades, a self-perpetuating mechanism fed by Hoxha's intense paranoia.

The dictator never relaxed his fear that frustrated ambition in the Party must lead to conspiracy. In 1981, his most trusted comrade, Mehmet Shehu, the man who built the Albanian People's Army and made the Sigurimi into the most feared secret police in Eastern Europe, 'committed suicide'. For forty years, Shehu and Hoxha had been blood brothers in the struggle against revisionism. Then,

* See chapter 3.

quite unexpectedly, Hoxha exposed Shehu's plan to marry his son to the daughter of a family of 'war criminals'. Unable to bear his own treachery, the world was told, the perfidious Shehu took his own life. Once his old comrade was buried, Hoxha was at liberty to reveal the terrible truth – Shehu had been working for the CIA, the KGB and KOS (Yugoslav military intelligence) throughout his career. Marrying his son into a family of 'war criminals' was the signal to begin the destabilization of Albania, a plan that had matured over almost half a century. '[I]t was done precisely with the aim of attracting public attention and causing a sensation', Hoxha later wrote. 'The Yugoslavs could use this to . . . discredit the leadership of the Party of Labour of Albania and especially Enver Hoxha.'[12]

The blood-letting inside the Party was often akin to a deadly family feud. After Hoxha had sided with Beijing in the Sino-Soviet split in 1960, Khrushchev's propagandists hit back in a Moscow radio broadcast:

> Half, or more, of the 53 members of the Central Committee of the Albanian Party of Labour are related. First, we have four couples: Enver Hoxha and his wife Nexhmije Hoxha; Mehmet Shehu and his wife Fiqrete Shehu; Hysni Kapo and his wife Vito Kapo; and Josif Pashko with his wife Eleni Terezi. The wives of Manush Myftiu, Politburo member, and of Pilo Peristeri, candidate-member of the Politburo, are sisters. Kadri Hasbiu, candidate-member of the Politburo and Minister of Internal Affairs, is the husband of Mehmet Shehu's sister.[13]

Notwithstanding Radio Moscow's factual errors (Hasbiu, for example, was not married to Mehmet Shehu's sister), the incestuous make-up of the communist elite in Albania was significant. Enver was a Tosk, born in October 1908 into a family of civil servants and Muslim clerics in the southern town of Gjirokastër. In the interwar years, this handsome young man went to study in France where, according to official communist histories, he wrote articles for the French Party newspaper *L'Humanité* (despite assiduous research, nobody has ever succeeded in tracking down any examples of his youthful journalism). Hoxha then returned to Albania to teach French at the *Lycée* in Korçë, also in the south. After its formation, the ACP drew virtually all its support from the down-trodden Tosk peasantry in the south and centre of the country. Almost all leading cadres were southerners, a pattern which sustained itself throughout the communist period. Ironically, the only Gheg who reached the Politburo and survived was Ramiz Alia, who assumed control of the Party of Labour following Hoxha's death in 1985. Hoxha made a concerted effort to include northerners in the Central Committee and Politburo. He also made clear gestures by sending teachers and doctors to the deprived areas of the north, and integrating the region into his industrialization programme. He went some way to overcoming suspicions between north and south by stressing his commitment to Albanianism.

Nonetheless, in some regions the Party still had difficulty in extending its influence. The strength of Catholicism is the Shkoder region and the exceptional courage of many Catholic clerics in the face of Hoxhaist repression meant that Tirana considered this an unreliable area throughout the communist period. Further, Ghegs in the north had supported the struggle of their brethren in Kosovo during the Second World War. The ACP was regarded as a creation of the Yugoslavs and therefore hostile to the interests of Kosovo Albanians. In addition, communist ideology made no secret of its contempt for the traditional social structure of the north. The atomized clan system; the blood feuds and the Canon of Lek; the miserable position of women in Gheg society; the greater religiosity in the north – these were all targets for the modernizing zeal of Hoxha and his comrades.

Once the borders with Yugoslavia were closed in 1948, Hoxha used the country's geographical isolation to implement a programme of unprecedented social engineering. The radical ambition of Albanian communism reflected 'the crushing poverty, the overwhelming illiteracy, rampant superstition, blood feuds, and ravaging epidemics, above all malaria and syphilis'[14] which Hoxha's régime inherited. In a population of just over a million in 1944, only 15,000 could be described as working-class in the Marxist sense. By 1976 the official figure stood at 370,000, a 24-fold increase. Male life expectancy in the late 1930s was forty-two. Thirty years later it had risen to sixty-seven. The programme of transformation had begun with the reclamation of large tracts of malaria-infested swamps. Arshi Pipa has written that 'the drainage of the Maliq marsh, from which Albania's sugar now comes, has been carried out mainly by political prisoners. "Our sugar smells of blood," they say in Albania'.[15] Then came Albania's electrification. The last village was attached to the national grid in the early 1970s although one experienced observer of Albania has pointed out that 'the system has been on the blink ever since'.[16] By 1955, textile factories and processing combines were working in several major towns and cities. With the assistance of Soviet technicians, Albania soon became one of the world's largest producers of chrome. Within less than two decades almost all children were attending secondary schools and illiteracy rates dropped to as low as 10 per cent.

The industrialization of Albania was astonishing but, like everywhere else in the Balkans, it was achieved at a heavy cost to agriculture and the peasantry. Unlike its neighbours, Albania was not self-sufficient in food production even though almost 90 per cent of the population made their living off the land in the late 1940s. With mountains covering almost three-quarters of the country, 'Albania has from 50 to 100 per cent less arable land per capita',[17] compared to other Balkan countries. In the 1950s, Albania was importing 50–60,000 tonnes of grain annually from the Soviet Union and other East European countries to meet its needs. Collectivization was postponed until the mid-1950s but it was then introduced mercilessly and without regard to the consequences. Intimidation of the *kulaks* surpassed even the ferocity of the Romanian campaign.

The combination of agricultural neglect and the ideological conflict with the Soviet Union almost proved fatal to Albania's fragile economy in the early 1960s. There was both an economic and a political aspect to its steady alienation from the Soviet Union in the late 1950s. Politically, Khrushchev's revisionism was anathema to Hoxha. The Albanian leader was especially offended by Khrushchev's denigration of Stalin, Hoxha's great hero, in the Secret Speech in 1956. More pragmatically, Khrushchev's policy implied an end to absolutist rule in Tirana which Hoxha would not contemplate. Mehmet Shehu best summed up Albania's attitude to the Soviet Union's collective leadership when he told Mikoyan with alarming candour: 'Stalin made two mistakes. First, he died too early and second, he failed to liquidate the entire present Soviet leadership.'[18]

On the economic front, Khrushchev's programme of a 'socialist division of labour', devised in the late 1950s, required Albania to concentrate on agricultural production. The Albanian leadership saw this as an attempt to roll back its industrial achievements. Hoxha later remembered one of his economic summits with Khrushchev:

> 'Fish,' he [Khrushchev] said, 'is another great asset for you. In the Scandinavian countries, in Norway, for example, they have created great wealth with fish . . . The question of citrus fruit is important for you,' he said. 'They, too, should become a great asset for you, because lemons, grapefruit, oranges, etc., are in great demand.'
>
> These were his instructions for the 'construction of socialism' in Albania . . .
>
> Now everything was becoming more clear. The Council of Mutual Economic Aid [Comecon] recommends that we solve the economic problems with Khrushchev. Khrushchev recommends that we solve them with cotton, sheep and with . . . the miracle of fish!'[19]

Insulted by these suggestions and fearful of what Soviet revisionism might do to his domestic omnipotence, Hoxha was quick to side with the resolute leadership of the Chinese. Every time Albania broke with a communist partner, however, severe consequences soon followed. The Soviet Union cut all economic cooperation with Albania. By the early 1960s, Tirana was importing almost 100,000 tonnes of grain annually from the Soviet Union. Much of Albania's industry, especially its only foreign-currency earner, mineral extraction, was dependent on Soviet engineers and technology. The Chinese provided ideological consolation for the Albanians but the technological and economic assistance they offered could not compensate for the stagnation and then decline of the Albanian infrastructure. As the standard of living fell in Albania during the 1960s, Hoxha began to feel unsure of his position. To restore confidence, he resorted to repression and, taking his lead from the Chinese, announced Albania's 'cultural revolution' in 1966. Elsewhere in Eastern Europe, the reduction in tension between the United States and the Soviet Union that followed the Cuban crisis led to a modest liberalization. But for Albanians, the mid-1960s heralded a period of grim ideological rectitude.

In 1967, Hoxha seized on a so-called 'popular demand', first made by school students in Durrës, to transform Albania into the world's 'first atheistic state'. This resulted in the closure of all churches and religious institutions and the arrest of clerics. A decade later, the Albanian leadership took this philosophy to an absurd conclusion:

> A decree, dated September 23, 1975, and published in *Gazeta zyrtare* in Tirana on November 11, 1975, stated: 'Citizens who have inappropriate names and offensive surnames from a political, ideological, and moral viewpoint are obliged to change them.' The decree added that persons affected by the edict were expected to comply with it voluntarily and that those who did not would be given 'appropriate names' by social organizations in their locality.[20]

No amount of state-organized repression, however, could resist the independent vigour of youth. The 1960s saw the maturation of a generation with no direct experience of the war. The Partisan struggle had been a key source of political legitimation for the communists, but its ubiquitous glorification meant little to young Albanians in the 1960s. Their rebellion was modest even by East European standards. By 1970, hair was growing a little longer; Beatles' records were played at parties, particularly those thrown by the children of the 'red bourgeoisie':

> It was . . . a sort of dissent and it started mainly among these communists' children. We wanted to hear foreign music. I started to write and to read foreign authors who were not allowed here like Sartre and Camus . . . Then I went to work in a factory among the working class. It was the first time that I have seen them with my own eyes. You must remember that at the time we assumed that the best people were the proletariat. Intellectuals, students, on the other hand, they were people with defects! And when I saw the workers – poor people, ignorant people, frightened people – I began to be in touch with Albania's reality and my first reaction was, 'I have been cheated!'[21]

There was no organized opposition in Albania, but the circles of café intellectuals and students quietly raising forbidden issues grew wider. At the same time, Hoxha had launched an attack on 'conservatism and bureaucratism' in the Party and among intellectuals. One consequence was a half-baked Maoist programme whereby writers and artists 'volunteered' to leave Tirana for the countryside in order to learn from the masses. But some dramatists, novelists and even Party members took it as a signal to experiment with progressive ideas. The ensuing liberalization in the arts, which lasted from 1969 to 1972, would have been imperceptible to all but the keenest observer of Stalinist systems. But it did appear that Hoxha was distracted temporarily, probably by illness, thereby allowing a gentle ferment of ideas. By 1972, he believed that matters were running out of control. In January 1973, he unexpectedly attacked the head of Albanian Radio and Television, Todi Lubonja, a Central Committee member and former President of Albania's Union of Labour Youth. Lubonja's crime had been to organize a music festival in Tirana which Hoxha labelled 'degenerate'. A campaign against liberalism was launched in the press, and in June, Lubonja and Fadil Paçrami, a highly respected dramatist and former Minister of Culture, were stripped of their Party membership and expelled from Tirana.

At 5 o'clock in the morning on 25 July 1974, a year after the expulsions, three men knocked at the door of the Lubonja household in Lezhë, 65 kilometres north of Tirana on the road to Shkodër. Instead of asking for Todi Lubonja, they asked for his twenty-three-year-old son, Fatos, a student of theoretical physics at Tirana university. 'They assured me nothing was wrong, that I was only required for some discussions in Tirana and that then they would bring me back',[22] Fatos recalled. They drove him in a Chinese-built jeep to a charmless modern building in Myslim Shyri street in central Tirana. Fatos had already begun to suspect that it was a serious matter because his minders would not even allow him to urinate on his own. When he met his two interrogators in the police station, it dawned on him how grave his situation was – they refused to shake his hand, a striking breach of custom. It emerged that in the Sigurimi's zeal to destroy his father, its agents had searched the attic of Fatos's uncle and found the young man's personal diaries. Here he detailed his clandestine thoughts and the books he had read. From this interrogation, he was taken to a solitary confinement cell where he was kept for five months before being sentenced to seven years for 'agitation and propaganda'.

Fatos, however, did not see outside the walls of a prison or labour camp for seventeen years, and had it not been for the collapse of communism he would have remained inside for even longer. With just over two years of his original sentence left to serve, Lubonja was embroiled as a 'defendant' in a bizarre trial. In 1978, at the labour camp where he worked in a coalmine, he heard how two inmates had sent a letter to Hoxha demanding a change in Party policy. He heard nothing more of the incident until six months later when he was taken without explanation from his prison camp to Tirana and again placed in solitary confinement. Within weeks, and with little idea what was happening, Lubonja found himself in the dock alongside the two letter writers, Fadil Kokomani and Vangjel Lezho, and accused of belonging to their 'counter-revolutionary organization'. In May 1979, two years before his release date, he was sentenced to another twenty years of forced labour in appalling conditions merely for being in the wrong labour camp at the wrong time. Hoxha had long since decided the fate of Lubonja's co-defendants, Kokomani and Lezho. Nothing testifies to the surreal insanity of Hoxhaism more than the two men's literal sentence: 'to be sentenced to death by shooting and deprived of electoral rights for five years'.[23]

'In Albania, dissidents did not exist', Fatos Lubonja explained after the collapse of communism led to his release. 'There is a difference between a dissident and a victim of the régime. A dissident is someone who has the possibility to enlighten other people, to express his opinions, maybe to go to prison but to inspire others and to make a choice. While in Albania, we were just victims which means we did not inspire others but were instead people whose experiences instilled fear into others.'[24] For those caught in the web of the Sigurimi, the experience was comparable with Stalin's Great Terror of the 1930s. Yet this régime of labour camps, arbitrary arrests, beatings and shooting continued until 1990, over three decades after Khrushchev's secret speech, five years after the death of the last old-style Soviet leader – and the Berlin Wall already a memory!

As Lubonja learned to his cost, Hoxha's fear of domestic enemies increased when relations with Albania's ally began to deteriorate.

The 1970s saw the end of the relationship with the Chinese. Just as Yugoslavia and the Soviet Union had withdrawn all aid and technological assistance overnight, the Chinese just disappeared in the late 1970s, leaving only bizarre traces of their once eternal friendship. In 1989, the language labs at Tirana University displayed row upon row of yellowing posters, each detailing the position of the mouth and tongue required to make a particular sound in Mandarin. These were by far the richest teaching aids available to the department for a language no longer taught there. Each time Hoxha rejected a father figure, he replaced him with one whose ideological credentials were more extreme but whose economy was even less well attuned to Albania's requirements. When the Chinese went, there was nobody left to meet Hoxha's esoteric ideological criteria.

Over a forty-year period, Albania's infrastructure became necessarily autarkic. Its detachment from world or even regional commerce and technological developments became more stark – its heavy industrial bases produced material and goods for which there was no market, either externally or internally. Travelling through the countryside for the first time in 1989, foreign visitors were confronted with rusting, Dickensian monstrosities, vandalized and purposeless – great monuments to Hoxha's twisted vision.

Albanians who lived either in the former Yugoslavia or in the United States were ambiguous in their attitudes to their homeland during the Hoxha period. The dictator had, after all, 'succeeded in making Albania a truly independent country – no mean achievement for a small state whose modern history was replete with examples of domination, perpetual insults, and repeated attempts at dismemberment by its more powerful neighbours'.[25] Yet as the extent of the trauma inflicted on Albanians under Hoxha became clear, and as the disastrous impact of his policies of terror and isolation on Albania's social psychology emerged during the 1990s, it became hard not to accept another Albanian's assessment that 'the chief mark of national sovereignty is the will to preserve and increase, within the framework of a truly independent state, those elements which make for the individuality of the nation. Communist Albania is the negation of that concept.'[26]

Broz vs. Djilas: Yugoslavia

Geo-politics and nationalism created profound differences in the nature of the communist régimes in the Balkans. This was not always obvious: on the surface they shared the grey bleakness characteristic of one-party states; but Yugoslavia was genuinely distinct – here the government and Party enjoyed a level of popular support unimaginable in its three Balkan neighbours.

After the break with Stalin in 1948, Yugoslavia developed a unique set of policies that, within a decade, transformed it into one of the most respected international actors outside the two power blocs. In 1955, the Soviet Union and Yugoslavia buried the hatchet by 'normalizing' their relations on the basis of full equality. After this, no communist country enjoyed such warm relations with the West while being acknowledged as a full, yet independent member of 'the socialist camp'. Yugoslavia added to its prestige five years later by founding the non-aligned movement, which brought together many countries of the developing world, initially in protest at the manipulative practices of the two superpowers.

This peculiar status bestowed unexpected benefits on Yugoslavs. Their passports allowed them to cross more borders without visas than any other passports in the world. Yugoslav construction and engineering firms competed successfully for contracts in Western Europe, Eastern Europe and the developing world. Westerners were welcomed along the Adriatic coast, where Croatia built up a lucrative tourist industry. In the 1960s, the gap in living standards between Yugoslavia and its Balkan neighbours, Romania and Bulgaria, grew ever wider – a fact that gave Yugoslavs enormous pleasure. The Americans and West Europeans looked favourably at Yugoslav applications for aid and loans. Yugoslav workers took jobs all over Western Europe, mainly in West Germany. The number of Yugoslavs using the freedom to travel to seek political asylum was negligible. The régime at home was liberal enough to prevent the mass alienation so obvious in Czechoslovakia or Romania. And when UDBa, the country's powerful secret police, did crack down on dissent (as it often did), the government easily escaped western censure thanks to its liberal reputation. The West turned a blind eye to human-rights abuses because its strategic planners were confident that

Yugoslavia would declare for NATO in the event of a war with the Soviet Union and its allies.

From afar, Yugoslavia appeared a remarkable success story – highly respected, stable and independent. All these qualities were embodied by the country's leader, President Tito. No European communist leader after Stalin projected authority like he did. His wartime heroism as chief of the Partisans was trumpeted not just by official propaganda but by ordinary Yugoslavs, and by distinguished British ex-SOE officers like Sir Fitzroy McLean. Alongside drab and inarticulate men like Zhivkov and Gheorghiu-Dej, Marshal Tito radiated self-confidence. Unlike them, he had not been installed by the Red Army. His forces had not only liberated Yugoslavia from the Germans, the new government had stood up to Stalin. Imre Nagy in Hungary and Alexander Dubček in Czechoslovakia enjoyed popularity as communist leaders for a few months. Tito boasted broad support among the Yugoslav peoples for almost four decades.

Tito was born Josip Broz on 7 May 1892 in Kumrovec, a Croatian village close to the Slovene border in Zagorje, Zagreb's northern hinterland. Although his family lived in the village's largest house, his father had difficulty making a living, like most Croatian peasants at the turn of the century. The endemic poverty of the region left a deep impression on Broz, which affected him for the rest of his life. His mother was from a wealthier peasant family over the border in Slovenia. During the long periods spent with his maternal family, Josip acquired fluent Slovene (a southern Slavonic language closely related to Croatian) and a taste for hunting and fishing. With only rudimentary education, Broz left Kumrovec in his mid-teens, and became an apprentice locksmith in Sisak, 40 kilometres south-east of Zagreb. He was seen as a skilled young worker, something of a dandy. He attempted to improve his social standing by buying a suit; later, in Vienna, he took dancing lessons. He was delighted by the variety of urban life and took great pride in his appearance.

Until the outbreak of war, Broz worked in many parts of the Austro-Hungarian Empire. During this time, he came into contact with socialist ideas and union activities. He received his call-up papers in 1913 and was serving as an NCO when war was declared. Until his death, he erased all mention from his official biography of his first posting on the Serbian front.* But he was soon transferred to the Russian front, where his courage and concern for the men under his command indicated a gift for leadership. Badly wounded, Tito spent the next two years in prisoner-of-war camps before escaping to witness the revolution in St Petersburg.

Tito entered the new Yugoslav state for the first time in late 1920 accompanied by his young Russian wife, who was exceptionally beautiful by all accounts, and a baby son, Žarko. His return coincided with the new Serb-controlled government's decision to ban the Communist Party and all its affiliate organizations. Tito drifted into cooperating with the illegal Party three years later. His quick thinking and his capacity for hard work made him an ideal conspirator. He contributed much to the survival of the Croatian Party before being tried for his illegal activity and sentenced to five years imprisonment in 1928. His carelessness in getting arrested probably saved his life, for after the imposition of King Aleksandar's dictatorship in January 1929 the authorities unleashed a brutal attack on the illegal Communist Party. Many of its leaders were killed while those who fled to Vienna or Moscow were swallowed up in destructive factional struggles.

By the time Tito was released in 1934, there was little left of the communist movement in Yugoslavia. He was eventually sent by the Party to join the émigré leadership in Moscow, where he attended lectures at the Comintern school. His time in the Soviet capital in the mid-1930s was among the most terrifying of his life. Fear stalked the long corridors of the Hotel Lux, the building which housed the members of fraternal parties attached to the Comintern. The NKVD watched and listened; nobody knew when they left the Lux in the morning whether they would be returning that evening. Stalin liquidated the leadership of the Polish Communist Party in its entirety. Apparently irritated by the incessant factional quarrels among the Yugoslavs, he also murdered most of their leadership. Tito was fortunately of peasant origin, free of the stigma associated with the intellectuals. In Moscow, he behaved with great caution and was diligent and modest in his opinions, all qualities which helped him escape the attention of the NKVD. By the time he returned to Yugoslavia in

* See chapter 5.

the late 1930s, he was among the few senior communist activists left alive by the Yugoslav and Soviet police.

In his mid-forties, on his arrival home, Tito gathered together a group of committed activists from several parts of Yugoslavia. The new leader soon came to depend on five comrades. The first was an exception in being Tito's contemporary – the Jewish newspaperman, Moša Pijade. But the others were all young and in awe of Tito, whom they nicknamed 'Stari', the Old Man. The paternal figure nurtured his brood and their particular skills – Edvard Kardelj, an energetic but meticulous lower middle-class achiever from Slovenia; Ivo Lola Ribar, a flamboyant free-spending upper-class Croat, passionate about the cause (had he not died during the Second World War, he would probably have been anointed Tito's successor); Aleksandar Ranković, whose round Serbian peasant face masked the organizational ability of a ruthless policeman; and Milovan Djilas, an enthusiastic young student and would-be man of letters from Montenegro.

Each acolyte made up for deficiencies that Tito perceived in himself. Tito had never been an intellectual. He had taught himself the classics of Marxism-Leninism-Stalinism sufficiently well to turn out propaganda brochures and inject socialist dogma into his speeches at Party meetings. But he relied on Kardelj and Djilas for the ideological stiffening of the Yugoslav régime, especially after the break with Stalin in 1948. Lola Ribar had style and social grace, something to which Tito aspired all his life but never properly achieved. He could rely on Ranković to get things done and to anticipate practical problems before they arose. For the duration of the war and immediately afterwards, these were Tito's family. After the loss of Lola Ribar, the three younger men Djilas, Kardelj and Ranković – vied for his affection and favour.

In the immediate postwar period, Tito and his inner circle diligently advocated Stalin's policies, assuring the Yugoslav people of the Soviet leader's omniscience. The break with Stalin in 1948 transformed the Yugoslav dictator from being a 'little Stalin' into a figure of genuine historical significance.

> By saying 'No!' to Stalin, Tito stood on his own two feet for the first time in the world of politics. And henceforth, his glittering political leadership was no longer a mere reflection of

> Stalin's sun . . . From that moment on, Tito now represented the sun for most Yugoslavs . . . *Serpens nisi serpentem comederit non fit draco* – a snake cannot become a dragon until it has eaten another snake.[27]

Standing up to the most powerful communist power in the world, however, did not turn Tito into a democrat. He was undeniably adored by many Yugoslavs, but he never considered putting his popularity to an electoral test. Had he done so, he probably would have won comfortably. The result might also have undermined his self-image, which demanded unquestioning approval: the entire political structure in Yugoslavia was dependent on Tito's belief in his own infallibility. And his achievements were real. In a short period after the war, he established a kind of harmony among communities emerging from the bloodiest imaginable civil conflict. He instilled pride in a small country that, even by European standards, had suffered inordinately during the first half of the century. And for the first time in the region's history, a majority of the population enjoyed economic prosperity under his rule.

Yet these advances were dearly bought. Yugoslavia's fratricidal conflict had left the new régime a national question of unprecedented complexity. By 1948, the country was involved in serious disputes about territory and minorities with five neighbours – Italy, Austria, Bulgaria, Greece and Albania. In addition, relations between Croats and Serbs and Albanian–Serb tensions in Kosovo posed a latent threat to domestic stability. National or regional conflict did indeed erupt in different guises during Tito's rule. But nationalism in Yugoslavia before his death in 1980 was not the blunt instrument seized on by Presidents Milošević and Tudjman of Serbia and Croatia to bludgeon their opponents in the late 1980s. Tito was, however, inclined to regard any form of national self-assertion as an inherent threat to the state. Instead of accommodating legitimate expressions of national identity, his preferred solution to the problem was to suppress it, or, worse still, to neutralize one nationalism by pitting another against it.

But nationalism was just one aspect of a more complicated problem. At its heart lay the impenetrable relationship between centrifugal and centripetal forces in the decision-making structures of the League of Communists and the Yugoslav state. After the break with the Soviet Union, two of Tito's closest advisers, Edvard Kardelj and Milovan Djilas, persuaded Tito that Yugoslav communism had to develop an ideology distinct from Soviet socialism. If it failed to do so, Kardelj and Djilas argued, then it must follow logically that the break with the Soviet Union was nothing more than an old nationalist or imperialist conflict. As such phenomena were foreign to socialism, the two men reasoned that the dispute must have been ideological in origin. They gave birth to 'self-management', Yugoslavia's unique contribution to socialist theory.

'Self-management' proposed the devolution of economic decision-making away from the political centre to the shop floor. Workers' councils should be involved in decisions concerning the distribution of investments and profits in an enterprise. The idea was reasonable enough, yet the implications of self-management were far-reaching and potentially subversive, for it appeared to undermine democratic centralism – the Leninist core of every communist dictatorship. It did not take long for liberals inside the League of Communists (LCY)* to appreciate that this theory could become a powerful instrument in pressing for reform. Tito always reacted cautiously to the prospect of major change. But at times he did embrace reform and democratization, only to reject them when he sensed that they might undermine his political power. This made Yugoslav politics a hazardous business. 'The people would just begin to adjust to the democratic euphoria of the leadership', the Croat reformer, Miko Tripalo, has observed, 'when the period of the "iron fist" would start. Then it would all get going again with utopian promises.'[28]

Devolution from the centre also raised the issue of the rights and powers of the six federated republics (Slovenia, Croatia, Serbia, Bosnia and Hercegovina, Montenegro, and Macedonia) in relation to central government. The national question frequently became entangled in the struggle between liberals and conservatives within the LCY. Until his death in 1980, Tito was the final arbiter in the countless clashes on this battle-scarred field. He had a remarkable political acumen and cunning, but he lacked the vision needed to find a long-term solution to the country's unique constitutional

* The Yugoslav Communist Party changed its name in 1952 to appear more open and to differentiate itself from Soviet-style parties.

problems. Self-management and autonomy were not sacred. Tito's power and prestige were.

Tito had already adopted some regal habits during and immediately after the war. Following his successful defiance of Stalin and the Soviet Union, these became more pronounced. In nineteenth-century Serbia, the Karadjordjević dynasty had introduced the practice of the monarch's becoming godfather to the ninth son of a family, in remembrance of the nine Jugović sons who died at the battle of Kosovo in 1389. Serbia at the time had less than three million inhabitants. Tito revived this in Yugoslavia, a country with almost twenty million inhabitants, still predominantly rural, and, in the spirit of emancipation, he accepted female children as well. He soon found he had more godchildren than he could count, all demanding special privileges and rewards. He became bored with this particular tradition after two decades and gave it up. But it illustrated how Tito's presidency owed more to the paternalistic relationship of peasant and master in the Balkans than it did to modern republican and civic culture.

A new constitution, promulgated in 1963, stipulated that no elective office, including the presidency, could be held for longer than two terms. In the proposal drawn up by the Constitutional Commission, 'there was one exception', as its Chairman, Kardelj, admitted, 'and that concerns comrade Tito whose period in office should not be limited by any electoral considerations. I must add that comrade Tito vigorously opposed this proposal but the Commission did not consider his objections. The Commission . . . was merely bestowing on comrade Tito in the name of the nation and the working people of Yugoslavia the deserved recognition . . . for the decisive importance which his work has had for our socialist society.'[29] It was not enough for Tito to be granted absolute power for life. He had to pretend that he assumed the responsibility reluctantly – another sacrifice for his beloved people.

Above all, Tito's megalomania manifested itself in his passion to acquire costly things. Tito accepted Rolls Royces, villas, paintings and jewellery and other gifts from the citizens of towns and regions throughout Yugoslavia; countless acres of choicest forest land were reserved for his hunting parties. At his magnificent villa on the Adriatic island of Brioni, Tito established his own zoo, where game was raised for his hunts. The more powerful he became, the more he withdrew into his castles and houses scattered in every republic – summer villas, winter residences, town houses, spa retreats. And walls were erected around all of them. As Tito became more convinced of his infallibility, he withdrew into a world of reclusive luxury.

Milovan Djilas and his new wife Štefica were watching *Citizen Kane* (of all films) at a Belgrade cinema on the evening of 5 January 1954. 'Suddenly Security agents came up to me in the darkness', Djilas wrote in his memoirs, 'and said softly that I was to step outside. Thinking my arrest imminent, Štefica came out, too. I was told to go and see Kardelj at once at his home on Užička Street.'[30] When he arrived at Kardelj's villa, Djilas found Ranković there too. The meeting turned into a perverse farewell from the two men with whom Djilas had made up Tito's trusted triumvirate since the war. Making it plain to his old comrade, Djilas, that he was finished, Kardelj contemptuously brandished a copy of the speech he would deliver in a few days to the Central Committee denouncing Djilas's supposed treachery.

Djilas's crimes were contained in a series of theoretical articles which first appeared in November 1953 in the Party's main newspaper, *Borba* (*The Struggle*). These had begun as the usual indigestible treatises on ideology, but after a month Djilas changed tack by raising the issue of self-management and what it implied for the Party. For self-management to work, Djilas concluded, the Party had to loosen its grip on the economy and society. Warming to his theme over the next few days, Djilas struck at the heart of communist dogma. He demanded that UDBa, Ranković's secret police, be held accountable for its actions. He even suggested the establishment of an opposition movement to the LCY. And he attacked the growing influence of the bureaucracy in uncompromising terms. His conversion to democratic principles appeared to take place over a matter of days but, as he later insisted, his disgust at the hypocrisy of Yugoslav communism had accumulated over several years.

Inspired initially by the search for an ideological justification of the break with the Soviet Union, Djilas had uncovered an obvious truth (but one which was hard for Yugoslav communists to admit): that Tito had broken with Stalin but not with Stalinism. While the dictator could allow a modest pluralism of ideas within the Party, he could not tolerate any real moves towards democracy. When challenged by Djilas, his brightest disciple, Tito had no choice but to destroy him. The warning to others was unambiguous. Tito humiliated his old friend in public at a specially convened Central Committee Plenum in January 1954, broadcast on Yugoslav radio, at which many of Djilas's friends and colleagues lined up to cast stones:

> Tito probably sensed that the atmosphere was fast turning into the sort of badgering and provocation that had characterized the Moscow trials. That is why, before the afternoon session on the first day, he said to me, 'We are going to behave humanely toward you, not vindictively.' But the speeches strung out, each more frenzied and bloodthirsty than the last. Tito's own brutal intransigence and Kardelj's theoretical underpinning had burgeoned to a level of savagery that perhaps even they had not wanted.[31]

The treatment of Djilas made it clear for the first time since the split from Moscow that Tito would not countenance democratization either of the Party or of society. He had a further reason for punishing Djilas. After Stalin's death in March 1953, both Belgrade and Moscow indicated a desire to 'normalize' relations between their two countries and restore some unity to the socialist world. Djilas 's radical proposals strengthened the conservative forces in the Kremlin around Molotov, who was arguing against normalization. Tito's tough reaction to Djilas bolstered Khrushchev and his supporters, who advocated the re-establishment of relations with Belgrade. Molotov conceded the point and later even suggested that each side name a scapegoat for the split of 1948. 'We'll blame Beria and you can blame Djilas!'[32] In the hot-house atmosphere of Stalinist communism, single personalities could be made to bear the weight of countries.

Before Djilas's expulsion, Kardelj had warned him that his articles and his assault on the Yugoslav Party were 'premature'. Other liberals in the Party attacked Djilas for putting back the cause of liberalism and democratization 'ten years' by alerting Tito too early to the growing momentum for change in the Party. Nonetheless, when the decade of political stagnation that followed Djilas's arrest ended, the banner of liberalism was raised once again and this time it was not just one man engaged in a lone struggle – entire republican leaderships had joined the fray.

Broz vs. Ranković: Yugoslavia

By the time he reached his fiftieth birthday in November 1959, Aleksandar Ranković's hair was two-tone in colour. It was dark black on the crown and silvery grey on the temples and sides. His posture was awkward and he had difficulty smiling. With his baleful features, his resemblance to Bela Lugosi in his most famous role as Dracula is striking. Ranković certainly had enough blood on his hands to qualify for the part. He had ordered the liquidation of thousands at the end of the war and had never flinched from wielding 'the sword of the Party', UDBa, in the service of communist orthodoxy. But, like Count Dracula, there was an element of tragedy to Ranković. Most who knew him well, including many he betrayed, were unable to hide a lingering affection for Comrade Marko, as he was known to his fellow Partisans. On occasions, it seemed as though he had taken on his role as Tito's chief executioner with a heavy heart, aware that as an uneducated tailor's apprentice from central Serbia, he did not have the intellect needed to grapple with the complex theory that exercised the mind of his colleague, Kardelj. When Yugoslavia's first strike broke out at the Trbovlje mine in Slovenia in 1957, Tito called Ranković and asked him to suppress the disgruntled workers by force. 'Oh yes', sighed Ranković after he had put the phone down, 'if the old man needs to have some ideological problem explained, he calls in Kardelj. But whenever he needs someone to get his hands dirty, it's always, "Go on, Marko! Off you go!"'[33]

Ranković may have had his private doubts but he carried out his tasks with exemplary diligence. By the mid-1960s, UDBa had files on the private and political lives of millions of Yugoslav citizens. Arbitrary arrest, torture and imprisonment were all part of UDBa's arsenal in the battle against subversion. In traditionally unruly areas like Bosnia and above all Kosovo, its writ was unchallenged and brutal. In the mid-1950s, Ranković deduced that Albanians in Kosovo were planning an uprising so he ordered a province-wide search for weapons. Like Ranković, most of UDBa's officers were Serbs. The confiscation of weapons soon turned into a violent Serb nationalist campaign which left a number of Albanians dead and many more in prison. Ranković's régime of state terror in Kosovo was the opening and most important move in a postwar game, characterized by dramatic changes in the province's political life. The relationship between Serbs and Albanians in Kosovo has a longer history of violence than any other in the former Yugoslavia. Serbs, Croats and Bosniaks got on tolerably well during the Titoist period, but in Kosovo violence was never far from the surface.

UDBa's Serbian nationalism was blatant in Kosovo. Elsewhere, there was an effort to disguise it by the employment of Croats, Slovenes and Muslims, but even so the percentage of Serbian officers was overwhelming in every republic. Ranković himself was less a Serb nationalist than a fanatical 'unitarist'. He believed that all power should remain in Belgrade (where possible, in his own hands) and that republican capitals, like Zagreb, Ljubljana or Sarajevo should act as cyphers charged with carrying out orders from the centre. 'Unitarism', or 'conservatism', therefore became readily associated with Serbian nationalism: both aimed to preserve a status quo that favoured the Serb elite. It is true that there was much cross- fertilization between Serb nationalists and conservatives in the Party, but the two were not synonymous. There was a strong band of conservatives in the LCY in both Slovenia and Croatia, and an important liberal faction in the Serbian party.

The presence of so many factions within the LCY showed how far the Yugoslav Party had moved compared to its counterparts elsewhere in Eastern Europe by the early 1960s. The modest economic liberalization of the late 1950s had bolstered pluralism in the Party. Soon, political change was moving faster than the economic reforms, which were in fact rather hesitant. The market was uncharted territory for a planned economy and Tito remained suspicious of capitalism. In 1961, after several years of encouraging expansion, the economy went into reverse. The news spread panic through Yugoslavia's elite, compounded by the emergence of such non-socialist phenomena as strikes, unemployment and inflation. Party leaders immediately asked the question, 'Was the crisis a consequence of too much reform or too little? Do we liberalize the economy still further, or do we apply the brakes?'

These questions triggered a great debate in the LCY which lasted almost three years. Ultimately Tito would decide the outcome but not before hearing out his many colleagues. Vladimir Bakarić, the most senior Croat in the Party (aside from Tito himself), urged a radical overhaul of the economy and a thorough implementation of self-management, with full decentralization. Croatia and Slovenia were the most developed republics and had the most productive industries. By the mid-1960s, Croatia's exports, its tourist industry and its migrant workers accounted for over 40 per cent of Yugoslavia's foreign-currency earnings. But in the centralized economy, foreign currency and revenue from taxes were collected and distributed by Belgrade. The banking system was dominated by three large Belgrade banks and foreign trade was regulated by import–export firms in the Serbian capital. The Croat liberals wanted individual republics to exercise greater control over earnings, and to wean Belgrade's central planners off large-scale projects that consumed the bulk of the country's investment resources. This was in effect a demand to impose local control over the transfer of wealth from the north-west of the country, Croatia, Slovenia, Vojvodina and northern Serbia, to the poorer regions – Bosnia, Montenegro, southern Serbia, Kosovo and Macedonia. The Croat proposals triggered lively discussions throughout the country. Factions lined up in every republic to applaud or attack the suggested reforms, or to put forward novel ideas of their own. Surprisingly, the Croat communists received warmest support from the Macedonians, represented by two dynamic young leaders, Krste Crvenkovski and Kiro Gligorov. Coming from an extremely poor part of Yugoslavia, the Macedonians were not motivated by economic imperatives but by a desire to balance Serbia's influence in the federation.

This policy debate in the Party and the republics challenged Yugoslavia's totalitarian power structure, which was dominated by Ranković. He ran the mighty UDBa, but he was also Organizational Secretary of the LCY, a position equivalent to the inspectorship which Stalin used in the 1920s to gain control of the Soviet state and Party. So confident was Ranković of his position that he barely followed the details of the reform discussions. He simply used his network to block practical moves towards reform, resulting in the continued stagnation of the economy. The democratizing principles of self-management were thus at odds, if not in full collision, with the Stalinist mechanisms that had survived the Tito/Stalin split. (Ironically it was during the Party purges against Stalin's supporters between 1948 and 1952 that UDBa and Ranković consolidated their grip on Yugoslav society.) Only Tito had the authority to break the logjam.

After a two-year period of reflection, Tito decided to move against Ranković. His decision was apparently influenced by the extent of UDBa's power. After receiving intelligence regarding UDBa abuses, Tito convened a commission, chaired by Crvenkovski, to investigate its activities. Most famously, it emerged that Ranković had been bugging the entire leadership of the LCY for years. From his home in the grand suburb of Dedinje, where the top Party hierarchy all lived, 'Ranković could listen in on all the telephone calls in the houses with lower numbers, including Tito's in number 15. With a switch in his bedroom, he could relax and simultaneously eavesdrop on his colleagues in the top leadership.'[34] News soon spread that he had placed a listening device in Tito's bedroom, a revelation which came to symbolize the whole affair. In fact, the investigating commission found no evidence that any device had been placed in Tito's house.

It did, however, uncover a staggering abuse of power. Ranković had Yugoslavia's entire foreign service under his control. Diplomats or businessmen who refused to cooperate with UDBa were recalled and sacked. Many of the smuggling rackets which channelled western consumer goods on to the black market were UDBa operations. Its officers were responsible for the 'misappropriation of public property for private uses, private gambling casinos and forced labour by prisoners in the construction of villas for UDBa officials'.[35]

A Central Committee meeting, still known in the former Yugoslavia as the Fourth Plenum, was convened on 1 July 1966. Here, the commission revealed Ranković's secret kingdom. In one closed discussion with top leaders, Kardelj apparently remarked, 'I had noted years ago that my telephone was being tapped.' 'Why didn't you tell me?' snapped Tito. 'I thought *you* might have ordered it,'[36] Kardelj replied quietly. His observation begged another question: how much did Tito actually know of Ranković's activities? Although he feigned ignorance, the evidence suggests that Tito was better informed about UDBa than most. Before Tito convened the Party commission to investigate Ranković, he had already ordered another organization to gather all the relevant material. This organization was KOS, the military intelligence service, UDBa's only serious rival, which happened to be run by Croats. As head of the Party commission investigating Ranković, Crvenkovski repeatedly requested that KOS be subject to investigation as well.

The Macedonian leader suspected that the military intelligence service was also too powerful and was involved in similar rackets to UDBa's. Tito categorically refused these requests. UDBa itself was purged, but Tito neither disbanded nor reorganized it, and after a few months, it was revived as the core of Yugoslavia's repressive state apparatus. Tito's purpose had never been to dismantle state security. His aim was to destroy Ranković, the second of his three 'sons' to betray him. No evidence suggests that Ranković was actually trying to oust Tito, but the secret police chief's accumulation of power was clearly designed to guarantee his position as Tito's unchallenged successor. The succession was a prerogative which Tito guarded jealously; Ranković paid the price for daring to encroach on it.

The Fourth Plenum was also Tito's final answer to the question of whether economic liberalization should be accelerated. The end of the arch unitarist, Ranković, was a clear signal in favour of economic reform – a decision of great moment. The next six years were the most crucial in the country's postwar history, offering the possibility of a historic compromise between Serbs and Croats and the other nationalities of Yugoslavia.

Broz vs. the liberals: Yugoslavia

On 2 June 1968, the *Caravan of Friendship*, a satirical review, rolled into Belgrade. Students at the city's university were invited to view the comedy along with a group of workers from a voluntary labour brigade. At the hall of the Workers' University in New Belgrade, however, there was insufficient room to accommodate both students and workers. A brawl broke out. Rocks were hurled, windows broken, there were injuries on both sides and general panic set in. Before long, forty riot police arrived and attacked the students:

> The crowd gathered in front of Bloc 1 gets larger all the time. The police hem them in this area with batons and water cannon from the fire engines. Suddenly the news spreads that a student has been killed. The students, outraged at the behaviour of the forces of law and order, push back the riot police and commandeer a fire engine . . . By now, there are some three thousand students in the square. Speakers atop the fire engine

say that they will formulate their demands and present them to the Federal Parliament that same night.[37]

The university was occupied within a matter of hours. After Paris, Berlin, Warsaw and Prague, Belgrade raised the banner of student rebellion: 'Bureaucrats: Hands Off Workers!', 'More Schools, Fewer Cars!', 'Workers – We Are With You!', 'Our Demands Are Your Demands!' Some slogans were specific to the East European experience – 'Down With the Red Bourgeoisie!' or 'There Is No Socialism Without Freedom, No Freedom Without Socialism!'[38] – but with minor adjustments they might have been heard and read anywhere across Europe that year. It was the very similarity of these demands to those made elsewhere that made them so astonishing – for the first time in Yugoslav history, a political protest movement took to the streets making no reference to the national question.

The feverish atmosphere of 1968 and the heavy influence of the new Left on the faculty of Belgrade University contributed much to the movement, but there were pressing domestic reasons for the students to raise issues of economic and social injustice. Yugoslavia was three years into a programme of radical reform. The exceptional discrepancy in development between the rich north and the poor south of the country meant that the economic liberalization unveiled in 1965 had to be accompanied by a devolution of political power from the centre to the republics. Devolution not only affected the state but the Party as well. The upshot was sheer chaos – nobody knew who was responsible for decision-making. Government virtually seized up. The only people benefiting from the reform were the Belgrade bankers and businessmen who retained a firm grip on the economic rudder. The government, by contrast, was hopelessly adrift, allowing this 'Red Bourgeoisie' considerable space for its money-making activities. In Belgrade's fashionable city centre the clothes and cars were reminiscent more of Milan than of Bucharest or Sofia. The stark inequalities of the new economic policy offended the students' idealism.

The workers resented them too. With government stagnating, the only person who understood the potential danger was Tito. He showed his charisma and political cunning to the full in a televised fireside chat – a '*tour de force* by an understanding but stern grandfather asking for help to build a better future for his family', as the

American scholar Dennison Rusinow described it.[39] Tito disarmed the rebellious students by backing their main demands. He adopted their youthful rhetoric in articulating his irritation with 'obstructionists from the Party, who are violating socialist norms of behaviour'. Appealing to the egalitarian instincts of the protesters, he called for 'immediate action to help the low income workers who had so far borne the heaviest burden of the economic reform. Such action would fulfil the students' justified demands.'

Tito had no intention of carrying out his promises. But that was not the point – he had defused the crisis, resurrected his prestige in the eyes of ordinary people and reminded all squabbling factions in the LCY where ultimate authority in Yugoslavia rested. He was especially concerned to underline this last point, as the country was in a state of confused transition of which the student strike was just one manifestation.

In March 1967, the first serious dispute between Serbs and Croats in over twenty years had broken out. A broad spectrum of Croat intellectuals had published the *Declaration concerning the Name and Position of the Croatian Literary Language*. This rejected the Novi Sad Agreement of 1954 which had regulated the literary language of Serbo-Croat or Croato-Serb. The Croat intellectuals argued that by choosing the Serbian variant as the literary language, the Agreement had relegated Croatian to the status of a regional dialect, thus ignoring its rich literary history. Serb intellectuals responded by conceding some of the points made in the *Declaration* but demanding special rights for Serbs outside Serbia, especially in Croatia.

Particularly awkward for Tito was the signature of the Croatian writer, Miroslav Krleža, arguably south-eastern Europe's greatest intellectual of the twentieth century. Tito invited Krleža to his villa in Belgrade and asked him to withdraw his support for the petition (Krleža was probably the only person in Yugoslavia whom Tito would feel uneasy ordering about). Refusing to change his mind, Krleža resigned instead from the Croatian Party's Central Committee. 'If I withdrew my signature', he told the Croatian leader, Miko Tripalo, 'they'll all say: "Look at the old monkey. Now he's making out that he didn't realize what he was signing!"'[40] Other leading intellectuals were purged or lost their jobs. The most prominent victim was the energetically abrasive director of Zagreb's Institute for the History of the Workers' Movement, Dr Franjo Tudjman.

The *Declaration* was a product of the euphoria that the fall of Ranković had occasioned in Croatia. It was a taste of things to come throughout Yugoslavia. In November 1968, it was the turn of the Kosovo Albanians. After years of humiliation and discrimination at the hands of Ranković and his UDBa operatives, Albanian students rioted and Priština, the provincial capital, rocked with violence. The security forces were ordered by the Serbian leadership (with Tito's approval) to quell the disturbances, but some of the Albanians' grievances were addressed. For the first time, Albanians were granted real representative powers on both Serbian and federal bodies. The Albanian language emerged from the ghetto and, before long, textbooks and other publications from Albania proper flooded the schools and libraries of the province. The assumption that Ranković's dismissal would be gratefully received by submissive Albanians was mistaken. An articulate younger generation dominated the university in Priština and was hungry to assert Albanian national rights.

The most important consequence for Bosnia of the erratic politics of the late 1960s was the opportunity it gave to a group of young Muslim scholars and communists to force the process which led to Muslims being granted the status of nationhood. Throughout Yugoslav history, the Muslims had been treated dismissively by both Serb and Croat ideologues as apostate members of the dominant Slav nations. The latest manifestation of this theory assumed that in a secular society like Yugoslavia, the Muslims would increasingly regard their religious identification as anachronistic and at last make the correct choice by joining either of the two larger nations. But like the Albanians in Kosovo, the Muslims were beginning to find a voice that corresponded to their growing maturity as a modern nation. The Yugoslav state first recognized the Muslims as a separate nation in the 1963 constitution, although the relevant clause was ambiguously formulated. It spoke of Bosnia as a republic inhabited by 'Serbs, Moslems, and Croats allied in the past by a common life'.[41] This definition excluded the Muslims of the Sanjak, the former Ottoman region divided between Serbia and Montenegro, but it was a start. It was not until 1968 that the Bosnian League of Communists finally recognized the Muslims as a constituent nation of Yugoslavia (as opposed to a minority), a move confirmed by the LCY a year later. At the time, the Muslims' campaign for recognition was 'part of an attempt to avoid the historical competition between Serbs and Croats for the loyalties of Muslim cultural, intellectual, religious and, especially, political leaders'.[42] Its authors could not have known that it would be turned around by Serb and Croat politicians two decades later as a way of trying to annihilate the Muslims.

In 1969, it was the turn of the Slovenes to take to the streets. The International Bank had given Yugoslavia a loan for a motorway network. The Slovene leadership had been led to expect that it would receive funds to build a motorway from Nova Gorica to Ljubljana, opening up the Italian market for Slovenia and for Yugoslavia as a whole. The Serbs and Croats instead diverted the funds for their own road-construction programmes. The entire reform programme seemed to be directed by the Serbs and Croats at the expense of all other republics. Above all, the fear that this was the case influenced the thinking of Edvard Kardelj, a Slovene and the last remaining member of Tito's triumvirate still in power. A strong coalition between Serbs and Croats might jeopardize Kardelj's position as successor to Tito. It might even jeopardize the position of Tito himself.

The sudden process of political fragmentation meant that economic problems, like the Slovene road-building crisis, also assumed a national dimension. Politicians soon discovered how easy it was to add to their popularity by appearing to defend national interests. As a consequence, those economic and social problems less readily associated with national grievances were neglected. Two of these, however, were to have a long-term negative influence on Yugoslavia's stability, and ultimately a big impact on the national question when the country collapsed in the early 1990s.

The first was the perennially insoluble question of the peasants which, by the late 1960s, had assumed a new guise. The successful expansion of industry and of employment opportunities in towns and cities had encouraged large numbers of younger peasants to leave the countryside for higher wages and a more stimulating social life. Yugoslavia was developing a sophisticated and cosmopolitan culture, especially in centres like Zagreb, Sarajevo and Belgrade. The films of the Belgrade director, Dušan Makavejev, were now appearing in European art houses while a new generation of Bosnian, Serbian and Croatian film-makers were returning from Prague armed with the technical and narrative secrets of the Czech new wave. Sarajevo, Belgrade, Ljubljana and Zagreb all produced musicians and rock bands, like Bijelo Dugme (White Button) and Atomsko Sklonište (Nuclear Bunker), whose influence would stretch beyond Yugoslavia's borders, attaining cult status in both Eastern and Western Europe. Yugoslavia became a key intellectual entrepôt between East and West, as the philosophers of the group around the journal *Praxis* invited their colleagues from Warsaw Pact and NATO countries to exchange critiques of Stalinism and capitalism over meals on the sunny Adriatic island of Korčula. Large sections of Western Europe's liberal intelligentsia took their holidays in Yugoslavia or participated in educational exchange programmes. For liberal westerners, this was a balmy communism which most felt they could support with a good conscience.

While hundreds of thousands of peasants were drawn to the cities, the new urban sophistication also served to underline the growing social gap between town and country. Mutual antipathy between rural and urban communities in Yugoslavia grew rapidly in the 1970s and 1980s. It was not a well-documented phenomenon, attracting little comment, but its impact on the wars of Yugoslav succession in the 1990s was enormous.

By 1967, over 2.5 million peasants had left the countryside but it was still home to 48 per cent of the Yugoslav population. With the emigration, productivity slumped and the peasant population began to age. Tax revenues in rural areas began to decline and with them locally financed social services. In the mid-1960s, the cities approached saturation point. Young peasants continued to stream towards them but the work began to dry up. 'The country's politicians, with the sociological ignorance or irresponsibility common in their profession, talked blithely of sending surplus labour back to the farms. Instead, as in many other Mediterranean countries, the surplus migrated to Western Europe in search of the urban employment it could not find at home, partly relieving the pressure at the critical moment but not solving the problem.'[43]

That emigration to the labour markets of Western Europe was welcome in many respects. It provided substantial hard-currency remittances for a country which was rapidly expanding trade ties with the European Economic Community but which did not have a convertible currency of its own. And it brought cultural benefits for the Yugoslavs, exposing its peoples to western culture. It also, of course, soaked up the surplus labour which the Yugoslav economy could not absorb. But it brought great dangers too. According to official Yugoslav statistics, there were 800,000 migrant workers in Western Europe by 1969, 'nearly 22 per cent of total domestic employment, both public and private'.[44] In the event of a downturn in western economies, particularly in West Germany, a large number of those workers would inevitably be thrown back on the Yugoslav labour market. This is precisely what happened after 1973 and, like all other East European countries except Czechoslovakia and Albania, Yugoslavia borrowed huge sums from western banks to tackle the problem. The national debt proved an especially mischievous ingredient in the pressure cooker which Yugoslavia became in the 1980s.

Vladmir Bakarić, Tito's most faithful and competent lieutenant in Croatia, bears more responsibility than any other politician for placing economic reform and decentralization on the agenda before and after Ranković's fall. Croatia's role in the developments between 1966 and 1972 was paramount. Its intellectuals suffered a defeat when Tito refused to accept the central tenets of the *Declaration concerning the Name and Position of the Croatian Literary Language*, but this turned out to be a temporary setback. The ferment of intellectual and political activity could not be stopped. Tito still publicly identified 'unitarism' (for many non-Serbs a code word for Serbian nationalism) as the greatest threat to Yugoslavia's harmonious development until the very end of 1971. Croatian cultural nationalism was *ipso facto* regarded as a valuable ally in the battle against 'unitarism'.

This was confirmed at the Tenth Plenum of the Croatian League of Communists' Central Committee held in January 1970. Miloš Žanko, a conservative, came under sustained attack from Party members for a series of articles he had written for the Belgrade-based Party newspaper, *Borba*, entitled 'There is Method in this Nationalist Madness'. Žanko argued that the groundswell of Croatian national sentiment was the first stage in a plan to destabilize Yugoslavia and bring down socialism. The Croatian Party was now led by an energetic young woman, Savka Dabčević-Kučar, while its representative in the Executive Committee of the LCY (effectively its Politburo) was a former teenage partisan and head of the Yugoslav Youth Movement, Miko Tripalo. These two had embraced the growing freedom of the press in Croatia and welcomed the participation of non-communist organizations in debates on economic and political reform. Chief amongst these groups was the Matica Hrvatska. This club had promoted Croatian culture since its creation in the 1840s, at roughly the same time as equivalents like the Serbian Matica Srpska and the Czech Matica Česká. Moribund for most of the communist period, the struggle over the *Declaration* imbued the Matica Hrvatska with a new sense of mission. At the Tenth Plenum, Žanko singled it out for particular criticism. But instead of being applauded, he was rounded on by fellow delegates, suggesting a historic victory for the liberals in the Party. Tito's attitude was decisive. Monitoring the proceedings by telephone, he gave Dabčević-Kučar specific authority to lead the charge against Žanko. There could be no clearer signal for the Croatian Spring to begin.

In many respects, the cultural and political renaissance which swept across Croatia from 1969 until December 1971 was comparable to the liberalization in Czechoslovakia that ended so dramatically with the Soviet-led invasion of August 1968. In Croatia, newspapers like *Vjesnik u Srijedu* (*Vjesnik on Wednesday*) were transformed from stodgy Party mouthpieces into vibrant investigative journals, full of critical articles about subjects considered taboo for more than two decades. *Hrvatski tjednik* (*Croatian Weekly*), the weekly newspaper published by Matica Hrvatska, which was founded in early 1971, soon had a circulation of over 100,000. After the Tenth Plenum, membership of the Matica reached over 40,000 by the end of 1971 with new branches opening every week.

The idiocies of communist dogma were a favourite target of intellectuals, journalists and even some radical Party members in Croatia. But it became quickly obvious that the national question encroached on the discussion of almost any issue. 'Unitarism', as a political ideology, had a cultural twin, 'Yugoslavism'. According to this, Yugoslavs' primary cultural identity was defined by their common experience of statehood in the twentieth century. This implied that one's narrow nationality – Croat, Serb or whatever – was secondary, an interesting regional adjunct to the Yugoslav identity. Croatian history which veered from Yugoslav ideology or the mythology of the Partisan struggle was simply not studied. This meant that the national question, the complex relations between Serbs and Croats in both Yugoslav states, had been systematically ignored.

Unmuzzled, newspapers like *Hrvatski tjednik* wanted to know why 'even in Zagreb, the capital . . . there were 56.5 Serbs and 40.8 percent Croats on the city police force in 1971',[45] when Serbs made up but 15 per cent of the republic's population. Awkward questions like these touched on the most delicate sensibilities. For the largely rural Serb population in Croatia, numerical supremacy in Croatia's security forces was a guarantee against any resurgence of Ustaše ideology. For the Croats, it was a permanent reminder that Yugoslavia had never escaped its Greater Serbian origins. This conundrum lay at the heart of Yugoslavia's national question: the status of Croats as a minority in Yugoslavia, and of the Serbs as a minority in Croatia.

After the Tenth Plenum in January 1970, participation in politics suddenly broke the narrow bounds of Party and intelligentsia. 'This development, the broad activation of all sections of the population in political life, took me and everyone else by surprise', admitted the Croatian communist leader, Miko Tripalo. 'It was particularly noticeable in 1970 when discussions on the changes to the constitution began. Ordinary people were simply no longer prepared to sit and listen to the wise words and advice of the leadership – they wanted to take part themselves in some way, just as the programme of the League of Communists claimed they could.'[46] It was a source of pride to the Croat leadership that they presided over and encouraged this intellectual flowering. This was democratic 'self-management' in action, Tripalo insisted. It was not an expression of struggle between Serbs and Croats. 'The origins of the conflict were socio-economic and the national problems emerged as a consequence . . . This was a battle between etatism and self-management, between dogmatism and democratic socialist ideas.'[47]

That was not, of course, how members of the Serbian League of Communists (LCS) viewed matters. Tito reprimanded the LCS leader, Marko Nikezić, for holding a closed meeting of the LCS leadership. This was not Tito defending openness – he simply assumed that he would be the subject of any closed meetings.

Nikezić dismissed Tito's concerns: 'if we had published what was said at that meeting, the Croats and ourselves would never be able to work together again'.

It was an article of faith among the reformist Croats that all obstacles in the way of progress had been put in position by the 'unitarists, Greater Serbs, or Rankovićites' in Belgrade. But this oversimplification ignored one crucial fact. In November 1968, control of the LCS had passed into the hands of two liberal Serbs, Marko Nikezić, a former foreign minister, and Latinka Perović, erstwhile chair of the Association of Yugoslav Women. They had accepted the logic of anti-unitarism and explicitly supported the encouragement of market principles in the economy; 'liberation from the ballast of Serbian Yugoslavism; the promotion of trained and competent Party cadres; and cooperation not confrontation with other republics'.[48] Furthermore, on a visit to Bosnia, Nikezić told a meeting of Bosnian Serbs that they should not address their grievances to him but to the Bosnian leadership, 'which is your leadership'. Certainly, Belgrade newspapers wrote disparagingly about the resurgence of Croatian nationalism but just as the Croatian communists had relinquished censorship so too had the liberal Serbian leadership. Nikezić and Perović could claim with justification that Serbia was not interfering in Croatia's republican affairs.

Disquiet about the Croat nationalist movement came from elsewhere. First, it came from unitarist Croats, like Žanko, but more significantly it came from Kardelj and hardliners in the military establishment, most importantly the federal Defence Minister, General Nikola Ljubičić. But by the middle of 1971, the activities of the Maspok, a contraction of the Croatian phrase meaning Mass Movement, had alienated the key figure in the Croatian communist establishment, Vladmir Bakarić. These three had little difficulty in persuading Tito that Tripalo and Dabčević-Kučar had lost control of the situation: policy in Croatia was now being dictated by the ideologues of Matica Hrvatska and the Croatian Party was limping behind. The so-called 'excesses', demands being made by extreme nationalists on the fringes of the Maspok, began to frighten liberal supporters of the Croats in other republics like Macedonia. Tito decided to act in December 1971, summoning the Zagreb leadership to his favourite hunting-lodge, Karadjordjevo in Vojvodina, denouncing their work and demanding their resignations. This was then followed up with a swift show of force by the police and army in Zagreb which led to hundreds of arrests and the subsequent imprisonment of 'ringleaders'. Tito had reverted to standard techniques of communist repression. The democratic experiment in Croatia was closed down but liberalism was still alive in other republics, though not for long. Tito applied his cherished principles of 'brotherhood and unity', elsewhere in Yugoslavia. The Serbian leaders, Nikezić and Perović, were forced out in October 1972.

The leadership's response to the Croatian Spring and the Serb liberals was a disaster for Yugoslavia's future. Free from external interference for the first time in twentieth-century history, the elites were presented with the possibility of resolving their national problems by a steady democratization of the entire system. The true villains of the period were Tito and Kardelj, neither of whom (the latter in particular) welcomed reconciliation between the Serbs and Croats. An examination of their tactics towards the Serb and Croat leaderships between 1966 and 1972 reveals that they were playing off Zagreb against Belgrade, stirring up animosities in order to consolidate their own authority. Less than two years after the crushing of the Serbian liberals, Tito introduced a new constitution, the longest such document in the world, baffling in its complexity. It further eroded Belgrade's constitutional dominance by devolving greater power to Kosovo and Vojvodina. But Croats did not regard this as a particular victory, as they had been denied their voice by what they believed was a Serbian conspiracy. Tito had driven both Serbian and Croatian nationalisms underground. When they emerged from hibernation in the mid- and late 1980s, they had lost their modernizing and liberal characteristics. It is hard to disagree with the prediction made in 1971 by the Serb communist, Dobrivoj Radosavljević, a Tito loyalist, who broke ranks on just one occasion: 'Tito committed a historical error by encouraging Albanian–Serb and Croatian–Serb conflict. Yugoslavia will pay a heavy price for it.'[49]

The Father, the sun and the demiurge: Romania

An entire people,
not yet born,
but condemned to birth
in columns before birth
foetus beside foetus,
an entire people
which does not see, does not hear, does not understand,
but moves forward.
Through writhing bodies of women,
through the blood of mothers
unconsulted.

Ana Blandiana, 'The Children's Crusade', 1984[50]

On 21 August 1968, troops from five Warsaw Pact countries violated Czechoslovakia's sovereignty, turning the Prague Spring into winter. As the Soviet-led forces were consolidating their positions, the leader of a sixth Warsaw Pact country, Nicolae Ceauşescu, mounted the podium in the Palace Square in Bucharest. The gawky General Secretary of the Romanian Communist Party was never a good speaker, even after he had overcome the heavy stutter of his childhood. His delivery was monotonous, except when his nerves led him to stress the wrong words. Self-conscious of his rustic accent, he attempted to disguise his dialect, producing a curious hybrid that made the sophisticated audiences of Romania's capital laugh. But on that sweltering August day in 1968, the large crowd before him was listening attentively to his every word. Their admiration and pride grew as he denounced the invasion of Czechoslovakia as 'a grave danger to peace in Europe, to the fate of socialism in the world . . . a shameful moment in the history of the revolutionary movement'.[51]

In his short, passionate address, Ceauşescu announced the formation of 'armed patriotic detachments of workers, peasants, and intellectuals, defenders of the independence of our socialist homeland . . . The entire Romanian people will not allow anybody to violate the territory of our homeland.'[52] The performance was genuinely felt. He had recently returned from a successful bilateral visit to Prague where, despite some private misgivings about the extent of the liberalization, he had publicly backed the Czechoslovak

Communist Party's right to map out its own road to socialism.

Over the next few days, Ceauşescu and his fellow Party and state leaders fanned out across the country to spread their message of resistance to the threat of Soviet invasion. The First Secretary himself went to Transylvania – first to Braşov, Romania's second industrial city, and then to Cluj. Everywhere in the mixed Hungarian/Romanian region, he was greeted with spontaneous enthusiasm by both communities. In Bucharest a group of young authors, notorious for their criticism of the Communist Party leadership, signed a declaration, expressing their 'complete agreement with the position of the Party and of the Romanian government, as defined by Comrade Ceauşescu'. They swore to do 'all in our power to defend our fundamental values, our country and the peaceful construction of socialism in our country'.[53] Three of them, including a gifted young novelist from Bessarabia, Paul Goma, joined the Party on the same day.

Thousands of Romanians volunteered for the Patriotic Guard, lending substance to Ceauşescu's promise that – in contrast to the Czechs and Slovaks – the Romanian people must resist aggression with force. In retrospect, a Soviet invasion of either Romania or Yugoslavia (whose leadership also felt threatened) seems most unlikely. But at the time, Romanian fears that they were next on the list were understandable. Relations with the Soviet Union were tense. Moscow had excluded the Romanians from two emergency Warsaw Pact summits before the Czechoslovak invasion. In such an atmosphere, Ceauşescu's call to arms and his defence of the Czechoslovaks' sovereignty transformed him almost overnight into one of the most popular figures in modern Romanian history.

Excoriated by the press of its Warsaw Pact allies, Romania took heart instead from the warm support offered by other countries. The United States indicated unofficially that NATO would go to war if the Soviets moved against Romania. The Chinese congratulated Ceauşescu for his principled stand. Even Enver Hoxha, who rarely had a good word for anyone, encouraged Bucharest to remain firm. Ceauşescu was careful not to push the Russians too far. He did not wish to give Moscow the impression that he was behaving provocatively by creating a pro-Chinese bloc in Eastern Europe. 'Nothing can hinder the good cooperation and friendship between Romania and the Soviet Union',[54] he reassured his ally just five days after the invasion. The Soviet leadership heard the message clearly – Romania would remain a loyal member of the camp. Ceauşescu had covered all bases: the Russians would not invade; the British Prime Minister, Harold Wilson, President de Gaulle of France and President-to-be Richard Nixon, were so impressed with his feisty independence that they all made the pilgrimage to Bucharest. At the age of fifty, his position in Romania was unassailable.

It was hard for the 'little Stalins' (or indeed the less tyrannical 'little Khrushchevs' of the 1960s) to establish political legitimacy in the people's democracies. Democracy itself was clearly out of the question and so, as dictators are wont to do, they expended much energy devising other schemes to justify their power – anything that would disguise the fact that these powers were in truth guaranteed by the Red Army and the local apparatuses of terror. Władysław Gomułka's appeal rested in his reputation as a victim of Stalinist persecution and as the reforming patriot of 1956. But as the 1960s wore on, Poland's crusty dictatorship became ever more visible underneath this veil of legitimacy. Todor Zhivkov played the tenuous card of Bulgarian wartime hero but such popularity as he enjoyed lay in the indisputable truth that he was less ghastly than his predecessor, Chervenkov. János Kádár was despised by his people for siding with the Russians to crush the Hungarian revolution of 1956. When his New Economic Mechanism, introduced in 1968, brought a little luxury into people's lives the hatred gradually dissolved into indifference. Only the soulless Antonín Novotný in Czechoslovakia had the honesty to behave openly as an unrepresentative dictator installed by the Russians. He was finally ousted in January 1968 by Alexander Dubček, the only East European leader prepared to submit his work to popular scrutiny.

The case of Ceauşescu was more complicated. He had inherited his post from Gheorghe Gheorghiu-Dej. In the early 1960s, Dej saw an opportunity to loosen the bonds that tied Romania to the Soviet Union. He was quick to understand how far-reaching the implications of the Sino-Soviet split were for the communist world; his primary reason for distancing Bucharest from Moscow was economic. According to Khrushchev's plan for establishing an 'international division of socialist labour', Romania, along with Bulgaria and Albania, was to produce food for the Soviet Union and the north-east European states, which would produce industrial goods. Romania would remain mired in peasant backwardness, or so Dej and his colleagues saw it; their dream was to modernize Romania through industrialization. The Prime Minister, Ion Gheorghe Maurer, is reported to have said 'Why should we ship our corn to Poland so that the Poles can fatten their pigs in order to buy machinery in the West, when we can sell our corn to the West and buy machinery that we need?'[55]

The people's democracies were dependent on the Soviet Union for most of their mineral resources, above all oil. But Romania had its own oil. It also had natural gas, timber, bauxite, coal, manganese, copper, lead, zinc and uranium. And, if managed correctly, it was a bread basket as well. As Khrushchev was not prepared to support Romania's industrialization, Dej looked beyond Comecon for support – to the socialist mavericks, China, Yugoslavia and Albania, and the imperialists in the EEC. The impact on Romania's foreign trade was dramatic. In the three years from 1964, Romania's trade with the Soviet Union dropped from 42 per cent of the total to 27 per cent while Comecon as a whole accounted for less than half of its trade by 1967.

To underline Romania's alienation from the Soviet Union, Dej ordered a spree of name-changing in the capital and other cities. One journalist recorded that 'the A. Popov movie theatre became the Dacia; the Maxim Gorky, the Union. A Russian language institute in the capital was closed and a large Russian bookstore demolished; the Rumanian edition of the Soviet propaganda monthly New Times was discontinued; schools dropped compulsory Russian-language studies; Rumanian orthography was "re-Latinized," eradicating the previous "Slavification" of the alphabet and of culture in general.'[56] More provocatively, a Bucharest publishing house brought out a collection of material by Marx, hitherto unpublished, under the title *Notes on Rumanians* in which the father of socialism denounced Russia's claim to Bessarabia (which had been incorporated into the Soviet Union in 1941 as the Soviet Republic of Moldavia).

Dej's flag-waving was popular with ordinary Romanians. They warmed to him still further in late 1964 when he ordered an amnesty for several thousand prisoners, including many political detainees. The jamming of the BBC, Radio Free Europe and Voice of America also came to a halt and Romanian writers addressed politically delicate subjects for the first time. Three days after Dej's death on 19 March 1965, Ceauşescu was elected First Secretary at a time of rising expectations. While appreciating the delicacy of the country's geo-political position, Romanians wanted the new leadership to continue the experiment with liberalization and independence. At forty-seven, Ceauşescu was the youngest Party leader in the socialist world. He was energetic and apparently aware of the travails of the average citizen. He was not, however, entirely in control of the Party and still had powerful enemies, none more so than the Minister of Internal Affairs, Alexandru Drăghici – the man who controlled the Securitate.

Even three years after Dej's death, Ceauşescu was not yet in command of the Party. Coalitions of ambitious colleagues in the Politburo and Central Committee made him feel insecure. In uncertain times, the Party became an arena of political struggle, and included elements of indirect democracy by reflecting differences within the dominant bureaucracy. The rival factions appealed to various constituencies for support. Ceauşescu flattered writers, journalists and other intellectuals. He spoke of the need for 'socialist legality', which implied an attack on corruption and cronyism, but also on the use of terror by the Securitate. He told the Youth Union that its meetings were too boring and it should make itself more appealing to young people. Above all, he seized the weapon of nationalism, and lavished praise on the military as the guardians of Romanian independence. The Party's popularity rose steadily with a notable improvement in the standard of living. Ceauşescu placed his own people in key Party positions, eroding little by little the power of Dej's contemporaries.

During seven months of intense political activity from October 1967, he succeeded in outwitting all his rivals. His victory was sealed at a Central Committee Plenum in April 1968 when he secured the rehabilitation of Party members purged by Dej, most notably Lucreţiu Pătrăşcanu. He used the 'revelations' about Stalinist distortions to force his most powerful enemy, Drăghici, from the Interior Ministry.

Before the showdown at the April Plenum, a special Party Conference was held in December 1967, and agreed on major economic changes, including the decentralization of decision-making. The discussions were peppered with references to self-management and other heresies such as incentive payments and profit maximization. But Ceauşescu himself pointedly refused to countenance any relaxation of central planning. This did not prevent a brief flowering of private enterprise at the end of the 1960s: some private shops and privately owned restaurants were allowed to open. From 1967 onwards, Romanians could even build their own houses. New regulations made it easier for Romanians to travel abroad, and police repression was relaxed.

As Ceauşescu's power increased, the focus of his vision sharpened. He saw a Romania transformed from supplicant peasant state into an independent industrial powerhouse dominating south-eastern Europe, and that it was his mission to realize this transformation. To succeed he would require complete control over the economy. The more convinced Ceauşescu became of his vision, the more remote was the prospect of economic liberalization.

On grounds of alleged efficiency, Ceauşescu also forced through a massive reorganization of Party and state administration at the December 1967 Conference. In principle, the duplication of posts at every level of government was, as Ceauşescu argued, a waste of time and money. But Ceauşescu's motivation for introducing the change was primarily a desire to consolidate his political monopoly. This was effectively a *Gleichschaltung*, stripping state organs of any modest autonomy they may have wielded. An outgrowth of the reorganization was the campaign to restore 'socialist legality', to restrict the abuse of power and rein in corruption. Ceauşescu had begun to raise disturbing questions about the Interior Ministry and the Securitate: 'It is no secret that certain outrages have been committed over the years', he wrote in *Scînteia* (*The Spark*), the Party newspaper. 'The Penal Code must ensure the strict observance of socialist legality, so that nobody may infringe upon it in any way or commit abuses.'[57] This was the preface to the assault on Drăghici. By opening an investigation into the purges carried out by the leadership in the middle and late 1940s, Ceauşescu compromised all his leadership rivals, who were implicated in the execution of Pătrăşcanu. The General Secretary himself, however, was appointed a candidate member of the Politburo two days *after* the murder of Pătrăşcanu in April 1954. He could reasonably claim that he was not involved in conspiracy to murder. When the Party later considered putting Drăghici on trial, the former Interior Minister issued a veiled warning that he would release material implicating Ceauşescu in a different but equally unsavoury murder case. Preparations for his arraignment were quietly dropped, the official explanation being that it fell outside the statute of limitations. This was only a minor setback, however. Drăghici's removal from office achieved two goals: there were no more serious challengers to Ceauşescu, and the Securitate was now in the General Secretary's hands.

With the exception of Czechoslovakia, where the reform had less than five months left to run, Romania was by far the most liberal country in the Warsaw Pact in April 1968. But in the guise of promoting reform, Ceauşescu had cornered immense power. Not so well known as his much-vaunted declarations of national independence were moves that hinted at the obsessive character of the Ceauşescu 'vision'. Most significant were a series of laws passed in 1966 and 1967 which banned abortion and made divorce and contraception extremely difficult to obtain. This legislation was prompted by a steadily falling birth rate that threatened to undermine the 'vision' of industrial growth dependent on a burgeoning young workforce. In the first two years after the ban on terminations, the birthrate leapt back up but began to decline thereafter as a widespread network of illegal and hence much less safe abortion clinics sprang up around the country. Campaigns against smoking and against the creeping influence of western culture on young people were also introduced, suggesting that Ceauşescu might not be as liberal as many Romanians and western journalists believed.

As we have seen, 1971 was a bad year for reform in Yugoslavia and Albania. Matters were no better in Romania. In June, Ceauşescu, accompanied by his ambitious wife, Elena, spent a month on an official visit to North Vietnam, North Korea and the People's Republic of China. For a man whose self-image was assuming messianic proportions, these societies were a revelation. In Pyongyang, 'he was impressed with the monumental buildings and the neat layout of the large boulevards with endlessly similar apartment blocs – all tied up with the deified name of Kim Il Sung. From that time, Ceauşescu dreamed not only of rebuilding Bucharest in his own image but also of erecting a single monumental edifice that would symbolize his glorious epoch and be his legacy.'[58] In China, seas of flag-waving children dazzled the Romanian leader, who loved the obsequious adulation bestowed on him and his hosts. Two aspects of the Cultural Revolution impressed him most: obedience and uniformity. The Czechoslovak crisis of 1968 was the height of Ceauşescu's popularity; his trip to the Far East in 1971 saw his descent into a form of political madness, an irrational belief in his ability to transform totally a rural Balkan society. A month after his return, he posted his seventeen 'theses' on the door of the Central Committee. This was the start of Romania's 'mini-cultural Revolution'. A decade later, this new programme culminated in a social-engineering experiment without parallel in postwar Europe.

The theses shocked the generation of Romanian writers and artists who had eagerly exploited the liberal atmosphere of the 1960s. They interpreted the new line, officially adopted by the Party in November 1971, as a return to the Zhdanovite principles of socialist realism. The theses were indubitably a call to place art in the service of the Party, but in them nationalism was emphasized over socialism. The General Secretary denounced 'cosmopolitanism' in art. In Stalin's day this had been a code word for anti-Semitism. In Ceauşescu's Romania, it sounded an ominous note for all ethnic minorities. The anti-Russian nationalism that had won support at home and abroad in 1968 was sliding steadily towards jingoism. Many prominent writers raised their voices in protest against the tightening of Party control over their work. But within a year, Ceauşescu had marginalized this opposition. A few, including Paul Goma, continued to speak out, marking the beginning of an isolated dissident movement.

A few months after the seventeen theses were enshrined in Party lore, Ceauşescu introduced his master stroke of political control – job rotation. Rightly fearful that he was despised by large numbers inside and outside the Party, Ceauşescu made it compulsory for functionaries to move to new positions on a regular basis. This ensured that nobody could build a power base from which he or she could launch an assault on Ceauşescu's leadership. Rotation had several side effects. Politicians were never in one job long enough to develop any specialist knowledge; rather the administration was plagued by inexperience and incompetence. Fear of demotion also played a bigger role in the Romanian Party than anywhere else in Eastern Europe; and the constant toing and froing turned the kremlinology of Bucharest politics into an esoteric art. Naturally, the Ceauşescu family was exempt from the principle of rotation.

In March 1974, in front of Romania's elite and with millions more watching on live television, Nicolae Ceauşescu, wearing a sash with the national colours and bearing a ceremonial mace, took the solemn oath of the newly created office of President of the Republic. The establishment of the presidential decree as Romania's supreme legislative act confirmed suspicions that Ceauşescu aspired to royalty in all but name. In fact, the ruling couple (Elena's influence had grown enormously) enjoyed powers which earlier Romanian monarchs would not have thought possible. As the cult of personality developed, fawning courtiers composed poems and meditations that described Ceauşescu as, *inter alia*, 'morning star', 'sun', 'omniscient father' and 'titan'. Corneliu Vadim Tudor, a ferocious anti-Semite and nationalist, anointed him both 'demiurge' and 'god'.

The extravagance of this dictatorship was without precedent in European communist history. With the exception of Tito (and even he was modest in comparison with the Romanian dynasty), the material aspirations of most Party leaders were bland and petit-bourgeois.

As Ceauşescu and his appalling coterie indulged its passions, life for ordinary people became progressively more miserable throughout the 1970s and early 1980s. Ceauşescu's determination to industrialize the country rapidly led to serious distortions in the economy. The programme was financed in three ways: by diverting investment from agriculture; by lowering consumption; and, when petro-dollars glutted the market from 1974 onwards, by borrowing heavily from western banks and governments. These policies victimized almost everyone – peasants, industrial workers and the intelligentsia.

In his novel *Refuges*, published in 1984 and which the censor's net inexplicably missed, Augustin Buzura portrays Romania in the late 1970s as a society whose members are so profoundly alienated and frightened that it can never be redeemed. 'I am afraid of running away, but also of staying, of roaring, but also of keeping silent, of living, but of dying too', the central character, Ioana, reflects as she attempts to come to terms with her collapsing life. 'I'm afraid of lying, but am unable to tell the truth. I'm afraid of the night, of light, of people . . . I fear everything! I'd stay here if I knew nobody would come . . . I'd leave if nobody looked for me, if they didn't recognize me, if I didn't have to answer questions. Fear! She heard her hoarse, turbid voice and at that moment she felt an urge to pray, to abandon herself to somebody's mercy, but no formula occurred to her.'[59]

Cowed by authority, the men in Buzura's Romania are chronic alcoholics and abusers of women. The women are engaged in a battle on two fronts. Obliged to find sufficient food and money to ensure their family's survival, on the one hand, they have to avoid their menfolk's anger on the other. Male ambition, frustrated by a submissive relationship to the state, is channelled into violence against women. The village, the mainstay of Romanian society, disintegrates as the Party's authoritarian hierarchy allows local bullies to tear apart the delicate network of social relations in the countryside. In the towns, the pressure from above to produce and expand turns the factory managers and their employees into lazy and corrupt cynics. Set mainly in the psychiatric ward of a regional hospital, the most insane patient, who insists on being addressed as 'Your Excellency', has developed a social theory which aims to overcome all human frailties:

> The FINAL UNIVERSE will avoid violence, criminality, alcoholism, gratuitous eroticism, indifference, dry, non-productive day-dreaming, idle time, doubt, delay, hesitation, meta-scientific desires, cowardice, abuse, terror, anarchy and all the other defects that have led us to the present crisis. The reduction of people's height (by genetic methods), physical equality – except for basketball players – which will allow the consumption of utilitarian goods to decrease; this will increase the chances of mankind's survival far beyond the limits compelled upon it by the almost exhausted sources of energy and the ever increasing population. This, of course, until they get used to the chlorophyll I have synthesized in the past years.[60]

'"Whenever I see this man," Ioana said, showing him [His Excellency] to the doctor, "I feel a chill creep up my spine. How many dead and maimed must be hiding in the darkness of his mind! How many consciences destroyed . . . And how many distorted, blinded infants doomed to psychic death stand in the shade of his apparently well-meaning laws?"'[61]

Apart from Ioana herself, Buzura includes one other redemptive character, Helgomar David, a loyal Party member since the war. An engineer, he rebels against the state on behalf of the workers in the mine where he is employed. His colleagues are the victims of regular accidents and, after one particularly unpleasant incident which leaves several dead, he fights for their families to be compensated. This was an elliptical reference to an extraordinary act of defiance in Ceauşescu's Romania, the Jiu Valley miners' strike of 1977.

From the early 1970s onwards, Ceauşescu expanded the role of the Securitate. By 1989, it employed an estimated 24,000 active service officers. But its foot soldiers were the tens and possibly hundreds of thousands of informers who reported on the activities of citizens in every nook and cranny of society. The prisons, psychiatric units and torture sessions represented the sharp end of the Securitate, but made up only a small part of its activity. For most people, the terror consisted in the certainty that one of your close friends or family was informing on you, contributing to the detailed files that the Securitate opened on every citizen. 'The first great socialist industry was the production of personal files', one Romanian writer reflected. 'In the socialist world, people and things exist only in personal files. The owner of [these] files is the owner of all existence.'[62]

The information could be used at any moment to have people sacked, to blackmail them into working for the police or simply to remind others that they were under constant surveillance. The only organization comparable with the Securitate was the Sigurimi in Albania. By the early 1980s, anybody owning a typewriter was obliged to register it with the secret police. The most insignificant conversation with a foreigner had to be reported to the Securitate. Failure to do so could have dire consequences – the loss of one's job, eviction from one's flat, one's children barred from higher education. The organization's invasion of private life even began to affect the bodies of Romanian women when, in March 1984, Ceauşescu announced a new campaign to increase the birthrate at a meeting of the National Women's Councils. He told the delegates that to 'breed, comrade women, it is your patriotic duty'.[63] Under the supervision of the Securitate, all women of child-bearing age were forced to undergo a gynaecological examination every month to establish whether they had conceived or not. If not, the Securitate wanted to know why.

In such an atmosphere, mounting a campaign of dissent was an enormous problem. Inspired by the Czechoslovak petition, Charter 77, Paul Goma decided to alert the President to the need to resist the Securitate's régime of fear. 'Mr. Ceauşescu', he wrote, inviting the President to add his name to a letter of protest, 'I realize that your august signature will never accept a place alongside the signature of a simple citizen . . . And even if this miracle occurred, what could be done *with just two signatures*? . . . But where are [the others] going to come from? I already told you: the Romanians are afraid of the Securitate. It emerges that in Romania, only two people are not afraid of the Securitate: you and me. But, as I already said, with only two signatures . . .'[64] Seven people did sign Goma's open letter to the Belgrade follow-up of the Helsinki Conference for Security and Cooperation in Europe. They paid a heavy price. Goma himself was beaten and imprisoned, and only released after a campaign that attracted the support of Eugene Ionescu, Arthur Miller and Jean-Paul Sartre. He was sent into French exile.

The Jiu Valley miners' strike was unrelated to the dissidents' lonely gesture, but it showed how deeply unpopular Ceauşescu's austerity programme had become. In the summer of 1977, miners were told that the pensionable age for their profession was to be raised from fifty to fifty-five. Working conditions were already atrocious, so when the decree filtered through to them 35,000 angry coalface workers occupied the plant.* They wanted the law rescinded and a reduction in working hours. A Politburo member and the Minister for Mines were sent to calm the men down but were taken hostage by them. They would only be released, the miners warned, if Ceauşescu himself came to talk to them. For the only time in his career, Ceauşescu had no choice but to respond to his subjects' wishes. On arrival in the Jiu Valley, one eye-witness recalled how 'Ceauşescu was totally taken aback by the sight of so many protestors. His eyes darted from right to left and he was clearly shaken by the scene . . . In an attempt to distort the reasoning behind the decision to extend [the working day], he claimed that it had in fact been the Party leadership which had resolved to

* The people of Bucharest can testify to just how angry Jiu Valley miners can become, as they stormed the capital almost fifteen years later in an inglorious repetition of their 1977 militancy.

reduce working hours but that this decision had met opposition from the miners. This insult to the miners' intelligence prompted the reply: "It is not us! Bandits, thieves!"'[65] Faced with a crowd of hostile, violent workers, Ceauşescu promised them the earth. Unwisely, the miners believed him. As soon as the President returned to the capital, he ordered a Securitate clear-up operation at the mines. Arrests, prolonged spells in psychiatric wards and a strategic 'suicide' soon brought the situation under control. Two years later, 200 people across the country joined SLOMR, a free trades union modelled loosely on Solidarność in Poland. It was a bold, short-lived attempt to coordinate opposition activities in Romania but it was not long before the 'ringleaders' suffered the same fate as the leaders of the Jiu Valley strike.

Romanians have debated long and hard why opposition to Ceauşescu was so weak. Many reasons account for it. First, the power of the ruling clique had a long lineage in modern Romania. The Phanariot princes of the Danubian Principalities* gave way to the powerful Brătianu dynasty and the Hohenzollern monarchs. Then, the overwhelming majority of the population were peasants or at most first-generation immigrants to the town, and had yet to shake off the submissive peasant attitudes to authority. Desperate though their lives were, they enjoyed a higher standard of living in the new urban environment than they had in their villages. In ideological terms, nationalism lent Ceauşescu's régime a certain legitimacy, tapping into the xenophobia that had always played an important role in Romanian intellectual life. There was depressingly little evidence of resistance among Romanian intellectuals to the open season declared in the late 1970s on the rights of the Hungarian minority in Transylvania.

Even granting all this, the role of the terror and the Securitate should not be underestimated. The Poles, the Hungarians and the Czechoslovaks never faced a police apparatus of such brutal effectiveness. Furthermore, Western Europe and the United States can rightfully be accused of appalling ambivalence towards Ceauşescu. Despite evidence to the contrary, the West was convinced that Ceauşescu would remain neutral in the event of conflict between

---

* See chapter 1.

NATO and the Warsaw Pact. This flirtation with one of the nastiest dictators in Eastern Europe climaxed with a state visit to Britain in 1978 when Ceauşescu was allowed to ride in the royal carriage with Queen Elizabeth II. The Royal Institute for Chemistry held a lunch in honour of Elena, who had constructed the fiction that she was a world-class chemist. In fact, she was barely literate. The Ceauşescus were received around the world as though they were enlightened royalty, the realization of their wildest dreams. (As late as 1987, I was told by the political officer at the US Embassy in Bucharest that the Reagan administration was determined to extend Romania's most-favoured-nation trading status as 'in the event of war, we think we can turn him'.) This cynicism on the part of NATO members had a deeply demoralizing effect on Romania's opposition.

In 1982, the International Monetary Fund demanded further austerity measures in Romania as a condition for rescheduling the debt, which had climbed by then to $13.2 billion. Western economic agencies were less convinced of Ceauşescu's reliability than their political counterparts. Ceauşescu deeply resented having to concede to external pressure, and resolved not only to meet the interest repayments but to pay off the principal by the end of the decade (he succeeded in doing so by March 1989, six months before his demise). This meant an even more concerted assault on living standards. With chronic food shortages plaguing the country, Ceauşescu introduced the 'Rational Eating Programme', which he justified by claiming that Romanians were eating too much. He 'set limits on per capita consumption for the period 1982–85. The programme reduced calorie intake limits by 9–15 percent . . . Following these guidelines, the dietary programme for 1984 . . . set allowances even lower than the "scientific plan".'[66]

In the winter of 1987, gas consumption in Bucharest was set at two hours a day. It was often not distributed at all. I recall visiting apartments where families were wrapped from morning till night in coats and blankets, teeth chattering in dark rooms. In the bleak city centre, the markets offered a few rotten potatoes and carrots while the largest showcase supermarket could supply only Portuguese anchovies and a processed cheese from France called 'La vache qui rit'. As the population scavenged for essentials, an architectural monstrosity, the House of the Republic, was emerging from the ruins of three historic districts in the centre. Some 40,000 people were evicted from their homes to construct this hideous folly, sired by Stalin out of Metropolis. With disarming honesty, Bucharest's chief architect explained to me in 1987 that 'people just get in your way when you are building – it is so much easier without them'.[67] Fourteen old Orthodox churches and a synagogue were among the structures razed to make way for the largest public building in the world after the Pentagon. 'Only the sixteenth-century Mihai Vodă church and bell-tower survived, being moved 225 metres in 1985 to be hemmed in by new tall blocks of flats.'[68]

In March 1988, Ceauşescu announced his plans for 'systematization', his scheme to destroy up to 8,000 villages and herd the inhabitants into purpose-built 'agro-industrial complexes'. Over 300 communities were uprooted – in some instances, villagers were given two days to demolish their own homes or wait for the bulldozers. If they chose the latter course, they received no compensation. 'Systematization' provoked an outcry both in the West and inside Romania itself. By this time, Romania's role in western strategy was diminishing rapidly because of the new influence of Mikhail Gorbachev in East–West relations. Indeed, on a visit to Bucharest in May 1987, Gorbachev had made clear his displeasure at Ceauşescu's now archaic policies of repression. Ceauşescu had lost his ability to read the international situation. Instead of attempting to adapt to the new spirit of cooperation and openness, he resorted to ever more extreme forms of authoritarianism. He failed to understand that he could only sustain his maverick Stalinist nationalism as long as there existed a fundamental hostility between East and West. Gorbachev's decision not to resist the revolutions in Hungary and Poland in the summer of 1989 ensured that Ceauşescu's independence became irrelevant. This was the supreme irony: the policy that had set Romania apart from its allies in the bloc was entirely dependent on the continued existence of the bloc. By the autumn of 1989, it was clear that the entire system was disintegrating throughout Eastern Europe.

Enosis – taksim: Greece and Turkey

> From the price of rice to roads and tourist sites, there is not a single problem in this country which is not related to national security. If

> you happen to be a very deep thinker, that too is a matter of national security.
>
> Orhan Erkanlı, fourteen years after he had taken part in the May 1960 *coup d'état* in Turkey[69]

Since the consolidation of Atatürk's revolution in the 1930s, Turkish politics ceased to be involved in the Balkans and the peninsula's regional concerns. Istanbul and Izmir remained the great commercial centres. But it was the swift growth in the size and importance of Ankara that emphasized the shift in Turkey's political culture as its people strove to fashion a post-Ottoman identity. Kemal had placed the capital in the interior as a snub to Istanbul, but also for strategic reasons. Later, the government ordered the construction of key primary and secondary industrial complexes deep inside Anatolia, away from the coast. This further underlined the Kemalist determination both to reduce Turkey's economic dependency on the great powers, and to stay aloof from armed conflict. The country harboured no active territorial desires against its neighbours; its army had been exhausted by the First World War and the Greek-Turkish war; and conflict would have placed further unwanted strain on an already lopsided economy. In this light, Turkey's neutrality during the Second World War was the crowning achievement of Atatürk's successor, İsmet İnönü.

But wartime neutrality allowed many Turks to scrutinize the single-party or 'mono-party' régime, as the rule of Kemal's Republican People's Party, the RRP (*Cumhuriyetçi Halk Partisi* – CHP), became known. On inspection, they found the RRP wanting in almost every respect. Despite being at peace, Turkey suffered from the same disease that had afflicted it during the Great War – rampant speculation. A small group of businessmen and bureaucrats made tremendous profits while most people toiled hard for scant reward – Turkey had to adjust to an external environment in which trade was hampered and distorted by the global struggle. İnönü's government made no attempt to tackle the chronic imbalance in the economy. Instead, he sustained this kleptocracy by expanding the police force and encouraging the widespread intimidation and repression of citizens, regardless of their ethnic origins. 'Everybody had problems with the police', remembered Yaşar Kemal, Turkey's best-known novelist. 'If one villager could not pay his road tax, or the taxes on his fields, the whole village would be punished. It had become a tradition.'[70]

It was as much the victory of the Allies as internal pressures that persuaded İnönü to announce a relaxation in the RPP's monopoly after the Second World War. The New Order of European fascism had been discredited and 'democracy' was the word favoured by both East and West, even if interpretations differed in Washington and Moscow. Unnerved by the Soviet Union's apparently aggressive attentions towards its territory, Turkey welcomed western aid; it became the main local recipient of such support together with Greece, under the Truman Doctrine of 1947.

Democracy was not included in the six principles of Kemalism – Republicanism, Nationalism, Populism, Statism, Secularism and Revolutionism/Reformism. These commandments had been added to the constitution in 1937 and were represented on the RPP's emblem by six arrows. Of course, such broad categories were sufficiently amorphous for the National Leader, or İsmet Paşa as İnönü was called colloquially, to accommodate democracy if need be. After the war, he followed Kemal's example and allowed the formation of a loyal opposition, the Democrat Party (DP), under the control of the RPP. In fact, the DP, originally designed to defend the country's nascent bourgeoisie and its landowners against state interference, proved much more popular than the régime expected. Within four years, it had gathered a huge following, including the impoverished peasantry and artisan classes. The DP's dramatic success in the vote of May 1950, in which they won 408 seats to the RPP's 39, can be ascribed in part to the winner-takes-all electoral system and in part to the political decrepitude of the RPP – people were simply fed up with it. After twenty-seven years of control during the crucial formative years of modern Turkey, Kemalism, not as an ideology but as an organized political force, was dead.

The first four years of DP rule were a celebration of this political death. Turkey revelled in its liberation from the shackles of the bureaucracy and the military. A dynamic young entrepreneurial class now joined forces with the big landowners to replace them as the two main pillars of the Turkish elite. The new philosophy of economic liberalism, promising to open Turkey to the outside world, was of course welcomed by the Americans. The new government was rewarded in several ways for its unabashed pro-western policies. Substantial aid continued to flow into the country, prompting an unprecedented mechanization and expansion of agriculture. The first half of the 1950s saw living standards rise for most Turks. Mechanization in the countryside encouraged further emigration to the cities. In a matter of years, the *gecekondu* (literally 'built-by-night'), sprawling shanty towns, altered an urban physiognomy that had remained stable for centuries. Along with American friendship came American influence. With the zeal of a convert, Adnan Menderes, Prime Minister for a decade from 1950, dispatched 25,000 Turkish troops to fight in Korea. Most Turks felt the sacrifice was justified. They had only to cast their eyes across the Black Sea to Romania and Bulgaria to observe that American influence was unquestionably preferable to the Soviet embrace. Given its strategic position in the Cold War, Turkey would have found continuing neutrality a difficult option in any case. Within a generation, the DP trumpeted, Turkey would be a 'little America . . . with a millionaire in every district'.[71]

After sending its troops to Korea, Turkey was admitted to NATO in February 1952. This move had an enormous impact on the country, giving a psychological boost to the modernizers. As well as providing security from Russia, it was a recognition of Turkey as an equal partner with the West. From the beginning, Kemalism as an ideology embodied a tension about Turkey's relationship with the Occident. Atatürk had been an unashamed admirer of western civilization and progress, the road that promised to lead Turkey out of agrarian backwardness and primitivism. But he also valued economic autarky and isolation as a way of protecting Turkey from the marauding economic practices of the West. This ambivalence was embedded deep in Turkey's cultural and political life. In the 1950s, however, the decision to join NATO and the early benefits of the DP's economic reform gave a decisive lead to the westernizers.

Some things did not change. For all the free-market ideology of the DP, most Turkish entrepreneurs, like their counterparts in Greece, were reluctant to invest in large projects, preferring instead the small business that would produce reliable if modest profits year in, year out before being handed down to the next generation. Nor did western capitalists show much interest in investing in Turkey. 'As a result, between 40 and 50 per cent of investment had to come from the state, all the liberal rhetoric notwithstanding.'[72]

The second stubborn legacy of RPP rule was political intolerance. Despite its name, the DP would not brook organized opposition. It began by humiliating the RPP and then stripping it of its financial assets. The DP's anti-state rhetoric, so important in winning electoral support, proved a fiction as the Party's most influential member, Prime Minister Adnan Menderes, passed legislation muzzling the press, placing severe restrictions on academic freedom and banning all political activity on the factory floor. These measures were introduced before the DP won its most spectacular election victory in 1954, reaping the rich harvest of the economic boom. With 56 per cent of the vote, the Party was allotted 503 seats in the Assembly to the RPP's paltry 31.

Menderes interpreted the victory as a mandate to govern without restraint. As production fell in both agriculture and industry, he opted to print money to continue funding the rise in living standards. He doggedly refused to tax his main backers, the landowners, 'who together earned more than a fifth of the GDP, [but] paid only 2 per cent of the total tax revenue'.[73] In order to offset the resulting inflation and the ever-widening trade deficit, Menderes visited the international money markets. By 1960 the debt was $1.5 billion, an enormous sum at the time. As Menderes lost control of the economic situation, the intelligentsia, the bureaucracy and, above all, the army began to lose patience. They had been politically sidelined by the DP, and their material circumstances had either stagnated or declined while the wealth of the country was growing so conspicuously.

It was Menderes' neglect of the army that sealed his fate. The very existence of a modern Turkish state was intimately linked to the military. Both Kemal and İnönü had made their reputations as soldiers, and during the war against Greece in 1922–23 the army had fashioned a clear image of modern Turkish identity. The army was the guardian of secularism, yet at the same time it was the one enduring and unquestioned link with Turkey's glorious imperial past. A visit to Istanbul's superb military museum (to judge by appearances, the best-funded in the city) makes clear that the Turkish army sees itself as the inheritor of the great Ottoman war machine. The young men who entered the army as a career in the 1930s and 1940s were sorely disappointed by the Menderes government. Not only did they earn comparatively little, they were treated with contempt. 'Everywhere they were treated like second class human beings', recalled Alparslan Türkeş, a junior officer during the DP's administration. 'In Ankara, people had labelled basement flats "Staff-Officer flats." In places of entertainment officers were nicknamed "lemonaders" because they could not afford to order expensive drinks and compete with the black-marketeers and profiteers.'[74]

Menderes wooed the generals of the High Command, the pashas as they are known, but neglected the lower ranks. After joining NATO, junior officers were able to see at first hand how backward the Turkish army had become. They admired the technical capability and the modern strategic thinking of their NATO allies. These were affairs in which Menderes showed little interest. The rift between the junior officer corps, on the one hand, and the High Command and civilian politicians, on the other, grew ever wider.

'Honourable fellow countrymen!' Alparslan Türkeş's gravelly voice announced over the radio on the morning of 27 May 1960. 'Owing to the crisis into which our democracy has fallen, in view of the recent sad incidents, and in order to avoid fratricide, the Turkish armed forces have taken over the administration of our country. Our armed forces . . . will hold just and free elections as soon as possible under the supervision and arbitration of a non-party administration.'[75] As he was talking, junior officers commanding key garrisons throughout the country were arresting DP leaders, including the respected elderly President, Celâl Bayar. Menderes was in western Anatolia when he heard the news. He tried to flee, but he was captured in Kutahya. The government and 400 leading supporters were transported unceremoniously to the island prison on Yassada in the Sea of Marmara. The *coup* was greeted with joyful demonstrations in Ankara and Istanbul. It received the vocal backing of intellectuals, students and businessmen, not to mention supporters of the RRP. But the countryside was sullen. The peasants revered Menderes as the first politician since the foundation of the Republic to have addressed their economic problems.

The *coup* had been long in gestation. The officers responsible knew that the High Command would disapprove as the plan undermined the strict hierarchy of the Turkish army. And before they could carry it out, they had to ensure that their supporters commanded all the key points in Istanbul and Ankara. In order to make the *coup* acceptable to the High Command, they persuaded a sympathetic general, Cemal Gürsel, to head it, rewarding him with the office of President. The putschists carried out the takeover meticulously, but once they had seized power, they discovered they had no idea what they wanted to do with it. In-fighting broke out among the thirty-eight members of the unwieldy National Unity Council, representing all the factions among the officer corps. By the end of the year, the hardliners who wished to rule the country for an extended spell had been forced out of the Council. The remainder, with the approval of the High Command, moved to re-establish civilian rule and in October 1961 new elections were called.

The 1960 *coup* was significant for two reasons. The first was the gruesome treatment of the DP government and the execution of Menderes on 17 September 1961, and his Finance and Foreign ministers a day earlier. To avoid the dishonour of hanging, the ousted Prime Minister tried to take his own life by swallowing the sleeping pills he had been carefully storing. He survived the attempt, giving the military the vindictive satisfaction of killing him. No Turkish politician could fail to register this warning. Despite his patchy record, Menderes became a martyr to many and his memory would be invoked on many occasions in the future.

Of even greater moment than this individual tragedy was the political arrangement that led to the re-establishment of civilian power. The army commissioned a group of academics to write a new constitution. The draft had some positive elements, including a new voting system that made the domination of a single party extremely difficult to achieve, thus preventing a repeat of the monopolies abused by the RPP and the DP. It also created a number of institutions designed to curb the power of the executive. The most successful of these was the Constitutional Court. But under the influence of the High Command, the academics also found a place for the National Security Council. This body institutionalized military interference in Turkish politics, effectively granting the *coup d'état* the status of a legitimate constitutional instrument, to be used as and when the High Command saw fit:

> The army had become an autonomous institution recognized by Turkey's ruling circles as the guardian and partner of the new order it had just helped to create. The High Command

> had become an integral part of the political and socio-economic life of the country. The new Assembly passed laws increasing pay scales and pensions and as a result the status and image of the officer improved sharply. Luxury homes were specially built for the pashas in the compound close to the presidential palace in the most exclusive part of the capital.[76]

But the army's involvement went even further than this. Using contributions from some 80,000 officers, the military established a fund in 1961 called the Army Mutual Assistance Association (better known by its Turkish acronym OYAK). This developed into an enormous holding company, acquiring interests in domestic and joint-stock enterprises all over Turkey. Run by civilian employees, OYAK became one of the most influential players in Turkish business. By 1972, its assets were estimated at roughly $300 million. Included in OYAK's portfolio were:

> controlling interests in the Turkish Automotive Industry, a company that assembles International Harvester trucks and tractors; MAT, a truck and tractor sales firm; the OYAK Insurance Company; Tukaş, a food canning firm and a $3,000,000 cement plant. OYAK also holds 20 per cent of the $50 million Petkim Petroleum plant . . . 8 per cent of the state owned Turkish Petroleum, and 7 per cent of the $5.6 million tire factory owned mostly by Goodyear.[77]

Its largest single investment was in OYAK-Renault, the joint venture with the French vehicle manufacturer, in which it retains a 42 per cent stake. By becoming one of the most dynamic capitalists in Turkey, the military's corporate interest in maintaining the status quo intensified. The burgeoning success of OYAK and industry in general during the 1960s was naturally accompanied by a rapid growth in Turkey's working class and the development of a labour movement. The military's involvement in the economy provided a further incentive to restrict the Left. During the 1960s and the 1970s, another crisis enabled the Turkish army to remain the ultimate arbiter of domestic politics – the situation on the island of Cyprus.

A few hours before dawn on 1 April 1955, units from a hitherto unknown organization attacked three installations in Nicosia, the Cypriot capital. One group inflicted extensive damage on the Cyprus Broadcasting Station. But elsewhere on the island the novice commandos enjoyed only limited success. In Famagusta, the bombs failed to detonate and one saboteur electrocuted himself when he lassoed a high-tension power cable with a damp rope. 'Dighenis', the self-styled leader of the guerrilla outfit, EOKA (*Ethniki Organosis Kyprion Agoniston* – National Organization of Cypriot Fighters), was disappointed with the indiscipline and incompetence of his foot soldiers. An inauspicious beginning perhaps but the surprise raids marked a turning point in relations between Greece and Turkey. Until then, the United States and Britain were reasonably confident that the two neighbours would act in harmony as the bulwark of NATO's southern flank. Ankara and Athens were indeed engaged in stuttering cooperation as NATO's two youngest recruits. But the fanatical commitment of Dighenis to *enosis*, the union of Cyprus with the Kingdom of Greece, would draw Britain, the United States, Greece, Turkey and the two Cypriot communities into one of the most intractable conflicts of the late twentieth century.

Dighenis's real name was Colonel Giorgios Grivas, a man with an unedifying past. As the Germans retreated from Greece in 1944, he founded the extreme right-wing paramilitary organization χ (khi), notorious for its brutality.* After the defeat of the Greek communists, EAM/ELAS, Grivas turned χ into a political party but failed in his bid to enter the Greek parliament. Even the right-wing cliques who ruled Greece with American backing after the Civil War treated Grivas as a pariah. Embittered, he looked for another outlet for his extremism and found it in his birthplace, Cyprus. Grivas was the Greek equivalent of Alparslan Türkeş, who was also from Cyprus. 'In the figures of these two febrile and narrow-minded men, one can discern the fanatical and violent mentalities which, apparently diametrically opposed to one another, . . . actually colluded in maiming Cyprus and in destabilizing democratic life and institutions in Greece and Turkey.'[78]

On the surface, Grivas's choice of Cyprus was a strange one. Cypriot society was not fertile territory for intolerant nationalist

---

* See chapter 7.

agitation – the Greeks and Turks on the island had a history neither of mixing nor of fighting. But in Makarios III, who had been elected Archbishop of Cyprus at the age of thirty-seven in 1950, the movement for independence from the British had found an able and energetic advocate. Independence implied self-determination which in turn implied *enosis*, as 80 per cent of Cyprus's population was Greek. Most of the remainder were Turks for whom *enosis* was completely unacceptable. Although Britain was conceding independence to its colonies elsewhere, it was determined to keep Cyprus for strategic reasons. Under pressure of these irreconcilable differences, political strains on the island multiplied after the Second World War. Makarios's most powerful weapon was the emotive appeals he made to mainland Greeks. Naturally, these appeals had an impact on the government in Greece – the more troubled the situation in Cyprus, the greater the temptation for politicians in Athens to play the nationalist card.

In 1952, the Greek Rally Party founded by Alexander Papagos, the hero of the Greco-Italian war of 1940–1, had won a comfortable electoral victory, leading to eleven years of stable, right-wing government in Greece. Like most members of the Greek establishment, Papagos was more concerned with establishing stable security arrangements with Turkey and NATO than with advancing the cause of *enosis*. He preferred to seek a solution to the Cyprus question through discreet discussions with the British. At his first bilateral meeting with Anthony Eden, the British Foreign Secretary dismissed the topic. Eden's counterpart, Stephan Stephanopoulos was outraged, 'Papagos came back and said to me in an outraged voice: "He told me *never* – not even *we shall see*!"'[79]

By refusing to enter into a diplomatic dialogue, Britain guaranteed that Cyprus's status would assume greater importance in Greek politics. Makarios understood this too. He wasted no time in lobbying not only Greek politicians, but also sympathetic opposition MPs in Britain, law-makers in Congress and the Greek community in the United States. Britain in turn quietly encouraged the Turkish government, hitherto little engaged in Cyprus affairs, to take a more active interest in the question. London's clumsy attempts to localize the problem succeeded only in internationalizing it.

After EOKA's first bombing campaign, the British government called a Tripartite Conference, with the Prime Minister, Harold

Macmillan, and the Greek and Turkish foreign ministers in attendance. While the conference was under way in London, a bomb exploded next to the house where Atatürk was born in Salonika (many observers believed it was a Turkish provocation). On hearing this news, a Turkish mob went on the rampage in Istanbul and Izmir. Businesses belonging to the 100,000 strong Greek community were plundered; Orthodox churches were set on fire; Greeks, Armenians and Jews were beaten up and killed on the street. The riots coincided with a World Bank meeting and a conference of Byzantine studies. As the historian, Nancy Crawshaw, has pointed out, nothing 'could have done more to harm Turkey's image in the mid-twentieth century than this spectacle of mass destruction and mob rule against an innocent Christian minority'.[80] The combination of EOKA and the riots ensured that Cyprus from then on exerted great influence on the governments of Greece and Turkey, offering a powerful lever to destructive nationalists in both countries. At the Tripartite Conference, Macmillan believed he could see common interests that ran 'like a vein of gold beneath the great overburden of misunderstanding and confusion'.[81] He had, alas, found only fool's gold.

One month after the Istanbul riots, General Papagos died, opening the way for Constantin Karamanlis to establish himself as one of the dominant political figures in postwar Greece. Surrounded by jealous rivals in the Greek Rally, Karamanlis created a new party, the National Radical Union (ERE), in order to strengthen his personal authority on the Right. The fusing of a single powerful individual with the fate of an entire political party had become a striking peculiarity of Greek politics. As liberals attempted to dent the apparently unbreakable monopoly enjoyed by the Right under Papagos and Karamanlis, their most combative representative, Giorgios Papandreou, fielded candidates belonging to the George Papandreou Party. There were profound ideological differences in Greek politics, but these were invariably reduced to the question of the charisma of the party leader.

Of course, the main reason for the electoral successes of the Right in the 1950s was the economy. Greece enjoyed the fruits of the worldwide upturn just as Turkey did. The *drachma* was stabilized for the first time in living memory, and in the thirteen years from

1951 the per capita income rose in Greece from $112 to over $500. The most spectacular success was the rationalization of agriculture and an increase in productivity so steep that in 1957 Greece became self-sufficient in food production. Given the paucity of arable land compared to all other Balkan countries except Albania, this was an impressive feat. The country remained heavily dependent on agriculture for its foreign-currency earnings. In the mid-1960s, tobacco, cotton, and fresh and dried fruits accounted for 51 per cent of all exports. Like the Turks, the Greeks were reluctant to invest in large-scale industries. As a consequence, employment prospects for the hundreds of thousands who swelled the slums of Athens were erratic. As in the past, many Greeks preferred to earn their money abroad although the favoured destination was no longer Australia or America but Germany.

The other significant source of remittances from abroad was Washington. From the start of the Truman Doctrine in 1947 until the *coup d'état* of the colonels in 1967, America donated almost $3.5 billion to a country with a population of just 8 million. Just under half of this was in the form of military aid.

> Unfortunately, American interference was often blatant. In addition, whereas the Soviet government was usually able to cover its activities in Eastern Europe with a veil of secrecy through the strict censorship enforced, American actions received full publicity, not only in the Greek opposition press, but throughout Europe and in the United States . . . Once the American embassy in Athens became involved in the making or breaking of cabinets, it could expect to carry the blame for the failures and weaknesses of the régimes it supported.[82]

The economic boom of the 1950s sustained the right-wing administrations but the scars of the Civil War were still visible and raw. The government retained undemocratic emergency powers from the late 1940s. These included the notorious Certificates of Social Beliefs – a document testifying to political reliability that each citizen had to produce in order to obtain a driving licence or passport, not to mention a job with Greece's largest employer, the civil service.

The end of stability in Greece was brought about by a mixture of anti-American sentiment, the Cyprus situation and Karamanlis's rigging of elections. In October 1961, he called premature elections to cash in on the rising temperature of the Cold War. The East Germans had built the Berlin Wall in August that year and a little later Khrushchev had threatened to 'blast the Acropolis out of existence' when it became known that nuclear weapons were being stored at US bases in Greece. But for Greeks, the most significant foreign-policy issue concerned the 1959 agreement that Karamanlis had negotiated with Adnan Menderes under British pressure over the heads of Archbishop Makarios and Dr Fazil Küçük, the leader of the Turkish Cypriots. Outmanoeuvred, Makarios reluctantly agreed to endorse the deal that seemed to exclude the possibility of *enosis* and also gave the Turkish community a constitutional role disproportionate to its size.

Karamanlis's resolutely pro-western policy was undermined by the Cyprus Agreement, and on the eve of the 1961 elections his popular support appeared to be dwindling. The results, however, gave his party, the ERE, an overall majority and 51 per cent of the vote. Papandreou, who had successfully forged a coherent centrist coalition, refused to accept the result, announcing he would wage 'a relentless struggle' against the government. Increasingly, Karamanlis's authority was brought into question by pro-*enosis* officers in the army and by the meddling of King Constantine. The Prime Minister was spending ever more time shoring up his position, and ever less time governing. He decided to resign and was finally defeated by Papandreou in February 1967. The new Prime Minister's Centre Union promised a new start for Greece's postwar politics, offering the possibility of healing the scars of civil war. Unfortunately, not all Greeks were ready for reconciliation. More regrettable still, most of those were in the army.

On Thursday morning, 21 April 1967, Greeks woke up to learn that a group of colonels had seized power in their country. King Constantine was particularly infuriated by the news as he had been planning a *coup* of his own with more senior officers. The *coup* was remarkably successful and no blood was shed during it. According to Constantine Kollias, the stooge civilian Prime Minister, 'the shameless and wretched horse-trading of the parties, the decay of a great part of the press, the methodical onslaught against all institutions . . . the paralysis of the state machine . . . more decline, confusions and uncertainty . . . and finally the ceaseless inflammatory declarations of conscienceless demagogues',[83] were a few in a long list of reasons that had provoked the military into taking power.

The real reason can be found in the jealousy of a large part of the officer corps that had seen its material and political circumstances decline steadily during the 1960s. The ideological inspiration behind the *coup* came from IDEA, the nationalist conspiracy formed at the end of the Second World War. This organization had been revitalized by Colonel Giorgios Papadopoulos, who saw in the rise of Papandreou (and in particular in the growing influence of his leftist son, Andreas) a threat to the dominance of nationalist and anti-communist ideas in the army.

The colonels' régime, which lasted seven years, was a shabby, vicious administration that subjected its opponents to persecution and torture. After the internment of several thousand suspect civilians, the new rulers purged their own ranks, dismissing several hundred officers and replacing them with less competent but politically reliable men from the lower orders. Their rhetoric of 'social justice' and a renewal of Greek society revealed itself as a hollow sham, as 'officers not forcibly retired benefited from higher salaries, loans for cars and houses, improved promotion prospects, and discounts in shops. They therefore had little incentive to return power to the civilians.'[84]

Greece became a pariah in Europe and the focus of a sustained human-rights campaign demanding the restoration of civilian rule. In Washington, Congress voted to halt military aid to the colonels, but the régime received persistent covert and overt support from Presidents Johnson and then Nixon, whose concern for the 'big picture' of security in the eastern Mediterranean and the Middle East overrode any concern about the democratic credentials of its ally.

The degeneracy of the colonels' régime was reflected in its demise. Its second strongman, Brigadier Dimitrios Ioannides, who had ousted Papadopoulos in a *coup* within the *coup*, used Grivas and EOKA to overthrow Archbishop Makarios and proclaim *enosis* in 1974. The immediate Turkish invasion of Cyprus, the prelude to partition, revealed the colonels' utter military and political bankruptcy.

They had subjected Greece to seven years of grim dictatorship, and had ensured an end to several centuries of co-existence between the Greeks and Turks of Cyprus.

The débâcle of the colonels' régime did bequeath one valuable gift to Greece: the military had so discredited itself that its capacity to interfere in Greek politics was henceforth negligible. The same was not true in Turkey where the invasion of Cyprus opened the door to *taksim*, partition, a phrase which by 1974 had become as much an article of faith in Turkish politics as *enosis* had been for the Greeks. By the 1950s, Greece and Turkey had succeeded in overcoming the legacy of enmity from the war of the early 1920s, but the confrontation of the Greek colonels and the Turkish generals in Cyprus in the 1970s plunged the eastern Mediterranean into a crisis from which it had not recovered thirty years later.

The hot house: Yugoslavia, 1981–9

After a long spell in hospital, Tito finally died in the Slovene capital, Ljubljana on 4 May 1980, at the age of eighty-seven. Yugoslavs of all nationalities went into demonstrative mourning, barely able to conceive how the country could govern itself without their stern grandfather at the helm. His funeral attracted government leaders from 122 states, the only absentee being the new American President, Ronald Reagan. The assembled dignitaries used the occasion for intense negotiations. Since the Soviet invasion of Afghanistan the previous December, the world had been in the grip of a Second Cold War. After the purges in Serbia and Croatia in the early 1970s, Tito and Kardelj had reimposed conservative policies at home and abroad. The Soviet intervention, however, led to an improvement in Yugoslavia's relations with the West. 'If Soviet troops could move across their border without international consultation or sanction,' an American historian has noted, 'what would protect Yugoslavia if relations [with the Soviets] soured again some day?'[85]

Warmer relations with western Europe and the United States were also important given Yugoslavia's parlous economic situation. In 1972, Tito and Kardelj had brought the economic reforms begun in 1966 to a halt. The small private industries encouraged during the reform were cut back in favour of the large, loss-making industrial enterprises characteristic of planned economies. But the earlier rationalization programme had increased unemployment levels throughout the country. This was now compounded by the return of hundreds of thousands of guest workers, victims of the recession of the early 1970s in western Europe. In the less developed parts of Yugoslavia – Kosovo, Macedonia, Bosnia and southern Serbia – the number of those without jobs made up 20 per cent of the workforce. To combat this problem and in order to meet the material expectations provoked by the reform, Yugoslavia followed the same path as Poland, Hungary and Romania – it borrowed heavily on the international money markets. By 1982, Yugoslavia's debt stood at $18.5 billion. Each year, the government had to find new loans merely to finance the interest repayments.

A third talking point at Tito's funeral was Yugoslavia's own political stability. Articles in the western press predicted the imminent demise of Yugoslavia and even a civil war between its constituent nations. Such alarmist views overlooked Yugoslavia's geo-strategic position in the early 1980s; they also assumed that Tito was the sole support of Yugoslavia's multi-ethnic unity. Neither NATO nor the Soviet Union were interested in the destabilization of Yugoslavia, and the most powerful domestic institution holding the country together was the Federal Army which, although dominated by Serbs in the officer corps, had not yet been infected by Serbian nationalism. In the absence of overt nationalist agitation, the majority of Slovenes, Serbs and Croats had no reason to bring down the federation.

They did, however, face enormous problems in interpreting Tito's confused political legacy. While he and Kardelj (who died in 1979) were still alive, the mechanisms of the 1974 Constitution were little more than window dressing. Policy was made by the two elderly leaders. Nobody felt they needed to establish in detail how the new system was supposed to work. It was based on a system of political musical chairs – senior positions would be rotated every year to prevent any single republic or politician from accumulating too much power. It succeeded in doing so for little more than five years and even then it was at the expense of proper continuity in government. The constitution in principle devolved powers to the federal units but the exact relationship between the centre of the republics was opaque – leading eventually to terrible confusion and corruption. Initially this problem was not so significant as the leadership of the eight communist parties (from the six republics and Serbia's two autonomous provinces, Kosovo and Vojvodina) were dominated by conservatives, united in the fight against liberalism. They also lacked the imagination required to deal with a number of crises which rocked the country in the early 1980s.

The first shock to the system came in March 1981 when Albanian students in Priština rioted over poor food at their university canteen. This disturbance spread through many parts of Kosovo and assumed an openly political character. The explosion in Kosovo was not caused by Serbian repression: under the 1974 Constitution Kosovo had gained an unprecedented measure of self-government. For the first time since the war, the Yugoslav authorities granted Kosovo's Albanians the right to travel to Albania proper. Newspapers, academic texts and schoolbooks printed in Tirana also became available in Kosovo. What the Kosovars wanted was equality with the other nationalities in Yugoslavia, and their movement was, in effect, a late-flowering national revival. They did not demand self-determination for the province, but they did call for the Socialist Autonomous Province of Kosovo to become a republic. The disturbances were put down by the army and the police, but this was a problem which could not be swept under the carpet using strongarm tactics alone.

The federal authorities were now faced with a very delicate situation. The call for a Kosovo republic set alarm bells ringing, particularly in Serbia and in Macedonia, where there was also a large Albanian minority. Granting Kosovo republican status would mean detaching it from Serbia and conceding that it had the right to secede from the federation. The special position that Kosovo held in Serbian mythology meant that any move towards a republican status for Kosovo might trigger a backlash of Serbian nationalism. The federal authorities decided to block contacts between the Kosovo Albanians and Albania proper, but they also ruled out the reimposition of central control from Belgrade, which some Serb communists were demanding. Instead, the Kosovo party (led after 1986 by a young Albanian communist, Azem Vllasi) agreed to stifle any manifestation of Albanian nationalism in the province.

The atmosphere in Kosovo in the early eighties was heavy with tension; secret policemen were ubiquitous. Nonetheless, the local state apparatus, including the police force, was staffed mainly by

Albanians, and they had no interest in provoking the Kosovars. Life was not easy, but it was free from nationalist violence. A minority of communists in Serbia, aided at times by the Belgrade media, claimed that the Serb and Montenegrin minority in Kosovo (roughly 10 per cent of the population) were subjected to systematic terrorism at the hands of Albanian 'irredentists'. They based these claims on the numbers of Serbs moving from the province to Serbia proper. There was indeed an exodus of Serbs in the early eighties, but they were economic migrants, not refugees. The stories of rape, murder and intimidation were without foundation.

The political problem of Kosovo coincided with deepening economic problems in the country as a whole. Slovenia and Croatia renewed their criticism of a system which saw a disproportionate amount of their foreign earnings directed into a Solidarity Fund for the development of the poorer, southern regions. The debt crisis was exacerbated by Yugoslavia's impenetrable banking system. Foreign loans were contracted not only by the Yugoslav National Bank but by the republican banks as well so that Yugoslavia's indebtedness was invariably higher than official figures admitted. In formulating macroeconomic policy, the federal government had to negotiate both with the western banks and with the banks of the six republics. The devolved banking system also encouraged corruption within the republics, on a huge scale. Any attempt by the federal authorities to interfere with republican financial arrangements was fiercely resisted. Popular mistrust of the federal and republican authorities began to grow by 1986; unemployment and strikes had become endemic. For different political and economic reasons, then, Yugoslavia's government was under siege in the mid-1980s from its constituent parts. Supported by the West, the military and, with growing reluctance, by public opinion, it continued its precarious existence, based on Tito's formula of 'brotherhood and unity'.

On 24 September 1986, a Belgrade newspaper published a document written by an anonymous team from the Serbian Academy of Sciences (SANU). The Memorandum, as it became known, was an inflammatory manifesto of Serbian nationalism. Its central claim was that the Serbs of Kosovo faced extermination at the hands of aggressive Albanians. But it also insisted that 'except during the period of the Independent State of Croatia, Serbs in Croatia have never been as endangered as they are today. The resolution of their national status must be a top priority.'[86] The communist authorities condemned the Memorandum in uncompromising terms. Ivan Stambolić, the head of the Serbian Party, called it 'Yugoslavia's obituary', warning the academicians that they were not just provoking other nationalities in Yugoslavia, but acting against the interests of Serbs, 'for Yugoslavia is the only solution to the Serbian question. Without Yugoslavia, the Serb nation is condemned to dismemberment.'[87]

Stambolić himself had requested SANU a year earlier to contribute to the process of reform. He had been expecting a series of ideas on political and economic reform. According to his memoirs, the secret police claimed to know nothing about the document, not even the identity of the main authors. It took the leadership by complete surprise. Only one leading Serbian communist, hitherto a resolute critic of nationalism, declined to condemn the document in public, restricting his criticism to a brief denunciation at a meeting of the secret police leadership. This was Stambolić's protégé and closest ally, Slobodan Milošević, who had been elected President of the Serbian League of Communists (on Stambolić's urging) in May 1986.

Parlour games: Yugoslavia

I spent much of 1989 as the BBC's Central Europe Correspondent, reporting events from Gdansk to Tirana. I was moved to tears when standing ten yards behind Václav Havel and Alexander Dubček as they walked onto a balcony overlooking Wenceslas Square to accept the adulation of almost a million Czechs and Slovaks. On Christmas Day, I watched Romanian television as it repeatedly broadcast the image of Nicolae Ceauşescu and his wife Elena lying prostrate on the ground after their summary execution. I have always opposed the death penalty, but on this occasion felt no compulsion to regret the severity of the sentence.

But my most vivid memory is of a warm early spring evening in Vučitrn, a small town north of Priština, the capital of Kosovo. The neat, oblong town square was bathed in dark yellow sunlight. In front of the town hall, a Serbian communist was emphatically denouncing Albanian 'separatists and terrorists', while praising the resolve of Slobodan Milošević. Before the speaker stood a few hundred Serbs. The majority were young men, most of them bussed in from Niš and Kragujevac in Serbia proper. Over and again, they chanted the phrase '*Srbija je ustala*' (Serbia has arisen). Watching the proceedings in bemused silence were thousands of Albanians (at the time 95 per cent of Vučitrn's population). They were hanging off walls, leaning out of windows, playing backgammon in the cafés and sipping viscous coffee from small cups. Cocooned in a self-referential world, the Serb demonstrators were oblivious to the quiet mass of Albanian spectators. Names and acronyms stirred in my mind – VMRO, Ustaše, Chetniks, the Iron Guard. Briefly I was transported back to the 1930s. Although it was a chaotic nationalist display, the demonstrators had a bullish, confident look that came with the full approval of a powerful state.

Almost two years later I found myself in a Zagreb housing estate on a miserable April afternoon, surrounded by what seemed to be the same people wearing the same denim jackets. As Franjo Tudjman, the newly elected President of Croatia, mounted a makeshift podium, I saw the same look on the faces in the crowd that I had seen in Vučitrn. Only one thing was different, the chant: '*Hrvatska je ustala*' (Croatia has arisen).

By this time, the spring of 1991, war between Serbs and Croats was all but inevitable. Two years earlier, the Serbian President, Slobodan Milošević, had stripped Kosovo of the autonomy that Tito had conferred on the province in 1974. Milošević's sudden conversion to the plight of the Serbian and Montenegrin minority of Kosovo in 1987 was cynical. When the Memorandum of the Serbian Academy of Sciences was published in 1986, Milošević formally distanced himself from its intemperate nationalism. Within less than a year, he had adopted its rhetoric as a coercive instrument within the Serbian Communist Party and had destroyed the political career of his mentor and longstanding friend, Ivan Stambolić.

Milošević's real aim was not to end Kosovo's autonomy. Before he unleashed his self-proclaimed 'anti-bureaucratic' revolutions in Kosovo, Vojvodina and in the Republic of Montenegro, Serbian representatives were a minority in Yugoslavia's collective leadership. The Federal Presidency had eight members, one from each republic, and one from the two autonomous provinces. Until the 'anti-bureaucratic' revolution, Serbia could be outvoted on any issue. 'By abolishing the autonomy of both provinces of Vojvodina and Kosovo,' Milan Kučan, the Slovene president, remarked, 'Serbia would control three out of eight votes in the Federal Presidency – in comparison with the other republics that had one vote each. That meant turning Yugoslavia into Serbo-slavia.'[88] Once Serbia also controlled Montenegro's vote, giving it four out of eight, Slovenia, Croatia, Bosnia and Macedonia had to maintain an informal alliance to prevent Milošević from bulldozing through any constitutional change he desired. Maintaining such an alliance was no easy matter.

For two years from 1987, Milošević had conducted a carefully orchestrated campaign of nationalist hysteria, focused on Kosovo but widening gradually to conjure up for Serb audiences an unholy alliance of Albanians, Slovenes and Croats. But once the Serbian president had won the extra votes in the presidency, he lost interest in Kosovo. This was the first example of Milošević's boundless opportunism. Kosovo ceased to be a problem, unless you were a Kosovo Albanian. With four members of the presidency in his pocket, Milošević felt able to attend to more important affairs than Kosovo. Overnight the conflict had mutated into something quite different – a struggle between the three most powerful republics, Slovenia, Croatia and Serbia over the nature of the Yugoslav state. The battle for Kosovo prefaced a revival of the problem that had beset the first Yugoslavia in the 1920s and the 1930s* which had led in 1966 to Aleksandar Ranković's downfall in the Second Yugoslavia; and which Tito had mistakenly attempted to solve by repression in 1971 and 1972. In essence, this was the question of Yugoslavia's identity – was it a unitarist state or a genuine federation?

But it was a variation of the old problem, not a mere repetition. Yugoslavia had not been in a historical deep-freeze under communism – on the contrary, it developed more rapidly than many European countries. There were decisive new elements present in the early 1990s: the political maturity and confidence of the Slovenes, in particular, but also of the Bosnian Muslims, the Kosovo Albanians and the Macedonians. In addition, Yugoslavia's exposure to western Europe had accentuated the cultural divisions between rural and urban life as nowhere else in the communist Balkans. This had unexpected consequences for another element in the equation, the Yugoslav People's Army (JNA). According to Ivan Stambolić,

---

* See chapter 6.

who was once the political superior of these men, the senior leadership and the officer corps were dominated by men from 'impoverished peasant families', who moved 'from city to city throughout their career, spending most of their time in barracks. They lived in cities but were never part of them, feeling isolated, rejected. They grew to hate cities and the people who lived in them.'[89]

The leaderships of the big three republics were united in their hostility to the federal government, albeit for different reasons. Faced with this hostility and the sudden dramatization of the national question, it is no surprise that the federal prime minister, Ante Marković, a commendably reformist Croat from Bosnia, stood little chance of rallying the dispersed forces of democratically minded citizens.

The conflict between the republics manifested itself in countless ways – a trade war between Serbia and Slovenia; an avalanche of nationalist and racist propaganda; battles over the control of tax revenues. Together these and other disputes suffocated rational political debate, opening the way for the propaganda of extremist organizations. They swamped the public arena with instrumentalized historical memories. In Serbia, most of these symbols, myths and martyrdoms recalled the Second World War, quite the most violent period of Yugoslav history. The identification of 'Croat' and 'Ustaše' was too often taken for granted in them. The Croats sought recognition for the victims of the Bleiburg massacre* but also began a process of rehabilitating the Ustaše state. The parties and movements that indulged in reviving the darker moments of Yugoslavia's recent past sought to instil fear less in 'enemy' ranks than in their own community. If ordinary Serbs believed that the Ustaše were about to return, or if Croats in the mixed areas of Croatia could be convinced that their neighbours were preparing for a Chetnik onslaught, then it would be much easier to mobilize them for war, according to the principle 'Kill before you are killed'.

Television played a seminal role in preparing people not just for war but for the spiral of massacre that was to come. Day after day, RTV Belgrade and Croatian Television (HTV) emitted images of atrocity, while historical documentaries and movies about the

* See chapter 7.

Second World War romanticized each nation's soldiery. Propaganda has always played an essential role in mobilizing for war, of course, and television can influence people quickly and effectively. But in Yugoslavia in 1991 it reached such a pitch that one friend from Belgrade described RTV Serbia and HTV as 'the two greatest war criminals of them all'.

On a political level, the constitutional battle was regulated through a series of meetings between the six republican presidents. Complex shifting alliances, communicated to the public in a bizarre hybrid language, obscured the intentions of Milošević and Tudjman, whose antagonism in turn obscured a more sinister mutual respect. Stipe Šuvar, the Croatian communist leader, recalled a lunch held after one round of discussions immediately before the outbreak of war:

> Around the lunch table sat Milošević, Ante Marković, and Tudjman. And they were all fooling around. Milošević said to Marković, 'Don't worry if Tudjman puts the screws on you in Croatia, we'll make sure you get elected as an MP there.' He was supposedly joking. I said to him, 'Slobo, are you sure that you still have that sort of influence in Croatia.' At this point Marković shouted at Tudjman, 'Franjo, how long are you lot going to keep this Šuvar in the Presidency?' Everyone joined in just making fun of everything and laughing and laughing. Who amongst us realized that the most bloody war was just about to start? I do not know for certain that Milošević and Tudjman were such monsters that they were planning for war but just keeping it to themselves. But maybe there exists a rule among these people that they can joke and laugh together before happily killing each other.'[90]

Inside Serbia and Croatia, the two presidents were playing the same game – consolidating control over the machinery of state through purges and intimidation. This posed few problems for Milošević, as he had inherited the communist bureaucracy. Most functionaries remained loyal after he transformed the party into the Socialist Party of Serbia. He did this by merging the communist Party with the Socialist Alliance of Working People of Serbia, the Communist front that included satellite organisations like the trade unions, the women's and youth movements. The fusion gave him copious financial resources and put the new Serbian opposition parties at an enormous disadvantage, with no money and no access to the media.

Tudjman faced a different situation. A disproportionately high number of Serbs were in positions of authority in Croatia. This was a consequence of the purge carried out by Tito after the suppression of the Croatian Spring in December 1971. Serbs replaced Croats as a way of insuring against a recrudescence of autonomist sentiment inside the Croatian Communist Party. So when Tudjman began sacking communists in the media, in the legal system, in factory management, and in the civil service, these included many hitherto influential Serbs. The transition from a one-party dictatorship to a democratically elected government in Croatia led to an immediate rise in tension between Croats and one of the most volatile Yugoslav minorities, the Serbs of the Krajina. This was greatly assisted by the overt racism of Tudjman's party, the Croatian Democratic Union (HDZ), and Milošević's policy of encouraging armed rebellion among Croatia's Serbs, especially in that old Chetnik heartland, Knin, the majority of the Krajina.

March 1991 was the point of no return. On Saturday the 9th, the Serbs finally found their voice when demonstrators took to the streets in protest against Milošević's manipulation of state television. Running battles broke out in the centre of town – one civilian and one policeman were killed. The next day hundreds of thousands converged on the centre of Belgrade to participate in a demonstration against the Serbian president that lasted a week and went on twenty-four hours a day. For the military, this was the last straw. Two months earlier, they had threatened a military *coup* in Croatia unless Tudjman disarmed his police force. The Croat government agreed but had not implemented the order, nor had the Slovenes obeyed a similar demand. As far as the JNA leadership was concerned, Tudjman was an Ustaša, bent on destroying Yugoslavia and exterminating the Croatian Serbs. In the Serb demonstrators of March, the crusty Stalinists of the JNA believed they saw the other side of the coin – Chetniks, right-wing nationalists hostile to the Partisan tradition of the Yugoslav People's Army. With Milošević's support, they decided to mount a *coup*. This would have liquidated the opposition in Serbia as well as the secessionists in Slovenia and

Croatia in one fell swoop. But the Federal Presidency was still functioning and it refused to sanction the *coup*. The army decided to seize power without the Presidency's approval, but at the last moment stepped back from the brink. Milošević's plans had been thwarted. In a conversation with the Serbian leader on 17 March, the joint chiefs-of-staff justified their change of mind. If they had mounted a *coup*, the generals solemnly explained, Croatia, Slovenia, Bosnia and Macedonia

> would have refused to carry out the orders of the General Staff . . . inciting citizens to resist and undermining the JNA by labelling it an occupying force. The four republics would finally secede, offering armed resistance and appealing for foreign military assistance . . .
>
> In Kosovo there would be an uprising of Albanians and a declaration of unification with Albania.
>
> In Bosnia-Hercegovina, the Croats would join the armed resistance movement of Croatia and probably the Muslims would too.
>
> The outbreak of extensive intercommunal fighting could not be excluded.
>
> In Serbia, the opposition would attempt to exploit the situation by bringing down the legitimate authorities . . .
>
> Abroad – one may expect condemnation from foreign powers, resolutions – condemnation at the UN and in European institutions . . . the imposition of sanctions.
>
> In the event of a civil war, an arms embargo is likely.
>
> The country would be bankrupted with a severe danger of hyperinflation . . . the democratic rights of citizens would be suspended.
>
> The international community would denounce us as a dictatorial régime.[91]

The only disaster the generals failed to predict was the NATO bombing campaign of 1999.

The presidency's refusal to sanction a military takeover marked the moment when Milošević ditched Yugoslavia as a vehicle for his ambition – he could not reliably control it. He appeared on television to announce that 'Yugoslavia has entered into the final phase of its agony . . . The Republic of Serbia will no longer recognize a single decision of the Presidency under the existing circumstances because it would be illegal.'[92] This meant war, but there were still some loose ends that the Serbian president needed to tie up before it could begin. Milošević and Tudjman had both decided to draw the boundaries of the new Serbia and the new Croatia by force. Before hostilities commenced, the two men met in secret to see whether there were areas of agreement between them. On 24 March, they convened at Karadjordjevo, Tito's hunting lodge in Vojvodina.* Bosnia-Hercegovina, they concurred, could be split along the lines envisaged in the Cvetković–Maček *sporazum* of 1939 – half going to Croatia, half to Serbia.

To the outside world, the two men seemed poles apart. They had succeeded in dividing the sympathy of other European countries along lines that were reminiscent of the alliances of the early twentieth century – Austria and later Germany were sympathetic to the secessionist goals of Slovenia and Croatia while Britain, France and Russia were firm supporters of the Yugoslav state and were more sympathetic to the Serbs.

Clearly, the Serbs and the Croats were in competition during the Croatian war that broke out in May 1991 and lasted until January 1992. But it is impossible to find examples of either President publicly criticizing the other. As events in Bosnia-Hercegovina were to confirm, Milošević and Tudjman were acting in harmony at the expense of both Yugoslavia and Bosnia.

---

* The location was replete with irony. Almost two decades earlier, Tito had called the top leadership there to denounce the liberal Croatian Party leaders and launch the crushing of the Croatian Spring, the move that ended hopes for a democratic solution to the national question.

CHAPTER 9

THE BALKAN VORTEX

Nationalism, war and NATO, 1989–99

The international community

In a report for the BBC filed in February 1991, I wrote, in somewhat lurid terms, that the leaders of Yugoslavia 'were stirring a cauldron of blood that would soon boil over'. My superiors reprimanded me for the piece on the grounds that it was 'alarmist'. This was the end of the 20th century, not the beginning, they told me, and there would be no war in the Balkans. When it came, news editors unfamiliar with the Balkans were surprised by the return of the Bosnian Question and of violence between Serbs and Croats; politicians were completely unprepared. This myopia, which affected many among the élites of western Europe and the United States, had two causes.

Europe celebrated the fall of communism in 1989 as the beginning of a new era. After half a century of division and Cold War, people from East and West could look forward to building 'the common European home', as Mikhail Gorbachev put it. Overnight, democratic rights and freedoms replaced censorship and dictatorship. But throughout Eastern Europe, the outgoing communist bureaucracies devised ways of adapting to the new conditions, preserving their privileges against the challenge of political or economic competition. In Poland and Hungary, communists emerged among the most dynamic capitalists. In Romania and Bulgaria, the renamed communist parties hung on to political power for several years by playing on people's fear of sudden economic change. In Yugoslavia, aggressive nationalism was the trump card. Milošević reinvented himself as a Serbian chauvinist, the sad addict of power finding a new drug. Where the communists failed to appropriate nationalism, as in Croatia, others stepped in.

The second reason the policy-makers were caught off balance was because they were distracted by another intractable regional problem. From August 1990 the world was gripped by war in the Gulf after Iraqi forces invaded Kuwait. In the same month, Croatian police and Serb rebels in Knin (encouraged and armed by Milošević's associates from Belgrade) exchanged fire for the first time, in a brief skirmish. The revival of an obscure Balkan squabble seemed trivial set against the rising tension in the Middle East. As the Bush administration deployed a huge military force in Saudi Arabia with a mandate from the UN Security Council, there was an alarming growth of paramilitary activity in Croatia. Ominously, the Serbian minority in Knin, after fruitless negotiations with President Tudjman, who ignored their fears of oppression in a triumphalist Croatian state, proclaimed the creation of SAO Krajina (the Serbian Autonomous Province of Krajina). Western diplomats and journalists in Belgrade sent increasingly urgent dispatches back home. Too often they went unnoticed.

The crisis in Yugoslavia in 1991–1992 was centred on the problem of Serb, Croat and Slovene relations. But the shattering implications for the rest of the country were barely appreciated. The international community repeatedly 'declared itself happy with what were only partial solutions, ignoring that the problems of all six republics were inextricably bound up with one another'.[1] If the Serbs and Croats went to war, the only Yugoslav region likely to remain unscathed was Slovenia, because of its distinct culture and history, its ethnically homogeneous population and its Alpine location, nestled between Austria and Italy. Everywhere else would be threatened.

Yugoslavia lasted as long as it did because its very existence offered an apparently workable solution to the two most complex problems in the Balkans – those of Bosnia-Hercegovina and Macedonia. Assessing the Congress of Berlin, convened to 'solve' the Great Eastern Crisis,* the British historian A.J.P. Taylor noted that 'Macedonia and Bosnia, the two great achievements of the congress, both contained the seeds of future disaster. The Macedonian question haunted European diplomacy for a generation and then caused the Balkan war of 1912. Bosnia first provoked the crisis of 1908 and then exploded the World war in 1914, a war which brought down the Habsburg monarchy.'[2]

It is no coincidence that after the Great War, both Bosnia and the most contested part of Macedonia found themselves in the one state that bucked the Wilsonian trend of self-determination after Versailles. Yugoslavia formed a protective layer around the two provinces, preventing either Serbia or Croatia from making exclusive claims on Bosnia as regional imperialists. It also diminished Slav-Albanian rivalry in Kosovo and Macedonia. When Serbo-Croat harmony collapsed in 1941, Yugoslavia's most violently contested regions were Bosnia-Hercegovina and Macedonia. In 1991, fifty years after the beginning of the Second World War, if the Serbs and Croats were to discard the united state in favour of strict Wilsonian principles of self-determination, then Bosnia and Macedonia would have the most to fear. Their respective presidents, Alija Izetbegović and Kiro Gligorov, clearly understood this danger. They realized that if Croatia were to become a nation state (one identified explicitly with the Croat people to the exclusion of others), then the Serbs of Croatia would refuse to participate, the Serbs of Bosnia would try to secede from Bosnia and the Albanians of Yugoslavia would demand to leave Serbia and Macedonia. Often those people who most fervently supported the secession of Croatia from Yugoslavia were also the loudest in supporting an independent Bosnia. Here, however, stability depended on all three nationalities, Serb, Croat and Muslim, actively supporting Bosnia's secession from Yugoslavia, a consensus that patently did not exist at the time of independence.

In contrast to most Balkan crises this century, the great powers (under their bland new title, the international community) did not cause the wars in Croatia, Bosnia and Kosovo. Once they did intervene from 1991 onwards, however, they frequently made matters worse. Germany and Russia allowed themselves to be drawn into the

---

* See chapter 3.

conflict first in 1990 and 1991. With their undoubted feel for Balkan history, both Tudjman and Milošević appreciated the need for a powerful international backer. Tudjman spent much time travelling abroad before and after his election as president. His aim was twofold – to mobilize Croatia's diaspora, chiefly for financial reasons, and to secure the sympathy of European powers, most importantly Germany. Milošević chose Russia, but for ideological rather than historical reasons. The Serbian leader had experimented with most ideologies but the one he understood best was neo-Stalinism. As the Croat lobby tried to convince Bonn to back Zagreb's claim for self-determination, the Serbs and the JNA approached the Soviet Defence Minister, Dimitri Yazov, for military guarantees.

The results were unexpected. In August 1991, conservatives in Moscow, including Yazov, launched an unsuccessful coup against President Mikhail Gorbachev. Boris Yeltsin rose from the ashes of a political career to become president. Milošević had publicly welcomed the coup, earning him Yeltsin's lasting antipathy and leaving him with very little support abroad.

Tudjman's strategy drove a wedge through the European Union just when it was trying to adjust to the unification of Germany. War in Yugoslavia broke out in early June 1991 as soon as the parliaments of Slovenia and Croatia voted for independence. As fighting intensified in the summer and autumn, Croatia convinced the German government that its cause was just by presenting itself 'as an integral part of a civilized Catholic, central European culture while denigrating its Serbian neighbour as a representative of the barbaric, despotic Orient. Moreover, the drive for independence was presented as an act of liberation from decades of Serbian oppression. This killed two birds with one stone – both Catholic conservative circles in Germany, and the Social Democrats and the Greens.'[3] By the autumn of 1991, Hans-Dietrich Genscher had made the recognition of Slovenia and Croatia his personal crusade.

The position of the French and British governments was almost diametrically opposed to that of Germany. Recognition, they argued, would stir a hornet's nest. It was preferable instead to pursue a negotiated way out of the crisis through the offices of the International Conference on Yugoslavia under the chairmanship of the former Foreign Secretary and NATO Secretary General, Lord Carrington. The United States reserved judgement, agreeing with the EU that this was a European affair and reluctant to encourage the break-up of a complicated federation. In the meanwhile, the United Nations became involved when the Secretary General, Perez de Cuellar, charged the former US Secretary of State, Cyrus Vance, with brokering a temporary settlement to allow the deployment of a UN peace-keeping force, UNPROFOR. In the event, the Germans won the battle in the EU but the peace-keeping force was also deployed in four regions of Croatia. The remaining republics were offered the possibility of independence, subject to a referendum. Until this point both Izetbegović and Gligorov had argued against a policy of recognition. It was sheer folly to introduce plebiscitary democracy in Bosnia-Hercegovina at a time of heightened tension between Serbia and Croatia, whose leaderships made little secret of their territorial ambitions in Bosnia.

By the beginning of 1992, it was obvious that the Yugoslav federation was dead. The question was not whether Croatia and Slovenia should be granted recognition; it was a matter of how and when. Immediate unconditional recognition increased the strain on Bosnia-Hercegovina enormously, and also sealed the fate of the Krajina Serbs in the long term. Beyond that it failed to take into account the implications for Kosovo and Macedonia.

Six months after the outbreak of the war, the Yugoslav crisis had assumed serious international dimensions. The United States, Germany, Britain and France, Greece, Turkey, Russia, Iran and a number of Middle Eastern countries all pursued widely different policies with regard to Croatia and Bosnia-Hercegovina. The difficulty in reconciling these became insuperable when violence broke out in Bosnia, three months after the peacekeepers arrived in Croatia in January 1992. With encouragement from the Americans, Izetbegović opted for independence on 5 April, an injudicious move for a government with limited military resources and two potential enemies. The Bosnian Serbs rejected the declaration and the fighting began. 'The Serbs, who until this point still enjoyed some sympathy among part of the international community, launched an offensive that would leave them isolated except for the tentative support of Russia and Romania and the unequivocal backing of Belgrade's Balkan ally, Greece.'[4] The atrocities perpetrated by Serbs against Muslim civilians had an immense impact on Western public opinion and policy. For the first time in Balkan history, the question of external intervention in the region revolved less around perceived strategic or economic issues than around humanitarianism. But although the terms of reference had shifted, the practical problems involved remained the same.

The first co-ordinated international response against Serbia took the form of UN sanctions. Russia had opposed the policy of recognition of Croatia, Bosnia and the other republics. It did not, however, veto the sanctions in July 1992. Despite misgivings, Russia backed most western policy initiatives in Yugoslavia until 1994 when the United Nations threatened to use air power against Serb positions around Sarajevo. Until that time, Serbia found that its 'traditional ally' (a persistent, if erroneous description in the western media) was either unable or unwilling to deliver practical support.

Objections to the sanctions regime came from other Balkan countries and from Hungary. Sanctions in any case only highlighted the difficulty of isolating Serbia, because of its central position on the peninsula. Romania, Bulgaria, Macedonia and Albania were all highly dependent on Serbia, both as a commercial partner and as their chief overland trading route to northern Europe. All these countries had emerged from half a century of communism with severe economic problems. Bulgaria had inherited a $10 billion dollar debt from the communist government. During the Gulf War, Sofia was compelled to write off $4 billion owed to it by Iraq as a consequence of sanctions. Bulgaria has estimated that since the sanctions on Yugoslavia were imposed in 1992, it has been losing revenue of about $2 billion per annum, money it can ill afford to do without. Greece exacerbated the regional tangle by imposing a blockade on Macedonia, accusing it of appropriating Hellenic cultural property by the very use of the state's name.

So although sanctions gave the international community a certain leverage in its diplomatic dealings with Belgrade, they also encouraged economic decline throughout the whole region, setting the peninsula further adrift from the rest of Europe.

Relations among the Western allies reached a nadir during the tortuous efforts of Cyrus Vance and the former British Foreign Secretary, Lord David Owen, to reach a peace settlement in the Bosnian war. In the spring of 1993, the two men produced a plan (the Vance Owen Peace Plan, known as the VOPP) that divided

Bosnia-Hercegovina into ten cantons. The Europeans, the Bosnian Croats, Tudjman and Milošević all supported the plan. A rather unlikely coalition lined up against the plan – the Americans, the Bosnian government, and the Bosnian Serbs. The Americans expressed reservations about the cantonal divisions. 'We're not happy with the maps,' as the Secretary of State, Warren Christopher put it. The Muslim-dominated Bosnian government was aggrieved because the VOPP denied its central war aim – a fully unified state. The plan's most bitter opponents were the Bosnian Serbs. After much hesitation, the Americans and Bosniaks finally agreed. Under enormous pressure from Milošević, Radovan Karadžić, the Bosnian Serb president, was the last to consent. But his parliament insisted on holding a referendum on the issue, confident that, when asked, the Bosnian Serb people would reject the VOPP. This they duly did.

The VOPP came in for much criticism from many in the western media but two experienced writers on Yugoslavia later offered a more accurate assessment:

> There was never a more comprehensive plan than Vance-Owen, which, despite criticism to the contrary, did preserve a multi-ethnic Bosnia within its internationally recognized borders. Once Vance-Owen was rejected by the [Bosnian] Serbs however, the US lost no time ditching it. It was cast aside ostensibly because of the Bosnian Government's complaints, but also because of fears that it was unenforceable. The fact that it would have required at least 50,000 ground troops, of which the US had already pledged half – was probably the overriding reason.[5]

The Clinton Administration's reluctance to consider any plan that might have involved the deployment of US ground troops contributed much to the development of the policy of 'lift and strike', the Americans' preferred option until late 1994. They sought to end the arms embargo on the Bosnian government and to assist it with some strategic bombing. While clothed in lofty rhetoric about the right of a nation to defend itself and the need to halt Serb atrocities, this was a device whereby the Americans could appear to be doing something without risking the lives of their service men and women. The division between Europe and the United States began to widen.

The British and the French, who had contributed most of the peace-keepers to the UN operation in Bosnia-Hercegovina, were incensed at what they regarded as American cowardice. Russia was also alarmed at the talk of air power being used in the Balkans. Moscow's hostility to unilateral western intervention against the Bosnian Serbs or indeed Serbia itself was not born of a particular affection for Serbia, and certainly not of any affinity between President Yeltsin and his Serbian counterpart. Western assumptions of brotherhood based on shared Slav and Orthodox values were wide of the mark. But with its imperial pride badly wounded by the collapse of the Soviet Union, Russia objected strongly to NATO deploying its power in the middle of Europe before Washington and Moscow had defined the contours of their post-Cold War security arrangement.

The failure of the VOPP was preceded by the outbreak of war between the Muslims and Croats. Until this point, the two communities had formed an uneasy alliance against the more powerful Bosnian Serb army. The Serbs had inherited the bulk of Yugoslav Army supplies in Bosnia and could call on the support of the Serbian army at will. The breakdown of the Croat-Muslim alliance was a catastrophe for the Muslims. Tudjman decided that the time had come to cash in the Karadjordjevo* agreement with Milošević and to split Bosnia down the middle. The Croats proved that they were as willing as the Serbs to perpetrate atrocities against Muslim civilians. At the height of fighting in the Hercegovinan capital, Mostar, UN observers registered up to 1,000 Croat shells a day fired at the eastern, Muslim side of the city.

For two years, the international community wrung its hands, its members hurling accusations of cowardice and incompetence back and forth across the Atlantic. Apart from lack-lustre negotiations, the only policy in operation was the protection of six 'safe areas' – Sarajevo, Goražde, Žepa, Srebrenica, Tuzla and Bihać. The supposed 'protectors' of these areas were the United Nations troops in Bosnia. Outgunned, demoralized, and subject to the most inflexible bureaucracy in military history, this force became a convenient scapegoat for everybody. But real responsibility lay with the governments of the great powers, in particular the five permanent

---

* See chapter 8.

members of the Security Council (although China was not directly involved in Yugoslav matters). They presented UNPROFOR with an imprecise mandate that was constricting, frequently amended and impossible to implement. The British and French at least had the decency to contribute a large force to UNPROFOR. The Americans carped from the sidelines.

Age of the parastate: Bosnia and Hercegovina

Until the last moment, Bosnians from all three communities cherished the illusion that there would be no war. This was not naivety but the knowledge that if war did break out it would be merciless. Gavrilo Grahovac was a remarkable man, a Serb from Sarajevo who ran Svjetlost, the most successful publishing company in the former Yugoslavia. Grahovac remained in the Bosnian capital throughout the war. As the noose was tightening around Bosnia's neck, I asked him why he insisted that war might still be avoided. Because when war begins, he explained, 'that is when the massacres begin. And what you are doing with your logic is leaving me with no hope. And you cannot take away my hope.'[6]

Unlike Grahovac, most Bosnian Serbs lived in villages spread sparsely across large tracts of countryside. These stretched in a rough crescent from eastern Hercegovina in the south and then along Bosnia's eastern border with Serbia and into the north-west, the so-called Bosanska Krajina bordering the predominantly Serb regions of Croatia. The Croats lived in two largely rural but compact territories in western Hercegovina and in Posavina in the extreme north, with a more dispersed community in central Bosnia. The Muslims lived throughout both provinces but were concentrated in the towns.

As with every other region of Yugoslavia, the prosperity of the Tito years had benefited Bosnia's cities more than the villages. The rapid departure of young Bosnians from the countryside to the cities after the Second World War dislocated the close relationship between town and country. The greatest number of migrants were Serbs, but the Muslims, whose urban roots went much deeper, continued to achieve higher levels of education and were more prominent in most professions. To encourage ethnic harmony, the Communists introduced a three key system in the Republic. If a

Croat was promoted in the administration, a Serb and a Muslim would also have to be advanced. If a Serb were arrested for political offences, it was only a matter of time before the police picked up a Muslim and a Croat and charged them as well.

For thirteen years, Radovan Karadžić worked at the psychiatric clinic at Koševo Hospital in Sarajevo. His superior and friend was a Muslim, Dr Ismet Cerić. Karadžić would occasionally moan that he would only ever be second-in-command at the clinic and never its boss because he was not from Sarajevo and because he was a Serb. Eventually in the late 1980s, Karadžić asked his colleague to use his influence to help him secure a post at the much larger psychiatric hospital in Belgrade. He told Cerić that he would be able to fulfil his ambition better in Belgrade where his nationality would not bar his professional progress. 'Radovan,' Cerić said, 'I will help you but I can't guarantee your old job back if it doesn't work out.'[7] To nobody's surprise but his own, the snobbish doctors in the Serbian capital patronized Karadžić as a peasant from the sticks. Before long, he was pleading with Cerić to take him back. With difficulty, Cerić persuaded the hospital authorities to allow Karadžić to return to Sarajevo.

When he became the president of the Bosnian Serb republic, Karadžić thanked his old friend by attacking the psychiatric clinic with mortars. Karadžić was typical of the Bosnian Serb leadership. Frustrated professionals (academics, businessmen, doctors, publishers and journalists), they had often moved to Sarajevo from other parts of Bosnia. Preferring to overlook their own shortcomings, they ascribed their professional failure to the supposed stranglehold of Muslims on Sarajevo society. Few had ever shown much interest in Serbian nationalism. After the one-party system began to collapse, Karadžić himself founded Bosnia's first ever Green Party on the assumption that this would be a powerful political force in the future. He soon lost interest, however, when he discovered that few Bosnians shared his passion for the environment.

His decision to co-found the Serbian Democrat Party (SDS) was motivated less by nationalism than by personal ambition. Nenad Kecmanović was a Serb member of the Bosnian government in Sarajevo. In August 1992, he left Sarajevo for Belgrade but stopped off in Pale, the Bosnian Serb headquarters just outside Sarajevo. Here he spent an evening with Karadžić's deputy, Nikola Koljević, a professor of English at Sarajevo University who hailed from Banja Luka. 'You know, you are all obsessed with Sarajevo,' Kecmanović remarked, 'none of you come from Sarajevo but you all feel rejected by it. You are all too personally involved with the city and I think that is why you spend so much time on it.' Koljević nodded his head, adding absent-mindedly, 'Of course with everybody worrying about Sarajevo, it means that they don't pay much attention to what's going on elsewhere.'[8]

And there was much going on elsewhere. The Bosnian Serb war aim was to establish control over a great arc of contiguous territory linking up the majority Serb rural areas. Although Serbs made up only a third of Bosnia's population, they sought to grab 70 per cent of the republic's territory. The main obstacle they faced was the Muslim-dominated towns like Bihać, Tuzla, Goražde and Srebrenica, which had often functioned as strategic fortresses during the Ottoman period. Karadžić and his forces, led by the notorious General Ratko Mladić, enjoyed substantial military superiority, logistical support from the army in Serbia, and political support from Milošević. In addition, most Bosnian Serbs genuinely wished to remain part of Yugoslavia. These circumstances allowed Karadžić and Mladić to prosecute the war with energy and without mercy. Despite encountering tenacious resistance from some Muslim defenders, the Serbs were able to sweep through large areas of Bosnia, murdering tens of thousands in the process.

The brutal policy of 'ethnic cleansing' provoked a rapid demographic shift inside areas still controlled by the Bosnian government. Many Serbs either left these areas voluntarily or themselves were cleansed by the Bosnian government. Their places were taken by traumatized Muslim refugees, often less cosmopolitan than their compatriots in Sarajevo or Mostar. For a long period, the Bosnian government was unable to exercise proper control over the semi-criminal élites that proliferated in Sarajevo and other cities. Muslim society, the core of multi-culturalism in Bosnia-Hercegovina, was itself becoming radicalized and its more parochial elements becoming more powerful.

From the very beginning, the Bosnian government found co-operation with its Croatian ally difficult. Alija Izetbegović's war aim was the establishment of a unitary state in Bosnia with a degree of centralized government. This was always incompatible with the

Croats' war aims. At best, they sought a Zagreb-dominated union between Croatia and Bosnia-Hercegovina. At worst, they wished to divide Bosnia with the Serbs. But neither the Croats nor the Muslims could realize their aims without first establishing Bosnia's independence from Yugoslavia and so at the start of the conflict they cooperated. Franjo Tudjman never disguised his antipathy towards Muslims. He often told diplomats that Serb leaders were right in claiming that Bosnia's Muslims were seeking to establish a bridgehead of Islamic fundamentalism in Europe. Herb Okun, Cyrus Vance's shrewd deputy, was often struck by Tudjman's condescending attitude towards Izetbegović, in theory his ally. 'Izetbegović always used the respectful form *Vi* when addressing Tudjman. But Tudjman would not reciprocate, using the familiar *Ti* contemptuously.'[9]

Even when allied to the Muslims, the Croats regularly obstructed military and food supplies to Sarajevo. Throughout most of the Bosnian war, the Bosnian Croats sold oil and other essential supplies to the Bosnian Serbs. The Bosnian Croat heartland was western Hercegovina. Amongst the very poorest regions of the former Yugoslavia, this had been an important recruiting ground for Ante Pavelić's Ustaše and for enthusiastic supporters of the wartime Independent State of Croatia (NDH).* As a Reuters journalist, Andrej Gustinčić, discovered in 1992, Croat rural fascism was blossoming again. On 10 April, the anniversary of the Pavelić state, he awoke in a small valley in western Hercegovina with celebratory guns and artillery audible a few miles away. On the hillside opposite the cottage he was staying in, he was confronted by three huge letters written in burning tires: NDH. As one western Hercegovinan put it, 'Only three things grow here: snakes, stones and Ustashas.'

Yet there was a fundamental difference between Tudjman's perception of Bosnia and the way it was seen in Ustaša ideology. Pavelić included Bosnian Muslims within Croatdom, considering them apostates but no less Croat for that. Tudjman's attitude was baldly racist. His most vociferous opponent was no democrat but the extreme right-winger, Dobroslav Paraga, who led the fascist Croatian Party of Rights (HSP) and its military wing the HOS, the

---

* See chapter 6.

direct ideological descendents of Pavelić. Paraga advocated a *Hrvatska – sve do Drine* (Croatia to the river Drina). It would include all of Bosnia-Hercegovina up to its border with Serbia. HOS considered the Muslims as brothers in the struggle against the single enemy, the Serbs. Under no circumstances could it tolerate the division of Bosnia between Serbia and Croatia. Notwithstanding his alliance with Izetbegović at the beginning of the war, Tudjman always preferred an alliance with the Serbs. Moreover, in political discussions he frequently demonstrated understanding for Milošević and the Serbian leader's tactics.

After Sarajevo's destruction by Serb shells, and the appalling suffering of its population, the Muslims had to watch the wholesale destruction of eastern Mostar at the hands of Hercegovina Croats supported by units of the regular Croatian army. On 9 November 1993, a group of Bosnian Croat soldiers videoed the climax of this orgy when the city's great symbol, the sixteenth-century arched stone bridge over the Neretva river, was obliterated. This single act seemed to represent the utter senselessness and misery of the entire conflict.

Apart from supporting the bumbling United Nations ground operation, the international community was at a loss to know how to respond to these events. The winter of 1993–4 was the darkest period for Bosnia and Hercegovina. On the morning of Saturday, 5 February, a mortar exploded in the middle of Markale, the main outdoor market in Sarajevo, when it was packed with people looking to buy scraps of extra food. The death-toll reached sixty-eight. The United States called an emergency meeting of NATO ministers who demanded that the Bosnian Serbs withdraw all their heavy artillery surrounding Sarajevo within ten days. Three days before the ultimatum expired, Boris Yeltsin made a surprise announcement that Russia would deploy troops around Sarajevo to ensure that the Bosnian government forces did not exploit the absence of Serbian guns to launch an infantry breakout from the city. This decision (an idea which Moscow had categorically ruled out six weeks earlier) defused the tension around the ultimatum. The Serbian and Bosnian government forces began handing in weapons to UN collection points. The Serbs never fulfilled their commitment, keeping a large number of weapons in place. But for several months, the people of Sarajevo enjoyed a breathing space. The shelling of the capital died down and a degree of normality returned.

At this point, the Americans and the Germans began an initiative that would eventually bring the war to a close. By exerting considerable pressure on Zagreb, they persuaded Tudjman and Izetbegović to form a Federation on 18 March 1994. This was an impressive achievement as it brought an immediate halt to the suffering of Croats and Muslims alike. The Federation was a shotgun wedding that amounted to a glorified cease-fire, but it also gave Croatia the right to interfere directly in Bosnian affairs. As such the Federation Agreement represented the beginning of one of the most curious forms of partition yet seen on the Balkan peninsula, which culminated eighteen months later in the Dayton Accords. The new Bosnia-Hercegovina was hailed as a triumph of the West's commitment to a multi-ethnic state but in reality confirmed its total partition.

With respect to American policy, the Federation also marked another turning point. Henceforth, the rhetorical support that Washington had always given to the Bosnian government would transmute into practical support for Croatia, encouraging the build-up of Croatia's armed forces as the only way of eroding Serbian military superiority. This was certainly effective, but while ensuring military equality between the Serbs and Croats, it made it still easier for Tudjman to dictate policy to the Muslims.

Dayton and beyond: Bosnia-Hercegovina, Serbia, Croatia, the international community

> Milošević is reinventing himself as a statesman. He's rather like a mafia boss who's gotten tired of doing drugs in the Bronx and now wants to move down to Palm Beach to get into junk bonds.
>
> *The late Robert Frasure,*
> *American special envoy to Yugoslavia*[10]

The creation of the Bosnian-Croat Federation coincided with a new plan put forward by the Five-Nation Contact Group (representatives from the US, Britain, France, Germany, and Russia). This proposed the division of Bosnia into two entities, the Federation and a Serbian entity called the Republika Srpska (RS) or Serbian Republic. The Federation was to control 51 per cent of Bosnian territory while the RS would ruler over the remainder. The Bosnian

Serbs remained obdurate, unwilling to give up the 20 per cent of Bosnia necessary for the plan to work.

There was no significant fighting during 1994 except for an autumn offensive by the Serbs in the Bihać pocket or Cazinska Krajina, the north-western edge of Bosnia that jutted into Croatia's armpit. The situation in the pocket was the most confused in all Bosnia, but also of critical importance to the eventual outcome of the conflict. At the start of the war, the Cazin district was governed by Fikret Abdić, a shrewd, if unscrupulous, Muslim businessman. Abdić's stronghold was Velika Kladuša, in which, as director of Agrokomerc, he had developed the largest food processing factory in Yugoslavia. Abdić commanded tremendous loyalty in the region where he was known as Babo (Daddy) or Fikret Paša. In the Bosnian elections of 1990, he polled more votes for the presidency than Alija Izetbegović, the eventual victor. Abdić rejected the office, preferring to remain the undisputed master of Cazin. Until 1993, this pocket was a haven of peace in Bosnia. Surrounded by rebel Serb armies in Croatia and Bosnia, Abdić struck deals with everybody – the rebel Serbs in Croatia and Bosnia, the Croatian government, and the UN – except the internationally recognized Bosnian government in Sarajevo. Abdić had become an authentic successor to Huska Miljković, the Second World War leader in the region who also ran his own personal army and cooperated with all sides in the fratricidal Bosnian war.* In late 1993, the Bosnian 5th army corps stationed in Bihać rebelled against Abdić. The pocket was split in half and two years of internecine warfare between the Muslims of Cazin followed – one of the bloodiest episodes in the Bosnian war.

In late 1994 and early 1995, Abdić's increasingly close cooperation with the Bosnian and Croatian Serbs against the 5th Army corps led to a dissolution of the boundaries that had divided the separatist struggles of the Croatian Serbs from the Bosnian Serbs. Croatia could not tolerate the prospect of a link-up between the two Serb armies through Bihać.

In February 1995, President Tudjman announced that Croatia would not agree to a renewal of UNPROFOR's mandate in the republic. The UN forces were at that time dispersed around the four rebel Serb zones in Croatia. International diplomacy now had

* See chapter 8.

six months to find a negotiated settlement or expect a Croatian assault on the Serb parastate in Croatia. In Bosnia, the cease-fire negotiated in December 1994 was breaking down and all three armies were stepping up their preparations for a renewal of hostilities. By this time, Richard C. Holbrooke, the US Assistant Secretary of State for European and Canadian Affairs, had assumed responsibility for finding a solution in Bosnia. He concluded that he would need to deal with Milošević in order to throttle the Bosnian Serbs. The Serbian leader had accepted the Contact Group plan which envisaged a sovereign Bosnia into two entities, one Serb, one Bosnian-Croat. Furthermore, he made plain his displeasure with Radovan Karadžić's stubbornness by imposing a blockade between Serbia proper and the Republika Srpska. The sanctions regime was beginning to hurt Serbia and Milošević was furious that Karadžić was threatening the economic well-being of the rump Yugoslavia for the sake of a mere 20 per cent of Bosnian territory.

In early summer 1995, Robert Frasure, Holbrooke's assistant, an unusually astute and good-humoured diplomat, struck a deal with Milošević. There was one problem. Milošević had agreed to a suspension (not lifting) of sanctions on Yugoslavia. But the two sides could not agree on the mechanism required to reimpose sanctions if Serbia and Montenegro failed to comply with their side of the bargain. The United States wanted to empower an independent commission of three UN member states with the task. Milošević insisted that only the UN Secretary General, Boutros Boutros-Ghali, should be able to reimpose sanctions. Privately, Frasure believed that Milošević's suggestion should be accepted but he was obliged to refer the matter back to his superiors in Washington. 'I am going to dump this file on the table,' he told this writer in Belgrade just before his return home, 'and on Thursday I am going down to my ranch in Shenandoah for a rest. I'll be back in the office on Monday or Tuesday and we'll see if they'll go with it. If they don't, it's out of my hands.'

The eyes of Milošević, Tudjman and Izetbegović were now turned to Washington. If the Frasure-Milošević deal failed, all three sides in Bosnia were preparing to do final battle. Within a week, Washington turned it down. Three days later, the Bosnian government began an infantry offensive aiming to break out of Sarajevo. In early July, Mladić attacked the safe Muslim haven of Srebrenica.

Bosnian Serb troops entered the city on the late afternoon of Tuesday, 11 July 1995, and began to commit the single biggest crime of the Bosnian war, the murder of some 8,000 unarmed Muslim men. Days later, Mladić turned his guns on the next safe area, Žepa. That town also fell. But at the third target, Goražde, Mladić stopped – under pressure from both Belgrade and the imminent threat of NATO air strikes.

In May, the Croatian army overran the weakest of the four rebel Serb areas in Croatia, western Slavonia, which lay astride the main motorway to Belgrade some 45 kilometres east of Zagreb. The Serb defenders, exhausted and without support from Serbia, crumbled in a matter of hours. This was a dry run for the big offensive against the two strongholds of Knin and Kordun/Banija launched in early August. Knin, the militant centre of the Serb frontier region, the Krajina, collapsed like a pack of cards. The fighting triggered a hurried mass exodus of 150,000 Serbs from Croatia, the largest single movement of refugees in Europe since the expulsion of the Sudeten Germans from Czechoslovakia in 1945. The entire operation was carried out by the authorities in Zagreb with the support of the US government. President Clinton himself welcomed Operation Storm, as it was called, suggesting that it would open the way to a solution of the Yugoslav conflict.

European diplomats were less enthusiastic. Carl Bildt, the former Swedish prime minister, who replaced David Owen as the European Union's mediator on the former Yugoslavia, called for the International Tribunal on War Crimes in The Hague to investigate President Tudjman for the shelling of Knin. Prophetically, he asked, 'If we accept that it is all right for Tudjman to cleanse Croatia of its Serbs, then how on earth can we object if one day Milošević sends his army to clean out the Albanians from Kosovo?'

Operation Storm had an immediate impact on the Bosnian war. As soon as the Krajina Serbs were attacked by the Croats, Fikret Abdić's defences melted away. So did his 'Republic of Western Bosnia'. This had been established only one week earlier, giving it the distinction of being the shortest-lived of the twelve states that have been proclaimed since Tito's Yugoslavia expired in 1991. The Croatian army had also succeeded in pushing the Bosnian Serbs out of the territory that separated the Bihać pocket from western Hercegovina. For the first time since the outbreak of war, the

Bosnian Serbs were taking significant territorial losses. Defeats on the battlefield, the flood of refugees from the Krajina and the acrimonious three-way political struggle between Karadžić, Mladić and Milošević combined to undermine the morale of the Bosnian Serbs.

Urged on by President Clinton, whose eye was on his forthcoming re-election campaign, Holbrooke resurrected the Frasure plan. Now Milošević was his most accommodating partner. The Serbian leader was ready to make even greater concessions than before to secure an end to sanctions. Karadžić and Mladić, however, were still prepared to fight. On 28 August, another mortar bomb smashed into Sarajevo's market place. This triggered a NATO bombing campaign against Bosnian Serb positions on 30 August 1995 that culminated in a strike of thirteen Tomahawk cruise missiles on the Bosnian Serb Army's command and control centre near Banja Luka. As a consequence, the Serb defences in western Bosnia collapsed and the Muslim and Croat armies filled the vacuum.

The Serbian leader made no attempt to defend the Bosnian Serbs against air strikes. He had agreed to the bombing before it began in order to cement the deal that Holbrooke had arranged between him, Tudjman and Izetbegović. Milošević did not acquiesce in the face of bombing – he wanted it to go ahead so that he might be relieved of the responsibility of bringing the Bosnian Serbs into line. The illusion that he had crumpled after a short sharp bombing campaign would lead to unreasonable expectations, on the part of statesmen who should have known better, four years later in Kosovo.

The presidents of Serbia, Croatia and Bosnia-Hercegovina signed the Dayton Agreement on 21 November 1995. Based on the Contact Group plan that gave the Federation 51 per cent of territory and the RS 49 per cent, Dayton brought the fighting to an end, in itself a considerable achievement. But as a model for reconciliation and for rebuilding a shattered society, it was and remains severely limited. The Dayton documents, which make up a thick book, are complex and contradictory. They have been interpreted both as a blueprint for partition and for the consolidation of a unitary state. The constitution included the most advanced provisions for the protection of human rights anywhere in the world. But it conspicuously omitted any reference to the role of the armed forces. Military Annexes Ia and Ib, a full third of the Dayton Agreement, regulate the country's military status. These make the bold assumption that the Croatian HVO and the Bosniak/Muslim Army of BH will eventually come together under a single command. They also concede, however, that for the foreseeable future there will be three armies operating independently in Bosnia (not to mention the NATO-led peace-keeping force).

The detailed provisions for the return of refugees to their homes have proved irrelevant. The presence of three hostile nationalist armies occupying territory defined by treaty means, in effect, that Bosnia is partitioned. The international community has preserved the constitutional fiction of a unified Bosnia by maintaining its own armed force in the country, but it refuses to use its military power to enforce the return of refugees. The Dayton Agreement is so fragile that the war will start again should the international troops ever leave. Bosnia is a military protectorate, but one for which the occupying force is reluctant to take political responsibility. The three local élites are comfortable with the arrangement as it guarantees their hold on power within their own communities. The way the maps defining Serb, Croat and Muslim-controlled territory are drawn undermines the economic development of all three communities, while the political arrangement discourages cooperation between them. The settlement is, in short, full of anomalies and frictions. The Bosnian question remains unanswered.

War in Europe: Serbia, Kosovo, Macedonia, NATO

> This war started in Kosovo and it will end in Kosovo.
>
> *The Kosovo Albanian writer, Shkelzen Maliqi*[11]

On the evening of Monday 22 April 1996, a small group of Serbs were enjoying a drink at the Čakor café in Dečani in western Kosovo. They represented a broad sweep of Serbdom – one was from Kosovo, a second from Belgrade, and one had only recently arrived in Kosovo from Drniš after the Croat Army had stormed the southern outpost of the late Republic of Serbian Krajina. At 8:25 PM, a group of masked men walked into the café and opened fire indiscriminately with semi-automatic weapons, throwing a grenade as they withdrew. Three Serbs lay dead, the first murder victims of the *Ushtria Çlimitare e Kosovës* – the Kosovo Liberation Army (KLA). In the next hour, there were three more attacks in different parts of Kosovo resulting in two further deaths – one of a policeman, the second of a female prisoner being transferred to Priština's main jail.

During the following months, the BBC Albanian service in London received several faxes from the KLA claiming responsibility for the attacks. These had been sent from Tirana, the Albanian capital. The moderate Albanian leader in Kosovo, Ibrahim Rugova, questioned the authenticity of the claim, suggesting that Serbian extremists might have carried out the shootings to ratchet up the tension and worsen the atmosphere of fear in the province.

The KLA's first murders were not, however, a Serb-inspired provocation. A section of the Albanian community in Kosovo had finally decided that enough was enough. Rugova and his Party, the Democratic League of Kosovo (LDK) had pursued a path of peaceful resistance to the rule of Belgrade since the province's autonomy had been rescinded in 1989. Rugova's policy of restraint ensured that Kosovo remained peaceful throughout the Croatian and Bosnian wars. But peace was accompanied by political stagnation and the continuing systematic repression of Albanians. Rugova's movement boycotted all Serbian institutions. Serbian opposition parties argued that the boycott of Serbian elections helped Milošević maintain his grip on the country as the Serbian minority in Kosovo, 10 per cent of the province's population, delivered all the parliamentary seats to Milošević and his allies. Younger, less patient Albanians became frustrated with the Rugova strategy and immediately after the events of 22 April 1996, one of Rugova's harshest critics in Kosovo, the maverick politician, Adem Demaqi, noted that the Kosovo Albanians were 'increasingly vociferously accusing their leaders of betraying national interests'.

The KLA attacks occurred five months after the signature of the Dayton Agreement. The Kosovo Albanians looked northwards to Croatia and Bosnia with envy. They observed that with the help of the international community, the Serbs had been defeated completely in the former and partially in the latter. In Bosnia-Hercegovina, the international community had pledged $5 billion to aid reconstruction. Despite being Milošević's first victims, the Albanians had received nothing. As long as they remained passive, the more radical Albanians reasoned, the outside world would ignore them and the Milošević regime could continue to deny

Albanian rights and his shabby regime of repression would continue undisturbed.

In spring 1996, the KLA was not an organized force. Its members belonged to small cells and were drawn from the large rural population that had little political influence in Kosovo; but by taking up terrorist methods, the KLA laid down a challenge to Rugova's leadership. The tactics of armed confrontation would inevitably lead to reprisals by the Serbian security forces, which in turn would boost support for the KLA. Tired of Rugova's apparent inaction, many young Albanians switched their allegiance to the men with the guns.

During the first year of its existence, the KLA failed to attract much attention outside Kosovo and Serbia. With the support of the United Nations and Russia, the West was engaged in putting the Bosnian jigsaw back together again. This was difficult and exasperating work. After five years of vicious conflict in the former Yugoslavia, the West had tired of the Balkan tragedy. The death of a few Serbs in Kosovo barely registered in diplomatic cables and no government was interested in pursuing the matter. The peace in Bosnia depended on the goodwill and cooperation of Slobodan Milošević. This was not the time, western politicians thought, to open a Pandora's box like Kosovo. Yet the clash between Albanian and Serb in Kosovo should not have come as a surprise. All intelligence suggested that at some point there would be a serious escalation of violence. April 1996 was that turning point. And true to form, the international community turned a blind eye.

In the summer of 1997, neighbouring Albania descended into chaos. The government of the right-wing President, Sali Berisha, collapsed after the failure of several huge pyramid investment schemes. Fighting broke out between supporters of Berisha's Democratic Party and those of the Socialist Party, led by Fatos Nano. Criminal gangs filled the power vacuum, unleashing a reign of terror on the civilian population and looting the weapons facilities of the demoralized Albanian army. Much of this hardware found its way into Kosovo via the western, Albanian areas of neighbouring Macedonia, where support for the KLA was growing.

Yet another development spurred the conflict in Kosovo. Throughout the Yugoslav crisis, Milošević had counted on unswerving support from Montenegro, Serbia's tiny sister republic in the rump Yugoslavia, the FRY. Many Montenegrins, however, considered the wars in Croatia and Bosnia to be purely Serbian affairs. Yet because of the federation with Serbia, the Montenegrins had to endure sanctions and isolation in the same measure as the Serbs. The Slavs of Montenegro, who speak a variant of Serbo-Croat, are divided between those who believe themselves bound to Serbs ethnically and historically, and those who regard Montenegrin identity as separate. The Prime Minister, a young reformer, Milo Djukanović, built a broad coalition powered by the growing resentment felt towards Milošević and the Federal government. In October 1997, Djukanović was elected President of Montenegro. For the first time since 1989, Milošević was faced with an opponent who could actually limit his room for manoeuvre. Djukanović's outspoken criticism of Milošević and his warm relations with the West irritated the Serbian leader, who toyed with the idea of provoking civil war in the republic to bring his rival down.

In Kosovo, the death toll mounted on both the Serbian and Albanian sides. The European Union and the United States were awakening to the possibility of war in the province. They sent delegations to investigate the situation but diplomacy consisted in warning both sides against the use of violence. Rugova's support was ebbing away in favour of the KLA whose operations were concentrated on its stronghold in west central Kosovo, the Drenica valley. On Thursday 5 March 1998, a large force of Serbian police launched an offensive in Drenica, killing 22 Albanian fighters and triggering a flight of the civilian population towards Vučitrn. The assault occurred three weeks before elections called by Rugova to Kosovo's unofficial government.

The Serb offensive in Drenica had three consequences that Milošević had almost certainly anticipated. First, the KLA became stronger by the day, as thousands of young Albanian men swelled its ranks. Second, western Europe and the United States stepped up their involvement in the conflict. Third, regional stability was unsettled by polarizing Montenegrin society and increasing tension in neighbouring countries, especially Albania and Macedonia.

Macedonia was the most fragile of the new states to emerge from the former Yugoslavia, less secure even than Bosnia-Hercegovina. Sixty-five per cent of its two million inhabitants are Slavs who are known to everybody except the Bulgarians and Greeks as Macedonians. The Bulgarian government refuses to recognize the modern identity of the Macedonians, insisting that they are western Bulgarians.* When Macedonia became independent in 1992, the Greek government claimed that the very name, Macedonia, had a Hellenic pedigree stretching back to Alexander the Great. The Macedonians, Greece warned, harboured territorial aspirations on Aegean Macedonia and its port of Thessaloniki. How this tiny, impoverished and effectively unarmed nation intended to invade Greece, a member of both NATO and the EU, was never explained. Macedonians themselves also feared that Serbia and Milošević would never reconcile themselves to losing their influence over Macedonia. Some worried that when Milošević had finished in Bosnia, he would turn his attentions to Macedonia.

Macedonia's greatest problem was its large Albanian minority, accounting for roughly 25 per cent of the population. Living in the compact territory of western Macedonia and in the capital Skopje, the Albanians of Macedonia had suffered worse treatment at the hands of the Macedonian communist authorities in the 1970s and 1980s than the Kosovo Albanians in Serbia. They expected the new government in Macedonia to demonstrate greater respect for their rights. The Macedonian state was weak and defenceless; successive governments had no option but to cooperate with the Albanians to avoid rebellion. To the credit of most Albanian and Macedonian politicians, the two élites worked hard to find a modus vivendi that was not always to the liking of their constituents. If the Albanians and Macedonians were to begin fighting, the security interests of the country's four neighbours – Albania, Serbia, Bulgaria and Greece – would be directly affected. War in Macedonia would destabilize the southern Balkans and risk spreading conflict beyond the borders of the former Yugoslavia. NATO (the United States in particular), with its vital interests in the eastern Mediterranean, could not tolerate this.

The conflict in Kosovo threatened Macedonia in two ways. The KLA's programme sought independence for Kosovo – nothing else would now satisfy the Albanians. But an independent Kosovo would act as a powerful magnet on the Macedonian Albanians – through the fog, Albanians could for the first time make out the contours of a Greater Albania. More immediate, however, was the

* See chapter 3.

effect that a large exodus of refugees from Kosovo into Macedonia would have on the country's fragile balance. For this reason, western governments refused to support the KLA's goal of independence.

Extensive autonomy from Belgrade was the most that the international community would sanction for the Kosovars. But it did agree to guarantee this autonomy with the presence of a NATO peace-keeping force. From the summer of 1998, a variety of western representatives hoped to persuade the KLA to drop its demand for independence. They also had to convince Milošević to accept the presence of a NATO force in Kosovo. Until the very last minute in March 1999, they failed on both counts. As western diplomacy faced total defeat, the KLA changed its mind at the Paris peace talks, accepting autonomy in place of independence. The Serbian authorities agreed with most of the political plan for autonomy but refused categorically to countenance a NATO presence in their hallowed territory of Kosovo.

Milošević had called NATO's bluff. As the western defensive alliance approached its 50th birthday celebrations in April 1999, it was confronted with a distasteful dilemma. It must embark upon a war against a country of 8 million inhabitants or renege on its public commitment to do so, in the event of Milošević refusing what came to be known as the Rambouillet agreement.

If NATO backed down, it would lose its vaunted 'credibility'. It had announced the bombing and so it must go ahead regardless of the consequences. The Pentagon, however, advised against an open-ended bombing campaign without properly-defined war aims. So did senior European diplomats involved in Balkan affairs, 'The only alternative to shooting yourself in the foot,' Carl Bildt told White House staff ten days before the bombing started, 'is not to do it.' The reply came back: 'Credibility.'

Soon after the bombing started on the evening of 24 March 1999, it became evident that the posture of 'credibility' did not amount to a clear war aim. NATO leaders had assumed that Milošević would capitulate within days of the start of an air campaign. His resolve to stand firm exposed the uncertainty of western strategy. In the first week of the bombing, NATO leaders offered a string of more precise goals that left nobody any wiser. The campaign aimed variously to force Milošević to accept the Paris peace deal; to prevent a humanitarian catastrophe in Kosovo; to degrade and destroy the Yugoslav army; to weaken Milošević's grip on power; and to stop the spreading of conflict beyond Kosovo.

Yugoslav air defences were no match for NATO bombers and cruise missiles. But NATO's astonishing public admission prior to the campaign that ground troops would be excluded from the operation gave Milošević an enormous tactical advantage. His only weapon of war was the two million Albanians in Kosovo. He lost no time in directing hundreds of thousands of refugees into Albania, Macedonia and Montenegro. Instead of preventing a humanitarian catastrophe, NATO's decision had contributed massively to a gathering disaster. A flood of biblical proportions threatened to drown Macedonia and Albania. The Serbs also channelled tens of thousands into Montenegro to encourage the destabilization of Milošević's rival, Djukanović. The influx of so many Albanians into Macedonia had the most severe consquences. It was as though the population of London or New York had been increased by a quarter overnight; as though over a quarter of a million people had been dumped on a region the size of Tuscany. Yet NATO had made no provisions for this outcome and sought instead to place the burden of coping with a huge refugee problem entirely on Macedonia. It will be many years before Macedonia may again be considered a stable country.

Far from deserting Milošević, as the West had hoped, Serbs initially rallied behind their president, enabling him to destroy most independent media overnight. The campaign severely undermined Mile Djukanović's hold on power in Montenegro, especially since NATO liberally bombed the republic in an effort to destroy federal military installations. Inasmuch as Milošević had any war aims, the subversion of Djukanović was probably the most important of them. Both Djukanović and Serbia's democratic opposition, which had been gaining in strength in the two years prior to the Kosovo crisis, have been weakened by the NATO campaign. From the start of the campaign, NATO leaders repeatedly gave assurances that it was fighting Milošević and his regime, not the Serbian people. Yet their refusal to risk their own troops in a ground war, preferring instead to pummel Serbia's economic infrastructure from the air, and thereby causing 'collateral damage' – that is, civilian casualties – looked to many like an act of general punishment. Of course, once the Alliance had embarked on the air campaign, it had no option but to intensify its operation until victory was secured. What would be the price of that victory?

The Balkan vortex

> There are equally important practical reasons for the West's final involvement in Yugoslavia. Most of them are prompted by extra-Balkan considerations: the place and future of NATO, the role of the United States as the global military superpower and especially its strategic stake in European affairs, and so forth. All of this is euphemistically enveloped in the favorite word in recent American diplomatic vocabulary: credibility. If ancient examples are any good, perhaps the most evocative is the behavior of the deities in the Trojan war who followed their own game when tipping the scales without, however, ever pretending they were doing it for the sake of humankind. But they were deities, after all.
>
> *Maria Todorova*[12]

The propaganda war accompanying the conflict in Kosovo was intense even by modern standards. In Serbia itself, Milošević's government likened the airstrikes to the Nazi bombardment of Belgrade in 1941. This was a cynical appeal from a regime that regularly used violence against its opponents at home and abroad. Yet the imagery reinforced the sentiment inside the country, shared even by many of Milošević's most bitter opponents, that the NATO campaign was at best inappropriate and at worst immoral.

The leaders of NATO claimed that the organization's first unilateral military intervention 'out of area' was a moral act, driven not by the strategic or economic interests of its members but by a commitment to humanitarian values.

The struggle for moral superiority during this war centred on two opposing concepts of international relations. Serbia relied on the long-established if frequently violated idea of sovereignty – that if a country had not actually threatened a third party, then there could be no justification for military intervention against it.

NATO was acting upon a new premise that had emerged during the conflicts in Bosnia and Croatia. Military intervention against sovereign states, so this embryonic doctrine proclaimed, is legitimate if it prevents or halts the abuse of human rights by a state against its own citizens, in this instance the Kosovo Albanians. Humanitarian considerations alone may justify war.

This represented a clear break with the morality of the Cold War, established at Yalta in 1945 and symbolized by the Brezhnev doctrine of limited sovereignty, during which NATO was not prepared to disrupt relations with the the Soviet Union and Eastern Europe over human rights abuses. NATO, of course, expected reciprocity on Moscow's part with regard to western complicity in human rights abuses, notably in Indo-China, Latin America and the Middle East.

The implications of the new doctrine of humanitarian intervention, still ill-defined, extend far beyond the Balkans, especially since the creation of the International War Crimes Tribunal on alleged crimes against humanity in the former Yugoslavia and Rwanda. They are intimately connected with the Spanish government's attempts to bring the former Chilean dictator, General Augusto Pinochet, to trial. If it is applied with any consistency in the future, the elevation of humanitarian issues to a central position in foreign affairs will necessitate a fundamental revision of international relations.

Both sides presented the war in Kosovo as a clash over the principle of sovereignty in order to bolster public support for their position and to obscure less convenient matters. Milošević made the simple calculation that his political position would be strengthened if he defied NATO's ultimatum. NATO's leadership highlighted the humanitarian issue, less to cover up any ulterior motives it may have had in waging war than to camouflage its own deep confusion regarding its aims and tactics.

A more serious consequence of framing the war in this language of sovereignty emerged after Yugoslavia had capitulated militarily. The bombing inflicted severe damage on Serbia and Kosovo, while their Balkan neighbours suffered collateral economic damage. Estimates of the losses sustained by Serbia, including Kosovo, during the three-month war range from $7–10 billion. Reconstruction of Serbia and Kosovo alone will cost some $10 billion over a three to five year period. But other countries also need assistance in the short term to offset the drop in GDP caused by the war, from 5 per cent in the two worst-affected states, Macedonia and Bosnia-Hercegovina, to 0.5 per cent in Romania and Hungary. This is quite apart from the much greater sums required for the long-term recovery of the region caused by ten years of instability in Yugoslavia. Early estimates from the Vienna Institute for Economics suggest that as much as $100 billion will be needed to create stability in the Balkans.

It is these issues of reconstruction and recovery that will in retrospect define the morality of the Kosovo war, rather than the Manichean battle proclaimed by NATO and the leadership in Belgrade. The West's claim to a moral victory in the Balkans when Yugoslavia surrendered in early June 1999 was unsurprising but irrelevant, within the larger historical context of relations between the great powers and the Balkans. To claim such a victory honestly would require the reversal of a pattern that has persisted for over a century. This has seen the great powers intervene massively in the region, either deploying or exciting violence, before beating a retreat and disclaiming any responsibility for the consequences of the original intervention.

Before 1999, the great powers had intervened three times in the Balkans. The first was at the Congress of Berlin in 1878 when European diplomats agreed to replace Ottoman power by building a system of competing alliances on the Balkan peninsula. The second began with the Austro-Hungarian ultimatum to Serbia in the summer of 1914 and culminated in 1923 with the Treaty of Lausanne and the Great Population Exchange between Greece and Turkey. The third started with Italy's unprovoked attack on Greece in March 1940 and ended with the consolidation of unrepresentative pro-Soviet regimes in Bulgaria, Romania and a pro-western administration in Greece.

These three interventions were so destructive that they that guaranteed the Balkans' relative economic backwardness, compared to the rest of Europe. And the violence that these interventions encouraged, often inflicted by one Balkan people on another, ensured the continuation of profound civil and nationalist strife. In the West, however, these events are rarely regarded as the result of external intervention. On the contrary, the Balkan countries are seen as culprits who force the reluctant outside powers into their unfathomable conflicts. This imagined Balkans – a world where people are motivated not by rational considerations but by a mysterious congenital bloodthirstiness – is always invoked when the great powers seek to deny their responsibility for the economic and political difficulties that the region has suffered as a consequence of external interference. 'The Balkans,' Theodore Geshkoff wrote in 1940, 'are usually reported to the outside world only in time of terror and trouble; the rest of the time they are scornfully ignored.' It is during these long periods of neglect that the Balkan countries have badly needed the engagement of the great powers. Yet the only country to demonstrate a sustained interest in the economic development of the Balkans was Nazi Germany during the 1930s.

The NATO assault on Serbia and Kosovo should be judged above all in this light. Should the West fail to address the effects, not merely of a three month air war in 1999, but of 120 years of miscalculation and indifference since the Congress of Berlin, then there will be little to distinguish NATO's actions from any of its great power predecessors. The NATO campaign can hardly claim either a moral or political victory if its sole achievement is the expulsion of Milošević's Serbia from Kosovo.

There is an unassailable case for political and economic restitution in the Balkans. Yet this is a daunting challenge. The lack of preparedness on the part of NATO was obvious during the air campaign. It was evident after victory, when the Alliance proved incapable of stopping the KLA from imposing a regime of intimidation and murder which provoked the departure of almost the entire Serbian minority population from Kosovo within weeks of the Albanians' return. If the greatest military machine in history is unable to impose law and order in a small province, one cannot help wondering what the future holds for the international community's other, larger Balkan protectorate, Bosnia-Hercegovina; and whether the great powers, above all, the USA, have the political and economic resources to deal with Serbia as it hovers between civil war, economic collapse and conflict with its sister republic, Montenegro. Yet if the great powers fail to seize the present opportunity by investing heavily in the region, the suffering of the Balkans will surely continue for several decades into the new millennium.

EPILOGUE

THE SWINGING DOORS

Europe, crime and economic crisis, 1999–2012

The fall of Milosević and the death of Djindjić

The twelfth of March 2003 was a bright morning which promised to end a cold winter. After a short delay, Serbia's Prime Minister, Zoran Djindjić, left his residence in Dedinje, in contemplation of the full day's work that lay ahead. High on his agenda was a meeting with Sweden's Foreign Minister, Anna Lindh. This was no formality. Stockholm had been a firm supporter of Serbia's modernization programme, which Djindjić had initiated after assuming office in January 2001. Central to his goals was Serbia's future membership of the European Union, and Sweden had proved to be one of Belgrade's most reliable backers.

At precisely 12:25 Djindjić's official car, a black BMW 7 series, drew into the courtyard of the Serbian Government building from Nemanjina street in the centre of Belgrade. The Prime Minister struggled to emerge from the car because a fortnight earlier he had damaged his Achilles tendon playing a game of football, and so his bodyguard, Milan Veruović, handed Djindjić a pair of crutches. As Djindjić started to take a step towards the building's entrance, a bullet, travelling at 700 metres per second, hit the right side of his chest. Two seconds later, a second bullet fired from the same Heckler & Koch G3 rifle went through Veruović's pelvis.

Djindjić's death was immediate. The bullet was a full metal jacket, and the vibrations it generated on impact shattered several organs. Veruović remained in a critical condition for several weeks but eventually survived.

The murder of Serbia's fifty-year-old premier stands out as the most damaging in a series of assassinations that were carried out across the Balkans in the fifteen years after the end of the Bosnian war in 1995. It was the defining moment of an elemental struggle. Emerging democracies throughout the region enjoyed fluctuating degrees of political support. They boasted much greater legitimacy than anything to have preceded them, but they were weak if not fragile. Against them stood a powerful, malignant coalition of mighty criminal syndicates and parts of a powerful oligarch class. Their influence extended into politics and the security services, the economic infrastructure and large parts of the print and broadcast media.

These syndicates had contributed much to the emergence of nationalist violence during the Yugoslav wars. Indeed, their members often made up the core of the notorious and brutal militias who were responsible for a disproportionate amount of the ethnic cleansing during the war years. Despite the association with violent nationalism throughout the conflicts, these groups had maintained close relations with one another across the very national divides they did so much to create and nurture. The benefits derived from pursuing a criminal enterprise, which quickly infected large parts of the region's economy, were sufficient, it appeared, to overcome even the most patriotic of passions.

In Serbia, the determination of the wealthiest criminal group to exert decisive control over the political process led both to the death of Djindjić and, in the wake of his assassination, to its own downfall (although it did not, of course, mean an end to organized crime in general).

The implications of the events of March 2003 went far beyond Serbia's borders. The response of the European Union to the Prime Minister's murder was paradoxical. On the one hand, the Greek Foreign Minister, George Papandreou, persuaded the European Union to make an unprecedented commitment to admit all Balkan states as members in June 2003 at a summit in Thessaloniki (although the EU stopped short of offering a firm timetable). This he did both to underline Europe's commitment to Djindjić's legacy but also because the accession process forced governments in the region to undergo a thorough reform of their institutions. In the long term, the theory went, this would prove invaluable in strengthening the rule of law in the postwar Balkans and provide the requisite, targeted support required to modernize the economies.

Yet not all constituencies in the Union welcomed this commitment. In particular, the Directorate of Justice and Home Affairs in Brussels sought to erect some daunting hurdles for aspirant members as fears about the perceived influence of Balkan crime and corrupt networks grew in certain EU member states. These fears also coloured attitudes to Bulgaria and Romania although the two states to the east of the former Yugoslavia were much further advanced down the road to membership.

The issues of organized crime and corruption, combined with the insistence that all former Yugoslav states fully cooperate with the International Criminal Tribunal for Yugoslavia (ICTY) in The Hague, presented the most fundamental challenge to the states of the Western Balkans (as the EU foreign ministries had now renamed the region). Criminals and indicted militiamen (often one and the same) had collaborators and supporters within most branches of the state, notably in the intelligence services and police force. Infiltrated by the very forces it needed to combat, the state's ability to overcome them was thus severely constrained.

This problem of criminal penetration was common to all Balkan states, including Greece, which had been inside the EU since 1981. But Serbia's geographical location as the transportation hub of the region meant that its underground networks were linked to their equivalents in all neighbouring countries.

The origin of the Djindjić assassination stretched back four years to the summer of 1999, when Serbia's then President, Slobodan Milošević, agreed to NATO's conditions for ending the Alliance's three-month-long bombardment of federal Yugoslavia (although this was largely a war between Serbia and NATO as Montenegro's President, Milo Djukanović, signalled clearly to both Belgrade and NATO at the start of the conflict that Montenegro had no interest in fighting history's most powerful military alliance).

NATO had launched its war on the remainder of Yugoslavia

(now down from the original six republics to just two, Serbia, including the provinces of Kosovo and Vojvodina, and Montenegro) in late March. Contrary to most western expectations, however, over three months later Milošević was still holding out. The primary reason for NATO's apparent failure lay in the refusal of the American President Bill Clinton to commit ground troops against the Yugoslav Army in Kosovo. Clinton still suffered from the consequences of a botched raid on Somalia ordered by his predecessor, George H. W. Bush, and the subsequent humiliation of American troops in Mogadishu in late 1993 and early 1994. So he resisted pressure from Britain's Prime Minister, Tony Blair, to mount a ground invasion from Kosovo and Macedonia.

As summer drew ever closer, there was evident unease among some NATO members, of which Germany (new to armed conflict after a break of half a century) was the most important. The longer the bombing of Serbia continued, the greater the popular resistance inside Germany to the campaign. This was symbolized in May when a participant at the Party Conference of the Greens, junior partner of the SPD in government, threw an ink bomb at Foreign Minister Joschka Fischer, damaging his ear. Along with Germany, the Czech Republic, Italy and Greece all indicated to Brussels and Washington that their support for the war had limits, and after two months, these were becoming visible.

It is hard to imagine the United States would have abandoned the campaign in any but the most extreme circumstances. A withdrawal would not only have represented an unbearable humiliation, it would most likely have led to the collapse of NATO. But the failure of the aerial bombardment led to a striking degree of panic at NATO headquarters in Brussels and in the alliance's capitals.

Unsurprisingly, the relentless bombing had a negative psychological impact on Serbian civilians. The first targets were military but after some two weeks, the economic, political and media infrastructures of Serbia were added to the list. Notorious incidents included the hit on Radio Television Serbia's headquarters in which fifteen civilians were killed and the bombing on 7 May of the Chinese Embassy, which resulted in the deaths of three diplomats and a rapid deterioration in Sino-American relations.

As for most Serbs, they were stranded. The American Serbian poet Charles Simic noticed the most apt piece of graffiti in Belgrade during the war: 'NATO in the air; Milošević on the ground.'[1] Nonetheless, popular support for Milošević in Serbia grew to an extent during the campaign as NATO's precision bombing raids targeted the heart of major residential centres, especially in the capital Belgrade (almost thirteen years later, some of the largest buildings in the city centre, such as the Defence Ministry, remain in ruins). Nonetheless, as long as the NATO campaign was restricted to the air, Yugoslav generals found they were able to maintain control of Kosovo and further assist Milošević's programme of violence and expulsion directed against the territory's Albanian inhabitants.

This in turn accentuated the huge refugee crisis that developed in neighbouring Albania but even more importantly in Macedonia, a country already suffering from growing mistrust between its Slav and Albanian populations.

As Milošević's position in Serbia strengthened, albeit temporarily, Bill Clinton and, in particular, the British Prime Minister Tony Blair, were elevated to the status of demigods among the Albanians. Indeed, one British commentator reviewing a selection of biographies about Blair argued that his embrace of the Kosovo cause was the turning point in Blair's prime ministerial career, and that this would have a major impact on global politics. Peter Wilby's essay from *The Guardian* is worth quoting at length as it places the British Prime Minister in the long line of Great Power politicians who have used intervention in the Balkans to enhance their domestic political standing. The Kosovo campaign, although less controversial than the succeeding decade's wars in Iraq and even Afghanistan, prepared much of the philosophical ground for the disasters which followed after the events of 11 September 2001. Noting the Prime Minister's frustration at dealing with the tedious bureaucracy associated with domestic issues such as health care reform, Wilby remarked that it was:

> No wonder Blair turned increasingly to foreign affairs. There, he found greater philosophical certainty, more opportunity to use his personal talents, and more capacity to achieve quick results. As Jenkins[2] puts it, 'he found it a satisfying theatre of power where orders are obeyed and things happened'. Stephens's[3] suggestion that Blair had long been a Gladstonian liberal interventionist has him waiting to leap on to the world

> stage, his Christian faith driving him to the view 'that civilised nations had the right and duty to confront suffering beyond their boundaries' . . .
>
> Blair thus discovered an arena in which he could act confidently and decisively. Each time he went to war, he did so against bitter criticism, but each time he survived. In Kosovo, he was the hawk, demanding ground troops be sent in and straining his friendship with Clinton near to breaking point. The war went badly at first and Blair told aides that it could be the end of him. But he held his nerve, took personal charge of the British effort . . . and emerged triumphant. . . .
>
> But Kosovo created a new Blair image: not a man, as Stephens puts it, 'tossed to and fro in the winds of public opinion', but one firm of purpose and resilient in adversity. The admiring Rawnsley[4] writes: 'He took a stance and, as others scurried for cover, he held to it'. In his insistence on stepping up the war and introducing ground troops, he was largely isolated both in the Western Alliance and in his government. The outcome, writes Seldon,[5] 'further increased his reliance on and trust in the small circle around him'. It also 'ingrained in Blair that he was the bridge between the United States and Europe, and that he uniquely could explain the one to the other'.
>
> The road to Baghdad therefore led directly from Pristina where, after the Kosovo war, Blair was acclaimed as a hero. . . .[6]

Eventually, Blair's advocacy of the use of ground troops in Kosovo convinced Clinton to threaten their deployment. That threat in turn played an important role in persuading the Yugoslav army leadership that this was not a fight they could win and that Milošević's insistence on holding out was becoming counterproductive.

But the decisive move was not on the battlefield. It took place on the diplomatic front. The Finnish President and subsequent Nobel Laureate Martti Ahtisaari had succeeded, with American backing, in suggesting to the Russian Government that it drop any support offered to Milošević. Together with the former Russian Prime Minister, Viktor Chernomyrdin, Ahtisaari visited Belgrade in early June and spelled out the options to Milošević – either he agree to sign NATO's peace plan or the Alliance, which had already flown close to 38,000 bombing missions, was determined to bring the regime crashing down by upping the aerial campaign and preparing for an invasion. Resistance, the Yugoslav Army leadership averred, was no longer an option.

The key to this outcome lay in Russia's decision not to extend any guarantees to Milošević. Still recovering from the crash of the ruble less than a year earlier, President Boris Yeltsin was in no position to confront NATO. With his political power waning almost in direct correlation to his rising alcoholism and senility, Yeltsin nonetheless remembered through the mist of vodka vapour surrounding him that Milošević had backed the organizers of the Russian coup in August 1991. He was not going to jeopardise his presidency still further by challenging NATO, a huge political risk, on behalf of an ungrateful cousin. One can but speculate how Yeltsin reacted to Milošević's extravagant and rather desperate offer at the eleventh hour to enjoin Serbia in a political union with Russia and Belarus.

Two notable long-term consequences resulted from the Kosovo war, one with serious local implications, the second with international ramifications.

There was no consensus among the victorious NATO allies as to the precise constitutional outcome of the conflict. The West had not gone to war specifically to create an independent Kosovo although the aim was implicit for some (but not all) of the Alliance's members. Clearly the Kosovo Albanians and their guerrilla forces, the Kosovo Liberation Army (KLA), understood independence as axiomatic. But instead of waging war in pursuit of an unambiguous political goal, NATO's political leadership was testing out Tony Blair's new doctrine of humanitarian intervention, the self-conferred right to intervene in the domestic affairs of a state which was engaging in the violent suppression of a part of its citizenry. It became clear fairly quickly that waging war in the name of a philosophy resulted in postwar political and constitutional problems.

At the same time, as the Yugoslav troops scuttled Kosovo in accordance with the Ahtisaari-Chernomyrdin agreement, the deployment of NATO and other forces (including Russian troops) inside Kosovo was carried out in a rather haphazard fashion. The Russians, who had also joined the Kosovo occupation as per the agreement, raced from Bosnia (where they were stationed as part of another Balkan stabilization force) to seize the airport in the capital Prishtina. At this point, General Wesley Clarke, NATO's Supreme Allied Commander in Europe, ordered Lieutenant General Mike Jackson, the British head of the Rapid Reaction Force in Kosovo, to block the Russian deployment at the facility. Jackson, renowned for his blunt manner, refused the order with undoubtedly the most memorable line from the war, 'I'm not having my soldiers responsible for starting World War III!'

In the north of the territory, French troops drew a line down the middle of Mitrovica – the Albanians lived south of the Ibar River while some 50,000 Serbs congregated on the other side right up to the border with Serbia proper some thirty miles to the north.

Elsewhere the occupying forces, who were soon transformed into the stabilization force KFOR, realized that they would have to throw protection rings around the rest of the Serbian population concentrated in enclaves to the south of Mitrovica. Parts of the KLA and the Albanian population were bent on revenge against their Serbian neighbours for the indignities and violence suffered at the hands of the Serbian state.

For the international community, the long-term importance of the Kosovo war lay in the uncertain constitutional status of the territory. Ambiguity was written into the UN Security Council Resolution 1244, the document that effectively regulated the post-conflict governance of Kosovo. Paragraphs 10 and 11 were at the heart of this:

> 10. Authorizes the Secretary-General, with the assistance of relevant international organizations, to establish an international civil presence in Kosovo in order to provide an interim administration for Kosovo under which the people of Kosovo can enjoy substantial autonomy *within the Federal Republic of Yugoslavia*, and which will provide transitional administration while establishing and overseeing the development of provisional democratic self-governing institutions to ensure conditions for a peaceful and normal life for all inhabitants of Kosovo;
>
> 11. Decides that the main responsibilities of the international civil presence will include:
>
> (a) Promoting the establishment, *pending a final settlement*,

> of substantial autonomy and self-government in Kosovo, taking full account of annex 2 and of the Rambouillet accords (S/1999/648). [*emphasis mine – MG*]

In the future, supporters of Serbia's claim to Kosovo would argue that paragraph 10 precluded independence while those backing the Kosovars would claim that paragraph 11 enabled it. It was entirely a matter of interpretation and a lot of arcane language would be expended arguing over this fine print in the following few years, to little effect.

UNMIK, the United Nations administration, charged with administering the territory until the self-governing institutions were up and running, had an exceptionally difficult job. In collaboration with KFOR, the multi-national military force, UNMIK was a small army of international bureaucrats who mostly spoke not a word of the local languages nor had they ever set foot in the region. Its members were expected to oversee everything from garbage collection to electricity and water provision. Its political wing was also charged with devising and then building instruments of political dialogue between the Albanians and the Serbs along with the other minority communities. To their credit, they were largely able to prevent major outbreaks of ethnic violence.

Beyond that, however, results were mixed at best. Failure was most obvious and disastrous in the economic field, for which the EU had assumed responsibility. Kosovo's unemployment rate was a catastrophe even when taking into account the territory's large informal sector. Most disturbingly youth unemployment stood at close to 70 per cent, leading Veton Surroi, the media owner, to remark that if that rate were repeated 'in London, then not a building in the British capital would be left standing',[7] as a consequence of the attendant social unrest.

At the height of the global economic boom in the first half of the first decade of the new millennium, Kosovo was Europe's only territory to register a negative growth in GDP from 2003 onwards. This was not helped by the uncomfortable circumstances whereby the territory, which was traditionally a net exporter of labour, was suddenly required to absorb large numbers of refugees returning from western Europe. As soon as Belgrade had capitulated to NATO, EU governments lost no time in expelling Kosovo Albanian asylum seekers, as their homeland was now deemed free and, therefore, safe.

In the absence of a functioning economy, organized crime found fertile ground to consolidate its influence over Kosovo. The BND, Germany's Federal Intelligence Service, compiled a detailed report in 2005 that explained the competitive relationship between three geographically distinct organized crime groups known as the Llap, Djukagini and Drenica groups. The document also described these groups' effective ownership of the three major Albanian political parties in Kosovo. The report read like a Who's Who of Kosovo politics and included an addendum on their counterparts among the Albanian community in neighbouring Macedonia.

Among other things, it intimated that organized crime groups had been instrumental in the most serious threat to Kosovo's stability during the immediate postwar period when armed Albanians attacked both Serbs from the village of Čaglavica and KFOR troops protecting the latter in March 2004. Dozens died in the unrest, which was in part caused by the frustration of Albanians who were unhappy at what they perceived was the slow progress towards independence for Kosovo. The BND report, however, offered a different interpretation:

> Various intelligence reports point to a role of regional OC [Organized Crime] structures in the unrest of March 2004. OC structures have no interest in the development of a functioning state order following the Western model as this would damage their flourishing smuggling activity. . . .
>
> At the beginning of April 2004, security circles in the Balkans let it be known that OC prepared the most recent unrest in Kosovo and carried it out at their behest. Members of *the Albanian (Kosovar) and Serbian mafia* organized the preparations on both sides. According to information we have received (still unconfirmed) whole trucks carrying heroin and cocaine moved across the border during the unrest.[8] [*emphasis mine – MG*]

What is striking in this is again the cooperation (repeated across the region) between organized crime groups from ethnic communities generally perceived to be hostile to each other. Furthermore, this mafia collaboration involved sparking inter-ethnic violence to which their innocent compatriots fell victim. The heroin trade was especially important in joining the criminal interests of the Kosovo Albanian and Serbian undergrounds.

Life to the north of the Ibar river in Kosovo's Serbian enclave was marginally more tolerable for ordinary people compared to the experience of most Albanians to the south. The economy in the north was almost entirely dependent on subsidies from Belgrade. Of course, the financial and political support which Belgrade offered the Mitrovica Serbs was at odds with the British and American plans to back Kosovo's independence.

This division between Serbia's determination to maintain at least nominal sovereignty over all Kosovo (and real control over the northern enclave), on the one hand, and the Kosovo Albanians' demands for nothing less than full secession from Federal Yugoslavia, on the other, would later find reflection in international attitudes towards the problem as both sides lined up their more powerful allies. This was accentuated once the Kosovars decided to move towards a unilateral declaration of independence in early 2008.

In the summer of 1999, however, Milošević was still in power and keen to present the UN's Resolution 1244 as confirmation of Serbian sovereignty over the territory even though any physical signs of it had disappeared (with the exception of the enclaves). The following months would suggest that Milošević's ability to assess his political position was increasingly delusional. But for those around him, it was very clear that under his leadership, Serbia had fought three wars (four, if one counts Slovenia, as many Serbs do) and lost them all. That made him vulnerable, and some of his oldest supporters in the security services and the economy began to wonder whether it was time for a change.

Ordinary Serbs felt atomized, demoralized and poor. Yet although they had not supported the NATO bombing campaign (unsurprisingly), they understood that Milošević had suffered a humiliating defeat and must stand weakened by it. The two most dynamic opposition parties, the SPO (Vuk Drašković's Serbian Renewal Movement) and the DS (the Democratic Party, led by Zoran Djindjić), lost no time in devising strategies to undermine Milošević's power structure. Milošević's reaction to this renewed activity betrayed both his fraying nerves and his readiness to resort to violence to deal with perceived problems. His first move was to order, indirectly, the murder of Drašković. The attempted assassination on Drašković's convoy travelling on the Ibar Highway (named after the same river that eventually dissects Mitrovica in Kosovo) resulted in four deaths but not in that of the primary target, Drašković himself.

This incident heralded an extraordinary twelve months in Serbian politics which culminated in the final end of Milošević and the start of a new yet still unpredictable era of Balkan politics.

The cold in January 2000 would break records, and on Saturday 15th, freezing fog had smothered Belgrade for most of the day. Night had fallen and the temperature had begun a downward slide past zero. The blackness was pierced by the intense dark green light emanating from the Hotel Intercontinental, a desolate rectangular block, which stands lonely over the Sava River in New Belgrade. Just inside the building, a group of tough-looking men were slouched in the reception area's hideous 1970s leather sofa enclaves, discussing football and filling out betting slips. At exactly 5:04 PM, a former Belgrade policeman, Dobrosav Gavrić, emerged from the elevator and walked towards them. As he reached reception, he pulled out a gun and started shooting. Pandemonium reigned for about two minutes as the men sitting down returned fire. Gavrić was hit in the back but saved from certain death by an accomplice who appeared from nowhere, hauled him through the entrance's revolving door and into a car which the thick fog soon swallowed up as it sped towards a rendezvous with a second getaway vehicle.

Back inside the Intercontinental amidst blood and wailing, the man filling in the betting slip, known to his many admirers as The Commandant, was breathing his last. He had received three bullets to the head, one of which had gone straight through his left eye into his brain. This was the inglorious end of Arkan, the most notorious crime boss in Belgrade, who was wanted throughout Europe on charges of murder and armed robbery – 'aggressive, armed and extremely dangerous', as the Interpol warrant described him. The Hague War Crimes Tribunal was also preparing a case against him for genocide, and even Milošević had a year earlier dubbed him 'my greatest enemy', despite the fact that during the Yugoslav wars of the 1990s Arkan had soaked himself in blood on Milošević's behalf.

But The Commandant had many friends, and indeed countless Serbs venerated him as the country's most glamorous celebrity. At the time of the killing, Zoran Djindjić, who was still in opposition, reacted to the assassination by declaring Arkan to have been a close friend. 'It was Arkan who warned me to flee to Montenegro during the Kosovo war because Milošević intended to murder me', Djindjić explained later. (Indeed, with an eye to Serbia's democratic political future, Arkan had organised and paid for Djindjić's evacuation.) Gangsters, oppositionists, entertainers, supporters of Milošević, opponents of Milošević, soccer hooligans, the business fraternity mourned Arkan in their hundreds of thousands.

Arkan's killer, Gavrić, fled Serbia in 2006, eventually ending up in South Africa, where in late 2011 he was caught up in another mafia shoot-out, then identified by the local police, thus enabling Serbia to request his extradition. Gavrić was merely a hit man – nobody ever discovered who ordered Arkan's murder or why. But the consequences were profound as the events that January afternoon triggered an unprecedented internecine battle among Serbia's gangs, known as Bloody Spring 2000. Less than a month after Arkan's death, the Yugoslav Defence Minister was exterminated while dining in a Belgrade restaurant. Thereafter assassinations and executions occurred on a weekly basis as Milošević's final months began to resemble the fearful denouement of an Elizabethan revenge tragedy.

At the time of his death, Arkan was the most powerful figure in Serbia's underworld. Believing himself to be invincible, he never seemed to walk but swaggered through Serbia's streets with minimal protection (which explained in part why he proved such an easy murder target). He controlled large parts of the country's mafia business, whether oil smuggling on an industrial scale, dealing in contraband cigarettes or transporting heroin (the only time the CIA almost managed to snatch this indicted war criminal was when he was scheduled to rendezvous with his main Albanian partner in the narcotics trade on the border between Kosovo and Serbia – he received a tip-off, however, and did not show at the meeting[9]).

In addition, he was investing much of his money into legitimate businesses as his long-term aim was to transcend his status as gangster and enter the elevated world of the oligarch, exerting monopoly control over various business sectors; in Arkan's case tobacco, sport and energy were of particular interest.

Thus when he was killed, disputes broke out between several of the other main mafia organizations in the country eager to grab a piece of his legacy. Over the following four years, three characters from the often indistinguishable worlds of organized crime and state security would have a decisive role to play in Serbian and Balkan politics. These men were Ljubiša Buha 'Čume' (The Bogey Man); Dušan Spasojević 'Šiptar' (The Albanian) and Milorad Luković Ulemek 'Legija' (The Legionnaire).

There were a host of other unsavoury characters in this milieu, like Marko Milošević, the dictator's son, who was a significant (albeit rather hopeless) player in the counterfeit and smuggled cigarette trade. One of Milošević Junior's hangouts was the Kotobanja Café in Surčin, the village which gave its name to Belgrade's airport to the west of the city. The Café was owned by a certain Čume, boss of the notorious Surčin clan, one of the two largest mafias in Serbia.

The UN sanctions on the remainder of Yugoslavia account for Čume's rise to economic and mafia power as he became the most successful smuggler of vehicles into Serbia (in collaboration with Croatian mafia groups) before expanding into other areas, including the importation of sugar.

Later he began cooperating with another major criminal group called the Zemun gang, which was named after the fashionable Belgrade suburb where its leader, Dušan Spasojević, had built an armoured mansion in Šiler Street. This gaudy building became for many Serbs a distressing symbol of their country's descent into criminality and corruption.

Spasojević was a small-time thug from the village of Veliki Trnovac in the far south of Serbia. Situated two miles east of the border with Kosovo and ten miles north of Macedonia, Veliki Trnovac had been a hub for heroin smuggling throughout much of the communist period. Albanians, Serbs, Macedonians and Bulgarians were all engaged in the activity – cross-border cooperation was vital at this juncture of the business. Spasojević's nickname in the Serbian underworld was 'Šiptar', which is otherwise the standard derogatory epithet that Serbs use for Albanians.

After moving to Belgrade in order to consolidate his growing status as a national organized crime figure, Spasojević became close to Milorad Ulemek Luković, known universally in the former Yugoslavia as Legija. Translated from Serbian, Luković's nickname means 'Legionnaire', a reference to the time he spent as a member of the French Foreign Legion in the late 1980s and early 1990s.

Luković's rise to prominence in the former Yugoslavia began in 1996 with the formation of the *Jedinica za specijalne operacije* (Unit for Special Operations, or JSO) under the auspices of the Serbian Intelligence Service (RDB), headed by Jovica Stanišić, one of the former Yugoslavia's master spies. Stanišić's original aim was to create an armed formation of highly trained men who would act as Slobodan Milošević's Pretorian guard.

The JSO was a critical node where the world of the state and that of organized crime intersected. Known colloquially as the Red Berets, the JSO and its godfathers in Serbian State Security acted as a protective shield for Spasojević and his fellow heroin dealers, kidnappers and extortionists from the Zemun clan. The revenues from the criminal business were distributed among the more privileged members of the JSO.

In 1999, Legija became the Commander of the JSO. As Spasojević and the Zemun clan started seizing much of the late Arkan's business following the militia leader's murder, large parts of Serbia, especially the capital, came under *de facto* control of organized crime and paramilitary operations.

Milošević, however, was becoming progressively weaker, and he took particular fright when rumours spread that his primary opponent in presidential elections would be Ivan Stambolić. This was the former Serbian communist leader who, more than anyone else, had propelled Milošević up the power structures of Titoist Yugoslavia in the 1970s and 1980s. Notwithstanding his one monumental error of judgement in selecting Milošević as a successor, Stambolić was a mild, moderate character who generated deep affection among Serbs. When it seemed ever more likely that he would challenge his erstwhile protégé for the presidency of Yugoslavia, Milošević's reaction was positively Shakespearean. He ordered the kidnapping and murder of his former mentor and father figure. Snatched during broad daylight in Belgrade, members of the JSO and Zemun clan took Stambolić to a wooded area in Fruška Gora in the northern province of Vojvodina. Here they shot him in the back of the neck and buried the body in a shallow grave.

Three years later, Stambolić's corpse would be identified by the sneakers he had been wearing on the day of his abduction. His disappearance in August 2000 did more to galvanize the opposition than any other single event that year. Once Stambolić had disappeared, the opposition persuaded Vojislav Koštunica, a lawyer and reluctant leader of a tiny political outfit, the Democratic Party of Serbia (DSS), to stand against Milošević for the presidency.

In late September, the Federal Election Commission announced that Koštunica had failed to win an outright victory against Milošević and that a run-off election would therefore be scheduled. The opposition refused to accept this, convinced that their candidate had received over 50 per cent of the vote.

In earlier years, many Serbs and most of the outside world would have shrugged their shoulders and ignored such chicanery at elections. But this time some strange things came to pass which should perhaps have alerted Milošević that all was no longer what it seemed. Most importantly, the Kolubara coal miners of central Serbia downed tools in late September saying they would stay out until Koštunica was proclaimed President. This was followed by the announcement of a general strike and messages of support that arrived from all parts of Serbia, including some of Milošević's strongholds. The opposition announced that it would hold a giant rally in Belgrade on Thursday 5 October to drive home their demand for Milošević to make way for Koštunica.

On the morning of the proposed showdown between Milošević and the opposition, an icy Košava wind whipped through the streets of Belgrade. Members of the youth movement, Otpor (Resistance), which had excelled in mobilizing the population against Milošević with their innovative techniques using new media, were throwing up barricades across the city as fast as the police could tear them down.

From across Serbia, peasants and workers were descending on Belgrade, some in convoys of tractors, some marching in military formation and others holding up the banners of their factories. Many had their hands raised showing two fingers and a thumb, the victory sign in Serbia that on occasions carries overtones of nationalism and which on 5 October symbolized opposition to Milošević.

Before long close to a million people were crammed into the

centre of Belgrade. At first the police responded by attempting to corral the demonstrators and disperse them using teargas. It soon became evident, however, firstly that the police were not using the full force of which they were capable and, secondly, that there was no sign of the army intervening. Somebody had leaked an internal poll of officers up to the rank of colonel that indicated a majority now held a negative opinion of Milošević. Whether the generals would be prepared to order their subordinates to open fire on the demonstrators remained unknown although some officers would have been aware that their own children were on the streets.

There were two images which came to symbolize the 5 October revolution as live pictures were disseminated through television around the world. An opposition supporter had led the assault on Radio Television Serbia (a bastion of Milošević's power) using his industrial wheel loader, quickly mistaken for a bulldozer. At the same time, thuggish opposition supporters had stormed the federal parliament in the heart of the city and set it on fire, the red flames bright against an overcast sky.

The question on most demonstrators' minds remained: will Milošević order the forces of law and order to attack? One incident during the events offered a clue:

> Around 17:30, several armoured Humvees manned by members of the JSO entered Belgrade from the direction of Banjica.[10] In total there were no more than fifty heavily armed men. . . . They headed towards Aberdarev Street [where] they removed their helmets and masks and began waving three fingers in the air while greeting the masses around them. They even found a priest to kiss in front of the TV cameras. After this they quickly disappeared. What was important was for Legija to fly his flag on the ground, on the winning side; it was an eminently political act with long-term consequences. The aim was to provide insurance for the JSO's and Legija's existing and future investments in organized crime against a damaging outcome of the 5 October revolution, which at that point was perfectly possible.[11]

The Red Berets and their criminal associates did not decide to join the revolution on the spur of the moment. The Pretorian guard had begun hedging its bets two months earlier when some of its soldiers had unexpectedly turned up to act as protection for opposition politicians at a rally in southern Serbia. This was a month before members of the same unit were to kidnap and kill the leading opposition symbol, Ivan Stambolić. Apparently, they were still gauging which way the wind would blow, but they had begun looking in earnest for new partners on the assumption that Milošević was losing control.

During August and September 2000, the JSO and their mafia friends established contact with the opposition. Reflecting on that period, Zoran Djindjić later remarked that 'the mafia had suddenly lost its state and it was looking for a new one'.[12]

In any event, on the evening of 4 October 2000, Djindjić met Milorad Luković Legija, the Commander of the JSO, in a building on Admiral Geprata, the very street from which the bullet that killed Djindjić would be fired two and a half years later. The deal was struck – the Red Berets and the other shadowy figures like Čume and Šiptar who lurked behind this capricious paramilitary formation would betray Milošević and join the revolution.

For Djindjić, it was of course a Faustian pact but at the time absolutely necessary. Had the JSO and its associated network remained loyal to Milošević, there was a genuine possibility of bloodshed and civil war on 5 October. The Red Berets were a very intimidating symbol of power – if they were to make a stand on Milošević's behalf, it would almost certainly have persuaded some in the Army's chief of staff, conservative and equivocating at best, to stand by the dictator. Djindjić's decision to meet Legija and strike a deal was the final blow against Milošević. Ultimately, it also proved fatal for Djindjić himself.

It was obvious almost from the first day of the successful revolution of 5 October 2000 that its two leaders, Vojislav Koštunica and Zoran Djindjić, could not abide each other, either politically or personally. Their coalition, DOS, easily won the parliamentary elections of 23 December 2000, and Djindjić became Serbian Prime Minister in January. But DOS was divided from the very beginning with the two main seats of power, Djindjić's prime ministerial office and Koštunica's Yugoslav presidency, constantly feuding.

Koštunica, crippled by a ponderous and legalistic mind, steadily revealed himself to be a dour and unimaginative leader, suffocated by a Romantic nationalism. Before long, he and Djindjić were fighting over a number of issues. The latter was concerned where possible to eradicate the lingering influence of the *ancien régime* by removing Milošević's consiglieri in the security forces. Rade Marković, head of intelligence and a central cog in the former dictator's machine of power, actually offered his resignation three days after 5 October. Koštunica turned it down, affording Marković two vital months to start cleansing his own reputation and ensure that his allies secured longer term roles in the organization.

But not even this matched the tension between Djindjić and Koštunica that broke over the International Criminal Tribunal on Yugoslavia's demand for the extradition of Milošević to The Hague. Despite opposition from Koštunica, Djindjić ordered Milošević to be flown out of Belgrade on 28 June 2001. It was Vidovdan, the most resonant date in Serbia's calendar, when the Battle of Kosovo took place in 1389 and when Gavrilo Princip fired the shot that killed Archduke Franz Ferdinand in 1914. The event was suitably dramatic as several of the actors prepared for a final shoot-out of the Milošević regime. Eventually, he was escorted from his grand residence in Dedinje to Surčin airport and on to The Hague, much to Koštunica's chagrin.

After Milošević's fall, prosecutors and police intensified their investigations into a number of serious crimes (including the attempted assassination of Vuk Drašković on the Ibar Highway). Dušan Spasojević and Milorad Luković started to feel uncomfortable as the enquiries came ever closer to home. In response, Legija launched an extraordinary campaign, using his extensive links in the media. This included an apparent recruitment drive for the Red Berets under the slogan *Terrorism is a disease. Call the doctor!* which was wrapped around the intimidating image of a wolf bearing its fangs and wearing a red beret. The campaign also hinted at the unacceptability of the cooperation with The Hague Tribunal which Djindjić had stepped up since the arrest of Milošević on Vidovdan. Legija's intention was to encourage the obvious hostility between Djindjić and Koštunica. He believed the former was driving the anti–organized crime campaign, which he understood was directed at him. The latter, he realized, was moving away from the policy of deepening ties with the West. The Hague, Koštunica argued, was an infringement of Serbian sovereignty and dignity.

Matters came to a head in November 2001, when Legija mobilized his troops in the JSO and sealed off parts of the roads entering Belgrade. To most observers, this looked like an armed *coup d'état*. But the Red Berets received backing from Koštunica and succeeded in replacing key members of both State Security and the criminal police who were the primary criminal investigators looking into Spasojević, Luković and their associates.

The democratic order in Serbia was being intimidated: the elected government was forced to make changes to its personnel under the threat of an armed formation (founded by Milošević's state security) which received backing from members inside the ruling coalition from Koštunica's Democratic Party of Serbia.

Not that the gangsters and paramilitary had it all their own way. There was growing discord between Belgrade's two largest gangs, the Surčin clan and the Zemun gang. At one point, Ljubiša Buha Čume was almost poisoned to death (at the hands of his own wife) and he decided that in order to survive he would need to make his peace with the government. He agreed to testify against Spasojević and Luković in open court and in exchange was granted immunity from prosecution and witness protection.

Čume's decision to testify in late 2002 was the real reason that Zoran Djindjić was killed. He was not murdered, as some would have it, because he was betraying his compatriots to the war crimes tribunal in The Hague but his Government was determined to call Luković and Spasojević to account for their crimes.

The official response to Djindjić's murder was unexpected. After imposing a State of Emergency on the country for forty days, the Interior Ministry ordered a series of mass arrests, which would eventually include over 11,000 suspects, suggesting that, while weak, the state was by no means entirely spineless. Among the main targets of Operation Sabre, as police called it, was Spasojević, shot dead after being surrounded by police.

Djindjić's funeral, held three days after his death, saw almost a million people follow the cortege, indicating how popular disgust with organized crime and paramilitary formations had reached new levels in Serbia. Foreign dignitaries from around the world came to pay their respects at the service held in Belgrade's enormous Sveta

Sava Cathedral. Most important for the region was the appearance of Ivica Račan, the Social Democrat Prime Minister of Croatia – his presence carried profound symbolic weight.

One absentee from Belgrade that day was Legija. The co-conspirator to the assassination who had frequently masqueraded as a great Serbian patriot was under the protection of one of his counterparts in Croatia, Hrvoje Petrač – a militia leader and militant Croat nationalist. Their friendship had been forged when they were both members of the French Foreign Legion, perhaps the strongest bond enjoining criminal elements from the former Yugoslavia through the war period.

The death of Djindjić was the defining moment in the first decade of the twenty-first century for the Balkans and the former Yugoslavia. Just a few days before the assassination, he claimed that 'if anyone thinks that they will stop the rule of law and implementation of reform by eliminating me, then they are badly mistaken'.[13] In the long term, Djindjić may yet be proved correct. But in the short term, his death had negative consequences for both economic and social progress in Serbia and, critically, for the region.

The Prime Minister had been engaged in clandestine contacts with the leadership in Kosovo. He had indicated his intention to find a resolution to a regional problem that was a serious stumbling block on the path to European Union membership. Furthermore, he was adamant that he would continue to cooperate with the Hague Tribunal to deliver the remaining indicted war criminals, including the notorious Bosnian Serb duo Radovan Karadzic and General Ratko Mladic.

There was nobody else in Serbia at the time who could muster sufficient authority to continue Djindjić's modernizing, and indeed the next four years were characterized by stagnation under the leadership of Djindjić's political nemesis, Vojislav Koštunica.

Djindjić's murder was the most dramatic consequence of the contest between corrupt networks and the Serbian state's drive for institutional reform demanded by the European Union. But the pattern was repeated across the region. Acts of group and individual violence with far-reaching implications punctuated politics not between states, as was during the case in the 1990s, but inside them. One might argue that Djindjić's death was the final trigger for the decision by Montenegro's dominant political figure, Milo Djukanović, to prepare the ground for his republic's secession from Yugoslavia, which was confirmed by referendum in May 2006. With Montenegro's departure, Yugoslavia came to a final end – each of the former state's constituent republics was now an independent country. Just eighty-nine years after its first appearance, the name Yugoslavia vanished from the map of Europe, probably forever on this occasion.

This did not signify the end of the fragmentation of the territory as Kosovo's status as part of Serbia remained contested. Two years after Montenegro's referendum, the government in Kosovo proclaimed its unilateral declaration of independence. But whereas all five members of the UN Security Council endorsed Montenegro's secession in quick succession, Kosovo's announcement in 2008 divided world opinion. At the time of this writing in 2012, Russia and China still refuse to recognize Kosovo as do other BRIC countries, India, Brazil and South Africa. Several influential members of the Islamic Conference Organisation, including Indonesia, have yet to acknowledge Kosovo's independence. Even within the European Union, Madrid (with an eye to the Basque country and Catalonia) was among five members effectively to back the Serbian position.

Of all these countries, Russia was the most significant. It withheld recognition in part to express its displeasure at western (especially American) support for Georgia, Moldova and Azerbaijan in the so-called 'frozen conflicts' affecting parts of the former Soviet Union.

Of equal significance, however, was Moscow's indication that although integration in the European Union remained the primary goal of Balkan states, Russia had its attractions of which energy (gas in particular) was undoubtedly the most alluring.

After Vladimir Putin visited Zagreb for the Balkan Energy Summit in October 2007, Russia sought to persuade as many Balkan countries as possible to take part in its South Stream gas pipeline, a direct challenge to the European Union's faltering Nabucco project. With most Balkan energy companies mired in debt, Russian companies began to increase their holdings in the gas and oil infrastructure of the region. There was nothing intrinsically sinister in this. Indeed, in many respects diversification of energy supplies away from Ukraine and into the Balkans would reassure the European Union that its members were less likely in future to be held hostage to the baffling disputes between Ukraine and Russia which regularly disrupted gas supplies to Europe from 2000 onwards. It served to remind the region, however, that the United States and the European Union did not hold a monopoly on influence in the Balkans.

Serbia's hope that it could cling to sovereignty over Kosovo received a severe blow in 2011 when the German Chancellor, Angela Merkel, told President Boris Tadić directly that if Serbia continued to support Kosovo's de facto independence, then it would not secure European Union membership. As the governments in Belgrade and in Prishtina pushed and pulled, Brussels slowly shoved them in the direction of an awkward resolution. By March 2012, Serbia was finally granted its much-prized candidate status for the European Union. To achieve this, it was compelled to concede that Kosovo's government could be represented at regional meetings and would not require the mediating signature of UNMIK for official agreements. In exchange, Prishtina accepted that its official name would carry the suffix * (a first in diplomatic history) which referred to the footnote '* This designation is without prejudice to positions on status and is in line with UNSC Resolution 1244 and the ICJ Opinion on the Kosovo Declaration of Independence'.

Despite this increasingly bizarre and winding path towards a solution to the Kosovo problem and, ultimately, the general recognition of another state in the former Yugoslav territory, the consensual desire of Balkan nations to join the European Union meant ironically that they were all pursuing a political strategy that would bring them closer together again in terms of pooled sovereignty, almost as soon as they had got rid of one another measured in historical terms.

This has been an especially striking development in Croatia, where the desire to establish a separate identity from its former Yugoslav neighbours had been such a powerful driver towards independence in the 1990s.

President Franjo Tudjman had invested considerable political capital in both highlighting the separateness of Croats from Serbs and dismissing what he considered the historical fiction of Bosnia-Hercegovina. Shrewd enough to forge a diplomatic alliance first with Germany and later with the United States before and during the wartime period, he continued to undermine Bosnia's cohesion after signing the Dayton Accords in 1995, a policy that was especially poorly received in Washington.

Tudjman's relationship with the European Union was similarly strained. Not only was he genuinely sceptical about the need to merge his newly independent country with a large supra-national organization (even if the EU was not associated with the hated epithet 'Balkan'), but also he quickly grew to dislike the International War Crimes Tribunal in The Hague.

If it is possible to identify a victor of the wars in the 1990s, it was Tudjman and Croatia. On the assumption that victors never have to face investigation for any war crimes they may have committed, Tudjman was initially a keen supporter of ICTY. This soured as he realised that prosecutors from The Hague were interested in Croat war crimes suspects as well as Serbs. Not only that, it soon became clear that Tudjman himself was probably under investigation.

He forestalled any personal difficulties with The Hague by dying at the age of seventy-seven in December 1999. It remains to be seen whether later historians elevate Tudjman to the pantheon of Croat national heroes like Stjepan Radić or whether he is excoriated like the wartime Ustaše leader Ante Pavelić. He will probably nestle somewhere between them, although his legacy is unlikely to find much favour outside Croatia. After his death, the HDZ Government lost its mandate in parliamentary elections, to be succeeded by a centre-left coalition comprising several parties. The social democrats (the reformed League of Communists) dominated under its leader, Ivica Račan. One new parliamentarian, Vesna Pusić, would later become probably the most elegant and astute Foreign Minister the Balkans has ever seen. The liberal coalition reversed Tudjman's central policies and vigorously courted the European Union. In this, they enjoyed strong backing from Tudjman's successor as President, Stipe Mesić, who was a key player at the birth of independent Croatia but had never been infected by Tudjman's extremism.

It was far from plain sailing as the HDZ under its new leader, Ivo Sanader, was determined to place obstacles on the path to European Union membership. Much of the HDZ's strategy involved creating difficulties in the Croat areas of Bosnia and Hercegovina. The EU insisted that Zagreb break the support it had consistently given to the tougher elements of the Croat leadership in Bosnia as they were deliberately hindering efforts to rebuild and reintegrate the state. The West through its diplomats in the Croatian capital and its High Representative in Sarajevo had been monitoring how HDZ's sister party in Bosnia, the HDZ BiH, had been colluding with the extremist militias from the war in throttling the political development of the Bosnian state that had been established in Dayton in 1995.

Just as the Red Berets and their criminal associates started to undermine the legitimate government of Serbia, so did the HDZ in Croatia and Bosnia try to destabilize the new policy of engagement with Europe in Croatia.

Central to this were the activities of the main Veterans' Association in the Bosnian Croat areas, known as HVIDRA. In a similar fashion to the JSO in Serbia, HVIDRA had been able to expand its criminal activities and its symbiotic relationship with the HDZ BiH to exert significant political control over the Croats in Bosnia and Hercegovina (BiH). They were powerful and popular.

In March 2001, the HDZ BiH announced that it would withdraw from the Bosniak-Croat Federation, one of the pillars of both the Dayton State and American policy in the region. Not only did this threaten the Agreement, which had ended the war in Bosnia, but also the move was a direct challenge to the new reformist government in Zagreb. Croat members of the BiH Army ratcheted up the tension still further when they walked out of their barracks and refused to serve. In early April, some of these Croat troops moved to claim the barracks as their own. The crisis seemed set to turn nasty.

The High Representative in Sarajevo, the Austrian diplomat Wolfgang Petritsch, and the NATO-led stabilization force, Sfor, reacted decisively, demonstrating an uncharacteristic willingness to deploy robust force. At the centre of the activities of HDZ BiH and HVIDRA was the main bank that serviced Croats in BiH, the Hercegovačka Banka. Not only was Hercegovačka Banka a central tool undermining the functioning of the Bosnian state, but also it was a vast money-laundering operation able to channel funds to a variety of corrupt instances, including those Croats sought by the War Crimes Tribunal in The Hague who were on the run.[14]

At about 3:00 AM on 6 April 2001, Sfor troops launched raids on the headquarters of Hercegovačka Banka in Mostar along with ten of its branches elsewhere. The Croats responded by rioting, looting and in some instances attacking Sfor troops. Dutch soldiers at the same time secured the barracks contested by the Croat rebels and the Bosnian army.

The Sfor raids had overcome the immediate crisis, but it was clear that Croatia faced political difficulties almost as overwhelming as those facing Serbia in its struggle between the government and the Red Berets. For Bosnia-Hercegovina, this was no idle matter. The presence of international troops ensured that a return to armed conflict in the fragile country was unlikely (although the events surrounding the Croat boycott of the BiH Army suggested that it was not inconceivable).

Political life, however, was effectively stagnant. The Dayton Accords had created a culture of dependency on the office of the High Representative. Countless governments at the national, entity, cantonal and municipal levels, each with their own ministers and bureaucracy, ruled over Bosnia's four million inhabitants. The further up the hierarchy, the more rewarding the ministerial sinecure. In many respects, the art of politics was reduced to a competition between those who might secure the ear of the High Representative as this European officer had the power to introduce and revoke laws. As a form of governance, it owed as much to the mandates of the late colonial period as it did to democratic accountability.

The countervailing force to Bosnian statehood was Serbian and Croatian nationalism. As long as pro-European governments were in power in Belgrade and Zagreb, secession would be beyond the capacity of even powerful nationalist forces among the Croats and Serbs of Bosnia. Meanwhile, the United States, and in particular its intelligence agencies, grew concerned about the radicalization of part of the Bosniak population and the burgeoning influence of jihadists. So as a consequence of the events of 11 September 2001 when Islamic militants attacked the World Trade Center's Twin Towers in New York and other targets, there was a shift of emphasis in American policy towards Bosnia. Whereas before it was unambiguously supportive, Washington started to apply pressure on the Bosnian government to increase their monitoring of suspected Islamists.[15]

If politics continued to stagnate in Bosnia, there was always the possibility that Islamist ideology could put down deeper roots, in part to weather harsher winds that might start blowing from the Serbian and Croatian capitals.

Such a wind indeed began to pick up first in Serbia after the assassination of Djindjić and the revival of Koštunica's political fortunes. The phenomenon appeared to repeat itself in Croatia when the HDZ triumphed once more in the general election in December 2003. There were considerable fears that Sanader intended to resurrect Tudjman's strategy of what was effectively isolationism both within Europe and within the former Yugoslavia. To her great relief, Vesna Pusić remembered how 'after they won . . . they turned around . . . or I would say I think more precisely, Sanader turned around . . . And he turned around and turned his party around on three issues: they were against Croatia's membership in the EU, now they were for Europe; they were against Serbs, now they were for Serbs – I mean in terms of having normal relations and respecting multi-ethnicity and respecting the institutions of the other ethnicities; and they were against cooperation with The Hague, now they were for cooperation with the Hague'.[16]

Confirmation of the HDZ's transformation occurred in 2005 when Ante Gotovina, among the most wanted Croat war crimes indictees, was arrested over his hotel dinner in the Canary Islands. Having stoutly defended Gotovina in the past, the HDZ government made not a sound on this occasion. After this, Zagreb's path to EU membership speeded up and the civil service embarked on an extraordinary effort to meet the stringent Copenhagen criteria, the mountainous documentation which stipulates what legislation an aspirant country must pass through its parliament and implement if it is to be granted EU membership.

By now, Slovenia had already become the first region of the Balkans affected by war in the 1990s to be granted membership. In many respects, especially economic, Croatia was far in advance of the other two countries closing in on membership, Bulgaria and Romania. But the war crimes issue had slowed down the accession process and only recently Croatia had been failing to comply in a number of highly visible and sensitive areas such as the treatment of ethnic minorities, notably the remaining Serb population in Croatia.

Over the decade, however, Croatia had leapfrogged over another advanced contender for membership, Macedonia. The EU's decision to grant Macedonia candidate status, which is just one step before full membership, was idiosyncratic and motivated by specific political calculations. Under normal circumstances a country as dysfunctional politically and economically as Macedonia would have expected to wait much longer before it were allowed inside the hallowed waiting room of candidate status.

But in the wake of the Kosovo war, circumstances conspired to destabilize Macedonia and push the country to the precipice of a civil war, which had the potential to be as bloody and destabilizing as any of the conflicts since 1991.

Before descending upon Macedonia, however, the locus of violence shifted eastwards from Kosovo, after NATO had occupied the territory, towards the neighbouring district of South Serbia, known by the name of its three largest towns, Preševo, Bujanovac and Medvedja. The line linking these skirted to the west of the regional capital, Vranje. In parts, it kisses the route of the E 57, the main arterial road connecting northern Europe with southern Europe through the mountains of Macedonia. Preševo boasts a sizeable Albanian majority; Bujanovac, with an equal number of Serbs, Albanians and Roma, sits next to the town of Veliki Trnovac from where hailed Dusan 'Šiptar' Spasojević, conspirator in the assassination of Zoran Djindjić; and Medvedja is a majority Serbian town.

As well as being the pivotal area for the Balkan heroin trade, South Serbia had always been extremely poor. Lack of investment combined here with the collapse of traditional markets and commercial infrastructure. Kosovo and northern Macedonia, with which South Serbia's economy had been integrated for five hundred years, were suddenly cut off by the imposition of borders associated with the break-up of Yugoslavia and the Kosovo war. Official unemployment rates were ferociously high even by former Yugoslav standards.

Among the Kosovo Albanians, especially in the Kosovo Liberation Army, this territory was designated Eastern Kosovo, and with Serbs controlling northern Mitrovica, Albanian militants began demanding that this area be absorbed by Kosovo as a guarantee against any eventual incorporation of Mitrovica into Serbia. In the five-mile demilitarized zone where Kfor troops were supposedly maintaining order, a new organization, the UCPBM or Liberation

Army for Presheve, Bujanovac and Medvejda, gathered large numbers of Kalashnikovs and other weapons from the KLA and ramped up a low-level insurgency in early 2000 that had been sputtering along for a year or so.

Both the Serbian Government and NATO were swift to recognize the significant danger of an ethnic-based war breaking out in South Serbia, and in an unprecedented example of cooperation (unimaginable under Milošević) and following astute negotiations run by the Deputy Prime Minister, Nebojša Ćović, soon came up with the Konculj Agreement signed in May 2001. Eventually this allowed for not only the return of Yugoslav (Serbian) forces back into the region but also the creation of a multi-ethnic police force, considerable investment in the economic infrastructure (largely by the EU) and the reintegration of Albanian political parties into local and national political structures. Subsequent implementation faced some serious challenges, but as agreements in the Balkans go, it has proved relatively durable.

Unhappily, just as the UCPMB was scaling down its operations in South Serbia, the conflict in Macedonia was warming up. Indeed, the two events are not unrelated. The impoverished Albanian village of Tanuševci, just inside Macedonia on the border with Kosovo, was one of the bases through which weapons from the Kosovo Liberation Army were channelled to the UCPMB. Otherwise, the main function of this remote settlement was as one of the several hubs for cigarette smuggling from Macedonia's tobacco factories into Kosovo.

On hearing reports that Tanuševci had become a conduit for arms destined for Albanian insurgents in South Serbia, a Macedonian television team from the capital Skopje headed there to film a report. Arriving on 17 February 2001, they were promptly seized by the local Albanian militia who later identified themselves as members of the National Liberation Army (known confusingly but intentionally in Albanian as the UÇK, the same acronym used by the Kosovo Liberation Army).

The Macedonian government responded by sending armed police into Tanuševci, leading to several skirmishes. The NLA then ordered its troops to open up a proper front close to Tetovo, the main city in north-western Macedonia with a large Albanian population. Before long, the leader of the NLA, Ali Ahmeti, who had worked with the KLA in a logistics role during the Kosovo war, had set up his headquarters in the village of Šipkovici, in the mountains above Tetovo.

It soon became clear that while the Albanians of Macedonia had genuine grievances due to the discrimination they had suffered at the hands of the Macedonian authorities (although this was not comparable with the treatment that Milošević had meted out to Albanians in Kosovo), there was more to the Macedonian civil war than met the eye. Ahmeti and his followers had a history of rivalry with the DPA, the political party that had dominated in Macedonia's Albanian community until this point.

Western intelligence services and Macedonian journalists soon established that this intra-Albanian competition was a powerful driver behind the NLA's insurrection and that this was inspired at least in part by an attempt by some of Ahmeti's supporters to gain control of the cigarette smuggling trade which key members of the DPA had dominated until this point.

Not that the Slav Macedonian elite were renowned for clean hands. As soon as the fighting began, the Interior Minister, Ljube Boškovski, looked to deploy his special unit, the Lions, who had been trained by Legija's Red Berets and appeared to have adopted the Serbian team's moral code as well. Boškovski became the only participant in Macedonia's civil war to be indicted as a suspected war criminal by the Hague Tribunal.

One magazine claimed with some compelling documentation that senior Macedonian Government officials had financial interests in some of the brothels run by Albanians in the notorious western town of Velešta.

The familiar complex of criminal interests and ethnic rivalry was a catastrophe as potentially damaging as the war in Bosnia had been, a fact which was at least recognized by the myriad western security, political and non-governmental organizations stationed in the region. In consequence, international instances reacted much more swiftly and decisively in Macedonia to prevent the spread of the violence, and within a matter of months, the warring parties had signed the Ohrid Agreement, which regulated the political, cultural and linguistic status of Albanians in Macedonia, apparently satisfactorily. Overnight, Ali Ahmeti, who had only a year before been denounced as a terrorist by the United States, was appointed Deputy Prime Minister in a new government and welcomed at receptions at the American embassy in Skopje.

The number of deaths in Macedonia by the time of the Ohrid Agreement in August 2001 was in the region of 140, about half Macedonians and half Albanians. By the standards of Balkan conflict, this does not really qualify it as a war.

Perhaps most important in the framing of the peace agreement was the European Union's decision to allow Macedonia to bypass many of the hurdles which everyone else in the Balkans was required to overcome in order to obtain membership of the Union. From being at almost the back end of the queue, Macedonia was hurled up front to obtain a Stabilization and Association Agreement, one of the many stages through which aspiring members now needed to pass, and then finally in 2005 the most prized Candidate Status. Since then successive Macedonian governments have proved incapable of capitalizing on this rare privilege. Nonetheless, the European Union's decision to confer it showed clearly that Brussels was prepared to override its bureaucratic mechanism in favour of a highly strategic political end if this was deemed strictly necessary.

By the middle of the decade, the European Union had fulfilled its promise from 2003. All Balkan countries were on the path to membership at some point in the short to medium term. While not carrying the burden of having been participants in war, Bulgaria's and Romania's efforts to join were hampered by widespread crime and corruption. Nonetheless, understanding the value of having these two countries inside the tent rather than out, the EU agreed to their full membership in 2007.

The approach of the European Union was beginning to have positive effects even if these manifested themselves only in the wake of further tragedy. In October 2008, assassins planted a bomb under the car of Ivo Pukanić, editor of the Croatian investigative magazine *Nacional*, which killed him and one other. In response, the Croatian, Serbian and Bulgarian governments launched a cross-border investigation on an unprecedented scale, leading to the arrest and conviction of some the most notorious gangsters in the Balkans. Events such as these brought several Balkan governments who only a few years earlier were at war much closer together and, astonishingly, cross-border cooperation on a whole range of issues has become more effective than it has ever been in the modern history of south-eastern Europe.

As governments began to make progress on several fronts, one European diplomat even came up with the bright idea that Brussels might strive to admit all the remaining south-east European states into the Union on 28 June 2014, exactly one hundred years after the assassination of Archduke Franz Ferdinand. The EU would be able to claim that it was putting its final armed conflicts to rest, a century to the day after Great Power machinations in the Balkans had plunged the world into the first of its two great twentieth-century nightmares. The idea could have been designed as one of the most powerful political statements imaginable. In all probability the idea was simply too creative for the often stultifying institutions of Brussels.

Alexander Rondos, the diplomat who had suggested that the Balkan aspirants should join the EU in June 2014, was Greek. Until this point, Greece, especially during George Papandreou's tenure as Foreign Minister, had played a vital role not just in advancing the cause of south-eastern Europe but also in promoting the interests of its age-old enemy, Turkey. Indeed, it was Papandreou who smashed the adamantine cornerstone of Greek Government policy by lifting Athens' permanent objection to Turkish membership in 1999, a move of immense symbolic and practical importance.

So notwithstanding the murder of the journalist, Pukanić, in October 2008, the prospects for the Balkans looked rosier than they had for a long time. That grim event in a Zagreb car park was overshadowed, however, by a rather different one elsewhere – the collapse of the Lehman Brothers private investment bank, a development which exposed the unfathomable venality of the western banking system as it had mutated since the collapse of communism. The chain reaction to Lehman was to have a big impact on the economies of Europe and then upon the European Union itself.

One of the effects of Lehman was to place further strain on the unified monetary system of seventeen EU member states, the Euro. This then turned into a full-blown Euro crisis and Greece's apparent insolvency was at the centre of what threatened to become a global economic meltdown. The European Union, which for several years had been regarded as the key to promoting peace, stability and prosperity in the Balkans, was about to become extremely unstable itself.

Turkey had first applied for membership of the European Union in 1987. The obstacles in Ankara's ways were many and varied, reflecting fluctuating levels of hostility and suspicion among existing member states. As noted, this changed in 1999 when George Papandreou lifted Athens' long-standing objections to Turkey opening full negotiations.

It soon became obvious that several other countries had been happily sheltering behind the Greek veto as Germany, France and Austria, *inter alia*, started muttering about how the absorption of a country with a large Muslim population into the EU would be inappropriate. Berlin raised the possibility of Turkey contenting itself with a special relationship to Brussels and its institutions. The Vatican and the former French President, Valéry Giscard d'Estaing, to name but two, argued that the Lisbon Treaty should stipulate the European Union to be founded on traditions of Christianity (implying, presumably, that all other faith traditions were allowed there by special dispensation – the Ottoman *millet* system springs to mind).

Thus despite the lifting of the Greek veto on negotiations, it appeared that Turkey's path to Europe would continue to be blocked, especially after Cyprus was admitted to the EU in 2004 (the Cypriots have resurrected the veto on Turkey if no solution to the divided island acceptable to Nicosia is found).

What few people had anticipated, however, was the astonishing upheavals that would transform Turkey in the first decade of the new millennium.

At the start of the decade, the country was sinking in a quagmire of inflation and economic instability when interest rates on the spiralling lira reached 5,000 per cent. The lifting of the Greek veto had changed the foreign policy landscape, but domestically Turkey looked as chaotic and unmanageable as ever. Under the guidance of one of Turkey's most gifted economists, Kemal Derviş, then the Minister of Economic Development, Turkey inaugurated a reform programme in May 2001 which addressed some of the country's deeply ingrained structural malignancies, not least of which was the banking sector and the opportunistic and corrupt control that politicians from across the ideological spectrum had exploited for personal and professional gain.

At the time, Derviş's impact was regarded as almost miraculous (indeed, it still looks that way a decade later). Within a year, inflation, a constant irritant in the previous decades, settled at a manageable 12 per cent level while most sectors quickly registered high growth rates leading to a rapid reduction in unemployment and rising tax revenues. Turkey's influence as a regional economic centre led to a deepening of ties with the European Union – they had already signed a Customs Union in 1995. But it also developed into the pivotal trading hub in a region that took in most of the former Ottoman Empire (including the Balkans) as well as Ukraine and southern Russia.

Of equal significance was the concurrent transformation in Turkey's political landscape. The results of the November general elections in 2002 were a sensation. Only two parties overcame the 10 per cent hurdle that permits parliamentary representation in Turkey's restrictive proportional representation system. Derviş's Republic People's Party gained 10.7 per cent of the vote. But it was the success of the moderate Islamist Justice and Development Party (the AKP), which received just over 34 per cent of the vote, that triggered a political earthquake in Turkey.

This was the nightmare that the Kemalist establishment, especially the so-called Deep State, the military and security apparatus, had always feared, the emergence of a ruling party that was motivated by religious principle rather than secular ideology or corruption. At the time of the victory, its leader, Recep Tayyip Erdoğan, was banned from holding public office. But as only two parties passed the 10 per cent hurdle, this ensured that the AKP now had a thumping majority in the Meclis, almost two-thirds – almost but not quite enough to change the constitution. It was certainly easy to lift the ban on Erdoğan, and he was duly appointed Prime Minister.

The fear that the AKP would immediately start reversing the liberal political policies designed to accommodate the EU's accession criteria proved unfounded. The AKP removed the death penalty, allowed the first expansion of language rights for the minority Kurdish population and introduced policies to combat crime and corruption in the police and civil service. It also, in accordance with EU demands, constrained the ability of the military to influence both political and economic life.

From the EU's point of view, Turkey was doing what it had promised. The AKP was swiftly rewarded with the announcement in December 2002 that the EU had granted Turkey Candidate Status. Less than three years later, negotiations on accession were opened.

The US, Nato and Israel were less enamoured of the new direction in Turkish politics. The warning shot was fired in March 2003 when the Meclis voted against participating in the Iraq war or allowing Turkey's NATO allies to launch offensive operations from Turkish territory. The leadership of the AKP had been more accommodating – it had actually supported NATO's request. But its members demonstrated that this was now a rather different Turkey in matters of foreign policy and military affairs.

Yet the constituency with most to lose in the wake of the AKP's rise was not to be found abroad but at home in Turkey. This was the feared 'Deep State', the network of vested interests at whose heart lay the leadership of the Armed Forces, parts of the Security Services who were assisted by Turkey's ultra-right nationalist movement and, indeed, organized crime.

The battle between the AKP and the Deep State burst into public during 2007. The year began ominously with the murder of Hrant Dink, the Armenian newspaper editor, by his office in Istanbul. This assassination along with other nationalist-inspired murders in previous and subsequent months appeared designed to destabilize the government and prepare the ground for some form of military intervention. At the same time, parts of the judiciary also linked to the Deep State moved to ban the AKP through the constitutional courts.

In previous decades, few would have bet against the Deep State achieving its desired outcome. But on this occasion, it was outmanoeuvred by the AKP, which called a snap general election in July. At the polls, the AKP increased its vote to a staggering 47 per cent, giving it a huge popular mandate.

In an unrelated incident just before the elections, police in Istanbul came across a huge arms cache, which triggered a six-month-long investigation. This culminated in January 2008 with the first arrests in what subsequently became the most extensive police and security operation in Turkish history. The case was dubbed Ergenekon, which referred both to an ancient Turkic national myth and, in 2008, an alleged Deep State conspiracy to mount a coup against the elected AKP Government.

Four years later on and thousands have been arrested for perceived direct or alleged involvement in the Ergenekon conspiracy. This has become a battle royale for the soul and future direction of the Turkish state, which has taken on more sinister aspects the longer it has gone on. What began as a serious examination of a probably treasonable underground network has itself become a tool for stifling legitimate opposition to the AKP. The criminal justice system, the media, the military, the security services, the opposition parties and the police have all been subject to something akin to a purge. Those even suspected of disloyalty are at risk while new members of the civil service are increasingly likely to be AKP sympathizers or adherents to a religious education movement known as the Gülen Community, after its founder and spiritual guide, Fehtullah Gülen, who despite wielding enormous political and social influence inside Turkey has lived in self-imposed exile in Pennsylvania for several decades.

The baffling contradictions within the country are both heightening and mesmerizing. The centre of Istanbul is a swinging European metropolis with dynamic young entrepreneurs and artists dominating cultural life, demanding ever-greater personal freedom and deeply attached to the secular traditions of Kemalism.

The outskirts of the city, however, are changing. In 1960, Turkey had a population of 27 million people, 68 per cent of whom lived in the countryside. By the year 2000 that had grown to 68 million, two-thirds of whom lived in cities, above all in Istanbul. The cultural differences between the immigrants from Anatolia and the urban elite of western Turkey run very deep. Conservatism and modernism sit cheek-by-jowl often quite uncomfortably.

Even as it struggles with an immense and complex crisis of identity, Turkey's influence as a regional power is growing. Few countries are surrounded by so many neuralgic areas as Turkey – a divided Ukraine, Russia and the violent Caucasus, central Asia and Iran, the Middle East and the Maghreb convulsed by the Arab Spring, not to mention the permanent Israeli-Palestinian crisis.

Turkey's influence in all these regions is growing economically, politically and strategically – not for nothing do people refer to its new engagement as the New Ottomanism. This extends to the Balkans as well where Turkey has mounted a vigorous diplomatic and economic campaign to strengthen its influence in the region after several decades of decline. The charm offensive is by no means restricted to its confessional partners among the Bosniaks and Albanians. Ankara's presence is felt equally in Belgrade, Bucharest and Sofia.

This has been happening outside the framework of European Union negotiations. The desire to accede to the EU remains strong but has been tempered as Turkey watches the Union sink into an existential crisis borne of political and economic mismanagement.

For three decades, Greece, Turkey's traditional rival since the beginning of the nineteenth century, has enjoyed considerable advantages over its neighbour by dint of its membership in the EU. In the space of a frenetic eighteen months, the tables appear to have turned as Greece finds itself at the epicentre of the European calamity. The impact has already been disastrous for Greek society, but it may also have very serious consequences for the rest of the Balkans.

In the year preceding the adoption of the Euro as a physical currency on 1 January 2002, only one of the twelve participating countries, Luxembourg, could claim to have flawlessly met the four so-called convergence criteria for the Euro. Some animals were more equal than others in their transgression but none more so than Greece.

In its original 1998 assessment, the European Commission had ruled that Greece failed to meet any of the criteria. In many respects, this was unsurprising. The new democracy when it emerged from the Colonels' regime was still carrying huge debts from the profligate period of the dictatorship. Membership of the European Union in 1981 had again persuaded western banks to open up their purses with cheap loans while the rush of money into the country was augmented by subsidies and new grants from the European Union.

The result was a huge expansion of the public sector in the 1980s and early 1990s that included a bloated defence budget. The perceived Turkish threat ensured that over 4 per cent of its annual spending went on the military, in particular the purchase of new weapons. This was almost twice as much as any other European country, including the big northern spenders, Britain and France, paid out for defence every year.

What successive governments were signally unable to do was to increase their tax revenues, as the wealthy elites of Greece were past masters at manipulating the financial system to their benefit. Such was their influence of the political classes and the civil service that to a great extent they did not even have to move their money overseas to mask it. The banking system was thoroughly corrupted, as were the major infrastructure sectors, notably energy importation.

Equally disturbing was the 'flexibility' and unreliability of economic statistics in Greece. Those politicians who did feel like confronting the traditions of clientalism in the Greek state had few weapons at their disposal to actually prove what was going on even though it was obvious to everybody living there. Furthermore, their peers and the influence of vested economic interests proved an insuperable barrier to anyone with a crusading zeal who might have wanted to reform the system. Government ministers, for example, enjoyed lifetime immunity from prosecution, so there was little disincentive against engaging in corrupt practices if all one's colleagues were.

Ironically, joining the Euro was also a chance to impose rules on the Greek economy and budget that, it was hoped, would curb corrupt practices, tax evasion and fraud. Opinion polls indicated that popular support for joining the Euro stood at exceptionally high levels because voters believed it would start to erode the inherent iniquities of the system.

When Greece requested that the Commission's ruling from 1998 barring entry into the Eurozone be rescinded in 2000, Brussels agreed even though the debt-to-GDP ratio was still over 60 per cent. (It should be pointed out that the debt ratio of countries such as Belgium, Italy and Spain were also well beyond 60 per cent.) Similarly, Greek inflation had been reduced to acceptable levels partly because the government had lowered VAT for that specific purpose. As the Government in Athens later admitted, the books had been cooked and some of the claims that had been made were simply fraudulent.

As a member of the Euro, the Greek Government was able to borrow money at extremely low rates, the same, of course, as everybody else in the Eurozone. Because it was a member of the common currency, banks in Europe and America regarded the country as low risk on the assumption that its debts were ultimately guaranteed by the rest of Europe, Germany in particular. Banks fell over themselves to lend money to Greece with French financial institutions leading the way. More cunning enterprises like Goldman Sachs persuaded the Greek Government to take on more debt by using masking techniques, variations on the complex speculative mechanisms which were simultaneously undermining the very foundations of global finance.

Perhaps the greatest beneficiary of this sudden float of cash in southern Europe was Germany, whose export-oriented economy received a huge injection as the once-impoverished southern tier of the Eurozone started buying German.

Around the world, European diplomats and politicians proclaimed the virtues of 'European' values – and in principle these were impressive and they included a commitment to transparency and rectitude in commercial and political dealings, i.e., obeisance to the rule of law.

Much of it, alas, was overblown rhetoric. Inside the EU, examples abounded of fraudulent behaviour. For years, member states refused to blow the whistle on characters like Silvio Berlusconi in Italy, whose near monopoly of televisual and print news media was a disgrace, as was his habit of introducing legislation in parliament to circumvent the latest corruption charges brought against him in court. The Common Agricultural Policy, one of the unhappiest European political imaginings, developed into an especially rich source of fraud across the Union.

But in light of subsequent events when Greece's budgetary infrastructure hurtled towards collapse, the Greek-German relationship as it developed soon after the millennium was one of Europe's most humiliating moments. Not only did the German Government encourage companies like Siemens to sell billions of Euros' worth of substandard telecommunications equipment to Greece in the late nineties and early noughties—but also the company paid almost one billion Euros in bribes to Greek politicians to ensure these sales went through. Well may have the German press excoriated feckless spendthrift Greek politicians a decade later as Athens sought vast bailout funds to prevent a massive default. But those same media outlets would have done well to remind their audience that it was Germans who were enticing them into corruption. Probably the most scandalous event was the sale of four submarines (complete with a defective electronic steering system) to the Greek navy for a staggering €1.8 billion.

What would prove to be the icing on the cake, barely appreciated at the time, were the Olympic Games. When Athens had won the right in 1997 to hold the 2004 Games, the Government estimated the cost to the state would be some $1.5 billion. Like all other governments which are awarded the Olympic Games, it argued that the event would recoup much of that and, furthermore, this would be a valuable Keynesian exercise in urban regeneration. In fact, Olympic Games habitually saddle the host nation with a debt that is still being paid off decades later – some organizers deploy the money more effectively with regard to its social value but all end up losing money. Greece was no exception – the final cost was almost $16 billion, the largest single item that went towards the construction of its disastrous debt mountain.

The first warning signals that something was seriously amiss in Greece appeared in 2006. Some local and international economists began warning that Athens and the European Union should start to address the problem of Greek debt. Had the Eurozone acted rationally and moved to cauterize the issue, the subsequent crisis could have been avoided – the bottom line was that Greece accounted for 2 per cent of European GDP and 2 per cent of its public debt. The fact that the European Union, by some chalk the world's largest economy, was unable to nip this problem in the bud was a mark of its political immaturity. Disturbingly for the future, it also suggested the ease with which member states would adopt defensive, nationalist policies as soon as the financial strain began to tell. Europe's much vaunted 'values' of solidarity and cooperation proved to be much less durable than its capitals had so often claimed.

But before the Eurozone threatened to bring the global banking system to its knees, the Anglo-American financial markets triggered an infarct throughout the financial system. Even though the US and European governments acted as lenders of last resort to save the banks from consequences of the outrageous losses they had sustained due to their long-term speculative activity, the banking system was now extremely fragile and liquidity a problem everywhere. As the western economies started recovering in 2010 from the recession begun in 2008, the looming threat of a Greek debt default began to spook the financial markets. It dawned on Brussels, Berlin, London, Paris and Washington that if Greece were to default then this would likely result in a domino effect, bringing down Portugal, Italy, Ireland, Belgium and even France. Banks like Société Généràl, heavily exposed to the Greek debt, ran a very serious risk of collapse. So the fate of a small Balkan country suddenly threatened the world with economic disaster.

When George Papandreou defeated Kosta Karamanlis in October 2009, he immediately instructed his cabinet colleagues to start examining the accounts of their ministries. The reports he received were hair-raising – the Prime Minister knew that he would have to engage with the European Union, with the banks and with the International Monetary Fund. But he also appreciated that he had no choice but to inaugurate a root-and-branch reform of Greece's economy and its entire public administration.

He was not helped by the patronizing tone struck by fellow Eurozone politicians and, very soon after, their media. The entire crisis, it was argued, was the result of Greek mismanagement and their penchant for living off the fat of others. Very soon, the influential countries of the Eurozone were demanding the most draconian reforms if they were to refinance the Greek debt with a series of bailouts (the word *bailout* is in some respects unfortunate because it implies that Greece would simply be given cash to pay off its debts – in fact, these bailouts are government-backed loans at commercial rates off which the donor country would make money, as more than one embarrassed Eurozone finance minister admitted).

There were two major thrusts to the reforms. The first concerned public expenditure and taxation. On the one hand, Athens was compelled to slash public spending in a fashion which hit the most disenfranchised social classes with the power of an express train. The middle classes, too, faced unprecedented attacks on their living standards. Painful though it was, Papandreou simply had no choice – an exit from the Eurozone would have had a yet more disastrous impact on the population. He also tackled the issue of Greece's excessive military spending by ordering a 30 per cent cut in weapons purchases—much to the private chagrin not just of German and

French ministers but to US officials as well, as American manufacturers were responsible for 42 per cent of arms sales to Greece.

Papandreou made a concerted effort to crack down on one of the great Greek evils – tax evasion. He highlighted the obscene wealth that various sectors of society had accumulated while successfully hiding this from the authorities. The health service was particularly open to abuse where senior medical staff, including countless doctors and consultants, would augment their modest official salary with a regime of bribes taken from patients, hospitals and pharmaceutical companies that conferred huge material privilege on them. In 2011, the largest single investor in the bloated property markets of Mayfair and other parts of central London was made up of individuals from Italy and Greece, seeking to stash their money away from the prying eyes of their home tax authorities.

The assault on tax evasion met predictable resistance. But Papandreou's determination to use the crisis to uproot the still more sinister influence of oligarchs and organized crime groups was a still riskier strategy. For over a year, Papandreou juggled with the demands for deep budget cuts made by the EU, especially Germany, and by the IMF; the dramatic social protests triggered by those cuts; and the machinations of the oligarch and criminal classes, represented in public life by corruption politicians and influential media outlets.

He finally fell on 9 November 2011 after he had shocked Chancellor Merkel and President Sarkozy by announcing that he could not continue with the programme of reform unless this was backed by the electorate in a referendum.

'Capricious', 'unpredictable', 'unreliable' and 'ideologically driven' were just some of the more printable epithets hurled at George Papandreou during his final week as Greek Prime Minister. In fact, Papandreou had achieved as much as was humanly possible in his last days in office to ensure implementation of the Brussels plan for Greece. In doing so, not only was he doing Greece a favour in the long term, but also he was saving the EU's face.

Included in his legacy were some important innovations in the Greek political system, notably the decision to deploy a computer programme, Hephaestus, that could monitor tax collection and prevent tax evasion. Vested interests in the oil, banking and media industries bitterly opposed the introduction of this system for understandable reasons. A week after Papandreou left office, two respected think tanks, Eliamep (the Hellenic Foundation for European and Foreign Policy) and IOBE (the Foundation for Economic and Industrial Research), released their findings on corruption and tax evasion in the Greek economy. According to their report, a full 5–6 per cent of the GDP (€10–13 billion) was being lost to tax evaders every year, a figure which does not include monies lost to corruption. The economy's informal sector at between 25–28 per cent was the EU's highest according to the Paris-based Organization for Economic Cooperation and Development. In his resignation speech, Papandreou revealed how a pan-Balkan fuel-smuggling operation was losing Greece an estimated €3 billion annually. Papandreou spelt out exactly how damaging such criminal activities have been, all but naming those involved.

Behind this lay the real fear that the oligarch class in Greece was promoting the economic collapse of the country in order to further its long-term interests. The aim, it seems, was to pounce on the state assets which, under the various bailout plans, the Greek Government were obliged to privatize. With the domestic economy in free fall, the share price of these hugely valuable entities like the electric grid and the national lottery had been collapsing steadily in the previous two years. For example, the final 10 per cent of OTE, the Greek telecoms provider, was sold to Deutsche Telekom for €7 a share over the summer of 2011, down 75 per cent on its price three years earlier. This pattern was being repeated across all industries earmarked for privatization.

The oligarch conglomerates were waiting to scoop them up at anything up to less than a fifth of their real value – a critically poor financial return for the state but in five to ten years' time a bonanza for the purchasers. Some even appeared to be banking on Greece exiting the Euro so that they could then deploy the billions of Euros they had transferred into safe havens to purchase the assets for knock-down drachma prices.

Papandreou's PASOK administration was replaced by a unity coalition of PASOK, New Democracy and the far-right LAOS party. At its head stood an apolitical figure, the former Greek Central Bank Director, Lucas Papademos. In February 2012, the new Government had agreed to the draconian programme of cuts which the EU had insisted upon. The future looked exceptionally grim for a population whose living standards were sinking in the sand.

But although the EU's Prime Ministers signed off on an agreement which guaranteed Greece a second huge bailout (loan) of €130 billion in March 2012, the country's economic catastrophe was by no means over. The Greek tragedy had already placed unprecedented strains on the European Union before the end of the first act.

The millennium had begun in the Balkans with what looked like a simple contest: defeat corruption and organized crime and enter Europe. Bulgaria, Romania and Croatia made sufficient progress to satisfy Brussels of their achievements. Albania and the remaining territories of the former Yugoslavia had not yet been convinced. Nonetheless in March 2012, the EU's decision to confer Candidacy Status on Serbia and Kosovo*'s admittance to discussions among regional bodies suggested that a solution to the Kosovo problem might be in sight.

But it was Greece, paradoxically the only long-standing Balkan member of the European Union, which turned the situation on its head by unwittingly exposing many of the political and economic inadequacies of the EU. Strikingly, this did not diminish the value of EU membership in the eyes of other Balkan countries. Even Turkey, with its growing self-confidence and influence in the region, remained keen to join if it were allowed.

But the debt crisis had long before ceased to be a Greek crisis. It was now a regional, a European and, indeed, a global crisis.

GLOSSARY

ağas	Muslim nobles of the Ottoman Empire
andartes	Greek guerrilla bands
Ausgleich	the 'compromise', the agreement of 1867 creating the Dual Monarchy of Austria Hungary
Ban	Viceroy
başi-bözök	Ottoman irregular
beg/bey	Ottoman landowner
besa	word of honour among Albanians; cessation of vendetta
bošnjak	Bosniak
bošnjaštvo	Bosniakdom
boyar	Romanian aristocrat
čaršija	market/gossip-mongers
četa, *čete*	Serbian and Bulgarian guerrilla bands
četnik	Serb/Bulgarian guerrilla
Chetniks	Serbian nationalist movement during the Second World War
chorbadjii	well-to-do Bulgarian peasants and traders
clacă	feudal labour obligation in Wallachia and Moldavia
dahi	janissary leaders in the Belgrade pashalik

devşirme	culling of Christian children to serve in the Ottoman bureaucracy
dragoman	interpreter at the Ottoman court
enosis	unification with Greece
EO	External Organization, pro-Bulgarian wing of VMRO at the turn of the twentieth century
firman	imperial Ottoman decree
gjakmarrje	blood revenge (Albanian)
hajduk, hadjuci	Serb outlaw/s
Honvéd	Hungarian army
IO	Internal Organisation, autonomist wing of VMRO
Kapetanios, oi	commander/s of the communist-backed ELAS army
Kapos/kapoi	guerrilla leader/s in the Greek War of Independence
kirçali	nomadic bandits
klepht	Greek outlaw
kmet	feudal peasant
knez	Serb chieftain/s
kum	marriage witness
Megali idea	the Great Idea –the programme of a greater Greece
millet	nation or religious community in the Ottoman Empire
načertanije	Plan – the programme of a greater Serbia
nagodba	'Agreement' negotiated in 1868 between the Hungarians and Croats to regulate the status of the Croatian crown lands
narodniki	Russian populists
Paşa	Ottoman governor
Pashalik	Ottoman province
raya	Christian peasantry
Sabor	parliament in Croatia and Bosnia
serasker	senior army commander
şeria	Islamic code of law
Sipahi	Muslim landlords of the Ottoman Empire
softa	Muslim students in Istanbul
Sonderkommando	special unit

ulema	elders of Islamic hierarchy
Ustaşe	Croatian fascist movement
Vatan	Fatherland (Turkish)
Vilayet	Ottoman administrative region
VMRO	Internal Macedonian Revolutionary Organization
vojvoda	Military leader or duke (Serbian)
zadruga	extended Serbian family unit

NOTES

1 A confederacy of peasants: rebellion and revolution, 1804–66

1 *The Memoirs of Prota Matija Nenadović*, ed. Lovett F. Edwards, Oxford, 1969, p. 51.
2 Michael Boro Petrovich, *A History of Modern Serbia*: 1804–1918, New York, 1976, vol. I, pp. 28–9.
3 Ibid., p. 27.
4 Leopold Ranke, *The History of Servia and the Servian Revolution*, London, 1853, p. 36.
5 Ibid., p. 36.
6 Quoted in Duncan Wilson, *The Life and Times of Vuk Stefanovic Karadzic, 1787–1864*, Oxford, 1970, p. 42.
7 *The Memoirs of Prota Matija Nenadović*, op. cit., p. 157.
8 Lawrence P. Meriage, *Russia and the First Serbian Insurrection, 1804–1812*, New York and London, 1977.
9 Traian Stoianovich, 'The Pattern of Serbian Intellectual Evolution', *Comparative Studies in Society and History* (March 1959), p. 243.
10 Petrovich, op. cit., p. 84.
11 Slobodan Jovanović, *Iz istorije i književnosti*, Belgrade, 1931, vol. I, p. 70.
12 Ibid., p. 53.
13 Petrovich, op. cit., pp. 118–19.
14 Photios Chrysanthopoulos Photakos, *Apomnemoneumata peri tes Hellenikes Epanastaseos*, ed. Stavros Andropoulos, Athens, 1899, I, pp. 33–4.
15 Richard Clogg, *A Short History of Modern Greece* (2nd edn), Cambridge, 1986, p. 47.
16 Dennis N. Skiotis, 'Ali Pasha's Last Gamble', in *Hellenism and the Greek War of Liberation (1821–1830): Continuity and Change*, ed. Diamandouros, Thessaloniki, 1976, p. 97.

17 George Finlay, *A History of Greece from Its Conquest by the Romans to the Present Time, BC 146 to AD 1864*, Oxford, 1877, vol. VI, pp. 218–19.
18 John S. Koliopoulos, *Brigands with a Cause: Brigandage and Irredentism in Modern Greece, 1821–1912*, Oxford, 1987, p. 33.
19 Cited in John Th. Kakridis, 'The Ancient Greeks of the War of Independence', *Journal of Balkan Studies*, 4: 2 (1963), p. 252.
20 Douglas Dakin, *British and American Philhellenes in the Greek War of Independence, 1821–1833*, Thessaloniki, 1955, pp. 51–2.
21 William Mure, *Journal of a Tour in Greece and the Ionian Islands*, Edinburgh and London, 1842, ii, p. 216.
22 Quoted in C.M. Woodhouse, *The Philhellenes*, London, 1969, p. 46.
23 Ibid., p. 43.
24 C.M. Woodhouse, 'The Untoward Event: The Battle of Navarino 20 October 1827', in *Balkan Society in the Age of Greek Independence*, ed. Richard Clogg, London, 1981, p. 13.
25 Ibid., pp. 74–5.
26 John A. Petropoulos, *Politics and Statecraft in the Kingdom of Greece, 1833–1843*, Princeton, NJ, 1968, p. 19.
27 Ibid., p. 135.
28 Clogg, *A Short History of Modern Greece*, op. cit., p. 61.
29 Rudolf Horvat, *Ban Jelačić. Hrvatski pokret 1848*, Zagreb, 1990, p. 52.
30 Ibid., pp. 127–8.
31 Quoted in Josip Horvat, *Politička povijest Hrvatske*, Zagreb, 1989, p. 126.
32 Barbara Jelavich, *History of the Balkans: Eighteenth and Nineteenth Centuries*, Cambridge and New York, 1983, p. 262.
33 Ibid., p. 96.
34 Quoted in Josip Horvat, op. cit., p. 102.
35 Jaroslav Šidak, *Studije iz hrvatske povijesti za revolucije 1848–49*, Zagreb, 1979, p. 21.
36 David MacKenzie, *Hija Garasanin: Balkan Bismark*, New York, 1985, p. 95.
37 Josip Horvat, op. cit., p. 47.
38 Djordje Stratimirović, *Was ich erlebte: die Errinerungen von General von Stratimirović*, Vienna, 1910, p. 39.
39 István Deák, *The Revolution and the War of Independance, 1848–1849*, in *A History of Hungary*, eds. Peter F. Sugar, Pétar Havák, Tibor Frank, Bloomington, 1990, p. 220.
40 Quoted in Anðelko Mijatović, *Ban Jelačić*, Zagreb, 1990, p. 169.
41 Josip Horvat, op. cit., p. 137.
42 Vlad Georgescu, *The Romanians: A History*, Columbus, Ohio, 1991, p. 78.
43 Georgescu, op. cit., p. 99.

2 The realm of ruins: reform and decay, 1839–78

1 Bernard Lewis, *The Emergence of Modern Turkey*, London and New York, 1961, p. 98.
2 Ivo Andrić, *Omerpaša Latas*, Sarajevo, 1977, p. 45.
3 Ferdo Šišić, ed., *Bosna i Hercegovina za vezirovanje Omer-Paše Latase*,

Belgrade, 1938, p. 27.
4 Ibid., p. 67.
5 Ibid.
6 Andrić, op. cit., p. 10.
7 Ahmed Muradbegović, *Omer Paša Latas u Bosni, 1850–1852*, Zagreb, 1944, p. 66.
8 Šišić, op. cit., p. 302.
9 Ibid., p. 320.
10 Ibid., p. 317.
11 Ahmed S. Aličić, *Uredjenje Bosanskog Ejaleta od 1789. do 1878. Godine*, Sarajevo, 1983, p. 63.
12 Šišić, op. cit., pp. 289, 301.
13 Roderic H. Davison, *Reform in the Ottoman Empire, 1856–1876*, Princeton, NJ, 1963, p. 4.
14 Lord Kinross, *The Ottoman Centuries: The Rise and Fall of the Turkish Empire*, New York, 1970, p. 502.
15 Donald C. Blaisdell, *European Financial Control in the Ottoman Empire*, New York, 1929, p. 27.
16 Stanford J. Shaw, *History of the Ottoman Empire and Modern Turkey*, vol. II: *Reform, Revolution and Republic: The Rise of Modern Turkey, 1808–1975*, Cambridge, 1977, p. 94.
17 Davison, op. cit., p. 110.
18 Blaisdell, op. cit., p. 43, n. 47.
19 Charles Morawitz, *Les Finances de la Turquie*, Paris, 1902, p. 29.
20 J. Lewis Farley, *The Decline of Turkey, Financially and Politically*, London, 1875, p. 14.
21 Lewis, op. cit., p. 156.
22 Davison, op. cit., p. 3.
23 Şerif Mardin, *The Genesis of Young Ottoman Thought: A Study in the Modernization of Turkish Political Ideas*, Princeton, NJ, 1962, p. 15.
24 Ibid., p. 18.
25 Davison, op. cit., p. 69.
26 Quoted in Mardin, op. cit., p. 19.
27 Shaw, op. cit., p. 117.
28 Mardin, op. cit., pp. 3–4.
29 Davison, op. cit., p. 221.
30 Ibid., p. 62.
31 Quoted in Davison, ibid., p. 305.
32 Alexander van Gilferding, *Poezdka po Gercegovine, Bosnii i Staro Serbii*, Petersburg, 1859, p. 431.
33 Vaso Čubrilović, *Bosanski ustanak, 1875–1878*, Belgrade, 1930, p. 55.
34 Quoted in Mardin, op. cit., p. 110, n. 60.
35 Quoted in Davison, op. cit., p. 298.
36 Davison, ibid., p. 342.
37 Ivan Vazov, *Under the Yoke*, London, 1912, pp. 152–3.
38 Janarius A. MacGahan, *The Turkish Atrocities in Bulgaria*, Geneva, 1956, p. 44.
39 Ibid., p. 18.

40 Shaw, op. cit., p. 162.
41 L.S. Stavrianos, *Balkan Federation: A History of the Movement toward Balkan Unity in Modern Times*, Northampton, MA, 1942, p. 1.
42 Vazov, op. cit., p. 40.
43 Thomas A. Meininger, *The Formation of a Nationalist Bulgarian Intelligentsia, 1835–1878*, New York, 1987, p. 70.
44 C.E. Black, *The Establishment of Constitutional Government in Bulgaria*, Princeton, 1943, p. 19.
45 Fyodor Dostoyevsky, *Früher oder später muß Konstantinopel doch uns gehören*, in *Politische Schriften*, Munich, 1923, p. 363.
46 Joseph Rothschild, *East Central Europe between the Two World Wars*, Seattle, 1977, p. 332.
47 Quoted in Nikolai Genchev, *The Bulgarian National Revival Period*, Sofia, 1977, p. 122.
48 Meininger, op. cit., pp. 397–8.
49 Quoted in Black, op. cit., pp. 41–2.
50 Michael Boro Petrovich, *A History of Modern Serbia: 1804–1918*, vol. I, New York, 1976, p. 316.
51 Ibid., pp. 381–2.
52 B.H. Sumner, *Russia and the Balkans, 1870–1880*, Oxford, 1937, p. 177.
53 Quoted in Imanuel Geiss, *German Foreign Policy, 1871–1914*, London, 1976, p. 26.
54 Sumner, op. cit., p. 74.
55 Ibid., p. 75.
56 Gale Stokes, *Politics as Development: The Emergence of Political Parties in Nineteenth-Century Serbia*, Durham, NC, 1990, p. 111.

3 A maze of conspiracy: the southern Balkans, 1878–1914

1 Iselin Gundermann, *Berlin als Kongreßstadt*, Berlin, 1878, p. 54.
2 W.N. Medlicott, *A Diplomatic History of the Near Eastern Settlement, 1878–1880*, London, 1938, p. 39.
3 Ibid., p. 57.
4 Ibid., p. 71.
5 Gundermann, op. cit., p. 103.
6 Robert Howard Lord, 'The Congress of Berlin', in *Three Peace Congresses of the Nineteenth Century*, Cambridge, MA, 1917, p. 62.
7 Ibid., p. 61.
8 *Der Berliner Kongress von 1878: Die Politik der Grossmächte und die Probleme der Modernisierung in Südosteuropa in der zweiten Hälfte des 19. Jahrhunderts*, ed. Ralph Melville and Hans-Jürgen Schröder, Wiesbaden, 1982, p. 400.
9 From Gjërgj Fishta, *The Mountain Lute*, quoted in Robert Elsie, *History of Albanian Literature*, Boulder, CO, and New York, 1995, vol. I, p. 407.
10 Fikret Adanir, *Die Makedonische Frage: Ihre Entstehung und Entwicklung bis 1908*, Wiesbaden, 1979, p. 84.
11 Stavro Skendi, *The Albanian National Awakening, 1878–1912*, Princeton, NJ, 1967, p. 54.

12 Ibid., p. 61.
13 *Documents on the Struggle of the Macedonian People for Independence and a Nation State*, Skopje, 1985, vol. I, p. 267.
14 Richard Crampton, *Bulgaria 1878–1918: A History*, Boulder, CO, 1983, pp. 28–9.
15 Quoted in A. Michael Radin, *IMRO and the Macedonian Question*, Skopje, p. 19.
16 Algernon Blackwood, *Jimbo: A Fantasy*, London, 1915, p. 207, both quoted in Keith Brown, 'Of Meanings and Memories: The National Imagination in Macedonia', unpublished Ph.D. dissertation, University of Chicago, 1995, p. 57.
17 Quoted in Evangelos Kofos, *Greece and the Eastern Crisis, 1875–1878*, Thessaloniki, 1975, p. 252.
18 Josef Koetschet, *Aus Bosniens letzter Türkenzeit*, Wien and Leipzig, 1905.
19 *Kako je branjeno Sarajevo od Austrougarskog okupatora 19. Augusta 1878. godine* in *Otpor Austrougarskoj okupaciji 1878. godine u Bosni i Hercegovina*, ed. Milorad Ekmecic, Sarajevo, 1979, p. 363.
20 Muhsin Rizvić, *Književno stvaranje muslismanskih pisaca u Bosni i Hercegovini u doba austrougarske vladavine*, Sarajevo, 1973, p. 5.
21 Quoted in Slobodan Jovanović, *Iz istorije i književnosti*, Belgrade, 1931, vol. I, p. 425.
22 Quoted in Slobodan Jovanović, *Vlada Milana Obrenovića*, Belgrade, 1927, vol. II, p. 180.
23 Ibid., p. 183.
24 Ibid., p. 196.
25 A.F. Golowine, *Fürst Alexander I. von Bulgarien*, Vienna, 1896, p. 89.
26 July 15, *The Times*, 1879.
27 Crampton, op. cit., p. 57.
28 Egon Caesar Corti, *Alexander von Battenberg*, London, 1954, p. 161.
29 Quoted ibid., p. 164.
30 Golowine, op. cit., p. 279.
31 Jovanović, *Iz istorije i književnosti*, p. 273.
32 Branislav Nušić, *Pripovetke jednoga kaplar*, Belgrade, 1966, p. 72.
33 Quoted in Vojdan Černodrinski, *Makedonska Krvava Svadba* (Macedonian Blood Wedding), Act II, Scene I, Sofia, 1900.
34 N.C. Moutsopoulos, 'Une ville entre deux siècles', in *Salonique, 1850–1918: La Ville des Juifs et le réveil des Balkans*, ed. Gilles Veinstein, Paris, 1993, p. 28.
35 From an 1875 description quoted in Walter F. Weiker, *Ottoman Turks and the Jewish Polity: A History of the Jews in Turkey*, Lanham, MD, and London, p. 177.
36 Leon Sciaky, *Farewell to Salonika*, London and New York, 1946, p. 31.
37 Ibid., p. 15.
38 H.N. Brailsford, *Macedonia: Its Races and their Future*, London, 1906, pp. 36–7.
39 Michael Boris Petrovich, *A History of Modern Serbia: 1804–1918*, vol. I, New York, 1976, p. 480.
40 Nikos Kazantzakis, *Freedom and Death [Ho Kapetan Michales]*, New York, 1955, p. 117.

41 Ibid., pp. 58–9.
42 Quoted in Douglas Dakin, *The Unification of Greece, 1770–1923*, London, 1972, p. 152.
43 Brailsford, op. cit., p. 102.
44 From the dispatch of the Austrian Consul in Monastir, August Kral, to Foreign Minister Goluchowski, 11 March 1903, in *The Events of 1903 in Macedonia as Presented in European Diplomatic Correspondence*, ed. Angelos A. Chotzids, Basil C. Gounaris and Anna A. Panayotopoulou, Thessaloniki, 1993, pp. 47–8.
45 According to Shatev's memoirs, which are quoted in *Salonique 1850–1918*, ed. Veinstein, op. cit., pp. 134–5.
46 Ibid., p. 135.
47 Brailsford, op. cit., p. 149.
48 Ibid., p. 57.
49 From Tevfik Fikret's famous ode, 'Sis' (Mist), to Sultan Abdülhamid II's rule, *c.* 1897, quoted in Bernard Lewis, *The Emergence of Modern Turkey*, London, 1961, p. 206.
50 Douglas Dakin, *The Greek Struggle in Macedonia 1897–1913*, Thessaloniki, 1966, p. 126.
51 Adanir, op. cit., p. 207.
52 Gustav Hubka, *Die österreichisch-ungarische Offiziermission in Makedonien 1903–1909*, Vienna, 1910, pp. 32–4.
53 Dakin, *The Unification of Greece*, p. 169.
54 Adanir, op. cit., p. 210.
55 Sciaky, op. cit., p. 142.
56 The letter is quoted at greater length in a riveting passage in Adanir, op. cit., pp. 236–8.
57 Richard Davey, *The Sultan and his Subjects*, New York, 1897, vol. I, p. 197.
58 Charles Roden Buxton, *Turkey in Revolution*, London, 1908, p. 44.
59 Ernest Edmondson Ramsaur, Jr, *The Young Turks: Prelude to the Revolution of 1908*, New York, 1957, pp. 18, 116–30.
60 Dakin, *The Greek Struggle in Macedonia*, p. 142.
61 Quoted in Ramsaur, Jr, op. cit., New York, 1957, p. 130.
62 Quoted in Philip Mansel, *Constantinople: City of the World's Desire, 1453–1924*, London, 1995, p. 346.
63 Ibid.
64 Quoted in Paul Dumont and François Georgeon, 'La Révolution commence à Salonique', in Veinstein, op. cit., p. 235.
65 Ibid., p. 236.
66 Quoted in Adanir, op. cit., p. 248.
67 Sciaky, op. cit., p. 164.
68 Ibid., p. 178.
69 Quoted in Emanuel Skatula, *Válka na Balkáně: Válečné taženi Bulharska, Srbska, Řecka a Černé Hory proti Turecku*, Praha, 1913, p. 394.
70 'The Bulgarian Army in the Balkan Wars', in *East Central European Society and the Balkan Wars*, ed. Béla K. Király and Dimitrije Djordjević, Boulder, CO, 1987, p. 35.
71 *Handbook of the Bulgarian Army, 1909*, in *Armies of the Balkan States*, The

War Office, London, 1915, p. 3.

72 S. Victor Papacosma, *The Military in Greek Politics: The 1909 Coup d'Etat*, Kent, OH, 1977, p. 21.

73 Richard Crampton, *The Hollow Detente: Anglo-German Relations in the Balkans, 1911–1914*, London, 1979, p. 13.

74 L.S. Stavrianos, *Balkan Federation: A History of the Movement Toward Balkan Unity in Modern Times*, Hamden, CT, 1942, pp. 153–6.

75 Crampton, *The Hollow Detente*, op. cit., p. 11.

76 Quoted in Stavrianos, op. cit., p. 160.

77 Leon Trotsky, *The Balkan Wars, 1912–1913*, New York, 1980, pp. 224–5.

78 Skatula, op. cit., p. 448.

79 *Report of the International Commission to Inquire into the Causes and Conduct of the Balkan Wars*, Carnegie Endowment of International Peace, Washington, DC, 1914, p. 17.

80 Quoted in Skatula, op. cit., pp. 484–6.

81 Ibid., p. 81.

82 Trotsky, op. cit., pp. 62–3.

83 Quoted in Skatula, op. cit., p. 392.

84 Ibid., p. 170.

85 Quoted in Trotsky, op. cit., pp. 267–8.

86 Bernard Lory, '1912, les Hellènes entrent dans la ville', in Veinstein, op. cit., pp. 247–8.

87 Skatula, op. cit., p. 446

88 Carnegie Endowment, op. cit., p. 131.

89 Crampton, *The Hollow Detente*, pp. 90–1.

90 Skatula, op. cit., pp. 615–16.

91 Ibid., p. 66.

92 Ibid., p. 94.

93 Quoted in Stavrianos, op. cit., pp. 173–4.

4 The empire of illusions: the northern Balkans, 1878–1914

1 Veselin Masleše, *Mlada Bosna*, Sarajevo, 1990, pp. 51–2.

2 *Letters of James Joyce*, ed. Stuart Gilbert, London, 1957, p. 57.

3 Srećko M. Džaja, *Bosnien-Herzegowina in der österreichisch-ungarischen Epoche (1878–1918): Die Intelligentsia zwischen Tradition und Ideologie*, Munich, 1994, p. 193.

4 Mirjana Gross and Agneza Szabo, *Prema hrvatskome gradjanskom društvu*, Zagreb, 1992, p. 459.

5 Ksaver Šandor Gjalski, *U noći: Svagdašnja povijest iz hrvatskoga života*, Zagreb, 1913, pp. 135–9.

6 Ibid., pp. 131–2.

7 Stjepan Radić, *Moj politički životopis* in *Politicki spisi*, Zagreb, 1971, pp. 53–4.

8 Josip Horvat, *Politička povijest Hrvatske*, Zargreb, 1989, pp. 222–34.

9 Nikola Pašić, *Sloga Srbo-Hrvata*, Belgrade, 1995, p. 54.

10 Quoted by Zvonimir Kulundžić in his introduction to Radić, op. cit., p. 25.

11 Horvat, op. cit., pp. 222–34.

12 Testimony of Dr Jovan Paču, a Serb doctor from Zagreb, quoted in Vasilije Krestić, *Istorija Srba u Hrvatskoj i Slavoniji, 1848–1914*, Belgrade, 1991, pp. 353–4.
13 Josip Horvat, *Živjeti u Hrvatskoj. Zapisci iz nepovrata 1900–1941*, Zagreb, 1984, p. 26.
14 Radić, op. cit., p. 12.
15 Quoted in Horvat, *Politička povijest Hrvatske*, op. cit., pp. 276–7.
16 Martha M. Čupić-Amrein, *Die Opposition gegen die österreichisch-ungarische Herrschaft in Bosnien-Hercegovina (1878–1914)*, Bern, 1986, p. 97.
17 Robert J. Donia, *Islam under the Double Eagle: The Muslims of Bosnia and Hercegovina, 1878–1914*, New York, 1981, p. 182.
18 Ferdo Hauptmann, ed., *Borba Muslimana: Bosne i Hercegovine za vjersku vakufsko-mearifsku autonomiju*, Sarajevo, 1967, pp. 116–17.
19 Ibid., p. 122.
20 Donia, op. cit., p. xii.
21 'Imperial Edict of February 28, 1880', Appendix I in Peter F. Sugar, *Industrialisation of Bosnia-Hercegovina, 1878–1914*, Seattle, 1963, p. 223.
22 R.W. Seton-Watson, *The Southern Slav Question and the Habsburg Monarchy*, London, 1911, pp. 331–2.
23 J.M. Baernreither, *Fragmente eines politischen Tagebuches: die südslawische Frage und Österreich-Ungarn vor dem Weltkrieg*, Berlin, 1928, p. 277.
24 Robert Musil, *Der Mann ohne Eigenschaften*, Hamburg, 1978, vol. I, pp. 33–4.
25 Henry Wickham Steed, *Through Thirty Years, 1892–1922: A Personal Narrative*, London, 1924, vol. I, p. 191.
26 Ibid., p. 188.
27 Ibid., pp. 195–6.
28 Ibid., p. 196.
29 Quoted in Richard S. Geehr, *Karl Lueger, Mayor of Fin de Siècle Vienna*, Detroit, 1990, p. 200.
30 From Hitler's *Mein Kampf*, quoted in Johannes Hawlik, *Der Bürgerkaiser: Karl Lueger und seine Zeit*, Vienna, 1985, p. 196.
31 Samuel R. Williamson, *Austria-Hungary and the Origins of the First World War*, London, 1991, pp. 20–1.
32 Peter Schuster, *Henry Wickham Steed und die Habsburgermonarchie*, Vienna, 1970, p. 13.
33 Musil, op. cit., pp. 32–3.
34 Williamson, op. cit., p. 179.
35 Leo Tolstoy, *On the Annexation of Bosnia and Herzegovina by Austria*, Bristol, 1965, Part I (no page numbering).
36 Dušan Lončarević, *Jugoslawiens Enstehung*, Zürich, 1929, pp. 85–6.
37 Quoted in Wayne S. Vucinich, *Serbia between East and West: The Events of 1903–1908*, Stanford, CA, 1954, p. 182.
38 Baernreither, op. cit., p. 74.
39 Rudolf Kiszling, *Erzherzog Franz Ferdinand von Österreich-Este: Leben, Pläne und Wirken am Schicksalweg der Donaumonarchie*, Graz, 1953, p. 83.
40 Ibid., p. 94.

41 Luigi Albertini, *The Origins of the War of 1914*, Oxford, 1952, vol. II, p. 3.
42 Robert A. Kann, *Erzherzog Franz Ferdinand Studien*, Vienna, 1976, p. 31.
43 Quoted ibid., p. 19.
44 Gunther E. Rothenberg, *The Army of Francis Joseph*, West Lafayette, 1976, pp. 141–2.
45 Quoted ibid., p. 143.
46 Ibid., p. 144.
47 Franz Conrad von Hötzendorf, *Aus meiner Dienstzeit*, Wien, 1921, p. 57.
48 'I. Mémoire von Aehrenthal, 05.02.1907', in Solomon Wank, ed., *Aus dem Nachlaß Aehrenthal: Briefe und Dokumente zur österreichisch-ungarischen Innen- und Außenpolitik 1885–1912*, Graz, 1994, vol. II, p. 451.
49 Ibid.
50 'Franz Ferdinand an Aehrenthal, Dokument. 624', in Wank, ibid., p. 624 (emphasis in the original).
51 Quoted in Lončarević, op. cit., p. 241.
52 Lončarević, op. cit., pp. 304–5.
53 Vladimir Dedijer, *The Road to Sarajevo*, London, 1967, p. 371.
54 Lav Trotski, *Sarajevski atentat*, Belgrade, 1989, p. 7.
55 Dragoslav Ljubibratić, *Mlada Bosna i Sarajevski atentat*, Sarajevo, 1964, p. 47.
56 Dedijer, op. cit., p. 187.
57 Ljubibratić, op. cit., pp. 59–60.
58 Čupić-Amrein, op. cit., p. 381.
59 Vladimir Dedijer, *Sarajevo 1914*, Belgrade, 1966, p. 336.
60 Steed, op. cit., p. 307.
61 Quoted in Ljubibratić, op. cit., p. 41.
62 Gaćinović's essay in Trotsky, op. cit., p. 12.
63 David MacKenzie, *Apis: The Congenital Conspirator*, New York, 1989, p. 98.
64 Quoted in Ljubibratić, op. cit., p. 68.
65 Ibid., p. 77.
66 Tyska Utrikesministeriets, *Balkankonflikten: Krigshändelsernas förhistoria i dokumentarisk belysning: Vita Bok nr. 7*, Stockholm, 1941, p. 9.
67 Masleše, op. cit., p. 53.
68 Quoted ibid., p. 37.
69 Quoted in Dedijer, *The Road to Sarajevo*, op. cit., p. 18.
70 Samuel R. Williamson, Jr, 'Influence, Power, and the Policy Process: The Case of Franz Ferdinand, 1906–1914', in *Historical Journal*, vol. 17 (1974), p. 434.
71 Martin Pappenheim, *Gavrilo Princips Bekenntnisse*, Vienna, 1926, p. 6.

5 A house of wars: war and peace, 1914–24

1 Karl Kraus, *Die lețzten Tage der Menschheit*, Frankfurt-am-Main, 1986, p. 741.
2 Martin Gilbert, *First World War*, London, 1994, pp. 299–300.
3 Milorad Ekmečić, *Ratni ciljevi Srbije 1914*, Belgrade, 1990, p. 14.
4 Quoted in Imanuel Geiss, 'Origins of the First World War', in *The Origins of the First World War: Great Power Rivalry and German War Aims*, ed. H.W. Koch, London, 1972, p. 64.

5 Quoted in Gilbert, op. cit., pp. 33–4.
6 Sveta Milutinović, 'Kako se u Beogradu živelo u prvim danima svetskoga rata', in *Golgota i vaskrs Srbije, 1914–1915*, ed. Silvija Djurić and Vidosav Stevanović, Belgrade, 1986, p. 36.
7 Živan Živanović, 'Rat', in ibid., p. 52.
8 Tadija Pejović, 'Dvadeset šesti Juli 1914 . . .', in ibid., p. 32.
9 Svetozar A. Djordjević, 'Cerska bitka', in ibid., p. 56.
10 Henry Barby, *Avec l'armée Serbe*, Paris, 1918, p. 101.
11 Ibid., p. 102.
12 Emil Ludwig, *Der Kampf auf dem Balkan: Berichte aus der Türkei, Serbien und Griechenland, 1915–1916*, Berlin, 1916, pp. 64–6.
13 Commandant M. Larcher, *La Guerre turque dans la Guerre Mondiale*, Paris, 1926, p. 43.
14 *Proclamation of the Jihad*, Istanbul, 23 November 1914, quoted in Ahmed Emin, *Turkey in the World War*, New Haven, CT, 1930, pp. 174–5.
15 Lewis Einstein, *Inside Istanbul: A Diplomatist's Diary during the Dardanelles Expedition, April–September 1915*, London, 1917, p. 1.
16 Quoted in Ulrich Trumpener, *Germany and the Ottoman Empire: 1914–1918*, Princeton, NJ, 1968, p. 19.
17 Quoted in Carl Mühlmann, *Das deutsch-türkische Waffenbündnis im Weltkrieg*, Leipzig, 1940, p. 41.
18 Quoted in Gilbert, op. cit., p. 124.
19 Ibid.
20 Quoted in Larcher, op. cit., p. 65.
21 Emin, op. cit., p. 89.
22 Einstein, op. cit., p. 2.
23 Quoted in Larcher, op. cit., p. 101.
24 Einstein, op. cit., p. 4.
25 Quoted in Gilbert, op. cit., p. 167.
26 Erich J. Zürchner, *Turkey: A Modern History*, London, 1993, p. 130.
27 Ibid., p. 136.
28 Quoted in Emin, op. cit., p. 182.
29 Ibid., p. 242.
30 Quoted in David Mitrany, *The Effect of the War in Southeastern Europe*, New Haven, CT, 1936, p. 79.
31 Einstein, op. cit., p. 122.
32 Quoted in Gilbert, op. cit., pp. 201–2.
33 Josip Jeras, *Kroz Albaniju 1915–1916*, Belgrade, 1968, pp. 192–3.
34 Stephen Constant, *Foxy Ferdinand: 1861–1948, Tsar of Bulgaria*, London, 1979, p. 290.
35 Quoted ibid., p. 297.
36 Alan Palmer, *The Gardeners of Salonika*, London, 1965, p. 57.
37 Živko Avramovski, *Ratni ciljevi Bugarske i centralne sile, 1914–1918*, Belgrade, 1985, pp. 224–5.
38 Quoted in Stephane Groueff, *Crown of Thorns: The Reign of King Boris III of Bulgaria, 1918–1943*, Lanham, MD, 1987, pp. 74–5.
39 Quoted in John D. Bell, *Peasants in Power: Alexander Stamboliski and the*

Bulgarian Agrarian National Union, 1899–1923, Princeton, NJ, 1977, p. 115.
40 Richard Crampton, *Bulgaria 1878–1918: A History*, Boulder, CO, 1983, p. 433.
41 Karel J. Vopička, *Taje Balkánu*, Prague, 1927, p. 75.
42 Nicolas Basilesco, *La Roumanie dans la Guerre et dans la Paix*, Paris, 1919, p. 183n.
43 Palmer, op. cit.
44 Commandant M. Larcher, *La Grande Guerre dans les Balkans*, Paris, 1929, p. 122.
45 Vopička, op. cit., p. 108.
46 Basilesco, op. cit., p. 185.
47 Ivo J. Lederer, *Yugoslavia at the Paris Peace Conference: A Study in Frontiermaking*, New Haven, CT, 1963, p. 22.
48 Palmer, op. cit., p. 70.
49 Ibid., pp. 150–2.
50 Alexandra Yerolympos, 'La Part du feu', in *Salonique, 1850–1918*, ed. Gilles Veinstein, Paris, 1993, p. 263.
51 Alexander S. Mitrakos, *France in Greece during World War I: A Study in the Politics of Power*, Boulder, CO, 1992, pp. 113–14.
52 N. Kaltchas, *Introduction to the Constitutional History of Greece*, New York, 1940, p. 137.
53 Palmer, op. cit., p. 105.
54 Evangelos Spyropoulos, *The Greek Military (1909–1941) and the Greek Mutinies in the Middle East (1941–1944)*, Boulder, CO, 1993, p. 16.
55 Mitrakos, op. cit., pp. 181–2.
56 Mihailo Vojvodić and Dragoljub Živojanović, eds, *Veliki rat Srbije 1914–1918*, Belgrade, 1970, p. 401.
57 General Alfred Dieterich, *Weltkriegsende an der mazedonischen Front*, Berlin, 1925, pp. 26–7.
58 Quoted in Palmer, op. cit., p. 217.
59 Erich Ludendorff, *My War Memoirs, 1914–1918*, London, 1919, vol. II, p. 679.
60 Dieterich, op. cit., p. 14.
61 Palmer, op. cit., p. 215.
62 Dieterich, op. cit., p. 124.
63 Ibid., p. 226.
64 Konstantin Milanov Dŭngŭrski, 'Ne ste veche nikakŭv general i ministŭr', in *1918, Vojniskoto Vŭstanie: Sbornik ot dokumenti i spomeni*, ed. Dimitŭr Tishev, Sofia, 1968, pp. 271–2.
65 Crampton, op. cit., p. 480.
66 Ibid., p. 482.
67 Quoted in Petko M. Petkov, *The United States and Bulgaria in World War I*, New York, 1991, p. 50.
68 Quoted ibid., p. 55.
69 Quoted in Bell, op. cit., p. 135.
70 Harold Nicolson, *Peacemaking* (2nd edn), London, 1943, p. xiii.
71 Ibid., pp. 34–5.
72 Quoted in George Goldberg, *The Peace to end Peace*, London, 1970, p. 196.
73 Josip Horvat, *Politička povijest Hrvatske*, Zagreb, 1991, vol. II, p. 19.
74 Ivo Banac, *The National Question in Yugoslavia: Origins, History, Politics*,

Ithaca, NY, 1984, p. 129.
75 Quoted in Lederer, op. cit., p. 37.
76 Slobodan Jovanović, *Iz istorije i knjizevnosti, Sabrana dela*, vol. II, Pt I, Belgrade, 1991, p. 174.
77 Horvat, op. cit., vol. I, p. 379.
78 Nicolson, op. cit., p. 274.
79 Michael A. Ledeen, *The First Duce: D'Annunzio at Fiume*, Baltimore, MD, 1977, p. 13.
80 Quoted in Goldberg, op. cit., p. 170.
81 Ledeen, op. cit., p. 2.
82 J.N. MacDonald, *A Political Escapade: The Story of Fiume and D'Annunzio*, London, 1921, p. 94.
83 Quoted ibid., p. 67.
84 Leeden, op. cit., p. vii.
85 Quoted in N. Petsalis-Diomidis, *Greece at the Paris Peace Conference*, Thessaloniki, 1979, pp. 198–9.
86 Quoted in Alexandros A. Pallis, *Greece's Anatolian Venture – and After: A Survey of the Diplomatic and Political Aspects of the Greek Expedition to Asia Minor (1915–1922)*, London, 1937, p. 22.
87 Ibid., pp. 23–5.
88 Quoted in Michael Llewellyn Smith, *Ionian Vision: Greece in Asia Minor 1919–1922*, London, 1973, p. 80.
89 Richard Clogg, *A Short History of Modern Greece*, Cambridge, 1979, p. 121.
90 Llewellyn Smith, op. cit., p. 89.
91 Quoted ibid., p. 89.
92 Quoted in Petsalis-Diomedes, op. cit., p. 208.
93 Quoted in Harold Temperley, ed., *A History of the Paris Peace Conference*, London, 1925, vol. VI, p. 72.
94 Vamik D. Voltan and Norman Itzkowitz, *The Immortal Atatürk: A Psychobiography*, Chicago, 1984, p. 152.
95 Llewellyn Smith, op. cit., p. 138.
96 Dimitri Pentzopoulos, *The Balkan Exchange of Minorities and its Impact on Greece*, Paris, 1962, p. 44.
97 Quoted in Llewellyn Smith, op. cit., p. 214.
98 Ibid., p. 276.
99 Quoted in Marjorie Housepian Dobkin, *Smyrna 1922: Destruction of a City*, New York, 1966, p. 173.
100 Ibid., p. 103.
101 Quoted ibid., p. 121.
102 Ibid., pp. 133–4.
103 Ibid., p. 150.
104 *Daily Mail*, 16 September 1922.

6 The palaces of deceit: the royal dictatorships, 1923–41

1 Quoted in Dimitri Pentzopoulos, *The Balkan Exchange of Minorities and its Impact upon Greece*, Paris, 1962, p. 96.

2 Quoted ibid.
3 Ibid., p. 101.
4 Joseph Rothschild, *East Central Europe Between The Two Wars*, Seattle, 1974, p. 210.
5 Quoted in Stephane Groueff, *Crown of Thorns: The Reign of King Boris III of Bulgaria, 1918–1943*, Lanham, MD, 1987, p. 77.
6 Ibid., p. 76.
7 Quoted in Franz Borkenau, *World Communism*, Ann Arbor, MI, 1962, p. 240.
8 Quoted in Groueff, op. cit., p. 131.
9 J. Swire, *Bulgarian Conspiracy*, London, 1939, p. 176.
10 Ivan Meštrović, *Uspomene na političke ljude i događaje*, Buenos Aires, 1961, p. 152.
11 Quoted in Josip Horvat, *Politička Povijest Hrvatske*, Zagreb, 1989, vol. II, pp. 303–4.
12 Ibid., p. 306.
13 Reproduced in full, ibid., pp. 318–19.
14 Quoted in Zvonimir Kulundžić, *Atentat na Stjepana Radića*, Zagreb, 1967, pp. 335–6.
15 Quoted in Ferdo Čulinović, *Jugoslavija između dva rata*, Zagreb, 1961, vol. I, pp. 525–7.
16 Ibid., p. 529.
17 Faik Konitza, *Albania: The Rock Garden of Southeastern Europe and Other Essays*, Boston, 1957, p. 150.
18 Bernd Jürgen Fischer, *King Zog and the Struggle for Stability in Albania*, New York, 1984, p. 119.
19 Quoted in Nicolas J. Costa, *Albania: A European Enigma*, New York, 1995, p. 34.
20 Quoted in Giovanni Zamboni, *Mussolinis Expansionspolitik auf dem Balkan: Italiens Albanienpolitik vom* I. *zum II. Tiranapakt im Rahmen des italienisch-jugoslawischen Interessenkonflikts u. der italienischen 'imperialen' Bestrebungen in Südosteuropa*, Hamburg, 1984, p. 4.
21 Quoted in Fischer, op. cit., p. 97.
22 Ramadan Marmullaku, *Albania and the Albanians*, London, 1975, p. 38.
23 Fischer, op. cit., p. 92.
24 Quoted ibid., p. 99.
25 Kočo Racin, 'Na Struga dukjan da imam . . .', from the collection *Beli mugri*, Skopje, 1953.
26 Derek H. Aldcroft and Steven Morewood, *Economic Change in Eastern Europe since 1918*, Aldershot, 1995, p. 53.
27 Dieter Petzina, 'Germany and the Great Depression', *Journal of Contemporary History*, 4: 4 (1969), p. 61.
28 Rothschild, op. cit., p. 23.
29 Meštrović, op. cit., p. 250.
30 Quoted in Bogdan Krizman, *Pavelić i ustaše*, Zagreb, 1978, p. 57.
31 Josip Horvat, *Hrvatski panoptikum*, Zagreb, 1965, p. 223.
32 Quoted in Meštrović, op. cit., p. 223.
33 Quoted in Krizman, op. cit., p. 118.

34 Aleksa Djilas, *The Contested Country: Yugoslav Unity and Communist Revolution, 1919–1953*, Cambridge, 1991, pp. 109–10.
35 Meštrović, op. cit., p. 262.
36 Quoted in D. Lukać, *Tre i rahj i zemlje jugoisto ne Evrope*, vol. I: *1933–1936*, Belgrade, 1982, p. 211.
37 Quoted in Groueff, op. cit., p. 243.
38 Lukać, op. cit., p. 337.
39 Paul D. Quinlan, *The Playboy King: Carol II of Romania*, Westport, CT, 1995, p. 69.
40 R.G. Waldeck, *Athene Palace: Hitler's New Order comes to Rumania*, London, 1943, p. 35.
41 Nicholas M. Nagy-Talavera, *The Green Shirts and Others: A History of Fascism in Hungary and Rumania*, Stanford, CA, 1980, p. 255.
42 Quoted in Nagy-Talavera, op. cit., p. 266.
43 Ibid., p. 247.
44 A.L. Easterman, *King Carol, Hitler and Lupescu*, London, 1942, pp. 229–30.
45 Quoted in Andreas Hillgruber, *Hitler, König Carol und Marschall Antonescu*, Wiesbaden, 1954, p. 9.
46 Waldeck, op. cit., p. 14.
47 Henry L. Roberts, *Rumania: Political Problems of an Agrarian State*, New Haven, CT, 1951, p. 201.
48 Quoted ibid., p. 199, n.
49 Quoted in Nagy-Talavera, op. cit., p. 292.
50 Quoted ibid., p. 295.
51 Dov B. Lungu, *Romania and the Great Powers, 1933–1940*, Durham, 1989, p. 220.
52 Waldeck, op. cit., p. 76.
53 Mario Cervi, *The Hollow Legions: Mussolini's Blunder in Greece, 1940–1941*, London, 1972, p. 7.
54 Quoted in P.J. Vatikiotis, *Popular Autocracy in Greece, 1936–41: A Political Biography of General Ioannis Metaxas*, London, 1998, p. 177.
55 Hugh Gibson, ed., *The Ciano Diaries, 1939–43*, New York, 1946, p. 300.
56 Ibid., pp. 301–2.
57 Vatikiotis, op. cit., p. 177.
58 Cervi, op. cit., p. 71.
59 Gibson, op. cit., 306.
60 Costas N. Hadjipateras and Maria S. Fafalios, *Greece 1940–41, Eyewitnessed*, Athens, 1995.
61 Ibid., p. 327.
62 Cervi, op. cit., pp. 194–5.
63 Quoted in Martin van Crefeld, *Hitler's Strategy 1940–1941: The Balkan Clue*, London, 1973, p. 46.
64 Corey Ford, *Donovan of OSS*, London, 1971, p. 100.
65 Joseph Goebbels, *Tagebücher*, ed. Ralf Georg Reuth, Munich, 1993, vol. IV, p. 1511.
66 Franz Halder, *Kriegstagebuch*, Stuttgart, 1963, vol. II, p. 183.
67 Quoted in van Crefeld, op. cit., p. 82.

68 Ibid., p. 86.
69 *New York Times*, 23 November 1940.
70 Winston Churchill, *The Second World War*, London, 1961, vol. V, pp. 148–9.
71 Quoted in Groueff, op. cit., p. 286.
72 Quoted in Ford, op. cit., p. 103.
73 Ferdo Čulinović, *27. Marta*, Zagreb, 1961, p. 258.
74 Ford, op. cit., p. 103, n.
75 Quoted in Čulinović, op. cit., pp. 278–9.
76 Quoted ibid., p. 305.
77 Ljubo Boban, *Sporazum Cvetković-Maček*, Zagreb, 1965, p. 378.

7 City of the dead: occupation, genocide, liberation, civil war, 1941–9

1 Quoted in Hagen Fleischer, 'Searching for the "Fruits of Victory"', in *Greece during the War*, ed. Ion Iatrides, Thessaloniki, 1976.
2 Walter Drechsel-Ritschel, *Erinnerungen an Griechenland: Kriegserlebnisse der Jahre 1941–1944*, Aachen, 1995, p. 13.
3 Quoted in Mark Mazower, *Inside Hitler's Greece: The Experience of Occupation, 1941–44*, London, 1993, p. 24.
4 Report of the Turkish News Agency, Ulus, 3 July 1941. Quoted in Janusz Piekalkiewicz, *Krieg auf dem Balkan, 1940–1945*, Munich, 1984, p. 123.
5 Jeanne Tsatsos, *The Sword's Fierce Edge: A Journal of the Occupation of Greece, 1941–1944*, New York, 1969, pp. 12–13.
6 Mazower, op. cit., p. 37.
7 Quoted in Hagen Fleischer, *Im Kreuzschatten der Mächte Griechenland 1941–1944*, Frankfurt, 1986, p. 116.
8 Ibid., p. 82.
9 Ibid., p. 134.
10 Quoted in Dominique Eudes, *The Kapetanios: Partisans and Civil War in Greece, 1943–1949*, London, 1972, p. 6.
11 Quoted in Piekalkiewicz, op. cit., p.129.
12 From Dr Stevan Moljević's memorandum on 'Homogeneous Serbia', quoted in Jozo Tomasevich, *The Chetniks: War and Revolution in Yugoslavia, 1941–1945*, Stanford, CA, 1975, p. 167.
13 Eyewitness quoted in Walter Manoschek, *'Serbien ist judenfrei': Militärische Besatzungspolitik und Judenvernichtung in Serbien 1941/42*, Munich, 1993, p. 157.
14 Ibid.
15 Zvonimir Vučković, *Sećanje iz rata*, London, 1980, p. 100.
16 Desanka Maksimović, *Pesme*, Belgrade, 1989, pp. 165–7.
17 Quoted in Tomasevich, op. cit., p. 148.
18 'Testimony of Derviš Bačića', quoted in Vladimir Dedijer and Antun Miletić, *Genocid nad Muslimana*, Sarajevo, 1990, pp. 138–9.
19 Milovan Djilas, *Wartime: With Tito and the Partisans*, London, 1977, p. 140.
20 Quoted in Milko Riffer, *Grad mrtvih: Jasenovac 1943*, Zagreb, 1946, pp. 19–20.
21 R.G. Waldeck, *Athene Palace Bucharest: Hitler's New Order Comes to Rumania*, London, 1943, p. 216.

22 Josef Goebbels, *Tagebücher*, Munich, 1994, vol. IV, p. 1524.
23 Frederick B. Chary, *The Bulgarian Jews and the Final Solution, 1940–1944*, Pittsburgh, 1972, p. xiii.
24 *The Crimes of the Fascist Occupants and their Collaborators against Jews in Yugoslavia*, ed. Zdenko Löwenthal, Belgrade, 1957, p. 65.
25 Quoted in Bogdan Krizman, *Pavelić izmedju Hitlera i Mussolinija*, Zagreb, 1980, p. 117.
26 From the Nuremberg trials, quoted in Ladislaus Hory and Martin Broszat, *Der kroatische Ustascha-Staat, 1941–1945*, Stuttgart, 1964, p. 101.
27 Manoschek, op. cit., p. 63.
28 Löwenthal, op. cit., pp. 41–2.
29 Quoted in Christopher R. Browning, *Fateful Months: Essays on the Emergence of the Final Solution*, New York, 1985, p. 51.
30 Ibid.
31 Ibid., pp. 79–80.
32 Löwenthal, op. cit., pp. 30–1.
33 Ibid., p. 32.
34 Chary, op. cit., p. 57.
35 Alexander Matkovski, *A History of the Macedonian Jews*, Skopje, 1985, p. 132.
36 Ibid., pp. 142–3.
37 Ibid., p. 151.
38 Chary, op. cit., p. 151.
39 Michael Matsas, *The Illusion of Safety: The Story of the Greek Jews during the Second World War*, New York, 1997, pp. 264–5.
40 Erika Kounio-Amariglio, *Damit es die ganze Welt erfährt: von Saloniki nach Auschwitz und zurück*, Konstanz, 1996, p. 37.
41 Ibid., pp. 37–8.
42 Ibid., p. 40.
43 Matsas, op. cit., pp. 34–5.
44 Kounio-Amariglio, op. cit., p. 47.
45 Ibid., p. 48.
46 Ibid., p. 52.
47 Ibid., p. 53.
48 Ibid., p. 57.
49 Ibid., p. 59.
50 Ibid., p. 71.
51 Ibid., p. 78.
52 Ibid., p. 71.
53 Ibid., p. 109.
54 Quoted in Diane Shaver Clemens, *Yalta*, New York, 1970, p. 33.
55 Quoted in Piekalkiewicz, op. cit., p. 228.
56 Hugh Seton-Watson, [check reference]
57 Hugh Seton-Watson, *The East European Revolution*, New York, 1951, p. 205.
58 Winston Churchill, *Triumph and Tragedy*, London, 1954, p, 198
59 Quoted in Geir Lundestad, *The American Non-policy towards Eastern Europe, 1943–47*, Oslo, 1978, p. 233.
60 Robert Wolff, *The Balkans in Our Time*, London, 1956, pp. 287–8.

61 Elizabeth Barker, *Truce in the Balkans*, London, 1948, pp. 84–5.
62 Ibid., p. 97.
63 *Dimitrov wastes No Bullets: Nikola Petkov: The Test Case*, 1948, London, p. [check reference]
64 Barker, op. cit., p. 49.
65 Seton-Watson, *The East European Revolution*, op. cit., p. 217.
66 Barker, op. cit., p. 78.
67 Quoted in Paul Vergnet and Jean Bernard-Derosne, *L'Affaire Petkov*, Paris, 1948, pp. 146–7.
68 Milovan Djilas, *Razgovori sa Staljinom*, Belgrade, 1990, p. 51.
69 Piekalkiewicz, op. cit., p. 309.
70 Dimitrije Djordjevic, *Scars and Memories: Four Lives in One Lifetime*, New York, 1994, p. 234.
71 Ibid., from the Preface (unpaginated).
72 John R. Lampe, *Yugoslavia as History: Twice There was a Country*, Cambridge, 1996, p. 234.
73 Djilas, *Razgovori sa Staljinom*,op. cit., pp. 59–60.
74 Seton-Watson, *The East European Revolution*, p. 347.
75 Djilas, *Razgovori sa Staljinom*, op. cit., p. 61.
76 Quoted in Fernando Claudin, *The Communist Movement from Comintern to Cominform*, Harmondsworth, 1975, p. 490.
77 C.M. Woodhouse, *Apple of Discord: A Survey of Recent Greek Politics in their International Setting*, London, 1948, pp. 204–5.
78 Ibid., pp. 55–7.
79 Eudes, op. cit., p. 190.
80 Daniel Yergin, *Shattered Peace: The Origins of the Cold War and the National Security State*, Harmondsworth, 1980, p. 280.
81 Ibid., pp. 281–2.
82 Djilas, *Razgovori sa Staljinom*, op. cit., p. 116.
83 David H. Close, *The Origins of the Greek Civil War*, London, 1995, p. 214.

8 Prisons of history: communism and militarism, 1949–89

1 Vera Kržišnik-Bukić, *Cazinska buna 1950*, Sarajevo, 1991, p. 3.
2 Ibid., p. 79.
3 Milovan Djilas, *Rise and Fall*, New York, 1985, pp. 72–3.
4 Quoted in Ghiţa Ionescu, *Communism in Rumania, 1944–62*, London, 1964.
5 Quoted in Dennis Deletant, *Communist terror in Romania: Çheorghiu-Dej and the Police State, 1948–1965*, London 1998, p. 139.
6 Gizella Hervay, quoted in *The Facts behind the Danube Black Sea Canal*, http://www.hungary.com/corvinus/genoci/genoci03.htm.
7 Deletant, op. cit., pp. 202–3.
8 Ibid., p. 206.
9 Georgi Markov, *The Truth that Killed*, London, 1983, pp. 46–8.
10 Quoted in J.F. Brown, *Bulgaria under Communist Rule*, London, 1972, pp. 253–4.
11 Quoted in Peter R. Prifti, *Socialist Albania since 1944: Domestic and Foreign*

Developments, Cambridge, 1978, p. 182.
12 *The Artful Albanian: The Memoirs of Enver Hoxha*, ed. Jon Halliday, London, 1986, pp. 333–4.
13 Quoted in William E. Griffith, *Albania and the Sino-Soviet Rift*, Cambridge, MA, 1963, pp. 319– 20.
14 Prifti, op. cit., p. 29.
15 Arshi Pipa, *Albanian Stalinism: Ideo-political Aspects*, Boulder, CO, 1990, p. 20.
16 Interview with Liam McDowall, Thessaloniki, 12 February 1999.
17 Prifti, op. cit., p. 64.
18 Quoted in Paul Lendvai, *Eagles in Cobwebs: Nationalism and Communism in the Balkans*, New York, 1969, p. 194.
19 Enver Hoxha, *The Khrushchevites: Memoirs*, Tirana, 1980, pp. 99–100.
20 Prifti, op. cit., p. 164.
21 Interview with Fatos Lubonja, Tirana, 14 July 1997.
22 Interview with Fatos Lubonja, Tirana, 9 February 1999.
23 Fatos Lubonja, *The Second Sentence*, New York, 1999.
24 Interview with Fatos Lubonja, Tirana, 14 July 1997.
25 Elez Biberaj, *Albania: A Socialist Maverick*, Boulder, CO, 1990, p. 15.
26 Pipa, op. cit., p. 5.
27 Kosta Čavoški, *Tito: Tehnologija vlasti*, Belgrade, 1990, pp. 18–19.
28 Miko Tripalo, *Hrvatsko proljeće*, Zagreb, 1989, p. 20.
29 Ibid., p. 22.
30 Djilas, op. cit., p. 349.
31 Ibid., p. 361.
32 Darko Bekić, *Jugoslavija u hladnom ratu*, Zagreb, 1988, p. 582.
33 Tripalo, op. cit., pp. 69–70.
34 Lendvai, op. cit., p. 161.
35 Dennison Rusinow, *The Yugoslav Experiment, 1948–1974*, pp. 187–8.
36 Lendvai, op. cit., p. 162.
37 *Jun-Lipanj 1968, Dokumenti*, Zagreb, 1968, pp. 56–7.
38 Rusinow, op. cit., p. 234.
39 Ibid., p. 236.
40 Tripalo, op. cit., p. 93.
41 Quoted in Francine Friedman, *The Bosnian Muslims: Denial of a Nation*, Boulder, CO, 1996, p. 159.
42 Steven L. Burg and Paul S. Shoup, *The War in Bosnia-Herzegovina: Ethnic Conflict and International Intervention*, New York, 1999, p. 41.
43 Rusinow, op. cit., p. 204.
44 Ibid., p. 250.
45 Ante Cuvalo, *The Croatian National Movement, 1966–1972*, New York, 1990, p. 45.
46 Tripalo, op. cit., p. 23.
47 Ibid., p. 29.
48 Slavoljub Djukić, *Slom srpskih liberala: Tehnologija politickih obracuna Josipa Broza*, Belgrade, 1990, p. 25.
49 Ibid., p. 40.
50 Quoted in Deletant, op. cit., p. 195, §71.

51 Quoted in Mary Ellen Fischer, *Nicolae Ceauşescu: A Study in Political Leadership*, Boulder, CO, 1989, p. 143.
52 Ibid., pp. 143–4.
53 Dennis Deletant, *Ceauşescu and the Securitate: Coercion and Dissent in Romania, 1965–1989*, London, 1995, p. 180.
54 Fischer, op. cit., p. 144.
55 Lendvai, op. cit., p. 302.
56 Ibid., p. 265.
57 Quoted in Fischer, op. cit., p. 127.
58 Silviu Brucan, *The Wasted Generation: Memoirs of the Romanian Journey from Capitalism to Socialism and Back*, Boulder, CO, 1993, pp. 108–9.
59 Augustin Buzura, *Refuges*, Boulder, CO, 1994, p. 160.
60 Ibid., pp. 44–5.
61 Ibid., p. 450.
62 From *Monarhia de Drept Dialectic: a doua versiune a memoriilor lui Belu Zilber*, quoted in Gail Kligman, *The Politics of Duplicity: Controlling Reproduction in Ceauşescu's Romania*, London, 1998, p. 42.
63 Quoted in Deletant, *Ceauşescu*, op. cit., p. 332.
64 Ibid., p. 235.
65 Deletant, op. cit., pp. 244–5.
66 Vlad Georgescu, *The Romanians: A History*, Columbus, OH, 1991, p. 260.
67 Conversation, December 1987.
68 Deletant, op. cit., p. 311.
69 Quoted in Feroz Ahmad, *The Making of Modern Turkey*, London, 1993, p. 130.
70 Nicole and Hugh Pope, *Turkey Unveiled: Atatürk and After*, London, 1997, pp. 86–7.
71 Ahmad, op. cit., p. 109.
72 Erik J. Zürcher, *Turkey: A Modern History*, London, 1993, p. 235.
73 Ibid., p. 239.
74 Quoted in Ahmad, op. cit., p. 123.
75 Feroz Ahmad, *The Turkish Experiment in Democracy*, London, 1977, pp. 160–1.
76 Ahmad, *The Making of Modern Turkey*, op. cit., p. 130.
77 Quoted ibid., p. 131.
78 Christopher Hitchens, *Hostage to History: Cyprus from the Ottomans to Kissinger*, New York, 1989, p. 53.
79 Ibid., p. 37.
80 Nancy Crawshaw, *The Cyprus Revolt: An Account of the Struggle for Union with Greece*, London, 1978, p. 137.
81 Quoted ibid., p. 132.
82 Barbara Jelavich, *History of the Balkans*, vol. II: *Twentieth Century*, Cambridge, 1983, p. 407.
83 Quoted in Richard Clogg, 'The Ideology of the "Revolution of 21 April 1967"', in *Greece under Military Rule*, ed. Richard Clogg and George Yannopoulos, New York, 1972, p. 37.
84 Thanos Veremis, *The Military in Greek Politics: From Independence to Democracy*, London, 1997, p. 161.

85 John R. Lampe, *Yugoslavia as History: Twice There Was a Country*, Cantab., 1996, p. 317.
86 Quoted in Silber, Little, op. cit., p. 30.
87 Ivan Stambolić, *Put u bespuće*, Belgrade, 1995, p. 120.
88 Laura Silber and Allan Little, *The Death of Yugoslavia*, London, 1995, p. 66.
89 See Chapter 5.
90 See Chapter 8.
91 Ivan Stambolić, in conversation with the author, June 1995.
92 See Chapter 7.
93 Interview with author, Zagreb, 4 June 1995.
94 See Chapter 8.
95 Borisav Jović, *Poslednji dani SFRJ: Izvodi iz dnevnika*, Belgrade, 1995, p. 309.
96 Misha Glenny, *The Fall of Yugoslavia*, London, 1992, p. 60.
97 The location was replete with irony. Almost two decades earlier, Tito called the top leadership here to denounce the liberal Croatian Party leadership and launch the crushing of the Croatian Spring, the move that ended hopes for a democratic solution of the national question.
98 See Chapter 6.

9 The Balkan vortex: nationalism, war and NATO, 1989–99

1 Marie-Janine Calic, *Der Krieg in Bosnien-Hercegovina: Ursachen, Konfliktstrukturen, Internationale Lösungsversuche*, Frankfurt, 1995, p. 225.
2 A.J.P. Taylor, *The Struggle for Mastery in Europe, 1848–1914*, London, 1954, p. 252.
3 Calic, op. cit., p. 17.
4 Glenny, op. cit., p. 165.
5 Silber & Little, op. cit., p. 319.
6 Glenny, op. cit., p. 158.
7 In conversation with the author, April 1993.
8 The author was present for this conversation. Koljevic committed suicide three and half years later.
9 In conversation with the author.
10 In conversation with the author, April 1995.
11 In conversation with the author, 1991.
12 Maria Todorova, *Imagining the Balkans*, New York, 1997, p. 185.

Epilogue: The swinging doors: Europe, crime and economic crisis, 1999–2012

1 Quoted in P. H. Liotta, Cindy R. Jebb, *Mapping Macedonia, Idea and Identity*, Santa Barbara, 2004, p. 35.
2 Simon Jenkins, columnist for *The Guardian*, consistently hostile to Blair.
3 Phillip Stephens, columnist for *The Financial Times*, generally sympathetic to Blair.
4 Andrew Rawnsley, political editor of *The Observer*.
5 Anthony Seldon, Blair's unofficial biographer, moderately sceptical.
6 Peter Wilby, 'Man Without a Shadow', *The Guardian*, London, 4 May 2007.

7 In conversation with the author.
8 BND Kosovo Intelligence Report, 22 Feb 2005, www.wikileaks.org/wiki/BND_Kosovo_intelligence_report,_22_Feb_2005.
9 Information furnished to the author by a senior American diplomat who had been briefed on the CIA operation.
10 In south Belgrade, the district housing the capital's largest military base.
11 Miloš Vasić, *Atentat na Zorana*, Belgrade, 2005, p. 25.
12 Ibid., p. 17.
13 Misha Glenny, 'The Death of Djindjić', *The New York Review of Books*, vol. 50, no. 12, 2003.
14 For more details on HVIDRA, see Vesna Bojičić-Dželilović, *Peace on Whose Terms? War Veterans' Associations in Bosnia and Hercegovina*, LSE 2004, www.brad.ac.uk/acad/twe/papers/BojicicDzelilovic,_Vesna_War_Veteran_Associations_in_Bosnia.pdf.
15 The one predominantly Muslim country anywhere in the world where 9/11 was greeted with spontaneous mass demonstrations in solidarity with the United States was Kosovo.
16 Interview with the NGO European Stability Initiative, 12 January 2012, www.esiweb.org/enlargement/?cat=110#awp::?cat=110.

BIBLIOGRAPHY

Adanir, Fikret, *Die Makedonische Frage: Ihre Entstehung und Entwicklung bis 1908*, Wiesbaden, 1979.

Ahmad, Feroz, *The Young Turks: The Committee of Union and Progress in Turkish Politics, 1908–1914*, Oxford, 1969.

Ahmad, Feroz, *The Turkish Experiment in Democracy*, London, 1977.

Aldcroft, Derek H. and Morewood, Steven, *Economic Change in Eastern Europe since 1918*, Aldershot, 1995.

Aličiæ, Ahmed S., *Uredjenje bosanskog ejaleta od 1789. do 1878.* godine, Sarajevo, 1983.

Albertini, Luigi, *The Origins of the War of 1914*, 2 vols., Oxford, 1952.

Aleksiev, Aleksandar, *Vojdan Černodrinski*, Skopje, 1974.

Andrić, Ivo, *Omerpaša Latas*, 1977, Sarajevo.

Armies of the Balkan States, The War Office, London, 1915.

Auty, Phyllis, *Tito: A Biography*, London, 1970.

Avramovski, Živko, *Ratni ciljevi Bugarske i centralne sile, 1914–1918*, Belgrade, 1985.

Baernreither, J. M., *Fragmente eines politischen Tagebuches: die südslawische Frage und Österreich-Ungarn vor dem Weltkrieg*, Berlin, 1928.

Balić, Smail, *Das unbekannte Bosnien: Europa's Brücke zur Islamischen Welt*, Vienna, 1992.

Banac, Ivo, *The National Question in Yugoslavia: Origins, History, Politics*, Ithaca, 1984.

Barac, Antun, *Pet Stoljeća Hrvatske Književnosti*, Zagreb, 1968.

Barby, Henry, *Avec L'Armée Serbe: De l'Ultimatum Autrichien l'Invasion de la Serbie*, Paris, 1918.

Barker, Elisabeth, *British Policy in South-East Europe in the Second World War*,

London, 1976.
Barker, Elisabeth, *Truce in the Balkans*, London, 1948.
Basch, Antonín, *The Danube Basin and the German Economic Sphere*, London, 1944.
Basilesco, Nicolas, *La Roumanie dans la Guerre et dans la Paix*, Paris, 1919.
Bauer, Otto, *Die Nationalitätenfrage und die Sozialdemokratie*, Vienna, 1907.
Bekić, Darko, *Jugoslavija u hladnom ratu: Odnosi s velikim silama 1949–1955*, Zagreb, 1988.
Bell, John D., *Peasants in Power: Alexander Stamboliski and the Bulgarian Agrarian National Union, 1899–1923*, Princeton, NJ, 1977.
Benbassa, Esther and Rodrigue, Aron, *The Jews of the Balkans: The Judeo-Spanish Community, 15th to 20th Centuries*, Oxford, 1995.
Biberaj, Elez, *Albania: A Socialist Maverick*, Boulder, CO, 1990.
Black, C. E., *The Establishment of Constitutional Government in Bulgaria*, Princeton, 1943.
Blaisdell, Donald C., *European Financial Control in the Ottoman Empire*, New York, 1929.
Blinkhorn, Martin and Veremis, Thanos, *Modern Greece: Nationalism and Nationality*, Athens, 1990.
Boban, Ljubo, *Sporazum Cvetković-Maček*, Zagreb, MI, 1965.
Borkenau, Franz, *World Communism*, Franz Borkenau, Ann Arbor, MI, 1962.
Brailsford, H. N., *Macedonia: Its Races and their Future*, London, 1906.
Braude, Benjamin and Lewis, Bernard, eds., *Christians and Jews in the Ottoman Empire: The Functioning of a Plural Society*, New York, 1982.
Brown, J. F., *Bulgaria under Communist Rule*, London, 1971.
Brown, Keith, *Of Meanings and Memories: The National Imagination in Macedonia*, unpublished Ph.D. dissertation, University of Chicago, 1995.
Browning, Christopher R., *Fateful Months: Essays on the Emergence of the Final Solution*, New York, 1985.
Brucan, Silviu, *The Wasted Generation*, Boulder, 1993.
Burg, Steven L. and Shoup, Paul S., *The War in Bosnia-Herzegovina: Ethnic Conflict and International Intervention*, New York, 1999.
Buxton, Charles Roden, *Turkey in Revolution*, London, 1908.
Buzura, Augustin, *Refuges*, Boulder, 1994.
Calic, Marie-Janine, *Der Krieg in Bosnien-Hercegovina: Ursachen, Konfliktstrukturen, Internationale Lösungsversuche*, Frankfurt-am-Main, 1995.
Carnegie Endowment for International Peace, *Report of the International Commission to Inquire into the Causes and Conduct of the Balkan Wars*, Washington, D.C., 1914.
Čavoški, Kosta, *Tito: Tehnologija vlasti*, Belgrade, 1990.
Černodrinski, Vojdan, *Makedonska Krvava Svadba*, Sofia, 1900.
Cervi, Mario, *The Hollow Legions: Mussolini's Blunder in Greece, 1940–1941*, London, 1972.
Chary, Frederick B., *The Bulgarian Jews and the Final Solution*, Pittsburgh, 1972.
Chirot, Daniel, ed., *The Origins of Backwardness in Eastern Europe: Economics and Politics from the Middle Ages until the Early Twentieth Century*, Berkeley, CA, 1989.

Choliolčev, Christo, Mack, Karlheinz and Suppan, Arnold eds., *Zeitgeist und Umfeld nationalrevolutionär Idelogien: Zur Typologie des Illyrismus*, Arnold Suppan in *Nationalrevolutionäre Bewegungen in Südosteuropa im 19. Jahrhundert*, Vienna, 1992.

Chotzidis, Angelos A., Gounaris, Basil C. and Panayotopoulou, Anna A., eds., *The Events of 1903 in Macedonia as Presented in European Diplomatic Correspondence*, Thessaloniki, 1993.

Churchill, Winston, *The Second World War*, 6 Vols., Harmondsworth, 1961.

Claudin, Fernando, *The Communist Movement: From Comintern to Cominform*, Harmondsworth, 1971.

Clemens, Diane Shaver, *Yalta*, New York, 1970.

Clogg, Richard and Yannopoulos, George, eds., *Greece under Military Rule*, New York, 1972.

Clogg, Richard, ed., *The Movement for Greek Independence*, London, 1976.

Clogg, Richard, ed., *Balkan Society in the Age of Greek Independence*, London, 1981.

Clogg, Richard, *A Short History of Modern Greece*, Cantab., 1986.

Close, David H., *The Origins of the Greek Civil War*, London, 1995.

Coppa, Frank J., *The Italian Wars of Independence*, London, 1992.

Corti, Egon Caesar Conte, *Alexander of Battenberg*, London, 1954.

Constant, Stephen, *Foxy Ferdinand: 1861–1948, Tsar of Bulgaria*, London, 1979.

Costa, Nicolas J., *Albania: A European Enigma*, New York, 1995.

Crampton, Richard, *The Hollow Detente: Anglo-German Relations in the Balkans, 1911–1914*, London, 1979.

Crampton, Richard, *Bulgaria 1878–1918: A History*, Boulder, 1983.

Crawshaw, Nancy, *The Cyprus Revolt: An Account of the Struggle for Union with Greece*, London, 1978.

van Crefeld, Martin L., *Hitler's Strategy 1940–1941: The Balkan Clue*, Cantab., 1973.

Cvijić, Jovan, *Remarks on the Ethnography of the Macedonian Slavs*, New York, 1906.

Čubrilović, Vaso, *Bosanski ustanak, 1875–1878*, Belgrade, 1930.

Čubrilović, Vaso ed., *Svetska ekonomska kriza, 1929–1934*, Belgrade, 1976.

Čulinović, Ferdo, *Dvadeset Sedmi Mart*, Zagreb, 1961.

Čulinović, Ferdo, *Jugoslavija izmedju dva rata*, Zagreb, 1961.

Čupić-Amrein, Martha M., *Die Opposition gegen die österreichisch-ungarische Herrschaft in Bosnien-Hercegovina (1878–1914)*, Bern, 1986.

Cuvalo, Ante, *The Croatian National Movement: 1966–1972*, New York, 1990.

Dadrian, Vahakn N., *The History of the Armenian Genocide*, Providence, RI, 1995.

Dakin, Douglas, *British and American Philhellenes in the Greek War of Independence, 1821–1833*, Thessaloniki, 1955, p. 51–52.

Dakin, Douglas, *The Greek Struggle in Macedonia 1897–1913*, Thessaloniki, 1966.

Dakin, Douglas, *The Unification of Greece, 1970–1923*, London, 1972.

Davey, Richard, *The Sultan and His Subjects*, New York, 1897.

Davison, Roderic H., *Reform in the Ottoman Empire, 1856–1876*, Princeton, 1963.

Dedijer, Vladimir, *Sarajevo 1914*, Belgrade, 1966.

Dedijer, Vladimir, *The Road to Sarajevo*, London, 1967.

Dedijer, Vladimir, *Književnost i istorija*, Belgrade, 1985.
Dedijer, Vladimir, and Miletić, Antun, *Genocid nad Muslimana*, Sarajevo, 1990.
Deletant, Dennis, *Ceauşescu and the* Securitate*: Coercion and Dissent in Romania, 1965–1989*, London, 1995.
Deletant, Dennis, *Communist Terror in Romania: Gheorghiu-Dej and the Police State, 1948–1965*, London, 1998.
Deretić, Jovan, *Kratka istorija srpske književnosti*, Belgrade, 1990.
Despatalović, Elinor Murray, *Ljudevit Gaj and the Illyrian Movement*, New York, 1975.
Diamandouros et al., *Hellenism and the First Greek War of Liberation (1821–1830): Continuity and Change*, Thessaloniki, 1976.
Dieterich, Alfred, *Weltkriegsende an der mazedonischen Front*, Berlin, 1926.
Dinev, Angel, *Ilindenskata epoja*, 2 vols., Bitola 1987.
Djilas, Aleksa, *The Contested Country: Yugoslav Unity and Communist Revolution, 1919–1953*, Cambridge, 1991.
Djilas, Milovan, *Wartime: With Tito and the Partisans*, London, 1977.
Djilas, Milovan, *Tito: The Story from Inside*, London, 1981.
Djilas, Milovan, *Rise and Fall*, New York, 1985.
Djilas, Milovan, *Razgovori sa Staljinom*, Belgrade 1990.
Djordjević, Dimitrije, *Scars and Memory: Four Lives in One Lifetime*, New York, 1997.
Djukić, Slavoljub, *Slom srpskih liberala: Tehnologija političkij obračuna Josipa Broza*, Belgrade, 1990.
Djukić, Slavoljub, *Izmedju slave i anateme: politička biografija Slobodana Miloševića*, Belgrade, 1994.
Djurić, Silvija and Stevanović, Vidosav, eds., *Golgota i vaskrs Srbije 1914–1915*, 2 vols., Belgrade, 1986.
Documents on the Struggle of the Macedonian People for Independence and a Nation State, Vol. I, Skopje, 1985.
Doklestić, Ljubiša, *Kroz Historiju Makedonije*, Zagreb, 1964.
Domanović, Radoje, *Stradije i druge satire*, Belgrade, 1963.
Donia, Robert J., *Islam under the Double Eagle: The Muslims of Bosnia and Hercegovina, 1878–1914*, New York, 1981.
Donia, Robert J. and Fine, John V. A., *Bosnia and Hercegovina: A Tradition Betrayed*, New York, 1994.
Dotoyevsky, Fyodor, *Politische Schriften*, Munich, 1923.
Dragnich, Alex N., *The First Yugoslavia: Search for a Viable Political System*, Stanford, 1983.
Dragoitschewa, Zola, *Von der Niederlage bis zum Sieg: Aufzeichnungen einer bulgarischen Revolutionärin*, Vienna, 1983.
Drechsel-Ritschel, Walter, *Erinnerungen an Griechenland: Kriegserlebnisse der Jahre 1941–1944*, Aachen, 1995.
Durham, Edith, *High Albania*, London, 1909.
Džaja, Srećko M., *Bosnien-Herzegowina in der österreichisch-ungarischen Epoche (1878–1918): Die Intelligentsia zwischen Tradition und Ideologie*, Munich, 1994.
Easterman, A. L., *King Carol, Hitler and Lupescu*, London, 1942.
Einstein, Lewis, *Inside Constantinople: A Diplomatist's Diary during the*

Dardanelles Expedition, April-September 1915, London, 1917.
Einzig, Paul, *Bloodless Invasion: German Economic Penetration into the Danubian States and the Balkans*, London, 1938.
Ekmečić, Milorad, *Ustanak u Bosni, 1875–1878*, Sarajevo, 1960.
Ekmečić, Milorad ed., *Otpor Austrougarskoj okupaciji 1878. godine u Bosni i Hercegovini*, 1979.
Ekmečić, Milorad, *Ratni ciljevi Srbije 1914*, Belgrade, 1990.
Elsie, Robert, *History of Albanian Literature*, Boulder, 1995.
Emin, Ahmed, *Turkey in the World War*, New Haven, 1930.
Esdaile, Charles J., *The Wars of Napoleon*, London, 1995.
Eudes, Dominique, *The Kapetanios: Partisans and Civil War in Greece, 1943–1949*, London 1972.
Evans, Arthur J., *Through Bosnia and the Herzegovina on Foot during the Insurrection, August and September, 1875*, London, 1877.
Fabius, J., *Zes maanden in Albanië*, Amsterdam, 1991.
Farley, J. Lewis, *The Decline of Turkey, Financially and Politically*, London, 1875.
Fischer, Bernd Jürgen, *King Zog and the Struggle for Stability in Albania*, New York, 1984.
Fischer, Mary Ellen, *Nicolae Ceauşescu: A Study in Political Leadership*, Boulder, 1989.
Finlay, George, *A History of Greece from Its Conquest by the Romans to the Present Time, BC 146 to AD 1864, Vol. VI The Greek Revolution, Part I, AD 1821–1827*, Oxford, 1877.
Fleischer, Hagen, *Im Kreuzschatten der Mächte: Griechenland 1941–1944 (Okkupation-Resistance-Kollaboration)*, Frankfurt-am-Main, 1986.
Ford, Corey, *Donovan of OSS*, London, 1971.
Frazee, Charles A., *The Orthodox Church and Independent Greece 1821–1833*, Cantab., 1969.
Friedman, Francine, *The Bosnian Muslims: Denial of a Nation*, Boulder, 1996.
Galbraith, J. K., *The Great Crash 1929*, New York, 1955.
Geehr, Richard S., *Karl Lueger, Mayor of Fin de Si cle Vienna*, Detroit, 1990.
Geiss, Imanuel, *German Foreign Policy, 1871–1914*, London, 1976.
Georgescu, Vlad, *The Romanians: A History*, Columbus, 1991.
Genchev, Nikolai, *The Bulgarian National Revival Period*, Sofia, 1977.
Gerõ, András, *Modern Hungarian Society in the Making: The Unfinished Experience*, Budapest, 1995.
Geshkoff, Theodore, *Balkan Union, A Road to Peace in South Eastern Europe*, New York, 1940.
Gibson, Hugh, ed., *The Ciano Diaries, 1939–43*, New York, 1946.
Gilberg, Trond, *Nationalism and Communism in Romania: The Rise and Fall of Ceauşescu's Personal Dictatorship*, Boulder, 1990.
Gilbert, Martin, *First World War*, London, 1994.
Gilbert, Stuart, ed., *Letters of James Joyce*, London, 1957.
van Gilferding, Alexander, *Poezdka po Gercegovine, Bosnii i Staro Serbii*, St. Petersburg, 1859.
Gjaski, Ksaver Šandor, *U noći: Svagdašnja povijest iz hrvatskoga života*, Zagreb, 1913.

Glenny, Misha, *The Fall of Yugoslavia*, London, 1992.
Goebbels, Joseph, *Tagebücher*, Vol. 4., Munich, 1992.
Goldberg, George, *The Peace to End Peace: The Paris Peace Conference of 1919*, London, 1970.
Goldsworthy, Vesna, *Inventing Ruritania: The Imperialism of the Imagination*, London, 1998.
Golowine, A. F., *Fürst Alexander I. von Bulgarien*, Vienna, 1896.
Gooch, G. P., *Before the War: Studies in Diplomacy*, London, 1936.
Griffith, William E., *Albania and the Sino-Soviet Rift*, Cambridge, 1963.
Gross, Hermann, *Die wirtschaftliche Bedeutung Südosteuropas für das deutsche Reich*, Berlin, 1938.
Gross, Mirjana and Szabo, Agneza, *Prema hrvatskome gradjanskom Društvu*, Zagreb, 1992.
Groueff, Stephane, *Crown of Thorns: The Reign of King Boris III of Bulgaria, 1918–1943*, Lanham, 1987.
Gundermann, Iselin, *Berlin als Kongreßstadt, 1878*, Berlin, 1978.
Güntekin, R. N., *The Autobiography of a Turkish Girl*, London, 1949.
Hadjipateras, Costas N. and Fafalios, Maria S., *Greece 1940–41, Eyewitnessed*, Athens, 1995.
Hagen, Walter, *Die geheime Front: Organisation, Personen und Aktionen des Deutschen Geheimdienstes*, Vienna, 1950.
Halder, Franz, *Kriegstagebuch*, Vol. 2, Stuttgart, 1963.
Halliday, Jon ed., *The Artful Albanian: The Memoirs of Enver Hoxha*, London, 1986.
Hauptmann, Ferdo, ed., *Borba Muslimana Bosne i Hercegovine za vjersku vakuf-sko-mearifsku autonomiju*, Sarajevo, 1967.
Hawlik, Johannes, *Der Bürgerkaiser: Karl Lueger und seine Zeit*, Vienna, 1985.
Hilberg, Raul, *The Destruction of the European Jews*, New York, 1985.
Hillgruber, Andreas, *Hitler, König Carol und Marschall Antonescu*, Wiesbaden, 1954.
Hibbeln, Ewald, *Codreanu und die Eiserne Garde*, Siegen, 1984.
Hitchens, Christopher, *Hostage to History: Cyprus from the Ottomans to Kissinger*, New York, 1989.
Hitchins, Keith, *Rumania 1866–1947*, Oxford, 1995.
Hoptner, J. B., *Yugoslavia in Crisis, 1934–1941*, New York, 1962.
Horvat, Josip, *Hrvatski panoptikum*, Zagreb, 1965.
Horvat, Josip, *Živjeti u Hrvatskoj. Zapisci iz nepovrata 1900–1941*, Zagreb, 1984.
Horvat, Josip, *Politička Povijest Hrvatske*, Zagreb, 1989.
Horvat, Rudolf, *Ban Jelačić. Hrvatski pokret 1848.*, Zagreb, 1990.
von Hötzendorf, Feldmarschall Franz Conrad, *Aus meiner Dienstzeit: 1906–1918, Erster Band: Die Zeit der Annexionskrise, 1906–1909*, Vienna, 1921.
Hory, Ladislaus and Broszat, Martin, *Der kroatische Ustascha-Staat 1941–45*, Stuttgart, 1964.
Hösch, Edgar, *Geschichte der Balkanländer: Von der Frühzeit bis zur Gegenwart*, Munich, 1995.
Housepian Dobkin, Marjorie, *Smyrna 1922: Destruction of a City*, New York, 1966.

Hoxha, Enver, *The Khrushchevites: Memoirs*, Tirana, 1980.
Hubka, Gustav, *Die österreichisch-ungarische Offiziermission in Makedonien 1903–1909*, Vienna, 1910.
von Huhn, Major A., *The Struggle of the Bulgarians for National Independence under Prince Alexander*, London, 1886.
Hünigen, Gisela, *Nikolaj Pavlovič Ignat ev und die russische Balkanpolitik, 1875–1878*, Göttingen, 1968.
Iatrides, John O. and Wrigley, Linda, *Greece at the Crossroads: The Civil War and Its Legacy*, University Park, PA, 1995.
Imamović, Mustafa, *Historija Bošnjaka*, Sarajevo,1998.
Ionescu, Ghita, *Communism in Rumania: 1944–1962*, London, 1964.
Istorija na Makedonskiot Narod, Institut za Nacionalna Istorija, Skopje, 1969.
Istorija na srŭbsko bŭlgarskata voyna, 1885, Ministerstvo na narodnata otbrana, Sofia, 1971.
Jelavich, Charles and Barbara, *The Establishment of the Balkan National States, 1804–1920*, Seattle, 1977.
Jelavich, Barbara, *History of the Balkans: Eighteenth and Nineteenth Centuries*, Cantab., 1983.
Jelavich, Barbara, *Russia's Balkan Entanglements, 1806–1914*, Cantab., 1991.
Jelić, Milosav, *Albanija: Zapisi o ljudima i dogadjajima*, Belgrade, 1933.
Jireček, Konstantin, *Dějiny ņároda bulharského*, Prague, 1876.
Jovanović, Slobodan, *Vlada Milana Obrenovića*, Belgrade, 1927, 2 vols.
Jovanović, Slobodan, *Iz istorije i književnosti*, Belgrade, 1931, 2 vols.
Jović, Borisav, *Poslednji dani SFRJ: Izvodi iz dnevnika*, Belgrade, 1995.
Jun-Lipanj 1968, Dokumenti, Zagreb, 1968.
Kaltchas, N., *Introduction to the Constitutional History of Greece*, New York, 1940.
Kann, Robert A., *Erzhog Franz Ferdinand Studien*, Vienna, 1976.
Karadjordjević, King Peter II, *A King's Heritage*, London, 1955.
Katadžiev, Ivan, *Sto godini od formiranjeto na VMRO; Sto godini revolucionerna tradicija*, Skopje, 1993.
Kazantzakis, Nikos, *Freedom or Death*, New York, 1955.
Kellog, Frederick, *The Road to Romanian Independence*, West Lafayette, Indiana, 1995.
Kent, Marian, ed., *The Great Powers and the End of the Ottoman Empire*, London, 1984.
Lord Kinross, *The Ottoman Centuries: The Rise and Fall of the Turkish Empire*, New York, 1977.
Király, Béla K. and Djordjević, Dimitrije, *East Central European Society and the Balkan Wars*, Boulder, 1987.
Király, Béla K. and Stokes, Gale, eds., *Insurrections, Wars, and the Eastern Crisis in the 1870s*, Boulder, 1985.
Kiszling, Rudolf, *Erzherzog Franz Ferdinand von Österreich-Este: Leben, Pläne und Wirken am Schicksalweg der Donaumonarchie*, Graz, 1953.
Kligman, Gail, *The Politics of Duplicity: Controlling Reproduction in Ceauşescu's Romania*, London, 1998.
Koch, H. W. ed., *The Origins of the First World War: Great Power Rivalry and German War Aims*, London, 1972.

Kočić, Petar, *Izbor*, Sarajevo, 1960.
Koetschet, Josef, *Aus Bosniens letzter Türkenzeit*, Vienna, 1905.
Kofos, Evangelos, *Greece and the Eastern Crisis, 1875–1878*, Thessaloniki, 1975.
Kofos, Evangelos, *Nationalism and Communism in Macedonia: Civil Conflict, Politics of Mutation, National Identity*, New York, 1993.
Koliopoulos, John S., *Brigands with a Cause: Brigandage and Irredentism in Modern Greece, 1821–1912*, Oxford, 1987.
Koljević, Svetozar, *The Epic in the Making*, Oxford, 1980.
Kolokotronis, Theodoros, *Memoirs from the Greek War of Independence 1821–1833*, London, 1892.
Konitza, Faik, *Albania: The Rock Garden of Southeastern Europe and Other Essays*, Boston, 1957.
Kounio-Amariglio, Erika Myriam, *Damit es die ganze Welt erfährt: von Saloniki nach Auschwitz und zurück 1926–1996*, Konstanz, 1996.
Kovačević, Aleksa, *Nevesinjski ustanak*, London, 1975.
Kraus, Karl, *Die letzten Tage der Menschheit*, Frankfurt-am-Main, 1986.
Kresnenskoto Vostanie vo Makedonia, 1878–79, Skopje, 1982.
Krestić, Vasilije, *Istorija Srba u Hrvatskoj i Slavoniji, 1848–1914*, Belgrade, 1991.
Krizman, Bogdan, *Pavelić i ustaše*, Zagreb, 1978.
Krizman, Bogdan, *Pavelić izmedju Hitlera i Mussolinija*, Zagreb, 1980.
Kržišnik-Bukić, Vera, *Cazinska buna 1950*, Sarajevo, 1991.
Kulundžić, Zvonomir, *Atentat na Stjepana Radića*, Zagreb, 1967.
Lampe, John R. and Jackson, Marvin R., *Balkan Economic History, 1550–1950*, Bloomington, 1982.
Lampe, John R., *Yugoslavia as History: Twice There Was a Country*, Cantab., 1996.
Larcher, M., *La Guerre Turque dans la Guerre Mondiale*, Paris, 1926.
Larcher, M., *La Grande Guerre dans les Balkans*, Paris, 1929.
Lederer, Ivo, *Yugoslavia at the Paris Peace Conference: A Study in Frontier-making*, New Haven, 1963.
Leeden, Michael A., *The First Duce: D'Annunzio at Fiume*, Baltimore, 1977.
Lendvai, Paul, *Eagles in Cobwebs: Nationalism and Communism in the Balkans*, London, 1969.
Lewis, Bernard, *The Emergence of Modern Turkey*, London, 1961.
Lewis, Raphaela, *Everyday Life in Ottoman Turkey*, London, 1971.
Liotta, P. H. and Jebb, Cindy R., *Mapping Macedonia, Idea and Identity*, Santa Barbara, 1994.
Littlefield, Frank C., *Germany and Yugoslavia, 1933–1941: The German Conquest of Yugoslavia*, New York, 1988.
Llewellyn Smith, Michael, *Ionian Vision: Greece in Asia Minor 1919–1922*, London, 1973.
Ljubibratić, Dragoslav, *Mlada Bosna i Sarajevski atentat*, Sarajevo, 1964.
Ludendorff, Erich, *My War Memoirs, 1914–1918*, Vol. II, London, 1919.
Ludwig, Emil, *Der Kampf auf dem Balkan*, Berlin, 1916.
Logoreci, Anton, *The Albanians: Europe's Forgotten Survivors*, London, 1977.
Lončarević, Dušan, *Jugoslawiens Entstehung*, Zürich, 1929.
Lord, Robert Howard, *Three Peace Congresses of the Nineteenth Century*, Cambridge, MA.

Löwenthal, Zdenko, ed., *The Crimes of the Fascist Occupants and Their Collaborators against Jews in Yugoslavia*, Belgrade, 1957.

Lubonja, Fatos, *The Second Sentence*, New York, 1999.

Lukać, Dušan, *Treći rahj i zelmje jugoistočne Europe, Vol. I. 1933–1936*, Belgrade, 1982.

Lundestad, Geir, *The American Non-policy towards Eastern Europe, 1943–1947*, Oslo, 1978.

Lungu, Dov B., *Romania and the Great Powers, 1933–1940*, Durham, 1989.

MacDonald, J. N., *A Political Escapade: The Story of Fiume and D'Annunzio*, London, 1921.

Macfie, A. L., *Atatürk*, London, 1994.

MacGahan, Januarius A., *The Turkish Atrocities in Bulgaria*, 1966, Geneva.

MacKenzie, David, *Ilija Garasanin: Balkan Bismarck*, New York, 1985.

MacKenzie, David, *Apis: The Congenial Conspiratorial – The Life of Colonel Dragutin T. Dimitrijević*, Boulder, 1989.

Magocsi, Paul Robert, *Historical Atlas of East Central Europe*, Seattle, 1993.

Makriyannis, Ioannis, *The Memoirs of General Makriyannis, 1797–1864*, tr. and ed. H.A. Lidderdale, London, 1966.

Maksimović, Desanka, *Pesme*, Belgrade, 1989.

Malcolm, Noel, *Bosnia: A Short History*, London, 1994.

Mamatey, Victor S., *The United States and East Central Europe, 1914–1918: A Study in Wilsonian Diplomacy and Propaganda*, Princeton, 1957.

Manchester, William, *The Arms of Krupp, 1587–1968*, Boston, 1964.

Manning, Olivia, *The Balkan Trilogy*, Harmondsworth, 1981.

Manoschek, Walter, *'Serbien ist judenfrei': Militärische Besatzungspolitik und Judenvernichtung in Serbien 1941–42*, Munich, 1993.

Mansel, Philip, *Constantinople: City of the World's Desire, 1453–1924*, London, 1995.

Mardin, Şerif, *The Genesis of Young Ottoman Thought: A Study in the Modernization of Turkish Political Ideas*, Princeton, 1962.

Markov, Georgi, *The Truth That Killed*, London, 1983.

Marmullaku, Ramadan, *Albania and the Albanians*, London, 1975.

Masleše, Veselin, *Mlada Bosna*, Sarajevo, 1990.

Matkovski, *A History of the Macedonian Jews*, Skopje, 1985.

Matsas, Michael, *The Illusion of Safety: The Story of the Greek Jews during the Second World War*, New York, 1997.

der Maur, Gilbert, *Die Jugoslawen Einst und Jetzt*, 3 vols., Berlin, 1938.

Mazower, Mark, *Inside Hitler's Greece: The Experience of Occupation, 1941–1944*, London, 1993.

McCauley, Martin, ed., *Communist Power in Europe, 1944–1949*, London, 1977.

Mears, Eliot Grinnell, *Modern Turkey: A Politico-economic Interpretation, 1908–1923*, New York, 1924.

Medlicott, W. N., *A Diplomatic History of the Near Eastern Settlement, 1878–1880*, London, 1938.

Meier, Viktor, *Wie Jugoslawien verspielt wurde*, Munich, 1996.

Meininger, Thomas A., *The Formation of a Nationalist Bulgarian Intelligentsia, 1835–1878*, New York, 1987.

Melville, Ralph and Schröder, Hans-Jürgen, eds, *Der Berliner Kongreß von 1878: Die Politik der Großmächte und die Probleme der Modernisierung in Südosteuropa in der zweiten Hälfte des 19. Jahrhunderts*, Wiesbaden, 1982.

Mendelsohn, Ezra, *The Jews of East Central Europe Between the World Wars*, Bloomington, 1983.

Meriage, Lawrence P., *Russia and the First Serbian Insurrection, 1804–1813*, New York, 1987.

Meštrović, Ivan, *Uspomene na političke ljude i dogadjaje*, Buenos Aires, 1961.

Mijatović, Andjelko, *Ban Jelačić*, Zagreb, 1990.

Milazzo, Matteo J., *The Chetnik Movement and the Yugoslav Resistance*, Baltimore, 1975.

Mitrakos, Alexander S., *France in Greece during World War I: A Study in the Politics of Power*, Boulder, 1982.

Mitrany, David, *The Land and the Peasant in Rumania: The War and Agrarian Reform (1917–21)*, London, 1930.

Mitrany, David, *The Effect of the War in Southeastern Europe*, New Haven, 1936.

Morawitz, Charles, *Les Finances de la Turquie*, Paris, 1902.

Mühlmann, Carl, *Der Kampf um die Dardanellen 1915*, Berlin, 1927.

Muradbegović, Ahmed, *Omer-Paša Latas u Bosni, 1850–1852*, Zagreb, 1944.

Mure, William, *Journal of a Tour in Greece and the Ionian Islands*, Edinburgh, 1842.

Musil, Robert, *Der Mann ohne Eigenschaften*, Hamburg, 1978.

Nagy-Talavera, Nicholas M., *The Green Shirts and the Others: A History of Fascism in Hungary and Rumania*, Stanford, 1970.

Nenadović, Prota Matija, *The Memoirs of Prota Matija Nenadović*, ed. Lovett F. Edwards, Oxford, 1969.

Neubacher, Hermann, *Sonderauftrag Südost, 1940–45*, Göttingen, 1956.

Nicolson, Harold, *Curzon: The Last Phase 1919–1925*, London 1934.

Nicolson, Harold, *Peacemaking 1919*, London, 1943.

Nikolić, Milan M. ed., *Timočka buna, 1883*, Belgrade, 1954.

Nissan, Oren, *Bulgarian Communism: The Road to Power 1943–44*, New York, 1971.

Nušić, Branislav, *Pripovetke jednoga kaplara*, Belgrade, 1966.

Pacepa, Ion Mihai, *Red Horizons*, London, 1988.

Padev, Michael, *Dimitrov Wastes No Bullets: Nikola Petkov, the Test Case*, London, 1948.

Palmer, Alan, *The Gardeners of Salonika*, London, 1965.

Pallis, Alexandros A., *Greece's Anatolian Venture – And After: A Survey of the Diplomatic and Political Aspects of the Greek Expedition to Asia Minor (1915–1922)*, London, 1937.

Pandevski, Manol, *Makedonija na balkanot*, Skopje, 1990.

Papers on the Eastern Question, The Eastern Question Association, London, 1877.

Papacosma, S. Victor, *The Military in Greek Politics: The 1909 Coup d'Etat*, Kent, OH, 1977.

Pappenheim, Martin, *Gavrilo Princips Bekenntnisse: Zwei Manuskripte Princips, Aufzeichnungen seines Gefängnispsychiaters Dr. Pappenheim aus Gesprächen von Feber bis Juni 1916 über das Attentat, Princips Leben und seine politischen und sozialen Anschauungen*, Vienna, 1926.

Pašić, Nikola, *Sloga Srbo-Hrvata*, Belgrade, 1995.
Pentzopoulos, Dimitri, *The Balkan Exchange of Minorities and Its Impact upon Greece*, Paris, 1962.
Perry, Duncan M., *The Politics of Terror: The Macedonian Revolutionary Movements, 1893–1903*, Durham, 1988.
Petkov, Petko M., *The United States and Bulgaria in World War I*, New York, 1991.
Petropulos, John A., *Politics and Statecraft in the Kingdom of Greece, 1833–1843*, Princeton, 1986.
Petrovich, Michael Boro, *A History of Modern Serbia, 1804–1918*, 2 vols., New York, 1976.
Petsalis-Diomidis, N., *Greece at the Paris Peace Conference*, Thessaloniki, 1978.
Photakos, Photios Chrysanthopoulos, *Apomnemoneumata peri tes Hellenikes Epanastaseos*, Vol. I, Athens, 1899.
Piekalkiewicz, Janusz, *Krieg auf dem Balkan: 1940–1945*, Munich, 1984.
Pinson, Mark, ed., *The Muslims of Bosnia-Herzegovina: Their Historic Development from the Middle Ages to the Dissolution of Yugoslavia*, Boulder, 1996.
Pipa, Arshi, *Albanian Stalinism: Ideo-political Aspects*, Boulder, 1990.
Pope, Nicole and Hugh, *Turkey Unveiled: Atatürk and After*, London, 1997.
Prifti, Peter, *Socialist Albania since 1944: Domestic and Foreign Developments*, Cambridge, 1978.
Quinlan, Paul D., *The Playboy King: Carol II of Romania*, Westport, 1995.
Račin, Kočo, *Beli mugri*, Skopje, 1953.
Radić, Štjepan, *Srbové a Chorvati: Několik kapitol k objasnění podstaty posledních událostí*, Prague, 1902.
Radić, Stjepan, *Politički spisi*, Zagreb, 1971.
Radin, A. Michael, *IMRO and the Macedonian Question*, Skopje (Undated).
Ramsaur, Ernest Edmondson, *The Young Turks: Prelude to the Revolution of 1908*, New York, 1957.
Ranke, Leopold, *The History of Servia, and the Servian Revolution*, London, 1853.
Recker, Marie-Luise, *Die Aussenpolitik des dritten Reiches*, Oldenbourg, 1990.
Redžić, Enver, *Bosna i Hercegovina u drugom svjetskom ratu*, Sarajevo, 1988.
Report of the International Commission to Inquire into the Causes and Conduct of the Balkan Wars, Carnegie Endowment of International Peace, Washington, D.C., 1914.
Riffer, Milko, *Grad mrtvih: Jasenovac, 1943*, Zagreb, 1946.
Rizvić, Muhsin, *Književno stvaranje muslimanskih pisaca u Bosni i Hercegovini u doba austrougarske vladavine*, Sarajevo, 1973.
Roberts, Henry L., *Rumania: Political Problems of an Agrarian State*, New Haven, 1951.
Rothenberg, Gunther E., *The Army of Francis Joseph*, West Lafayette, 1976.
Rothschild, Joseph, *East Central Europe between the Two World Wars*, Seattle, 1977.
Rusinow, Dennison, *The Yugoslav Experiment, 1948–1974*, London, 1977.
Schevill, Ferdinand, *A History of the Balkan Peninsula*, New York, 1933.
Schmitt, Bernadotte E., *The Annexation of Bosnia, 1908–1909*, Cantab., 1937.
Schorske, Carl E., *Fin-de-Siècle Vienna: Politics and Culture*, New York, 1961.

Schuster, Peter, *Henry Wickham Steed und die Habsburgermonarchie*, Vienna, 1970.
Sciaky, Leon, *Farewell to Salonica: Portrait of an Era*, London, 1946.
Seton-Watson, Hugh, *The East European Revolution*, New York, 1951.
Seton-Watson, R. W., *The Southern Slav Question and the Habsburg Monarchy*, London, 1911.
Seton-Watson, R. W., *Disraeli, Gladstone, and the Eastern Question*, New York, 1972.
Sharp, Alan, *The Versailles Settlement: Peacemaking in Paris, 1919*, London, 1981.
Shaw, Stanford J., *Between Old and New: The Ottoman Empire Under Selim III, 1789–1807*, Cambridge, 1971.
Shaw, Stanford J., *History of the Ottoman Empire and Modern Turkey: Vol. II: Reform, Revolution and Republic: The Rise of Modern Turkey, 1808–1975*, Cantab., 1977.
Sherman, David Spector, *Rumania at the Paris Peace Conference: A Study of the Diplomacy of Ioan I. C. Brãtianu*, New York, 1962.
Šidak, Jaroslav *et al.*, *Povijest hrvatskog naroda g. 1860–1914*, Zagreb, 1968.
Šidak, Jaroslav, *Studije iz hrvatske povijesti za revolucije 1848–49*, Zagreb, 1979.
Šidak, Jaroslav, *Hrvatski narodni preporod, Ilirski pokret*, Zagreb, 1990.
Silber, Laura and Little, Allan, *The Death of Yugoslavia*, London, 1995.
Šišić, Ferdo, *Bosna i Hercegovina za vezirovanja Omer-Pase Latase*, Subotica, 1938.
Skatula, Emanuel, *Válka na Balkáně: Válečné taženi Bulharska, Srbska, Řecka a Černé Hory proti Turecku*, Prague, 1913.
Skendi, Stavro, *The Albanian National Awakening, 1872–1912*, Princeton, 1967.
Slijepčević, Djoko, *Pitanje Bosne i Hercegovine u XIX veku*, Cologne, 1981.
Slijepčević, Pero, *Napor Bosne i Hercegovine za oslobodjenje i ujedinjenje*, Sarajevo, 1929.
Šljivo, Galib, *Omer-Paša Latas*, Sarajevo, 1977.
Smith, Denis Mack, *Mussolini's Roman Empire*, London, 1976.
Sowards, Steven W., *Austria's Policy of Macedonian Reform*, Boulder, 1989.
Spyropoulos, Evangelos, *The Greek Military (1909–1941) and the Greek Mutinies in the Middle East (1941–1944)*, Boulder, 1993.
Stambolić, Ivan, *Put u bespuće*, Belgrade, 1995.
Stavrakis, Peter, *Moscow and Greek Communism, 1944–49*, Ithaca, 1989.
Stavrianos, L. S., *Balkan Federation. A History of the Movement toward Balkan Unity in Modern Times*, Northampton, MA, 1942.
Stavrianos, L. S., *The Balkans since 1453*, New York, 1958.
Stefanović, Miladin, *Drugi srpski ustanak*, Belgrade, 1990.
Stoianovich, Traian, *Balkan Worlds: The First and Last Europe*, New York, 1994.
Stojančević, Vladimir, *Srbija i Bugarska od Sanstefanskog Mira do Berlinskog Kongresa*, Belgrade, 1986.
Stojanovski, Aleksandar, ed. *Turski dokumenti za ilindenskoto vostanie*, Skopje, 1993.
Stokes, Gale, ed., *Nationalism in the Balkans: An Annotated Bibliography*, New York, 1984.
Stokes, Gale, *Politics as Development: The Emergence of Political Parties in*

Nineteenth-Century Serbia, Durham, 1990.

Stratimirović, Djordje, *Was ich erlebte: die Erinnerungen von General von Stratimirović*, Vienna, 1910.

Sugar, Peter F., *Industrialisation of Bosnia-Hercegovina, 1978–1914*, Seattle, 1963.

Sugar, Peter F. and Lederer, eds., *Nationalism in Eastern Europe*, Seattle, 1969.

Sugar, Peter F. ed., *Native Fascism in the Successor States, 1918–1945*, Santa Barbara, 1971.

Sugar, Peter F., Hánák, Péter, Frank, Tibor, *A History of Hungary*, Bloomington, 1990.

Sumner, B. H., *Russia and the Balkans, 1870–1880*, Oxford, 1937.

Swire, J., *Albania: The Rise of a Kingdom*, London, 1929.

Swire, J., *Bulgarian Conspiracy*, London, 1939.

Swire, J., *King Zog's Albania*, London, 1941.

Taylor, A. J. P., *The Struggle for Mastery in Europe, 1848–1914*, London, 1954.

Tejchman, Miroslav, *Válka na Balkáně: Balkánské státy v letech 1941–1944*, Prague, 1986.

Temperley, H. W., ed., *A History of the Peace Conference of Paris*, 6. vols., London, 1920.

Tishev, Dimit r, *1918, Vojniskoto Vŭstanie: Sbornik ot dokumenti i spomeni*, Sofia, 1968.

Todorova, Maria, *Imagining the Balkans*, Oxford, 1997.

Tolstoy, Leo, *On the Annexation of Bosnia and Herzegovina by Austria*, Bristol, 1965.

Tomasevich, Jozo, *The Chetniks: War and Revolution in Yugoslavia, 1941–1945*, Stanford, 1975.

Tripalo, Miko, *Hrvatsko proljeće*, Zagreb, 1989.

Trotsky, Leon, *The Balkan Wars, 1912–1913*, New York, 1980.

Trotsky, Lav, *Sarajevski atentat*, Belgrade, 1989.

Trumpener, Ulrich, *Germany and the Ottoman Empire: 1914–1918*, Princeton, 1968.

Tsatsos, Jeanne, *The Sword's Fierce Edge: A Journal of the Occupation of Greece, 1941–1944*, New York, 1969.

Vasić, Dragiša, *Devetsto treća (majski prevrat)*, Belgrade, 1925.

Vatikiotis, P. J., *Popular Autocracy in Greece, 1936–41: A Political Biography of General Ioannis Metaxas*, London, 1998.

Vazov, Ivan, *Under the Yoke*, London, 1912.

Veinstein, Gilles ed., *Salonique, 1850–1918: La 'ville des Juifs' et le réveil des Balkans*, Paris, 1993.

Verdery, Katherine, *National Ideology under Socialism: Identity and Cultural Politics in Ceauşescu's Romania*, Berkeley, 1991.

Vergnet, Paul and Bernard-Derosne, Jean, *L'Affaire Petkov*, Paris, 1948.

Veremis, Thanos, *The Military in Greek Politics*, London, 1997.

Vickers, Miranda, *The Albanians: A Modern History*, London, 1995.

Vita Bok nr. 7: Balkankonflikten: Krigshändelsernas förhistoria i dokumentarisk belysning, Tyska Utrikesministeriets, Stockholm, 1941.

Vojvodić, Mihailo and Živojinović, Dragoljub, *Veliki rat Srbije, 1914–1918*, Belgrade, 1970.

Volkan, Vamik D. and Itzkowitz, Norman, *The Immortal Atatürk: A Psychobiography*, Chicago, 1984.

Volkan, Vamik D. and Itzkowitz, Norman, *Turks and Greeks: Neighbours in conflict*, Huntingdon, Cambridgeshire, 1994.

Vopička, Karel J., *Taje Balkánu*, Prague, 1927.

Vražinovski, Tanas, *Ilindenski prozen revolucioneren folklor*, Skopje, 1981.

Vucinich, Wayne S., *Serbia Between East and West: The Events of 1903–1908*, Stanford, 1954.

Vucinich, Wayne S., ed., *The First Serbian Uprising, 1804–1813*, New York, 1982.

Vucinich, Wayne S. and Emmert, Thomas A. eds., *Kosovo: Legacy of a Medieval Battle*, Minneapolis, 1991.

Vučković, Zvonimir, *Sećanja iz rata*, London, 1980.

Waldeck, R. G., *Athene Palace Bucharest: Hitler's 'New Order' Comes to Rumania*, London, 1943.

Wank, Soloman, *Aus dem Nachlaß Aehrenthal: Briefe und Dokumente zur österreichisch-ungarischen Innen- und Außenpolitik 1885–1912*, 2 vols., Graz, 1994.

Weiker, Walter F., *Ottomans, Turks and the Jewish Polity: A History of the Jews of Turkey*, Lanham, 1992.

White, Leigh, *Balkan Caesar: Tito versus Stalin*, New York, 1951.

Wickham Steed, Henry, *Through Thirty Years, 1892–1922: A Personal Narrative*, 2 vols., London, 1924.

Williamson, Samuel R. Jr., *Austria-Hungary and the Origins of the First World War*, London, 1991.

Wilson, Duncan, *The Life and Times of Vuk Stefanović Karadžić, 1787–1864*, Oxford, 1970.

Wolff, Larry, *Inventing Eastern Europe: The Map of Civilization and the Mind of the Enlightenment*, Stanford, 1995.

Wolff, Robert, *The Balkans in our Time*, London, 1956.

Woodhouse, C. M., *Apple of Discord: A Survey of Recent Greek Politics in Their International Setting*, London, 1948.

Woodhouse, C. M., *The Philhellenes*, London, 1969.

Yergin, Daniel, *Shattered Peace: The Origins of the Cold War and the National Security State*, Harmondsworth, 1980.

Zamboni, Giovanni, *Mussolinis Expansionspolitik auf dem Balkan: Italiens Albanienpolitik vom I. zum II. Tiranapakt im Rahmen des italienisch-jugoslawischen Interessenkonfliks u. der italienischen 'imperialen' Bestrebungen in Südosteuropa*, Hamburg, 1984.

Zarnowski, J., Dictatorships in East-Central Europe, 1918–1939, Warsaw, 1983.

Živulović, Žika, *Najveće bitke prvog srpskog ustanka*, Belgrade, 1965.

Zografski, Dančo, *Za makedonskoto prašanje*, Skopje, 1990.

Zürcher, Eric J., *Turkey: A Modern History*, London, 1993.

INDEX